The Baseball Filmography, 1915 through 2001

SECOND EDITION

The Baseball Filmography

1915 through 2001

SECOND EDITION

by HAL ERICKSON

McFarland & Company, Inc., Publishers
Jefferson, North Carolina, and London

To my sons, Brian and Peter,
who years ago made their own special pilgrimage
to the "Field of Dreams" in Dyersville, Iowa

Library of Congress Cataloguing-in-Publication Data

Erickson, Hal, 1950–
The baseball filmography, 1915 through 2001 / by Hal Erickson.—
2nd ed.
p.   cm.
Includes bibliographical references and index.

ISBN 0-7864-1272-0 (illustrated case binding : 50# alkaline paper) ∞

1. Baseball films—History and criticism.
I. Title.
PN1995.9.B28E7   2002   791.43'655—dc21   2002002699

British Library cataloguing data are available

On the front cover: Robert Redford
plays Roy Hobbs in *The Natural* (1984)

Manufactured in the United States of America

*McFarland & Company, Inc., Publishers
Box 611, Jefferson, North Carolina 28640
www.mcfarlandpub.com*

Table of Contents

v

Preface and Acknowledgments

When I was asked by McFarland to update and revise my 1992 book *Baseball in the Movies: A Comprehensive Reference*, I could not help but think of Roy Hobbs, the "rookie" pitcher played by Robert Redford in *The Natural* (1984). Those who saw the film will remember that Hobbs, whose burgeoning baseball career had been tragically nipped in the bud 16 years earlier, returned to pinstripes at the age of 35, determined to resurrect the talent, energy and mental acuity of his youth. Undoubtedly, Roy approached his mission with mixed feelings of enthusiasm, anticipation, and stark, raw fear—just as I did when I began work on what came to be titled *The Baseball Filmography: 1915 through 2001*. (And I must confess that I will never see 35 again, so if anything I have even *more* trepidation than Roy Hobbs!)

In my foreword to the first edition, I noted that while researching the project I learned a little more of film history than I'd already known, and a whole lot more about baseball. That statement still stands, pertaining not only to the 29 new feature films that have been added to this text, but also to the 81 films covered in the first edition. Or perhaps I should say 82 films: the 1978 *Goodbye Franklin High*—which I'd been unable to analyze in the 1992 edition because I never could track down a copy of the film

or any other pertinent information—now, thanks to the generosity of the film's screenwriter, has been included. Also, I have been able to screen full, uncut versions of several silent and pre–1950 talkie baseball films which were unavailable to me (uncut or otherwise) in the early 1990s, among them *Hit and Run* (1924), *The Battling Orioles* (1924), *Slide, Kelly, Slide* (1927) and *They Learned About Women* (1930). The practical effect of my admission in the first edition—that I had not actually seen all of the films discussed in these pages—is considerably less now than it was then.

In addition to revising several of the entries from the earlier book, I have expanded upon my introductory overview of baseball movies to include those films produced between 1991 and 2001, and to add a handful of new notes and observations. Likewise, the closing chapters on "Baseball Short Subjects" and "Baseball in Non-Baseball Films" have undergone significant revisions.

I had hoped to include a chapter on Japanese baseball films, but time and space restrictions made this impossible. However, a representative cross-section of these Japanese efforts—among them *Anata Kaimasu* (*I'll Buy You*, 1956), *Gishiki* (*The Ceremony*, 1971), *Kata Ashi No Ace* (*One Legged Ace*, 1971), *Sado* (*A Boy Called Third Base*,

1978), and, best of all, *Setouchi Shonen Yakyu Dan* (*MacArthur's Children*, 1985)—are superbly documented in Rob Edelman's *The Great Baseball Films* (Citadel Press, 1994).

In limiting my book to baseball films produced and released in the United States (while some were filmed in Canada for economic reasons, these are essentially "American" pictures), I also confined my text to "fictional" films. Thus, I was compelled to exclude the prolific field of baseball documentaries, ranging from the modest but captivating *Little Giants* (a 1958 Mexican theatrical feature focusing on the world-champion Monterrey Little League team) to Ken Burns' exhaustively researched, thorough, and endlessly fascinating 18½-hour PBS miniseries *Baseball* (1994). This genre is truly worthy of a book of its own, as are such baseball-oriented American TV series as *Ball Four*, *The Bay City Blues* and *Hardball*—not to mention the scores of appearances by professional ballplayers on such weekly TV sitcoms as *The Phil Silvers Show*, *Leave It to Beaver*, *The Beverly Hillbillies*, *Mr. Ed* and *The Simpsons*.

Although the 1994 Major League strike cut into the sales and profits of several baseball books, including mine, the original *Baseball in the Movies* somehow took on a life of its own, and I am immeasurably gratified that it has brought pleasure, entertainment and edification to so many people, ranging from print journalists to radio talk-show hosts to college professors. I was especially honored when, in 1993, my book was one of ten nominated for the Casey Award, bestowed annually by the Cincinnati-based *Spitball: The Literary Baseball Magazine*. Although the Casey ultimately went to another author (and a very deserving one), my wife and I had a wonderful time at the awards ceremony, surrounded by friendly and convivial baseball enthusiasts and enveloped in the warm and inviting aroma of hot dogs and fresh-roasted peanuts.

Helping to fill the gaps in my research in a variety of ways were many friends and fellow historians. I now take pleasure in bestowing extra special thanks upon George Callahan of American Movie Classics, Woodbury, New York, actor Frank Coghlan, Jr., Pat Hansen and Eli Savada of the American Film Institute, radio personality Dr. Robert R. Hieronimus, screenwriter Stu Krieger, and film historians Jim Neibaur and Ted Okuda, each of whom personifies the phrase "above and beyond the call of duty." Ditto to the ever diligent, ever courteous staff of the Wisconsin Center for Film and Theatre Research, Madison, Wisconsin, and the Academy of Motion Picture Arts and Sciences, Beverly Hills, California.

Additional praise and thanks are due the following persons and business establishments: The Acme Movie Poster Company, Glastonbury, Connecticut; the late John Bierman; Carl, Cari and David Bobke; Cinema Collectors, Hollywood; Cinemagraphics, Denver; Steve Cummings and Mike Shannon of *Spitball* magazine; Eddie Brandt's Saturday Matinee, Van Nuys; Gary Elfe; The Family Channel, Virginia Beach, Virginia; Sandy Fast; Jim Feeley of WCGV-TV, Milwaukee; Film Favorites, Canton, Oklahoma; Wayne and Rita Hawk; Tom Herricks; Jerry Ohlinger's Movie Material Store Inc., New York; The Jimmy Stewart Museum, Indiana, PA; Larry Koellner; Lee Matthias; Metro Golden Memories, Chicago; The Negro Leagues Baseball Museum, Kansas City, Missouri; The Nostalgia Factory, Boston; Henry Osier; Photoworld, Houston; Press Kits Plus, Williamstown, Mass.; Corky Savely; David Seebach; Bill Sprague; Turner Broadcasting, Atlanta; Debby Tzortzos of the Oriental-Landmark Theatre, Milwaukee; West Coast Video; Yesterday's Memories, Milwaukee; and Mark Zimmerman.

Last but never least, a big warm gust of gratitude to my parents, Pudge Erickson and the late Pete Erickson, who, in addition to the obvious forms of support, kept an eagle eye on the TV-cable services; to my marvelous wife, Joanne, who even after seven published books won't let me veer toward William Faulkner in my run-on sentences that never seem to end and don't quite get to the point until you're practically at the end of ... oops, sorry, Joanne; and to the dedicatees of this book, my sons, Brian and Peter, both of whom love sports, and both of whom I love without limit.

Hal Erickson
Milwaukee
February 2002

Introduction

What is it about America's Pastime that so often prevents it from successfully combining with America's Second Pastime? Why is it that, since 1914, there have been only a little over a hundred American feature films about baseball?

Can all those "truths" perpetuated throughout the years actually be truths? Do baseball movies regularly lose money? Do they all have the same plot? Are they habitually inaccurate? Are they poor substitutes for actually attending live baseball games? Let's break these arguments down.

Baseball Movies Regularly Lose Money. Tell that to the producers of *Slide, Kelly, Slide*, one of MGM's biggest hits of 1927. Tell that to Joe E. Brown, whose 1935 *Alibi Ike* put him back on the list of moviedom's top ten moneymakers after a three-year absence. Tell that to Samuel Goldwyn, whose 1942 production *The Pride of the Yankees* was his most profitable feature up to that time (and that was after three decades in the business!). Tell that to the folks responsible for *The Stratton Story, Take Me Out to the Ballgame, Damn Yankees, The Bad News Bears, Bull Durham, Major League, Field of Dreams, A League of Their Own* and *Rookie of the Year*—all of which ended up very comfortably in the black at the box office, some of them even more than just comfortably.

Baseball Movies All Have the Same Plot. *Babe Comes Home* (1927) was the story of a slugger who couldn't perform unless he had a plug of chewing tobacco embedded in his mouth. *Fireman, Save My Child* (1932) was about an itinerant inventor and part-time fireman who only reluctantly became a full-time major leaguer. *Death on the Diamond* (1934) had an exploding baseball, *Girls Can Play* (1937) had a poisoned baseball, and *It Happens Every Spring* (1949) had a wood-resistant baseball. *Damn Yankees* (1958) opined that the New York Yankees were the unwitting tool of Satan; *The Natural* (1984) suggested, conversely, that baseball and sainthood were one and the same. The troubled hero of *The Slugger's Wife* (1985) got his act together, but his team lost all the same. The troubled hero of *Bull Durham* (1988) guided his team to victory, but he was fired all the same. *Field of Dreams* (1989) considered the possibility that Iowa was heaven. *A League of Their Own* (1992) managed the neat trick of qualifying simultaneously as a "Chick Flick" and a "Guy Thing." And *Ed* (1996) suggested that it was high time the majors began recruiting from the animal world. Few other film genres can boast as much variety of plot.

Baseball Movies Are Habitually Inaccurate. Check out *Big Leaguer* (1953), *Eight Men Out* (1988), *Bull Durham* (again!)

or *Cobb* (1994) some time. They're so accurate it hurts.

Baseball Movies Are Poor Substitutes for Attending Actual Live Games. You've got me there, pal. But three out of four isn't bad.

Working in reverse order, let's take this last point first. Yes, it's true that it's difficult to re-create the feel of a real game: The crack of the bat, the texture of the glove, the smell of the turf, and all those other overworked sensory experiences. The same can be said of any other filmed sport, but there are certain aspects of non-baseball activities which can be handled successfully on a cinematic level to pump up audience excitement. For one thing, many sports victories hinge upon a single performer or single play. We can empathize with, say, a prizefighter or race-car driver, because it's a one-on-one deal where the viewer can pull for an individual combatant.

Baseball doesn't work that way—not in real life at any rate. The home run in the third inning can be scuttled by the bonehead play in the ninth. A team's best player can find himself benched halfway through the game. The team that plays badly until the seventh-inning stretch can emerge victorious as much through an error on the other side as through a single miracle catch. Despite star player publicity and salaries, baseball is a game won collectively.

The team concept inherent to baseball conflicts with Hollywood's tradition of building films around the talents of individual stars. Until recently, few "name" players would be satisfied with scripts which suggested that they couldn't handle ball game–related crises alone. Thus, Gary Cooper was the sole savior of the Yanks in *The Pride of the Yankees*, Ronald Reagan alone won the World Series for the Cardinals in *The Winning Team* (1952), and Robert Redford was the prime mover for the fictional "New York Knights" in *The Natural*.

Not only was this rugged individualism expected of these stars, it was most likely in their contracts. That's why *Major League*, a film largely lacking in surprise and nuance, can still seem fresh in the eyes of many viewers—clichéd it was, to be sure, but the emphasis was on teamwork rather than isolated grandstanding (though even here, it was the teamwork of the four leading actors—Tom Berenger, Charlie Sheen, Corbin Bernsen and Wesley Snipes—more than the contributions of the rest of the team which saved the day).

Rooting for a team rather than an individual doesn't always work if the team is a fictional group whom you've never seen before the film and who you'll never see afterward. Films like the 1951 version of *Angels in the Outfield* and the aforementioned *Major League* solved this problem somewhat by naming real teams—respectively, the Pittsburgh Pirates and the Cleveland Indians—but then posed the new problem of losing those filmgoers who didn't happen to like the actual Pirates or Indians. As for *Eight Men Out*, the attempt to literally make a star out of a whole team resulted in audience confusion and resistance when it was realized that there were no heroes on the 1919 White Sox, singular or plural.

Hollywood's general aversion to the team format does not, however, completely explain away the relative paucity of films about baseball, especially considering the overabundance of football movies—which, if anything, are even more group dominated than baseball pictures. Remember, though, that football is governed by the clock, and, indeed, so are most of the other sports that have enjoyed wide cinematic exposure. Baseball is a sport that can go on forever. In baseball films there are no ticking clocks, no two-minute warnings, no whistles, no guns. This open-ended quality is at odds with the notion that your average movie should run a hard-and-fast two hours, and even more contrary to the strictures of earlier films made during the "double feature" era, when it was unofficially decreed that the "A" picture on the bill would run 90 minutes, and the "B" cofeature an average of 65 minutes, with time to spare for the newsreel, cartoon, travelogue and coming attractions.

The suggestion has been made (not by this writer) that the ideal baseball film would be one which uninterruptedly records a single game, from the national anthem to the bottom of the ninth inning, allowing all the time in the world to unravel that game's own inner drama without the adornments of voiceover narration, subplots or character motivations. Were this the case, then such marathon filmmakers as David Lean, Andy Warhol, Marcel Ophuls or Bernardo Bertolucci would have been the sole directorial candidates whenever a baseball film was conceived. Frankly, unless this "ideal" film happened to be the story of Bobby Thompson's miracle home run in the cliff-hanging 1951 Giants-Dodgers pennant race, I can't think of anyone who'd pay money to sit through an uninterrupted game re-creation. The fact is, no one who goes to a big-league ballpark these days really sees any such "unbroken" game; thanks to tight TV and sponsor contracts, the end of each inning constitutes a "station break," followed by a parade of advertisements, sports trivia and such displayed upon the scoreboard to allow for 90 seconds' worth of commercials on the home screen. Each interruption is a miniature "seventh-inning stretch" which permits the spectator some welcome breathing room during a good game and a merciful break in the monotony of a bad one.

Thus, it's no crime to toy with reality in a baseball film by whittling a game down to its highlights. Even 1999's *For Love of the Game*, which *did* attempt to focus almost exclusively on a single, solitary baseball game from start to finish, cunningly used an arsenal of cinematic diversions—time compression, flashbacks, interior monologues, off-field cutaways, etc.—to keep the nonfans from dozing off (though, judging from some of the reviews, it didn't totally succeed in this respect).

It's quite true that attending a baseball film can't compare with attending a game in the flesh, a truth that has resulted in relatively few baseball pictures being made over the years. It isn't true, however, that this precludes any baseball film from turning out successfully.

So let's now take a glance at that argument about inaccuracy. Oddly, some of the most painstakingly accurate baseball pictures are not necessarily the best. *Eight Men Out* is meticulous in its re-creation of time, place and sport, but it seems more like a doctoral thesis than a film, and just plain isn't as entertaining as something like *Bull Durham*. And while we're on that subject: *Bull Durham* has probably the best handle of any film on what it's really like to survive a season in the minor leagues, but would it have been as enjoyable without the constant cutaways to its romantic subplot, which, to put it mildly, is exaggerated for comic and erotic effect?

Baseball purists howl at such dramatic digressions, complaining that they lessen the authenticity of baseball pictures. Maybe so. But look at 1953's *Big Leaguer*: It is pure baseball, with as accurate a representation of the training process as has ever been put on film. But does anyone care? Five minutes after the picture is over, you can't remember "feeling" for any of the ballplayers, because they are merely types, not human beings. The only character in the film who really touches the audience is the Giants' coach, played by Edward G. Robinson, who utilizes every dramatic trick at his considerable disposal to guarantee that you pull for him and his contribution to the plot. The trouble is, the film isn't supposed to be about Robinson but about the aspiring ballplayers under his wing—and since they can't get you to worry about them, consequently you don't really worry about anything that happens in *Big Leaguer*, accuracy or no accuracy.

Few fact-based films of any kind, baseball or otherwise, are completely faithful to those facts. This hasn't lessened the value of such Oscar-winning films as *The Great Ziegfeld, The Life of Emile Zola, A Man for All Seasons, Patton, Gandhi, Amadeus* and *Titanic*, so it seems a little petty to pillory "true story" baseball films for occasionally misrepresenting matters of personalities, places and events. Any number of right-handed actors have played left-handed ball-players, but this is a hazard one must face when determined to make a film about a sport where southpaws figure more prominently than in most walks of life. The period of time between Monty Stratton's crippling accident and his moderately successful return to the minor leagues is shortened by several years in *The Stratton Story*, but this serves to heighten the punch of the finale. It may be misleading to suggest in *The Winning Team* that Grover Cleveland Alexander's strikeout of Tony Lazzeri was the very last play of the 1926 World Series, but it works for the dramatic structure of the film. It isn't likely that a sportscaster would make ominous commentary upon Lou Gehrig's pulling himself out of his last Yankees game in *The Pride of the Yankees*, especially in view of the fact that Gehrig frequently played only a few innings before heading for the bench; but the fictional broadcaster's comments are vital so far as precipitating the "shadow of death" sequences which wrap up the screen play. And although the Rockford Peaches, the all-female team dramatized in *A League of Their Own*, was not truly in imminent danger of being disbanded after only a single season in operation, this script-imposed deadline added an extra layer of urgency to the film's climax. (As for *The Babe Ruth Story*'s suggestion that Mel Allen was the NBC sports-

caster on hand when Babe hit a homer for a hospitalized kid—an event that occurred in 1926, when Allen was still in his teens and nowhere near a network booth—this was a mere misdemeanor compared to the other atrocities committed by this sorry excuse for a movie).

In one way the powers that be in baseball have subverted total cinematic accuracy. It's probable that many filmmakers would have given anything to film an honest to goodness major league game in the 1920s, 1930s and 1940s, with a rich variety of camera angles and close-ups at their disposal. But there was a hard and fast rule during that period which prohibited the on-field filming of any game in progress. This left filmmakers no choice but to shoot from a distance, stationed either in the grandstands or at an overhead vantage point in the press box—hardly conducive to maintaining immediacy and excitement in a medium devoted to zeroing in on individual "big moments."

Not content with this, filmmakers of an earlier age had to reenact games in ballparks more amenable to the setting up of camera equipment, and, to keep budgets from bursting at the seams, those ballparks had to be closer to the studios than the majority of big-league stadiums, which were concentrated in the East. This usually would require making a trek to one of two Hollywood (actually Los Angeles) locations. The first was Wrigley Field, built on the corner of Avalon and Forty-Second by Chicago chewing gum magnate William Wrigley, Jr., in 1925 for his Pacific Coast League–affiliated Los Angeles Angels (for many years a farm team for Wrigley's Chicago Cubs). With its 22,000 seating capacity and its major-league dimensions, Wrigley Field was an acceptable stand-in for many a big-city park like Chicago's Wrigley, Forbes Field, Yankee Stadium and so forth. From *Babe Comes Home* (1927) through *Damn Yankees* (1958), whenever a baseball game materialized on film, it was usually originating from L.A.'s Wrigley. (Don't go looking for the park today; it was torn down in 1966 to make room for Gilbert Lindsay Park, a public playground.)

Hollywood's other oft-filmed ballpark was Gilmore Field, a 12,000-seater named for oil millionaire Earl Gilmore and located at Beverly Boulevard and Fairfax Avenue, more recently the site of the Farmers' Market and CBS Television City. Used chiefly as the home turf of the Hollywood Stars, a Pacific Coast League aggregation bankrolled in 1935 by several big movie names (including Walt Disney, Bing Crosby, Gary Cooper, Burns and Allen, William Frawley, Cecil B. DeMille and George Stevens), Gilmore Field was an ideal smaller park for the staging of the minor-league and "bush" games employed to chart the professional progress of the main character in many a baseball biopic filmed in the 1940s and 1950s.

It probably disturbed filmgoers of that period less than it disturbs film historians nowadays that being limited to shooting in Wrigley and Gilmore lessened the credibility of many baseball films. Until the emergence of television in the 1940s and baseball's westward expansion in the 1950s and 1960s, most Americans in nonmetropolitan communities had never seen a genuine major-league game, so they weren't aware that those minor-league Hollywood ballparks didn't really resemble the "big" stadiums all that closely. Nor were film fans of that bygone era preoccupied with spotting such gaffes as the Los Angeles style bungalows and West Coast topography surrounding what were supposed to be the playing fields of New England, or those giant floodlight towers which loomed over the Wrigley outfield making anachronistic appearances in film biographies that were supposed to be taking place in the years before night baseball. And given the fact that virtually all L.A. location shooting had to take place

very early in the morning to avoid traffic noises and large crowds of curious onlookers, filmgoers in years past took it for granted that movie actors who appeared in exterior shots tended to cast inordinately long, spiderlike shadows on the ground—even in baseball movies, where the action was supposed to be transpiring sometime in the middle of the afternoon.

The binding rule against cameras on the playing field during games has been relaxed over the last three or four decades, thanks in great part to the smaller, less cumbersome and (to the players) less distracting photographic equipment that has been developed in that time period. Also, once movies began to drift away from the studios and to indulge in extensive location filming outside California, local chambers of commerce have welcomed the presence of movie people as a publicity-building, tourist-grabbing ploy. And since there were more ballparks at the filmmakers' disposal once new teams began springing up in the 1960s, movie crews could simply pack up and move to a new city if banned from a specific genuine park, a luxury not afforded in the days when there were only a handful of major-league stadiums. Even so, the paucity of big-league cooperation and available locations did not prevent the successful completion of several baseball pictures during Hollywood's so-called Golden Age—even when the accuracy of those films suffered due to restrictions imposed upon them during filming.

Despite the virtual elimination of those old restrictions in recent years, there are still certain basic problems in logistics which make it hard to stage a filmed baseball game with total authenticity. David S. Ward, writer-director of the 1989 hit *Major League*, addressed this matter in a 1994 interview: "Baseball is just so difficult to film! The main problem is the distance between players and between the points of action. The bases are 90 feet apart, and even the pitcher and batter are 60 feet 6 inches apart, so it's sometimes hard to contain them in the same shot without one of them looking like they're—literally—out in left field." Ward compared his *Major League* experience to the relative lack of difficulties he encountered while shooting the 1993 football drama *The Program*. "In football, the players are right next to each other. You can move along the line and in and out of the action. In baseball, you don't have that luxury."

Now, let's return to the "Baseball pictures all have the same plot" conceit.

There's some truth in this. Despite the rundown of different plot devices that were tallied in an earlier paragraph, in general these devices were secondary to the main storylines, which in many cases have tended to cover the same well-worn path in film after film.

The archetypal baseball movie could at one time be encapsulated thusly: A young rube fresh off the farm with a great deal of natural talent but with a shy or goofy demeanor is whisked away to the big city to play Major League baseball, often as not leaving his hometown sweetheart to await his promised return. Once in the city, the rube is (1) mercilessly ribbed by his teammates; (2) seduced (or nearly so) by the pleasures of nightlife and strung along by a mercenary femme fatale; (3) so taken with himself that he alienates everyone around him with his arrogance; and either (4) seriously injured (or else someone close to the hero is seriously injured) or (5) approached by gamblers or mobsters and finagled, pressured, or extorted into fixing a couple of games. Whatever the case, something dreadful compromises the player's talent and integrity and gets him into deep, hot water by the fifth reel.

Even supposing that none of the above occurs, the quintessential baseball flick finale has still remained fairly consistent: the winning play at the bottom of the ninth

in the Big Game. In its generally favorable review of *The Busher*, *Variety* noted that the film veered toward cliché at the climax by offering "the usual 'save the game in the ninth'" routine. And that was in May 1919.

This religious adherence to formula was not something created from whole cloth by the movies. Early filmmakers, ever hungry for story material, turned to the printed page, serving up adaptations, imitations or outright swipes of popular novels and magazine pieces. Most sports stories were written by a relatively tiny group of authors. Among these were Edward Stratemeyer (who, using the pen name of Arthur M. Winfield, created the collegiate Rover Boys and Motor Boys stories), Gilbert Patton (who achieved fame for his Frank Meriwell stories, and who, like Stratemeyer, employed a nom de plume, in this case Burt Standish), Charles E. Van Loan, Gerald Beaumont and, best of all, Ring Lardner. With the notable exception of Lardner, these authors wrote with their juvenile and young adult readers in mind; thus, cynicism or disturbingly original plot twists were not in their repertoire. Their audiences expected, and got, the hero who conquered enormous odds and who won the Big Game when victory seemed beyond his grasp. And since these predictable plotlines "sold," filmmakers followed suit when assembling their own sports stories.

When someone did have the nerve to stand up and suggest a new story slant, that someone was often hooted down by professional baseball itself. This was particularly true in any story involving dishonesty. While Ring Lardner could include a cheating ballplayer as a marginal character in his short story "Hurry Kane" (and its subsequent stage adaptation *Elmer the Great*), it would never do to see a crooked player—or any other baseball "professional"—up there on the screen; otherwise, the filmmaker could kiss goodbye any Major League cooperation of any kind. Thus, the villainous

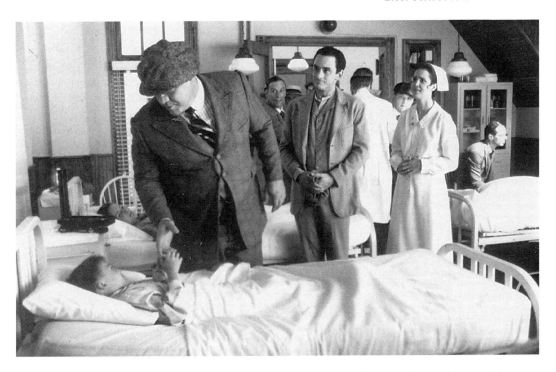

Probably the most famous of all baseball-movie setpieces: Babe Ruth promises to hit a home run for a hospitalized child. This celebrated anecdote has not only been dramatized in three different baseball biopics (this still is from 1992's *The Babe*, with John Goodman as Ruth), but has also been retooled as a key scene in the non-biographical *The Fan* (1996), and mercilessly lampooned on such television sketch-comedy series as *Saturday Night Live* and *SCTV*.

baseball scout in *Casey at the Bat* (1927) is a phony scout, the culprit in the 1934 murder mystery *Death on the Diamond* was a man denied a big-league coaching job, and the 1929 and 1933 film versions of *Elmer the Great* centralized all dishonest activity solely within the machinations of non-ball-playing gamblers. As for the 1919 "Black Sox" scandal, dramatizations of this incident were effectively blocked for nearly six decades by the higher-ups in pro baseball, notably commissioner Ford Frick, who ordered that a 1959 TV re-creation of the event be scuttled because it wasn't in the best interest of the game.

So it was that most baseball films played it safe. And it's quite correct to observe that, regarded as a group, baseball films do tend to look and sound alike. But if you recall, we've already observed that

these films were not released as a group; with rare exceptions (the years 1927–28, 1949–50, 1988–89, and 1993–1994, for example), baseball movies were doled out approximately one per year. On this basis, the clichés and traditions of baseball stories have been spaced far enough apart to make them easier to digest—at least until cable television enabled the casual viewer to experience a century of filmmaking within the space of a few months.

Now we come back to the principal case against baseball films: "They never make any money." We've previously listed the exceptions to this rule. But we must also note that such pictures as *They Learned About Women* (1930), *The Babe Ruth Story* (1948), *Big Leaguer* (1953), *The Great American Pastime* (1956), *Bang the Drum Slowly* (1974), *The Bingo Long Travelling All-Stars and Motor Kings* (1976), *The Slugger's Wife* (1985), *Pastime* (1991) and *Cobb* (1994) have all played to less than capacity crowds. The fact that some of these were mediocre movies, and that at least three of them were given virtually no prerelease publicity at all, was not taken into consideration when assessing their anemic box office performance. They were baseball films; they lost money; therefore, logic dictates that baseball films lose money.

Film producers who've proffered this argument can't always be taken at face value. Frequently, when a studio mogul would prophesy that no one would sit still for a baseball film, he meant that *he* wouldn't sit still for that film. While most film moguls in the first half of the century acknowledged the popularity of baseball, many of them couldn't really fathom why it was so popular. After all, most of these producers were European immigrants who'd spent the better part of their lives working long, backbreaking hours at a series of menial jobs before hitting it big in Hollywood; and after attaining studio ownership, they devoted virtually all their time and energy to running their little fiefdoms. The sports of preference to these men were games in which they themselves could excel and dominate, as they did at their studios, sports such as golf or polo. These pioneer film titans were not well versed in American traditions, nor were they by nature sideline spectators, so baseball was never a priority issue.

But if studio executives only filmed what they immediately understood, 90 percent of all movies would never have been made. Thus, that knee-jerk verbal rejection of proposed baseball pictures often served a purpose other than shutting up a minion. "It'll never make a dime" was as much a challenge as a reaction. These producers could sense that if a director or writer was willing to put his job on the line and defy the boss' veto, then that person wasn't going to do a halfhearted job on a pet pro-

ject. It's true that Sam Goldwyn was initially resistant to *The Pride of the Yankees*, and was convinced of its potential only after his story editor Niven Busch talked Goldwyn into screening a newsreel of Lou Gehrig's farewell speech. But note that Busch was able to talk Goldwyn into that screening. Had the producer been as ignorant or stubborn as some Hollywood historians have made him out to be, he would have kicked Busch out of his office at the beginning. Sam Goldwyn was willing to be convinced—you just had to be equally willing to state your case without allowing yourself to be cowed by his gruffness before Goldwyn would respect your judgment.

Once a baseball project was "sold," the creator was not only faced with the aforementioned physical and subject matter limitations imposed by professional baseball, but was required to include as many of the popular elements as possible to attract filmgoers not particularly fond of baseball. In the more archaic 1920s, 1930s and 1940s, "popular elements" referred to those qualities which would entice women moviegoers who—as all males told themselves back then—just hated baseball. To draw the ladies (and, presumably, their male escorts) into the theater, it was decreed that a baseball picture had to have a love story subplot. Well and good, except that America's most fervent baseball fans, the kids, would automatically be put off by the mushy stuff. Thus, each new baseball film became a juggling act, trying to please everyone and offend no one. This is a hard enough stunt to pull off in an average film which already contains all the so-called popular elements; it's a stunt requiring superhuman strength when dealing with as narrow a subject as baseball.

We can, therefore, regard the argument that baseball films were automatic money losers as an argument composed of equal parts truth and caution. A baseball film can be successful—but a lot of extra work has to go into that film to make it successful. Too often, "extra work" is a phrase that has nullified a project when it was perceived that there wasn't enough time or interest to expend the additional effort: "We've got fifty-two pictures to get on the docket this year. You're asking me to write (or direct or produce) a picture where we've gotta spend six weeks training a bunch of actors to throw a ball around, and also try to wedge in a romance between innings? Forget it. Let's do a western."

And often, baseball alone just isn't enough. As the song says, you've gotta have a gimmick. To further explore that point, it might be useful to take a chronological journey through the world of baseball films.

The earliest silent baseball movies (described in fuller detail in the chapter on short subjects) simply recorded the game, since the sheer novelty of moving images was enough to draw a crowd at the turn of the century. Thus gimmickry was not needed in the first filmed representations of major-league ball games. Motion pictures were the gimmick.

The dawn of American cinema history occurred not in Hollywood but in the laboratories of the East—in New Jersey, New York and Philadelphia. Gradually filmmaking moved as far west as Chicago, but no one got the bright idea of exploiting the year-round good weather of California until 1907. Being located in the proximity of the existing major-league teams of the era, the first filmmakers had full access to the leading baseball stars—the sort of stellar players to whom the later Hollywood-based filmmakers would have to pay great sums of money in order to get them to head west during the off-season to make faces in front of the camera. And since everyone regarded movies as a passing fad with no staying power, legends like Christy Mathewson and Home Run Baker could make low-cost, vanity serving appearances without having to clear permission from their teams or their

press agents, all of whom would later want a piece of the action when the movies became a big-bucks industry.

Those baseball greats who appeared in one-reelers of the pre–1910 era didn't need to do anything more than show up. They weren't expected to emote in a story because there wasn't any story. They weren't expected to play spectacularly since they were coasting on the thrilling prospect of appearing in front of a camera for the benefit of people who'd probably never see them in the flesh. Once more, the gimmick was in being there.

As filmgoers tired of just seeing people move about on a big screen, filmmakers strove to maintain interest in the infant medium by strengthening story values, adding trick photographic effects and the like. Comedies were the most popular subjects in the years 1904–10, so most baseball pictures (and most other pictures) strove for laughs. And when melodramas began to take hold around 1908, baseball films went along for the ride. Baseball started becoming secondary to story genres. Stories with baseball as an ingredient were interchangeable with stories about farmers, gypsies, newlyweds and cowboys. Baseball films happened to be made because films of all kinds were being made by the hundreds; but baseball was now icing on the cake, rather than a film's sole reason for being. And after 1911 producers like Thomas Ince, and directors like D. W. Griffith and Mack Sennett, began imposing their personal stamps on their films, rendering the storyline less important than how the story was told. The gimmick now was showmanship. If a group of subjects from a particular company resulted in more positive audience response than the product of another company, this was the selling point—not the stories themselves.

The rise of the feature film and the star system happened almost simultaneously about 1915. If audiences would accept their favorite star in a particular type of film, the star would oblige. Actor-director Hobart Bosworth was known for his rugged action films; thus it was natural that he'd get around to baseball sooner or later, which he did in 1915 with *Little Sunset*, the first feature length dramatic baseball film. And since melodramatic gesticulations were expected of Bosworth, *Little Sunset* was as heavy on the dramatics and pathos as it was on ballpark activity.

The Bosworth film set the standard for subsequent baseball features in the years before 1920: using the game as window dressing for a star's established screen personality. Charles Ray's two baseball films, *The Pinch Hitter* (1917) and *The Busher* (1919), were tailored to the two most successful variations of this very popular star's film persona; Ray was a gangling country boy who allowed people to walk all over him until time came to call upon his inner reserves in *The Pinch Hitter*, while in *The Busher* Charlie was a braggart who had to be taken down a peg or two before achieving victory both on the field and over his own bad judgment. Charles Ray used, reused, and re-reused the character traits seen in *The Pinch Hitter* and *The Busher* in virtually all of his films; like any other plot device, the baseball angle took a back seat to what Ray's audience expected of him.

DeWolf Hopper was another case entirely. A celebrated Broadway musical comedy star, Hopper was brought to films as part of an industry-wide effort to add culture and class to a still unrespectable medium. The theater was more legitimate than the movies, so a bona fide stage star could elevate a mere film to a higher artistic plane. Since DeWolf Hopper's most famous stage turn was his recital of "Casey at the Bat," it seemed quite natural in 1916 to star him in a photographic representation of that comic ballad. The fact that Hopper looked like a sack of wet laundry in a baseball uniform and played with the dexterity

of a pregnant octopus didn't matter. Here was New York star DeWolf Hopper, condescending to appear in a humble movie titled *Casey at the Bat*. Bow, you infidels, bow!

The two Charlie Ray baseball films were successes, but the DeWolf Hopper film was a dog. The message was evidently loud and clear: baseball movies would make money only if featuring a top film favorite, which Ray was and which Hopper was not. Already Hollywood was holding baseball itself responsible for the failure of a film, rather than the quality of the film itself. The same thing happened when *One Touch of Nature* (1917) neglected to turn a profit. It couldn't have been the second-rate performances or the hackneyed storyline. Baseball had to be to blame. It was more convenient to claim that the film died because of its subject matter instead of its inherent awfulness. To admit that a film could be bad on its own was to cast aspersions on the efficiency of the whole Hollywood system of moviemaking. Thus baseball movies had another gimmick imposed upon them—this time the requirement of a major name in the credits before a project would get off the ground.

The major name mindset was established in another manner by New York Giants player "Turkey Mike" Donlin, who in 1915 took it upon himself to become the first baseball star to headline a feature film. *Right Off the Bat* was several lengths removed from a classic, but it got bookings, proving that a baseball film would click if it incorporated the gimmick of featuring a real live ballplayer in the lead. That's how we wound up in 1916 with *Somewhere in Georgia*, starring Ty Cobb of the Detroit Tigers, and *Headin' Home* (1920), starring that most prolific of ballplayer-actors, Babe Ruth. All three films did business, but they made it harder and harder to produce a simple, unadorned baseball picture. Once a subject becomes synonymous with gimmickry, it will seldom be filmed without that gimmickry.

On to the 1920s, when we had westerns

with ballgames (*Hit and Run, Out of the West*), domestic dramas with ballgames (*Life's Greatest Game*), police stories with ballgames (*Trifling with Honor, Catch-as-Catch-Can*), real estate boom satires with ballgames (*The New Klondike*) and slapstick farces with ballgames (*The Battling Orioles*)—but baseball movies pure and simple were hard to come by. All of this changed, ever so briefly, in 1926. This was the year that Babe Ruth, after enduring an illness which proved disastrous to his own game and nearly fatal to the fortunes of the New York Yankees, made one of the most remarkable comebacks in baseball history, returning to top form and guiding his team into the World Series. The Yanks lost that series, but this didn't alter the fact that baseball was suddenly on the lips and in the consciousness of practically every sports fan in America— thanks not only to the ceaseless publicity flackery in the newspapers, but also to those newfangled radio machines which brought big-league games to people who never dreamed they'd be allowed to share such an experience.

In the wake of Ruth's comeback, Hollywood responded with no fewer than four big-budget baseball pictures in 1927. First National brought forth *Babe Comes Home*, starring Guess Who taking full advantage of the afterglow of his World Series performance. Warner Bros.' *The Bush Leaguer* was the story of a bespectacled intellectual (Monte Blue) who happens to be a dynamite ballplayer. Wallace Beery starred in a rollicking, diligently nonartistic new version of *Casey at the Bat* for Paramount. And William Haines led the pack with the most profitable baseball epic of the year, MGM's *Slide, Kelly, Slide*. Though each of these films gave their stories substance with a gimmick or two (the female team owner in *Bush Leaguer*, the period setting of *Casey at the Bat*, etc.), this 1927 quartet came as near as possible to a cycle of films wherein baseball appeared for its own sake.

The cycle didn't last and, given the transitory nature of fads in the fad-conscious 1920s, it probably would have withered even without the 1928 appearance of Paramount's *Warming Up*, a film conspicuously lacking in credible baseball scenes or anything else of much worth. There was hope for a new spate of ballpark movies after the positive financial reaction to *Fast Company* (1929), though it became clear within a few months that people attended this first film version of the Ring Lardner and George M. Cohan play *Elmer the Great* due to the novelty of its being "all talkie" (another gimmick!) rather than out of any deep affection for baseball. The poor showings of *They Learned About Women* and *Hot Curves* (both in 1930), released after the bloom was off the rose for talking pictures, confirmed this suspicion.

The best thing to happen to baseball pictures in the 1930s was comedian Joe E. Brown, whose status as a premiere moneymaker for Warner Bros. resulted in his getting several contract perks. Brown did not ask for full script approval, opportunities to direct, or a dressing room the size of the Beverly Hills Hotel. All he demanded was that Warner's organize a baseball team composed of topnotch athletes, with Brown himself as captain. The studio would have been foolish not to capitalize on this well-publicized aspect of Brown's popularity, so Joe E. set a Hollywood record by starring in three high-grossing baseball pictures during his hitch at the studio. And there was a bonus: while most actors couldn't play ball, and practically all ballplayers couldn't act, Joe E. Brown was expert in both fields of endeavor. Thus, Warners didn't have to make up excuses to keep Joe away from either diamond activity or tricky plot convolutions.

The Joe E. Brown baseball trilogy, consisting of *Fireman, Save My Child* (1932), *Elmer the Great* (1933) and *Alibi Ike* (1935), may have contained a shade of gimmickry in terms of novel and unusual stagings for the climactic Big Game sequences, but they were as close to being pure baseball pictures as Hollywood would ever get. *Alibi Ike*, the best and most lucrative of the three, had the added lagniappe of being released just after the arrival on the scene of pitcher Dizzy Dean, possibly the most talked about baseball personality since Ruth. With baseball on the brain, the average audience member was preconditioned to enjoy *Alibi Ike* with more abandon than might otherwise have been the case.

Other studios, lacking a double threat man like Warner Bros.' Joe E. Brown, tended to ignore baseball in the 1930s. When it was used at all, baseball was either gimmicked up with a murder mystery (*Death on the Diamond, Girls Can Play*) or became the gimmick itself to breathe new life into an old-fashioned tearjerker (*Swell Head*).

The game seemed to be on the verge of a cinematic renaissance with the 1942 release of *The Pride of the Yankees*. This most successful baseball film to date was the harbinger of two new trends in the genre: it was the first of the baseball biopics (earlier films starring the likes of Ty Cobb and Babe Ruth could hardly qualify as biographical), and it was the first film to use baseball to promote a philosophy outside the confines of baseball. In the case of *The Pride of the Yankees*, that philosophy was "courage in the face of death and adversity"—a very timely concept in that first year of World War II. The fact that *The Pride of the Yankees* was a box office bonanza, and the two other baseball films of the 1942–43 period, the rather pleasant *It Happened in Flatbush* and the execrable *Ladies' Day*, didn't exactly set any records, bolstered the Hollywood theory that a ballpark picture had to be dressed up with a "deeper meaning"—a New York film critic's term that can be roughly translated to "gimmick."

The wartime manpower shortage precluded the production of big-budget, male

dominated baseball films—and besides, most viewers would have wondered why those fine physical specimens weren't off the fields and in military uniforms. In real life, baseball was in the doldrums (again the victim of depletion in the civilian ranks), a period aptly summed up in the title of a book by William Mead: *The Ten Worst Years in Baseball*. Life became zestful again with the 1945–46 return of several star players from the war, and the game bounced back to public favor in 1947 with the best World Series since 1941. Also in 1947, the good news was that Babe Ruth was busy with his long awaited autobiography. The bad news was that Babe was dying of cancer, prompting Allied Artists to slap together a Ruth biopic as quickly as possible to get it in theaters before Babe expired—and since one of the writers was Ruth's principal "mythmaker," Grantland Rice, why bother with the facts? *The Babe Ruth Story* (1948) was so deplorable a piece of film "craft" and such an unremitting bombardment of lies that it almost single-handedly destroyed all hope for any future baseball movies.

Fortunately, salvation was around the corner in the form of James Stewart, whose portrayal in *The Stratton Story* was a thoroughly credible and entertaining hit for MGM in 1949. That same year, 20th Century–Fox scored with a comedy, *It Happens Every Spring*, which constituted the first film to combine baseball and fantasy, or at the very least whimsy (Ray Milland invents a wood-resistant formula which he rubs on a baseball and uses to pitch St. Louis toward a pennant).

Now the Hollywood higher-ups figured they had it right. Baseball films worked only if they were biographies in which the protagonist had to face a handicap of some sort (Monty Stratton had his amputated leg, and Lou Gehrig his fatal neurological disease) or if baseball was utilized as the foundation of a fantastic, unbelievable comic story. Subsequent baseball movies of the late 1940s to late 1950s were fairly evenly divided into the "against all odds" biography category or the "fantasy/improbability" genre. In the former camp, we had the hero's battle against race prejudice in *The Jackie Robinson Story*, Grover Cleveland Alexander's bout with epilepsy and alcohol in *The Winning Team*, Dizzy Dean's comeback as a broadcaster after being sidelined by an injury in *The Pride of St. Louis*, and Jimmy Piersall's struggle with mental illness in *Fear Strikes Out*. In the latter camp we had a cat inheriting a ball club in *Rhubarb*, the titular spirits in *Angels in the Outfield*, the kid with the "magic" pitching arm in *Roogie's Bump*, the devil himself manipulating a World Series outcome in *Damn Yankees*, and, stretching a point, *Take Me Out to the Ballgame*, which can pass as fantasy since people in the real world don't regularly burst into song with full orchestral backup.

Once more, the box office receipts of the 1950s legitimized Hollywood's theories on baseball films. Movies designed to exploit baseball without a surfeit of deeper meanings or extra shtick—*The Kid from Cleveland, Big Leaguer,* or *The Great American Pastime*—made no impression at all financially. Again, to suggest that these pictures would have done better if they'd been better was not a sufficient argument. Including baseball wasn't enough of a surefire method to pep up an otherwise mediocre film: ergo, baseball films were box office poison.

The 1960s brought baseball to cities that never had major-league activity before. Television, already installed as the principal method through which America was inundated with the game, dropped the exclusivity rules of the 1950s which dictated that major-league cities could not receive network telecasts of any teams other than their own. So it was that in addition to having new ballparks and fresh new teams, America in the 1960s had greater access to free baseball activity. The consequence of this upsurge in home entertainment was a downsurge in baseball movies. From 1960 through 1972 there was precisely one theatrical baseball film—and that film, a 1962 vehicle for Mickey Mantle and Roger Maris titled *Safe at Home!*, wouldn't have existed had not the whole of America witnessed Maris's sixty-first home run on network television, either live or on videotaped recaps.

The 1969 release and unexpected success of *Easy Rider* suddenly forced the major studios to give special consideration to smaller, personal statement films. This atmosphere made it feasible for Paramount in 1974 to release *Bang the Drum Slowly*, a low-budget film light on star names, which used the framework of baseball to illustrate the undying power of friendship, and which was an extension of the screenwriter's perspective of the world rather than Paramount's. *Bang the Drum Slowly* had been around in book form since 1956, but it didn't fit the blockbuster mentality of Hollywood in the 1950s and 1960s, nor did it have the popular elements of a happy ending and a romantic subtheme. A different Hollywood made possible a different sort of baseball picture.

The socially conscious 1970s tended to employ baseball as a forum for the various personal agenda of the filmmakers. *The Bingo Long Travelling All-Stars and Motor Kings* came about mainly because producer Rob Cohen wanted to make a statement about black survival in a white dominated society—though its message was softened by its reliance upon slapstick. *The Bad News Bears* was on the surface a "gonzo" comedy about junior-league baseball, but was actually a continuation of director Michael Ritchie's satiric overview of the phony, self-serving qualities indigenous to self-styled liberals and affluent suburbanites. About the only baseball project to confess flat out that most people came to movies strictly for entertainment was the R-rated *Squeeze Play* (1979), not by any means a good film, but

How to promote a baseball film without actually mentioning anything about baseball.

not a self-congratulatory "message picture" either.

The market for baseball biopics diminished in the 1970s, only to be given a shot in the arm by the burgeoning made-for-TV movie market. While many theatri-

cal film concerns wouldn't consider bankrolling such chancy projects as *It's Good to Be Alive* (the story of Roy Campanella's life as a paraplegic), *A Love Affair: The Eleanor and Lou Gehrig Story* ("It's been done already!"), and *One in a Million: The Ron LeFlore Story*, the TV movie industry needed a product several times per week. It also helped if these projects were politically correct in the manner of *A Love Affair*, which characterized Eleanor Gehrig as a feminist long before anyone had ever used that word; or *Don't Look Back: The Story of Leroy "Satchel" Paige*, which took Paige's admittedly mercenary practice of hopping from team to team in the Negro Baseball leagues and redefined that practice as Paige's personal protest against white supremacy.

The first half of the 1980s saw the baseball film as a conduit for ego-tripping. *The Natural* (1984) was by and large worthwhile, but still came across as a vanity production for Robert Redford. *The Slugger's Wife* exuded showbiz arrogance from every orifice: Neil Simon is a great writer, Hal Ashby is a great director, Ray Stark is a great producer, so how dare you intimate that *The Slugger's Wife* isn't a great film? *The Natural* was good but occasionally ponderous, *The Slugger's Wife* was continually worthless, and the audience was by and large indifferent to both projects (though *Natural* did post a modest profit). Pure ego as a gimmick failed as an added ingredient to baseball pictures in the 1980s.

The filmgoer of this decade was more inclined to pull for an underdog story than root for a slick, affluent Robert Redford or Neil Simon package. The average 1980s film fan was a baby boomer who grew up in the 1950s and 1960s with promises of a better, brighter future than had greeted the previous generation. When this better, brighter future didn't materialize, many boomers felt cheated and betrayed, and commenced to cast themselves in the roles of the downtrodden and put-upon generation. Even those who'd successfully climbed the corporate ladder felt that they could have moved farther in life had they not been held down by those all-knowing "suits" higher up that ladder. This was the audience ripe for the "misfit makes good" pictures which proliferated in the middle to late 1980s. This was the audience that responded so positively to *Major League*, in which the poor, tired, huddled masses hired to turn the Cleveland Indians into a "joke team" runs rings around the millionaire owner exploiting them for her own nefarious purposes. And this was the audience that made a cult classic of the cable TV baseball movie *Long Gone*, in which another band of surefire losers revs itself up to ultimately throw victory in the faces of those rich and powerful ogres who don't want them to succeed.

Yes, these films were gimmicky in their unabashed manipulation of audience emotions. But they were also radically different from many of their earlier counterparts. *Major League* and the made-for-TV *Long Gone* were Baseball Movies, not psychological dramas, fantasies, disease of the week affairs, or political broadsides which treated baseball as an adjunct or afterthought. At long last, Hollywood wasn't afraid of filming the game on its own merits.

Why? Several reasons for the recent increase in pure baseball movies have been proposed by various observers. It's been noted that the new men in charge of Hollywood are mostly American bred, born in the mid–20th century, who are more likely to have grown up following baseball than their 19th-century-born immigrant predecessors. There's even a theory floating about that the latter-day onslaught of baseball films is due to corporate takeovers of Hollywood studios by Japanese businessmen, who have imposed Japan's near-obsessive fascination with baseball on their own movie-project proposals.

This "teaser" campaign for Universal's *The Bingo Long Travelling All-Stars and Motor Kings* (1976) also sidesteps the fact that the film is about *black* ballplayers.

The best reasons I can come up with are that (1) the newer, more flexible photographic equipment made it possible to get up close and personal with a game that in the past could only be viewed from a safe distance, and (2) there has recently emerged a whole flock of star actors—the Charlie Sheens, the Mark Harmons, the Kevin Costners—who can actually play baseball, or are at least quickwitted and athletic enough to rapidly absorb the game with the aid of big-league technical advisers. This new breed prides itself on never relying upon stunt doubles unless forced to do so by the insurance companies, and even then finding a way to sneak in its own ballplaying on-screen.

And there's something else, a gimmick new to movies that has characterized such late 1980s films as *Bull Durham, Eight Men Out* and *Field of Dreams.* Hollywood has discovered that baseball can function as a metaphor for life itself; and in its typical "day late, dollar short" fashion, Hollywood has unearthed this metaphorical quality several decades after it was first realized by American poets and novelists. In his 1989 *Films in Review* critique of *Field of Dreams,* Kenneth M. Chanko has noted, "As rich a history as it is, baseball lends itself to symbolism and myth like no other sport. Using baseball to somehow define ourselves and our country is an undeniable lure; many of America's best 20th century writers at one time or another wrote about baseball—not football, basketball or hockey."

Earlier filmmakers had sometimes caught on to this, notably director George Stevens, who in his 1942 *Woman of the Year* used a baseball game to put man-of-the-people sportswriter Spencer Tracy and nose-in-the-air foreign affairs correspondent Katharine Hepburn on the same democratic level. But until the 1980s no pure baseball film had really used the game metaphorically.

Kenneth M. Chanko's *Field of Dreams* review continues with the observation that both this film and *The Natural* ended with the image of father and son playing catch: "the archetypical across-the-generations connection." This hands-across-the-years notion was developed further in Terence

Mann's curtain speech in *Field of Dreams,* where he proclaims with fervor that the one clean, pure constant in an ever deteriorating world has always been baseball. Governments have toppled, wars have been lost, economies shattered, but baseball endures and shines bright.

In his essay in the summer 1990 edition of *Journal of Popular Film and Television,* Frank Ardolino suggests that *Field of Dreams* "equates belief in baseball with religious conviction; belief in the innocent values of baseball will produce regeneration and purification." Annie Savoy, the superliterate baseball groupie in *Bull Durham,* and a character who cannot by any stretch of the imagination be labeled "innocent," reaffirms Ardolino's thesis by insisting that "the only church that truly feeds the soul is the Church of Baseball."

In an era where it was increasingly difficult to find anything to believe in or latch onto, filmgoers embraced the sentiments of returning to basics proposed by *Bull Durham* and *Field of Dreams.* There are those who find this retrogressive, linking this fond glance backward at past values to the Reagan era, wherein civil and personal rights were often made secondary to a restoration of the status quo of the past—when the country was not so much all pure as all white, and when things were less complex because people were willing to let the government tell them that things were less complex.

Some observers have preferred the bleaker implications of *Eight Men Out* which, like *Field of Dreams,* places the game in the context of a so-called simpler time, but which finds not sinless innocence but corruption and betrayal at the hands of those older, wiser, and wealthier than the little ballplayer or littler fan. Frank Ardolino characterizes *Bull Durham* and *Eight Men Out* as seeking out the same goal but arriving at diametrically opposite destinations; *Bull Durham* traces a move from innocence into experience as something good for the game of baseball and those who play the game, while in *Eight Men Out* the journey from innocence to experience spoils the purity of baseball and shatters the illusions of its disciples.

The public, which is the Court of Last Resort in such matters, responded by turning out in droves to see *Bull Durham* and *Field of Dreams* and virtually disregarding the existence of *Eight Men Out*. Give the moviegoing public baseball as a metaphor for life, and it seems that the metaphor of preference is an idealized good life over an unvarnished bad life.

As the 1980s segued into the 1990s, baseball was finally deemed "box office"— a fact affirmed in a loud, clear voice when 1992's *A League of Their Own* surpassed all expectations by becoming the most financially successful baseball picture of all time (a record still unchallenged ten years after its release). The popularity of this film has been attributed to a number of factors: a larger number of movie fans of both sexes who were willing to accept the depiction of strong, positive female characters triumphing over adversity on their own terms; an impressively crafted screenplay which, to paraphrase *Bull Durham*'s Crash Davis, knew how to "use the clichés," but used them so adroitly that audiences are blissfully unaware that they *are* clichés; or simply the downright likeability of stars Geena Davis and Tom Hanks.

In the long run, it didn't matter how or why the film succeeded; it was enough that it *did* succeed, thereby spawning a fresh and prolific new cycle of baseball films, both theatrical and made-for-TV.

Overall, the most satisfying aspect of this new crop was the ever-increasing amount of ballpark authenticity. It was not so long ago that a film in which the leading actors actually knew how to play the game, and in which the game scenes themselves were staged with more than a passing nod to re-

ality, was the exception rather than the rule. After 1992, it was rare indeed to see a film in which the key baseball sequences were *not* totally believable in concept and execution—so much so that audiences came to take this believability for granted, just as they learned to accept the sight of living, snarling dinosaurs in *Jurassic Park* and airborne martial-arts combatants in *Crouching Tiger, Hidden Dragon* without giving the matter a second thought. In a 2001 *Sports Illustrated* interview, *Bull Durham* director Ron Shelton said it best: "The old films didn't have to get it right because, for the most part, nobody had ever been to a game or watched one on TV. Television made film directors get better. You now have a very sophisticated audience watching sports films. They're used to seeing action sequences from nine different angles. Making a sports film these days is like taking a string quartet to Vienna."

More baseball movies were produced in the ten years following *League of Their Own* than in any other comparable period; indeed, of *all* the feature-length ballpark films produced since movies began, approximately 25 percent came out between 1992 and 2002. With so much material on hand within this rather limited genre, we are able to divide the results into a number of subgenres, if only to get a handle on what sort of cinematic trends were considered saleable during this crowded decade:

Baseball biographies. *The Babe* (1992), trumpeted by its producers as the first authentic, no-holds-barred filmed biography of Babe Ruth, admittedly did go farther than any previous film in delivering the unvarnished truth about the Sultan of Swat (showing him to be neither total hero nor thorough heavy, but instead a paradoxical combination of both), with John Goodman delivering an almost intimidatingly on-target portrayal of the title character. Even so, the screenwriters, knowing

By 1993, baseball was a saleable enough movie angle to be promoted without any of that *Bingo Long* obfuscation; there can be no doubt as to the subject matter of 1993's *Rookie of the Year*.

what audiences weaned on past baseball biopics expected, served up several of the old familiar setpieces, including the sick kid to whom Babe promises a home run, and the controversial "called shot" of 1932. And despite its much-touted historical accuracy, *The Babe* minted several brand-new misconceptions and anachronisms, among them the curious notion that newsreels came fully equipped with soundtracks and narrators in the early 1920s.

The relative box-office failure of *The Babe* was attributed in many quarters to its biting off more than it could chew—trying to crowd the events of an entire lifetime into 113 minutes of screen time. Significantly, subsequent baseball biographies (all made for television) concentrated solely on a single, life-altering event: the postwar jockeying among Satchel Paige, Jackie Robinson and Josh Gibson to be the first black player in Major League baseball in *Soul of the Game* (1996), the resurrection of the New York Yankees during the 1996 season in *Joe Torre: Curveballs Along the Way* (1997), and the 1961 race between Mickey Mantle and Roger Maris to break Babe Ruth's home-run record in *61** (2001). Even more minimalist was the theatrical feature *Cobb* (1994), which, though based upon Al Stump's all-inclusive biography of Ty Cobb, offered only the briefest snatches of Cobb's actual baseball career, choosing to focus almost exclusively on Ty's tempestuous final two years on earth. (*Cobb* also demonstrated the pitfalls of iconoclasm; in accurately portraying its subject as the nastiest son of a bitch who ever drew breath, the film scared off viewers in droves).

Comedies and Fantasies. Beyond the inevitable sequels to the surprise hit *Major League* and the Albert Brooks-ing of a noncomic Roger Angell magazine article in *The Scout* (1994), the 1992 through 2001 period produced a remarkably high number of lighthearted baseball comedies told from a child's point of view, reflecting the fact that kids aged 12 to 18 constituted a healthy percentage of the moviegoing and TV-watching public. The 1993 theatrical release *The Sandlot*, the made-for-TV *Man from Left Field* (1993), the direct-to-video *Perfect Game* (2000) and other films made a laudable effort to capture the thrills and nuances of the game as seen through younger eyes. A goodly portion of these youth-oriented films harked back to the "fantasy/whimsy" cycle of the 1940s and 1950s: 1993's *Rookie of the Year* (a kid becomes a pro ballplayer) and 1994's *Little Big League* (a kid inherits a baseball club); the 1994 remake of *Angels in the Outfield* and its TV-movie spinoff *Angels in the Infield* (2000); 1995's *The Last Home Run* (a senior citizen is transformed into a ballplaying youngster); and 1996's *Prisoner of Zenda Inc.* (the old Anthony Hope swashbuckler revamped into contemporary Little League terms).

Baseball as a Metaphor for Life. Examples include 1993's *Cooperstown*, in which a truculent old ballplayer embarks upon a pilgrimage to the titular Hall of Fame town, learning a lot about life—especially his own—en route; 1995's *Past the Bleachers*, wherein a thirtyish businessman, grieving over the loss of his son, shakes off self-pity and finds fulfillment by coaching a team of junior-league misfits; Kevin Costner's third baseball film, *For Love of the Game* (1999), the story of a veteran ballplayer whose dogged determination to pitch a perfect game on the eve of his retirement coincides with his efforts to reassemble the pieces of his shattered personal life; and 2001's *Hardball*, starring Keanu Reeves as a disillusioned, burned-out gambler whose life takes on new meaning when he is pressed into service to coach a team of youngsters in a grim South Chicago housing project.

Star vehicles. The aforementioned *Man from Left Field*, *The Scout*, and *For Love of the Game* were all brought into being essentially to showcase the talents of their leading men (respectively, Burt Reynolds,

Albert Brooks and Kevin Costner)—frequently at the expense of everything, and everyone, else.

Baseball Outside the American Mainstream. The year 1992 offered two films within this subgenre: the long-delayed *Mr. Baseball*, with Tom Selleck as an over-the-hill Major Leaguer who finds the proverbial New Lease on Life when he is signed by a top Japanese baseball club; and the made-for-TV *Comrades of Summer*, with Joe Mantegna, likewise playing a ballplayer at the end of his Major League tenure, thrust into greatness of sorts when he becomes the manager of the first Olympic baseball team from the former Soviet Union.

Quirky Independent Projects. Entries in this category included the aforementioned *Last Home Run* and *Prisoner of Zenda Inc.*; the made-for-cable drama *Finding Buck McHenry* (1999), all about a septuagenarian janitor who may or may not be a long-lost champion of the old Negro Leagues; and the obscure 1997 oddity *The Marksmen* (reissued in 2000 as *Sliding Home*), the tale of a disgraced New York Yankee who reinvigorates himself as a softball-team coach in his Wisconsin home town.

The embarrassment of riches in the last decade of the 20th century and first year of the 21st expectedly yielded its share of disappointments (*The Scout, For Love of the Game*), but only a handful of out-and-out stinkers, the most pungent of which were the "chimpanzee in pinstripes" fiasco *Ed* and the "psycho in the stands" extravaganza *The Fan* (both unleashed in 1996). With no fewer than five baseball films in 1994 alone, we might have had even more to choose from had not the bitter Major League strike of that same year—which succeeded in canceling the World Series for the first time since World War II—caused consumers to lose most of their interest in anything even peripherally connected with a ball or a bat. Fortunately, the market for All Things Baseball began to rebound a couple of years later, then took a huge leap forward with the Mark McGwire–Sammy Sosa race to beat Maris' 61-homer record in 1998. As the millennium came and went, it was a sure bet that there would be many, many more baseball films to come.

Would these future films follow the past trends of fantasy and gimmickry? Would they, like 2001's *Summer Catch*, consign baseball to the back seat while promoting a love story or a subplot off the field? Would they grind their own ideological axes at the expense of baseball? Or would they merely "play the game"? Whatever may come to pass, baseball pictures will continue to be made, sometimes in clusters, sometimes one by one, year by year.

And there's no real point in further analyzing the results. Too many words have been written, here and elsewhere, pontificating on the appeal of baseball and its previously skimpy, recently overabundant treatment by Hollywood. But remember that films are essentially entertainment, and so is baseball, so have fun and send intellectualization back to the showers. Actor Stephen Lang, star of the 1991 TV movie *Babe Ruth*, has summed things up in words that could apply equally to baseball and the film business: "It's been intellectualized, poetized, computerized, idealized, but it's just a game, yet something to care about on a day-to-day basis, small headaches and some victories leading up to bigger ones."

Baseball Movies

The films listed in this section represent all feature length, English-language baseball movies released in the United States from January 1915 (the year of the first such feature, *Little Sunset*) through December 31, 2001. Movies made for television are covered in the regular alphabetical listings, rather than in a separate section. The distinction between theatrical and made-for-TV features has in recent years been all but obliterated by the direct-to-video movie market, and by the tendency to ignore any differences between the two genres in the home-video and DVD industry.

One TV effort you won't find here is Disney's *Moochie of the Little League* (1959), directed by William Beaudine and spotlighting Kevin "Moochie" Corcoran as a preteen ballplayer who bamboozles a crusty English gent (Reginald Owen) into organizing a kid's team. A recent reacquaintance with this effort confirms my memory of its being an above-average endeavor, with an offbeat climax wherein Moochie blows the Big Game by running the wrong way around the bases. *Moochie of the Little League* might have been included had it not been for the fact that it really isn't a feature film. It was first telecast as a two-parter on *Walt Disney Presents* in 1959, and thereafter reedited for release as a feature film in Europe. Most subsequent American showings have been in short, serialized vignettes on Disney's various syndicated editions of the *Mickey Mouse Club*. Had I included this production, I would have been compelled to list such non–feature length TV projects as Shelley Duvall's cable TV production of *Casey at the Bat*, and the 1962 one-hour-long drama *Flashing Spikes*, directed by John Ford—projects of definite merit, but essentially outside the realm of this book.

At the risk of breaking this self-imposed rule, I have included one 10-part serial, *Play Ball* (1925). That's because the film ostensibly *could* have been exhibited as a feature, though at 200 minutes it certainly would have been an assault on the kidneys.

One final note: For this revised and updated edition, I have listed the domestic box-office earnings of selected films. The casual reader will notice a few apparent discrepancies; for example, whereas 1942's *Pride of the Yankees* was considered a hit with a profit of $3,000,000, the 1994 *Little Big League* was regarded as a disappointment because it earned "only" a little over $12,000,000. It seems unnecessary to point out that a dollar went considerably further in 1942 than it did 54 years later, and that movie admission prices escalated dramatically in that same space of time. Though it would have been possible to go through this book and adjust all dollar amounts to reflect inflation rates (according to the consumer price index of the Bureau of Labor and Statistics, *Pride of the Yankees'* $3 million would be the equivalent of $32,670,000 in 2001, when these notes are being written), I decided that it would be more expedient to let the "original" earnings stand.

Alibi Ike

Warner Bros.; released July 1935

Produced by Edward Chodorov. Directed by Ray Enright. Screenplay by William Wister Haines, from the story by Ring Lardner, first published in *The Saturday Evening Post*, July 31, 1915. Photography: Arthur Todd. Edited by Thomas Pratt. Art director: Esdras Hartley. Musical direction by Leo Forbstein. 72 minutes; black and white; sound.

Cast: Joe E. Brown (Francis X. Farrell, also known as "Alibi Ike"); Olivia de Havilland (Dolly); Roscoe Karns (Carey); William Frawley (Cap); Ruth Donnelly (Bess); Joseph King (Owner of Cubs); Paul Harvey (Crawford); Eddie Shubert (Jack Mack); G. Pat Collins (Lieutenant); Spencer Charters (Minister); Gene Morgan (Smitty); Jack Norton (Reporter); Jack Riley (Ballplayer); Cliff Saum (Kelly); Joseph Crehan (Conductor); Jed Prouty (Jewelry Merchant); Jack Cheatham (Operator); Eddie Chandler, Bruce Mitchell (Detectives); Fred "Snowflake" Toones (Elevator Operator); Selmer Jackson (Announcer); Adrian Rosely (Valet); Frank Sully (Player); Huey White (Crawford's Henchman); Wilfred Lucas (Umpire at Night Game); Bill Elliot, Milt Kibbee (Fans); George Stovall (Coach); Ed Wells, Archie Campbell, Mike Gazella, Bob Meusel, Cedric Durst, Dick Cox, Wally Hood, Ray French, Lou Koupal, Irish Meusel, Herman Bell, Walter Galvin, Pat O'Shea, Don Hurst, Frank Shellenback, Wes Kingdon, Wally Hebert, Jim Levy, Guy Cantrell, Wally Rehg, Smead Jolley, Babe Pinelli, Johnny Bassler, Gene DeSautels (Ballplayers). And Mushy Callahan, Jim Thorpe, Julie Bescon, Renny Fagin and Bob Lee.

Francis X. Farrell, rookie pitcher for the Chicago Cubs, is undeniably talented, and would be the first person to tell you so. He is also known as "Alibi Ike" because of his inability to make a move on or off the field without making an excuse about it. When he's late for spring training, he claims his calendar didn't work, and when he loses a game, his excuse is that he doesn't play his best on Wednesday. Cap, the Cub's manager, says that Farrell probably apologizes to the fork every time he takes a bite to eat. When Farrell falls in love with Dolly, Cap's sister-in-law, he can't admit that he's smitten with her. This nearly gets him arrested when he tries to buy a wedding ring but "alibis" to his pals that he's not *really* buying it, leading the jeweler to believe he's got a loony in the store. Ultimately, Dolly overhears Farrell's alibi that their upcoming marriage is only because he feels sorry for her. She walks out, and Farrell goes into a slump during the World Series—which coincides with the attempts of a crooked gambler, Crawford, to intimidate Farrell into throwing several games. Accused of cheating, Farrell won't hurt Dolly by admitting that she's the cause of his slump, and the Cubs' owner, thinking that the pitcher is merely providing an alibi for taking a bribe, kicks him off the team. When the real reason for Farrell's doldrums is learned, it is suggested that Farrell pretend to agree to the gambler's plans, the better to catch the crooks red-handed. But the bad guys get wind of this plan and kidnap Farrell on the day of the deciding World Series game. Farrell makes a spectacular escape, utilizing both an ambulance and a car-carrying truck, and makes it to the game just in time to score the winning run—and to win back Dolly in the bargain.

The last and best of Joe E. Brown's three baseball pictures of the 1930s (see also *Elmer the Great* and *Fireman, Save My Child*), *Alibi Ike* is also the best baseball picture made during that decade, period. It is jam-packed with comedy, ranging from sit-uational humor to farce to out-and-out slap-stick, and its ballpark scenes, particularly the climactic night game, are first-rate. The biggest advantage *Alibi Ike* has over the handful of other baseball films of its era is that its star unabashedly adored the game, and this love permeates the movie's every frame.

If Joe E. Brown had not been in show business, he would most likely have gone into pro baseball. At one point during his Broadway days in the 1920s he was seri-ously scouted by the New York Yankees; after his tryout, Yank manager Miller Hug-gins reportedly muttered, "Well, he's not the first comedian I've seen in a Yankee uniform." A contract was offered, but at this juncture of his life Brown was more in-terested in stage success, though he did play for fun on the National Vaudeville Artists team, managed by fellow comedian Joe Schenck (see *They Learned About Women*). When Brown was signed by Warner Bros. Pictures in 1930, one proviso of his contract was that the studio organize a ball team, with himself as captain. Buster Keaton had a similar setup at MGM, but while Keaton's team was made up of studio personnel, Brown's was composed of bona fide ath-letes, both professional and scholastic; one member of Joe E.'s team was college ath-letic champ Mike Frankovitch, who later evolved into a powerful Hollywood film producer.

Joe E. Brown became something of an executive himself when, in 1933, he became part owner with baseball legend Tris Speaker of the Kansas City Blues, a top-notch American Association minor-league team. Joe kept a hand in baseball into the 1950s, when he provided pre- and postgame "color" for televised Yankee games; and nothing could have pleased Brown more than when his son Joe L. became manager of the Pittsburgh Pirates in 1955. The elder Brown's fascination with the game followed

him into his posh Beverly Hills home, where he maintained his "Room of Love," a trophy den chock full of memorabilia from his career and artifacts given him by some of pro sports' greatest participants. Brown's home was tragically destroyed by a fire which decimated Beverly Hills in the summer of 1961, but thankfully a great deal of Joe E.'s baseball material had been do-nated earlier to UCLA.

Though baseball films were not proven moneyspinners in the 1930s, Joe E. Brown's popularity, and the agreeable box office re-turns from Brown's 1933 *Elmer the Great*, induced Warner Bros. to purchase another Ring Lardner baseball story for their pre-miere comedian. The rights for "Alibi Ike," which had first appeared in print in 1915, were bought from Lardner's widow Ellis for $3,500. Lardner's story concentrates on Francis Farrell's elaborate alibis and the ad-verse result they have on his romance with Dolly, and this was interpolated almost verbatim into William Wister Haines's screenplay, though certain dated elements, among them a whiff of the casual racism so common to stories of that period (Farrell, asking why he's been nicknamed Ike, re-marks "I ain't no Yid"), were sifted out. The crooked gambler angle appears nowhere in the original, but was borrowed from the plot of *Elmer the Great* to add a little spice to the screenplay. Farrell's liaison with Dolly afforded little opportunity for the physical humor that fans had come to expect from Joe E. Brown pictures; a run-in with the criminal element was rife with knockabout possibilities.

Brown himself injected some ideas into the script, among them an incident borrowed from the career of Phillies pitcher Harry Frank Covaleskie. Covaleskie had a particularly eccentric pitching windup, and during one game he was so involved in winding up that he failed to notice an op-posing player stealing second base. When brought to task for this by manager Billy

Murray, Covaleskie cheerfully explained that he didn't know the base was occupied. With measured sarcasm, Murray rallied the rest of the team members and said to them, "I want you to have no secrets in this club, understand? If there's a man on first, *I want the pitcher to know about it.*" Whereupon Covaleskie replied ingenuously, "That's the stuff, Bill. Give 'em hell. They deserve it." This event, virtually unchanged, is reenacted in *Alibi Ike*, with William Frawley as the manager—the first in a long line of such roles for diehard baseball nut Frawley.

While Covaleskie was a prime inspiration for Brown's performance, the movie version of Lardner's Francis X. Farrell was based more than a little on Dizzy Dean (see *The Pride of St. Louis*), whose unlimited bravado and limited intellectual capacity were already quite famous. Warner Bros. did nothing to dispel the Dean tie-in; a throwaway reference to Ol' Diz is heard in the film, and the publicity campaign for *Alibi Ike* included the advertising tag line, "He's Dizzy! He's Daffy!"

Unlike many Hollywood baseball pictures which force the game to take a back seat to the story, the five revisions of the *Ike* script show more and more baseball action being added as work progressed. An early expository scene, originally set in a hotel room, was moved to the ballpark during a training session; and the final scene, in which Farrell was to have merely tagged an opponent out, was punched up by allowing Joe E. Brown, as Farrell, to hit the deciding run, sprint around the bases (followed by the camera in what is almost a full 360-degree pan) and then leap over the opposing catcher to grab home plate.

In the film Farrell makes his first appearance by crashing through the spring training camp fence in his rickety old car and swerving out of control onto the diamond. This bit of business, inspired by Christy Mathewson's habit of driving his

flashy new roadsters onto the field ten minutes before game time for the benefit of his cheering fans, does not appear in the script until its third revision. Up until then, Farrell's entrance was a garden variety climb over the fence.

The climax was planned from the beginning to have Farrell, wearing a hastily improvised and ill-fitting baseball uniform covering his pajamas, win the game. In the first draft Farrell's bizarre uniform was put together while the rest of the team huddled around him. The huddle was rendered unnecessary when the final sequence was rewritten to take place during a night game, allowing Dolly to douse the ballpark's lights so that Farrell could dress somewhat more discreetly. Changing the final game from day to night was inspired by two elements: the fact that the major leagues announced in 1935 that night games would become commonplace (the first such game was played in Cincinnati on May 24), and by the fact that Los Angeles's Wrigley Field, where the scene was shot, had been exhibiting *minor*-league night games since July 1932, and thus the illumination equipment was all in place and just waiting to be utilized. Ironically, the scene was supposed to be taking place in *Chicago's* Wrigley Field, which wouldn't install lights until over half a century later.

The closing gag of *Alibi Ike*, with Francis X. Farrell kissing the minister instead of Dolly at his wedding, was cute enough, though some of the earlier versions—among them a bit in which Farrell would mistakenly plant a kiss on his manager's cheek at the ballpark when the lights were turned off—were equally amusing. The original ending had Farrell, surrounded by reporters after winning the game, being grilled as to why he hadn't shown up until the last minute. For once, "Alibi Ike" had no alibi, but his hitherto demure fiancée Dolly suddenly launched into an elaborate, mile-a-minute alibi for her future husband's behavior. Astounded at Dolly's sudden burst

Olivia de Havilland flashes a starlet smile at Joe E. Brown in *Alibi Ike.*

of verbiage, Farrell was to have turned to the camera and let forth what the script described as "the famous Joe E. Brown cry."

Perhaps this ending wasn't used because it gave the closing gag to the ingénue rather than the star—or perhaps the actress playing Dolly, newcomer Olivia de Havilland, didn't yet have the comic know-how to pull off the routine. Although this was her second picture, *Alibi Ike* was released before editing was finished on de Havilland's first film *A Midsummer Night's Dream*, and thus was Olivia's introduction to movie audiences. While the pressbook of *Alibi Ike* had the nineteen-year-old actress state that she preferred her "modern" role in this picture to the classics, in real life Olivia de Havilland didn't want to appear

in what she considered an insignificant role; she was told bluntly that she was under contract and would do what she was told, or else. (de Havilland was, of course, the prime mover of the legislation that would render illegal the studios' prisonlike contract system, but that was a decade or so into the future.) To her credit, Olivia de Havilland exhibits as much energy and eagerness to entertain in this film as does Joe E. Brown and his male costars William Frawley and Roscoe Karns, both of whom were borrowed from Paramount Pictures to enhance the sports dominated ambiance of *Alibi Ike.*

As with all of Brown's sports pictures, the supporting cast of *Alibi Ike* was crammed with genuine sports figures. In addition to Frank Shellenback, a pitcher-manager for the Pacific Coast League's Hollywood Stars who showed up in all three of Brown's baseball movies, *Alibi Ike* was graced with the presence of ballplayers Archie Campbell, Cedric Durst, Mike Gazella, Bob Meusel and Ed Wells, all former Yankees; Dick Cox, Ray French, Wally Hood and Lou Koupal, late of the Brooklyn Dodgers; Herman Bell and Irish Meusel, ex–New York Giants; Walter Galvin, Don Hurst and Pat O'Shea, recently of the Cubs; Wally Hebert and Jim Levy, graduates of the St. Louis Browns; Guy Cantrell, Wally Rehg and Smead Jolley, alumni of the Red Sox; Wes Kingdon, onetime Washington Senators player; George Stovall, former manager and first baseman of the Indians; and, drawn from old rosters of the 1934 pennant-winning Tigers, Johnny Bassler, Gene DeSautels and Babe Pinelli.

Other athletes, most of them pals of Joe E. Brown, also turned up in *Ike*, including track star Bob Lee, basketball celebrity Renny Fagin, USC athletic captain Julie Bescon, and two faded stars who would appear time and again among the ranks of Warner Bros.' supporting casts: boxing trainer Mushy Callahan and the legendary but luckless Jim Thorpe. The presence of all these real-life athletes gave *Alibi Ike*'s action scenes a vivid reality that wouldn't have been possible if the ballpark had been populated merely by extras in uniform. The fact that Joe E. Brown did all his own ballplaying also bolstered a film that, for all the expertise director Ray Enright displayed in its sports sequences, might have fallen flat had the star been some contract-player Romeo cast more for good looks than for ability.

Alibi Ike helped Joe E. Brown return to the list of top-ten moneymaking stars after a three-year absence but did not convince studio executives that the film's success was due as much to its enthusiastic and accurate treatment of baseball as to Brown; so but for the Columbia "B" melodrama

Girls Can Play (1937), *Alibi Ike* would be the last baseball picture of the 1930s.

Angels in the Infield

Roger Birnbaum Productions/Walt Disney Television/Pacific Motion Pictures, Inc.; first telecast April 9, 2000

Executive producer, Roger Birnbaum. Produced by Fitch Cady. Directed by Robert King. Teleplay by Robert King and Garrett K. Schiff; story by Robert King and Holly Goldberg Sloan. Based on characters in the motion picture *Angels in the Outfield* from the Turner Entertainment Co. Library. Photography: James Gardner. Edited by Corky Ehlers. Co-producer/Production manager: Deb Lefaive. Co-producers: Gary Stutman, Irby Smith, Holly Goldberg Sloan. Music: Ira Newborn. Production designer: Dennis Davenport. Casting: Gary M. Zuckerwood (US), Stephanie Gorin (Canada). 1st Assistant Director: Wendy Ord. 2nd Assistant Director: Debby Crewe. Set decorator: Gordon Zim. Script supervisor: Daniele Simon. Choreographer: Jocelyn Snowden. Production coordinator, Alexandra MacKenzie Carter. Costumes: Sherry McMoran. Makeup: Warren Schneider. Hair stylist: Mary Lou Green. Baseball consultant: Rick Johnston. Stunt coordinator: Branko Racki. Special effects: Malivoire Pictures. Visual effects: Dome Audio Video Effects. Sound Mixer: Stuart French. Color. 89 minutes; sound.

Cast: Patrick Warburton (Eddie "Steady" Everett); David Alan Grier (Bob Bugler); Brittney Irvin (Laurel Everett); Kurt Fuller (Simon); Rebecca Jenkins (Claire Everett); Duane Davis (Randy Fleck); Colin Fox (The Devil); Beau Starr (Gus Keeler); Peter Keleghan (Dexter Deeken); David Duran (Rex Lumbar); Leif Anderson (Student); Jennifer Boland (Pretty Baseball Groupie); Joe Bostick (Soren); Tannie Burnett (Dejected Fan); Laura Catalano (Ballet Teacher); Rufus Crawford (Assistant Manager); Shane Daly (Indians Base Catcher); Adam David (Jay Snodgrass); Neil Girvan (Angels Catcher); Miko Graham (Celine Dion Wannabe); Tamara Hickey (Pretty elevator woman); Kyle Kassardjian (Piano Playing Kid); Culjo Kurkurugya (St. Peter); Hannah Lochner (Young Laurel); Paul A. MacFarlane (Babe

Ruth); Jamie McRoberts (Opera Singing Kid); Brian Paul (Umpire); Jeanette Roxborough (Lily Hart); Peter Simtic (Jacob); Rachel Sharsten (Brigitte); David Sparrow (Taxi Driver); David Talbot (Valet); Wayne Ward (Male Ballet Dancer); Scott Watson (Hot Dog Vendor); Rudy Webb (Usher); Zoltan Buday (Devil's Minion); Michael Segovia (Dejected Fan's Son).

The Anaheim Angels are mired waist-deep in a long, *long* losing streak. One of the principal reasons is the dismal perfor-mance of onetime star pitcher Eddie "Steady" Everett, who has never quite got-ten over bungling the Angels' chances to win the Pennant several years earlier. Com-pounding Eddie's woes is the fact that his college-teacher wife Claire is in the process of divorcing him, mainly because he has been a poor and distant father to their 13-year-old daughter Laurel, an aspiring balle-rina. Laurel insists upon being temporarily left in Eddie's care, even though the two have literally nothing in common except their last name. Realizing that all Eddie needs to put his life together is a renewal of self-confidence, Laurel prays to Heaven to give her father "one more chance." In a twinkling, Laurel's prayers are answered in the form of apprentice angel Bob "The Bungler" Bugler, a former big-league ball-player who was scooped up into the Here-after before being able to redeem himself for the bonehead play that ruined *his* ca-reer. Alas, Bob turns out to be little more than a Heavenly "bench-warmer"—and the battery of fellow angels that he has sum-moned to earth, ostensibly to guide the Anaheim team to victory, are even more inept! As if this isn't bad enough, Eddie Everett's hated rival Randy Fleck has just signed a lifetime contract with The Devil Himself, who has materialized on earth for the express purpose of keeping the Angels out of the Pennant race. But with the help, input and overall moral support of little Laurel—not to mention Eddie's glad-hand-ing agent Simon—Eddie Steady and Bob

the Bungler are given the Second Chance that they both so richly deserve.

Angels in the Infield premiered in April of 2000 as a two-hour TV movie (actually 89 minutes, minus commercials), part of ABC's *Wonderful World of Disney* anthology. The highly imaginative title, and the fact that Holly Goldberg Sloan was among the screenwriters, would seem to suggest that the film was a sequel to, or even a carbon copy of, Disney's highly successful 1994 the-atrical-feature remake of *Angels in the Out-field* (q.v.). This suggestion was curtly dis-missed by the Disney publicists, who worked like beavers to assure potential viewers that, while *Infield* may have been inspired by *Outfield* (this much was affirmed in the clos-ing credits), it was an entirely separate en-tity, and as such should be judged solely on its own merits.

Underlining this was a comment by the film's director/cowriter Robert King, who, stressing the difference between the highly skilled celestial ballplayers in *Angels in the Outfield* and their clumsy *Angels in the Infield* counterparts, noted that, "These an-gels are much less physical. For one thing, they aren't very good at playing baseball, so they bumble around a lot." To King's credit, the scene in *Infield* wherein Bob's fellow angels make a triumphant, special effects–generated entrance (replete with offscreen Heavenly Choir), only to shatter any illusion of competence by royally screw-ing up an easy catch—and rendering them-selves unconscious in the process!—is one of the funniest bits in the picture.

Still, it is truly funny only in the con-text of *Angels in the Outfield*; had it not been a meticulously constructed lampoon of the similar scene in *Outfield* in which the film's angels performed brilliantly on the dia-mond after *their* descent from the clouds, the laugh would have been cut in half. In this and so many other ways, *Angels in the Infield* cannot possibly be judged separately from *Angels in the Outfield*, since it owes its very existence to its predecessor. Virtually all the script devices that worked so well in *Outfield* were dutifully trotted out in the TV film: The child protagonist prefacing her prayer to God with "If You really exist," or words to that effect; the antagonistic sportscaster who is made to look ridiculous as the objects of his scorn continue to exceed expectations; the oft-repeated "Believe! Believe!" to spur on the skeptical hero; and the climactic moment in which every person in the stadium makes a "flapping wing" motion to confirm his or her faith in Divine Intervention. Even some of the throwaway gags can be traced back to *Outfield*, especially the silliness which takes place while the team stands at attention for the National Anthem.

Nor was *Outfield* the only source tapped by the screenwriters; at times, it seems as if *every* feel-good movie made since the Birth of Talkies—baseball-related or otherwise—has been recycled for this film. The premise of an angel earning his wings only after proving his mettle on Earth was, of course, a key plot point in *It's a Wonderful Life* (1946). The pathetically understaffed stadium "cheering section" in the opening scene was lifted bodily from *Major League* (q.v.). The strategic utilization of classical music to chart the Angels' upward progression (in this instance, Rossini's "Thieving Magpie" Overture and Beethoven's Ninth Symphony) had its roots in the *Bad News Bears* films (q.v.), while a related scene in which a pitcher's-mound conference turns into a debate over the relative merits of Beethoven and Schubert was a blatant swipe from *Bull Durham* (q.v.). The "Devil" subplot was beholden not only to *Damn Yankees* (q.v.) but also *Oh God!, You Devil* (1984). The scene in which Laura's audition for the starring role in an upcoming ballet recital magically metamorphoses into a lip-synched production number built around the Tokens' recording of "The Lion Sleeps Tonight" (an all-but-exclusive Disney

property since *The Lion King*) had as its genesis the "Banana Boat Song" sequence in *Beetlejuice* (1988). When the angelic Bob Bugler artificially speeds up Laura's recital so that Eddie can attend his daughter's stage debut and still make it to a crucial game on time, one cannot help but be reminded of the hyperaccelerated "Bolshoi" number in the 1963 film version of *Bye Bye Birdie*. Claire Everett's bottom-of-the-ninth appearance in the stands during the Big Game, providing extra incentive to her estranged husband Eddie, was not only derived from the finale of *The Natural* (q.v.), but staged and framed in exactly the same way. Even Jerry Lewis' *Visit to a Small Planet* (1960) was referenced for the scene in which obnoxious ESPN sportscaster Dexter Deekin, under the spell of the capricious Bob, begins uncontrollably picking his nose before an audience of millions.

So much for what *Angels in the Infield* has; what it does *not* have is the sweet, disarming simplicity that enabled viewers to go along with the more fantastic elements of *Angels in the Outfield*. The earlier film was able to indulge in multiple special effects and goofy slapstick because it was built on a situational foundation that was both realistic and recognizable to the audience: A lonely boy's wish to be a member of a loving family again, and a grown man's realization that you don't necessarily have to act like an S.O.B. to be a winner. *Infield*, however, has so many crises that must be solved and so many life lessons that must be learned that the audience is confused as to which of the film's situations is the most important, and the one most worth caring about. It was as if the filmmakers were so insecure about the success of *Infield* that they tossed in everything they could think of, desperately hoping that at least one or two of their ideas would click—a problem that never seemed to plague the folks responsible for *Outfield*. An end-of-tether ballplayer given a chance to renew himself, two

See if you can spot the star of the show in this *TV Guide* ad for *Angels in the Infield* (2000).

different teams of bunglers who have to get it together, an angel-in-training earning his wings, a little girl who wants to bring her family back together again, that same girl aspiring to success as a dancer, the long-time enemy who must be defeated—any one of these plot situations would have made a workable film on its own, but throwing the whole batch in the same stew ultimately renders them all unsatisfying.

With those warring subplots already cluttering up the film, it was entirely unnecessary to drag the Devil into the proceedings! But as gratuitously as it plays, this plot strand might have worked had it been handled with a modicum of cleverness and nuance; instead, it suffers from the same let's-try-everything overkill as all the other elements in the film. Compared to *Angels in the Infield*'s depiction of Satan—it isn't enough to show him with a reddish complexion, we have to see those cute little horns as well—the musical-comedy excesses of *Damn Yankees* are as subtle and restrained as Milton's *Paradise Lost*. For all of the sledgehammer gags and bloated special effects attending His Satanic Majesty's every appearance, it is the simplest gag that registers best: When three of the Devil's handpicked demonic ballplayers stand side by side on the ballfield, the numbers on their uniforms ever so briefly form the designation "6-6-6".

If one can get past its many shortcomings, *Angels in the Infield* yields a few small pleasures. The special effects are actually much smoother here than in *Outfield*, with more convincing flying-angel sequences and a particularly good use of rotoscoping (creating animated cartoon versions of live actors) to avoid having the "human" characters overlap with the angels when both are sharing the same screen. One reason for the improvement over the earlier film's special effects was director King's decision to generally avoid actual ballpark locations, where camera trickery and wired-up stunt

flying is harder to control. Virtually all of the baseball diamonds and grandstands seen in this film were specially designed to accommodate the action and the more elaborate sight gags. The results, which could have come off as disappointingly artificial, were quite pleasing to the eye, conveying a sense of vast space and realistic perspective far more successfully than the rather claustrophobic Heaven which shows up at the beginning and end of the film.

The acting is pretty good, too. Patrick Warburton, best known to *Seinfeld* fans for his recurring appearances as New Jersey Devils–obsessed auto mechanic David Puddy, is generally effective as Eddie Everett, even though his ballplaying skills are largely a product of clever editing and photography. Brittney Irvin, who had just spent a year playing Nan Harding on a TV-series version of Louisa May Alcott's *Little Men*, gets the most out of her role as the sensitive-but-resilient Laura without resorting to cloying cuteness or professional-kid slickness. And until he begins to wear out his welcome, Kurt Fuller delivers some bona fide laughs as Eddie's neurotic agent Simon, who is bound and determined to emulate the hands-on sensitivity of legendary sports agent Jerry Maguire (from the 1997 Tom Cruise film of the same name)—even if it kills him.

Though technically he is not billed first, comedian David Allen Grier (one of the more distinguished alumni of the Wayans Brothers' groundbreaking Fox Network variety series *In Living Color*) is the true star of the proceedings, and indeed the film is most successful when the plot is cast aside and Grier's talent for mimicry and improvisation is allowed to hold sway. Like Patrick Warburton, Grier does not entirely convince us that he could go nine innings in an actual ball game, but his comic versatility is ample compensation for the skimpiness of his baseball scenes.

One of several 1990s baseball films

economically lensed in Canada for U.S. consumption (see notes for *Joe Torre: Curveballs Along the Way, Finding Buck McHenry* and *Prisoner of Zenda Inc.*), *Angels in the Infield* proved an agreeable timefiller for those viewers who weren't distracted by two other, more aggressively advertised TV-movies which were broadcast on the same April evening, *Fail-Safe* and *Don Quixote*. Since that time, the film has done tolerably well in the home-video market, where it often shares the same Blockbuster shelf as its predecessor *Angels in the Outfield* and Disney's "interim" football fantasy *Angels in the Endzone*. We believe that the Republic will stand if we are spared *Angels in the Locker Room*.

Angels in the Outfield

MGM; trade shown in August 1951; general release in October 1951

Produced and directed by Clarence Brown. Screenplay by Dorothy Kingsley and George Wells, from a story by Richard Conlin. Photography: Paul H. Vogel. Edited by Robert J. Kern. Music by Daniel Amfitheatroff. Art direction: Cedric Gibbons. 98 minutes; black and white; sound.

Cast: Paul Douglas (Guffy McGovern); Janet Leigh (Jennifer Page); Keenan Wynn (Fred Bayles); Donna Corcoran (Bridget White); Lewis Stone (Arnold J. Hapgood); Spring Byington (Sister Edwina); Bruce Bennett (Saul Hellman); Marvin Kaplan (Timothy Duncey); Ellen Corby (Sister Veronica); Jeff Richards (Dave Rothberg); John Gallaudet (Reynolds); King Donovan (McGee); Don Haggerty (Rube Robinson); Paul Salata (Tony Minella); Fred Graham (Chunk); John McKee (Bill Baxter); Patrick J. Molyneaux (Patrick J. Finley); Lawrence Dobkin (Rabbi); Douglas Fowley (Cab Driver); Harry Hayden (Doctor); Barbara Billingsley (Hat Check Girl); Bing Crosby, Ty Cobb, Joe DiMaggio, Harry Ruby (Themselves); James Whitmore (Voice of Gabriel).

Guffy McGovern, manager of the basement-dwelling Pittsburgh Pirates, is loud,

profane, abusive, and pugnacious. At least that's the situation until, while prowling the second-base line of a deserted Forbes Field at midnight in search of a lucky trinket he's lost, Guffy is accosted by the voice of the Archangel Gabriel. The invisible, tough-talking spokesman of the "Heavenly Choir Nine"—a team made up of deceased baseball greats, with a batting average of .321—Gabriel tells McGovern to look for a "miracle" in the next day's game. The miracle is that the Pirates win; thereafter, McGovern is willing to follow Gabriel's advice, which includes a personal ban on swearing and brawling. A ten-game winning streak and a chance at the pennant results. This coincides with the visit to the ballpark of two nuns from St. Gabriel's Parish and the orphans in their care. One of the children, Bridget White, insists that she can see an angel standing behind each Pirate player—as well she should, since it was Bridget's prayers to her patron saint, Gabriel, which prompted the angels to come to McGovern's aid in the first place. Newspaper "household hints" reporter Jennifer Page, assigned by her paper to write on baseball from the woman's angle, blows the angel yarn into a national headline event. McGovern, sensitive when it comes to public ridicule, stays mum about his own relationship with angels until he's beaned by a line drive. His dazed admission that he's spoken with Gabriel plays right into the hands of vindictive sportscaster Fred Bayles, who is still sore that McGovern had had him fired from the Pirates' announcers booth. Bayles starts a smear campaign that brings about a commissioner's hearing on the very day of the deciding pennant game. With the help of such character witnesses as little Bridget and an ecumenical lineup of clergymen, McGovern proves to the commissioner's satisfaction that there's nothing wrong with believing in or conversing with angels. Alas, this happy turn of events is tainted when McGovern is goaded into socking Fred Bayles, which causes Gabriel and his fellow angels to abandon the Pirates. But Guffy's celestial experience has taught him to manage with his heart as well as his head, so he takes a chance during the Big Game by putting veteran player Saul Hellman on the pitcher's mound; though Hellman is considered to be washed up, McGovern, who has learned from Gabriel that Saul will be "signed up" by the Heavenly Choir Nine come next spring, wants to give the pitcher one last grandstand play on earth. Thanks to his sentimental gamble with Hellman, plus the overall change in his nature, McGovern wins not only the pennant, but the love of Jennifer Page, whom he marries, and little Bridget, whom he adopts, as well as the respect of fans and players both here and in the hereafter.

Onetime pro football player (with the Philadelphia-based Frankford Yellow Jackets) and former radio sports announcer Paul Douglas had, since his 1948 screen debut in *A Letter to Three Wives*, carved himself a comfortable cinema niche, playing variations of the gruff, boorish middle-aged blowhard with a heart of gold. Douglas's athletic background, coupled with the self-assured air he demonstrated whenever ambling around a playing area of any kind, was immensely valuable in bringing realism to his sports-oriented pictures. Just two years before *Angels in the Outfield*, Douglas made his baseball movie debut in *It Happens Every Spring* (q.v.), stealing the film from star Ray Milland with his on-the-money portrayal of a grizzled, worldweary ballplayer. As the Durocher-like Guffy McGovern in *Angels*, Paul Douglas gives a terrific performance, successfully bridging the realistic aspects of professional sports with the fantastic elements of the plotline; Douglas is as believable when conversing with the unseen Gabriel as he is when chewing out umpires on the ballfield. And since Douglas seems to believe that those angels are really out there, so does the audience—

although, in the tradition of the six-foot rabbit in *Harvey*, there isn't one on-screen wing or halo in the whole film.

Douglas is, in fact, so convincing in the role—even pulling off a scene in which, abstaining from profanity, he argues with an ump by using quotes from Shakespeare—that it's astonishing to discover that the actor disliked *Angels in the Outfield*, describing it in a *TV Guide* interview as "really a pretty crummy picture." This attitude may have been shaped by the fact that the film was one of the favorites of President Dwight D. Eisenhower—whose politics the outspokenly liberal Douglas abhorred. For the record, Douglas' widow, actress Jan Sterling, would insist after her husband's death in 1959 that Paul was just kidding, and that Guffy McGovern was really his pet role.

Aiding Paul Douglas in getting the viewers to swallow the film's premise was MGM's decision to shoot a generous portion of the film on location, in and around Forbes Field in Pittsburgh (it's been reported that the film made a great deal of money in the Pittsburgh area because the local citizens would rather watch the fictional Pirates win than see the actual Pirates lose, which they were doing with alarming regularity in 1951). Location shooting was a comparative rarity in major-studio productions of the period, and the use of genuine exteriors (which were extremely well matched with studio mockups and medium shots filmed at Los Angeles's Wrigley Field) gave the film a semi-documentary quality unusual to fantasy stories. Some of the ballfield scenes also gave the world outside Pittsburgh some fleeting glimpses of the genuine Pirates team of 1950 and 1951, including Ralph Kiner, who was the biggest draw in the team's history thanks to his homerun skill, and for whom a space between two left-field fences where those homers frequently landed was named Kiner's Korner.

Irascible Pittsburgh Pirates manager Guffy McGovern (Paul Douglas, left of the umpire) is about to pay his daily visit to the showers. The original studio caption for this still from *Angels in the Outfield* [1951] stated that the film was based on "the original story by Father R. F. Grady." On screen, however, story credit was bestowed upon one "Richard Conlin"—a non-sectarian alias, perhaps?

Of particular help in keeping things credible both in and out of Forbes was the careful direction of Clarence Brown. A top-notch craftsman since the silent days, Brown had never had occasion to direct a baseball picture before, what with his preoccupation with such nonathletic luminaries as Greta Garbo and Mary Pickford, and such nonsports subject matter as *The Yearling* and *Intruder in the Dust.* Brown's particular gift in *Angels* was his ability to take potentially syrupy, sentimental material and toughen it up by directing each scene as straightforwardly as possible and by not allowing the actors to do the bug-eyed double takes and tremulous vocal inflections that frequently botched up many "ghost comedies" of the 1930s, 1940s and 1950s. The only time that Brown's no-frills approach fails to work is in the baseball game climax. By staging the scene in a matter-of-fact manner, Brown makes the game look quite authentic, but also robs the audience of the tension of imminent loss relieved by the euphoria of victory that a swifter pace, a few tighter closeups and a clever camera angle or two might have accomplished.

One aspect of the plot that did not fit into Clarence Brown's realistic approach—

not in 1951, at any rate—was Guffy McGovern's nonstop swearing in the earlier scenes. The MGM sound department came up with the witty idea of having Paul Douglas mouth the offensive epithets, but having them emerge on the soundtrack recorded backward, sounding more like Martian than Anglo-Saxon oaths. Incidentally, MGM was taking no chance that some clever projectionist might flip the "reverse" switch, treating an unsuspecting audience to a stream of obscenities. This author once taped a scene from *Angels* on a reel-to-reel audio recorder, only to discover that, when played in reverse, the lines *still* sounded like gibberish.

The supporting actors of *Angels*, from 8-year-old Donna Corcoran as the orphaned Bridget White to 72-year-old Lewis Stone as a baseball commissioner, all match Paul Douglas's performance and Clarence Brown's direction by keeping things from getting too cute or farfetched. A particularly compelling note is struck by Bruce Bennett, cast as veteran Pirate relief pitcher Saul Hellman, whose days are numbered, both professionally and literally. Wisely, Bennett, like the film itself, plays away from the sentimental goo by portraying Hellman as rather cranky and aloof, allowing the audience to realize that he is a good man through his ballplaying prowess and his perseverance rather than through any attempts by the actor to wheedle sympathy.

The guest star cameos by Bing Crosby (who owned 15 percent of the Pittsburgh Pirates), Joe DiMaggio, Ty Cobb and Harry Ruby (the latter a popular songwriter whose love of baseball bordered on the obsessive) are all the more effective because they appear without buildup or warning. Each celebrity is interviewed during a newsreel sequence for their opinions on the existence of angels. None of these vignettes could have taken any extra effort from the participants—Crosby's scene takes place on a golf course, his usual habitat when away

from the cameras—but the four real-life characters are welcome additions to the proceedings. Even Ty Cobb looks halfway human.

Angels in the Outfield did respectable business, though it would have to wait until its television release in 1961 to gain its reputation, and until 1994 before it was regarded as enough of a "classic" to warrant a remake (see separate entry). Selling the film overseas using its original title was considered out of the question, so MGM distributed the picture to England and Europe as *The Angels and the Pirates*. Imagine the reactions of foreign filmgoers as they sat through a film that many of them thought would be a celestial swashbuckler!

Angels in the Outfield

Angels Productions, Inc./Caravan Pictures/ Walt Disney Pictures; released July 13, 1994

Executive producer: Gary Stutman. Produced by Irby Smith and Joe Roth. Directed by William Dear. Screenplay by Dorothy Kingsley & George Wells, and Holly Goldberg Sloan. Based on the motion picture "Angels in the Outfield" from the Turner Entertainment Co. Associate producers: Richard H. Prince, Holly Goldberg Sloan. Photography: Matthew F. Leonetti. Production designer: Dennis Washington. Edited by Bruce Green. Original music: Randy Edelman. Costumes designed by Rosanna Norton. Associate producer: Holly Goldberg Sloan. Second unit director: Irby Smith. Library. Production manager/associate producer: Richard H. Prince. 1st assistant director: L. Dean Jones, Jr. 2nd assistant director: Jay Smith. Art director: Thomas T. Targownik. Set decorator: John Anderson. Camera operators: Robert LaBonge, David E. Diano. Sound mixer: Willie Burton. Casting: Pam Dixon. Key makeup: Scott H. Eddo, Diane Hammond. Key hairstylist: Paul Abascal. Production associate: Aida Gaboyan. Baseball technical advisor: Carney Lansford. Script supervisor: Joanie Blum. Supervising sound editor: John A. Larsen. Special effects coordinator: Frank W. Tarantino. Production coordinator: Lark W. Bernini. Senior illustrator:

Mike Swift. Junior illustrator: Oliver Dear. Steadicam operators: Gregory Lundsgaard, Peter Jensen. Film editor: Paul Dixon. Angel costume designer: Susan Nininger. Men's costumer: Joseph Roveto. Women's costumer: Barbara Kassal. Assistant baseball advisors: Mitchell Page, Steve McCatty, Wayne Gross. Special effects flying: James K. Friedburg, Glenn Thomas. Dialect coach: Suzanne Celeste. Stadium entertainers: Mollie Allen, Jerry Saslow. Visual effects by Pacific Data Images, Inc. Visual effects supervisors: Andrew Adamson, Giedra Rackauskas. Visual effects consultant: Robert Dyke. Visual Effects Producer: Jennifer Bell. Visual Effects Art Director: Carlos Arguello. Character technical supervisor: Dick Walsh. Animators: Steve Braggs, Mike Collery, Jamie Dixon, Phillipe Gluckman, Roger Guyett, Rebecca Marie, Michael Necci, Amie Slate, George Bruder, Aliza Corson, Terry Emmons, Rex Grignon, Betsy Asher Hall, Cleveland Mitchell, Karen Schneider, Larry Weiss. Motion animation producer: Doug Nichols. Character animator: Glenn McQueen. Music editor: Joanie Diener. Main titles designed and supervised by R/ Greenberg Associates West, Inc. End Title Design: Susan Bradley. Opticals: Buena Vista Imaging. Soundtrack available on Hollywood Records. Technicolor. 102 minutes; Dolby Stereo Sound. Rated PG.

Cast: Danny Glover (George Knox); Brenda Fricker (Maggie Nelson); Tony Danza (Mel Clark); Christopher Lloyd (Al the Angel); Ben Johnson (Hank Murphy); Jay O. Sanders (Ranch Wilder); Joseph Gordon-Levitt (Roger); Milton Davis, Jr. (J.P.); Taylor Negron (David Montagne); Tony Longo (Triscuitt Messmer); Neal McDonough (Whitt Bass); Stoney Jackson (Ray Mitchell); Adrien Brody (Danny Hemmerling); Tim Conlon (Wally); Matthew McConaughey (Ben Williams); Israel Juarbe (Jose Martinez); Albert Alexander Garcia (Pablo Garcia); Dermot Mulroney (Roger's Father); Robert Clohessy (Frank Gates); Connie Craig (Carolyn); Jonathan Proby (Miguel); Michael Halton (Hairy Man); Mark Conlon (Photographer); Danny Walcoff (Marvin); James C. King (Home Plate Umpire); Tony Reitano (Singing Umpire); Diane Amos (Woman Next to J.P.); Christopher Leon DiBiase (Teenager); Robert Stuart Reed (Guard); Ruth Beckford (Judge); Victoria Skerritt (Social Worker); Devon Dear (National Anthem Singer); O.B. Babbs (Mapel, Angels player);

Mitchell Page (Abascal, Angels player); Mark Cole (Norton, Angels player); Chuck Dorsett (Usher); Carney Lansford (Kesey); Pamela West (Ms. Angel); Oliver Dear (Rookie Angel); Lionel Douglass (Brother Angel); Bundy Chanock (Umpire); John Howard Swain (First Base Umpire); Marc Magdaleno (Home Plate Umpire no. 2); Ron Roggé (Angels Coach); Steven Meredith (Toronto Player); Bill Dear (Toronto Manager); Rocky Capella (Stunt Coordinator); Kevin Bailey, Lisa Dempsey, Eversley Forte, Johnny Martin, Mike Martinez, Tim Meredith, Jeff Mosley (Stunts); David Maier (Batboy); Theodore S. Maier, Lew Temple (Baseball Players).

Left in the care of a foster home by his ne'er-do-well father, 11-year-old Roger Bomman is told bluntly that there is about as much chance of his family reuniting as there is for the Anaheim Angels to win the pennant. Though this remark gives Roger a ray of hope, it was meant sarcastically: After half a season under the management of the misanthropic, hot-tempered George Knox, whose decade-long winning record with the Cincinnati Reds was supposed to guarantee a turnaround for the Anaheim team, the Angels are in last place only because there's nowhere lower to go. When the team's fourteen-game losing streak expands to fifteen, Roger turns to Heaven for assistance, praying for a "miracle" to save the Angels and bring him a family again. Somebody Up There must like Roger, for within the next 24 hours a genuine angel named Al appears to the boy (and *only* to the boy), informing him that a heavenly squad of baseball stars is ready, willing and able to help guide the earthbound Angels to victory—but on condition that Roger continues to *believe*, despite all logical challenges to his beliefs. Before long, even the cynical George Knox realizes that something divinely wonderful is happening to his ballplayers, as they clamber out of the cellar and race headlong to a Pennant win. Gradually, Knox also comes to accept, sight unseen, that there really are angels behind the Angels, though Roger warns him not to reveal this publicly lest Al and his Heavenly team return whence they came. Unfortunately, Roger's best friend J.P. accidentally lets slip the secret about the angels to radio sportscaster Ranch Wilder, who, bearing a long-standing grudge against Knox, venomously uses this "ridiculous" statement to destroy the Anaheim skipper. Called on the carpet by team owner Hank Murphy, Knox is told that he will be fired unless he firmly denies the presence of angels at a press conference. Instead, Knox is emboldened to reassert his faith in Greater Powers when virtually everyone in attendance at the conference—including such skeptics as Roger's foster-caregiver Maggie Nelson, priggish team publicist David Montagne, and aging but rejuvenated Angels pitcher Mel Clark—insists that if athletes and sports managers are within their rights to acknowledge their belief in God, then what in the heck is wrong with angels? Capitulating to popular opinion, Murphy keeps Knox on the payroll and cans the mean-spirited Wilder. Though Al the Angel and his winged colleagues keep their promise to help shepherd the Anaheim club to the Pennant race, the Rules of Heaven state that the ballteam has to win the deciding game by itself. This happily is just what happens, thanks in large part to the indefatigable Mel Clark, but also because the earthbound Angels, united by faith in themselves, have become an honest-to-goodness team at last. It appears, however, as if no such happy ending awaits Roger, whose father has run out on him permanently, leaving the boy with the bleak prospect of spending the rest of his youth as a ward of the State. But by fadeout time both Roger and his buddy J.P. have been adopted by the now-lovable George Knox, who may never have *actually* seen those angels in the outfield, but has at last learned that some things must be accepted—and can be accomplished—on Faith alone.

Disney's 1994 version of the 1951 MGM baseball fantasy *Angels in the Outfield* (q.v.) is not so much a remake as a rethinking of the original. Nevertheless, enough material was retained from the earlier film to earn its screenwriters, Dorothy Kingsley and George Wells (both still alive when the Disney film was in production), a full "screenplay by" credit in the opening titles of the 1994 version rather than the usual "suggested by" or "based upon" tag—even though neither Kingsley nor Wells was actively involved in the later film.

Carried over from the original were several of the basic story elements: A cantankerous baseball manager who becomes a winner, and is humanized in the process, with the help of a band of ballplaying angels; a little kid who can see the angels, complicating matters for both kid and manager; a spiteful sportscaster who tries to discredit the manager by turning the "angels" story against him; an over-the-hill pitcher who is allowed one last spectacular stand in the final game of the pennant race; and the exit of the angels during that crucial game, obliging the team to stand on its own fifty feet and still emerge victorious.

The success of 1993's *Rookie of the Year* (q.v.) persuaded Morgan Creek Productions executive Gary Stutman that another baseball fantasy might perform just as well. According to the pressbook for *Angels in the Outfield*, Stutman elected to purchase the film rights of the 1951 version from Ted Turner, then the owner of the entire MGM backlog, because Stutman recognized "its enduring value and universal appeal" and also hoped to "introduce a new generation to this timeless story." There is also a big advantage to recycling a property that had worked before, rather than risk several million dollars on something entirely New and Different, though the pressbook didn't go into this matter.

Once the remake rights were in the bag, Stutman contacted Irby Smith, co-executive producer of *Rookie of the Year* and

Angels in the Outfield (1994): Roger Bomman (Joseph Gordon-Levitt) demonstrates the wing-flapping gesture that will tip off Anaheim Angels manager George Knox (Danny Glover) whenever the stadium is visited by *genuine* angels.

the earlier baseball-oriented blockbuster *Major League* (q.v.). Likewise convinced that a new version of *Angels in the Outfield* would (if you'll pardon the expression) fly, Smith shopped the property to Joe Roth and Roger Birnbaum of Caravan Pictures—who, after securing the services of actor Danny Glover, a hot property thanks to his costarring assignments in the *Lethal Weapon* series with Mel Gibson, were able to arrange a release setup with Walt Disney Pictures. The studio's TV division had for several years been humming along profitably with remakes of such earlier Disney classics as *The Parent Trap* and *The Absent-Minded Professor*, proof enough that the Public had a healthy taste for warmed-up leftovers.

Assigned to do that warming was screenwriter Holly Goldberg Sloan, whose script for the 1993 Whoopi Goldberg vehicle *Made in America* had resulted in a three-picture deal with Caravan. As mentioned, Sloan kept the fundamentals of the original *Angels in the Outfield*, making several noteworthy eliminations along the way. First to go was the character of the "gal reporter," played in the 1951 film by Janet Leigh, who fell in love with the acerbic ball-club manager despite her monumental lack of baseball expertise; it was no longer compulsory for a film to have a romantic angle to draw in female viewers. Also deemed expendable was the scene in the earlier film in which the manager's faith in angels was "sanctified" by the combined efforts of a minister, a priest and a rabbi; the religious pressure groups who held Hollywood in thrall back in 1951 no longer wielded enough power to demand that a character's belief in Divine Intervention be given on-screen ecumenical approval—and besides, if a minister, priest and rabbi showed up together in a 1994 picture, audiences would be waiting for the punch line. Finally, with the MPAA rating system in force, it was possible to get by with a modest amount of swearing and questionable language in a family-oriented film so long as the "PG" label was affixed; thus, all those chucklesome scenes in the censor-dominated *Angels in the Outfield* of 1951, wherein the baseball manager's cuss words were recorded backwards, were (more's the pity) unnecessary.

Sloan's major changes in the original included the renaming of all the characters, beginning with the transformation of Guffy McGovern (the character played by Paul Douglas in the 1951 version) into George Knox. The little orphan girl who saw the angels in the first film became a little boy named Roger—not orphaned, though he might as well have been—in the remake; he no longer resided in a Catholic orphanage but in a shabby but comfortable foster home, presided over not by a baseball-happy nun but by a warmhearted but pragmatic "civilian" caregiver. In addition to the youthful leading character, Sloan dreamed up a best friend for Roger, a cute little African American foster child named J.P.; the screenwriter claimed she was inspired to increase the number of child protagonists by the relationship between her own two sons. The ballteam saved by the heavenly angels, originally the Pittsburgh Pirates, became the Anaheim Angels in the remake, the result of Sloan's forgivable unwillingness to resist a play on words ("Angels" helped by "angels"—no duh!), and also the fact that Disney had a sizeable financial interest in the Anaheim team (is it necessary to remind the reader of the name of the California city that was elevated from a *Jack Benny Program* running joke to a major tourist attraction by the advent of Disneyland?).

The antagonistic sportscaster, played by Keenan Wynn in the first film, was reborn in the form of Jay O. Sanders in the 1994 version. The reason for the sportscaster's dislike of the manager was revised: In the earlier film, the Wynn character was sore because the Paul Douglas character had gotten him fired; in the remake, Sanders' Ranch Wilder had once been manager of the Angels himself, but had been supplanted after one losing season too many by Danny Glover's George Knox. Much more so than in the earlier film, the animosity was two-sided: Knox despised Wilder for having spiked him during a ball game, thereby forcing Knox to give up an extremely promising playing career for the less fulfilling position of manager.

Since the new *Angels* was for all intents and purposes a Disney picture, Sloan was careful to load the script with as much Disneyesque slapstick as traffic would allow; when characters weren't getting knocked out by flying objects, they were being pelted by a wide and colorfully messy array of food items. It was the sort of glorious nonsense that only Disney could pull off so well, and it would have been totally out of place in the MGM original (with such spectacular exceptions as the studio's Marx Brothers and Red Skelton pictures, the "old" MGM was not suited to the demands of broad, low comedy). And a new character was added, conceived in the tradition of such earlier Disney comic foils as Elliot Reid, Don Knotts and Tim Conway: Prissy, purse-lipped Angels public relations man David Montagne. Doomed to be the target of unintentional (and clothes-ruining) persecution by youngsters Roger and J.P. the moment he is assigned to look after the boys during the Angels home games, David is also predestined to prove by film's end that he is really a nice guy beneath all those slow burns, delayed double-takes and gimlet-eyed glares.

The single most significant deviation from the original (beyond a technical consideration that will be discussed later) was manifested in the film's narrative point of view. In the 1951 *Angels*, the story revolved around Pirates manager Guffy McGovern, who could hear but not see the angels. Bridget, the little orphan girl who *could* see the angels, was an important plot device, inasmuch as it was she who prayed to her patron saint Gabriel to save the Pittsburgh Pirates from oblivion; but since Bridget had no real stake in whether the Pirates won or lost, the story was motivated and driven by McGovern's slowly dawning realization that he'd better realign his curmudgeonly behavior if he was going to be truly on the side of the angels and pull his team out of the cellar. In the 1994 version of *Angels in the Outfield*, the story's central focus and prime mover is young Roger Bomman. To be sure, Angels manager George Knox' career is on the line, but the audience cares more about the plight of Roger—who, sincerely believing that the only way he and his estranged father will be brought back together is if the Angels win the Pennant, is left with no choice but to beg God to deliver unto Anaheim a miracle. The climactic reformation of George Knox and salvation of the Angels are crucial to the story, but are of less importance to the audience than what will ultimately happen to Roger Bomman. In keeping with this shift of focus in the remake, it was decided that only Roger would be able to see or hear the angelic ballplayers—at least until the very end of the picture.

Engaged to direct the new *Angels* was William Dear, who like so many other film directors of the 1990s had learned his trade in the field of rock videos. In fact, Dear was on the ground floor of the MTV "revolution," having directed Michael Nesmith's pioneering comedy/music video *Elephant Parts* (1981). He was also well grounded in comedy-fantasy, as one of the house directors of the Steven Spielberg–produced TV anthology *Amazing Stories*, and as helmsman of the 1987 theatrical feature *Harry and the Hendersons*.

Two weeks before principal photography began in October 1993, the actors playing the ballplayers commenced training at a genuine baseball camp under Carney Lansford, former Oakland Athletics' all-star third baseman and the film's technical advisor (Lansford also appears in the film as the tobacco-gobbing White Sox batter whom Mel Clark must strike out in the deciding Pennant game). Helping out during the training process were three other members of the Oakland team, Wayne Gross, Steve McCatty and Mitchell Page (likewise seen in the film as Angels player Abascal). Though the producers were worried that the actors seemed a bit stiff and tentative during their first scenes, Lansford felt that these qualities worked well to establish that the Angels were in dire need of Godly assistance at the beginning of the picture! He also praised the baseball skills of actor Tony Danza (Mel Clark), noting that Danza "was also a little older than the rest of the team so they looked up to him as the veteran. It was right in sync with his character."

Though the Disney people could have moved right into Anaheim Stadium without the least little bit of red tape, that particular ballpark was being used by the L.A. Rams; thus, while the Stadium was seen in exterior shots, most of the baseball scenes were shot at Oakland Coliseum. Other filming locations included a bungalow at the corner of Foster and Hale in Oakland (for Roger's foster home), and the Old Federal Reserve Bank building in San Francisco (for the Anaheim courthouse).

Two technicians conspicuous by their presence during the baseball sequences were "flying consultant" Loree Lee Harper and stunt coordinator Mike Martinez, who joshingly referred to himself as a "test dummy." These were the people who, with the help of a crack team of on-set special effects wizards, made it seem as if the "live" Angels were being lofted through the air and navigated around the field by the "heavenly" angels. This was a major stylistic break from the original *Angels in the Outfield*, in which the presence of the angels was left to the audience's imagination, save for one tiny piece of concrete evidence: a tiny feather which floated from the sky at two or three junctures in the film.

But the producers didn't merely stop at the *Topper*-like suggestion that the ballplayers were being moved and manipulated by Forces From Beyond. Unlike the first *Angels in the Outfield*, in which the title characters were never actually shown on screen, the remake offered a full phalanx of transparent-but-visible "guys in sparkling pajamas," as Roger Bomman describes them. And not only sparkling pajamas, but wings and shimmering halos—and accompanied by the sort of celestial "Disney music" one normally associates with the Blue Fairy or Tinkerbell.

Some film purists have condemned *Angels in the Outfield* for forsaking the "imagination" of the original and for truckling to the "lowest common denominator" with gaudy special-effects spectres. This would seem to be a knee-jerk reaction, since the original *Angels*, entertaining though it is, has never been designated a "classic" of the sort immune to tampering. Besides, audiences of the 1990s were accustomed to special effects in fantasy features, and to withhold those effects might well have been regarded as a contemptuous cheat. Whether or not this robs younger filmgoers of the joy of using their imaginations to the fullest is an argument best left to aesthetes.

Clearly prepared for a certain measure of criticism, the production staff of the new *Angels in the Outfield* articulately laid out their reasons for "literalizing" the angels in the film's pressbook. After getting off to a shaky start by explaining, "It was a creative decision [in the original] not to depict the angels, based in part, on the technical limits of the day" (only half of that statement is completely accurate), the Disney publicity folks noted that, "the great advances made in filmmaking and computer technology" all but obligated the producers to show the angels instead of just talking about them. Nor were the visualizations conceived haphazardly: "With so many people having preconceptions of what angels look like, the filmmakers were challenged to create a visual concept that would be both realistic and ephemeral, pleasing to traditionalists and yet surprising, and free of sentimental clichés." What finally showed up on screen was, according to producer Irby Smith, the result of innumerable meetings and late-night sessions. "There was a point when we said we can't have any angels at all. But eventually we made our decision and we're secure with it."

The angels in *Angels* are indeed bereft of "sentimental clichés," and are genuinely funny and endearing, even when their faces are stamped with grotesque grins. But they are never entirely convincing—and if this seems like asking too much, take a look at the made-for-TV sequel *Angels in the Infield* (q.v.), which, though an inferior film, contains infinitely more credible-looking angels, avoiding the nervous shimmers and occasional out-of-register alignment which often plague the *Outfield* spirits. In truth, the film's best and most accomplished special effects can be found in the scenes *outside* the baseball diamond, notably the "de-li-quification" of head angel Al after he materializes in Roger's king-sized Coca Cola.

When the film's critics weren't grousing about the angels, they were bemoaning the Disneyfication of the original film by hoking the early baseball scenes with hyped-up visual effects and *Home Alone*-style stuntwork. Admittedly, one tends to worry after the third or fourth angelic intervention if we will ever see any *real* baseball played instead of an extended live-action cartoon. But all of this gimmickry takes place only when it is necessary to the plot.

The film's final 25 minutes, in which the Angels, led by pitcher Mel Clark, must win the Pennant all by themselves, is (even allowing for a few spurts of slow-motion photography) one of the finest and most realistic stretches of "pure baseball" filmed to date—and all the more compelling and believable when contrasted with the tricked-up sequences that have gone before.

This sequence (which, incidentally, is much better staged and photographed than its counterpart in the original *Angels in the Outfield*) also contains one of the precious few "sentimental" baseball-movie moments that does not play like fingernails across the blackboard. With two men out and the bases loaded at the bottom of the ninth (yes, *that* one again), manager Knox is being urged by the higher-ups to replace the visibly tiring pitcher Mel Clark—but Knox won't, knowing how important the game is to Clark. Yet without Roger's assurance that Clark is being "backed" by one of those heavenly angels, Knox may have no choice but to put in a relief pitcher. Instead, however, Knox and Roger opt for a bit of psychology: They lead Clark to believe that angels *are* present by using the arm-waving gesture established earlier in the film as Roger's "cue" to Knox that the Celestials have arrived on the field. At this point, everybody in the stands picks up the arm-waving movement, and it is this boost of confidence which gives Clark the will to go on and win the game with a fabulous showboat play. Beyond the fact that it is virtually impossible to watch this scene without a lump in one's throat, the climax of the *Angels in the Outfield* remake verifies the message implicit in both versions of the film: It is unimportant whether or not angels actually exist—the important thing is to believe in *something*, and by extension to believe in oneself.

At first, Danny Glover seems all bluster and no substance as George Knox, but as his character mellows, the believability factor increases. Paul Douglas may have been more likeable in the early reels of the original *Angels in the Outfield* than Glover, but he played the role the same way he played all of his screen roles; forever the old grump with the golden heart, Douglas never really "grew" as a character on screen because the viewer always knew what to expect. In the remake, Glover sticks out his neck artistically by playing a thoroughly repellant fellow early on, so that his gradual conversion to humanity would carry more dramatic weight—and it does.

As veteran pitcher Mel Clark, Tony Danza invests a great deal of depth and humanity in his role, which might come as a pleasant surprise to those weaned on his glib and flippant sitcom characterizations in such TV series as *Taxi* and *Who's the Boss?* His character is warmer and more accessible than his counterpart in the 1951 version, the taciturn Saul Hellman (played by Bruce Bennett); both interpretations are viable, and both equally convincing. On the other hand, Jay O. Sanders, as vitriolic sports announcer Ranch Wilder, comes off better than *his* 1951 counterpart Keenan Wynn, not because his villainy is any more amusing or menacing, but because he actually sounds like an authentic radio sportscaster, which Wynn did not.

The other adult characters are equally well cast. Taylor Negron neatly underplays his role as the long-suffering, mustard-splattered David Montagne, while Christopher Lloyd magnificently overplays Al the Angel, though not so much as to become a repetitious drag. In the small role of Roger's worthless father, Dermot Mulroney is both loathsome and pathetic, a rare specimen of the "dark side" in the otherwise sunny world of Disney. Two former Oscar winners are also well represented: Brenda Fricker (best supporting actress, 1989's *My Left Foot*) does a nice Ann B. Davis impression as foster caregiver Maggie Nelson, and Ben Johnson (best supporting actor, 1971's

The Last Picture Show) offers a sly Gene Autry imitation as team owner Hank Murphy.

In the best Disney tradition, the two main child actors are natural, unaffected, and casually charming. Joseph Gordon-Levitt, who'd previously played a key part in director Robert Redford's *A River Runs Through It* and a recurring role on TV's *Roseanne*, strikes a happy medium between happiness and pathos without ever descending into grinning idiocy and bathos. Similarly effective is Milton Davis, Jr., as the troubled J.P.; though he'd never made a film before, Davis had climbed to TV fame via a well-circulated Pepsi Cola ad in which, spoofing the classic "Mean Joe Greene" spot, he snatched a bottle of pop from the thirsty Shaquille O'Neal and barked "Don't even *think* about it."

Since practically everything works in *Angels in the Outfield*—even the surprisingly shoddy "angel" effects serve their purpose in keeping the audience entertained—it may seem nitpicky to make any complaints, but nitpick we must. While the plot device of having Guffy McGovern hauled before the baseball commission to "justify" his belief in angels is acceptable in the original 1951 film—the Commission didn't want any basket cases running their teams back then!—the similar scene in the remake, in which team owner Hank Murphy threatens to kick George Knox out of Major League baseball if he doesn't renounce *his* belief in angels, rings false. Since the film has already established that the avuncular Murphy tolerates George's prolonged losing streak and his violent outbursts on the field, why would the old guy object to so benign a quirk as exhibiting faith in winged ghosts—and especially with only one game separating the Anaheim Angels from the Pennant?

This writer's other complaint about the film is tied in with an overall objection to having Political Correctness clumsily shoehorned into popular entertainment. In order to establish Ranch Wilder and Roger's father as disreputable characters, both men are shown smoking cigarettes, with obscene close-ups of mashed-out cigarette butts. And when Roger learns from Al that Matt Clark has only a short time to live, the explanation is that Matt "has been a smoker all his life!" Nag, nag, nag.

Opening to reviews ranging from raves to pans, *Angels in the Outfield* proved an unqualified winner where it counted most, at the box office. Grossing $50,200,000, the film ended up the fifth most profitable baseball picture of the 20th century. To Disney, the message was loud and clear: SEQUEL TIME!!!!!!!! (see notes for *Angels in the Infield*).

As the World Rolls On

Andlauer Productions/Elk Photo Plays; released September 10, 1921

Photographed by Walter A. Andlauer. 6 reels/5,600 feet, black and white; silent.
Cast: Jack Johnson, Blanche Thompson.

Boxer Jack Johnson, playing himself, enables a young black street gang member to escape an ignoble future by teaching the youth to box and play baseball. The young man joins the Kansas City Monarchs and leads them to victory.

Jack Johnson's checkered career as a proud black athlete enduring a white dominated society disinclined to appreciate black pride has been well documented in Howard Sackler's *a clef* stage play (and subsequent motion picture) *The Great White Hope*. The ultra-cheap *As the World Rolls On* was one of four silent films featuring Jack Johnson, each of them targeted to the black-only audiences that the segregation system created in major cities. It was filmed in 1921, six years after Johnson lost his world championship to Jess Willard, and was released only five months after the aging champ had finished serving a rather lengthy prison term in Leavenworth on a decade-old morals charge of questionable authenticity. Despite his reversals of fortune, Johnson's refusal to be subservient to his white persecutors had sustained his enormous fan following among African-Americans, guaranteeing that his film would enjoy wide distribution to what were then designated as "colored" movie houses.

The Kansas City Monarchs represented in the closing scenes of *As the World Goes On* were the superlative Negro National League baseball team that would ultimately yield such power players as Satchel Paige and Jackie Robinson (see *Don't Look Back* and *The Jackie Robinson Story*). Neither the team members nor the action surrounding them were filmed with anything resembling showmanship; as with Jack Johnson, it was enough for producer-cameraman Walter Andlauer that the Monarchs showed up to be photographed.

Aunt Mary

Henry Jaffe Enterprises; originally telecast December 5, 1979.

Executive producers: Henry Jaffe and Ellis A. Cohen. Produced by Michael Jaffe. Associate Producer: Jann Dutmar. Directed by Peter Werner. Teleplay by Burt Prelutsky. Photography: Hugh Gagnier. Edited by John Farrell. Music by Arthur B. Rubinstein. 100 minutes; color; sound.

Cast: Jean Stapleton ("Aunt" Mary Dobkin); Martin Balsam (Harry Strasberg); Harold Gould (Dr. Hoxley); Dolph Sweet (Amos Jones); Anthony Cafiso (Nicholas Rocco); Robbie Rist (Vernon); K. C. Martel (Billy); Steven Cafiso (Tony Rocco); Dago Demster (Tommy); Barney Pell (Sam Jessup); Tim Gemelli (Andy Steinwald); DeVoreaux White (Wally); Robert Emhardt (Berwick); Phillip Bruns (Detective Lamonica); Clyde Hopper (Hap Lawrence); Gerry Black (George Hazel); Marilyn Coleman (Grace Hazel); Lula Boxer (Suzie Martin); Mitch Carter

(Man on Street); Rick Corsola (Chester); Christopher Ciampa (Hank); Roger Hampton (Cop Sokowitz); Natalie Sibna (Nurse Abbott); Ted Duncan (Man in Stunt Car); Ernie Harwell (Announcer); Julia Jennings (Nurse Sokowitz); Kristopher Marquis (Mickey); Annie O'Neill (Woman on Street); Steve Pollack (Dennis); Stuart Rogers (Jaguar Fielder); Tom Stern (Hawk Coach); Jesse Joe Walsh (Randy); Terry Wills (Jessup).

Mary Dobkin, a physically handicapped Baltimore woman living on welfare, decides in the early 1950s to stem the tide of juvenile delinquency afflicting her neighborhood. With little more at her disposal than sheer tenacity, Mary organizes the "Dobkin Dynamites," a little-league baseball team made up of disadvantaged children and the few "hoods" that she's able to reach. Over a period of several years, and despite several operations that eventually result in the amputation of her left leg and right foot, Aunt Mary provides nearly 35,000 boys the opportunity to play baseball and find something positive in life. Many of these children are black, even though the story is set at a time when most civic activities in Baltimore were strictly segregated.

Aunt Mary was a "Hallmark Hall of Fame" production, first televised over CBS in 1979. It afforded Jean Stapleton one of the first opportunities she'd had since the premiere eight years earlier of *All in the Family* to portray a person outside her Edith Bunker characterization, and she was superb, capturing the essence of a disabled woman to whom the word "no" was simply not in the vocabulary.

The story of "Aunt Mary" Dobkin was a true one, though its real-life time span of twenty-five years was telescoped in this film for dramatic effect. Peter Werner's direction overcame some of the clichéd pitfalls inherent in Burt Prelutsky's script; Prelutsky fared rather better in blending disability drama, sports, sentiment, and truth six

TV Guide ad for *Aunt Mary* (1979).

years later with his teleplay for *A Winner Never Quits* (q.v.), a biographical study of one-armed ballplayer Pete Gray.

Since the emphasis in *Aunt Mary* was on its heroine rather than her youthful charges, the drama contained far more hospital scenes than it did ballfield activity. The baseball sequences bore the influence of the 1977 movie *Bad News Bears* (q.v.), with the street kids indulging in a great many insults and wisecracks involving ethnic origins and physical shortcomings—though never using the expletives so prevalent in *Bears*. What baseball there was in *Aunt Mary* was staged with acceptable authenticity.

Additional verisimilitude was provided by the appearance of sportscaster Ernie "Voice of the Tigers" Harwell. To many latterday Detroit fans, Harwell may seem out of place in a story set in Baltimore, but be assured there's no mistake: from 1954 to 1960 Ernie Harwell was the man behind the mike for the Baltimore Orioles.

The Babe

Waterhorse/Finnegan-Pinchuk Productions/ Universal; released April 17, 1992

Executive producers: Bill Finnegan, Walter Coblenz. Written and produced by John Fusco. Directed by Arthur Hiller. Associate producer: Erica Hiller. Photography: Haskell Wexler. Edited by Robert C. Jones. Music: Elmer Bernstein. Production designer: James D. Vance. Art director: Gary Baugh. Costume designer: April Perry. Production Manager: Michael Polaire. 1st Assistant Director: Jim Van Wyck. 2nd Assistant Director: Mark Cotone. Music supervisor: Michael Simmons. Camera operator: P. Scott Sakamoto. Sound mixer: John K. Fundus. Set decorator: Les Bloom. Set designers: Michael Merritt, Karen Fletcher-Trujillo, Linda Buchanan, J. Christopher Phillips. Graphic artists: Joe Nieminski, Susan Wexler. Make-up supervisor: Kevin Haney. Hair stylist supervisor: Werner G. Sherer. Casting: Valerie McCaffrey,

Nancy Nayor. Location manager: John J. Healey. Script supervisor: Judi Townsend. Production coordinator: Margi Newquist. Helicopter pilot: Al Cerullo. Visual effects supervisor: Chuck Comisky. Director of photography, visual effects: Christopher Nibley. Supervising sound editors: John Leveque, Bruce Stambler (for Gordon Ecker Productions). Foley artists: John Roesch, Katie Rowe. Digital compositing and computer animation by Pacific Data Images. Animators: Ira Shain, Kevin Rafferty, Jamie Dixon. Matte Paintings by Illusion Arts, Inc., Syd Dutton, Bill Taylor. Main title sequence designed by Saxon/Ross Film Design. Choreographer: James Petrakis. Color by DeLuxe. 113 minutes; Dolby Stereo Sound. Rated PG.

Cast: John Goodman (George Herman "Babe" Ruth); Kelly McGillis (Claire Ruth); Trini Alvarado (Helen Ruth); Bruce Boxleitner (Jumpin' Joe Dugan); Peter Donat (Frazee); James Cromwell (Brother Mathias); J.C. Quinn (Jack Dunn); Joe Ragno (Miller Huggins); Richard Tyson (Guy Bush); Ralph Marrero (Ping); Bob Swan (George Ruth, Sr.); Bernard Kates (Colonel Ruppert); Michael McGrady (Lou Gehrig); Stephen Caffery (Johnny Sylvester at 30); Gene Ross (Brother Paul); Andy Voils (Young Jidge); Dylan Day (Johnny Sylvester at 10); Laura Whyte (Mrs. Ballister); James Andrelin (Asa); Guy Barile (Torrio); Bernie Gigliotti (Capone); Michael Nicolosi (Jimmy Colosimmo); W. Earl Brown (Herb Pennock); Barbara Faye Wallace (Mrs. Pennock); Shannon Cochran (Flapper); Michael Papajohn (Heckler); Thom C. Simmons (McKechnie); Gene Weygandt (Mr. Sylvester); Steve King (Fuchs); Matt Doherty, Brandon DeMay (Boys in Car); Brendan Hutt, Beep Iams, Jeffrey Wiseman (Boys at St. Mary's); Rick Reardon (Ernie Shore); Randy Steinmeyer (Ty Cobb); Stevie Lee Richardson (Tommy the Batboy); Elizabeth Greenberg (Dorothy); Wayne Messmer (Yankee Announcer); Larry Cedar (Forbes Field Announcer); John Webb (Eddie); Tanner King (Joey); Erika Baltonado (Shoeless Girl); Stavon Lowell Davis, Tom Guarnieri (Boys with Radio); Ken Gildin (Hot Dog Vendor); Alan Johnson (Orphanage Reporter); Michael Kendall (Jack Warhop); Harry Hutchinson (Tris Speaker); Michael Krawic (Theater Goer); Sonny Mann (Scoffer); Johanna McKay (Yankee Wife); Cory Grant (Inmate); Jim Ortlieb, Scott Haven (Scribes); James Deuter (Society Man); Ralph Foody (Pittsburgh

Man); Meg Thalken (Johnny's Nurse); Ron West (Spectator); Irma P. Hall (Fanny Baily); Dana Lubotsky (Julia); Patrick Clear, William J. Norris (Fedoras); Ron Dean (Umpire Owens); Brett Hadley (Umpire no. 1); Ken Kells (Umpire no. 2); Jeff Still (Umpire no. 3); Hank Robinson (Umpire no. 4); Peter Siragusa (Umpire Hildebrand); Vern Hazard (1st Baseman); Harris Kal (Pirates Catcher); Christopher Beacom (2nd Baseman); Donald Bagley, Richard Kingdon, Timothy McShane, Chuck Sisson ("The Chiefs of Staff," Barbershop Quartet); Mark Ingram, Chuckie Anderson, Tyrone Blair, Thaddeus Exposé, Roger Harris, Albert Smith (Speakeasy Band); Marysue Redmann (Mansion Harpist); Ari Brown (New Orleans Clarinetist); Joe Huppert (Ansonia Pianist); Steve Jensen, Daniel Anderson, William Findlay, Michael Kocour, Brian Naylor, Russell Phillips, Paul Wertico (Bistro Band); John S. Green, Melody Rae, Joan Elizabeth (Verbal Spectators); Kara Zedicker (Redhead); Nicholas Rudall (Brother Malcolm); John T. Miltes (Brother Lewis); Tricia Munford (Ida, Jump's wife); Alison Groh (two-year-old Dorothy); Jane Rodell Tipton (Baby Dorothy); Andrew Bendel (Radio Announcer); Patrick Nugent (Pittsburgh Announcer); James "Ike" Eichling (Cigar Smoker); Shirley Spiegler-Jacobs (Woman in Coffee Shop); Roy Hytower (Elevator Operator); Amy Carlson (Girl on Stairs); Michael Chesler (Combs); Ron Marino (Combs II); Brooke Linthicum (Jump's Child); Randy Moll (Bob Meusel); Nicholas Satriano (Tony Lazzari); Ned Schmidtke (Hospital Reporter); Rick LeFevour, Frank P. Calzaura, James Fiero, Mark Harper, Conoor LeFevour, Matthew LeFevour, Randy Popplewell, Stacy Logan, George Aguilar, Lori Petitti, Rich Wilkie, Jeffrey Martin Williams (Stunts); Greg Brooks (first Base Coach in Babe's Final Game).

This filmization of the life of Babe Ruth (1895–1948) gets under way in 1902. Written off as "incorrigible," seven-year-old George Herman Ruth is unceremoniously deposited at St. Mary's Industrial School for Boys, a Baltimore reform school, by his disgruntled father. Taunted by his schoolmates and cruelly disciplined by his Xaverian teachers, little "Jidge" despairs that he will never be accepted by anyone. Then one day, under the tutelage of kindly Brother

Matthias, Jidge discovers that he has a natural talent for baseball, with awesome home runs a specialty. By age 19, Ruth is St. Mary's best all-around ballplayer, a fact that comes to the attention of Jack Dunn, manager of the minor-league Baltimore Orioles. Agreeing to become Ruth's official guardian, Dunn signs the boy for his team, and within five months "Babe" Ruth, as he is now known, has been traded to the big-league Boston Red Sox, owned by theatrical entrepreneur Harry Frazee. Now earning more "jack" than he ever thought existed, the childlike Babe indulges in his every whim, all the while lavishing expensive gifts on the people he likes and showering affection upon his adoring throngs of youthful fans. While downing one of his famously gigantic meals at Lander's Coffee Shop, Babe meets and falls in love with shy waitress Helen Woodford, whom he weds after a riotous three-month courtship. Though he loves Helen, Babe soon tires of married life at the couple's Massachusetts farm, and before long he is carousing his nights away back in Boston. In 1920, Harry Frazee sells Ruth to the New York Yankees for a record $125,000. While Babe thrives on the no-holds-barred nightlife in the Big Apple, Helen grows to despise Babe's libertine friends and hedonistic lifestyle, and before long she heads back to the farm—all by herself. Feeling just as "deserted" as he'd been back in 1902, Babe turns his attentions to Claire Hodgson, a widowed Ziegfeld Follies girl whom he had previously met in Boston. Though Babe begins an affair with Claire, she advises him to "patch up the fences" with Helen, which he does by adopting a cute baby girl named Dorothy. Because of his spectacular ballfield performance as a power batter and left-handed pitcher, Babe's peccadilloes are tolerated by the Yankees staff—but there are limits, as proven when manager Miller Huggins fines Ruth $5000 for unbecoming conduct *off* the field. Meanwhile, Babe's marriage to Helen completely

John Goodman as the "Sultan of Swat" in 1992's *The Babe*.

deteriorates, driving him back into the arms of Claire. Going into a severe slump in 1925, Babe not only loses the devotion of his fans but also the will to win. With the encouragement and support of both Claire and his longtime pal and teammate Jumpin' Joe Dugan, Babe pulls himself together, and by 1926 the "Sultan of Swat" is back and better than ever. He celebrates his comeback by taking Claire as his second wife, a union that brings Ruth both happiness and (thanks to the business-savvy Claire) lifetime financial solvency. In 1927, while engaged in a friendly home-run rivalry with fellow Yankee Lou Gehrig, Babe knocks out 60 homers, a single-season record destined to remain unbroken for the next 34 years. Still another career high occurs at Chicago's Wrigley Field in 1932, when Babe pulls off the legendary "called shot." Triumph quickly turns to tragedy when Babe is told that first wife Helen has perished in a fire. Adding to his woes, Babe is unable to convince Yankees owner Col. Ruppert to fulfill his lifelong dream of becoming the team's manager. Leaving the Yanks in 1934, Babe signs with the Boston Braves in 1935 as both player and assistant manager, on the understanding that a promotion to full manager is just around the corner. But Babe is in for another letdown when he discovers that he has been signed as a mere publicity ploy, and will never be given the opportunity to manage. Even worse, the public—and many of his teammates—now regard him as a washed-up buffoon. But 40-year-old Babe Ruth shows everyone that he still has the old Moxie when he swats out his 712th, 713th and 714th home run—all during the same game!

Of the three films based on the life of George Herman "Babe" Ruth (see separate entries for *Babe Ruth* and *The Babe Ruth Story*), *The Babe* is unquestionably the best and most entertaining. Which is not to say that the film is exactly a masterpiece, nor that it is 100 percent faithful to the facts.

Universal Pictures originally conceived *The Babe* in 1989, the year that *Field of Dreams* and *Major League* had proven that baseball pictures were Big Cheese at the box office. During its two-year development period, the project picked up a front-rank director, a gifted young screenwriter, and an A-list star. Best known for his 1970 megahit *Love Story*, director Arthur Hiller had many another excellent film to his credit, including *The Americanization of Emily* (1964), *The Hospital* (1971), *Silver Streak* (1971) and *The In-Laws* (1977). His only previous biopic was *W.C. Fields and Me* (1976), which, though not a box office success, is generally regarded as several notches above the usual Hollywood life story, making up for its many inaccuracies with its strong period atmosphere and the flawless performance of Rod Steiger as Fields.

Not surprisingly in the light of his biggest film hit, Hiller characterized *The Babe* as "a love story" which operated on many levels. "It's about a man's love for the game of baseball, the adoration of his fans—especially children—they for him and he for them, his irrepressible love for life—overcoming his own very difficult childhood—and the love between him and his two wives."

The Babe's screenwriter (and "Creative Producer") was 31-year-old John Fusco, a former jazz musician and New York University Film School graduate whose first important scripting project was *Crossroads* (1986), the story of the uneasy friendship between an arrogant young musician and a legendary blues performer. With this in mind, one can readily understand why so many scenes in *The Babe* establish their historical time-frame through the use of sidelines musical performers, from the ebullient barbershop quartet singing a ballpark hosanna to Babe Ruth's slugging skills, to the authentic-sounding jazz combos figuring prominently in each of the nightclub sequences. Prior to and during pre-production for *The Babe*, Fusco had written a brace of all-star westerns, *Young Guns* (1988) and *Young Guns II* (1990), demonstrating a facility for blending fact, folklore and fancy, and a gift for combining the attitudes and vernacular of the past with the sensibilities of the present. And with his concurrently-filmed script for *Thunderheart* (1992), the fact-based yarn of an FBI murder investigation on an Ogala Sioux reservation, Fusco not only again proved his talent for inter-weaving truth and fiction, but also that he could conceive an epic-scale film on an economy-level budget.

Quoted in the film's pressbook, John Fusco said, "The name Babe Ruth to me always fell under the same category as a Paul Bunyan or a John Henry, a figure in folklore. I thought of Ruth as some mythological giant. My interest in American folklore in general had been growing over the years and when Universal approached me with the idea for this two years ago, I said I was interested but I'd like to do a little research before committing to it."

"Once I started reading about him, I couldn't believe the life that this guy had. And I couldn't believe that a film—a fact-based film (not the one with William Bendix)—hadn't been made from the rich, deep well of reality there."

From the moment he agreed to tackle the project, Fusco knew exactly who he wanted to play Babe Ruth: "...John [Goodman] was the only person I had in mind when I wrote this movie. It's pretty rare to sit down and have somebody in mind from page one but I think he's the only guy out there who could've pulled this off." Boasting a remarkable list of stage and film credits, 39-year-old John Goodman enjoyed a built-in fan following thanks to his lengthy costarring stint on the top-rated TV sitcom *Roseanne*. He had also proved that he could open a picture as star of the wackily whimsical comedy *King Ralph* (1991), written and directed by David S. Ward of *Major League* (q.v.) fame. Of more importance to the current project, the bulky, muscular Goodman *looked* the part of Babe Ruth—and in this respect the actor had an enormous advantage over both Bill Bendix in *The Babe Ruth Story* and Stephen Lang in *Babe Ruth* even before he'd started memorizing his dialogue.

"It was a tremendous challenge to play this guy who's bigger than life," observed Goodman at the time. "He was a complex, multidimensional human being, strong and cocky and also very childlike and needy. I'm a baseball fan—I've been a lifelong Cardinals rooter—but it was the man himself that really intrigued me in doing this. And it was a great script." Incidentally, it was not the *only* script: John Goodman had previously been approached to star as the Bambino in the aforementioned made-for-TV *Babe Ruth*, but he turned that one down in favor of the theatrical-feature version.

Determined to bring Ruth to life, Goodman read every piece of literature about the ballplayer that he could get his hands on, then screened all available films of The Babe in action—from newsreels to *Pride of the Yankees* (1942)—in order to capture Ruth's voice, mannerisms, pitching and batting stance, and that famous lumbering trot around the bases. In January of 1991, Goodman went into training, learning to bat and throw left-handed with the assistance of two former ballplayers. Next came wardrobe fittings for 44 different costume changes, and finally a prosthetic facial transformation supervised by makeup-crew head Kevin Haney, who had previously earned an Academy Award for *Driving Miss Daisy* (1989).

In May 1991, filming began in Chicago, where Wrigley Field was redressed as the Polo Grounds and Yankee Stadium before reverting to Wrigley for the "called shot" scene. The nearby campus of DePaul University was "cast" as St. Mary's School for Boys, the lobby of the Rialto Theater in Joliet appeared as the Boston hotel lobby in which Babe is introduced to his future best friend Jumpin' Joe Dugan, and three city blocks in Chicago's Southport district were made over as the Boston street where Lander's Coffee Shop, the first meeting place of Babe and future wife Helen, was located—and where the impulsive Babe nearly breaks his neck taking a motorcycle ride (a bit of stunting which almost put John Goodman out of commission for real!). Stately Dewse Mansion showed up as backdrop for the society party where Babe makes a fool of himself and is introduced to the woman who will become his second wife; the Norwood Historical Society was transformed into Babe and Helen's Massachusetts farm; Lake Forest Academy was used for the 1922 Spring training sequence in which Babe meets Lou Gehrig for the first time; and the Illinois Railway Museum (which that same year served as one of the locales for another period baseball picture, *A League of Their Own*) provided the vintage train station, stretch of track, and observation car for the scene in which Babe and Helen bitterly call it quits. In July, the producers journeyed some three hours south of Chicago to Danville, Illinois, where the town's venerable stadium was used for the early scenes in Boston's Fenway Park and the climactic sequence in Pittsburgh's Forbes Field. Such is the level of the crew's expertise that only when we see the closing-credits acknowledgement do we realize that the entire film was made within a 150-mile radius of Chicago.

The location shoot was probably regarded as an extended Old Home Week by multi–Oscar-winning cinematographer Haskell Wexler, a Windy City native whose disturbingly authentic footage of the 1968 Democratic Convention riots had found its way into his 1969 directorial effort *Medium Cool*. Having previously worked on many period films (*Matewan, Bound for Glory, Blaze*), Wexler was a past master in the art of nostalgically evoking a specific historical era. His deft utilization of color and shadings also contributed mightily to *The Babe*'s many (and ofttimes abrupt) shifts of mood. The Dickensian orphanage scenes are drenched in somber blues and dusty browns; once Babe discovers his latent baseball talent, the on-screen images ever so gradually brighten; an amber-toned

motif (resembling hand-tinted postcards of the era) pervades the pre–1920 scenes, giving way to rich, full, sunlit colors when Babe hits his stride in the early 1920s; things subtly darken again when Babe goes into his slump, only to once more lighten up during his comeback; thereafter, the lenswork alternates between brightness and darkness, culminating in an awesome combination of *both* in the bittersweet finale. A decade later, Haskell Wexler would apply his photographic genius to another, equally nostalgic baseball biopic, director Billy Crystal's *61** (q.v.).

While *The Babe* was going through its lengthy post-production phase, the rival TV movie *Babe Ruth* made its debut on October 6, 1991. Many of the real-life elements in *The Babe* which had previously not been touched upon in any dramatic film—notably Ruth's first marriage to Helen Woodford—were covered in the TV production, which also followed roughly the same chronology, coming to its conclusion with Babe's three-homer career finale in 1935. Thus, Universal could not go through with its original plan to publicize its film as the first Ruth biopic to offer a thorough, warts-and-all portrayal of its subject, even though technically the Universal version was completed some time before *Babe Ruth* had even started. On the other hand, *The Babe* used incidents that were not covered in *Babe Ruth*, and vice versa, so it was still possible to judge each film on its own merits.

Sneak-previewing *The Babe* in early 1992, Universal trimmed or eliminated several scenes that weren't working, and also cleared up the more confusing moments in the chronology by adding superimposed titles which helped the viewer determine when and where certain sequences were taking place. Finally, in mid–April of 1992, *The Babe* was given widespread theatrical release, hot on the heels of a modest Universal effort called *Beethoven*, which the studio hoped would coast along on the reputation of its co-writer, John Hughes. The poster for *The Babe* showed a smiling John Goodman hoisting a beaming young boy on his shoulder, indicating that the picture would be ideal PG-rated family fare—and also giving baseball historians their first inkling that the film would not precisely offer the unvarnished R-rated truth.

In his book *Field of Screams*, Richard Scheinin described Babe Ruth as "the very prototype for the modern athlete, drunk on headlines, who can't get enough money, enough drink or drugs, enough women. These characters had been in the game all along, but Ruth truly delivered the whole ball of wax. He set the standard." These words could easily have described such brazen sports stars of the 1990s as Dennis Rodman and Mike Tyson, who used their talent and celebrity clout as an excuse to behave any way they damn well pleased without ever feeling the need to justify or explain themselves. Screenwriter John Fusco sensed that while the public accepted such outrageous excesses from contemporary athletes, they might not be so kindly disposed toward seeing the same negative traits in a legendary sports figure—and that the average viewer, weaned on TV "highlight" programs in which the more contentious celebrities' misbehavior was distilled into a mere 60 or 90 seconds, might not be inclined to sit still for two hours' worth of Babe Ruth's egotistical rampages. Thus, while never entirely condoning Ruth's behavior, Fusco sought to provide it with motivations that would be understandable to the viewer—and at the same time command the viewer's sympathy, if not outright approval. And what better way to do this than to show that for all his faults, Babe Ruth was simply a lost soul who spent his entire lifetime desperately searching for love, approval and acceptance?

The first time we see Ruth (accurately nicknamed "Jidge" at this point, a derivation of his real name George) he is an ugly,

oversized seven-year-old, rejected by his parents, left in the custody of unsympathetic older disciplinarians who immediately begin beating him into submission, and surrounded by jeering, relentlessly cruel "normal" youngsters. He continues to be denied any sort of friendship or affection until he proves his mettle with a baseball bat. For Ruth, the conclusion is inescapable: As long as he can slug out those long homers, people will love and accept him, no matter what he looks like or how he behaves; baseball will not only be his life, but also his ticket into the human race.

When signed by the Boston Red Sox, Babe realizes that he will be able to make a fabulous living playing a kid's game. Having never had any real money before, he doesn't know any better than to spend it profligately on rich food and expensive playthings, two commodities that had been in short supply at St. Mary's. Since money makes him feel good about himself, it naturally follows that others will feel the same way if he lavishes his money upon them. If people will not naturally gravitate to him, he will buy his friends. And if he happens to fall in love with a girl like Helen Woodford, surely expensive gifts will win her over; if he can buy friends, he can certainly buy love.

Like many another person suffering from arrested emotional development, Ruth allows most of his desires and ambitions to be dictated by others. When his pal Joe Dugan expresses interest in meeting a few "dames," so does Babe. When Dugan shows up with his family in tow and declines Babe's invitation to go out on the town, Babe figures that if Joe is willing to reject his company in favor of the wife and kiddies, there must be something in this family racket—so he proposes to Helen Woodford. When Helen casually expresses a fondness for cuddly farm animals, it is only natural for Babe to shell out good coin for a 200-acre farm, and never mind that he

Babe Ruth (John Goodman) "calls his shot" in that fabled 1932 game against the Chicago Cubs.

himself doesn't know a rooster from a duck. When his casual girlfriend Claire suggests that he should find a way to patch up his relationship with Helen, Babe impulsively rushes out and adopts the baby that Helen has yearned for; he may not be cut out to be a father, but it sure seems like a swell idea at the time. And when Babe is traded to New York, he immediately embraces the city's wicked *demimonde*—bootleg hootch, painted women, multiple sex partners—because it is readily available, and hell, everyone else is doing it. By characterizing Ruth as an easily led man-child, screenwriter Fusco takes much of the curse off his bad behavior; after all, what else can one expect from a big overgrown kid?

Also, the harsh treatment endured by the young Babe at the hands of older authority figures is used to explain his petulant refusal to bow to authority in later years. This is established in the early scene where Jack Dunn tries to convince the

Xaverian brothers in charge of St. Mary's School to release the 19-year-old Ruth to the Baltimore Orioles. Intending to send Dunn on his way, the head priest scowlingly points out that Ruth has been smoking and drinking since childhood, and that his discipline record is miserable. All true—but then Babe's champion, Brother Matthias, gently observes that a boy who has been abandoned by his family, run ragged by his teachers and ostracized by other children could not be expected to behave any differently. Later on, the adult Babe shows up late at the Yankees' spring-training camp, ostentatiously drives his roadster onto the playing field, and loudly browbeats diminutive manager Miller Huggins in full view of the rest of the team. Anyone else would probably come across as a boorish bully; but thanks to what we have already seen, we understand that Babe is just getting even for all those knocks he was forced to take when he was powerless to knock back—and while we don't like his behavior, it is still possible to go on liking *him*. Similarly, the disturbing scene in which Babe slaps his wife Helen might in other circumstances have caused the audience to automatically turn against him *en masse*. But that doesn't happen here: Fed up with his adulterous behavior, Helen angrily calls Babe "incorrigible"—the very word used by his father just before Babe was locked behind the grim gray walls of St. Mary's. Thus, Babe isn't really striking out at Helen, but at his unloving parents; and the instant he realizes what he's done, he pathetically chases after her, apologizing and begging her forgiveness with as much sincerity as he is capable of mustering. It may be an obvious dramatic device, but Fusco has managed to make the audience "feel" for Babe as much as for the long-suffering Helen.

Even if these narrative and dramatic devices had failed, Fusco could always rely upon what movie critic Pauline Kael once disdainfully dismissed as the "Blind Beggar for Luck," referring to the recurring scene in several early gangster films in which the criminal hero revealed a heart of gold by dropping a few coins in the cup of a blind beggar—generally just after knocking over a bank. But whereas Kael was referring to a phony and contrived method of purifying an impure character, Fusco's "Blind Beggar" was genuine: Babe Ruth's unequivocal, unconditional love of children. Though some revisionist historians have burrowed deep to dredge up isolated incidents in which Babe was less than cordial to one of his youthful fans, the evidence is overwhelming that his fondness for kids was bed-rock real—and that is how it is played in *The Babe*. Once we've seen him giving a bunch of street urchins a joyride in his new sedan, or handing out shoes to a bunch of dewey-eyed orphans ("Are you Santa Claus?" chirps one sweet little girl), it is all but impossible to think ill of Babe Ruth, no matter how reprehensibly he's behaved in earlier scenes.

This sentimentalizing and "explaining" of Ruth does not compromise the historic facts in the film, but merely places them in a context which takes some of the bite out of Babe's darker side. John Fusco's approach is hokey at times, but infinitely preferable to the shameful distortions found in 1948's *The Babe Ruth Story*, where every one of the "bad" incidents in Babe's life is falsified and twisted about so that he invariably emerges as the hero. The title character in *The Babe* is a hero only on the ballfield; the rest of the time, he is a flawed but essentially redeemable human being.

According to director Arthur Hiller, "Everything in this picture happened. When you're working with a figure whose life and deeds strain credulity, one wants to have a message flash every ten minutes that says, 'this is true, this really happened.' But in drama, one often rearranges sequences and settings for impact, which we've certainly had to do. Still, there is far more fact contained in this film than people unfamiliar with his life might be inclined to believe." And at the very beginning of the film, a title card assures us, "The following incidents are based on true events that occurred between 1902 and 1925." Note the careful choice of words in both of these quotes. Yes, most of what takes place in *The Babe* really did take place—but not necessarily in the same order, nor to the same people, that we see in the film. And in certain cases, facts were ignored for the sake of dramatic convenience or in favor of romanticized hearsay.

When we first meet the young Ruth in 1902, it is suggested that one of the reasons he is an outcast is because of his obesity. In truth, Ruth was an unusually large youngster, but not a fat one. Even in his early adult years he was comparatively slender, as opposed to the porcine Ruth we see walking out of St. Mary's in 1914. The decision to show Babe Ruth at his "fighting weight" throughout the picture was made because of John Goodman's casting in the role. Had the actor been svelte to begin with, it would have been possible to outfit him with a fat-suit for Babe's later years. But there was no way that Goodman could have realistically been squeezed into a "thin-suit," even if such a costume existed; also, there was no time for the actor to go on a crash diet for the earlier sequences. Moreover, the image of Babe Ruth as a heavy man was too deeply ingrained in the public's conscious-ness to confuse the issue with scenes of fluctuating weight.

Likewise, the image of Ruth as a home-run king tends to overshadow his skills as a fielder and a pitcher. In keeping with this, *The Babe* suggests that Ruth's strength as ballplayer lay solely in his ability to knock 'em out of the field; only in one scene do we see him pitching. Though we'd never know it from this film, Babe didn't even hit a big-league homer until 1915, his sec-ond season with the Red Sox. Similarly, while Ruth's capacity for hot dogs was awe-some, no one has any incarnate proof that he actually downed the doggies while on the playing field, yet *The Babe* offers us this epicurean spectacle as if it really happened before unimpeachable eyewitnesses. Ditto the "called shot" at Wrigley Field in 1932, which, though still a matter of intense de-bate amongst baseball historians, is pre-sented here as if Babe truly, deliberately and beyond all doubt pointed to where that ball would end up.

This presentation of Legend as Truth reaches its pinnacle in *The Babe*'s retelling of the "Little Johnny" story, in which Ruth purportedly rallied a youngster from his sickbed by promising to knock out a home run in the boy's honor. The full story of Johnny Sylvester, who actually did exist (though accounts vary as to how seriously ill he actually was) can be found in the entry on *The Pride of the Yankees*, which even after six decades still contains the best-ever filmic interpretation of this heartwarming anecdote. Still, the version offered in *The Babe* is touching without being overplayed, though it takes as many liberties with the facts as did the treacly version of the same yarn in *The Babe Ruth Story*.

Most experts have pinpointed Babe's promise to Johnny as occurring during the World Series of 1926. In *The Babe*, how-ever, the incident takes place during Ruth's first Series appearance with the Yankees in 1921. On a purely dramatic level, this is where the "Johnny" story belongs in the film's chronology—but by predating the event, John Fusco wreaked a bit of havoc with the timeline of the rest of *The Babe*. In the film's very last scene, Fusco emulates *The Pride of the Yankees* by having the grown-up, fully recovered Johnny Sylvester appear at Babe's "last stand" Forbes Field game in 1935 (the script states outright that this was Babe's farewell appearance with the Boston Braves, and his final day in baseball; of course, it was neither). After confounding his detractors by knocking out three home runs in the same afternoon, Ruth wearily trudges to the showers. En route he is stopped by Johnny, who tells Babe that he's "the greatest," then reverently hands back the precious baseball that Babe autographed for him many years before.

But wait. According to the film's clos-ing credits, the younger Johnny (Dylan Day) is 10 years old, while the older Johnny (Steven Caffery) is 30. If Johnny was 10 in 1921, he'd be 24 in 1935—but if he was 30 in 1935, then the incident of Babe promis-ing to knock out a homer for the boy oc-curred in 1915, when Babe was still with the Red Sox and nowhere near a World Se-ries. Or looking at it from another angle, if Johnny was 10 in 1921 and 30 the day Babe made his last stand at Forbes Field, then the final scene actually occurs in 1941, by which time Ruth wasn't even playing anymore. (Besides, what is Johnny Sylvester doing in Pittsburgh on this particular day anyway? Was he privy to inside information that Babe was going to knock three out of the park? And why would Babe Ruth want a baseball with his own autograph on it?)

Time and again, historical events are juggled or telescoped in *The Babe*. After correctly noting that Ruth met his wife-to-be Helen at a Boston restaurant in 1914, the script has him meet his *second* wife Claire within the next few days. The staging of the scene is meant to show that the boisterous Babe and the worldly Claire are kindred spirits, and that he would have been better off wedding her from the outset rather than entering into a mismatch with Helen. According to the script, Babe and Claire are reunited in New York in 1920, at which time they inaugurate a clandestine romance—though Claire is wise enough to realize that Babe still cares for Helen and urges him to go back to her. Only after the Babe-Helen union has ended in divorce does Claire come back into Babe's life, at which point she lifts up his spirits and enables him to pull out of a lengthy and demoralizing slump. This, according to the film, takes place in 1925; one year later, Babe and Claire are married, and we are supposed to breathe a collective sigh and declare, "At long last, he's with the *right* girl."

The facts: Babe did not meet Claire until 1923. His marriage to Helen had by that time deteriorated, but he would not divorce her because it would have gone against the grain of his Catholic upbringing. According to those baseball historians in the pro–Helen Woodford, anti–Claire Hodgson camp, Babe's doldrums of 1925 had as much to do with his extramarital romance with Claire as with the intestinal abscess (officially attributed to overeating, though it was just as likely a side effect of syphilis) which kept him benched during most of the season. And Babe did not wed Claire until 1929, shortly after Helen died in a fire—a tragedy which *The Babe* blithely moves up to 1933, as if to suggest that

his grief over Helen was the principal reason for his professional downward spiral after the "called shot" high point of 1932 (Strangely enough, the film's pressbook recounts these same milestones in Ruth's life, but in the *correct* order).

In its treatment of that 1925 slump, *The Babe* ignores Ruth's medical ailments, choosing instead to recreate the events surrounding his earlier and far more serious slump in 1922: Thus we see Babe charging after a hostile fan, throwing dirt at a booing crowd and screaming "You're all yellow!" three years after these embarrassing incidents took place. This was apparently done to suggest that Babe gradually fell apart after breaking things off with Helen, requiring him to be rescued by Claire's love after a respectable length of time—dramatically justifiable, but historically irresponsible.

Quite often, the film uses composite characters, rolling several different people in Babe's life into one single person for the sake of dramatic expedience. Unlike other films which used fictional composites, *The Babe* utilized actual individuals as distillations of two or more *other* actual individuals. A minor example of this can be found in the film's treatment of Pittsburgh Pirates pitcher Guy Bush, better known as "The Mississippi Mudcat," who gave up Ruth's last-ever home run at Forbes Field on May 25, 1935. In the film, it is suggested that Bush (played by Richard Tyson, former semipro ballplayer with the Gulf Coast league) pitched all three of Babe's homers on that fateful day, though in fact Ruth hit his first four-bagger off another Pirates pitcher, Red Lucas. Additionally, the film's pressbook indicates that the character of Guy Bush was to have had a more prominent role in the proceedings, as "one of Babe's principal tormentors throughout their years as Big League competitors." Since Bush was with the Chicago Cubs during Babe's called-shot game in 1932, the filmmakers may have originally intended to have their version of Bush pitch the ball in question—though as everyone knows, it was Charlie Root who gave up *that* homer. As it stands, Guy Bush shows up only in the final Forbes Field sequence, with a mere handful of lines to indicate that he and Babe don't much care for each other.

The film's most prominent composite is Babe's teammate Jumpin' Joe Dugan, well played by Bruce Boxleitner. Dugan's function in the story is to represent all of Babe's bemused roommates, who, like Yankees outfielder Ping Bodie (fleetingly played in the film by Ralph Marrero), were prone to comment that they spent less time with Babe than with his suitcase. Dugan also serves an expositional purpose by providing a willing and receptive audience for Babe's innermost thoughts before Claire Hodgson usurps that responsibility in the later reels. And like Claire, Dugan is always available to help Babe get through the tough times, when it seems as if everyone else has deserted the big lug. Ruth clearly regards Dugan as a surrogate father or big-brother figure, an older and wiser guide through the thorns and thickets of adulthood.

The career of the real Jumpin' Joe Dugan was so clouded in obscurity by 1992 that many reviewers assumed the character had been invented for *The Babe*. But the more knowledgeable critics remembered that Joe Dugan was a third baseman with the New York Yankees in 1927, the year of "murderers' row," and that he invariably sat next to Ruth on the Yankees bench. The film adheres to *some* of the facts surrounding Dugan, notably the origin of his nickname. Early in his career, he had a habit of "jumping" from the Philadelphia Athletics and joining other teams whenever he got homesick or restless; this idiosyncrasy was so well known that fans invariably greeted Dugan with derisive shouts of "I wanna go home." And, as depicted in *The Babe*, Dugan

shed his nomadic tendencies the minute he joined the Yankees (though this occurred in 1923, and not 1920 as the film suggests).

While the choice of Joe Dugan as Babe's best buddy and Good Right Ear works within the context of the film, it does not always hold water in terms of accuracy. Of all Ruth's fellow Yankees, Dugan would seem to have been the *least* likely selection for bosom companion and confidante. Whenever interviewed about the Babe, Dugan invariably made a trenchant comment suggesting that the Bambino was somehow less than human; a typical Jumpin' Joe quip usually went along the lines of "Hell! Babe Ruth wasn't born! The son of a bitch fell from a tree!" As for being an older mentor to Babe Ruth, Joe Dugan could not have qualified for this position even if he'd wanted to. For one thing, Dugan was two years younger than Babe; for another, he didn't even enter the Major Leagues until 1917, by which time Ruth was a three-year veteran and could easily have acted as *Dugan's* mentor—had he actually been his teammate at the time.

Though John Fusco tends to rely upon the Whole Truth only when it suits his needs, his screenplay for *The Babe* does an admirable job invoking the period in which it takes place, particularly in its use of such colorful slang phrases as "banana oil" (an archaic term for "nonsense"), "johnny flusher" (toilet), "swacked" (drunk) and "ducats" (dollars). Even so, the film tosses in a few modernistic touches to make things more accessible to a 1990s audience. Had *The Babe* been made in the 1940s or 1950s, the scene in which Ruth embarrasses himself in front of a gathering of blueblooded Boston socialites (so broadly drawn that they seem to have escaped from a Three Stooges pie fight) would have had him commit a social gaffe along the lines of eating his peas with his knife, or taking off his shoes while dancing. Ah, but *The Babe* came out at a time when gross-out humor was all the rage; thus, Babe proves that he is socially retarded by inviting a bejeweled dowager to "pull my finger"—with the expected loud and aromatic report!

The scenes in which Ruth's baseball accomplishments are reported to a radio audience of millions likewise betray a 1990s sensibility. Instead of the clipped, declamatory style preferred by radio broadcasters of the 1920s and 1930s, the Yankees Announcer speaks in the casual, intimate cadence that wouldn't gain widespread popularity until the 1960s and 1970s. We can live with this little anachronism because the man playing the ubiquitous announcer is one of the best sports broadcasters in the business. Known as "The Voice for All Seasons," Wayne Messmer was for ten years the National Anthem singer for Chicago's Wrigley Field, and the announcer for the final two Major League All-Star Games held in Chicago in the 20th century. Already a celebrated figure in the Windy City, Messmer achieved worldwide fame when he sang the US and Canadian anthems at the 1991 NHL All-Star Game, which was beamed to the troops of Operation Desert Storm. In fact, Wayne Messmer's own life story might make a great movie in itself. Two years after appearing in *The Babe*, he was robbed at gunpoint and shot in the throat. Though fans despaired that his golden tones and flawless tenor voice would never be heard again, Messmer made a remarkable recovery, capping his professional comeback with an inspirational autobiography and a bestselling series of motivational audio tapes.

While Wayne Messmer's presence enables us to accept the notion that sportscasters of Years Gone By sounded just like their contemporary descendants, it is harder to accept the clumsy handling of the film's expository newsreel sequences. Just having the action sped up and filmed in black and white does not make these scenes look authentic, nor are they helped along by the subtitles ("Ruth hits 60 Home Runs—Sets a Record"), which are far too contemporary in design to pass muster as products of their era. Even worse, several newsreel vignettes, ostensibly occurring in the early 1920s, are equipped with tinny voiceover narration—long before talking pictures had arrived!

On balance, the good outweighs the bad in *The Babe*, and the film works best on a level of solid, old-fashioned entertainment, packing a surprising amount of incident, and some beautifully crafted baseball scenes, into 113 minutes without any feeling of rush or strain (though the postproduction cutting tended to leave a few plot tangents unresolved, such as the now-pointless sequence in which Claire Hodgson is seen dining with four of Chicago's top gangsters). Even when the script or the direction falters, the film is brought back on track by its superb cast. John Goodman's performance in the title role is nothing short of amazing; one has to keep reminding oneself that this is the same actor who played Roseanne's husband, so thoroughly does he submerge his own distinctive personality into the indelible public persona of Babe Ruth. Beyond perfectly capturing Ruth's singular combination of childlike ingenuousness and casual debauchery, and serving up an admirable approximation of his ballplaying technique, Goodman also accurately recreates Ruth's unique Baltimore bray and bullhorn-like voice. Put John Goodman's portrayal of Babe side by side with the real Ruth's appearance in *Pride of the Yankees*, and we defy you to tell the difference!

Likewise excellent are the performances by Trini Alvarado and Kelly McGillis as the two women in Babe's life. Alvarado's interpretation of Helen Woodford as a simple, unpretentious girl who had the misfortune to hitch her star to a man who thrived on thrills and constant attention is first-rate, never becoming too mousy in the scenes in which she is browbeaten by Babe nor too shrill when she finally turns upon him. In the showier of the two roles, McGillis carries off Claire Hodgson's transitions from pragmatic woman-of-the-world to loving nurturer and back again without a ripple on the water. (For a rare unsympathetic characterization of the controversial Claire Hodgson Ruth, see the notes for 61*.) Of the supporting players, James Cromwell makes a good impression in the brief role of Brother Matthias, though his tall and slender presence perpetuates the false impression (created by Charles Bickford in *The Babe Ruth Story*) that the real Brother Matthias was trim and muscular-looking instead of being some 200 pounds overweight! Less effective are Peter Donat as Harry Frazee and Bernard Kates as Colonel Ruppert, but only because these two characters are written as sterile cardboard figures to contrast with the warmth and humanity of Babe Ruth.

Unfortunately, *The Babe* brought in only $17,530,000 domestically at the box office; conversely, *Beethoven*, the "little" Universal release which snuck into the theaters just before *The Babe*, raked in over $57,000,000, indicating that the future of family pictures would not be manifested in baseball biographies but instead in films with lots of kids, funny animals and gratuitous slapstick. Plus, the fact that *The Babe* didn't perform as expected discouraged other producers from coming up with "full" biographies, covering the subject from cradle to grave. The typical baseball biopic produced in the decade following *The Babe*—*Joe Torre: Curveballs Along the Way, Soul of the Game, 61**—would focus on an isolated incident in the life of its subject, rather than the entire lifespan.

What prevents *The Babe* from being a great film, rather than merely a very good one, are the same intangibles that weaken the two other Ruth biopics. Try as they might, the filmmakers fall short of recreat-

ing the historical circumstances which placed Babe Ruth head and shoulders above the rest. Generations removed from the Roaring Twenties era in which Ruth flourished, *The Babe* simply cannot replicate a period in which the American public, disillusioned by a devastating world war, sociopolitical unrest at home and any number of spectacular public scandals, needed and demanded celebrity deities like Babe Ruth, Rudolph Valentino and Charles Lindbergh.

Perhaps recognizing this, John Fusco inserted a brief scene near the end of the film which attempted to explain Ruth's full impact on the business of baseball. Appalled that Colonel Ruppert has so disdainfully refused to grant Babe's long-cherished dream of becoming a manager, Claire Ruth confronts Ruppert and angrily reminds him of how Babe literally saved baseball from the ignominy of the 1919 Black Sox scandal (see notes on *Eight Men Out*). Claire is right on target, and for a few seconds the viewer can almost appreciate just how important Babe Ruth was to the survival of the Game. But without an elaborately staged retelling of the Black Sox brouhaha (which would admittedly have doubled the film's running time!) to put Claire's powerful and eloquent words in context, they remain just words. Watching *The Babe* is like staring at a photograph of the most exciting ballgame in history rather than actually being there; you can see it, you can appreciate that the crowd was thrilled, but you will never truly feel it. (Nor does Elmer Bernstein's derivatively "heroic" musical score—which, when not emulating Aaron Copland's "Fanfare for the Common Man," is desperately striving to imitate Randy Newman's compositions for *The Natural*—enable the viewer to even vicariously experience the euphoria of being in the presence of Babe Ruth).

And despite the terrific performance of John Goodman, the essence of the real Babe Ruth was summed up by *The Babe*'s advertising slogan: "There was only one." In the words of his biographer Robert Creamer, "Nobody else ever looked like Babe Ruth. Or behaved like him. Or did all the things he did in his repressed, explosive, truncated life." And nobody ever will.

Babe Comes Home

First National; released May 22, 1927

Produced by Wid Gunning. Directed by Ted Wilde. Scenario by Louis Stevenson, from the short story "Said with Soap" by Gerald Beaumont, published April 1925 in *Redbook* magazine. Photography: Karl Struss. 6 reels/5,761 feet; black and white; silent.

Cast: Babe Ruth (Babe Dugan); Anna Q. Nilsson (Vernie); Louise Fazenda (Laundry Girl); Ethel Shannon (Georgia); Arthur Stone (Laundry Driver); Lou Archer (Peewee, third Baseman); Tom McGuire (Angels Manager); Mickey Bennett (Mascot); James Bradbury, Jr., Guinn "Big Boy" Williams, James Gordon (Ballplayers); James Toman (Umpire); Doc Crandall (Pitcher); Patsy File, Mitch Southerville, Joe Cotrell (Genuine Ballplayers); Helen Parrish (bit).

Babe Dugan, home run king of the Los Angeles Angels, is a demon on the diamond and equally demonic in his devotion to chewing tobacco. Babe's stained uniform is practically a resident at the Snow White Laundry, where laundress Vernie makes it her mission to find out what sort of a man is so careless with his habits. She attends a ballgame, where one of Babe's fly balls tags her in the eye. Babe heads over to the laundry to apologize, and before long he and Vernie are double dating with Babe's fellow player Peewee and Vernie's chum Georgia at the local amusement park. When a wild roller coaster ride jostles Babe and Vernie together, they become soul mates. Once engaged, Vernie tries to cure her future hubby of tobacco—but on the wedding night, a row develops between the newlyweds over the preponderance of spittoons and ash-

trays that turn up as wedding gifts. Vernie walks out, and Babe's game suffers mightily. During the inevitable Big Game, Vernie reappears in the stands and concedes defeat by tossing Babe a fresh plug of tobacco. With a wad in his mouth the size of Gibraltar, Babes hits a homer with the bases loaded. At the end, both hero and heroine "win" because Babe realizes that it was Vernie's love that helped him succeed, so he swears off chewing tobacco for good.

Babe Comes Home, filmed in the winter of 1926-27, was George Herman "Babe" Ruth's second starring feature film (see *Headin' Home*), and the first of Babe's several picture assignments in Hollywood. Producer Wid Gunning (owner of the hardnosed Hollywood trade publication *Wid's Daily*) and First National Studios hoped to capitalize on Ruth's 1925 comeback after his nearly career smashing slump, and on his participation in the 1926 World Series (had they waited another year, the production team could have received infinitely greater advance publicity for their film thanks to Babe's sixty homer record breaker). Having been burned by the creative bookkeeping that left him with less than promised for his first film venture in 1920, Babe demanded that First National pay him $50,000 before he'd set one foot on the westbound train. The studio cheerfully complied.

Babe loved Hollywood. He loved the zany publicity photo sessions, such as the one in which he had his makeup applied by Gloria Swanson; he loved hobnobbing with the coast-based sports celebrities; and he especially loved the nonstop parade of luscious movie starlets. This last perk almost compensated for the studio's insistence that Babe undergo an exhausting athletic training regimen before shooting started—which included a strict no-sweets diet and a nightly 9 P.M. curfew!

Babe's costar was Anna Q. Nilsson, a seasoned actress who'd recently recovered from a riding accident which left her immobile for a year, and who was, understandably, not keen on compounding the pains that still plagued her by trying to act with an athlete who'd probably have to be led around the set with a carrot on a string. Nilsson was markedly cold to Babe, despite publicity stories that had Ruth declaring how much fun it was to make love to such a classy lady and get paid for it to boot. To allay friction, director Ted Wilde (who'd later put Ruth through his guest star paces on the Harold Lloyd picture *Speedy*) filmed most of his costars' scenes separately, on different days, seeing to it that Ruth and Nilsson would endure each other's company *only* on the days that they had scenes together.

Babe Comes Home was a comedy, so there were plenty of scenes in which Ruth was called upon to do something funny, like accidentally slamming someone with a door when entering a locker room, finding himself crouched under the leading lady's bed, or mugging broadly while careening on a roller coaster. Taking into consideration that Babe's comic expertise was rudimentary at best, Louis Stevenson's script provided ample scenes for not one but two comedy relief characters: Babe's buddy Pee-wee, played by veteran vaudeville laugh getter Lou Archer; and a laundry drudge, portrayed by proven audience favorite Louise Fazenda. And since most comedies of the silent era were counterbalanced by moments of pathos, the scriptwriter made sure that the heavy dramatics were in the hands of Anna Q. Nilsson, confining Babe to such fleeting histrionic moments as his smashing a "Home Sweet Home" sign with his fist after his bride walks out. (The publicity machine "quoted" Babe as saying that this was the hardest scene for him to do since he deeply believed in the sentiment of a Home Sweet Home, a statement that must have been a source of belly laughs to Babe's past roommates, one of whom insisted that he roomed not with the habitually absent Ruth but with Ruth's suitcase.)

The film's baseball scenes were among the first to be photographed at Los Angeles' Wrigley Field, built only one year before shooting commenced. Wrigley was known for being a park where home runs were achieved with comparative ease, so one tends to believe the claim in the pressbook of *Babe Comes Home* that Ruth hit nearly seventy homers during the course of the production to accommodate retakes. The ballpark was the home of the Pacific Coast League's Los Angeles Angels, who not only provided uniforms and equipment for the game scenes but also several team members as bit players and extras, including Doc Crandall, Patsy File, Joe Cotrell and Mitch Southerville. Even the park's umpire, James Toman, showed up on screen, playing—get a grip on yourself—the park's umpire!

When Ruth's fellow Yankees attended the preview of *Babe Comes Home* in February 1927, they hooted and hollered at its various inaccuracies, most notably the rings worn on the fingers of the catchers. Most newspaper reviewers were kind but condescending to the picture; one Detroit critic observed that though Babe's performance was fun to watch, there was "no reason for John Barrymore or any other noted thespian to become agitated about the matter." Latterday witnesses to the film would generally observe that Ruth's much heralded charisma seemed to melt before the cameras, making him appear less like a glad handing crowd pleaser and more like a truculent child reciting poetry during a school pageant. Yankee player Mark Koenig cut closer to the bone when he stated that "[Babe] couldn't act worth crap."

Koenig was evidently not on the payroll of the First National publicity team, which went out of its way to sell the picture to the female fans that might otherwise shun a baseball story by rhapsodizing on Babe Ruth's hitherto untapped acting talent and

Anna Q. Nilsson and Babe Ruth oblige the still cameraman for *Babe Comes Home* by staring in wide-eyed fascination at absolutely nothing.

his persuasiveness as a romantic lead. This sort of elaboration was typical of a promotional campaign that included a big gun advertising a tie-in with Star Chewing Tobacco, the brand masticated by Babe throughout the film; a press kit that offered to local theater owners a giant cardboard baseball for the lobby and the material with which to convert the movie house's ticket booth into an ersatz ballpark box office;

and such hometown hype tips as suggesting that the theater ushers dress up in baseball uniforms. Not without justification, First National declared to its exhibitors that, "More publicity has been given this picture than any you've ever played!"

It certainly needed that extra push. Though well mounted and lightly entertaining, *Babe Comes Home* was utterly undistinguished, save for the appearance of its leading player. The picture made some money, but generated "no new business," a term used by *Variety* to describe the fortunes of a film that would attract few viewers other than the fans of the star. First National could have used more fans like the fellow who saw the picture ten times—every time he hit a town where it was playing. In other words, they could have used more fans like Babe Ruth himself.

Babe Ruth

Lyttle Productions/Warner Bros. Television; first telecast October 6, 1991

Executive producer: Lawrence A. Lyttle. Producer and second unit director: Frank Pace. Directed by Mark Tinker. Teleplay by Michael de Guzman, from the books *Babe Ruth: His Life and Legend* by Kal Wagenheim, and *Babe: The Legend Comes to Life* by Robert W. Creamer. Photography: Donald M. Morgan. Edited by Stanford C. Allen. Music by Steve Dorff. Production designer: Donald Light Harris. Production manager: Bob Jeffords. Assistant directors: Ken Ornstein and Tim Lonsdale. Supervising sound editor: Michael C. Gutierrez. Music editors: Chris Ledesma and Music Works. Set decoration by Bill Vail. Makeup by Michael Jones; special makeup design by Michael Westmore. Hairdresser: Julie Fehl-Bontier. Costume supervision by Darryl Levine. Location manager: Terry Gusto. Production coordinator: Bari Halle. Assistant to producer: Karen Ragan. Production supervisor: Lloyd Arnold. Baseball consultant: Rod Carew. Baseball coordinator: Danny Hall. 98 minutes; color; sound.

Cast: Stephen Lang (Babe Ruth); Brian Doyle-Murray (Marshall Hunt); Donald Moffat (Colonel Ruppert); Yvonne Suhor (Helen); Bruce Weitz (Miller Huggins); Lisa Zane (Claire); William Lucking (Brother Matthias); Neal McDonough (Lou Gehrig); John Anderson (Judge Landis); Pete Rose (Ty Cobb); Cy Buynak (Eddie Bennett); William Flatley (Emil Fuchs); Stephen Prutting (Jimmy Walker); Frankie Thorn (Lady in Hotel); Thomas Wagner (Bill Killefer); Gregory Adams (Orphan Boy); Jeff Blanchard (Jimmy Barton); Brandi Chrisman (Dorothy); Dana Craig (Umpire); Charles J. Fick (Waite Hoyt); Matthew Glave (Joe Dugan); Adam Goldberg (Vendor); Deborah Anne Gorman (Julia); Thomas B. Hall (Reporter); John Kolibab (Hod Lisenbee); Nathan Lisle (Fan); Mickey Manners (Reporter); Andrew May (Wally Pipp); Clint Nageotte (Young Babe); Jerry O'Donnell (Fan); Fred Ornstein (Reporter); Joe Schratz (Umpire); Troy Startoni (Charlie Root); Philip L. Stone (Graham McNamee); Rohn Thomas, Tom Tully (Reporters); Annabelle Weenick (Mrs. Woodford); Gary Wilbanks (Reporter); Dale Young (Fred Lieb).

This biopic of George Herman "Babe" Ruth covers the years 1920 through 1935, from Babe's freshman year with the New York Yankees to his retirement. On the field, we see Ruth's remarkable home run prowess as Babe sets and breaks several major league records all by himself. We also see Ruth's ongoing battles with authority, centralized on his love-hate relationship with Yankees manager Miller Huggins and his hate-hate relationship with team owner Jacob Ruppert. Babe's tumultuous "wine, women and more women" private life is explored, with special emphasis on his star-crossed first marriage to Helen Woodford and his happier alliance with showgirl Claire Hodgson, whom he weds after Helen's death in 1929. With Babe's considerable input, the Yanks win pennant after pennant in the 1920s, but Ruth never realizes his dream of becoming a manager. After an acrimonious parting of the ways with Ruppert in 1934, Babe is signed on by the Boston Braves, with the assurance that he'll eventually get that coveted managerial post. But his year with the Braves is an exercise in dullness and mediocrity, making it all too clear to everyone that Ruth is past his prime. Still, Babe finishes big on May 25, 1935, with three homers in a single game at Pittsburgh's Forbes Field, and it is at this high point in the fortunes of Babe Ruth that this TV movie tactfully comes to an end.

First broadcast over NBC in October of 1991, *Babe Ruth* seems determined to purge the sour aftertaste left by the unlamented 1948 William Bendix movie *The Babe Ruth Story* (q.v.). While it isn't exactly a "warts and all" yarn (Babe comes off more like an ingenuous child-man than a conscienceless carouser), the 1991 film is far closer to the real thing than the Bendix version—and, in fact, is in general one of the few baseball biopics that can boast of more than casual fidelity to the truth. The fact that Michael de Guzman's teleplay contrives to have all the characters speak fluent exposition can in this instance be forgiven, because the facts and statistics articulated by everyone at least *are* facts and statistics, and not the usual Hollywood fabrications and half-truths. It's also helpful to give 1991 audiences a handy shorthand guide to a career and time frame that is not the common knowledge it once was.

Film and TV star John Goodman, who certainly had the right build for the part, was originally approached to play Ruth, but the TV people couldn't come to the right financial terms, so Goodman opted to portray the Sultan of Swat in the theatrical picture *The Babe* (q.v.). It's just as well, since Goodman's replacement was in no way second best. Stephen Lang, a prestigious Broadway actor with limited TV and movie credits (his most memorable showing was in the 1985 CBS production of *Death of a Salesman*, which starred Dustin Hoffman), may not be Babe Ruth to the letter, but he successfully and consistently conveys the spirit, the swagger, the petulance, the gregariousness, and the weather-vane shifts from temperament to tenderness that were so much a part of the real Bambino.

Stephen Lang's home run scenes (shot mostly in an old-style stadium in Ontario, California) rank as some of the best baseball re-creations ever committed to film. Under the careful tutelage of Hall of Famer Rod Carew, who spent the better part of a month showing the right-handed actor how to play leftie with conviction, Lang made all the familiar Babe Ruth mannerisms his own: The circular warm-up motion, the pigeon-toed stance, the upward tilt of the head to check the progress of the batted ball, and the heavy-hoofed gallop around the bases. Michael Westmore's makeup design for Lang was another master stroke, providing the *Babe Ruth* star with a more than passable pug nose. And in a fit of "Robert De Niro," Lang also gained thirty-five pounds to match Ruth's hulking physique. (It's a filthy job, but somebody's got to do it!)

So many things work in *Babe Ruth* that it's a shame that quite a few things don't work. To its credit, the film tries to squeeze as many aspects of Ruth's life as is possible within a ninety-eight-minute space (one notable deletion is Babe's hitting a homer for a sick kid, though that chestnut was amply covered in the like-vintage *The Babe*). We get reasonably accurate representations of such heretofore undramatized vignettes as New York mayor Jimmy Walker's public reprimand of Ruth at an Elks Club tribute to the 1922 Yankees, Babe's cavalier attitude toward his first wife, the mystery surrounding the unheralded appearance of Ruth's infant daughter Dorothy, and Babe's 1925 collapse due to an intestinal abscess. But in its desire to include everything, the film has only enough room left over to offer sketchy, surface portraits of most of these incidents.

This insubstantial quality carries over to the supporting performances. With the

Babe Ruth: An autographed production still of Stephen Lang as the Bambino.

exception of Bruce Weitz's fleshed-out turn as Miller Huggins (the film proposes that Huggins and Ruth had something of a father-son relationship, a notion that would have come as quite a surprise to both men), the other characters exist only as single dimension types, in the manner of a medieval morality play. Thus, Ruth's first wife Helen is merely The Mousy One, second wife Claire is The Brassy One, Yankees teammate Lou Gehrig is The Shy One, and so forth. Nowhere is this truer than in Donald Moffat's single-note interpretation of Ruppert, who seems to have no other line to say but "Ruth, you didn't win me my Series." Perhaps to induce some self-interest in portraying this character, Moffat adopts a martinet posture and Teutonic accent straight out of a Wartime propaganda film. It's amazing that he overlooked the monocle and dueling scar.

Perhaps more breathing room for the actors and the incidents would have been made possible had the teleplay not wedged in a couple of "it never happened" moments. There might have been time to explore Ruth's pre–Yankees career with the Boston Red Sox had film not been expended on an imaginary confrontation between Babe and baseball commissioner Judge Landis (played by John Anderson, re-creating his role from *Eight Men Out* [q.v.]), in which Ruth calls Landis a "white-haired old bastard" to his face. And we might have had time for Ruth's 1930s feud with Lou Gehrig if *Babe Ruth* hadn't thrown in a fabricated, wholly arbitrary hotel room conversation between Babe and Ty Cobb.

This last scene evidently existed so that the producers could drum up viewers by publicizing the "special guest appearance" by onetime Cincinnati Reds star Pete Rose as Ty Cobb—a neat casting choice, in that it was Rose who broke Cobb's lifetime hits record. After all the ballyhoo in the press, you'd think it would have behooved the makers of *Babe Ruth* to give Pete Rose

more to do than recite five measly lines (which he does with considerably more finesse than the lines deserve) and take a few swigs of "bootleg hootch." He doesn't even get to appear in a baseball costume, since Rose's recent lifetime ban from baseball (for gambling, if you need to be reminded) prohibited his ever donning a uniform in public again.

One of *Babe Ruth*'s plusses indirectly works against the film. Director Mark Tinker immediately grabs the audience with an action-packed opening twenty minutes, making certain that no one will leave the room for a quick snack before the story's groundwork is laid out. Unfortunately, it's too much, too soon. Tinker is unable to sustain the rapid pace of the early scenes, rendering most of the film's later highlights—including Babe's record sixtieth home run during the 1927 season—repetitious and anticlimactic.

Remember, however, our original affirmation that a lot of *Babe Ruth* works, and works beautifully, resulting in a perfectly respectable TV "life story of the week." Television critics, apparently perceiving this film as a hastily assembled project to cash in on the upcoming John Goodman theatrical movie on Ruth, were unduly hostile to the Stephen Lang version. *Entertainment Weekly* gave *Babe Ruth* a "D" grade, itemizing the film's occasional clichés, remarking that poor Pete Rose played his cameo "like he just stepped into shoes filled with tobacco juice," and writing off the whole project as "tediously simple-minded." Hey, what's the problem? *Babe Ruth* may not have been Class A, but it could have been far, far, worse. Just keep reading and you'll see why.

The Babe Ruth Story

Allied Artists; released July 26, 1948; general release, September 6, 1948

Produced and directed by Roy Del Ruth. Associate producer: Joe Kaufman. Screenplay by Bob Considine and George Callahan; story by Grantland Rice, adapted from the *The Babe Ruth Story* by Babe Ruth and Bob Considine. Photography: Phillip Tannura. Music by Edward Ward. Vocals by Gertrude Niesen, The King's Men, and The Mitchell Boychoir. Assistant director: Mel Dellar. Edited by Richard Heermance. Art direction by F. Paul Sylos. Set decoration by Ray Robinson. Costume design by Lorraine MacLean. Makeup by Otis Malcolm. Technical director: Pat Flaherty. Special baseball assistance by Lew Fonsesca. Assistant to producer and 2nd unit director: D. Ross Lederman. 2nd unit photography: James Van Trees. 2nd unit assistant directors: Art Black, Mel Dellar. 106 minutes; black and white; sound.

Cast: William Bendix (Babe Ruth); Claire Trevor (Claire Hodgson Ruth); Charles Bickford (Brother Matthias); Sam Levene (Phil Conrad); William Frawley (Jack Dunn); Gertrude Niesen (Nightclub Singer); Fred Lightner (Miller Huggins); Stanley Clements (Western Union Boy); Bobby Ellis (Babe, age eleven); Lloyd Gough (Baston); Matt Briggs (Colonel Ruppert); Paul Cavanaugh (Dr. Menzies); Pat Flaherty (Bill Corrigan); Tony Taylor (Johnny); Warren Douglas (Young Player); Mark Koenig (Himself); Richard Lane (Boston Coach); Ziggy Sears, Bucky Harris, Harry Wismer, Mel Allen, H. V. Kaltenborn (Themselves); Knox Manning (Narrator); Ralph Dunn (George Herman Ruth, Sr.); Harry Cheshire (Cap Huston); Frank Ferguson (Father of Crippled Boy); Francis Pierlot (Brother at St. Mary's); James Flavin (Sailor); Bennie Bartlett, Frankie Darro, David Gorcey (Newsboys); Eddie Dunn (St. Louis Coach); Mary Field (Nurse at Orphanage); Ann Doran, James Arness, Eddie Fetherston (Reporters); George Lloyd (Prisoner); Bess Flowers (Nightclub Patron); Joseph Crehan (Johnny's Father); Ed Gargan (Policeman); John Harmon, Frank O'Connor (Men in Bar); Al Hill (Cab Driver); Sam McDaniel (Janitor); Charles Sherlock (St. Louis Player); Tom Stevenson (Headwaiter); Frank Wilcox (Doctor Who Refuses to Treat Dog); and Bob Meusel, Oliver Crawford.

Once upon a time, there was a wonderful young Baltimore boy by the name of George Herman Ruth. While attending St. Mary's Industrial School for Boys in 1914, young George's prowess at baseball brought him to the attention of Baltimore Orioles manager Jack Dunn, who upon meeting the gangly nineteen-year-old Ruth immediately nicknamed him "Babe." The phenomenal Babe Ruth became a pitching star for the Orioles, then later for the major-league Boston Red Sox, with no more enthusiastic supporter than his mentor at St. Mary's, Brother Matthias, who talked of nothing but baseball to anyone who would listen. For a brief period Babe went into a pitching slump, which was cured when a lovely young lady informed him that he tipped off the opposing team by sticking out his tongue each time he'd prepare to throw a curve ball. That lovely lass was nightclub performer Claire Hodgson, to whom bachelor Babe took an immediate liking, culminating in his writing a proposal to her on the very ball that he'd batted for his sixtieth home run in 1927. Along the way, Babe found time to perform a miracle; shortly after slugging the longest recorded home run in baseball history, he waved to a crippled child, causing the beaming youth to stand up and walk! There *were* dark times wherein Babe got himself into trouble, most of these events occurring after Ruth left Boston for the New York Yankees. But Babe would never have misbehaved had not the misguided Yankees manager Miller Huggins fined and suspended Ruth in 1925—all because Babe skipped a game when he rushed an injured dog to the hospital. Happily, Ruth and Huggins patched up their differences shortly before Huggins's death.

But this was not the end of the "Bambino's" story. Perhaps you've heard the legend of Ruth pointing to the direction where he planned to hit a homer during the 1932 Yankees-Cubs World Series. But what you might not know is that Babe was doing this on behalf of little Johnny, a bedridden boy with a near-fatal disease—and when Babe smacked that ball for Johnny, the lad obligingly rallied and survived. Alas, came the inevitable day when Ruth's career began to ebb. He took an executive job with the Boston Braves, only to learn that he was expected to play, though he knew he was past his prime. An insulting remark from a fellow Brave caused Ruth to revive his strength to hit three home runs in 1935; within ten minutes after this feat, he announced his retirement, and within ten seconds of this announcement, he received word that the Braves had fired him. After several aimless years, Babe contracted an unnamed but deadly illness, but he remained a champ, allowing himself to be guinea pig for a dangerous experimental drug that would ultimately save the lives of millions.

It was no crime in the 1940s to make a biographical film that played fast and loose with the truth; one need only look at the George M. Cohan biopic *Yankee Doodle Dandy* (1942) to see how people, places and events could be twisted, distorted and sometimes dispensed with entirely in order to come up with a good story. But the operative word here is "good." *The Babe Ruth Story* is not good. In fact, it would have to undergo a great deal of improvement to qualify as mediocre.

Rather than launching immediately into a tally of the film's shortcomings, let's delve a bit into its background. In 1946, a decade after Babe Ruth's retirement, Howard Hughes Productions purchased the movie rights to his life story for $150,000. One year later, Allied Artists, the newly formed "prestige" division of bargain-basement Monogram Pictures, was casting about for a surefire hit, and felt they'd found it by buying the Ruth story from Hughes. Allied Artists was aware that Ruth was working (in collaboration with Bob Considine and Considine's researcher Fred Lieb) on his long awaited autobiography, and the studio hoped to capitalize on the book's imminent publication. Babe was offered a percentage of the profits on the upcoming

film, and was promised that he'd be made technical adviser, with full script approval.

But Ruth, already weakened by the cancer that would ultimately kill him, was exhausted by the effort to get his book finished for the Christmas trade, and thus wasn't up to traveling to Hollywood until after Easter 1948. By that time, most of *The Babe Ruth Story* had already been shot, so whatever technical advice that Babe might have to offer was purely academic. He did become acquainted with William Bendix, star of the film, and spent at least one day giving Bendix pointers on his batting technique. It was evident by this time that Babe's days were numbered, so the film's final scenes were hastened before the cameras with little thought given to script rewrites, accuracy, or production polish; the studio wanted to get the picture to the public before Ruth succumbed to cancer. (There was a nasty rumor, still prevalent in some circles, that Allied Artists planned to release the film on the very day of Babe's demise—one of the few lapses of taste that *The Babe Ruth Story* had failed to incorporate into its screenplay.)

The picture debuted at New York's Astor Theatre on July 26, 1948, with a full cadre of celebrities, headed by Mayor O'Dwyer, in attendance. Babe Ruth was also there, at least physically. According to some reports, he became so ill that he left in the middle of the screening, while other witnesses asserted that Ruth was so heavily medicated that he slept through the whole affair. It is not true that Babe's disappointment with the picture led to his death less than one month later, but judging by the quality of *The Babe Ruth Story*, it's easy to see how a story like that could take shape.

In a way, the film's blissful disregard for facts is understandable. Sports columnist Grantland Rice, who is given sole story credit, was, after all, one of the chief newsprint fabricators of the Babe Ruth legend. To eradicate the bitter taste left after the

Black Sox scandal of 1919 (see *Eight Men Out*), Rice and his fellow reporters were anxious to create a hero who would save baseball in the eyes of the public. Babe Ruth came along at just the right time as the object of this media idolatry, and Rice worked day and night inventing the larger than life image of Babe that fans would be subjected to for the next 25 years.

It would not have been in Grantland Rice's best interest to clutter his screen story with facts that would make Rice look like a long-term liar, hence *The Babe Ruth Story* bends over backward whitewashing its subject. If Babe missed a ballgame that resulted in his 1925 fine and suspension, it was because he'd conked a mangy little pooch with a line drive and was speeding it to the hospital, not because of the real-life reason that Babe just didn't feel it was necessary to offer an explanation for his chronic tardiness. If Babe landed in jail, as indeed he did in 1922, it was not due to his assumption that a traffic ticket could be fixed (actually the case), but due to his nobly punching out a shady character who'd asked Babe to throw a game. And if Babe was in reality a shameless carouser who regularly cheated on his first wife, it was simple enough for Grantland Rice and his coconspirators to utterly ignore the existence of Wife Number One—who'd been dead since 1929 anyway, so who's to sue?—and suggest that Claire Hodgson was the only woman in Babe's life (Babe's daughter Dorothy claimed in 1988 that Claire Ruth was responsible for the script's distortions of Babe's private life—though if this were the case, it was surprising that the second Mrs. Ruth would characterize the film as "an obscenity, a ridiculous charade").

Actually, a great many plot points in the film were based upon fact. Babe really did promise an ailing youngster that he'd hit a home run on the kid's behalf, though this occurred during the 1926 World Series, not in the series of 1932 as the film would have you believe (see *The Pride of the Yankees* for more on this famous incident). Babe was actually fired after only one year with the Boston Braves, though the script elaborated on this by having him canned on the very day that he enjoyed his three homer "comeback" at Pittsburgh's Forbes Field. Ruth did referee a wrestling match in 1945, and this is dutifully related in *The Babe Ruth Story*, albeit with the added fiction of the match being between two fearsome-looking women. And toward the end of his life, Babe did undergo treatment with an experimental drug named Teropterin that had been successful in checking cancer in laboratory rats. While the drug lacked the fatal side effect threat that the "miracle cure" in the film was supposed to have posed, it was temporarily successful in assuaging Babe's illness, leading to a write-up on the efficacy of Teropterin in a paper for the International Cancer Congress—wherein Ruth was identified only as "a nationally famous fifty-two-year-old man" because he didn't want the facts of his cancer to be made public.

Any inherent credibility in the story was unfortunately undercut by the tendency of its scriptwriters to forget they were writing for the movies and not the printed page. Every line of dialogue is so painfully stilted that one wonders whether Grantland Rice, Bob Considine and George Callahan had ever heard two human beings actually carry on a conversation. Whenever baseball is discussed in the film, it's as though the speaker is quoting from a press release; Babe's mentor Brother Matthias speaks of Christy Mathewson as "the famous Christy Mathewson" to a group of boys that would have known Mathewson was famous without Matthias' help. Worst of all is the moment when, after Babe is urged to file charges against the Boston Braves for firing him, he replies that suing baseball would be "like suing the church." Perhaps Susan Sarandon could get away

Proof that all the art directors and makeup artists in Hollywood couldn't make Bill Bendix pass for a teenager (*The Babe Ruth Story*).

with referring to "the Church of Baseball" in 1988's *Bull Durham*, but *Bull Durham* was funny on purpose.

Much has been written of William Bendix's unsuitability for the role of Babe Ruth (reportedly, Claire Ruth had wanted the part to go to Paul Douglas, but Douglas had not yet made his film debut, while Bendix was a proven commodity both in films and in his *Life of Riley* radio series). Beyond the fact that the actor was right handed and Babe was a southpaw, Bendix's raspy Brooklyn flavored voice was nothing like Ruth's flat but deeply resonant vocal pattern, nor was the notoriously chunky Babe nearly as paunchy in his prime as Bendix. Not that Bill Bendix ever pointed to this film with pride; he later described *The Babe Ruth Story* as "[the] worst picture I ever made. It could have been great, I think.

But it didn't work out that way. I remember going to the preview in Los Angeles. In the early part of the picture, when I'm discovered in the orphanage, the scene was full of sixteen- and seventeen-year-old kids. Do I have a kid playing me? No. I have to do it with makeup. And I'm thirty-eight years old at the time." [He was actually forty-one!] "The audience laughed. I would have laughed, too, but I felt too bad."

That makeup work by Otis Malcolm was one of the film's biggest drawbacks. William Bendix tried on 75 false noses—evidently looking for one that wouldn't start growing when he quoted from the script—but the end result made him look more like character actor Lionel Stander than Babe Ruth. Nor was the makeup any more convincing on the rest of the cast. Once it is established what the characters look like, their looks are unaltered throughout the time span of the screenplay. Charles Bickford, who plays Brother Matthias, appears to be at least forty-five in his first appearance during a scene set in 1906; he steadfastly remains forty-five up to the final scene, set in 1948.

The film's anachronisms are too numerous to mention here, but it's worth noting that the inaccuracies go beyond the realm of baseball. A knowledgeable film buff with no interest in sports would find fault with Babe dancing on a nightclub stage to the tune of "Singin' in the Rain" during a scene taking place in 1919—ten years before "Singin' in the Rain" was written! And anyone with even a cursory knowledge of history would howl at the scene in which Babe's sixtieth home run is re-created. Allied Artists went to the expense of filming the scene at Yankee Stadium, apparently before or after a real game. Unfortunately, the studio overlooked the prominent ad for Ballantine Beer on the stadium's outfield billboard; it was fairly unlikely that Ballantine would be advertising in 1927, a Prohibition year.

All the film's shortcomings might have been forgiven had *The Babe Ruth Story* been expertly directed. Roy Del Ruth, not only director but producer of the picture, had an admirable track record of successful films, most of them made at such major studios as Warner Bros. and MGM. Away from the majors, however, Del Ruth seemed to flounder. Whenever a scene in *The Babe Ruth Story* required extra players, those people would not mill about and behave naturally as they would in a big-studio picture (where the burden of handling crowds was in the hands of the assistant directors), but would stand or sit absolutely still while Del Ruth busied himself putting the principal players through their paces. This is most noticeable in the opening scene at Babe's father's saloon; supposedly a rowdy, lawless joint, the saloon is populated with such lifeless patrons that it is about as boisterous as the Russian Tea Room. And without a guiding "front office" hand to let him know when his picture's pace was dragging, Roy Del Ruth allowed every scene to run on interminably. Babe's deathbed speech lasts so long that the less sentimental viewer is apt to shout, "So *die* already!"

The film comes to life briefly during a nightclub fight sequence, and even more briefly during a few of the baseball scenes in which William Bendix is reasonably well matched up with long shots involving stunt doubles. Without further comment, it should be noted that the film's second unit director was B-picture veteran D. Ross Lederman, who, according to film historian Leonard Maltin, had two specialties: a genius for staging fight scenes, and the uncanny ability to perfectly match stuntmen in long shots with the stars in close-up.

When all is said and done, the greatest failure of *The Babe Ruth Story* is that the film never tells us just what it was that made Babe Ruth's life worth filming. We see nothing of the salvation of baseball's soiled image that Ruth's talent brought about, nor do we learn that Babe single-handedly converted the home run from a mere display of bravado into a method of winning pennants. Instead, we see 106 minutes' worth of a clumsy ox who spends half his time being chewed out and the other half being praised beyond reason. And this particular clumsy ox is deadly, deadly dull.

We've wasted enough space on *The Babe Ruth Story*, so we'll close here by advising you to avoid this bow-wow and hold out for either the 1991 TV movie *Babe Ruth* (q.v.), starring Stephen Lang, or 1992's *The Babe* (q.v.), a theatrical Ruth biopic starring John Goodman. Despite their own shortcomings, both later films are infinitely better than the Bendix version; for that matter, watching wallpaper peel is better than the Bendix version.

THE BAD NEWS BEARS FILMS

The trio of films constituting the *Bad News Bears* "series" are best analyzed chronologically rather than alphabetically; thus, they will be discussed under the above umbrella heading.

1. *The Bad News Bears*

Paramount; released April 6, 1976

Produced by Stanley R. Jaffe. Directed by Michael Ritchie. Screenplay by William Lancaster. Photography: John A. Alonzo. Production design: Polly Platt. Music adapted and conducted by Jerry Fielding (from Bizet's *Carmen*). Edited by Richard A. Harris. Unit production manager and assistant director: Jack Roe. Second assistant director: Blair Robertson. Set decoration by Cheryal Kearney. Sound mixer: Gene Cantamessa. Costumes by Tommy Dawson and Nancy Martinelli. Makeup by Jack Obringer. Hairstylist: Caryl Codon. Lenses and panaflex camera by Panavision. Color by Movielab. 102 minutes; sound. Rated PG.

Cast: Walter Matthau (Morris Buttermaker); Tatum O'Neal (Amanda Whurlitzer); Vic Morrow (Roy Turner); Joyce Van Patten (Cleveland); Ben Piazza (Bob Whitewood); Jackie Earle Haley (Kelly Leak); Alfred W. Lutter (Albert Ogilvie); Brandon Cruz (Joey Turner); Chris Barnes (Tanner Boyle); Erin Blunt (Ahmad Abdul Rahim); Gary Lee Cavagnaro (Engelburg); Scott Firestone (Reggie Tower); Jaime Escobedo (Jose Agilar); George Gonzales (Miguel Agilar); Brett Marx (Jimmy Feldman); David Pollock (Rudi Stein); Quinn Smith (Timmy Lupus); David Stambaugh (Toby Whitewood); Timothy Blake (Mrs. Lupus); Bill Sorrells (Mr. Tower); Shari Summers (Mrs. Turner); Joe Brooks (Umpire); George Wyner (White Sox Manager); David Lazarus (Yankee); Charles Matthau (Athletic); Maurice Marks (Announcer); Kenny Pollack, Dan Harmetz (Yankees).

Morris Buttermaker, a former major league ballplayer reduced to cleaning swimming pools in a wealthy California suburban community, is hired by councilman Bob Whitewood to coach an inept junior-league baseball team called the Bears. Whitewood, who fancies himself a liberal, has filed a class action suit to get the Bears into the top-level North Valley League, even though the team is so bad that the only business who'll sponsor the Bears is Chico's Bail Bonds. The kids are clumsy and out of shape; worst of all, they have such a low opinion of themselves that it doesn't look as though they'll even come close to being winners at anything, on or off the field. Buttermaker, who has wasted his life by walking away from adversity instead of facing it, is determined not to let his Bears end up failures like himself. He talks Amanda Whurlitzer, the daughter of Buttermaker's onetime lady friend, into becoming star pitcher for the team, and manages to get the local hard-case punk, a motorcycling terror named Kelly Leak, into the lineup as a power hitter and outfielder. Rallying behind Amanda and Kelly, and whipped into shape by Buttermaker's incessant drilling, the Bears start playing to win, making it into the playoffs with the league-leading Yankees. The final game of the season brings out the best and worst from both parents and kids. Roy Turner, the smug, arrogant coach of the Yankees, reveals himself to be a childish bully when facing possible defeat; Buttermaker, realizing in the midst of haranguing his team that he has lost sight of the avowed purpose of the Junior League— to play for fun rather than blood—relents and allows his whole lineup, including the weakest players, into the game. The Bears lose, but the confidence and esprit de corps that they've gained is worth a lifetime of championships.

Ask anybody who hasn't seen *The Bad News Bears* since its 1976 release and they'll tell you that this is the picture in which little kids swear like stevedores, drink beer, and play guerrilla baseball. Or they might remember that this is the film where a prepubescent Tatum O'Neal offers her "services" to a young hoodlum in exchange for his playing on her team. Most of all, they'll remember how much they laughed at the antics of drink-besotted Walter Matthau and his youthful team of reprobates. What they won't remember—unless they've seen the film recently—is that *The Bad News Bears* is a brilliant, relentless attack on the world of frustrated adults who play out their fantasies through their children, then punish those children either physically or mentally because the kids can't fulfill their parents' dreams. And, when confronted, these adults will insist that they're doing all this for their kids' benefit and that the youngsters love what they're doing. Since most films made in the last two decades have featured kids who curse freely and colorfully, smoke and drink, and are well versed in sexual matters, the various "hooks" that brought audiences into *The Bad News Bears* twenty-five years ago are no longer effective, leaving the present-day viewer with a stinging exposé of suburban values and "conditional" love. And the laughs are fewer and more bitter.

Michael Ritchie, the film's director, spent most of the early 1970s building a reputation upon a group of films demonstrating the dark side of pursuing the American dream. *Downhill Racer* (1969) offered a champion skier (Robert Redford) who gained his championship status by losing his soul; *The Candidate* (1972) featured an idealistic politician (Redford again) whose liberal bubble was burst by the Machiavellian machinations of a senatorial campaign; and *Smile* (1975) was a superb dissection of the local beauty contest ritual and the winners and losers who make up that ritual.

The Bad News Bears was an extension of Ritchie's view of a society obsessed with winning at the cost of humanity, even though its ending was a lot more upbeat than those of his previous films. But Ritchie, ever the cynic, was not convinced that he was hired to direct the picture because of the unifying theme of his earlier work. As

the director observed to writer James Monaco, "[Paramount] had seen *Smile* and they'd seen the kids talking dirty and they figured, well, he can direct kids talking dirty. They don't look much beyond your last project."

The film had been given the go-ahead based on the bankability of stars Walter Matthau and Tatum O'Neal (a child actress who'd recently become the youngest ever Oscar winner via her work in 1973's *Paper Moon*). To make certain that the script would be as box office as the stars, screenwriter William Lancaster (son of Burt) concocted a tale with all the surefire ingredients. As conceived, Morris Buttermaker was much younger than Matthau, the better to make credible the affair he was going to be conducting with the wife of the Yankees manager. Kelly Leak, the town tough guy, was originally written as a drug dealer, and it was planned that his mother (a character deleted from the film) would be carrying on a clandestine romance with the councilman who'd organized the Bears. The shock of this plot point was to have compelled Kelly Leak to steal the councilman's limo, thereby embarking on a wild, audience pleasing car chase with the police. Somewhere in this concoction was the notion of a losing little-league ball club transformed into a squad of winners. Although he took no screen credit, Michael Ritchie completely reshaped Lancaster's story, retaining and emphasizing the plot elements that would satisfy what *The Bad News Bears'* production designer Polly Platt described as Ritchie's obsession "with humiliation and exhilaration." The upshot of Ritchie's efforts must have brought a sardonic smile to his face: William Lancaster was honored with a Writers' Guild Award.

As was his customary procedure, Michael Ritchie used a mixture of professionals and amateurs when casting the ball-playing children. In the former category was, of course, Tatum O'Neal, who was paid $350,000 plus eight percent of the film's profits for her five weeks of work. This caused no end of resentment among the other children, who had to make do with anywhere from $25 per day to the union minimum of $604 per week. Nor did it soothe their feelings any when it turned out that Tatum never could learn to pitch as well as her screen character, and had to be extensively doubled by two boys. Thus it's understandable if not condonable that O'Neal was pretty standoffish during filming, choosing her friends among those who shared her intellectual interests and deriding most of the others with such sobriquets as "Fatty" and "Squirt." One of Tatum's few friends on location was Alfred W. Lutter, who'd played Ellen Burstyn's son in *Alice Doesn't Live Here Anymore* (1975) and was here cast as the Bears' bespectacled team statistician Albert Ogilvie.

Other pros included Brandon Cruz, who'd recently starred in the TV series *Courtship of Eddie's Father* and who was cast (against his usual lovable type) in *Bears* as the bullying star pitcher of the Yankees (and son of the Yankee manager); Jackie Earle Haley, who'd made a big impression as a tantrum-tossing kiddie movie star in *Day of the Locust* (1975) and who brought some of that venom to his *Bears* role of cigarette smoking, loan sharking Kelly Leak; and advertising models Erin Blunt and George Gonzales, cast respectively as the sensitive black team member Ahmad Rahim and the monolingual Hispanic ballplayer Miguel Agilar.

Prominent among the nonprofessionals was Gary Lee Cavagnaro, who played the Bears' obese, unkempt Engelberg. Gary Lee got wind of the part because his mother was working at a California shopping mall where auditions for the film were being held. Michael Ritchie had been having trouble finding a fat kid who could be funny without being self-conscious, and Cavagnaro fit the bill. The youngster's ten-

dency toward surliness in the early days of shooting was incorporated into his screen character, though it's possible that this quality was a bit wearing on the nerves, since the role of Engelberg was played by a different child actor in the subsequent *Bad News Bears* sequels. To ensure his heaviness, crew members fed Cavagnaro before, during, and after shooting—one of the few instances in which one of the kids was unduly manipulated into a convincing performance.

The kids playing the Bears were cast more for their comic potential than their ballplaying skills, and though it wasn't admitted during auditions, Ritchie was looking for children whose athletic prowess was on the insubstantial side (this became a drawback when Ritchie couldn't get the Bears to improve their game once the script called for the team to start winning!). Conversely, the youngsters cast as the league-leading Yankees were drawn from the ranks of real-life championship ball clubs in the Mission Hills and Northridge communities of California. Ritchie wanted these first-rate players to appear arrogant and humorless, almost robotlike, in contrast to the scruffy, funny, extremely human Bears. Unfortunately, the "Yankees" took their roles so seriously that they were unable to loosen up and speak lines, nor were they able to "lose" a few plays convincingly during the film's climactic game. Thus some of the Yankees' lines and bits of business were assigned to Dan Harmetz, the son of *New York Times* fine arts critic Aljean Harmetz, and to David Lazarus, cast because he was physically the same "type" as young Harmetz. These boys weren't quite in the same ballplaying class as the rest of the Yankees, but they could at least deliver dialogue without looking constipated, and were able to fumble a play or two without contemplating running away from home in disgrace.

Some of the kids, notably thirteen-year-old Tatum O'Neal and fourteen-year-old

The coach is waiting for his next beer.
The pitcher is waiting for her first bra.
The team is waiting for a miracle.
Consider the possibilities.

WALTER   TATUM
MATTHAU   O'NEAL

BEARS 1976
NORTH VALLEY LEAGUE

Paramount Pictures Presents
A STANLEY R. JAFFE PRODUCTION   A MICHAEL RITCHIE FILM

"THE BAD NEWS
Bears"

Also Starring VIC MORROW Written by BILL LANCASTER
Produced by STANLEY R. JAFFE Directed by MICHAEL RITCHIE
Music Adapted by JERRY FIELDING In Color A Paramount Picture

PG PARENTAL GUIDANCE SUGGESTED
Some material may not be suitable for pre-teenagers

The engaging slovenliness of *The Bad News Bears* is superbly captured in this poster art by the inimitable Jack Davis.

Jackie Earle Haley, were either too old or too large to qualify for the real-life little leagues. To convey the illusion that the ballplayers were younger and smaller, the film's baseball diamond, constructed in the San Fernando Valley near the familiar movie locale of Chatsworth, was built proportionately larger than normal, right down to a thirty-six-foot-high backfield wall. That this trickery didn't make the adult actors look similarly small was due to the skill displayed by director of photography John A. Alonzo in coming up with camera angles that hid the discrepancy.

The principal adult player, Walter Matthau, had actually been a baseball coach during his teenage years and was a rabid sports fan in real life. The utter credibility of his performance as Morris Buttermaker—profane, boozing, fiercely competitive, embittered by life's bad breaks but basically a decent guy who does right by the kids at the end—was strengthened by his own lifelong love affair with baseball. Walter Matthau's thorough professionalism is all the more remarkable when one realizes that the actor spent most of his shooting time beneath a blazing sun during the summer of 1975, with its triple digit temperature, despite a heart condition that had resulted in an attack less than a decade earlier. In contrast to the rough treatment he puts his team through in the film, Matthau couldn't have been more patient and cooperative during shooting, befriending many of the children and inviting them and their parents over to his home. "He was like a pied piper during the filming," noted producer Stanley R. Jaffe. "A wonderful, lovely man." The only time the legendary Matthau temper flared was when Tatum O'Neal showed up for filming fifteen minutes late.

Walter Matthau's performance was enhanced by his refusal to play the obvious—we learn to like him because of the circumstances, not because he uses any actor's devices to make us like him. A similar refusal to take the easy way out characterized the rest of the adult actors. Ben Piazza's councilman, a bleeding-heart liberal who turns tightly conservative when the results of his liberality rain on his own parade, and Joyce Van Patten's "never kid a kidder" baseball equipment manager, whose pasted-on smile belies her dislike of the Bears and of Buttermaker, could have been stock villains, but here they come across as recognizable real-life types who have actually convinced themselves that every move they make is for the good of the children. Even the film's nominal "heavy," Yankee coach Roy Turner, who baits Buttermaker by mispronouncing his name and who, during the climactic ballgame, strikes his own son in full view of the spectators because the boy failed to follow instructions, is enacted by Vic Morrow as a man whose obsession with winning has made him more hollow and pathetic than wholly evil. When Morrow's son (Brandon Cruz), hitherto an unsympathetic reflection of his father, rejects Dad's false values by walking off the field in the middle of the game, the expression on Morrow's face is that of a man who realizes that he's trapped by his own self-deceptions, and that it's too late to save himself by walking away from those deceptions as his son has just done.

The Bad News Bears' baseball scenes, shot primarily with a hand-held camera, have the happy tendency to look spontaneous and realistically disorganized at times, a quality missing from many films about adult ball teams. In keeping with the tenor of Ritchie's direction and the actors' performances, the game scenes are also devoid of clichés. It would have been so easy to rouse the audience by having the Bears play brilliantly in the last scene in contrast to their incompetence at the beginning of the film, but instead it's made clear that while the team's *spirit* has improved enormously, and that the addition of two star players has enabled them to be contenders, the Bears' basic talent pool is still a far cry from "league standard." A crucial play in the last game, a catch made by previously ignored player Timmy Lupus (Quinn Smith), is handled so swiftly and casually that it genuinely takes the audience by surprise, just as such a catch would in a real game. This sequence is doubly effective because it avoids that curse of latterday sports films, slow-motion photography—making the viewer realize how much the movies lost when they started favoring special effects over the simple recording of events. Most refreshing is the fact that the Bears do not win the final game. The whole point of the film is that they finally believe in themselves enough to play ball for sheer enjoyment, and not to be devastated for life by an occasional loss or two on the ball field.

And besides, it makes for a better cinematic moment when Bears player Tanner Boyle (played with the manic intensity of a Richard Dreyfuss by seven-year-old Chris Barnes) disrupts the stiff formality of presenting the second-place trophy, and the Yankees' self-righteous congratulations to the Bears for being good sports, by shouting an obscenity-peppered warning to wait until *next* year.

Released with a modicum of fanfare, *The Bad News Bears* began building its following through the word of mouth of teen and preteen moviegoers, many of whom attended the movie to hear the kids swear on screen but who were soon swept up into the sheer energy and honesty of the story. The film wound up grossing over $25 million domestically—the fourth biggest moneymaker of the summer of 1976, and one of the most profitable baseball films of all time. Given the usual Hollywood "they liked it once, they'll love it twice" mentality, a *Bad*

News Bears sequel was inevitable. That this sequel failed to maintain the quality of the original was probably equally inevitable; it's just a shame that *The Bad News Bears in Breaking Training* was so diligent in its avoidance of that quality.

2. The Bad News Bears in Breaking Training

Paramount; released September 1977

Produced by Leonard Goldberg. Directed by Michael Pressman. Screenplay by Paul Brickman. Photography: Fred J. Koenekamp. Music by Craig Safan. Lyrics by Norman Gimbel. Musical score based on Tchaikovsky's *1812 Overture*. Edited by John W. Wheeler. Art director: Steve Borger. Set decoration by Fred R. Price. Costumes by Jack Martell. Assistant director: Michael Daves. Unit production manager: Fred T. Gallo. Location casting by Liz Keighley and Shari Rhodes Associates. Song "Looking Good" sung by James Rollerston. Filmed in Panavision. Color by Movielab. 100 minutes; sound. Rated PG.

Cast: William Devane (Mike Leak); Clifton James (Si Orlansky); Jackie Earle Haley (Kelly Leak); Jimmy Baio (Carmen Ronzonni); Chris Barnes (Tanner Boyle); Erin Blunt (Ahmad Rahim); Jaime Escobedo (Jose Agilar); George Gonzales (Miguel Agilar); Alfred W. Lutter (Albert Ogilvie); Brett Marx (Jimmy Feldman); David Pollock (Rudy Stein); Quinn Smith (Timmy Lupus); David Stambaugh (Toby Whitewood); Jeffrey Louis Starr (Mike Engleburg); Fred Stuthman (Lester Eastland); Dolph Sweet (Coach Manning); Lane Smith (Officer Mackie); Pat Corley (Coach Morey Slater); Ira Gilbert (Motel Manager); Gene Rader (Grocery Clerk); Ronnie Thomas (Indian Pitcher); Douglas Anderson (Carl Rutherford); Jerry Lawson (Chip Roberts); G. G. Lively (First Patrolman); Martha Turner (Francine); Maggie Burns (Ruth); Michelle Fruge (Janet); Leigh Manley (Janet's Girlfriend); Jason Cooper (Leon Waterson); Yvonne McCord (Sheila Lansing); Charles Krohn (TV Newscaster); Viki Kilstrom (Hitchhiker); John W. Goyen, Jr. (Locker Room Official); Ted Dawson (Astrodome Announcer); Robert J. Watson, Enos Cabell, Roger Metzger, James Richard, Joseph W. Ferguson, Kenneth R. Forsch, William C. Virdon, Cesar Cedeno (Houston Astros); Richard McKenzie (Councilman Whitewood).

The Bears have a chance to participate in a junior-league match to be played between double header games at the Houston Astrodome, with the winner going on to play an all-star team in Japan. Alas, our heroes are short of their pitcher Timmy Lupus, who has broken his leg. This gap is filled by star player Kelly Leak, who provides a fast-talking "hotshot" pitcher named Carmen Ronzonni. A second stumbling block to the team's getting to Houston is the absence of an adult coach, the last of whom, a Patton-like martinet, was literally chased off the diamond by Kelly Leak's motorcycle. Convincing their parents that the ballpark's retarded caretaker is their new coach, the kids get their folks to put up money for their trip and head off to Texas on their own, with Kelly at the wheel of a van that, unbeknownst to him, was stolen by Carmen Ronzonni. En route, the kids learn that self-styled baseball whiz Carmen can't pitch worth spit—he's so determined to imitate his idols that he can't relax into a style of his own. More trouble awaits the boys in Houston, where they park their hot van illegally and wind up in the hands of the law. A desperate Kelly promises the authorities that he'll produce the Bears' adult coach, and shortly thereafter arrives with his estranged father Mike Leak—who fortuitously has a hard-hat job in the area—in tow. Though Kelly is hostile to his dad for divorcing his mom and walking out eight years earlier, Mike obligingly gets the Bears in shape for their upcoming match with the Houston Toros. The day of the big Astrodome game arrives and, despite the superior skill of the Toros, the Bears hold their own; even Carmen shines, having been urged by Mike to be himself and not a cheap copy of someone else. Things look bleak when the game is called on account of time in the third inning with the Bears trailing 5–0, but the team, egged on by Mike Leak, urges the spectators—and such real-life Houston Astros as Enos Cabell, Cesar Cedeno and Bill Virdon—to chant "Let them play!" Not only does this get the officials to resume the game, but it serves to reunite Mike with his son Kelly. The game is played to conclusion, and lest you have any doubts regarding the final score, remember that the title of the Bears' next film is *The Bad News Bears Go to Japan.*

An early scene of this rushed-through sequel tries to gets laughs by having a mentally retarded adult learn phrases like "Hello, how are you?" and "Goodbye" by rote. The remainder of *The Bad News Bears in Breaking Training* fails to live up to the standard set by this scene.

Reasoning that the first *Bears* picture had done so well because of its appeal to youngsters, producer Leonard Goldberg, who'd built his career in the salt mines of weekly series television, decided to aim *Breaking Training* exclusively at teens and preteens. Thus we are treated to a lot of jokes on how stupid and pigheaded adult authority figures are, several slapstick vignettes involving pillow fights and such, a plentitude of humor involving anatomy and body functions, and, of course, the traditional four-letter words spewing forth from the mouths of babes.

Asking this exercise in raw commercialism (distinguished by the raw commercializing within the film, what with its shameless plugs for Budweiser beer, Hilton hotels and the Astrodome itself) to have

"More bad news" is right.

any of the point or poignancy of the initial *Bears* picture is a bit much. It is not much at all to ask that *Breaking Training* make sense. If these kids are bright enough to finagle their parents into letting them travel to Texas alone, why aren't they bright enough to stay out of a no parking zone once they reach their destination? If Carmen Ronzonni is such an erratic pitcher, why wasn't this figured out before the team set out on their journey to what is, after all, a very important game? And if we're supposed to believe that there's friction between Kelly

Leak and his father, why does actor William Devane, normally a specialist in steel-hearted villainy, choose this opportunity to play Mike Leak as a 100 percent Mr. Nice Guy—making Kelly, ostensibly the hero of this picture, come off like an unmotivated paranoiac?

The actors carried over in this film from the first *Bad News Bears*—Jackie Earle Haley, Chris Barnes, Erin Blunt, Alfred W. Lutter, Jaime Escobedo, George Gonzales, David Pollock, Brett Marx, David Stambaugh and, very briefly, Quinn Smith—are no longer the multifaceted problem children we saw in the original. Characterization has given way to caricature. In the earlier film Tanner Boyle (Barnes) was a race-baiting, pugnacious little twerp because he had a lousy self-image. Here, he's a lot more self-assured; yet he still spits out his racial slurs and picks fights at random, all for the sake of a few cheap laughs. More injurious is the deterioration of Ahmad Rahim (Blunt); an intelligent kid, overly sensitive to the athletic abilities of his older brothers in the original, Ahmad is reduced in *Breaking Training* to a jive talking buffoon who hasn't got the sense to realize that a "sanitized for your protection" label doesn't mean that a motel toilet is out of order. We won't even discuss the allegedly hilarious shenanigans of fat kid Engelburg (played here by Jeffrey Louis Starr, who is twice as porcine as Gary Lee Cavagnaro in the first *Bears*) except to say that his particular comic pinnacle consists of his eating a bucket of chicken while sitting on the john.

Beyond the cliché-ridden performances, the film is rife with giggle-inducing continuity gaffes. In the climactic Astrodome scene, the spectator seats go from being full to half-empty and back again with whimsical abandon. And in one of the travel sequences the sun apparently sets in the East.

Before we forget, the kids *do* play a little baseball here. There is one reasonably

entertaining impromptu game with a group of young Native American ballplayers in New Mexico; the big climax, however, is fatally ill conceived. Using the Astrodome as the locale may have been worthwhile in avoiding the weather problems attendant upon outdoor filming, but the enormity of the structure—coupled with some badly chosen camera angles—makes the Bears look so tiny that they're microscopic, rather like a museum display of dead fleas dressed in uniforms. And because there is nothing more at stake here than a trip overseas, we don't really care who wins and who doesn't; thus the game, sluggishly directed to begin with, is as boring as the season finale of a tenth place home team.

Since the potential audience of *The Bad News Bears in Breaking Training* was cut in half by the decision to target its appeal to younger viewers, the film grossed only a bit more than half the money earned by its predecessor. But a sequel to *Breaking Training* was already in preparation and had already been promised to theater owners; once again, the sure thing syndrome was at work, despite the fact that there is nothing less sure in Hollywood than a sure thing.

3. The Bad News Bears Go to Japan

Paramount; released June 1978

Produced by Michael Ritchie. Directed by John Berry. Written and coproduced by Bill Lancaster. Photography: Gene Polito (U.S.A.) and Kozo Okazaki (Japan). Edited by Dennis Virkler. Production design by Walter Scott Herndon. Music by Paul Chihara; score adapted from Gilbert and Sullivan's *The Mikado*. Songs arranged by Mike Meldvin. Unit production manager and Associate producer: Terry Carr. Assistant director: Jerry Ziesmer. Set decoration by Cheryal Kearney. Makeup by Robert Mills. Production services in Japan by Toei Company Ltd. Filmed in Panavision. Color by Movielab. 91 minutes; sound. Rated PG.

Cast: Tony Curtis (Marvin Lazar); Jackie Earle Haley (Kelly Leak); Tomisaburo Wakayama [Kenzaburo Jô] (Coach Shimizu); Hatsume Ishihara (Arika); Antonio Inoki (Himself); George Wyner (Network Director); Lonny Chapman (Louis the Gambler); Mathew Douglas Anton (E.R.W. Tillyard, III); Erin Blunt (Ahmad Rahim); George Gonzales (Miguel Agilar); Brett Marx (Jimmy Feldman); David Pollock (Rudy Stein); David Stambaugh (Toby Whitewood); Jeffrey Louis Starr (Mike Engelburg); Scoody Thornton (Mustapha Rabin); Abraham Unger (Abe Bernstein); Dick Button (Himself); Regis Philbin (Harry Haim); Kinichi Hagimoto (Game Show Host); Hugh Gillin (Pennywall) Robert Sorrells (Locke); Tak Kubota (Referee); Don Watters (Network Man 1); Tim P. Sullivan (Network Man 2); Dick McGarvin (Network Man 3); James Staley (Network Man 4); Dennis Freeman (Network Man 5); Michael Yama (Usher); Clarence Barnes (Mean Bones Beaudine); Gene LeBell (Mean Bones's Manager); Kyoto Fuji (Madam); Hector Guerrero (Stunt Double); Marjorie Jackson (Waitress); Bob Kino (Moderator); Yangi Kitadani (Fight Announcer); Jerry Maren (Page Boy); Ginger Martin (Directors' Aide); Dean A. Okinaka (Manager); Daniel Sasaki (Band Leader); Victor Toyota (Interpreter); Bin Amatzu (Arika's Father); Jerry Ziesmer (Eddie of the Network).

It looks as though the Bears aren't going to make it to that ballgame in Japan after all; the Junior League has pulled out of the game because they think the Japanese All-Stars are "too competitive." The Bears go on television to plead their case, which attracts the interest of Marvin Lazar, a seedy showbiz agent who's looking for a quick financial turnover and lots of promotional commercial tie-ins. Lazar agrees to represent the boys, and it's off to Japan for the whole caboodle. Before long, Lazar has managed to offend All-Star coach Shimizu with his ceaseless hustling and his attempts to stir up a publicity-baiting "deadly rivalry" between the Japanese and American kids, who happen to like each other; the shifty agent also loses the opportunity of an international telecast when the Amer-

ican network executives see how outclassed the Bears are. Having overextended his credit to the point that a hotel clerk starts scissoring his credit cards before his eyes, Lazar desperately tries to get network coverage by involving himself in a highly touted televised wrestling match. The ruse works, and for a while it looks as though the Bears–All-Stars match will go on without a hitch. But Lazar's old gambling buddies have bet heavily on the game, forcing Lazar to take on three overaged, unscrupulous players to improve the odds on the Bears. The game is a farce, and culminates in both teams walking off the field. The boys finish their game in a sandlot far from the crowds and the TV cameras, playing for the love of baseball rather than the lust for gold, and Marvin Lazar at long last sees the error of his ways.

The Bad News Bears Go to Japan isn't really about junior-league baseball at all. It's a tale of two hustlers: Marvin Lazar, whose escapades are recorded in the above synopsis, and Bears' star player Kelly Leak, who spends the greater number of his scenes in pursuit of a comely young geisha girl. The Bears have been reduced to being supporting players in their own movie; if we hadn't been introduced to most of these kids in their earlier films, we'd be hard put to discern any distinctive personalities in them. The script makes an effort to humanize these cardboard characters in ways that are typical of films in the 1970s: Ahmad Rahim has become a streetwise cynic with a heightened sense of his own racial pride, Toby Whitewood is now a born-again Christian, and so forth. Like most such 1970s script devices, these added touches seem more patronizing than humanizing and appear to have been squeezed into the proceedings with a shoehorn.

Nonetheless, *The Bad News Bears Go to Japan* is a definite improvement over the previous year's *Breaking Training*. Some of this upgraded quality is due to the presence of the original *Bad News Bears* director Michael Ritchie as producer of *Go to Japan*, and of the first film's author, Bill Lancaster, in the two-hat position of *Japan*'s coproducer and screenwriter. Unlike *Breaking Training*, which has "B Quickie" written all over it, *Go to Japan* is carefully and often elaborately put together, with some particularly gorgeous location photography and not just a few well-crafted comedy sequences. Once the picture does get around to baseball, the Big Game is very well staged, and the "clean" sandlot game set up in protest by the Bears and the All-Stars at fade-out time is a surefire—and marvelously handled—method of touching off cheers from the audience.

The film also has the advantage of a first-rate performance by star Tony Curtis, who puts a fresh coat of paint on his patented characterization of a ruthless entrepreneur with a deep-down streak of decency. It's to Curtis' credit that he survives such wheezy routines as not knowing when to stop exchanging bows with his Japanese hosts and disguising himself as a "mystery" opponent in order to talk business with a surly wrestler, with his integrity as a performer of stature intact. The *New York Times*' movie critic Vincent Canby, characterizing this film as "not a movie to see unless you're on a transatlantic flight and have gone through all available reading matter, including the timetables," singled out Tony Curtis' performance as the only reason the nonflying viewer should fritter away ninety-one minutes with *The Bad News Bears Go to Japan*.

One of the nicer aspects of the film is that it doesn't try to extract cheap laughs at the expense of the Japanese. *Go to Japan* refreshingly avoids the old gag of using slangy, scatological subtitles to translate the non–English dialogue. In fact, there are many scenes in which very little English is spoken, but the audience has no trouble following the story because of the actions of the players. This sensitivity to the Japanese characters stemmed from the fact that the film was designed for both American and Japanese audiences; American baseball films seldom do well overseas, but have always been enthusiastically received in Japan, where our national pastime is practically a state religion. In consideration of the Oriental fans, a generous slice of footage is devoted to the performance of Japanese film favorite Tomisaburo Wakayama, who'd risen to prominence as star of the internationally popular *Lone Wolf and Cub* martial arts films. As Coach Shimizu, Wakayama is every bit the consummate comic craftsman that Tony Curtis is in the two actors' scenes together.

But *The Bad News Bears Go to Japan* has a number of blemishes, chief among them its tendency to overload each scene with so much incident that the viewer loses track of story, characters, and humor. The wrestling match involving real-life Japanese sports celebrity Antonio Inoki is very amusing, but the attempts to build joke upon joke by incorporating not only Tony Curtis as Inoki's opponent but the uncalled for participation of the Bears themselves, and the bemused play by play commentary of Dick Button (who can't talk of any sport without pulling in his pet event, figure skating), results in the laughs from each comic canceling the other laughs out.

Similarly, a scene set at a Japanese TV musical talent contest has some appealing moments, not the least of which features the local All-Stars singing "Take Me Out to the Ballgame" in their own language; but the scene is far too busy and far too long to maintain its comic energy. In addition, Kelly Leak's romance, the chicanery of the gamblers, and other such plot convolutions serve only as roadblocks to the baseball climax that the audience is awaiting with ever-decreasing patience. The cluttered overkill of Bill Lancaster's script for *Go to Japan* would seem to indicate what Lancaster's first *Bad News Bears* project might have looked like had not director Michael Ritchie pared down and simplified the story.

While far from perfect, however, *The Bad News Bears Go to Japan* is far from worthless, and it performed well at the box office in Japan. But American audiences were tiring of the Bears, thus the film grossed only $6.5 million domestically—less than half the take of *Breaking Training* and a mere 25 percent or so of the gross of the first *Bad News Bears*. This heralded the end of the series, but not quite the end of the story.

Two events occurred in 1979 that kept the Bears before the public, the first being a lawsuit brought against Paramount by Walter Matthau. The actor had been paid $750,000 for his work in the first *Bears* film, and had been guaranteed 10 percent of the film's first $8 million gross, 12–12.5 percent of the next $5 million, and 15 percent of anything over $13 million. In 1978 Paramount sold the three *Bears* films to the ABC television network for $18.5 million, with the profits divided approximately equally among all three properties. This meant that Matthau, who appeared in the most profitable of the three films, would receive a slim percentage from about $6.2 million of the TV sale.

Matthau was furious, reasoning that, had Paramount sold the picture for an amount proportionate to its box office success, he could have made at least twice as much from the ABC deal. A courtroom date was inevitable. If this appears to be just another example of movie star greed, remember that Walter Matthau literally put his health—and possibly his life—on the line beneath a blazing California sun to get *The Bad News Bears* committed to celluloid.

The second 1979 event was Paramount's decision to milk every bit of profitability out of *The Bad News Bears* and its progeny by converting the property to a television series.

The television version of *The Bad News Bears* premiered over CBS on March 24, 1979, barely squeaked through to the fall of that year, and limped to cancellation in October, resurfacing in rerun form in the summer of 1980.

The series returned to basics by bringing back Morris Buttermaker (now played by Jack Warden), who once again was a washed-up ballplayer making a living as a swimming pool cleaner. In a plot twist typical of TV writers who can't fathom something like regaining one's self-respect as a motivational device, Buttermaker angrily drove a client's car into his pool when the client refused to pay him, and was then given the choice of going to jail or coaching a bumbling junior high school team (guess which one he chose). Had Buttermaker gone to the slammer, Jack Warden might have gotten two years' TV work instead of one.

Though the movie-to-TV carryover characters on *The Bad News Bears* included Kelly Leak, Amanda Whurlitzer, Tanner Boyle, Rudi Stein, Ahmad Rahim, Timmy Lupus, Ogilvie, Engelburg, and the Agilar brothers, none of the originators of these roles appeared in the series. Precious little time was spent on the ballfield, with most of the plots trodding the weary road of standard sitcomery. The series' soundtrack was disfigured with the sort of canned laughter that had been used back in the days of *Father Knows Best*, and the kids were so sanitized that the show should have been retitled "The Bad News Brady Bunch." This incarnation of *The Bad News Bears* is best forgotten, provided it isn't again exhumed for cable–TV exposure as it was in the early 1990s.

Bang the Drum Slowly

Rosenfield Productions/BTDS Partnership/Paramount; released January 1974

Produced by Maurice and Lois Rosenfield. Associate producer: Bill Badalato. Directed by John Hancock. Screenplay by Mark Harris, adapted from his novel. Photography: Richard Shore. Edited by Richard Marks. Music by Stephen Lawrence. Song "Look Before You Weep" by Claude Stoeber. Production design by Robert Guadlach. Costume design by Domingo Rodriguez. Script supervisor: Kay Chapin. Wardrobe by Yvonne David. First assistant director: Alan Wertheim. Baseball adviser: Del Bethel. Color by Movielab. 97 minutes; sound. Rated PG.

Cast: Michael Moriarty (Henry "Author" Wiggen); Robert De Niro (Bruce Pearson); Vincent Gardenia (Dutch Schnell); Phil Foster (Joe Jaros); Ann Wedgeworth (Katie); Patrick McVey (Mr. Pearson); Heather MacRae (Holly Wiggen); Selma Diamond (Tootsie); Barbara Babcock (Mrs. Moor); Maurice Rosenfield (Mr. Moor); Tom Ligon (Piney Woods); Andy Jarrell (Ugly Jones); Marshall Efron (Bradley Lord); Barton Heyman (Red Traphagen); Donny Burks (Perry); Hector Elias (Diego); Tom Signorelli (Goose Williams); James Donahue (Canada Smith); Nicholas Surovy (Aleck Olson); Danny Aiello (Horse); Hector Troy (George); Tony Major (Jonah); Allan Manson (Dr. Loftus); Ernesto Gonzales (Dr. Chambers); Jack Hollander, Lou Girolani (Tegwar Players); Arnold Kapnick (Detective); Jean David (Dutch's Wife); Bea Blau (Joe's Wife); Herb Henry (Keith Crane); Dorothy Neubert (Bruce's Mother); Pierrino Mascarino (Sid Goldman); Kaydette Grant (Gem); Del Bethel (Third Base Coach); Vince Canuto, Jeff Sartorius, Willie Lemmy, Doug Major (Ballplayers); Forrest Wynne (Bat Boy).

Henry Wiggen, pitcher for the New York Mammoths, accompanies his roommate, dimwitted catcher Bruce Pearson, to the Mayo Clinic in Minnesota, where they learn that Bruce is dying of Hodgkin's disease. Though he's not overly fond of Bruce, Henry nonetheless decides to protect the big lug during his last months. When negotiating his own contract, Henry adds the proviso that Bruce stays on the team as long as he does, and if Henry is traded, so is Bruce. Because Henry keeps mum about Bruce's disease—he doesn't want to see

Bruce bumped from the team, nor does he wish to endure a lot of crocodile tear sympathy directed toward the doomed man— no one can understand why the Mammoths' star pitcher is so devoted to a catcher who's the object of everyone's ragging because he's "a million dollars of promise worth two cents on delivery." This quandary is one of many elements that keeps the team at each others' throats and not working toward a common pennant goal. Word eventually gets out about the illness, and this, together with a plaintive vocal rendition by relief pitcher Piney Woods of the old song "Streets of Laredo" (about a dying cowboy giving instructions for his funeral), serves to unite the team, rallying their spirits and getting them into the pennant race. Once the season is over, however, everyone's got his own fish to fry, and when Bruce ultimately dies, the only New York Mammoth at his funeral is Henry Wiggen.

Bang the Drum Slowly, "by Henry Wiggen; certain of his enthusiasms restrained by Mark Harris," was first published in 1956. It was the second in a trilogy of novels by Harris about Wiggen, the colloquially articulate, amazingly perceptive and shamelessly self-promotional pitcher for the New York Mammoths: the others in this series were *The Southpaw* and *A Ticket for a Seamstitch* (Harris returned to the character in 1979 for *It Looked Like Forever*, a wistful look at life after baseball). Hollywood wouldn't touch the book in the 1950s, not with its "box office poison" mixture of baseball and disease, but an enjoyable version of the novel pared to the bone was telecast live over CBS on *U.S. Steel Hour* on September 24, 1956. The broadcast, still available in kinescope form on home video, featured Paul Newman as a rather more intelligent and emotionally overwrought Henry Wiggen than we find in the novel, and Albert Salmi doing a great job as the childlike, guileless, and "doom-ded" Bruce Pearson (loosely based on Zeke Bonura, a

The "doom-ded" Bruce Pearson (Robert De Niro) in a moment of tobacco-stained solitude in *Bang the Drum Slowly*.

fine White Sox player of the 1930s whose amiable inability to follow or fully comprehend instructions prompted manager Jimmy Dykes to dub Bonura "my pet ox"). Also featured was young and callow George Peppard as gangly country boy Piney Woods. This version of *Bang the Drum Slowly* was faithful to its first person source by having Wiggen step "out" of the drama from time to time to face the camera and narrate the story; there's a nice touch at the end, with Wiggen reciting the final speech of the book about how Bruce Pearson wasn't really a bad guy or really that bad a ballplayer, while behind him the lights dim on Pearson sitting on his hospital bed, awaiting the inevitable with the same simpleton expression that he'd displayed throughout the drama.

By 1973, fatal disease stories were "in,"

thanks to such hit films as *Love Story* (1970) and such top-rated TV movies as *Brian's Song* (1969). Paramount had released *Love Story* and was raking in gold from its recent *The Godfather*, so the studio felt it could afford to release Rosenfield Productions' *Bang the Drum Slowly*, confident that even if it wasn't a blockbuster (and it wasn't), it wouldn't kill the company and might even attract enough of the *Love Story* crowd to turn a little profit.

Mark Harris adapted the script from his own book—which is to say that he transposed the novel virtually verbatim to the screen. Except for modifying some of the "inside" baseball jargon so that viewers uninterested in sports wouldn't require an interpreter (the novel, which seems to have been sired by Ring Lardner out of Damon Runyon, is no quick read for people who haven't grown up around a professional ballpark), and for eliminating such antiquated plot points as having a character try to beat Babe Ruth's sixty homers, the movie is as faithful an adaptation of a sports novel as you're ever likely to find.

All the grace notes that gave the book its humanity and authenticity can be found in the film version of *Bang the Drum Slowly*: Bruce's mispronunciation of Henry's nickname "Author" as "Arthur"; Henry's negotiation of his own salary, with the inflation of the 1970s requiring the $19,000 in the book to balloon to $70,000 in the movie; the Herculean efforts by manager Dutch Schnell to find out just what Henry and Bruce were doing in Minnesota; Henry's white lie that Bruce is suffering from syphilis, resulting in drop-your-pants exams for the rest of the team; Schnell's hilarious locker-room speech comparing teamwork with the capture of a fly (if the fingers don't work together, there ain't no fly in that fist); mercenary goodtime girl Katie, who plans to marry Bruce for his life insurance; the ongoing card game called "Tegwar"—an anagram for "The Exciting Game Without Any Rules"—which Henry and team coach Joe Jaros deploy to pick up pocket money from any and all suckers; and, best of all, Henry's bittersweet closing speech about how the team didn't send anyone to Bruce's funeral and that Bruce was a fellow worth having around, concluding with, "From here on, I rag nobody."

What the film lacks is the one thing that the book is saturated with: the perception of the baseball season as a single, continuous game occasionally interrupted by the outside world. While the aroma of horsehide, pine and freshly mown grass oozes from every page of *Bang the Drum Slowly*, the most lasting impression in the movie is of a series of brilliantly acted hotel and locker-room sequences. Director John Hancock may have gone to the trouble of filming his exteriors at New York's Shea and

Yankee stadiums, and he may have had his cast train at the Yankees' spring quarters in Florida and then spend two hours before shooting each morning playing a quick ballgame, but *Bang the Drum Slowly* is essentially an indoors film, with baseball as a backdrop rather than an all-encompassing cyclorama.

Perhaps this is just as well, since the ballgame scenes come nowhere close to the excellence of the dialogue sequences. Limited by its smallish budget, the film confines the game scenes to a few long shots, most of them filmed from an uninspiring overhead vantage point between home plate and first base. Though the scenes purportedly represent vignettes chosen from games played throughout the season, many of the shots look as though they were all filmed on the same day, with one particular shot of Bruce Pearson running to first, and losing his helmet in the process, popping up in two different games!

The close-ups of Henry pitching and Bruce catching are quite convincing, as are the grandstand shots wherein director Hancock makes the seventy-five extras he hired per day look like thousands of fans, but these are undermined by some raggedly inserted grainy stock shots of genuine ballgames. The most damaging aspect of these scenes (and the most surprising, considering the straightforward directorial approach utilized in the rest of the film) is the excessive use of slow motion. Not only does this smack of the sort of self-indulgence that has badly dated many a fine film from the 1970s, but the slow motion occurs at all the wrong times—most glaringly during an argument between Dutch Schnell and an umpire which, when reduced to a snail's pace, looks more like an underwater shot of two drowning boaters.

The disappointing sports sequences aside, *Bang the Drum Slowly* is a funny, moving, memorable experience—its most memorable element being that it served as the breakthrough film for Robert De Niro who, after several years of supporting parts in "A" pictures and an occasional "B" lead, was finally awarded a starring role in a major release. The stories of De Niro's consummate craftsmanship, of his literally losing himself in his parts, are now part of Hollywood folklore. As Bruce Pearson, De Niro followed his usual pattern of learning skills he'd never before been called upon to perform—in this case, catching and batting—by immediately jumping into the deep end rather than first treading water. He began working out with his catcher's mitt three weeks before filming, strapping on the full gear and encouraging his trainers to throw fast balls at him without holding back. He pored over a book about the game by CCNY coach Del Bethel, who was brought onto the film as technical adviser and who can be seen in the film as a third base coach. De Niro squirreled himself away in his hotel room each evening, taking notes and watching televised ballgames and filmed highlight shows. And as director Hancock noted, once De Niro put on that uniform, he "lived" in it, and probably would have slept in it had it been hygienically feasible.

This dedication went beyond the mere playing of the game. For a scene in which he had to vomit off a hotel terrace, De Niro spun himself around to nauseate himself, then stuck his fingers down his throat; he did this forty times, once for each time the scene was rehearsed and filmed. But De Niro didn't find simulating illness nearly as hard as learning to chew the bulbous wad of tobacco that his character had stuffed in his cheek in almost every scene. "It was a bad experience," the actor observed later. "Somebody told me to mix the tobacco with bubble gum. Then I got sticky *and* sick. Finally a local doctor told me that chewing tobacco would make my teeth white. That gave me the courage to keep chewing. I got so I could *look* like I enjoyed it. But it didn't do a thing for my teeth."

Nowadays the media covers every move Robert De Niro makes in piecing together a performance. In 1973, however, he was just another character actor; all the press attention for *Bang the Drum Slowly* was being concentrated on the man playing Henry Wiggen. Michael Moriarty had the movie star looks and casual charm that seemed to indicate that his career would benefit most from his exposure in the film. *Bang the Drum Slowly* author Mark Harris, who was on the set for much of the shooting, would later note that while De Niro was absenting himself from the rest of the cast and crew and preparing himself for the next day's shooting, Michael Moriarty played the star game, graciously granting interviews and autographs and attending all the right parties and events. When the film came out, most spectators agreed that both Michael Moriarty and Robert De Niro were eminently believable as pitcher and catcher (Pete Bock, the tough to please baseball adviser on *Bull Durham* [1988] noted that Moriarty "seemed to be able to really throw strikes"), and that Moriarty in particular was a pleasing, handsome screen presence.

But once the film was over, the viewers couldn't shake the memory of Robert De Niro—and while it was Moriarty who made the Sunday magazine photo spreads, it was De Niro who made the film. Within a few years, Robert De Niro was a major name making prestige pictures like *The Godfather II* and *Taxi Driver*; meanwhile, Michael Moriarty would have to wait until landing a choice supporting role in the 1978 TV miniseries *Holocaust* to regain the ground he'd lost by becoming a movie star before honing his craft as an actor.

So many ingredients—from Robert De Niro's performance to the unbounded wit of Mark Harris's dialogue—are so precisely on the money that one really wants *Bang the Drum Slowly* to be perfect. Its lackluster ballpark sequences prevent that perfection, but otherwise, *Bang the Drum Slowly* is a respectable highlight in the fitfully rewarding history of baseball movies.

The Battling Orioles

Hal Roach/Pathé, October 1924

Directed by Ted Wilde and Fred Guiol. Story by Hal E. Roach. Titles by H.M. Walker. Photography: Floyd Jackman and George Stevens. Assistant director: Bert Currigan. Editor: T. J. Crizer. 6 reels/5,000 feet: black and white; silent.

Cast: Glenn Tryon (Tommy Roosevelt Tucker); Blanche Mehaffey (Hope Stanton); John T. Prince (Cappy Wolfe); Noah Young (Sid Stanton); Sam Lufkin (Jimmy the Mouse); Robert Page (Inspector Joslin); Gus Leonard ("Hoppy" Hopkins); Eddie Baker (Cop); Martin "Tonnage" Wolfkeil (Sailor); and, from "Our Gang": Joe Cobb, Jackie Condon, "Sunshine Sammy" Morrison and Mickey Daniels.

Back in 1874, the Orioles were "the wildest pack of gosh-awful, two-fisted, he-man baseball players that ever ripped the shirt off an umpire's back." Fifty years later, the former teammates are old, rich and cantankerous, vegetating in the red plush chairs of a stuffy Manhattan men's club. Small-town barber Tommy Tucker, son of a former Oriole, is invited by onetime star player Cappy Wolfe to bring some youthful vigor to the old team. Tommy's efforts to cheer up and rally the rheumatic ex-ballplayers—consisting mainly of corny sleight-of-hand tricks—only cause the oldsters to get mad and resentful. But when Tommy's sweetheart Hope gets innocently mixed up in a crooked scheme concocted by her Uncle Sid, a notorious speakeasy proprietor, the suddenly regenerated Orioles come to the rescue of both Hope and Tommy.

The Battling Orioles is a rambling, nonsensical farce significant only as the first feature length comedy made by the Hal Roach Studios which didn't feature Roach's onetime leading player Harold Lloyd, who'd left the studio by 1924 to become his own producer. The film's storyline had the suspicious feel of a scenario that had been originally prepared for Lloyd, but was handed over to the handsome but nondescript Glenn Tryon in Harold's absence. Ted Wilde, the film's codirector, would soon leave Roach as well, to become a gagman for Lloyd, eventually earning his first solo directorial credit on the 1927 Babe Ruth vehicle *Babe Comes Home* (q.v.). Interestingly, the climax of *Battling Orioles*, wherein the ancient teammates beat up a gang of much-younger hooligans, was reworked as a key action sequence in Harold Lloyd's 1928 feature *Speedy*, Ted Wilde's final directorial credit.

A disappointingly small amount of time is spent on the diamond in *Battling Orioles*. The film's opening reel is devoted to a boisterous, delightfully disorganized game set during baseball's roughneck era of the 1870s. There are some good, solid gags here—an umpire is bullied into calling strikes and outs where none exist, a player confuses the opposition by attaching a string to first base, another player majestically slides into home with the assistance of the special-effects department—but thereafter, baseball is totally shunted to the background, save for an occasional allusion to the game in the subtitles (which are decorated with a "coat of arms" comprised of home plate and a brace of crossed bats) and the climactic gag in which a wizened old ballplayer pitches empty beer bottles at the heads of the villains, awarding himself a cigar whenever he scores a direct hit.

Evidently, the film had been planned as an all-out baseball comedy, as indicated by the statement in the "official" studio synopsis that Glenn Tryon's character, Tommy Turner, is hired to be the Orioles' new pitcher, when in fact he is merely invited to pay a social call to the team's exclusive New York club. It was even suggested by some reviewers that the septuagenarian Orioles were still playing baseball fifty years after their peak; would that this were true!

Alas, the Hal Roach people abandoned the possibilities of building the whole film around ballpark slapstick after the first reel, opting instead for such surefire laugh-getting devices as having all of the Orioles' hats fly off in unison when the aging athletes down a convivial glass of moonshine, and the old gag (old even in 1924!) of using suspenders to project bottles into the air during the climactic battle with the heavies.

Better Times

Brentwood Film Corp./Robertson-Cole/ Exhibitor's Mutual; released June 13, 1919

Written and directed by King Vidor. Photography: Arthur Thornley. 5 reels/4,900 feet; Black and white; silent.

Cast: ZaSu Pitts (Nancy Scroggs); David Butler (Peter Van Slantyne); Jack McDonald (Ezra Scroggs); William DeVaulle (Whitaker); Hugh Fay (Jack Ransom); George Hackathorne (Tony); Georgia Woodthorpe (Young Old Lady); and Julianne Johnstone.

Nancy Scroggs, inspired by an upbeat motto on a calendar, resolves to revitalize the once thriving but now rundown health resort owned by her father. One of the resort's new clients, a wealthy young man named Peter Van Slantyne, has been advised by his doctor to stay on medication, restrict his diet and curtail his athletic activities; Nancy takes one look at Peter, sizes up the situation, and tells him to think positively, get some exercise, and eat what he wants. This self-healing program works, and Peter stays on to help Nancy run her hotel, but then mysteriously disappears after receiving a telegram, which Nancy assumes was sent by another girlfriend. Soon afterward, Nancy's father kills himself over his gambling debts, but leaves a substantial insurance settlement, allowing Nancy to enroll herself in a fancy finishing school. Weary of taunting by her schoolmates because of her lack of a sweetheart, Nancy begins carrying on a fake correspondence with a famous baseball player. To show her up, Nancy's chums take her to a ballgame where the ballplayer is performing, and who should be the star player but Peter Van Slantyne (that telegram had been a summons for him to get back in uniform). Peter jumps into the bleachers upon setting eyes on Nancy, and all's right with the world.

Had the viewers known that *Better Times* would end up in a ballpark the suspense would have been over, so for most of the film's five reels there was nary a ball or bat in sight. The film represented the first starring role for twenty-year-old ZaSu Pitts, who'd spend much of the rest of her long career playing variations of the fey, homely girl who yearns for (and frequently finds) true love; she would essay a similar part in the 1927 baseball yarn *Casey at the Bat*. The director of *Better Times*, the great King Vidor, had started his career directing two-reel comedies starring Edward Sedgwick, who would himself mature into a director with a special fondness for baseball stories. Vidor used *Better Times* less as a sports story or romance than as a podium whereupon to preach the good word of the Christian Science Movement, of which Vidor was a lifelong disciple.

Big Leaguer

MGM; released August 19, 1953

Produced by Matthew Rapf. Directed by Robert Aldrich. Screenplay by Herbert Baker, from a story by John McNulty and Louis Morheim. Photography: William Mellor. Edited by Ben Lewis. Musical direction by Alberto Colombo. Art direction: Cedric Gibbons and Eddie Imazu. Sound by Douglas Shearer. Assistant director: Sid Sidman. Technical adviser: Hans Lobert. 73 minutes; black and white; sound.

Cast: Edward G. Robinson (John B. "Hans" Lobert); Vera-Ellen (Christy); Jeff Richards (Adam Polachuk); Richard Jaeckel (Bobby Bronson); William Campbell (Julie Davis); Carl Hubbell (Himself); Paul Langton (Brian McLennan); Lalo Rios (Chuy Aguilar); Bill Crandall (Tippy Mitchell); Frank Ferguson (Wally Mitchell); John McKee (Dale Alexander); Mario Siletti (Mr. Polachuk); Robert Caldwell (Pomfret); Donald "Chippie" Hastings (Little Joe Polachuk); Al Campanis, Bob Trocolor, Tony Ravish (Themselves).

Hans Lobert is the scout in charge of the Florida training camp of the New York Giants, where each aspirant is given a two-week tryout before the team's final decisions are made. Lobert's new crop of rookies includes Adam Polachuk, son of an immigrant Polish miner who hopes that Adam will become a lawyer; Tippy Mitchell, whose ballplayer father wants him to be a first baseman but who'd rather be an architect; Julie Davis, a tough guy from 9th Avenue; Bobby Bronson, a showboating pitcher from Massillon, Ohio; and Chuy Aguilar, whose broken English is the source of endless hilarity amongst his peers. The focus of the story is on Adam, who is in Florida on the pretense that he's away at college, and who falls in love with Lobert's niece Christy, the camp secretary. When Adam's dad learns the truth about his "college" term and shows up at camp to watch his son play, old man Polachuk cheerfully okays baseball as a career move for his son.

Big Leaguer was the first theatrical feature directed by Robert Aldrich, a graduate of low-budget TV fare whose best known later work included *Kiss Me Deadly*, *Whatever Happened to Baby Jane*, *Flight of the Phoenix*, *Hush Hush Sweet Charlotte*, *The Longest Yard* and *The Frisco Kid*. Aldrich got his *Big Leaguer* assignment through screenwriter Herbert Baker, with whom Aldrich had worked as part of producer Carl Foreman's Enterprise Productions in the late 1940s. Baker was working for a new B-picture unit

at MGM known with a mixture of jocularity and disdain as "The Sons of the Pioneers" because it was chiefly composed of the offspring or younger relatives of longtime MGM executives. This unit was on the prowl for bright, young, directing talent, most of whom had turned down *Big Leaguer* because it was going to be unglamorously location shot and doggedly budget conscious; since he was eager to break into feature production and was already well acquainted with shoestring quickie production methods, Robert Aldrich was deemed the right man for the job.

Big Leaguer star Edward G. Robinson, playing real-life Giants scout and former Phillies manager Hans Lobert, would probably have turned down this undemanding B-picture assignment during his glory days at Warner Bros. But Robinson was, in the early 1950s, under the scrutiny of the House Un-American Activities Committee for allegedly being a communist sympathizer. Though the actor prepared a thorough inventory of his liberal activities in the 1930s and 1940s in an effort to clear himself, he was effectively "graylisted" from Hollywood—which, as Robert Aldrich would later observe, was even more insidious than "blacklisting" because, since Robinson was not overtly accused of anything, the HUAC would not give him a chance to publicly defend himself and thus encourage producers to hire him. *Big Leaguer* was Edward G. Robinson's first major-studio opportunity in three years, and while it was far from a prestige assignment, the actor eagerly grasped at the straw that might revitalize his career. Robinson did his usual excellent job as Lobert, though it wasn't until Cecil B. DeMille (ironically one of Hollywood's most virulent "Red-baiters") cast the actor in *The Ten Commandments* that Edward G. Robinson was restored to "A" productions.

Big Leaguer's rookie-camp scenes, shot at the Giants' winter grounds in Melbourne, Florida, have the appropriate gritty feel of the rigors of training, though more could have been made of the cutthroat competition that goes on in such camps. Aldrich adopted a documentarylike approach to these scenes, eschewing for the most part the clever staging and camera angles that distinguished his later work. Richard Jaeckel, who played the obligatory swellhead type in *Big Leaguer* and who later became an Aldrich regular, has recalled that the director, tied to a fourteen-day schedule, "couldn't emphasize quality. He had to do as many set-ups as possible." Yet it is this very lack of polish that gives *Big Leaguer* its sporadic jolts of realistic vitality. Further adding to the authenticity were the brief appearances of real-life ballplayers Al Campanis, Bob Trocolor and Tony Ravish, as well as the lengthier cameo by the great Giants star of yore (who was then a scout for his old team), Carl "The Meal Ticket" Hubbell. During the final exhibition game scene, the film's emphasis on the ways that some young players are pressured by their parents hit close to home with many male moviegoers (at one point, Hans Lobert growls that "this camp is lousy with fathers"), and possibly influenced *The Bad News Bears* screenwriter Bill Lancaster to pen his own, much harsher tale of athletes at the mercy of their elders. It's worth noting that the Hispanic character in *Big Leaguer* is named Aguilar, which, except for the letter "u," is the same last name of the two young Spanish-speaking players in *The Bad News Bears*.

Where *Big Leaguer* falls apart is in its strict adherence to stock characters and situations, especially in the "World War II bomber crew" diversification of backgrounds and attitudes among the young rookies. Further hurting the film is its corny dialogue and its syrupy references to the Great Game, never more prevalent than in the obtrusive, golly-gee voiceover narration by Paul Langton. *The Monthly Film Bulletin* noted succinctly that the film "treats its subject with an almost hushed reference and its appeal is restricted almost entirely to baseball enthusiasts."

Big Leaguer was considered by exhibitors to be so low in drawing power that the film had the distinction of being the first ever Edward G. Robinson picture not to be given a regular playdate in Manhattan. It did serve to prove that Robert Aldrich was capable of handling a feature film, but all in all, *Big Leaguer* was a mild to lukewarm affair, reasonably satisfying for baseball fans but not really good enough to stick in the memory of anyone else.

The Bingo Long Travelling All-Stars and Motor Kings

Motown/Pan Arts/Universal; released July 1976

Executive producer: Berry Gordy. Produced by Rob Cohen. Associate producers: Michael Chinich, Janet Hubbard and Bennett Tramer. Directed by John Badham. Screenplay by Hal Barwood and Matthew Robbins; based on the novel by William Brashler. Photography: Bill Butler. Edited by David Rawlins. Music by William Goldstein. "Steal on Home" and "Razzle Dazzle" by William Goldstein and Ron Miller; performer of "Razzle Dazzle": Thelma Houston. Production design by Lawrence G. Paull. Set decoration by Leonard A. Mazzola. Assistant directors: Tom Joyner, L. Andrew Stone and Richard Wells. Production manager: Robert Mayer. Title design by Michael Hamilton and N. Lee Lacy. Stunt coordinator: Jophery Brown. Filmed in Panavision. Color by Technicolor. 110 minutes; sound. Rated PG.

Cast: Billy Dee Williams (Bingo Long); James Earl Jones (Leon Carter); Richard Pryor (Charlie Snow); Rico Dawson (Rainbow); Sam "Birmingham" Briston (Louis); Jophery Brown (Champ Chambers); Leon Wagner (Fat Sam); Tony Burton (Isaac); John McCurry (Walter Murchman); Stan Shaw (Esquire Joe); Ted Ross (Sallison Porter); Mabel King (Bertha); Sam Laws (Henry); Alvin Childress (Horace); Ken Force (Honey); Carl Gordon (Mac); Ahna Capri (Blonde Prostitute); Joel Fluellen (Mr. Holland);

Sarina C. Grant (Purline); Jester Hairston (Furry Taylor); Emmett Ashford (Umpire); Ted Lehmann (Lars Borstrum); Fred Covington (Auctioneer); Greg Oliver (Sheriff); John R. McKee (White Stranger); Brooks Clift (Older Gentleman); Morgan Roberts (Kiosk Man); Marcia McBroom (Violet); Lidia Kristen (Nurse); Steve Anderson (One-Armed Ballplayer); Dero Austin (Midget Catcher).

It is 1939; major league baseball is segregated, compelling talented black ballplayers to make the rounds of the Negro leagues. Bingo Long, dynamite pitcher for the Ebony Aces, is fed up with working for team owner Sallison Porter, who takes every opportunity to cheat his players out of their rightful financial share. When Porter fires the seriously injured Rainbow Mikes, leaving the hapless player stranded without a cent, it's the last straw. Bingo bolts the Ebony Aces and, together with his friend Leon Carter, catcher for the Elite Giants, forms his own barnstorming ball club, the Bingo Long Travelling All-Stars and Motor Kings—so named because the whole team bounces from town to town jammed into two roadsters. The maverick team draws so many quality players out of the Negro leagues that Sallie Porter organizes a boycott against the Motor Kings, forcing them to play with amateur white clubs (for whom they have to joke around in order to be accepted as anything other than a threat) and House of David–style "clown" teams. Despite hardships imposed by Porter in particular and White Society in general, the Motor Kings persevere, until finally Porter offers Bingo a deal. If the Kings can win one last Big Game with the Negro All-Stars, the barnstormers will be allowed in the leagues; if Bingo's boys lose, they all have to go back to their old teams. The shifty Porter pulls more than a few strings to prevent the Kings from winning, not the least of which is having Leon Carter kidnapped, but Bingo Long and his compatriots win the game. Shortly after this victory, Esquire Joe, one of Bingo's top players, is signed by the Brooklyn Dodgers in an effort to break the "color line" in the majors—a forewarning that the great days of the Negro League are coming to an end.

When film producer Rob Cohen finished reading *The Bingo Long Travelling All-Stars and Motor Kings*, a novel written two years earlier in 1973 by former Chicago journalist William Brashler, he set his mind to transferring that book to the big screen. Cohen, the recently appointed head of the new film division of Motown Records, insisted that Motown chieftain Berry Gordy buy outright, rather than merely option, Brashler's book: "Optioning shows you're not confident," Cohen remarked later. "In this business it's knowing that makes the difference." Brashler was assigned to convert his book into a screenplay, but the results were so faithful that the picture would have run three hours. Rob Cohen thereupon hired Hal Barwood and Matthew Robbins, the screenwriters of the 1974 road movie "sleeper" *The Sugarland Express*, which Cohen had admired for its "balance between humor and truth."

Motown offered *Bingo Long* to a number of studios for distribution, but it was Universal which evinced the most interest. The only snag in the Universal deal was that Cohen had foreseen a $10 million budget for the picture, but the studio, wary of the salability of a film that dealt not only with baseball but with *black* baseball, imposed a ceiling of $3 million (at that, it was still one of the highest budgeted films with a black theme ever made). This meant that Motown's first choice as director for *Bingo Long*, Mark Rydell, was out of the picture, since Rydell had wanted not only a larger budget but a longer shooting time than the thirty-nine days allotted by Universal. The studio pitched young Steven Spielberg, who'd directed *Sugarland Express*, to Motown, but Spielberg became less and less available as more and more money rolled

The Bingo Long Travelling All-Stars and Motor Kings **enter a small town with their usual sense of moderation and sobriety.**

in from the director's most recent feature, *Jaws. Bingo Long* finally was awarded to John Badham, an Emmy-winning TV director who'd never been in charge of a theatrical feature. Despite his nervousness over handling an elaborate project with a minimum of time and money, and with only a moment's concern over the fact that, as a thirty-one-year-old Englishman, Badham's understanding of Southern black baseball in the 1930s was pretty sketchy, the director tackled the problem with élan, bringing in the project only four days over schedule and 10 percent over budget—no small achievement for *any* American-made film.

In William Brashler's novel, Bingo Long was a catcher based upon the phenomenal Josh Gibson (the subject of an earlier biography by Brashler), who spent his entire professional life in the Negro leagues

and who, according to legend, hit the only home run ever to go over the fence at Yankee stadium. Bingo's friend Leon Carter was a pitcher, created in the image of Satchel Paige. When Motown contractee Billy Dee Williams was cast as Bingo, positions were switched, with Bingo pitching and Leon catching. After all, Williams had done some pitching in school, while James Earl Jones, who played Carter, had spent less time in his youth participating in sports than he had overcoming a childhood stutter. Besides, Billy Dee was the star—no way was he going to spend half the picture with his face obscured by a catcher's mask.

Richard Pryor's character, a ballplayer named Charlie Snow who is determined to make it into the white majors by posing first as a Cuban and later as an Indian, doesn't appear in the novel. Pryor was added to attract theatergoers who may not have been interested in baseball but who were doling out money hand over fist to purchase Pryor's enormously popular comedy record albums. At this point in his career, Pryor was weary of playing supporting best-friend parts and comic cameos, but Rob Cohen made the deal financially attractive and even offered to rearrange the picture's shooting schedule to accommodate Pryor's full roster of personal appearances. Richard Pryor's limited availability resulted in his being on-screen a comparatively brief period of time—virtually disappearing at the film's halfway mark (*Ebony* magazine reviewer Martin Weston suggested that Pryor's part was cut down less to allow him to honor his other commitments than to give more screen space to Billy Dee Williams).

After viewing the end result, author Brashler was a little nonplussed that some of his favorite events in the novel were missing, but allowed that he was "happy as an author could be" about the adaptation. He was much happier than several of the novel's fans, and a whole lot happier than many Negro League veterans who saw the film. While *Bingo Long* follows the basic chronology of its source material, the "feel" of the movie is radically different from that of the book, while the "balance of humor and truth" that Rob Cohen had hoped to achieve is tipped rather too far in the direction of humor. Old-time black ballplayers were not happy to see the entire history of their teams reduced by the film version of *Bingo Long* to the level of Harlem Globetrotter slapstick.

Some of the film's embellishments are for the good. The novel is a rambling, picaresque affair, a series of anecdotes bounded at the beginning by Bingo's defection from the league and at the end by Leon Carter's arm going bad and Esquire Joe's sign-up with the major leagues; the film tightens this structure, providing the story with a

rousing conclusion by having the future of the Motor Kings rest upon a single Big Game. It's also beneficial to give the story focus by having the major adventures—a near-fatal confrontation with a white prostitute, an episode in which the Motor Kings steal back their car after it has been appropriated by a white auctioneer as a debt settlement, the climactic kidnapping—occur not to various minor members of the team but to Billy Dee Williams, James Earl Jones and Richard Pryor. Altering the full-time profession of villain Sallison Porter from restaurant owner (the livelihood of the real-life model for Porter, Gus Greenlee, the nicer but still ethically suspect head of the Negro National League in the 1930s) to funeral parlor operator at first seems like one of those "irreverent" gags so common to 1970s comedies. Only toward the end do we realize that the job change is there to set up the film's funniest sequence: Leon Carter's escape from Porter's henchmen by first hiding in a coffin, then commandeering a hearse to drive onto the diamond just in time to score the winning run.

Certain amendments to Brashler's original indicate that scenarists Barwood and Robbins had done their baseball homework. Pitcher Bingo Long calls in his outfield just before striking out the opposition, a little bit of bravado frequently performed by Satchel Paige, especially when someone on the other side had cast aspersions on Paige's ancestry. And when Charlie Snow, ever trying to crash into the white major leagues, shows up at the end sporting an Indian haircut and calling himself "Chief Tokohama," it's an affectionate invocation of John McGraw's attempt in 1901 to pass off light-skinned black ballplayer Charlie Grant as a Cherokee Indian to sneak him into the majors—using exactly the same phony monicker.

The inescapable issue of racial prejudice was treated in the novel as status quo for 1939, a "given" that the Motor Kings had to work around in order to survive. Standard procedure in films of the 1960s and 1970s was to have black characters adopt a more militant attitude toward the inequities imposed upon them by whites, and to magnify each incident of prejudice as though it were the eruption of Krakatoa. The makers of *Bingo Long*, both before and behind the cameras, took special pride in *not* making their film a tract. Each temptation to preach was deflected by the script; when Bingo and his

Billy Dee Williams as the guider of the destinies of *The Bingo Long Travelling All-Stars and Motor Kings*.

team are compelled to help pick potatoes to raise the money to buy back their car (another incident invented for the film), only to be paid half the wages that a white picking crew would have made, there was supposed to have been a bit of dialogue indicating that Roosevelt had put an end to the Depression only for white folks. The dialogue was cut; it was decided that the facial expressions of the black workers told the whole story without resorting to words. In another instance, the novel's vicious white Klansman who cheats the Motor Kings out of their automobile in order to add it to his own used car lot is softened in the film by becoming a cloddish hotel owner, who is still shifty but decidedly no cross burner. The character is further lightened up by being given an absurdly exaggerated Scandinavian accent.

The hotel owner's musical comedy dialect does, however, point out a major flaw in *Bingo Long*. The book was essentially a straight story with comic undertones; the film tries to sustain audience enthusiasm by making the story comedy through and through. In the tradition of the popular Mel Brooks films of the era, *Bingo Long* works so relentlessly for laughs that there's no time for the characters to become fully flesh and blood. As Sallison Porter, Ted Ross (who'd won a Tony Award for his Broadway performance as the Cowardly Lion in *The Wiz*) seems to be under the impression that he's "The Kingfish" from the old *Amos 'n' Andy* show, while Mabel King, cast as the female owner of a ball club (yet another character not in the novel) who sleeps with her best players and who terrorizes the male club owners even to the point of bursting in on them as they take a steam bath, has all the subtlety of a nuclear warhead. These performers who were over the top should have emulated the more disciplined character studies of veteran actors like Alvin Childress, the onetime "Amos" of TV's *Amos 'n' Andy*, here cast as a natty and articulate team owner; Jester Hairston, playing a washed-up old ballplayer reduced to begging in front of Sallie Porter's stadium;

and especially Joel Fluellen, who is outstanding as the grocery store owner who books the Motor Kings' games and gives them pointers on how to strut and preen when they march down small-town Main Streets to herald those games.

Viewers hoping for the baseball scenes to provide respite from the ceaseless barrage of pig-bladder comedy were in for a disappointment. The ballgames are excellently staged in two Georgia minor-league parks, Savannah's Grayson Stadium (you can spot Grayson by the ninety-foot light tower in left field) and Macon's Luther Williams Field. John Badham, unfamiliar with baseball and not sure of how best to direct the action, shot the games with multiple cameras, hoping to have lots of good material to choose from during the editing process. The result was plenty of choice baseball activity, most of it courtesy of former pro ballplayers Jophery Brown, Sam "Birmingham" Briston, and Leon Wagner, all of whom were cast as Motor King teammates. Alas, the postproduction crew of *Bingo Long* felt it was their bounden duty to "juice up" the games with a lot of special effect gimmickry, from a cartoon fastball to an outfield catch "improved" by first stretch-framing and then speeding up the action. The product looks more like cartoon director Tex Avery's *Batty Baseball* than a sport conducted by human beings. Curiously, the use of slow motion, often the least palatable aspect in filmed ballgames, is handled with relative expertise, especially when Bingo pitches the crucial strikeout in the final game.

When watching the ballgame scenes, one can appreciate the complaints made by Negro League survivors about the false impression given that black baseball was all goofing around and no nuts-and-bolts gameplaying. It's understandable that the Motor Kings would clown for "whitey," since the prevalent opinion of Southern whites in 1939 was that black players (and

blacks in general) weren't to be trusted if they didn't make fools of themselves. But the Kings continue behaving like court jesters during the final game, which is played against a black team before a black crowd. One has trouble buying the argument that the Motor Kings are larking about only to defuse race hatred; maybe these guys really *enjoy* wearing giant-sized catcher's mitts and dressing up in gorilla costumes.

But after all, this film was made to get laughs, not to change the world. *The Bingo Long Travelling All-Stars and Motor Kings* still retains some of its infectious exuberance when seen today, though, as in 1976, most viewers would rather see more horsehide and less horseplay. As Universal expected, the film did not exactly break records at the box office, meaning that it would be a long time—over twenty years, in fact—before a truer picture of the black baseball experience would reach the screen (See separate entry for *The Soul of the Game*).

Blue Skies Again

Lantana/Warner Bros.; released July 1983

Produced by Arlene Sellers and Alex Winitzky. Executive in charge of production: Elliot Schick. Directed by Richard Michaels. Screenplay by Kevin Sellers. Photography: Don McAlpine. Edited by Danford Greene. Music by John Kander; conducted by Donald Pippin. Art director: Don McIvey. Assistant directors: Michael Daves, Robert Doherty and Jeffrey Stacy. Florida casting by Dee Miller. Filmed in Panavision. Color by Technicolor. 91 minutes; Dolby Stereo Sound. Rated PG.

Cast: Harry Hamlin (Sandy Mendenhall); Mimi Rogers (Liz West); Kenneth McMillan (Dirk Miller); Dana Elcar (Lou Goff); Robyn Barto (Paula Fradkin); Cylk Cozart (Wallstreet); Andy Garcia (Ken); Joey Gian (Calvin); Doug Moeller (Carol); Ray Negron (Jeffrey); Tommy Lane (Roy); Rooney Kerwin (Mike Ross); Marcos Gonzales (Brushback); Joel Lindberg (Andy); Julian Byrd (Coach Lindburne); Jeff Rosenberg

(Devils Second Pitcher); Bill Hindman (Blues Manager); Julio Oscar Mechosa (Blues Translator); Frank Schuller (Umpire); Susan Hatfield (National Anthem Singer); Jeff Gillen, Jan Oniki (Couple in Stands); Will Knickerbocker (Redneck in Stands); Florence McGee (Elderly Lady); Bernie Knee (Fred Gandil); Frank Umont (Second Base Umpire); Fred Buch, Toni Crabtree, Bobby Gale (Reporters); Ralph Weintraub (Vendor); Robyn Peterson (Crystal); Phil Philbin (Policeman); Brody Howell, Tommy Barone (Intercoastal Duck Players); Earl Houston Bullock (Publicity Man); Carol Nadell (Motel Desk Clerk); Patrick Marie (Maitre d'); Gregg Gilbert (Bellboy); Jay Amor (Stunt Double).

Determined to be the first female second baseperson in the major leagues, Paula Fradkin journeys to the Fort Lauderdale winter training camp of the Denver Devils. Players' agent Liz West, fascinated with the boost for feminism that Paula embodies, offers to represent the girl. There is a great deal of resistance to the idea of making baseball coed, none stronger than from the new owner of the Devils, obnoxious millionaire Sandy Mendenhall. A preliminary tryout results in the rest of the team—at Sandy's bequest—taunting Paula with every sexual profanity in their repertoire, causing the girl to almost give up her dream. But with the conspiratorial aid of Liz West, team manager Dirk Miller, and former Devils star Lou Goff, Paula is sneaked into the opening exhibition game against the Memphis Blues. The Blues walk off the diamond in protest, but Paula shames the opposition's super-macho star pitcher into resuming the game. Paula scores a run to first base, the crowd goes wild, and the once recalcitrant Sandy Mendenhall welcomes Paula Fradkin to the Denver Devils.

Blue Skies Again is what is known in Hollywood as "lightweight summer entertainment." This one's so lightweight it's practically a meringue.

Director Richard Michaels, a veteran of TV sitcoms (*Bewitched, The Brady Bunch*) and miniseries (*Once an Eagle, Sadat*), de-cided to use a newcomer in the role of Paula Fradkin, and in so doing posed himself the nice problem of finding a girl who could both play ball and act. Robyn Barto, a collegiate softball ace, could play ball. One out of two wasn't bad. In truth, though Barto wields a mean bat, her second-base skill is never enough to convince the audience that she would ever get any farther than a school softball team—which doesn't hurt the film as much as you'd expect, since the Denver Devils aren't so hot either. Faced with the dual whammy of a star of bush-league abilities both as athlete and actress, *and* a "professional" ball club which looked like a group of refugees from an Idaho dinner theater, director Michaels performed wonders with the game scenes, utilizing adroit camera angles and fast-paced editing to sustain the illusion of a team that had some clue of what it was doing. What little energy *Blue Skies Again* has is concentrated on the ballfield (located at Florida's Fort Lauderdale complex, home away from home for the New York Yankees), with the rest of the picture adopting a sleepwalker's pace; one can only wonder what this film, which runs 90 minutes in videocassette form, looked like when it was trade shown at a length of 110 minutes.

Many old standbys from the Amalgamated Cliché Factory (sports movie division) are in attendance: the crusty manager with the fourteen-karat heart, the studdish athletes whose eyes grow into cantaloupes whenever there's a woman around, the desperate star player who's staring the end of his career in the face, the foreign-born pitcher who carries an interpreter with him at all times, the male spectator exasperated at the baseball illiteracy of his female companion, the old lady in the stands who clobbers the loud-mouthed redneck sitting next to her, the kindly ex-ballplayer turned caretaker who fortunately isn't named "Pop," the financial-whiz team member who unfortunately *is* named "Wall Street," and everyone's favorite, the slow-motion final pitch. But wait, there's more! As a special bonus to our special customers, there's a cliché in the making. Team owner Mendenhall is a Southern-based millionaire who pokes his nose into baseball matters of which he knows nothing, steps all over the feelings of others, delivers videotaped memos, consistently compromises his efforts to move gracefully through high society with his basic immaturity, and owns a yacht. It doesn't take a NASA scientist to figure out who this crudely drawn caricature is based on; the script leaves no Turner unstoned.

One supposes after a few minutes' viewing that *Blue Skies Again* is a comedy. One would also suppose that scenarist Kevin Sellers had previously worked as a gagman for bubble gum wrappers and cocktail napkins. It's awe-inspiring that any movie made in A.D. 1983 would resurrect the one about a man trying to impress his girl by pretending to be able to read the menu at a French restaurant, only to discover that he's just "ordered" the manager. And let us draw a veil of charitable silence over the sequence in which Devils manager Dirk Miller, portrayed by barrel-bellied Kenneth McMillan, dances an Irish jig in the locker room. About the only comedy setpiece that really works is the scene in which Paula Fradkin is taught how to chew tobacco.

It might have been funnier if we'd cared anything about Paula as a human being. She loses audience empathy early on with her grim insistence that she be given a chance with the Devils without the usual nicety of previous professional training. The script tries to get us to pull for her in the tryout scene by having the filthy-pig Devils shout sexual slurs and obscenities at her. But when she storms off the field after only a couple of minutes of this, we are thoroughly unconvinced that she really wants a baseball career so much that she can taste it. Witnessing Paula's humiliation, agent Liz West complains that, "nobody could be expected to perform with that kind of harassment"—whereupon the audience is sorely tempted to stand up and shout, "What about Jackie Robinson?"

The "insult" scene brings up *another* problem. We're never sure just what the filmmakers' definition of "sexist" entails. Paula wants to be accepted on the same terms as the male players, yet she makes girlish goo-goo eyes at poor Lou Goff to wear down his resistance. And in her efforts to keep Mendenhall from knowing that Paula has been entered in the seventh inning of the opening game, Liz West keeps the owner trapped in his office with the promise—and implied fulfillment—of sexual favors.

Blue Skies Again is another in an endless parade of low-budget films with excellent premises laid low by muddled execution. The film went nowhere financially in 1983, but has enjoyed a healthy second life in video rentals, thanks to the pre–*LA Law* presence of Harry Hamlin as Mendenhall, and the novelty of seeing future stars Mimi Rogers and Andy Garcia in their very first film roles. Perhaps, some day, some enterprising video store manager will offer a free rental to anyone who can figure out the meaning of the title *Blue Skies Again*.

Bull Durham

North State Films/Orion; released June 15, 1988

Produced by Thom Mount and Mark Burg. Executive producer and production manager: David V. Lester. Associate producer: Charles Hirschorn. Written and directed by Ron Shelton. Photography: Bobby Byrne. Edited by Robert Leighton and Adam Weiss. Music by Michael Covertino; "Goin' to the Show" by Bernie Wallace and Mac "Dr. John" Rabenack. Popular songs on soundtrack by various original artists. Musical supervision by Danny Abramson. Production design by Armin Ganz. Art director: David Lubin. Set decoration by Kris Boxell and David Brace. Costumes by Louise Frogley. Casting by Bonnie Timmerman. Sound: Kirk Francis and Michael Boudry. Assistant director: Richard J. Kidney. Production coordinator: Janice E. Sperling. Makeup by Cynthia Barr. Special effects by Vern and Jeff Hyde. Stunts by Webster Whinery. Baseball adviser: Pete Bock. Color by DeLuxe. 108 minutes (previewed at 115 minutes); sound. Rated R.

Cast: Kevin Costner (Crash Davis); Susan Sarandon (Annie Savoy); Tim Robbins (Ebby Calvin "Nuke" LaLoosh); Trey Wilson (Skip); Robert Wuhl (Larry); Max Patkin (Himself); William O'Leary (Jimmy); David Niedorf (Bobby); Danny Gans (Deke); Tom Silardi (Tony); Lloyd Williams (Mickey); Rick Marzan (Jose); George Buck (Nuke's Father); Jennie Robertson (Millie); Greg Avalone (Doc); Carey "Garland" Bunting (Teddy, Radio Announcer); Robert Dickman (Whitey); Timothy Kirk (Ed; also one of the Core Ballplayers); Don Davis (Scared Batter); Stephen Ware (Umpire); Tom Eshelman (Bat Boy); C. K. Bibby (Mayor); Henry G. Sanders (Sandy); Antoinette Forsyth (Ballpark Announcer); Shirley Anne Ritter (Cocktail Waitress); Pete Bock (Minister); Alan Mejia (Chu Chu); Sid Aikens, Craig Brown, Wes Currin, Kelly Heath, Mo Johnson, Todd Kopeznski, John Lovingood, Eddie Mathews, Alan Peternoster, Bill Robinson, Dean Robinson, Tom Schultz, Sam Veraldi, El Chico Williams (Core Ballplayers).

A year in the life of the Durham Bulls, a Class A team in the Carolina League. Specifically, this is the story of that year as experienced by three people: Ebby Calvin LaLoosh, a pitcher with major league potential whose control could use a lot of fine tuning (in his first game he beans the team mascot, the radio announcer, and the girl in the public address box); Crash Davis, an aging catcher with ten years in the minors behind him, hired by the Bulls principally to straighten LaLoosh out; and Annie Savoy, a beauteous college English teacher to whom baseball is a deeply metaphysical and spiritual experience, and who singles out one young Durham Bull player per year to sleep with and to "nurture." After choosing

LaLoosh over Davis as her steady of the season—or, rather, having the choice made for her when rejected by the worldweary Crash—Annie nicknames the kid "Nuke" because his wham-bam style of both baseball and lovemaking reminds her of a nuclear meltdown. As the Bulls' 142-game roster is played out, Annie gives Nuke pointers on poise and concentration both on the field and in the sack, while Crash gets Nuke to go with the flow and stop thinking so much about being a hotshot, to not be afraid of the occasional failure, and to listen to the advice of others. Davis also prepares Nuke for "The Show"—that's baseball talk for the big leagues—by teaching him his media interview clichés ("Ya gotta play the game one day at a time," "I just wanna give it my best shot"), and advises Nuke during a winning streak to abstain from sex with Annie, lest the kid think that his success is totally the result of external forces rather than the excellence within himself. Ultimately, Nuke gets his chance in The Show—while Crash, his usefulness to the Bulls at an end, is let go. Seeking solace, Crash knocks on Annie's door, and the two spend an exquisite night together. But just as Annie has a "mission" in life—expanding the horizons of younger ballplayers—so does Crash, and in the morning he's left for a new catching job in Asheville, determined to finish out the season, set a lifetime home run record of 247, and perpetuate the only life he knows. When Annie heads home after the last Bulls game of the year, however, Crash is waiting for her. He's decided to bid adios to baseball, at least as a player. Annie, who's missed Crash in a way she's never missed anyone before, resolves to give up her annual dalliances with green young kids and stick with someone closer to her own age and intellect. Crash Davis and Annie Savoy have come to realize that they're exactly the same, two seasoned players nearing the end of their rather ethereal careers, both in

Crash Davis (Kevin Costner, right) sizes up the opposition in *Bull Durham*.

need of something that will last. And as for Nuke LaLoosh, he's achieved the big-league status that he was always destined to have, thanks largely to the experience he's gleaned from both Crash and Annie.

The above cold-print synopsis does precisely no justice to *Bull Durham*. Things just don't get any better than this film. Sports fans and movie buffs alike have singled out *Bull Durham* as the best baseball picture ever made; certainly it's one of the most original, and one of the few to approach Absolute Truth—truth about baseball, truth about life. Writer-director Ron Shelton knew whereof he spoke in *Bull Durham*. He'd spent five years as a player in the Baltimore Orioles' farm system, closing out his baseball career at age twenty-five with the Rochester Red Wings in 1971. Unlike Crash Davis, Shelton was hardly a spectacular player; like Crash, however,

Shelton had the sagacity to take stock of himself and look for other avenues in life. After raising a family and holding down a variety of jobs, Shelton got a Master of Fine Arts degree from Arizona State, and set out to write short stories and screenplays. One of his early efforts, written in 1979, was titled *A Player to Be Named Later*, and in it were the embryonic characters of a veteran utility player and a wild newcomer. Neither this script nor the many others churned out by Shelton sold until he got a position in 1983 as rewrite man for *Under Fire*, a film directed by Robert Spottiswoode. The director liked both Shelton's work and his cheerful insouciance to multiple personal setbacks, and hired the ex-athlete to concoct the screenplay of Spottiswoode's next project, a tale of a middle-ager trying to reverse an old high school football defeat, titled *The Best of Times*. Shelton was also given a second-unit job on this film, and was allowed to direct the entire gridiron sequence himself. It was through *Best of Times* that Shelton earned his reputation in Hollywood as a man who could make sports events come to life on-screen (no small achievement, as we all have seen), and at long last, Ron Shelton got the chance to direct his pet project, *A Player to Be Named Later*—now renamed *Bull Durham* (The film's original title pops up in Crash Davis's first scene as his caustic opening line).

The Fates must have been smiling upon Ron Shelton when Thom Mount chose to coproduce *Bull Durham*. Mount was part owner of the Carolina League's real-life Durham Bulls, giving the filmmakers access to the team's home diamond at Durham Athletic Park, El Toro Stadium. Considered by minor-league followers as a "model" ballpark, El Toro was big without being too big, professional looking (its scoreboard clock had originally "done time" at Brooklyn's Ebbets Field) without losing its small-town charm, and user friendly both to its players and its spectators; the team could play a good game without worrying about an overly enormous outfield, while fans could luxuriate in good seating and the superb concession stand foodstuffs. El Toro, used for the lion's share of the ballpark scenes (there are a few shots of Crash Davis playing at Asheville's McCormick Field), becomes as much a "character" in the film as any of the human actors. The audience learns to accept the park as a gathering place for various character quirks of the leading players; as a clearing house for such plot devices as Crash's ongoing efforts to get Nuke to follow advice, Annie's ceaseless passing of advisory notes to her favorite players during games, and the wonderful moment where a midgame conference on the pitcher's mound turns into a discussion of what to buy one of the players for a wedding present; and as a "bulletin board" for sundry municipal activities

in the Durham-Raleigh area. The most memorable aspect of El Toro stadium, the giant bull in the outfield which spews forth smoke from its horns whenever hit by a ball, was specially constructed for the film, and has remained there to this day by popular demand of the fans.

Adding flavor to the stadium sequences is the antic presence of Max Patkin, "Clown Prince of Baseball." Patkin had been in the clowning business since 1946, and had once been made a uniformed "coach" by Bill Veeck to pack the fans in at Cleveland Indians games; the funster even got himself thrown out of a game by making a broad (but clean) gesture suggesting that the umpire was favoring the visiting team. A highly respected and thorough professional, Max Patkin was rewarded for forty years' faithful service by being given a full-fledged featured role in *Bull Durham*, including a post game dance session with Susan Sarandon at a Durham tavern. (As originally written, Patkin's character was to have died in harness, and his ashes were to have been sprinkled on the pitcher's mound.)

Just having a genuine ballpark and ballpark clown wouldn't have been worth the smoke coming out of those El Toro bullhorns had the rest of Ron Shelton's film not been every bit as genuine. *Bull Durham* is peopled not by tanned and tailored Malibu types whose athletic shortcomings are covered up with stunt doubles, but by actors who look, talk, move, play, and think like members of a pro ball club. Of star Kevin Costner, the film's baseball adviser Pete Bock said bluntly, "I'd sign Costner tomorrow if he quit acting. Kevin can hit from both sides of the plate with power. You believe the guy in closeups." Costner, who'd played some high school ball, showed off his switch-hitting talent after having a few drinks with Shelton one evening, inspiring the director to demand a baseball "tryout" from the rest of the potential cast members. There was no room on this club for any marshmallow thespians who began interviews with, "Well, I've never played the game before, but—" One of the actors, Robert Wuhl (who, as the Bulls coach Larry, spends most of the film rattling off a splendidly incomprehensible stream of sidelines chatter), was so knowledgeable in baseball lore that he was invited to write the chapter on Roger Maris's sixty-first homer in Danny Peary's 1989 book of hero-worship essays, *Cult Baseball Players*.

As a onetime pro himself, Ron Shelton was sickened by the usual clichés and half-truths attendant to baseball movies, so he avoided the old bromides with a vengeance and revealed facts about how the game is really played that caused audible gasps in the audience. None of the games are won in the last of the ninth with two outs and the bases loaded, and in fact the only homer hit out of the park by Crash in the picture is *not* the winning run. We see line drives, pop flies, grounders, fouls, errors, bonehead plays. We see the glamorous veneer of baseball stripped away with a procession of bumpy charter bus rides from game to game. We see Crash so keen on getting know-it-all Nuke to obey his signals that he tips off the opposition's batter as to what sort of ball Nuke will pitch—and so sure handed is Ron Shelton that he successfully pulls off this bit of business *twice*.

Bull Durham is a visual encyclopedia of minor-league baseball strategy. Drawing upon his intimate knowledge of such things, Shelton offers the sort of "tips for starters" that you won't find in the rule book, among them a foolproof method of how to spook the other team. Crash tells Nuke to deliberately throw a pitch at the Durham mascot (a man in a cumbersome bull costume), then warns the opposing batter that Nuke is so crazy and uncontrollable that no one knows who'll be bonked next—which frightens the hapless batter into striking out.

Shelton's handling of his main characters is also a wellspring of nuance. An example: the script's casual observations of various forms of spirituality—Annie's worshiping at the altar of baseball, ballplayer Jimmy's deeply felt fundamental Christianity, and teammate Jose's equally deep faith in voodoo and witchcraft—would in any other film have been the source of derision (indeed, Christianity and Voodoo are both fodder for easy laughs in *Major League*). But Shelton never sneers; he respects the beliefs of his characters, and even rewards them for sticking to their beliefs. When the virginal Jimmy marries town trollop Millie in a lovely ceremony at home plate, not one of his teammates has the slightest intention of bursting Jimmy's illusions by telling him the truth about his blushing bride.

Bull Durham is right up there with *Casablanca*, *All About Eve* and *Annie Hall* in its abundance of quotable dialogue. One is tempted to simply repeat every line in the picture as illustration of its wit, and undoubtedly there are *Bull Durham* junkies in the land who can recite the whole film from memory. (Well, why not? Kevin Costner endeared himself to costar Susan Sarandon by acting out every scene from his own favorite film, *How the West Was Won*.) Some of the best examples include Crash Davis's litany of his beliefs (among them that Lee Harvey Oswald acted alone, that the novels of Susan Sontag are "self indulgent, overrated crap," that "there ought to be a constitutional amendment outlawing Astroturf and the designated hitter," and that there's nothing finer than "long, slow, wet kisses that last three days"); the aforementioned lesson in clichés conducted by Crash for the benefit of Nuke; the labeling of strikeouts as "fascist," and of groundballs as "democratic"; Crash describing a home run by observing "anything that travels that fast oughta have a stewardess on it"; and Crash's lyrical description to his admiring teammates of his twenty-one days in "The Show," outlining such luxuries as hotels with room service and "ballparks like cathedrals." If these passages seem disproportionately relegated to Crash Davis, we must observe that Annie Savoy has the picture's single funniest line: when Nuke describes her as "cute," Annie's apoplectic response is "Cute? Baby ducks are cute! I *hate* cute!!!"

Annie Savoy is the film's single most fascinating character. Ron Shelton created Annie in hopes of dramatizing at least one "living male fantasy" who doesn't resort to the traditional last

In *Bull Durham*, Kevin Costner first exuded the "star quality" that was kept under wraps in his previous film work.

scene cop-out of apologizing for herself. We are in the palm of Annie's hand the moment we see her shrine, replete with candles, to Thurman Munson, and hear her voiceover narration outlining her credo that, "the only church that truly feeds the soul day in and day out is the Church of Baseball."

To Annie, sex, philosophy, intellect and baseball are interdependent and inseparable. She is able to talk of seduction, paraphysics and ant colonies in the same sentence; at the end of the film she manages to invoke both Walt Whitman and Casey Stengel in virtually the same breath. She can discuss relationships with Crash while joining him—and matching him—at batting practice. And she may well be the only female character in mass entertainment history who would even consider ad-

vising her boyfriend to improve his pitching by breathing through his eyes in the manner of the Galapagos lava lizard—and suggesting that he wear garters to throw his testicles out of alignment, thereby keeping his brains "slightly off center."

Slightly off center is the best way to describe the sublime performance of Susan Sarandon as Annie Savoy, one of the few baseball movie heroines who's as stimulating as the game itself, if not more so. (This aura of stimulation certainly must have been operative for the actor playing Nuke, Tim Robbins, whose on-screen love scenes with Sarandon were a contributing factor to his off screen romance with the actress.)

As an added fillip, Sarandon extended her screen character to a whimsical 1988 *TV Guide* article titled "My Annie Savoy's Red-Hot Rules for Better World Series

Viewing." In it, Annie/Susan advises the reader never to root for teams who play on plastic grass or under a roof, or whose uniforms have no belt loops; never switch channels during the game, as it betrays a "lack of respect"; never place the TV in opposition with the magnetic pull of the earth; and to wear loose clothing so as not to faint in the heat of excitement. And *always* believe in your own team, no matter what: "Miracles can happen—You've just gotta believe in the Church of Baseball."

If Annie Savoy is a wish dream, Crash Davis is what happens when you're wide awake. Kevin Costner was attracted to the role because Crash, unlike so many other baseball movie heroes, is not forced into rechanneling his life by a debilitating disease, a crippling injury, a last-minute win or a wonderful long-term contract with a top-rank team. His decisions are not borne of plot contrivance—they are based on his taking a good, sober look inside himself. Costner explained to *Rolling Stone* magazine that the film was "about deciding what kind of person you're gonna be. Are you gonna turn into an alcoholic 'cause you never made it?—. Are you gonna change your life? And that's about as powerful and heroic as covering a grenade."

The actor also discovered a lot of himself in Crash Davis: the flashes of humor, the knowledgeability in matters of history and culture, the willingness to share his expertise in practical matters, the flaws, the temperament. Some of Costner's character quirks even found their way into the script. In shooting an early scene, Ron Shelton tried to get a taciturn Costner to loosen up by saying, "It's fun, goddamnit." That line made it to the screen as a bit of advice given by Crash Davis to an uptight Nuke La-Loosh.

The contributions of Kevin Costner, Susan Sarandon, Tim Robbins and the rest of the cast, together with the razor-sharp perceptions of Ron Shelton and the almost nonchalant realism of the game scenes, make *Bull Durham* an unforgettable experience, one of the very few baseball films that can be watched over and over again with no lessening of enjoyment. Shot on a cautious $7 million budget in only eight weeks, the film was the surprise hit of the summer of 1988; it grossed nearly $51 million, making baseball bankable at the ticket office and bestowing full stardom upon Kevin Costner. Perhaps it might have had an even broader appeal had it gone for a "PG" rating and toned down its steamy (and often hilarious) sex scenes and its graphic banter on the diamond and in the locker room— Aw, leave it alone. Stop *thinking* so much. *Bull Durham* is a classic.

The Bush Leaguer

Warner Bros.; released August 20, 1927

Directed by Howard Bretherton. Screenplay by Harvey Gates, from a story by Charles Gordon Saxton. Photography: Norbert Brodine. Assistant director: Eddie Sowders. 7 reels/ 6,281 feet: black and white; silent.

Cast: Monte Blue (Buchanan "Specs" White); Clyde Cook (Skeeter McKinnon); Leila Hyams (Alice Hobbs); William Demarest (John Gilroy); Richard Tucker (Wallace Ramsey); Brad Marshall (Stetson); Tom Dempsey (The "Parson"); Wilfred North (Stokes); William Wilson (Lefty Murphy); Violet Palmer (Marie, Alice's Maid); Rodney Hildebrand (Detective).

Garage owner Specs White (that's the sort of nickname you used to get if you wore glasses) is the local ball team's star pitcher, but he's more interested in inventions; his current project is an ultra-improved gas pump. Lefty, a scout for the Los Angeles Angels, offers Specs a job, which the young mechanic takes in order to finance his invention. While in training, Specs is spurred to success by a newspaper photo of his dream girl, whom he's never met. When he learns that this girl is Alice

Hobbs, the owner of the ball club, the revelation not only sets his heart atwitter, but it helps Specs overcome his debilitating fear of big crowds. Specs almost loses Alice when she's led to believe that he's been bribed by a ring of game-fixing gamblers, but our hero routs the bad guys, sells his invention, reclaims his girl, and hits a winning home run seemingly in one fell swoop.

Although not mentioned at the time (not even in the studio legal files), *The Bush Leaguer* was partially remade by Warners in 1932 as *Fireman Save My Child* (q.v.), with Joe E. Brown as a small-town baseball champ preoccupied with inventing a new kind of fire-extinguisher. Both *Bush Leaguer* and *Fireman* featured baseball sequences filmed at Los Angeles's Wrigley Field, home of the genuine L.A. Angels (who were also prominently featured in *Babe Comes Home* [q.v], which, like *Bush Leaguer*, was a 1927 release). The 1932 film had an edge so far as the credibility of its ballpark scenes were concerned, thanks to Joe E. Brown's bone-deep baseball prowess. Monte Blue, star of *Bush Leaguer*, was an actor very much in the mold of future Warners stars like Jeffrey Lynn and Ronald Reagan; he was a reliable bread and butter performer, one whose films satisfied the audiences and made money, but who lacked the sort of dynamic personality that prompted screenwriters to create vehicles with Blue specifically in mind. Though an accomplished athlete (he was a former stuntman), Monte Blue was no more a baseball player than he was a society doctor, dam builder, or Northwest Mountie—roles that he'd essayed in other films. Consequently, *Bush Leaguer*, which was lackadaisically paced to begin with, lacked the extra sparkle it might have had with a baseball expert in the lead.

A comic subplot in *Bush Leaguer* concerned the byplay between the team's backup pitcher and the manager. These roles were filled by diminutive Clyde Cook and hulking William Demarest, who had been paired in an earlier Warners film, *Simple Sis*. The studio was evidently planning to build up Cook and Demarest as a comedy team in the manner of Paramount's Wallace Beery and Raymond Hatton or MGM's Karl Dane and George K. Arthur, but the later popularity of such teams as Laurel and Hardy and the Marx Brothers effectively put an end to these studio-fabricated "Mutt and Jeff" duos.

The Warner Bros. pressbook for *The Bush Leaguer* emphasized that the picture was "clean entertainment." In retrospect, this pressbook contained a far more significant message to movie exhibitors, printed at the bottom of the last page: "Coming Soon: *The Jazz Singer*."

The Busher

Thomas H. Ince/Famous Players-Lasky/Paramount; released May 25, 1919

Supervised by Thomas Ince. Directed by Jerome Storm. Screenplay by Earl Snell, based on a story by R. Cecil Smith. Photography: Chester Lyons. 5 reels/4,768 feet: black and white; silent.

Cast: Charles Ray (Ben Harding); Colleen Moore (Maizie Palmer); Jack [John] Gilbert (Jim Blair); Jay Morley (Billy Palmer); Otto Hoffman (Deacon Nasby); Margaret Livingston (Temptress); and Jack Nelson, Louis Durham.

Ben Harding, pitcher for the Brownsville bush club, takes on a big-city team when their train is stalled in Minneapolis. He helps his teammates trounce the visitors, then discovers that the losers are the major-league Pink Sox. Ben is invited to join the Sox and, as he leaves for the big city, he promises his girl Maizie that he'll return with a fortune and marry her. But Harding becomes cocky and undisciplined, takes to liquor, and becomes an insufferable snob, even snubbing Maizie at one point. A gorgeous gold digger relieves Ben of his bankroll, and shortly thereafter the headstrong player is sent back down to the bush leagues by the exasperated Pink Sox management. He returns home in disgrace and vows never to play again, but Maizie's brother has bet heavily on the outcome of the next Brownsville game. Ben relents, joins the game, wins, saves Maizie's family, marries Maizie, and regains the respect of his community. The Pink Sox executives, who've been waiting all along for Ben to straighten himself out, offer the player a new contract—but Ben turns them down, opting to settle in Brownsville with his new bride.

The Busher was the second in a brace of baseball stories (see also the 1917 version of *The Pinch Hitter*) starring the prototypical "all–American boy" Charles Ray, who actually was a fairly decent ballplayer. Some drably handled baseball sequences aside, *The Busher* is arguably the better of the two films, highlighted by Ray's eccentric delivery at the pitcher's mound, several amusing subtitles (some of them animated!), and a wealth of intelligently composed camerawork. It is, however, hard for modern-day audiences to understand the remarkable popularity of Charles Ray (besides *The Busher*, he made six more feature films in 1919, earning $35,000 per picture); most of the time, he played a character so emotionally retarded by his "niceness" and his unwillingness to step on toes that he comes across to modern viewers as a jellyfish. *The Busher* was one of a handful of Ray performances wherein he altered his bumpkinish persona by playing a swellheaded jerk who engineers his own downfall. Ironically, this scenario was to be Ray's real-life story: Refusing to listen to the advice of others, the actor was bankrupted by a disastrous, self-produced 1923 screen version of *The Courtship of Miles Standish*; his career never fully recovered, and Ray spent the last decade of his life in bit parts and extra roles.

The Busher is typical of the product being churned out by Paramount in the years following World War I. The film was, and is, reasonably entertaining, but its "rubber stamp" quality doomed it to forgetability. Its chief distinction is the presence of two superstars-to-be of the silent cinema: Colleen Moore and John (then billed as Jack) Gilbert.

Casey at the Bat

Fine Arts/Triangle; released July 2, 1916

Directed by Lloyd Ingraham. Screenplay by William Everett Wing, inspired by the poem by Ernest Lawrence Thayer. 5 reels, black and white; silent.
Cast: DeWolf Hopper (Casey); Kate Toncray (Casey's Sister); May Garcia (His Niece); Carl Stockdale (Hicks); William H. Brown (Judge Blodgett); Marguerite Marsh (Blodgett's Daughter); Frank Bennett (Her Sweetheart); Robert Lawler (The Politician); Bert Hadley (Casey's Brother-in-Law); Hal Wilson (Doctor); Frank Hughes (Casey's Admirer).

Casey, ace player for the Mudville team, is devoted to his sister and his little niece. The poor child falls ill on the day of the Big Game, but Casey won't leave her side until the demands of the spectators compel him to do so. Entrusting the care of his niece to a friend, Casey heads off to the ballpark, where it's the ninth inning, the score stands 4 to 2 in favor of the visitors, and the bases are loaded. Casey lets two strikes by, preparing to tear the cover off pitch number three. But just as the ball is thrown, the friend who'd been left with Casey's niece shows up in the stands. Fearing the worst, Casey lets his concentration crumble and strikes out. It develops that the friend is there to tell Casey that his niece has recovered—but the ex-champ has been disgraced in joyless Mudville, and at fade-out time Casey heads disconsolately out of town.

"Casey at the Bat: A Ballad of the Republic, Sung in the Year 1888" first appeared in the *San Francisco Examiner* on Sunday, June 3, 1888. Flanked on one side of the page by an editorial and on the other by a weekly column by Ambrose Bierce, it was the last in a series of comic poems written by Ernest Lawrence Thayer, who'd been hired in 1886 to compose a weekly *Examiner* piece by the paper's owner (and Thayer's college chum), William Randolph Hearst. The author collected his standard $5 fee, moved on in life, and forgot about "Casey."

Two months later, on August 14 or thereabouts, rising young Broadway performer DeWolf Hopper (later the husband of gossip queen Hedda Hopper and father of actor William Hopper) was appearing at Wallack's Theatre in New York, in a comic opera titled *Prince Methusalem*. It was the custom of the day to insert a special song or monologue in musical plays to honor whatever celebrities happened to be in the audience; on this particular evening, the guests of the house were the members of the New York Giants and the Chicago White Stockings. The story goes that a novelist friend of DeWolf Hopper's, one Archibald Clavering Gunter (whose name was probably funnier than anything in *Prince Methusalem*), pulled from his pocket a tattered clip of "Casey at the Bat" as a possible piece between acts. Hopper read the poem with his customary vocal calisthenics, and by the time the fabled final line of the poem rumbled through the auditorium, the crowd was earsplitting in its approval— a reaction Hopper would later attribute to the vainglorious Casey's defeat, which he suggested brought out the "malicious glee" within the heart of each ballplayer.

At that moment, the fate of "Casey at the Bat" was sealed. It became the single most famous piece of baseball literature of all time, outstripping its then contemporary contender for that title, "Slide, Kelly, Slide" (a song written in 1884), garnering printings and reprintings in big-city dailies and tank-town monthlies, and inspiring sequels, parodies (one written by T. S. Eliot!), "slang" versions, and updates well into the next century. Snatches of the ballad have been used in at least one sports page article in every American city during every baseball season for the past hundred years—and beyond that one need only mutter "No joy in Mudville" to describe succinctly the conditions that prevail in everything from the state of urban blight to the instability of Wall Street. That's a pretty fair track record for a bit of doggerel which its author openly despised; Thayer refused to demand any royalties for "Casey," commenting tersely, "All I ask is never to be reminded of it again."

As for DeWolf Hopper, he found that he'd suddenly inherited a comic piece that would serve him well through countless encores, vaudeville tours, and testimonial dinners (the actor once tried to count the "countless times" and gave up at around ten thousand, or at least that's *his* story). He committed "Casey" to an Edison phonograph record in 1906, and—though he wasn't involved in the first two one-reel motion pictures bearing the title of his most famous recitation (the first filmed by Edison in 1899, the second by Vitagraph in 1913 with Harry T. Morey in the lead)—it was inevitable that DeWolf Hopper would star in a feature length version of *Casey at the Bat*.

The film was produced in early 1916 by Fine Arts, the apex of the Triangle Film Corporation controlled by D. W. Griffith (the other two Triangle chieftains were Thomas H. Ince and Mack Sennett). Feature length films at the time had been standardized to a minimum five reels, which translated to about one hour when projected at silent speed. Fine. Director Lloyd Ingraham and scenarist William Everett Wing had to figure out how to get an hour's entertainment out of a poem that DeWolf Hopper regularly delivered on stage in less than six minutes. The solution? To squeeze the story dry of all its sly humor and offer in place a maudlin melodrama about a sweet little niece (who wasn't named Nellie but should have been) and the sickness that kept her loving uncle from fulfilling the hopes and dreams of the townspeople. There was also a banal romance involving Casey and the daughter of the local magistrate. And finally, there were a few baseball scenes that were as stodgy and stagy as the rest of this epic.

Then there was the problem of DeWolf Hopper—a problem not in his acting, which was serviceable, but in the plain fact that he'd been reciting *Casey at the Bat* for some twenty-eight years by the time he stepped before the cameras. He was no spring chicken when he performed that first reading in 1888, and given the state of makeup and lighting effects in the cinema of 1916, the merciless camera lens only served to emphasize that Hopper was in the deep end of middle age—and worse, that he was wearing an unbecoming toupee and patently false eyebrows, having recently lost all his hair during a bout with typhoid fever. The venerable trouper looked like the mighty Casey might have looked after being mummified for two thousand years. Through no real fault of his own, DeWolf Hopper joined the ranks of legendary *fin de siècle* actors like Sarah Bernhardt, James O'Neill, and Minnie Maddern Fiske for whom technology was a tad too late to provide a more flattering immortalization in celluloid.

Many of the assets of Triangle Corporation were eventually absorbed by Paramount, which meant that Paramount inherited the rights to the title *Casey at the Bat*. The studio waited over ten years to unleash its newest version of the old standard on a breathless world, but this time the results were well worth the wait. There was also a "happy ending" to the marriage of DeWolf Hopper and the movies. In 1922 Hopper was one of several artists who appeared in Dr. Lee DeForest's "Phonofilms," a series of experimental one-reel talking pictures. Though his advanced years were even more pronounced than in 1916, Hopper displayed the effervescence of a schoolboy as he delivered "Casey at the Bat" while standing before nothing more elaborate than a stage curtain. The actor's oration was as brilliant as it had been nearly forty years earlier; and after the customary five minutes and forty seconds were done, the modest bow and the winning grin offered to the camera by DeWolf Hopper seemed to say to those Hollywood "experts," "See, you clods? I did it *my* way!"

Casey at the Bat

Famous/Lasky/Paramount; released March 8, 1927

Presented by Adolph Zukor and Jesse Lasky. Directed by Monte Brice. Screenplay by Jules Furthman. Titles by Sam Hellman and Grant Clarke. Adapted from the Ernest Lawrence Thayer poem by Reginald Morris and Monte Brice. Photography: Barney McGill. 6 reels/6,040 feet; black and white; silent.

Cast: Wallace Beery (Mike Xavier Aloysius Casey); Ford Sterling (O'Dowd); ZaSu Pitts (Camille); Sterling Holloway (Elmer Putnam); Spec O'Donnell (Spec); Iris Stuart (Trixie, a Floradora Girl); Sidney Jarvis (McGraw); Lotus Thompson, Rosalind Byrne, Anne Sheridan [no, not *that* Ann Sheridan], Doris Hill, Sally Blane (Floradoras).

The time is the 1890s; the place, the minimetropolis of Centerville. Casey, the local junk dealer, is the most popular player on the local ball team. With his bat (his "old waggin' tongue") in one hand and a glass of beer in the other, Casey hits a home run during every Sunday afternoon game, showboating for the crowd by letting two pitches fly by before connecting. O'Dowd, who claims to be a scout for the New York Giants, invites Casey to sign for the big leagues: "Pack up your other suit, big boy,

Wallace Beery, Sterling Holloway and Ford Sterling strike an Armour-Star pose in this publicity shot for *Casey at the Bat* (1927).

New York's paging you. You'll forget Tanktown Tillie when you see the Broadway beauties." Truer words were never spoken. Once he signs for the Giants, Casey is New York's premiere carouser, forever squiring the lovely "Floradora Girls" of the stage and ordering drinks on the house wherever he goes—although those libations are actually paid for by Elmer Putnam, Centerville's barber, who is Casey's rival for the affections of hometown girl Camille and who hopes to discredit the boobish ballplayer in the girl's eyes. Putnam and O'Dowd, the latter hoping to win a few bets, conspire to convince Casey that he's too sick to show up at the Big Game. Spec, the team mascot, learns of the hoax and manages to get Casey to the game just in time. As recorded in the famous poem, however, Casey strikes out. But all is not lost; it turns out that the crooked O'Dowd had substituted a trick ball for the last strike. O'Dowd is exposed, the game is replayed, and Casey wins the ever patient Camille from the disgruntled Putnam. And to think this all happens in fifty-nine minutes of screen time.

Casey at the Bat was originally conceived as a "team" film, costarring husky Wallace Beery with diminutive Raymond Hatton; it was to have been the latest entry in Paramount's profitable Beery-Hatton series, which included such titles as *Behind the Front* and *Now We're in the Air.* The studio sent out preproduction publicity shots of Beery and Hatton attired in baseball uniforms, suggesting that Hatton was to have played a teammate of Casey's. Ultimately, Raymond Hatton was dropped from the cast, and *Casey at the Bat* became Wallace Beery's first solo starring vehicle at Paramount.

The film was hardly the studio's most important release of 1927 (*Wings* took care of that), but it was raw, raucous entertainment with Wallace Beery—well into his famous screen persona of the lumbering lug with good intentions but weak impulses—a particular treat in the title role. Beery was matched in his thespian efforts by Ford Sterling, a onetime Keystone Kop who specialized in foxy uncle types during the balance of his career, here playing the duplicitous O'Dowd; by ZaSu Pitts, whose brief (and successful) fling into heavy dramatics vis-à-vis Erich Von Stroheim's *Greed* would ever after take a back seat to her school-marm-type comedy roles; and by twenty-two-year-old newcomer Sterling Holloway, who launched a lifetime career of country bumpkins with his performance as Casey's rival for ZaSu Pitts' affections. (The Broadway-trained Holloway was none too happy with his first film, however, nor was he encouraged to continue before the cameras when a studio executive described the actor's countenance as "repulsive"; his best work lay ahead of him in the sound era, when he supplemented his acting income with his superb cartoon voice work for Walt Disney.)

Marching the actors through their paces with a minimum of the pathos and sentiment that often bogged down film comedies of the period was director Monte Brice, a veteran gag writer who ended his days as a career adviser for Bob Hope; it was Brice who, while picking through his remembrances of things past, provided film historian Kevin Brownlow with the title of Brownlow's first book on Hollywood in the silent era, *The Parade's Gone By*.

Casey at the Bat was banking on a general wave of nostalgia for the 1890s that was reflected in several films made between 1927 and 1933—a nostalgia principally centered on the fact that people back in the gay nineties could buy a five cent schooner of beer without having the Prohibition agents breathing down their necks. While *Casey* does its best to accurately pinpoint its period with such trappings as the Floradora Girls and early models of horseless carriages, there was a tendency (as with most nostalgia) not to contradict one's memory with the truth. The baseball sequences in the film, photographed and edited with the seemingly effortless expertise that 1927 film comedy fans had come to expect, were cheerfully vulgar, but nowhere near as down and dirty as actual baseball could become in the 1890s—a decade in which one could count the number of "clean" players on the fingers of one hand.

One decidedly vintage element in the film was its visual humor. No opportunity to score a low, long laugh with a timeworn bit was left untapped. Casey loses his trousers; Casey suffers the consequences of straying too close to a tin of limburger cheese; and both Casey and the duplicitous O'Dowd don several false beards and outlandish disguises in the closing reels. In its April 7, 1927, review of *Casey at the Bat*, the *New York Times* noted that the film "dodges any suggestion of keenness or subtlety." But the *Times* never said that the film wasn't funny.

While the 1927 version of *Casey at the Bat* was an enjoyable outing (and a moderately profitable one), it was no closer to the actual Ernest Lawrence Thayer ballad than the 1916 tear-jerking DeWolf Hopper version of *Casey* had been. Devotees of the poem would have to wait until the Walt Disney animation staff tackled the story in 1946 for a *Casey at the Bat* that thoroughly captured the satirical spirit of the Thayer original.

Catch-as-Catch-Can

Gotham/Lumus Film Corporation; released June 1, 1927

Produced by Sam Sax. Supervised by Sam Bischoff. Directed by Charles Hutchison. Story by L. V. Jefferson. Photography: James Brown. 5 reels; black and white; silent.

Cast: William Fairbanks (Reed Powers); Jack Blossom (George Bascom); Rose Blossom (Lucille Bascom); Larry Shannon (Phil Bascom); Walter Shumway (Ward Hastings); George Kotsonaros (Butch); George Chapman (Slippy Schnitzel).

Reed Powers manages a small-time ball club. His star player Phil is coerced into throwing a game by political "fixer" Ward Hastings. To protect Phil, the brother of his sweetheart Lucille, Reed allows himself to be accused of cheating, even though he's witnessed the payoff. Reed is fired, but soon after lands a job at a newspaper, which he uses to expose Hastings and Hastings's confederate, a wrestler named Butch, who are plotting to overthrow the mayor who—as these things sometimes happen in Grade-Z quickies—is the father of Lucille and Phil. There's a big chase through the streets, during which Hastings is killed, Reed punches out Butch, and Phil finally confesses. Reed is appointed chief of police, and in the excitement of finishing the picture before the sun went down, everyone has forgotten that this whole megillah started with a ballgame.

Gotham was a poverty row outfit specializing in cheap action melodramas with occasional sports themes. Its stars and directors were drawn from the ranks of has-beens and almost-weres. The director of *Catch-as-Catch-Can*, Charles Hutchison, was a notch above the usual Gotham level; a past master at fast-paced, intricately plotted serials, Hutchison was able to bring a touch of pep to an otherwise yawn inducing effort, particularly during the climactic chase. The star of *Catch-as-Catch-Can* was William Fairbanks, one of several western actors who adopted (or were given by their studios) stage names that suggested some sort of familial relation with a more famous star, in this case Douglas Fairbanks (other performers in this vein included Neal Hart and Art Mix). William Fairbanks was a slightly better actor than most of these pretenders to the throne, though as historian William K. Everson has pointed out, audiences were generally resistant and resentful toward second-string screen personalities who clutched at the coattails of established success.

Like many independent productions of the 1920s, *Catch-as-Catch-Can* was released on a States' Rights basis—meaning that the film, lacking a major distributor, was offered for circulation to various local entrepreneurs throughout the country. The picture usually played on the bottom half of double bills, during a period in which most movie theaters didn't *have* double bills.

Chasing Dreams

A Conte/Brown Film for Nascent Productions; released to video by Prism in 1989.

Produced by Therese Conte and David G. Brown. Executive producer: Marcus Robinson. Coproducer: Marc Schwartz. First unit director: Sean Roche. Second unit director: Therese Conte. Screenplay by David G. Brown; screenplay additions by Theresa Conte, Sean Roche and Kevin Kilnoy. Photography: Connie Holt. Edited by Jerry Weldon and Robert Sinise. Sports editing by Mike Renaud. Production design and art direction by Bobbi Peterson Himber. Music by Gregory Conte; park theme composed by Christopher Conte. Music performed by Shepherd. Makeup by Pamela Westmore. Wardrobe by Nancy Flaherty and Greg Morrison. Production manager and assistant director: Tim Silver. Sound mixer: Ken Wiatrak. Stunt coordinators: Scott Cook and Jimmy Monore. Assistant directors: Simon Barron and Dawn Kirk. Color by CFI. 91 minutes: sound. Rated PG.

Cast: David G. Brown (Gavin); John Fife (Parks); Jim Shane (Father); Claudia Carroll (Mother); Mathew Clark (Ben); Cecilia Bennett (Pam); Kelly McCarthy (Cindy); Lisa Kingston (Sue); Don Margolin (Coach Stevens); Marc Brandes (Gaylord); Dan Waldman (Nick); Henry Dunn, John Sullivan, Ken Straus, Terence O'Malley, Arthur Tonna, Jr., Dave D'Arnal, Joey Bell, David Christopher, Elliot Tonna, Martin Katz, Brian Bird (Cougar Players); Charles Craig (Angry Cougar); Kevin Costner (Ed); Jim Birge (Sports Announcer); Stanley Gurd, Jr. (Scout); Joe Benson (Owner of Club); Patrick Cameron (Pro Ball Player); Doug Cronin (Sheriff); Marilyn Korones (Teacher); Janet Levy (Renee); Chuck Himber (Reporter); Michael Downing (Doctor); Simon Barron (Priest); Robert Morrison, Mary Tobias, Gerry Munn (Umpires); Tim Robinson (Billy in Batting Cage); David and Mitzi Strollery (Grandparents); Scott Cook, William Barbour, John Naginey, George Hale, Lee Blitzstein (Stunts); Craig Hammill, Jr. (Boy in Park); Darryl Stroh (Bulldog Coach); Bill Cassesse (Bartender); The 1981 Granada Highlanders (Bulldogs); 1981 Canyon Cowboys, Moorpark College and K. and R. Baseball Teams (Opponents).

Teenaged Gavin, a California farmer's son, discovers an aptitude for baseball while attending junior college—even though he stubbornly refuses to "choke" the bat like any normal player. Gavin's independent streak is prompted by the lad's idolatry of his older brother Ed, who has left the farm to pursue his own life. In turn, Gavin is idolized by younger brother Ben. Although Ben is confined to a wheelchair, he gleefully helps Gavin practice his batting. The farm where the boys live is in dire financial trouble, and Gavin's dad wants his son either to stay at home to help out or to pursue a more substantial future than a career in sports. But Gavin finds that his ballplaying prowess has been noticed by a scout for the St. Louis Cardinals. Just before Gavin signs a contract, younger brother Ben dies, plunging Gavin into an orgy of guilt and self-doubt. He is talked back into utilizing his skill in sports by his girlfriend, who

points out that this is how Ben would have wanted things to be. In the bottom half of the ninth inning of the big game, Gavin is beaned by a wild pitch and suffers a concussion. It appears as though the attendant brain damage will turn Gavin into a mute, listless automaton. But when Gavin wanders into the fields and picks up the baseball which he and Ben had once tossed back and forth together, Gavin instantly snaps out of his lethargy and resumes his life.

We'd bet the ranch that when this turkey was filmed in 1982, its title wasn't *Chasing Dreams.* But it just so happened that the actor playing the hero's older brother was 27-year-old Kevin Costner, who in 1989 would star in the well-received baseball picture *Field of Dreams* (q.v.). Note the similarity in titles of these two ballpark films, and note also that *Chasing Dreams* languished on someone's shelf until released directly to videotape in—that's right—1989. It's possible, and I'm just spitballing here, that Prism Video was hoping that the wafer-thin resemblance between the two films would attract the more insatiable Kevin Costner fans. To this end, the artwork on *Chasing Dreams'* cassette box displayed an enormous picture of Costner, looming over a ballfield—quite an honor for an actor whose performance in the 1982 film lasts exactly 82 seconds, and who, despite his grafted-on "special appearance" screen credit, had originally been billed *twenty-fourth*—after each and every member of Gavin's college baseball team.

Kevin Costner's legal representatives sought to have the videocassette removed from shelves on the grounds of misleading advertising and unlicensed reproduction of the actor's likeness. If Costner was motivated in this action out of any fear that his reputation would suffer, he needn't have worried. Kevin Costner packed more professionalism into his fleeting opening-scene appearance in *Chasing Dreams* than can be found anywhere else in this ponderous project.

It would be nice to say that Costner is the only reason for watching *Chasing Dreams*, but this would suggest that there is any real reason at all. The film is so dreadfully photographed (save for an effective ground level shot or two of the climactic ballgame) and miserably directed that its awfulness is positively spellbinding. If this weren't enough, the film boasts the all-time worst leading actor in baseball movie history: David G. Brown. It probably isn't entirely the star's fault, since he is forced to speak the banalities written for him by the screenwriter, David G. Brown. But it's unfair to hold either star or writer totally responsible, since the ultimate failure of this film must rest upon the shoulders of its producer—David G. Brown.

Chasing Dreams is the sort of motion picture that makes one wish Thomas Edison had stuck to light bulbs.

Cobb

Regency Enterprises/Alcor Films/Warner Bros.; released December 2, 1994

Executive producer: Arnon Milchan. Produced by David Lester. Written and directed by Ron Shelton. Based upon the book *Cobb: A Biography* by Al Stump. Photography: Russell Boyd. Production designers: Armin Ganz and Scott T. Ritenour. Edited by Paul Seydor and Kimberly Ray. Original music: Elliot Goldenthal. Costume designer: Ruth E. Carter. Associate producer: Tom Todoroff. Production manager: Pat Kehoe. First assistant director: H. Gordon Boos. Second assistant director: K.C. Hodenfield. Second unit directors: Jerry J. Gatlin, Eugene Corr. Art directors: Troy Sizemore, Charles Butcher. Set decorator: Claire Jenora Bowin. Camera operator: Stephen St. John. Key makeup: Ve Neill. Key Hairstylist: Sterfon Demings. Script supervisor: Karen Golden. Special effects supervisor: Jim Fredburg. Sound mixer: Kirk Francis. Supervising sound editor: Bruce Fortune. Supervising music editor: Daniel Allan

Carlin. Illustrator: Trevor Goring. Billboard Illustrator: Ted Haigh. Special visual effects supervisor/second unit photographer: Mark Vargo. Foley artists: John B. Roesch, Hilda Hodges. Titles and opticals: Pacific Title. Special optical effects: Stokes/Kohne Associates Inc., Optical Illusions Inc. Digital effects supervisor: Brad Kuehn. Animation technical supervisor: Derek Spears. Technicolor; Panavision. 128 minutes; Dolby Stereo Sound. Rated R.

Cast: Tommy Lee Jones (Ty Cobb); Robert Wuhl (Al Stump); Lolita Davidovich (Ramona); Lou Myers (Willie); Bradley Whitford (Process Server); Stephen Mendillo (Mickey Cochrane); Eloy Casados (Louis Prima); William Utay (Jameson); J. Kenneth Campbell (Prof. Cobb); Tommy Bush (Rogers Hornsby); Ned Bellamy (Ray); Scott Burkholder (Jimmy); Allan Malamud (Mudd); Bill Caplan (Bill); Jeff Fellenzer (Sportswriter no. 1); Doug Krikorian (Sportswriter no. 2); Gavin Smith (Sportsman's Lounge Bartender); Rhoda Griffis (Ty's Mother); Tyler Logan Cobb (Young Ty); Rev. Gary Morris (Baptist Minister); Jerry J. Gatlin (Train Engineer); Harold Herthum (Gambler); Jay Chevalier (Gambler no. 2); Roger Clemens (Opposing Pitcher); George Rafferty (Teammate); Jay Tibbs (Teammate no. 2); Rodney Max (Umpire); Gary D. Talbert (Opposing Catcher); Fred Lewis (Philly Fan); David Hodges (Philly Fan no. 2); Joy Michiel (Last Chance Hotel Clerk); Mitchell "Mitch" Hrushowy (Harrah's Club Manager); Paula Rudy (Keely Smith); Artie Butler (Harrah's Bartender); Robert Earl Berkbigler (Croupier); George P. Wilbur (Casino Security Man); Steven Brown (Husband at Motel); Dana Y. Hill (Wife at Motel); Tony L. McCollum (Texas Motel Manager); Bobby Holcombe (Texas Motel Security Guard); Tom Todoroff (Hall of Fame Announcer); Ernie Harwell (Hall of Fame Emcee); Reid Cruikshanks (Pie Traynor); Rath Shelton (Paul Waner); Jim Shelton (Lloyd Waner); Stacy Keach Sr. (Jimmie Foxx); Clive Rosengran (Hall of Fame Director); Larry "Crash" Davis (Sam Crawford); Tracy Keehn-Dashnaw (Cobb's Wife); Jimmy Buffett (Heckler); Michael Moss (The Lover); Janice Certain (Cobb's Daughter); Jeanne McCarthy (Nurse no. 1); Patricia Forte (Nurse no. 2); Toni Prima (Hospital Receptionist); Michael Chieffo (Young Doctor); Don Hood (Older Doctor); Jennifer Decker (Sportsman's Lounge Waitress); Bill Wittman ("Cavalcade of Heroes" Narrator); Brian

Mulligan (Charlie Chaplin); Jerry Hauck (Handicapper); Bill Bates, Cliff Happy, Gene Hartline, John Hateley, Ethan Jensen, Les Larson, Tom Morga, Jeff Smolek, Patricia Tallman (Stunts).

The year is 1960: Though Al Stump basks in the knowledge that he is the highest-paid freelance sportswriter in America, he also knows he lacks the name recognition for literary superstardom. This, more than any other reason, is why he leaps at the opportunity to collaborate on the autobiography of Tyrus Raymond "Ty" Cobb, the greatest player in the history of baseball. Timorously advised by his fellow scribes that Ty Cobb is unpredictable at best, dangerously insane at worst, Stump laughs off these warnings, reminding his pals that Cobb is way past seventy years old, and at death's door to boot: "What's he gonna do, wheeze on me?" Upon arriving at Cobb's baronial hunting lodge in Lake Tahoe, Nevada, Stump is quickly made to understand why several other writers have turned his present assignment down: Not only is Al treated to a violent, race-baiting verbal exchange between Cobb and his ex-employee Willie, but he himself nearly has his head blown off by the gun-wielding baseball icon! Overcoming his initial impulse to turn tail and run, Stump elects to stay with Cobb and help him complete his autobiography—this despite the fact that Cobb, legally armed with total editorial control, intends to foist a thorough whitewash job upon the public, celebrating his own greatness while totally suppressing the darker, more sinister aspects of his life and career (including the mystery-shrouded death of his politically prominent father). It is during a riotous road trip to the Baseball Hall of Fame in Cooperstown, where Cobb is to be given a testimonial dinner, that the disillusioned Stump becomes fully aware of "The Georgia Peach"'s rampaging egomania, all-encompassing hatred of mankind (he's truly an equal-opportunity bigot!)

and unbridled rage. While appalled by Cobb's behavior, Stump is too fascinated—and though he won't admit it, too anxious to have some of Ty's fame rub off on him—to give up the job. Only after witnessing Cobb's brutal, humiliating treatment of a sexy cigarette girl in a Reno hotel bedroom does the infuriated Stump vow to tell the true story about the misanthropic ballplayer. So as not to tip his hand, Stump actually prepares two books: Ty Cobb's mythical version, which the writer leaves conspicuously in his typewriter, and a profane, unvarnished tell-all tome, which he furtively scribbles on cocktail napkins and tissue paper. As Cobb slowly, and sometimes sobbingly, begins to place his complete trust in Stump—even going so far as to designate the nonplussed writer as his only true friend—Al suffers a profound crisis of conscience, realizing that he has become the one thing Ty Cobb never was: a hypocrite. But just before Cobb dies in the summer of 1961, he manages to so thoroughly alienate Stump that the disgusted writer decides to proceed with the "real" story and to chuck Cobb's fantasy-land version. In the end, however, Al Stump publishes "My Life in Baseball" exactly the way Ty Cobb wanted: as a celebration rather than a hatchet job. "Finally, I lied to myself," explains Stump years after the fact. "I needed [Cobb] to be a hero. It is my weakness."

Tyrus Raymond Cobb (1886–1961) was by popular consensus the greatest baseball player who ever lived. Launching his career at age 17 with the newly formed South Atlantic League, Cobb was signed by the Detroit Tigers in 1905, spending the next 22 years with that organization. Between 1910 and 1919 he won seven of his twelve batting championships, and from 1921 to 1926 he doubled as player and manager for the Tigers, closing out his career with the Philadelphia Athletics in 1928. He set dozens of baseball records, many of which remained unchallenged not only during his lifetime, but for many years thereafter: a lifetime batting average of .367; 4,191 lifetime hits (a record finally broken by Pete Rose in 1985); 3,033 games played; 2,234 runs scored; and 1,901 RBIs. In addition to these accomplishments, Cobb was in the vanguard of a new breed of players who brought respectability to baseball; his fierce dedication and strong work ethic helped convince the public that The Game was in the hands of serious professionals and not just a bunch of drunken hooligans. He refined the concept of "scientific" baseball, favoring field strategy over the mere batting out of home runs; during his career he stole a record 896 bases—96 of those in a single season. Among many other examples of his shrewd, analytical approach to baseball, Cobb was the first hitter to warm up by lofting more than one bat, which helped lighten the feel of his swing when he finally stepped up to the plate. He also understood and appreciated the value of ballpark psychology; for example, although he never spiked as many players as has been claimed, he made certain that the *threat* of a spiking was always present in order to keep the opposition off balance.

Off the field, Cobb was blessed with an almost uncanny business sense. Though he was earning $70,000 per year at the time of his retirement, his personal fortune, estimated at over $12 million, was largely the result of smart investments in such going concerns as General Motors and Coca-Cola—not to mention scores of commercial endorsements. His wealth and his prestige enabled him to hobnob with film stars, American presidents and captains of industry.

With all this in mind—plus the fact that he was the first player elected to the Baseball Hall of Fame in Cooperstown—Ty Cobb should by rights have been a perfect candidate for a motion picture biography. Yet outside of his starring appearance

in the obscure 1917 baseball drama *Somewhere in Georgia* (q.v.), a guest cameo in the 1951 version of *Angels in the Outfield* (q.v.), a handful of newsreel interviews, and fleeting ersatz appearances in two of the three Babe Ruth biopics—he was played by Pete Rose in 1991's *Babe Ruth* (q.v.), and by Randy Steinmeyer in 1992's *The Babe* (q.v.)—Cobb was for many years ignored on the Big Screen. And understandably so: The man known to his fans by the cheery appellation "The Georgia Peach" was, by every existing account, the meanest, orneriest, most vicious and most vindictive human being that ever wore a baseball uniform.

It has been customary for Hollywood to gloss over the more negative or controversial aspects in the life of a celebrated athlete, either by stressing the person's positive attributes (*Pride of the Yankees*, *The Babe Ruth Story*) or his triumph over adversity (*The Stratton Story*, *The Winning Team*, *Fear Strikes Out*). Even as late as the 1990s, by which time audiences were more receptive to seriously flawed screen characters, most baseball biopics still counterbalanced the bad with the good: *The Babe* opined that Babe Ruth's grotesque self-indulgences stemmed from an insatiable need to be loved; *Soul of the Game* (q.v.) noted that the self-destructive personality of Josh Gibson did not prevent him from becoming a role model for the first generation of black Major League ballplayers; and *61** (q.v.) stressed the likeability factor in the personal makeup of Mickey Mantle, and his love of baseball, over his drinking and womanizing.

The problem with Ty Cobb was that his performance on the ballfield was practically the *only* admirable facet of his personality. Ferociously competitive and arrogant beyond belief, he often as not used his fists to settle differences of opinions with his fellow players, and kept himself well armed with handguns at all times. A loner by choice and disposition, he made only a handful of friends, virtually all of whom had turned against him—or he against them—by the time of his death, with many longtime relationships (such as his friendship with fellow ballplayer Ted Williams) severed over the most trivial of disagreements. A rabid racist, he not only despised African Americans—even his loyal and long-suffering servants—but seldom let an opportunity pass to mercilessly pummel a black man (or black woman) for the heinous crime of "insolence." As for his treatment of fans, we need only cite the infamous incident in which he charged into the stands and punched out a legless man. His relationship with his immediate family was no more harmonious; domineering and verbally abusive to his wives and his children, he was on speaking terms with only one of his daughters at the time of his death.

Nor was his baseball career completely spotless. Never mind the brawls and brouhahas in locker rooms and elsewhere; Ty Cobb came dangerously close to sullying the reputation of Major League Baseball with his compulsive gambling—specifically, by betting on games in which he played. In 1926, Boston Red Sox pitcher Hub Leonard accused Ty and four other Detroit players of fixing the outcome of a game between the Tigers and the Cleveland Indians. It turned out that Cobb had placed bets on a few "friendship games" played after Detroit was out of the running for the World Series, so as to improve the odds for Cleveland's pennant win—games that Cobb and his fellow Tigers didn't exactly try to lose, but didn't work very hard to win. This was a common practice in the 1920s, and though not quite ethical, it was not out and out illegal (the rules that banished Pete Rose from baseball merely for betting on games in which he hadn't even played were not yet on the books). Not wishing to have pro baseball weakened by another scandal of "Black Sox" dimensions, and at the same time acknowledging Cobb's popularity and clout, commissioner Kenesaw Mountain

Landis ultimately let the whole affair blow over, though Ty was forced to resign from his managerial position with the Tigers and seek out a new job with the Athletics.

Faced with these and other unsavory facts, is it any wonder that the average Hollywood screenwriter would rather have had his hair transplant pulled out by its roots than attempt to transform Ty Cobb into the traditionally sympathetic biopic subject? Admittedly, there were a *few* straws that a potential writer could have grasped. Misanthropic though he was, Cobb generously provided financial support to several indigent ex-baseball players, on the condition that they never reveal their source of income. He also founded the Cobb Memorial Hospital in 1948, and established the Ty Cobb Educational Foundation, a scholarship fund for impoverished college students (he might have done this just to see his name carved in stone, or, to quote one observer, he might been trying to buy his way into Heaven; the fact remains that he did do it). The screenwriter could also have gone the "psychological motivation" route, following the lead of author Paul Gallico, who suggested that Cobb became soured on Humanity after his father, a prominent Georgia educator and politician—and reportedly the only man whom Ty admired without qualification—was shot and killed by Cobb's own mother, who escaped prosecution when it was determined that she had mistaken her husband for a burglar. (Surprisingly, Cobb harbored no resentment toward his mother, making sure she was well provided for until the end of her days.) Or perhaps Cobb's reprehensible behavior could be explained away by the unbearably mean-spirited and sadistic hazing he received at the hands of his teammates during his first year in the Big Leagues. Even if all this unpleasantness was bypassed by the writer, something could have been made of Cobb's youthful recklessness—jumping off barn roofs, darting around railroad tracks in the paths of oncoming trains, walking on makeshift tightropes—suggesting that Ty's capricious disregard for conventional behavior (to say nothing of his own safety) spilled over into his adulthood. And in case the script needed a dash of humanizing humor, our hypothetical screenwriter could have expanded upon the fabled letter-writing campaign which brought young Ty to the attention of New York sports columnist Grantland Rice—letters that bore a variety of signatures but were all penned by Ty Cobb himself.

Even assuming that anyone wanted to make a Cobb biography in the 1940s or 1950s, these plans would have been torpedoed by Cobb himself, who had no intention of allowing the "true" story of his life to be written or filmed unless he was in total control of the project. Fully aware of his monstrous reputation—even his most devoted fans harbored no illusions about the man's prickly personality—he was determined to set the record straight by making sure that *his* side of the story was the only one to gain popular coinage. Cobb intended to prove that reports of his outrageous behavior were either exaggerated or grossly falsified by his legions of enemies; for every horror story, he would provide what he considered a logical explanation or a good excuse. So far as he saw it, everyone was out to get him, and he was a lifelong victim of persecution, crucified for the transgression of being better than anyone else in the baseball business. Somehow he would reshape the events in his life so that everyone else around him would be cast in a villainous light: If he couldn't be a hero in fact, he'd be one by default.

But Cobb did not agree to pen his autobiography until 1960, by which time his health had so deteriorated that he knew he'd have to get the story out as quickly as possible. Though he can hardly be said to have mellowed—getting even was still foremost in his mind—he figured that his book would reach a wider readership if he adopted a pose of All Passions Spent, magnanimously "forgiving" his enemies—while hanging them out to dry. Cobb also planned to devote a sizable portion of his book to a compendium of his baseball strategies and secrets. This would stand as a legacy to his athletic genius—and, he hoped, as proof that in his heyday he was infinitely superior to the young and pampered pups who were currently playing the Game.

More than anything, Cobb wanted an epitaph comparable to what Robert E. Lee had said of Ty's great-uncle, Confederate war hero Brigadier General Thomas Reade Rootes Cobb, who died in 1862 during the Battle of Fredericksburg: "Know ye not there is a prince and a great man fallen this day?" The title Cobb chose for his autobiography, *My Life in Baseball: The True Record*, said it all. His life story would be defined strictly within the boundaries of his unassailable string of record-setting baseball achievements, and not by his hellish temper, his rampant bigotry, his brutalities, his vendettas, his domestic failures. No mention at all would be made of his wives or his children; and while his father was a prominent figure in the book's early chapters, the elder Cobb's violent death would not be spoken of even in passing. If few were willing to characterize Ty Cobb as a "prince and a great man" in life, he would force them to do so after his death, by revealing only what he wanted them to know and ignoring all the rest.

Hired to ghostwrite Ty Cobb's autobiography (albeit with a byline) was Al Stump, who had already written in-depth profiles on other major sports figures for a variety of publications. Stump spent fourteen months with Cobb during 1960 and 1961, conducting interviews in person and by correspondence, consulting those few Cobb associates and family members who were willing to contribute to the project, and poring through printed baseball records and contemporary newspaper accounts to verify Cobb's claims. There is virtually nothing in the book that can be classified as an outright lie, but the "truth" was always filtered through Cobb's own self-glorifying, self-protective viewpoint. Having gone into the project with the understanding that Cobb had final editorial approval, Stump knew that he was expected to turn out a sanitized version of the ballplayer's life; but he also knew how to get maximum value from the limited facts at his disposal, and how to surreptitiously insert a few "greater truths" between the lines.

My *Life in Baseball* is at its most fascinating whenever Ty Cobb goes into detail about his ballplaying techniques. Clearly, Cobb was at his most open, relaxed and revelatory when discussing the mechanics of the game that had brought him worldwide fame, and Al Stump, seizing the opportunity to put down words that hadn't been carefully cleansed and censored beforehand, masterfully translated Cobb's "voice" to the printed page. While the movie *Cobb* suggests that Al Stump felt the pure-baseball chapters in *My Life in Baseball* were dull and unsaleable, they remain the most vivid and invigorating passages of the entire book. Say what one might about Ty Cobb, he knew and respected the game of baseball, and he was able to articulate his knowledge and respect even while his strength was rapidly eroding.

Published shortly after Ty Cobb's death in July of 1961, *My Life in Baseball* was well received, though many critics and readers expressed the wish that Cobb had revealed as much about himself as he did about his game. One of those readers was a 16-year-old Californian named Ron Shelton, who years later remembered, "*My Life in Baseball* was the first hardback I ever bought with money I earned from mowing lawns. When I read the book, I thought it was great, but I had a vague notion that there was more to the story."

Also dissatisfied was Al Stump, not so much because he'd been denied the opportunity to "tell all," but because he felt that there was even greater dramatic potential in the story of the terminally ill Cobb's struggle to finish the book—and to live his life as he'd always lived it—while staring death in the face. A few months after *My Life in Baseball* hit the stalls, Stump published a three-part article in *True* magazine, titled "Ty Cobb's Wild Ten-Month Fight to Live," focusing on the ailing ballplayer's defiant and volatile efforts to ignore the ravages of illness, and his stubborn refusal to take the medicines and adhere to the physical restrictions prescribed by his doctors. In the words of Salon.com movie critic Charles Taylor, the Ty Cobb of 1960–61 was "an ornery son of a bitch daring death to come and get him."

Finally catching up with Stump's *True* magazine article in 1980 was Ron Shelton, who in the intervening years had played minor-league baseball and dabbled in painting and sculpting before testing the waters of a film career under the tutelage of director Roger Spottiswoode. Shelton was impressed by the contrast between Stump's posthumous portrait of Cobb and the more guarded version in *My Life in Baseball*. "[The article] told about a Cobb that wasn't in the book." To Shelton, the 1961 autobiography was "a baseball book," while the later account was the story of "a reckless, incorrigible man who was refusing to die quietly. And I thought about the writer who had written both versions of a truth." Shelton was also intrigued by the "something unknowable" about Cobb, and the fact that he never let anyone get truly close to him. There was, said Shelton, "something compelling about him, about his excellence, his refusal to accommodate and the sheer bullheadedness of his will."

Some thirteen more years would pass before Al Stump and Ron Shelton, at first independently and then in concert, would elect to tell the whole story of Ty Cobb, with all the warts, open sores and carbuncles intact. During those years, Stump had written six books, countless magazine articles and definitive profiles of such sports luminaries as Eddie Arcaro, Magic Johnson, Johnny Longden, Joe Louis and Bobby Matthias, and had twice won the "Best American Sports Story Award." Meanwhile, Shelton had ascended to Hollywood's elite as the writer and director of such filmic exercises in Americana as *Blaze* (1989), *White Men Can't Jump* (1992), and, of course, *Bull Durham* (1988; see separate entry), which many regard as the finest and most perceptive baseball film of all time.

The success of his most recent projects enabled Shelton to interest Warner Bros. in releasing his proposed Ty Cobb biopic, and to give him a free hand in approach and content. Reportedly, Warners was nervous about Shelton's intention to tell the whole, horrible truth; if a laundered and idealized baseball biography like *Babe* could not earn back its cost, what hope was there for a film that made no compromises whatsoever? But the studio executives knew that similar "iffy" Shelton projects like *Bull Durham* and *White Men Can't Jump* had exceeded expectations, so Warners decided to take a chance.

While Shelton was preparing to bring Ty Cobb's life to the screen, the ballplayer's biographer Al Stump was putting the final touches on a new biography, titled *Cobb: The Life and Times of the Meanest Man Who Ever Played Baseball*—which, as the title indicated, would reveal all the dirty little secrets that Stump had been obliged to eliminate from the earlier book. Shelton's inspiration for his film had originally been *My Life in Baseball* and Stump's three-parter for *True* magazine; now he could pick Stump's brain, comparing research notes and interviewing the author on his own personal insights regarding Cobb, while Stump was likewise engaged in the process

of creation on the very same subject. And if the resultant film was successful, so much the better for Stump's biography, which was slated to be published shortly before the film's release.

Though, as we shall see, Shelton's treatment of the facts was often far afield of Stump's, the two men agreed on a number of crucial points. Both were of the opinion that, as Shelton put it in the pressbook for his film, "Cobb was a fabulous set of contradictions." They also concurred that Cobb was maddeningly impossible to figure out; every time either Shelton or Stump was prepared to write Ty off as irredeemably evil, or depict him as being pleasanter than suspected, they came across "some new contradictory information about his generosity or meanness." The most dramatically compelling aspect of Cobb was that, "his whole life, he didn't care what people thought of him. Yet facing death, he seemed to care too much." This aspect, which appears only at the beginning and end of Stump's *Cobb*, would be sum and substance of the plot in Shelton's film version, which, like Stump's *True* magazine piece, focused almost exclusively on Cobb's final days.

While writing his script, Shelton constantly referred to three notes that he'd hung above his typewriter: "Sam Peckinpah is Ty Cobb" (film director Peckinpah was, of course, the troubled, often violently combative genius behind such eloquent orgies of cinematic bloodletting as *The Wild Bunch* and *Straw Dogs*); "What if Samuel Johnson had hired Boswell at gunpoint?"; and, perhaps the most important of the three, "*Richard III* as a comedy." There aren't too many laughs in Al Stump's *Cobb*, but both Stump and Shelton agreed that certain of the incidents in Cobb's life were so outrageous that they might seem ludicrous if played seriously; hence, the film *Cobb* is constructed and paced like a comedy, albeit a *very* black one. Tommy Lee Jones, the actor engaged to play the title role, recognized this from the start of filming: "The first thing that Mr. Shelton and I spoke of when we met was the humor of the story. I said, 'I have an idea that this movie is an examination of the value of American athletic desire, am I right?' He said, 'You're right.' I said, 'I have the idea that it better be funny.' He said, 'You're right on that, too.'"

The "Johnson-Boswell" comparison came into play via Shelton's decision to frame the action of *Cobb* within the relationship between the aging ballplayer and his own "Boswell," Al Stump—played by Robert Wuhl, with whom Shelton had previously worked on *Bull Durham*. Though Wuhl consulted with Stump on various character details, the role was written with the actor rather than the author in mind. "Robert is bright, quick with words and doesn't have a mean bone in his body," explained Shelton. He's a perfect personality to take us to this man [Cobb] who almost doesn't have a sweet bone in his body." As for the Sam Peckinpah allusion, we need look no further than Shelton's insistence upon having his version of Ty Cobb fire off his handguns at the slightest provocation, graphically cough up blood in moments of stress, and sadistically hold the threat of rape over the trembling head of cigarette girl Ramona—a character who appears nowhere in Stump's book, but was written by Shelton specifically for Lolita Davidovitch, who'd starred in the director's previous biopic *Blaze*.

Nevada was the first location stopover for the *Cobb* production crew. Ehrman Mansion near Lake Tahoe became Ty Cobb's fortresslike hunting lodge. The notorious Donner Pass served as the locale for the wild downhill car chase between Stump and Cobb, while Lake Tahoe's Cal-Neva Lodge was used for the casino and nightclub scenes set in Reno. The real Reno was used for exteriors, with the long-dismantled "Biggest Little City in the World" arch restored so that the town would look as it did back in 1960 (though in a surprising oversight, the special effects people neglected to matte out the 1980s-style highrise buildings which presently dominate the Reno skyline). As was the case with the huge "smoking bull" cutout built in the outfield of Durham's El Toro Stadium for Shelton's earlier *Bull Durham*, the resurrected Reno arch remained intact after shooting wrapped on *Cobb* by popular demand of the local citizens.

The filmmakers then moved to Ty Cobb's home town of Royston, Georgia, where Cobb is buried in a family mausoleum with his mother, father and sister. The mausoleum appeared in the film, as did a few scattered locations in nearby Lavonia and Athens. The next stop was California, where Boardners, a Hollywood watering hole, was redressed as Sportsman's Lounge, the favored hangout of Al Stump and his fellow sports scribes. The façade of the Baseball Hall of Fame in Cooperstown was replicated in front of a Los Angeles elementary school, a stone's throw from Dodgers Stadium, while the Hall's interiors were recreated within the walls of an LA synagogue, Wilshire Temple. Finally, it was off to Birmingham, Alabama, where the film's baseball scenes were shot at Rickwood Field, the oldest active ballpark in America. The choice of the 84-year-old Rickwood undoubtedly had the racist Cobb spinning in his grave: The ballpark was for many years home of the Negro League's Birmingham Black Barons, and in this capacity hosted such black baseball legends as Satchel Paige and Josh Gibson (see notes on *Soul of the Game*, which used the same park for several scenes). For four days, Rickwood stood in for Tiger Stadium in Detroit, Shibe Park in Philadelphia and Forbes Field in Pittsburgh.

What ultimately emerged on screen was what Ron Shelton described to interviewer Robert J. Ellsberg as "my version of Al Stump's version of Ty Cobb's version of

Cobb: 47-year-old Tommy Lee Jones as 74-year-old Tyrus Raymond Cobb.

Ty Cobb." We're glad *he* said that; it saves us the trouble.

Cobb is the evil twin of 1992's *The Babe*. Whereas the earlier film went to considerable length to "explain" and thereby soften the sting of Babe Ruth's flaws and peccadilloes, *Cobb* succeeds in making its title character come off even *worse* than he appeared to be in real life. This is not to suggest that most of the outrages seen in the film weren't based on fact, merely that they were intensified and compounded for full shock value. Did Ty Cobb go around brandishing and firing off his arsenal of weapons as a means of threatening and scaring off anyone he didn't like? Sometimes, yes—but we beg leave to doubt that he "introduced" himself to Al Stump by shooting several rounds over Stump's head, or that he fired point-blank at Stump's typewriter when the latter expressed displeasure over having to write down falsehoods.

Was Cobb totally cut off from all his friends and family members at the time of his death? Pretty much so, but the film overstates the case when narrator Stump claims that none of Ty's associates were willing to be interviewed for the ballplayer's autobiography, and that Cobb was completely alone when he died (in truth, his daughter Beverly—estranged, but not entirely detached—was at his side). Did Cobb frequently make an embarrassing public spectacle of himself? It was known to happen, but nowhere in Stump's written memoirs is there anything comparable to the scene in the film in which Cobb, invited to take a bow from the stage of Harrah's Lounge by entertainer Louis Prima, perversely proceeds to insult not only Prima and the audience, but also blacks, Italians, homosexuals, and basketball players—all within a space of thirty seconds! (Louis Prima does not appear in Stump's biography of Cobb;

it just so happened that while working on the early drafts of the script, Ron Shelton relaxed by listening to old Prima records.) Was Cobb abusive to his wives? No doubt, but it was more a matter of neglect and mental cruelty, despite the merciless battering that we see him administering to the first Mrs. Cobb in the film. And were Cobb's sexual escapades as shockingly flamboyant as everything else in his life? By the standards of their time, yes—yet no evidence exists that the aging and impotent Cobb ever held a terrified cigarette girl at gunpoint, and after first threatening to ravish her against her will, ended up doing nothing more than offering her $1000 if she agreed to lie to her friends that Ty Cobb was "the greatest she ever had."

There was at least one incredible sequence lifted from Stump's *Cobb* that couldn't have been exaggerated even if Shelton had tried. This was the scene early in the proceedings in which, hell bent on driving to Reno for one last fling, Cobb piled into his own expensive car and began chasing Stump's vehicle down a long, treacherous, and very slippery Nevada mountain pass in the midst of a blinding snowstorm. This happened almost exactly as it is seen in the film, with a few snatches of Elliot Goldenthal's musical score from *Alien 3* thrown in to heighten the thrills. In most other instances, Shelton reserved the right to fabricate and hyperbolize certain events as "a dramatically realized point of view, inspired and informed by certain historical material." The same dramatic considerations motivated Shelton's decision to telescope the fourteen months that Stump actually spent with Cobb into the couple of weeks surrounding Cobb's testimonial dinner at Cooperstown.

On its own merits, Shelton's ability to compress several events and plot points into the briefest conceivable amount of screen time is astonishing. An especially outstanding example occurs directly after Stump's first meeting with Cobb. In a virtuoso display of cinematic shorthand, Shelton informs the audience that Ty Cobb is a cantankerous bigot and bully, a shameless glory-grabber, a financial wizard, a keen judge of human nature, and in full possession of his wits and faculties despite his myriad of physical infirmities. On top of that, by having Cobb adamantly insist that he has shot a passing deer from his bedroom window with no evidence to support his claim, we are treated to the spectacle of Ty Cobb the Mythmaker—only to discover a few moments later that Cobb really *did* bag that deer, and thus Myth seamlessly segues into Fact, as it will so often throughout the film.

Disregarding previous desultory efforts by baseball historians to explain Cobb's lifelong contentiousness, Shelton could not resist seeking out an underlying, deep-set motivation, in much the same manner that the reporter played by William Alland sought out a key to the contrary behavior of the enigmatic central figure in Orson Welles' *Citizen Kane*—which might be why *Cobb* bears so many echoes of *Kane* in its plot construction. Opening with a hero-worshipping newsreel comprised of Ty Cobb's career highlights, the film then shifts to a lone reporter (Al Stump) embarking on an odyssey into the psyche of the title character, beginning with a stopover at Cobb's Xanadu-like mansion. In his search for answers, the reporter interviews an elderly, heavily-made-up eyewitness to the event; but where *Citizen Kane* relied upon second-hand information from such Kane associates as Jed Leland, Ty Cobb is his *own* Jed Leland.

And throughout the narrative, several different versions of the same incident are presented in a prismatic fashion, each version revealing a bit more than the one that preceded it. In *Cobb*, the incident in question is the death of Ty Cobb's father, recounted by Cobb in flashback on three

Even during a brief R-and-R stopover in Reno, Ty Cobb (Tommy Lee Jones) cannot resist settling a dispute at the point of a gun.

separate occasions. First, we are told that the senior Cobb was killed by gunfire, nothing more nor less. Then we learn that Cobb was shot by his wife, who apparently thought he was an intruder. Finally, Cobb lets Stump in on what he thinks *really* happened; that Cobb Sr. was killed by Mrs. Cobb's clandestine lover. Despite Ty Cobb's protestations in the film, this tragic event qualifies as *Cobb*'s "Rosebud"—the single defining psychological reason that Cobb went through life convinced that people were no damned good, and thus were unworthy of any polite or considerate treatment on his part. (It should be noted that Al Stump's book also covers the various theories surrounding the elder Cobb's shooting, but rejects the more lurid versions and adheres to the official conclusion of accidental death; nor does Stump suggest that

Cobb ever doubted his mother's explanation of the event).

Cobb also shares the same structural flaw as *Citizen Kane*; namely, that events are recalled in flashback by people who could not possibly have witnessed those events. But in this instance, the "flaw" may have been intentional on Shelton's part. Two of the film's most controversial scenes—Cobb's "virtual rape" of cigarette girl Roberta, and the moment in which, upon finding out that Al Stump is writing his own alternate version of the autobiography, Cobb pulls out his gun and comes perilously close to blowing Stump's brains out—occur while Stump, from whose viewpoint the story is told, is unconscious. As if to deflect criticism of these fabrications, Shelton stages the scenes so that they can be rationalized thusly: "Sure, Stump didn't *see* these events, but he certainly must have *heard* about them, so who's to say they didn't really happen?"

Though Shelton's Ty Cobb is unrepentant in his behavior and intransigent in his philosophy that the rest of the world deserves nothing better from him, the director evinces the same desire held by Al Stump, to somehow get "inside" the inscrutable Cobb and root out the cause of his hostility. At several junctures, Shelton suggests that Cobb truly believed that everyone else on earth would behave just as he did if given the chance—and that he relished the opportunity to prove this theory. Thus, when his disgruntled African-American ex-employee Willie holds a gun to Cobb's head and defiantly rattles off the accomplishments of baseball's greatest black players, Cobb actually seems to enjoy having the tables turned, and appears to be reveling in Willie's display of Cobb-like behavior. Similarly, after wearily enduring Al Stump's wistful longings to be reunited with his estranged wife, Cobb is positively exultant when, confronted by a process server delivering his wife's divorce papers, Stump goes berserk, grabs a gun, and threatens to blast the poor server into the next world—just as Cobb himself might have done. At the same time, however, Cobb expresses fear over the possibility that he has unleashed a Frankenstein monster; though he has proven that Al Stump has "Cobb" potential, he really doesn't like what he sees!

To some degree, Shelton empathizes with Cobb by showing that the old man may be right after all: People *are* no damned good. Though the script does not touch upon the cruel hazing Cobb was forced to endure early in his career, nor the legitimate gripes that he had against certain of his enemies, Shelton finds other ways to vilify the people within his subject's orbit. During the Cooperstown Testimonial sequence, we are introduced to Mickey Cochrane, a washed-up ballplayer whom Cobb

has been financially supporting for years. Later, during the testimonial itself, Cobb is glad-handed by several of his contemporaries, including Rogers Hornsby and Pie Traynor. But after the festivities, when Cobb tries to attend a wild hotel-room party being held by his fellow baseball veterans, he is rudely informed that he has not been invited. As we peek into the room, we see that many of the aging ballplayers, who earlier arrived at Cooperstown accompanied by their wives, are grabbing and cosseting an assortment of flashy young call girls. By the time the viewer has absorbed the implications of the scene—How dare these old drunken reprobates judge the character of Ty Cobb?—Shelton deals his final blow by having none other than Mickey Cochrane shove Cobb out of the room, slamming the door in his benefactor's face!

Shelton additionally opines that Cobb occasionally harbored regrets over his failures as a human being, something the man never expressed during his lifetime. In one bravura sequence, Cobb watches a congratulatory newsreel encapsulating his fabulous baseball career—the same newsreel that the audience has already seen during the opening credits. But as the film-within-a-film rolls on, Cobb begins experiencing seconds-lasting flashbacks of his past cruelties and misdeeds. Ever so gradually, the newsreel itself begins recapping those same unpleasantries, while the film's stock "march" music grows eerily discordant—and the newsreel narrator, never altering the effusive tone of his voice, starts rattling off the shameful facts about Cobb's violent outbursts on and off the ballfield, his shabby treatment of his family, and other such revolting revelations. Of course, the newsreel has never actually deviated from its superficially upbeat approach, but the half-truths espoused by the narrator have unleashed a maelstrom of self-hatred and remorse within Cobb's tortured soul.

In these and other speculative scenes, Ron Shelton seems to be desperately seeking out something sympathetic or admirable about Ty Cobb to latch onto. Actor Tommy Lee Jones was likewise looking for this, as he articulated in a 1994 interview with Roger Ebert. "Does a guy like that have any redeeming qualities? Well, yes. No one's entirely beyond redemption. Otherwise they wouldn't call it redemption, would they?" As a result of this digging by Shelton and Jones, Cobb often comes across as a man who achingly yearns for proof of the fundamental decency of mankind, only to be betrayed at every turn. During his sojourn with Al Stump, Cobb occasionally lets down his guard, sobbingly declaring that Stump is the only real friend he has ever had. Upon realizing that Stump has been writing a vitriolic "alternate" autobiography, Cobb bellows like a wounded animal and goes so far as to aim his ubiquitous revolver at the head of the slumbering Stump. Once he has calmed down, Cobb steps behind his veneer of cynical indifference, insisting that he admires Stump for his act of treachery—but by now, the audience knows a pose when it sees one.

Overall, as roughly as Ty Cobb treats his fellow man, he is at his roughest when dealing with himself. In a harrowing sequence, Cobb begins hacking up blood, and, terrified that he is about to drop dead at any moment, launches into an act of attrition, reciting a prayer over and over. Suddenly he stares at himself in the bathroom mirror, and with an angry shout of "No!" he literally wills himself not to die—not just yet. In the end, Ty Cobb, who has never suffered weaklings at any point in his life, will not tolerate a single ounce of weakness within himself. "Cobb is a complicated man. I think that's a fair statement," noted Tommy Lee Jones to Roger Ebert. "Mr. Cobb is thought of as essentially a rattlesnake, but you have to conclude he was a pretty tough guy." Do Jones, and Ron Shelton,

want the viewer to admire Cobb's unswerving toughness, or to pity his inability to relax into basic, fundamental humanity? Like Ty Cobb himself, the film *Cobb* is a riddle wrapped in a mystery inside an enigma.

One of Ron Shelton's "signatures" as a filmmaker is his jaunty refusal to *have* a signature; put simply, the man is loath to repeat himself. He had already made his baseball picture, *Bull Durham*, and he had already made his "nice" biopic, *Blaze*, in which the far from admirable traits of Louisiana governor Earl Long and his mistress, striptease artist Blaze Starr, were outweighed by the characters' positive qualities. *Cobb* would be neither *Blaze* nor *Bull Durham*; it would neither dry-clean its subject, nor would it be a "real" baseball film— at least, not one in which the Game was played on and off throughout the film.

There is only one out-and-out baseball sequence in *Cobb*, a five-minute vignette filmed as a flashback in sepiatone. The sequence is a montage of several different games, with emphasis on a single confrontation between Cobb and an unnamed pitcher who hates Ty's guts. The point of the scene was to show how Cobb was able to get under his opponents' skin by being, in the words of the old novelty T-shirt, "The Meanest Sonofabitch in the Valley." The man playing the contentious pitcher was three-time Cy Young Award winner Roger Clemens, late of the Boston Red Sox—and ironically, it was Tommy Lee Jones as Cobb who was a bit intimidated by the formidable Mr. Clemens when time came to film the scene. Out of respect for Jones, Clemens held back while pitching to him, but when the script called upon him to react in anger to Cobb's taunts, Clemens went "method" and almost knocked the poor actor's block off! "I threw it too hard," Clemens later confessed sheepishly. "I have more control that way but, for a second there, I was afraid we were going to be doing the Ray Chapman story" (a reference to the only player in Major League history to be killed by a pitch).

By severely limiting the film's baseball action, Shelton remained faithful to his intention of showing us Cobb-the-Man rather than Cobb-the-Legend. But in doing so, he dealt his film a blow from which it never quite recovers, and which the film's detractors were never able to get past. Though the earlier *The Babe* is incapable of fully conveying the greatness and influence of Babe Ruth, the film at least offers evidence of those qualities with its generously apportioned baseball highlights. The lack of such scenes in *Cobb* leaves the average viewer of 1990s, who never saw Ty Cobb in action and knows of his accomplishments only from second- and third-hand information, almost completely in the dark as to what made Cobb the greatest of them all. Without some tangible proof of Cobb's baseball genius as a frame of reference, the viewer sees only a nasty, profane old man who, under normal circumstances, would not be worthy of the time of day.

Also, Shelton's aforementioned talent for amalgamating the events of several months into a period of two weeks unfortunately works as much against *Cobb* as it does in the film's favor. By the time the film has reached the 40-minute mark, we know all we really need to know—or want to know—about Ty Cobb. Beyond the fascination inherent in watching outrage pile upon outrage, there is really no place else to go; the rest of the film is plagued by repetition and scenes that are dragged out beyond their worth. Even such highlights as the "Newsreel from Hell" and the climactic verbal battle between Stump and Cobb at the latter's family mausoleum wear out their welcome rather quickly.

This Johnny-One-Note quality occasionally affects the performances of the actors, especially Robert Wuhl as Al Stump. There are just so many times that Stump can react with gape-mouthed astonishment at Cobb's latest assault on decency before the character begins to appear more half-witted than nonplussed. Wuhl's performance is also undermined by Shelton's decision to make Stump the "everyman" from whose point of view the story unfolds. It is quite understandable, for example, that the average viewer would not be aware that Cobb's father was killed by his mother. But having Al Stump "speak" for the viewer by expressing surprise at this revelation merely suggests that America's Highest-Paid Freelance Sportswriter doesn't know how to do his basic homework.

Fortunately, Robert Wuhl rises above the limitations placed on him by the script in his final scene, in which Al Stump's fellow scribes eagerly demand that he tell them the "whole truth" about Ty Cobb. Many observers have suggested that Stump's decision to impart Legend rather than Fact is an homage to the similar finale in John Ford's *The Man Who Shot Liberty Valance* (1962); but as staged by Shelton and acted by Wuhl, the message is completely different. Looking around at his drinking buddies, none of whom have written the Great American Novel as they'd hoped, or achieved the fame to which they all aspire, Stump realizes that, by virtue of the information imparted to him and his willingness to stick to Ty Cobb despite his initial impulse to turn down the assignment, he, like Cobb, has been "set apart" from his contemporaries. So he tells them the Lie, secure in the knowledge that he *could* tell the Truth whenever he chooses, and as *much* of the Truth as he deems necessary. In this way he will always possess something that his colleagues do not—and that is Ty Cobb's definition of Greatness. It might have been on the strength of this one scene that the real Al Stump was moved to remark, "I recognize that there are many dramatic conventions in the script, but it articulated how I felt towards Ty Cobb. It got to the heart of why I couldn't leave."

In the title role, Tommy Lee Jones also weathers the repetitious nature of the script, investing his characterization of Ty Cobb with nuance and variety even when none existed on paper. Though he seems too youthful and robust to be a man in his mid-seventies, Jones uses this essential spryness to make Cobb's bouts of bloody coughing all the more compelling by contrast. While he doesn't really carry himself like a baseball player, Jones has Ty Cobb's peculiarly aristocratic bearing and manner down pat—just as he brilliantly captures Cobb's speech patterns, that odd blend of elegant erudition and trailer-trash scatology, without ever actually sounding like the real Cobb. And though the craggy-faced Jones' facial resemblance to the wizened Cobb countenance is somewhat remote, the actor's age makeup was faultless, even unto Cobb's full head of skin. (Who could forget Jones standing on the podium of the Dorothy Chandler Pavilion to receive his 1994 Academy Award for *The Fugitive*, simultaneously thanking the Academy and explaining his *Cobb*-dictated appearance by exclaiming, "The only thing a man can say at a time like this is, 'I'm not really bald.'") So persuasive was Tommy Lee Jones' overall performance that the viewer completely overlooks a glaring lapse in accuracy: While Ty Cobb plays baseball left-handed, he is consistently *right*-handed in everything else he does.

In smaller roles, Lolita Davidovitch invests her 20-minute assignment as cigarette girl Roberta with the same virago energy as in her earlier starring role in Ron Shelton's *Blaze*; whether or not this approach is appropriate is a matter of taste, though she does shine when uttering the typically Shelton-esque epigram "Genius is overrated." Lou Myers is right on target in the "worm-turns" role of Ty Cobb's beleaguered servant Willie, while Bradley Whitford is equally memorable as the hapless process server (one of many "corporate prig" parts that Whitford would essay before his as-

cension to stardom as Josh Lyman on TV's *West Wing*). And in his brief appearance as Louis Prima, Eloy Casados makes it abundantly clear why he has become a good-luck charm in such Shelton-scripted efforts as *Under Fire*, *The Best of Times*, *Blaze*, *White Men Can't Jump* and *Play It to the Bone*, in much the same way that Hector Elizondo always shows up in the films of director Gary Marshall.

Given a limited premiere on December 2, 1994, *Cobb* was mercilessly—some would say murderously—lambasted by the major reviewers, who seemed to hold it against Ron Shelton personally that his latest film wasn't *Bull Durham* or *White Men Can't Jump*. The critics also panned the picture for presenting so unmercifully honest a portrayal of its title character—though many of these worthies had previously taken *The Babe* to task for not being honest enough. As a result of this drubbing, the executives at Warners (several of whom, it can be whispered, were lying in wait for the maverick Ron Shelton to fall on his face) scuttled plans for a general release of *Cobb*. Sneaking into local theaters with but a bare minimum of fanfare, the film was never given a chance to build an audience, and ended up posting a piddling $1,007,583 domestic gross—not even enough to cover Tommy Lee Jones' salary.

Perhaps *Cobb* was doomed to failure from the start; in the words of critic Charles Taylor, most of its detractors "seemed to resent being talked to as adults," and filmgoers traditionally feel the same way, especially when dealing with iconic characters. Though the film has as many faults as virtues, and admittedly does require a certain measure of intestinal fortitude to sit through from start to finish, *Cobb* does not deserve to be consigned to the refuse heap. Even at its worst, the film represents a courageous directorial vision that never falters—and in this respect, the movie emulates Ty Cobb himself, who for good or ill marched to his own drummer from birth to death, never really worrying what people thought. For our part, we'd rather munch on a risky failure like *Cobb* once in a while than limit ourselves to an exclusive diet of "safe" successes.

The Comrades of Summer

Grossbart Barnett Productions/HBO Pictures; originally telecast July 11, 1992

Produced by Tim Braine. Directed by Tommy Lee Wallace. Written by Robert Rodat. Photography: David Leiterman, Richard Leiterman. Edited by Stephen E. Rivkin. Original music: William Olvis. Production manager: Andrew McLean. Production design: David Fischer. Art direction: Gary Myers. Set decoration: Linda Vipond. First assistant director: Patrice Leung. Second assistant director: Colleen Neill. Costume design: Larry S. Wells. Makeup artist: Jayne Dancose. Hair stylist: Sherry Linder. LA casting: Vicki Huff. Canadian Casting: Sid Kozak. Production supervisor: Matthew O'Connor. Sound mixer: Rick Patton. Script supervisor: Jean Bereziuk. Production coordinator: Gretchen Goode. Baseball consultant: Doug Abrahams. Dialect coach: Michael Levykh. Special effects coordinator: Stewart Bradley. Stunt coordinator: Betty Thomas. Miniatures: Alan Munro, Bret Alexander, Barbu Marion. Opticals: VCE/Peter Kuran. Russian sequences produced in association with Soyuzkinoservice: A. K. Surikov, executive producer. CFI Color. 108 minutes; stereo sound. Rated R.

Cast: Joe Mantegna (Sparky Smith); Natalya Negoda (Tanya Buclova); Michael Lerner (George Kennan); Mark Rolston (Vladimir Voronov); John Fleck (Milo Milov); Eric Allan Kramer (Boris Breavitch); Ian Tracey (Andrei "Andy" Gareichov); Jay Brazeau (Tom); Dwight Koss (Jack); David Berner (Commercial Director); Gary Chalk (Ump); Roark Critchlow (Petra Rostoff); Mitchell Davies (Igor); Todd Duckworth (Leonid Kurutzov); Grant Forster (Vasily Verlich); Jano Frandsen (Meyers); David L. Gordon (Scoop Reporter); Doc Harris (Bud); Ken Kirzinger (Ivan Starkowsky); Kim Kondrashoff (Nikita); Jim Lampley (Radio Announcer); David Lovgren (Sasha); Michael Levykh (Leather Worker); David Lewis (Marine Pitcher); Celia- Louise Martin (Media Maven); Sharlene Martin (Connie); Gary Moten (Ortega); John Oliver (Hamill); Laurie Paton (Cynthia); Roman Podhora (Vlad); Wren Robertz ("Jarhead"); Raimund Stamm (Russian Ump); Don Thompson (Media Moe); Ken Tremblett (Jones); Lloyd T. Williams (Bobby Sims); Michael Dobson (Marine Ball Player).

There is no love lost in the Summer of 1991 between Sparky Smith, egotistical player/manager of the Seattle Mariners, and bombastic team owner George Kennan, but Sparky's insolence is tolerated because of his excellence on the ballfield. All this changes when Sparky is injured while filming a car commercial. His playing days over, Sparky is abruptly fired and blacklisted from Major League Baseball by the vindictive Kennan—and this, combined with the loss of all his product endorsements and the vulture like convergence of his two rapacious ex-wives, leaves Sparky utterly broke. Thus, he is in no position to turn down an offer from the Russian Sports Ministry to coach the former Soviet Union's first National Olympic Baseball team. Arriving in Moscow, Sparky finds that his team consists of hockey players, shot-putters and 100-yard-dash runners—champions all, but nary a baseball player in the bunch except for shortstop Andrei Gareichov, who learned the game while his father was a Soviet diplomat stationed in New York. Sparky's first major stumbling block is the abstinence of assistant coach Vladimir Voronov, who refuses to deviate from the ultra-restrictive baseball rules established years earlier by the mysterious "Manuel." Vladimir is but a minor irritant compared to the fact that the team has no facilities and no decent equipment, thanks to the rusticated wheels of Russian bureaucracy and red tape. With the help of enterprising black marketer Milo Milov, Sparky manages to requisition the proper number of uniforms, bats, balls and gloves, and even wangles a playable ballfield and backstop.

As the Russian "baseballists" slowly get their act together, Sparky finds that he is once again enjoying baseball as much as when he was a youngster—and as a fringe benefit, he has fallen in love with attractive Sports Ministry functionary Tanya Buclova. As winter turns to spring, the Ministry grows impatient and threatens to disband the team, but changes its tune when the Russians score an impressive victory over a tough Cuban ballclub. This, alas, proves to be a mixed blessing when, as a morale-boosting move, the Ministry demands that Sparky's Boys play five games with five top American baseball clubs during the Spring Training season—a challenge which the fledgling Russian team is woefully unprepared to meet.

The premise of the made-for-cable *The Comrades of Summer* was set forth in the film's opening title: "In 1991, in the midst of tremendous change in the Soviet Union, an incident occurred that may have long-term ramifications for America's National Pastime." As these words flashed upon the screen, there were no doubt a few Hollywood insiders who chuckled sarcastically and suggested that the film's written prologue should have read something like this: "In 1990, a film about the culture clash between Japanese and American baseball titled *Tokyo Diamond* began filming. Now it is 1992, and that film, retitled *Mr. Baseball*, is still languishing on the shelf, giving HBO and Grossbart-Barnett productions ample time to rush out their *own* culture-clash baseball comedy, *The Comrades of Summer*."

Well, maybe no one ever *really* said that (does anyone even *talk* like that?), but comparisons between *Mr. Baseball* (q.v.) and *Comrades of Summer* are unavoidable. Both films revolve around a burned-out American ballplayer who is given a second chance in a strange and faraway country; both are "culture shock" comedies, with the American protagonist confounded at every turn by old, deeply entrenched foreign tra-

ditions, customs, and taboos, and with the foreign characters equally stymied by American manners and mores; both films chronicle the adaptation-and-maturation process undergone by the American and his foreign counterparts as they glean important life lessons from each other; and both films include a "Twain Shall Meet" romance between the American and an attractive, intelligent and ambitious local girl. Otherwise, *Mr. Baseball* and *Comrades of Summer* could not be further apart—and we're not simply talking about the distance between Moscow and Tokyo.

First and foremost, where *Mr. Baseball* studiously avoided offending Japanese film fans by making the "Ugly American" lead character the butt of the humor, virtually every joke in *Comrades of Summer* is at the expense of the Russians. The country's tentative efforts to adjust to Western Democracy after centuries of feudalism, Czarism and Communism are played for laughs. Typifying this approach are those scenes where heroine Tanya Buclova, armed with a printed-in-Moscow book of American slang, comes up with such howlers as "Spit or get off the pot." (Not that Tanya needs a book to lead her astray; when trying to express her intention to "play ball"—that is, cooperate—with protagonist Sparky Smith, she declares somberly, "I wish to ball with you".) The average Russian's deeply ingrained inclination to blindly follow orders, whether they seem logical or not, is manifested in assistant coach Vladimir's rigid adherence to the convoluted rules of baseball as set down by one "Manuel." This leads to another example of Soviet misinterpretation and mispronunciation when "Manuel" turns out to be nothing more than an outdated baseball manual, cowritten by a team of Russian and Cuban "baseballists" who had clearly gotten their information second-, third- or even fourth-hand. (Tossing the manual aside, Sparky Smith scores a big laugh by establishing his *own* rules, explaining "It's in Sparky's Manual.")

The Russian necessity, born of never-ending shortages and economic privations, to make do with whatever happens to be handy is also mercilessly satirized. Dismayed upon discovering that his team's "playing field" is a desolate patch of land between a pig farm and a smoke-belching factory, and that the locker room is a dingy World War II–vintage bomb shelter, Sparky is further appalled when he learns that the team's "equipment" consists of only nine battered and bruised baseballs (forcing the players to wade knee-deep in a nearby pond to retrieve pop flies and fouls), a few splintery bats, and a mismatched array of goalie's gloves and oven mitts. In the same vein, the script has a lot of fun with Russia's "shadow economy," as explained by resourceful black-market specialist Milov. In order to obtain a much-needed backstop wall for the team, Milov has to appropriate Sparky's Walkman, which in a series of dizzying transactions is traded for a set of windshield wipers, a carton of shampoo and toothpaste, an electric nail driver and 244 condoms.

Also in for a great deal of ribbing is the Russian bureaucracy's adherence to the old party line: "From each according to their abilities, to each according to their needs." Just as people under the previous Communist regime were assigned their lifelong professions while still in childhood, with no room for flexibility or advancement, so too does the Sports Ministry "construct" its team by compartmentalizing. Boris Breavitch is an Olympic hockey champion, so it somehow meets efficiency standards to assign Boris to third base, where his defensive skills will presumably do the Greater Good for the Greater Number. Likewise, shot-putter Ivan Starkowsky is made the left infielder, handball champ Vasily Verlich is ordered to pitch, and 100-meter sprinter Leonid Kurutzov is appointed "base-stealing specialist." It takes the American Sparky Smith to cut through all this governmental preordainment and determine the strengths and weaknesses of his players on the basis of actual performance.

Another fundamental difference between *Mr. Baseball* and *Comrades of Summer* is that, while in the first film the hero stepped into a pre-existing condition when he began playing Japanese baseball, the hero of the second film has to literally build Russian baseball from the ground up (though in real life, the game had been introduced to Russia in 1988, during the waning days of the Old Guard). The scenes in *Mr. Baseball* where protagonist Jack Elliot is forced to adjust to a whole new set of ballfield rules could not be duplicated in *Comrades of Summer*, where Sparky Smith is literally the only person who actually knows what the rules are. Thus, while in *Mr. Baseball* Jack is benched for refusing to follow orders, in *Comrades* Sparky is the "bencher," sending Boris Breavitch to the showers for hitting a homer when he was ordered to let two pitches pass so as to assess the weaknesses of the pitcher.

The issue of celebrity endorsements, prevalent in both *Mr. Baseball* and *Comrades of Summer*, is given entirely different treatment in both films. Jack Elliot in *Mr. Baseball* is told in no uncertain terms that he is not only expected to do Japanese commercials to capitalize on his celebrity, but his contract *demands* that he do so. Conversely, the Russians in *Comrades of Summer* have not quite gotten over their distaste for American capitalism: When Sparky Smith films a Coca-Cola commercial in the middle of Red Square, it is perceived as an act of betrayal by Sports Ministry officer Tanya, who believes that a true "baseballist" should play for the love of the game rather than for any crass promotional consideration.

Also separating the two films is the casting. It would have been ludicrous (and positively fatal on a public-relations level) to cast Occidental actors as the Japanese characters in *Mr. Baseball*. But it is not quite as big a credibility stretch to have non–Russian actors play most of the Russian characters in *Comrades of Summer*, especially since their Slavic accents were flawless, thanks to Russian-born dialect coach Michael Levykh (who appears in the film as the leather worker who transforms a closet full of obsolete KGB jackets into eighteen baseball gloves!). It would also have been less practical to seek out an all–Russian cast for *Comrades of Summer* than it was to use a predominantly Japanese lineup in *Mr. Baseball*. Unlike the earlier film, which was largely lensed in Japan, *Comrades* was filmed primarily in Canada, with scale-model sets and miniatures (and the incessant cigarette smoking of the main characters) invoking the proper Russian atmosphere. Only a few background scenes of the Kremlin and other Moscow landmarks were shot for the film through the facilities of Soyuzkinoservice, and these required only the presence of stars Joe Mantegna and Natalya Negoda— one of the few *genuine* Russians in the picture.

Above all, *Mr. Baseball* is a star-driven film, focusing on the relationship between the characters played by top-billed Tom Selleck and Ken Takakura, and the effect that the film's outcome has on the lives of both these characters. Though Joe Mantegna is unquestionably the star and catalyst of *Comrades of Summer*, this is essentially an ensemble film: It is what happens to the team, rather than Sparky Smith, that commands the audience's attention and sympathies. Accordingly, the characters of the individual Russian team members are more thoroughly developed than their *Mr. Baseball* counterparts. It should not be surprising that the later credits of *Comrades of Summer*'s scriptwriter, Robert Rodat, included the ultimate "teamwork" picture, Steven Spielberg's *Saving Private Ryan* (1998).

One can only express admiration for Rodat's ability to stay "on program" throughout the film. With only a few side-trips into generic sports-movie gags (a group of Mariners players, armed with cell phones, closing financial deals while suiting up in the locker room) and standard sitcom humor (told that the Russian team is his only job option, Sparky screams, "I'm not going!"— followed by an instant jumpcut to an American plane touching down in Moscow), all of the humor in *Comrades of Summer* flows naturally from the situation and the characters. Equally admirable is the straightforward, gimmick-free direction of Tommy Lee Wallace, a protégé of John Carpenter who had previously specialized in horror films like *Halloween III* and the made-for–TV er *Stephen King's 'It'*. Even when Wallace deviates into directorial self-indulgence, he remains faithful to the film's basic premise. During the brief sequence in which a group of government craftsmen build a temporary ballfield for the Russian team, Wallace deftly launches into a spoof of all those exuberantly propagandistic "tractor musicals" (*The Jolly Fellows, Volga-Volga*, etc.) directed by Grigori Alexandrov during the Stalin regime.

The baseball scenes are logically and believably staged, detailing the tortuous birth pangs of Sparky's team, the players' initial clumsiness in adapting to a game that to them makes as little sense as *Mad* magazine's "43-Man Squamish," the team's coming together as a unified whole, the slow but steady improvement and building up of confidence, and the ultimate realization that there can be more than one definition of the word "victory." Two sequences stand out: The Russians' morale-boosting win over the fabled Cuban National Team, and their climactic face-off against Sparky's old team, the Seattle Mariners, in an exhibition game. Rather than take the easy-out of having the Russians defeat the Cubans through superior skills, the filmmakers set up a collection of circumstances showing how luck and psychology are as important as field performance. True, the Cubans are better equipped and better staffed—but they are not prepared for the bone-chilling Russian weather, and as the Castro Brigade shivers and shakes in their flimsy uniforms, the well-upholstered Boys from Moscow effortlessly dominate the game. More important to the outcome of the match, Sparky has arranged for all of his players' mothers to be in attendance—and if there is one thing that any Russian male fears worse than death, it is making a fool of himself in front of his own mother!

The buildup to the closing Russia-Mariners game is sublime. True to Sparky's fears, the Russians are no match for the four North American teams preceding the Mariners, and they are handily defeated in each instance. However, with each successive game, the margin of loss becomes smaller: 19–0 against the Yankees, 17–2 against the Red Sox, 13–5 against the Royals and 11–6 against the Blue Jays. Sparky and his players learn to console themselves with the fact that if they can't win, at least they're not losing as badly as they did at the beginning of the series—and somehow, this straw-grasping inspires a modicum of confidence.

By the time the team meets Seattle, Sparky has figured out why they haven't been doing any better; the presence of domineering assistant coach Vladimir has had an intimidating effect on the Russians, keeping them from truly excelling on the field. Using a diabolically clever strategy, Sparky maneuvers the umpire into throwing Vladimir out of the game—and suddenly the team loosens up enough to give Seattle a real run for its money. But then it dawns upon Sparky that the team has become too reliant upon *his* leadership, and are afraid to think for themselves on the field—and at this point, self-reliance is practically the only way to come close to defeating Seattle. In an uncharacteristic self-sacrificial ges-

ture, Sparky gets *himself* sent to the showers by the umpire, leaving his boys to fend for themselves, which they do magnificently.

Still, *Comrades of Summer* is grounded in reality, and though the Russians seem poised to win the game, Seattle emerges triumphant with one extra run. An unhappy ending? Not on your life! Everyone in the baseball park realizes that the Russians have truly "come of age" as ballplayers, and that even if victory has eluded them, they have proven themselves worthy of their uniforms. But the Russians *themselves* do not realize this until the Seattle Mariners walk onto the field and spontaneously burst into applause in honor of their courageous opponents—applause that is echoed by every man, woman and child in the stadium.

In addition to providing an upbeat denouement, this climax serves another purpose. Throughout the film, it has been carefully established that, whenever the Russian players are left to their own devices, they enjoy getting together for impromptu practice sessions; one of these is observed unnoticed by Sparky, who is touched that his boys are displaying the youthful enthusiasm for baseball that he thought he had left behind in childhood. This through-line has its payoff a mere few seconds before the final fadeout: Hours after the game with Seattle has ended, we see the Russians again having fun playing baseball amongst themselves—whereupon several of the Mariners clamber onto the field and ask if they can join in on the fun, just like a bunch of sandlot kids. We cannot imagine this scene playing as well as it does without the impetus of that earlier moment in which the Mariners led the cheers for their bloody but unbowed Russian opponents.

As Sparky Smith, the astonishingly versatile Joe Mantegna—a devout Chicago Cubs fan who had previously earned his place of honor in the annals of baseball fiction by cowriting and starring in the TV play *Bleacher Bums*—pulls off the not inconsiderable feat of conveying the essence of a big-buck baseball player without ever actually being shown playing the game. It is especially gratifying to watch Mantegna subtly transform Sparky's take-charge attitude from one borne of arrogance to an outgrowth of genuine affection and respect for his players. Mantegna is also most engaging in his scenes with Russian leading lady Natalya Negoda, here demonstrating the same consummate professionalism which she brought to her most celebrated role in director Nikita Mikhalkov's *Little Vera* (1988). The actress' best scene has her articulating her excitement and pride in being Russian at a time of profound social change, comparing the experience to that of a typical American in 1776. More amusingly, Nagoda's Tanya Buclova spends several scenes primly persuading Mantegna's Sparky Smith, whose F- and S-words come thick and fast in the early reels, that "profanity is unnecessary"—a cute in-joke referring to Mantegna's previous profanity-peppered appearances in the films and plays of David Mamet. In the same spirit, the makers of *Comrades of Summer* did not forget that Natalya Negoda was internationally famous for being the first Russian film actress to appear nude in an R-rated love scene, which may explain the slightly gratuitous but undeniably eye-catching *au naturel* bedroom scene between Sparky and Tanya.

In the supporting cast, Michael Lerner, previously seen as "Black Sox" instigator Arnold Rothstein in *Eight Men Out* (1988), does wonders with the stock-villain role of Mariners owner George Kennan, convincing us that he simultaneously abhors and admires his nemesis Sparky Smith. Also delivering standout performances are John Fleck (best known in show-business circles as one of the four independent performance artists who filed a lawsuit against the Na-

tional Endowment of the Arts in 1991) as the wheeling-dealing Milov, and Eric Allan Kramer (whose other roles included Little John in Mel Brooks' spoof *Robin Hood: Men in Tights*) as the thick-eared hockey player-cum-batter Boris Breavitch. The scene in which the towering Boris withers under the baleful glare of his diminutive mother is one of the singular comic highlights of the 1990s.

Like most other HBO movies, *The Comrades of Summer* was given repeated showings in the weeks following its television debut on July 11, 1992. Typical of the critical reaction was the assessment by *TV Guide*'s resident reviewer: "After it gets past its stale Commie clichés, *Comrades* becomes a small delight." In the years since its original release, with the collapse of the Soviet Union ever receding into the collective memory and the novelty of Russian baseball having long since worn off, *The Comrades of Summer* has lost much of its "torn from the headlines" edge—but absolutely none of its sheer entertainment value.

Cooperstown

Brandman Productions Inc./Amblin Television/ Majestic Films International/ TNT Screenworks; originally telecast January 26, 1993

Executive producer: Michael Brandman. Produced by Steven J. Brandman and Leanne Moore. Directed by Charles Haid. Written by Lee Blessing, from his stage play. Original music: Mel Marvin. Photography: William Wages. Edited by Andrew Doerfer. Production design: Vaughan Edwards. Art direction: Chris Cornwell. Set decoration: Sara Andrews. Costume design: Betty Madden. Makeup: Davida Simon. Hair stylist: Frankie Campbell. Production supervisor: Dan Kaplow. Casting: Juel Bestrop, Risa Bramon Garcia. Voice casting: Leigh French. Production manager: Leanne Moore. First assistant director: Jerry Grandey. Second assistant director: Bruce Carter. Martial arts choreographer: Danny Gibson. Music editor: Jeff Charbonneau. Dialogue editor: Pat McCormick. Sound mixer: Richard Schexnayder. Sound editors: Richard Taylor, Dave Weathers. Sound effects editor: Richard Thomas. Special effects: John C. Hartigan. Stunt coordinator: Terry James. Steadicam operator: Guy Norman Bee. Color. 93 minutes; Stereo Sound.

Cast: Alan Arkin (Harry Willette); Graham Greene (Raymond Maracle); Hope Lange (Cassie Willette); Josh Charles (Jody); Maria Pitillo (Bridget); Ed Begley, Jr. (Dave Cormeer); Ann Wedgeworth (Lila Kunznick); Paul Dooley (Sid Wiggins); Joanna Miles (Louise); Charles Haid (Little Eddie McVee); Ernie Harwell (Baseball Announcer); Miles Perlich (Young Eddie); Byron Thames (Young Harry); Robbie T. Robinson (Umpire); Jason Orman (Young Pitcher); Juarez Orman (Catcher); Lori Sebourn (Pam); Dan Chambers (TV Reporter); Zahn McClarnon (Young Raymond); Alexander Bookston (Raymond Maracle, Jr.); Jim Elk (Herbert Maracle); Jules H. Desjarlais (Young Native American); Victoria Racimo (Isabel); George Kee Cheung (Mr. Mastunaga); Gailard Sartain (Georgia State Trooper); Penelope Windust (Receptionist); John Capodice (Morelli); Tom Ashworth (Employee); Bill Feeney (Official); Harry Stanback (Security Guard); Brittany Haid (Fan).

If ever there was a prize given for the nastiest, most vituperative man in baseball, Ty Cobb would undoubtedly win—but ex-pitcher Harry "The Wing" Willette would be a shoe-in for second place. Thirty years after retiring from active duty as "a meal ticket for a team that never made its way past breakfast," Harry is still bitter over giving up a crucial home-run pitch during a tight pennant race, a bungle for which he has always held his Native American catcher Raymond Maracle responsible. Since that time, Harry has earned a respectable living as a major-league scout in Florida (his skills in this capacity are so well-honed that he can gauge a prospect's pitching speed *without* a radar gun), but nary a day has gone by that he hasn't cursed Maracle's memory. Adding insult to injury, Ray Maracle is about to be inducted into the Baseball Hall of Fame at Cooperstown, an honor that

has eluded Harry for years. Ironically, Maracle dies a scant few days before the induction ceremony. This minor inconvenience does not prevent Ray's ghost from visiting Harry and goading him into making the long northward journey from Florida to New York—there to demand that he, too, be fêted by the Hall of Fame. Leaving his perplexed wife Cassie behind, our curmudgeonly hero begins his pilgrimage to Cooperstown, accompanied not only by the spectral Ray Maracle (whom only Harry can see and hear), but also by several other eccentric characters: Harry's cycle-riding, Zen-spouting, martial arts–fancying nephew Jody; a smarmy club owner named Dave Cormeer; a faded but still buoyant "Baseball Annie" named Lila Kunznick; an abrasively iconoclastic sportswriter named Sid Wiggins; and Bridget, a punkish hitchhiker whom Jody picks up (and falls in love with) along the way—and who turns out to be the granddaughter of *another* man whom Harry has despised for years! Before his odyssey culminates in a surprising turn of events at Cooperstown, a considerably mellower Harry Willette has learned a lot more about life—and himself—in three days than he ever had in the previous three decades.

Except for a lengthy flashback sequence, a vignette involving Harry's latest pitching discovery, and a cameo appearance by "voice of the Tigers" Ernie Harwell, the visual baseball content in the made-for-cable *Cooperstown* is minimal. But that doesn't stop the characters from *talking* about the Game, and talking about it a lot. More than one TV critic observed that the film's dialogue contained more baseball statistics and folklore than any film outside of Ken Burns' multipart documentary on the subject.

Playwright Lee Blessing, whose other works include *A Walk in the Woods* and several episodes of TV's *Picket Fences*, had warmed up for this project with an existentialist theatrical piece called *Cobb*, which outside of its title and protagonist had lit-

ALAN ARKIN ★ GRAHAM GREENE

Two great
players.
Two best
friends.
But only
one spot in the
Hall of Fame.

COOPERSTOWN

TNT
Screenworks
GREAT STORIES FROM GREAT STORYTELLERS

TONIGHT   7PM/9PM encore

Artwork © 1993 Turner Pictures, Inc

An age-enhanced Alan Arkin (foreground) and an ethereal-looking Graham Greene in a
magazine ad for *Cooperstown* (1993).

tle in common with the 1994 film of the same name (see separate entry). Written in 1989, the play required three different actors to play the contentious Ty Cobb at different stages of his life. There was also a ghostly fourth character in the form of Negro League first baseman Oscar Charleston, generally considered the best black player of the 1920s. Materializing at various junctures in the play, Charleston, who in his heyday was known as "The Black Ty Cobb," haunted the three white incarnations of the *real* Cobb, mercilessly needling them about their flaws, failures and missed opportunities. Blessing had not chosen Charleston arbitrarily; an intense, fearless giant of a man who once tore the hood off a Ku Klux Klansman, he would certainly have given the racist Ty Cobb something to chew on had the two ever actually crossed paths. *Cobb* stressed the same three elements that would pervade *Cooperstown*: "Regret, Bigotry and Baseball," to quote one pithy Internet observer.

Likewise beginning life as a stage play in 1992 (though apparently it was never presented theatrically), *Cooperstown* features a distinctively Cobb-like leading character, who in the twilight of his years finds his lifelong values and prejudices challenged by a phantom representative of a persecuted minority group. *Cooperstown* also had the usual earmarks of Blessing's best works, notably the author's quirky blending of fact, mythology and mysticism.

The play was committed to film through the good graces of producer Mike Brandman, the creator of The Writer's Cinema, an ambitious project designed to revivify TV's "Golden Age" by bringing original works by top playwrights to the small screen. Brandman's project was put together in association with Steven Spielberg's Amblin Productions and with media mogul Ted Turner, over whose TNT cable network *Cooperstown* premiered on January 26, 1993. Lensed on location in Florida

and Georgia, the film was directed by actor Charles Haid, who also appears on-screen in the cameo role of Little Eddie McVee, the opposing batter whose home run "destroyed" Harry Willette's career. Unlike Daniel Stern's similar double duty assignment in the like-vintage baseball picture *Rookie of the Year* (q.v.), Haid's acting is every bit as good as his directing.

Since the film was essentially a two-man show, the proceedings were dominated by Alan Arkin, who earned an Emmy nomination for his performance, and by Graham Greene, an accomplished Native American character actor who skyrocketed to stardom in the 1990 Oscar-winner *Dances with Wolves*. While virtually the only time Harry Willette and Ray Maracle actually play baseball is during a flashback in which younger actors assume the roles, both Arkin and Greene are so thoroughly convincing as veteran ballplayers that it is never really necessary to see them in action. Because the byplay between the two stars is so compelling, the sidelines characters aren't quite as interesting, though this is in no way meant to belittle the performances of Hope Lange, Josh Charles, Anne Wedgeworth, Maria Pitillo, Paul Dooley and Ed Begley, Jr.; besides, it is perversely amusing to see the staunchly pro-ecological Begley play a role that requires him to be in close proximity to a pollution-belching automobile.

In his February 1, 1993, *New York Magazine* review, critic John Leonard cited the "odd pacing and peculiar emphasis" of Haid's direction, but allowed that all the "right" ingredients for baseball-movie success were in place: "Lots of stats, a couple of tears, and everybody behaving like an eight-year-old." *TV Guide*'s "couch critic" Jeff Jarvis took a more jaundiced view of *Cooperstown*: "It's cute, but there were times when I wanted to scream at the screen: 'It's only a game!'" Even so, it is hard to dislike a film with lines like "Baseball is the sport that's closest to life because so much of it's comprised of failure"—or better still, "Baseball is completely Zen!"

Given multiple showings when it first aired on TNT, *Cooperstown* not only engendered strong audience support, but ended up winning Lee Blessing a Humanitas Award "for humanizing achievement in television writing." Unfortunately, the film has seldom been revived since 1993, and its videocassette version has long been out of circulation. If cable-TV programmers can continue inflicting reruns of such negligible baseball epics as *The Fan, Ed* and *Major League II*, it certainly behooves them to put the unjustly forgotten *Cooperstown* back in the regular rotation immediately.

Damn Yankees*

Warner Bros.; released September 1958

Produced and directed by George Abbott and Stanley Donen. Associate producers: Frederick Brisson, Robert Griffith and Harold Prince. Screenplay by George Abbott; adapted from the musical play by George Abbott, Douglass Wallop and [uncredited] Richard Bissell, based on the novel *The Year the Yankees Lost the Pennant* by Douglass Wallop. Music and lyrics for "Six Months Out of Every Year," "Goodbye Old Gal," "(You've Gotta Have) Heart," "Shoeless Joe from Hannibal Mo.," "A Little Brains, a Little Talent," "Empty Chair," "The Good Old Days," "Whatever Lola Wants," "Who's Got the Pain?" and "Two Lost Souls" by Richard Adler and Jerry Ross. Photography: Harold Lipstein. Edited by Frank Wright. Art director: Stanley Fleischer. Set decorations by John W. Arthur. Choreography by Bob Fosse. Fosse's assistant: Patty Ferrier. Makeup by Gordon Bau. Production and costume design by William and Jean Eckart. Assistant director: Ivan Volkman. Color by Technicolor. 110 minutes; sound.

Cast: Tab Hunter (Joe Hardy); Gwen Verdon (Lola); Ray Walston (Mr. Applegate); Russ Brown (Van Buren); Shannon Bolin (Meg); Na-

thaniel Frey (Smokey); Jimmie Komack (Rocky); Rae Allen (Gloria Thorpe); Robert Schafer (Joe Boyd); Jean Stapleton (Sister Miller); Albert Linville (Vernon); Bob Fosse (Mambo Dancer); Elizabeth Howell (Doris Miller); William Fawcett (Hawkins); Phil Arnold (News Vendor); and Nesdon Booth, Lee Theodore, Art Passarella.

Joe Boyd, a married, middle-aged real estate salesman, is a diehard fan of the Washington Senators, a team that hasn't won an American League pennant since 1924. One night a mysterious stranger named Applegate pops up on Boyd's doorstep, offering Joe a chance to win for the Senators and chase those "damn Yankees" out of the American League series race. While it doesn't take Joe long to ascertain the true identity of Applegate—not after the little stranger lights a cigarette without benefit of a match—he signs his soul away in exchange for a young body and a crack at joining the Senators. But though Joe Boyd has now become strapping young athlete Joe Hardy, he's still a real estate man at heart, and insists that Applegate include an escape clause, one that will allow Joe to get out of his contract if he voluntarily walks off the Senators team before midnight, September 24. After joining his favorite team, Joe bats out homer after homer in game after game, accomplishing the pennant bid he'd wanted for the Senators. This, however, is all part of a master plan of Applegate's to place the series within reach of the hungry Washington fans, then pluck it away by claiming Joe's soul before the deciding game, resulting (he hopes) in apoplexy, heart attacks, and suicides. Joe throws a curve in these plans by moving in with Meg Boyd—his wife in his previous life—as a tenant, out of Applegate's sphere of influence; but our demonic friend conjures up a temptress named Lola to seduce

*The British title for this film was What Lola Wants, to avoid the misrepresentation that the picture was an American Civil War epic. The ongoing assumption that Britons would shun pictures with titles invoking that war was responsible for such other name changes over the years as the conversion of the 1949 William Holden–Lucille Ball comedy Miss Grant Takes Richmond into Innocence Is Bliss!

the hapless Joe back into Applegate's fold. This fails, so Applegate engineers the accusation that Joe Hardy had once cheated while in the Mexican League, a delaying tactic that plants Joe in the chambers of an investigating commissioner—just as the clocks toll midnight on September 24. All seems lost, but Joe can still win the deciding game and foil Applegate's plans. Enlisting the aid of Lola (who's fallen for the ballplayer), Joe keeps Applegate away from the stadium long enough for the Senators to win an early lead. Applegate appears at the last minute and vengefully changes Joe Hardy back to Joe Boyd before the eyes of the fans—which proves to be the nasty fellow's undoing, since not only does this break his contract with Joe, but Joe still pulls off the winning catch. A sadder but wiser Joe Boyd returns to the arms of his wife Meg, while Applegate is left to stew in his own juices.

Douglass Wallop's 1954 novel *The Year the Yankees Lost the Pennant* is such an engagingly light read that one can finish the whole book in a single day and still feel entertained. The novel, set in a vague but not too distant future (on some pages it's 1958, on others 1968), is predicated on a theory to which many baseball fans outside the Manhattan area had always subscribed— that the invulnerable, insufferable New York Yankees were a tool of the devil. Douglass Wallop's Applegate finagles Joe into the Senators as a diversionary tactic that will lead to a Yankee win, not simply because he wants to cause mass disappointment, but also because His Satanic Majesty is himself the Yankees' biggest fan. Among the plot points in the novel that didn't make it to *Damn Yankees* was included the strategy of hiding Applegate's shoes so he can't make it to the last game—concrete is hard on those cloven hooves. The most significant difference between the book and its stage and screen counterpart can be found at the end of *The Year the Yankees Lost the Pennant*,

after Joe Hardy has reverted to Joe Boyd. Applegate is momentarily stymied, but he affably informs Joe—whom he's grown to genuinely like—that he's created a brand new Joe Hardy to take Boyd's place at the World Series. And *this* Joe Hardy is destined to win. Now that the Yankees are out of the running, Washington is slated to play the series against the Brooklyn Dodgers—and as much as he loves the Yankees, Applegate hates the Dodgers even more.

It's to the everlasting credit of Broadway producer-director George Abbott that he was able to see musical comedy potential in such a slight piece. Abbott worked in collaboration with Douglass Wallop to convert *The Year the Yankees Lost the Pennant* into a two-and-one-half-hour evening at the theater; and the result, *Damn Yankees*, ran at New York's 46th Street Theatre from May 5, 1955, to October 12, 1957—a total of 1,019 performances. The success was due in no little part to the outstanding music and lyrics by Richard Adler and Jerry Ross, who one season earlier had collaborated on *The Pajama Game*, another musical based on a novel with a "working class" theme (in *The Pajama Game* the story involved union negotiations). There's no telling how many more excellent scores Adler and Ross would have turned out had not Jerry Ross died suddenly during the run of *Damn Yankees*.

Abbott, Adler, Ross and Richard Bissell (the author of the book upon which *Pajama Game* was based, and an uncredited contributor to this project) decided during out-of-town tryouts to build up the part of Lola as the principal female lead. In the novel Lola is described as the most beautiful woman in the world, but she's no slinky seductress. The coupling of the Adler-Ross classic "Whatever Lola Wants" with the athletic striptease developed by actress Gwen Verdon and her choreographer (and future husband) Bob Fosse resulted in the hot-to-trot Lola that audiences have come to know and lust after. Another major female

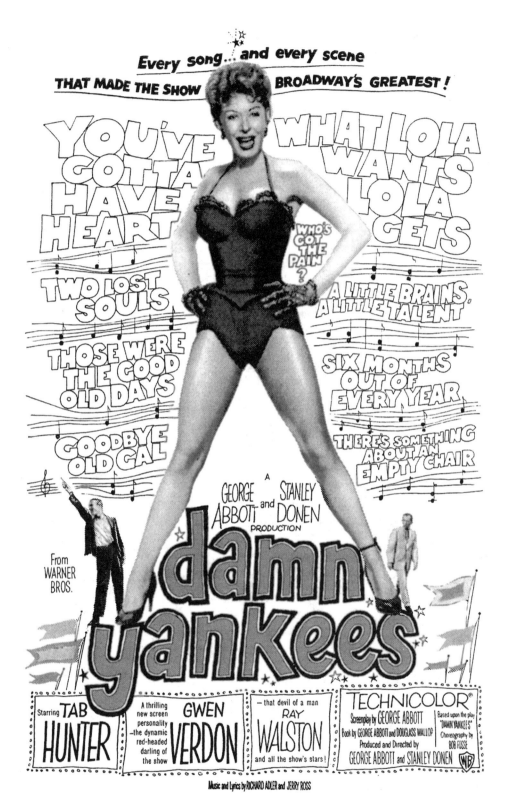

No baseball to speak of, but plenty of "selling power" in this ad for *Damn Yankees* (courtesy of Ted Okuda).

character—albeit one of less spectacular dimensions—was concocted for the play in the form of newspaper reporter Gloria Thorpe, who smells a rat when Joe Hardy appears out of nowhere to play for the Senators, and who has her suspicions fueled by the scheming Applegate in order to get Joe before the commissioner on the night of his "escape clause." The novel's counterpart to Gloria is a male sports columnist by the name of Luster Head, who is somewhat prissy and possibly sexually ambivalent (the implication seems to be that anyone who would question the capabilities of Joe Hardy would have to be less than a man!). But Luster Head was a limited character who wouldn't have translated well to the play; besides, having Gloria Thorpe on the ballfield gave Adler and Ross the opportunity to compose the obligatory "Ethel Merman" piece: a big production number, led by Gloria and danced by the ballplayers, titled "Shoeless Joe from Hannibal, Mo."

Another major character in the novel was Roscoe Ent, a seedy burlesque comic hired by the Senators' management as a "clown player" to improve attendance, who is embittered when Joe Hardy's signing results in his own loss of prominence. Roscoe was loosely based upon Jackie Price, an acrobatic comedian engaged by Bill Veeck as an "infielder" who was known to stand on his head at first base while playing for Veeck's Cleveland Indians. Ent existed in the book as a character to whom Joe Hardy, sensing that Roscoe is about to sign one of Applegate's contracts, confesses about the pact with the devil. This turns out to be a thread in the fabric that Applegate is weaving to keep Joe in the commissioner's office at deadline time; Roscoe Ent offers himself as star witness against Joe, but delays his entrance, and as midnight approaches causes the hearing to go into overtime by suddenly withdrawing his testimony—after losing his Senators job to Joe, Roscoe has found the love of a good woman to keep him happy.

Perhaps one might regret the deletion of Roscoe Ent in *Damn Yankees* on the basis that a burlesque comedian would likely have a great specialty number in him, but including Roscoe in the play would only have drawn comic focus away from the splendid performance of Ray Walston as Applegate.

Warner Bros. bought the rights to *Damn Yankees* for $750,000, splitting potential profits 50–50 with the play's producers. When time came to film *Yankees*, Warners opted for the decision they'd made with their lucrative 1957 adaptation of Adler and Ross's *Pajama Game*—to film the musical virtually as written, retaining as many of the Broadway cast members and original songs as possible. Of the three excised tunes, the robustly ribald second-act curtain raiser "The Game" (the inclusion of which would have posed serious censorship problems back in 1958) can be heard as an instrumental during the film's opening credits.

Though he had been the nominal director of a handful of films in the 1930s and 1940s, George Abbott was less familiar with the ins and outs of filmmaking than he was with the ways and means of the stage, so Stanley Donen, a seasoned hand at movie musicals, codirected with Abbott, as he'd previously done on *Pajama Game* (Donen was well versed in baseball musicals, having been one of the guiding forces in 1949's *Take Me Out to the Ballgame* [q.v.]). Judging by the results, it's fairly clear to see where Abbott deferred to Donen's judgment. Songs like "Heart," "Whatever Lola Wants," "A Little Brains, a Little Talent" and "Empty Chair," while superbly performed, are played out as though being enacted on the stage, and overprojected as if the actors are worried that the folks in the cheap seats can't hear the lyrics; on the other hand, "Shoeless Joe," "Two Lost Souls," and—to a lesser extent—Applegate's solo "Those Were the Good Old Days" take full advantage of the location work, lighting effects, and technical trickery indigenous to the movies. "Shoeless Joe," generally put down by disciples of Bob Fosse as being one of his lesser efforts, is on a cinematic level particularly appealing, with its wide variety of camera angles, its lightning-paced editing, and its corps of dancers in Senator uniforms stirring up dust clouds around the diamond of Los Angeles's Wrigley Field.

One bit of stage direction inherited by the film illustrates both the movie's comic charm and one of its drawbacks. When Joe Hardy tries out for the Senators, we never see the balls he slams out of the park; their flights are represented by the old "tennis game" gag of having the other ballplayers, in medium shot, turn their heads and eyes heavenward in unison. While the routine earns its laugh, it is unfortunately representative of the actual amount of real ballplaying in the film; the most action we're allowed to see occurs in a montage, and then it's only a batted ball or two and a couple of slides into home. No one was asking for *Damn Yankees* to eschew its score and become a baseball picture through and through, but moviegoers more fond of ballgames than they were of people suddenly bursting into song were left a little wanting.

Movie fans who liked stories with clear-cut climaxes were nonplussed by the abrupt ending in *Damn Yankees*. It's nice that Joe gets back to normal and Applegate is thwarted, but events happen so suddenly—and without a really rousing closing song—that the viewer walks out of the picture with the impression of having missed something. This unsatisfying "second act curtain," though slightly less glaring in the stage version of *Damn Yankees*, was a typical shortcoming of many musical comedies, and might have been remedied had Douglass Wallop's original, ironic coda of Applegate creating a second Joe Hardy been retained.

One aspect of the movie that has been routinely trounced upon since its release is the box office insurance casting of Tab Hunter as Joe Hardy. The usual comment is something like, "How *dare* the producers sully such a wonderful piece by casting an inexperienced zero like Hunter in the lead?" These tongue cluckers would be best advised to take a second look at the picture. Though Tab Hunter is doubled in many of the baseball scenes, he both moves and comports himself like a young big-leaguer in the Mantle mold. He did not come into this movie "cold," having been in films since the early 1950s, nor was he a total stranger to the diamond; Hunter had played Jimmy Piersall in the 1956 TV adaptation of Piersall's autobiography *Fear Strikes Out*, and, from all accounts, his interpretation knocked Anthony Perkins's film performance of Piersall out of the box. It might be instructive for latter day critics to observe Hunter's *Damn Yankees* performance closely. Marvelous though they are, Gwen Verdon and Ray Walston are reprising their Broadway performances, employing little bits of stage business and pauses for laughter that seem arch and contrived on the big screen. Tab Hunter is a *movie* actor giving a perfectly acceptable, seemingly spontaneous, and wholly winning *movie* performance. As for his singing, well, Rex Harrison was no Jan Peerce either. And think a moment; given the rest of the leading man crop in 1958, who would *you* have cast as Joe Hardy? Rock Hudson? Jeffrey Hunter? Aldo Ray?

It isn't necessary to analyze the misfire 1967 NBC television production of *Damn Yankees*, with Phil Silvers playing Applegate like Sergeant Bilko from hell, and Lee Remick coming across like Florence Henderson in the role of Lola. The 1958 screen version of *Damn Yankees* is the only authentic filmed record of this Broadway hit; and while it has its faults, the film is well worth rewatching today, even though the current hot-and-cold status of the New York Yankees and the 1961 transformation of the old Washington Senators into the Minnesota Twins have relegated *Damn Yankees* to the status of a period piece. In fact, when the musical was revived on Broadway in 1994 with Victor Garber as Applegate and Bebe Neuwirth as Lola, an offstage narrator was added at the beginning of the proceedings, the better to reaffirm the dominance of the 1950s Yankees and to establish the existence of the Senators for those too young to remember.

Death on the Diamond

MGM; released September 1934

Produced by Lucien Hubbard. Directed by Edward Sedgwick. Screenplay by Harvey Thew, Joseph Sherman and Ralph Spence, from a novel by Cortland Fitzsimmons. Photography: Milton Krasner. Edited by Frank Sullivan. Assistant director: Eddie Wohler. Second unit director: John Waters. Art directors: Cedric Gibbons, David Townsend. Second unit photography: Ray Binger, Leonard Smith. Recording director: Douglas Shearer. 69 minutes; black and white; sound.

Cast: Robert Young (Larry Kelly); Madge Evans (Frances Clark); Ted Healy (Terry O'Toole); Nat Pendleton (Truck Hogan); C. Henry Gordon (Joseph Karnes); Paul Kelly (Jimmie Downey); David Landau (Pop Clark); Dewitt Jennings (Patterson); Edward Brophy (Grogan); Willard Robertson (Lieutenant Cato); Mickey Rooney (Mickey, the Ballboy); Robert Livingston (Frank Higgins); Joseph Sauers [Joe Sawyer] (Dunk Spencer); James Ellison (Sherman, Cincinnati Pitcher); Ray Mayer (Sugar Kane); Pat Flaherty (Coach); Ralph Bushman [Francis X. Bushman, Jr.] (Jan Brisco); Sam Flint (Baseball Commissioner); Charles Sullivan (Taxi Driver); Tom McGuire (Chief of Police); Franklin Farnum (Fan); Jack Norton (Gambler); Hector Sarno (Barber); Harry Semels (Barber's Customer); Carl Stockdale (Hotel Clerk); Pat O'Malley (Cashier); Dennis O'Keefe, Bobby Watson, Sherry Hall, Garry Owen (Radio Announcers); Walter Brennan, Heinie Conklin, Max Wagner (Hot Dog Vendors); John Hyams (Henry Ainsley); Fred "Snowflake" Toones (Porter); Bert Lindley, Ward Bond (Policemen); Allen Wood (Newsboy); Alice Lake (Mrs. Brisco); Herman Brix [Bruce Bennett], Kane Richmond, Don Brodie, Sumner Getchell, Jack Raymond (Men on Ticket Line): Fred Graham (Card Player); James C. Morton (Husband); Jules Cowles (Farmer); Frank Marlowe (Cameraman); Billy Watson (Boy); Brooks Benedict (Game Reporter); Marc Lawrence (Bookie's Doorman); Members of the Cincinnati Reds, the Chicago Cubs, and the St. Louis Cardinals (Themselves); and Gertrude Short, Ernie Alexander, Eddie Dunn, Walter Clinton, Wilbur Mack, Al Richmond, Larry Steers, Baldwin Cooke, Les Goodwin, Frank Layton, Ed Philips, William Griffith, and Louis Natheaux.

Someone is sabotaging the pennant chances of the St. Louis Cardinals. First, the pitchers' mitts are doctored with a skin damaging chemical. No sooner has this been dealt with than the Cardinals are plagued by a series of murders: catcher Dunk Spencer is shot to death while rounding third base, pitcher Frank Higgins is strangled in the locker room, and another catcher, hot dog fanatic Truck Hogan, is poisoned by a frankfurter laced with arsenic. Star pitcher Larry Kelly barely escapes death himself when shot at from a moving automobile. Kelly finds himself one of the murder suspects because he'd been Dunk Spencer's rival for the affections of team secretary Frances Clark, daughter of manager Pop Clark. Other suspects include shady businessman Henry Ainsley, who stands to obtain the St. Louis franchise should the Cards fail to win the pennant; gambler Joe Karnes, who's bet heavily against St. Louis and has already tried to bribe Kelly; and a couple of vengeful ex–Cards thrown off the team by Pop Clark for gambling. Before the killer is revealed, Larry Kelly, who has joined forces with sports reporter Jimmie Downey to solve the mystery, is very nearly blown to bits by a tiny bomb hidden in his uniform. It is then we learn that the murderer is the elderly groundskeeper in charge of stadium security, who is bitter over not having been appointed a Cardinals coach.

Little knowing that a poisoned hot dog will spell his doom, Nat Pendleton (right) describes his fatal frankfurter fascination to an exasperated Ted Healy in *Death on the Diamond*.

Murder mysteries abounded in the early days of talking pictures, simply because it was easier for the microphone to stay rooted in one place when all the suspects were gathered in a single room for the denouement. As talkies matured, so did the audiences; they grew weary of the same accusations of murder made by the same stiff, declamatory actors in the same dinner jackets. "Gimmick" mysteries began to pop up, with killings committed in exotic settings by unusual weaponry. And just to break the monotony of the standard private eye or city cop authority figure, many mysteries featured an amateur sleuth, usually a flippant reporter or an innocent bystander drawn into the intrigue and forced

to figure out the solution lest he or she be accused of murder or end up as the killer's next victim. Thus it was that *Death on the Diamond* was created not so much to capitalize on baseball as to provide a typical mystery programmer with a few fresh angles.

Some energetic game playing scenes (shot at L.A.'s old reliable Wrigley Field) aside, the baseball in this film is rather perfunctory. Leading man Robert Young, who was featured in nine pictures in 1934, hardly had the luxury of time to train for his role as an ace pitcher; in fact, he'd been a last-minute replacement for the original star, Franchot Tone. Accordingly, Young was doubled in most longshots. And although

MGM went to the expense of sending a second unit to St. Louis, headed by director John Waters (who later helmed an MGM short subject titled *Donkey Baseball*), to film background footage of real games, it is clear that Robert Young wasn't present for all those exterior shoots; whenever Young is seen pitching, he's always standing before the grainiest and most obvious of back-projection screens.

Still, *Death on the Diamond* works as a fast paced, satisfying whodunit. Director Edward Sedgwick displays the same love of and familiarity with baseball that was evident in his silent film ballpark endeavors *Hit and Run* (1924) and *Slide, Kelly, Slide* (1927), and in the brief "dream game" routine in Buster Keaton's *The Cameraman* (1928). The characters in *Diamond* are enacted with the usual MGM stock company efficiency, with some particularly choice work by Nat Pendleton and Ted Healy playing, respectively, a catcher and an umpire who are perpetually at each other's throats. For a comic usually associated with blunt, disagreeable roles, Ted Healy is surprisingly moving in a sobbingly emotional scene after his "friendly enemy" Pendleton is killed.

On a film history level, *Death on the Diamond* is a fascinating way station for several actors who would be seen again in baseball stories in later years. Walter Brennan, who went on to portray Lou Gehrig's reporter chum in *The Pride of the Yankees*, has an unbilled role in *Diamond* as a ratchet-voiced hot dog vendor; likewise uncredited in the role of a spectator is Herman Brix who, after changing his name to Bruce Bennett, essayed the memorable part of the terminally ill Pittsburgh Pirates veteran in *Angels in the Outfield* (1951). Cast as a St. Louis Cardinal is actor-stuntman Fred Graham, who would don a ballplayer's uniform in such later pictures as *Angels in the Outfield* and *The Pride of St. Louis* before becoming director of the Arizona Motion Picture Development office in Phoenix. And acting in

Death on the Diamond as a Cardinals coach is the ubiquitous Pat Flaherty, a professional ballplayer turned performer who graced a number of baseball epics before his death in 1970, among them *The Pride of St. Louis*, *It Happened in Flatbush*, *The Jackie Robinson Story*, *The Stratton Story* and *The Winning Team*. In 1948 Pat Flaherty was awarded with the credit of "technical advisor" on *The Babe Ruth Story*, which in retrospect seems about as much of a prize as that poisoned hot dog in *Death on the Diamond*.

Don't Look Back: The Story of Leroy "Satchel" Paige

TBA/Saties/Triseme Productions; originally telecast May 31, 1981

Executive producer: Danny Arnold. Produced by Stanley Rubin and Jimmy Hawkins. Associate producer: Robert Stevens. Directed by Richard A. Colla. Teleplay by Ronald Rubin, adapted from the book *Maybe I'll Pitch Forever* by Satchel Paige and David Lipman. Photography: Hector Figueroa. Additional photography: George Spiro Dibie. Edited by Bud S. Isaacs and LaReine Johnson. Music by Jack Elliot and Norman Gimbel; title song performed by Andrae Crouch. Art director: James D. Bissell. Set decorator: Jim T. Hassinger. Executive in charge of production: Jordan Davis. Production supervisor: Mark Bull. Production manager: Fred Slark. Assistant directors: Charles Washburn, John D. Benson, Ray Roman, and Roger Carlton. Production coordinator: Susan Whittaker. Painting of Satchel Paige by Ernie Barnes. Casting by Eleanor Ross. Technical consultant: Leroy "Satchel" Paige. Color by CFI. 98 minutes; sound.

Cast: Louis Gossett, Jr. (Leroy "Satchel" Paige); Beverly Todd (LaHoma Brown Paige); Cleavon Little (Rabbit Thompson); Ernie Barnes (Josh Gibson); Clifton Davis (Cool Papa Bell); Jim Davis (J. L. Wilkenson); Ossie Davis (Chuffy Russell); Taylor Lacher (J. B. Munger); John Beradino (Jake Wells); Hal Williams (Carl Roberts); Tommie Stewart (Mama Paige); J. R. Horne (Mr. Andrews); Donnie Walker (Sugar Boy Porter); Donald Blakely (Bartender); Candy

Ann Brown (Ramona); Gloria Gifford (Darlene); Leopoldo Mandeville (Chester); Earle Willoughby (Dizzy Dean); Colin LaFayette (Mrs. Parker); Milton Stafford (Young Satchel); James Unger (Wilson Paige); Lawrence Johnson (Judge); Bobby Angelle (Outfielder); Bubba Phillips (Coach Hardy); Jim B. Smith (White Batter); Satchel Paige (Himself, introducing the film).

Dirt poor Alabama boy Leroy Paige, nicknamed "Satchel" while working at the local depot toting satchels for the freight and mail trains, is sent to reform school in 1918 after robbing a toy store. While institutionalized, Satchel is encouraged by the school's athletic coach to develop his natural skill as a baseball pitcher, and once released, it's a logical hop to semipro ball. But Paige is black, it's the early 1920s, and the only teams that will hire him are the all-black teams which play throughout the South; whenever a white manager or scout is impressed by Paige's talent, the accolades always conclude with, "If only you were white." Satchel is lavishly praised by Dizzy Dean after the two play opposite each other in a black-white "all-star" exhibition game, but it's still the same old story so far as getting into the white majors is concerned. To make ends meet, Satchel barnstorms from team to team, taking advantage of the far from binding contracts in black baseball, and is feted as a hero while playing in Cuba and Trinidad. Paige's arm fails him in the mid–1930s, but he's given a second chance by the Kansas City Monarchs, and soon he's one of the highest paid black players in the country, pitching in exhibition games and in the Negro World Series in the best of the white ballparks. The matriculation of Jackie Robinson into mainstream ball in 1946 opens doors for other black players. In 1948 Satchel Paige is engaged by the Cleveland Indians, becoming the first black pitcher in the American League and attaining the title "Rookie of the Year" at the tender age of 42.

Don't Look Back, an "ABC Theatre"

TV movie, was based upon Satchel Paige's 1962 autobiography (as told to David Lipman), *Maybe I'll Pitch Forever* (the film's title was drawn from Paige's famous credo, "Don't look back—something may be gaining on you"). The book, written in a vernacular style with a plethora of double negatives and an Anglo-Saxonism or two, surprised many junior high school kids of the 1960s who'd bought it through their Scholastic book clubs and were unprepared for Paige's uncompromising view of what it was like to grow up black in the 1910s and 1920s, and of the rocky trail trodden by Negro baseball in the years before Jackie Robinson. Paige did nothing to make himself lovable, nor did he offer any excuses for his team hopping (which almost got him banned from playing professionally) or his party animal lifestyle; and he emphasized that he was no "boy" for white society, reminding the reader that he took every opportunity to stick it to the Man by taunting white players in the press and on the diamond, and by refusing to give autographs to whites who, but for Paige's celebrity status, would otherwise have given him the backs of their hands. Many of the stories in *Maybe I'll Pitch Forever* were restructured and fictionalized by William Brashler for his black baseball novel *The Bingo Long Travelling All-Stars and Motor Kings*; as mentioned in the notes on the film version of *Bingo Long*, Brashler's character Leon Carter was a Satchel Paige clone, right down to the injured arm at the end of the story.

With such surefire material, the life story of Satchel Paige should have made a crackerjack movie. Such was not the case with *Don't Look Back*. Instead of utilizing the honest human drama inherent in the source material, Ronald Rubin's teleplay pulls from thin air conflicts and crises which transform Paige's life story into an artifice-laden "movie of the week" melodrama.

Typical is the space given to Satchel's arm injury. One would think that this serious threat to Paige's career, and his subsequent recovery from this setback, would be sufficient dramatic material in itself. But the script hokes this all up by alleging that the injury coincided with Paige's "lifetime ban" from baseball, a ban imposed due to his defying his "ironclad contract" by playing in Trinidad (Paige was banned from time to time, true, but it was always hard to make things stick because there was no such thing as "ironclad" in the realm of black baseball contracts). Satchel thus can't get any sort of baseball job anywhere, and is compelled to beg a job from a manager who'd wronged the pitcher early in his career. After this imaginary character laughs in Paige's face, Satchel considers joining up with an old reform school buddy, now a prosperous criminal, as a "courier" for moonshine liquor. When J. L. Wilkenson (Jim Davis), white manager for the Kansas City Monarchs, seeks out Satchel to give him a second chance, he finds Paige humiliating himself as a freak attraction in a baseball circus. Given this chain of fabrications, one wonders why the film's producers bothered to engage the real Satchel Paige as technical consultant, since it's obvious that precious little consultation took place.

At other times the facts were toned down so much that the film came across like an installment of *The Andy Griffith Show*. It's no secret that Paige carried a lot of anger with him, nor was it any secret to Paige that white baseball was closed to him in the formative stages of his career. According to *Don't Look Back*, however, Paige is an easygoing fellow who is not galvanized into demonstrating his anger against the white establishment until urged to do so by an older black baseball "great" (well played by Ossie Davis), who has been forced to take a job washing dishes. And in an early scene, when a white manager (John Beradino) states flat out that no white team will hire Paige, Satchel's openmouthed reaction

implies that such a restriction had never occurred to him!

Weakest of all were the baseball scenes, especially the yawn-provoking sequence in the middle of the film depicting an exhibition game between Paige's and Dizzy Dean's "All-Stars." The editing looks like it has been accomplished with a vegetable slicer; the action always seems to be taking place just before the camera focuses on that action or just after there's a cutaway to something else. Adding insult to injury, there's a hopeless attempt at demonstrating the racism common in the mid–1930s by emphasizing the biased commentary of a "good ole boy" sportscaster (overacted to the rafters by Taylor Lacher) and by contriving such moments as Dean's teammates mocking their black opponents by rolling a watermelon onto the field—something that would hardly have occurred with any team commandeered by Dizzy Dean, who in real life admired Satchel Paige and who went on public record saying that it was ridiculous *not* to allow black players into the major leagues. The phoniness of this sequence was doubly obvious when *Don't Look Back* was first telecast on May 31, 1981— immediately following a repeat broadcast of *Roots: The Next Generation*, an unsparing view of black America that could never be accused of distorting the truth.

Due partly to legal complications, many of the colorful real-life personalities who helped shape Paige's life and career were sketchily portrayed in *Don't Look Back*, or were completely absent or represented by nondescript "composite characters." The viewer is treated to a reasonably three-dimensional portrayal of J. L. Wilkenson, the white owner of the Kansas City Monarchs who gave Paige a new lease on life after the pitcher's arm went temporarily bad. Otherwise, the film offers superficial characterizations of black baseball legends Josh Gibson and Cool Papa Bell, and of Dizzy Dean (who looks and pitches nothing at all like the real Dizzy), while other important personalities, such as the Cleveland Indians' Bill Veeck and Lou Boudreau, are reduced to unbilled bit parts. Where, however, was Alex Herman, who got Paige his first pro job with the Chattanooga Black Lookouts? Where was Bill Gatewood, who hired Satchel for his first living-wage engagement with the Birmingham Black Barons? Where was Gus Greenlee, the inimitable wheeling-dealing owner of the Pittsburgh Crawfords, with whom Paige perpetually locked horns due to the ballplayer's team defections and barnstorming? Where was Neil Churchill, the car agency manager who owned the Bismarck, North Dakota, team wherein Satchel played shoulder to shoulder with white players for the first time? And where, other than the walk-on character of Satchel's brother Wilson and the uncredited presence of three actresses portraying his sisters, were Paige's ten siblings?

Representative of the liberties taken with real-life characters is the teleplay's depiction of Paige's wife LaHoma, who is described in the film as the "special kind of woman" that "a traveling man has got to have." This would suggest that LaHoma was Paige's "special woman" during the barnstorming years, an impression the teleplay does nothing to dispel. In fact, we see Satchel proposing to LaHoma just after his comeback from his injury, which the film places around 1939. But Paige's wife during the 1930s was Janet Howard, a woman who eventually got fed up with her husband's peripatetic existence and ultimately broke up with him (this first marriage was alluded to in *Don't Look Back* with an easily lost throwaway line). Satchel didn't meet La-Homa Brown until 1942, by which time he'd settled down with a single team, the Kansas City Monarchs. And he didn't marry LaHoma until 1947, a year after his divorce from Janet Howard was final and one year before he made it to the big time as a member of the Cleveland Indians.

(Fortunately, many of the aforementioned inaccuracies would be avoided, and several previously deleted or downplayed characters restored to their rightful prominence, in the 1996 cable–TV movie *Soul of the Game* [q.v.], which dramatized the three-way race between Satchel Paige, Josh Gibson and Jackie Robinson to be first to break the Big League color barrier in the late 1940s.)

Brooklyn-born Louis Gossett, Jr., does a convincing job with Satchel's Alabama dialect, exhibits his customary thorough professionalism while portraying Paige at a variety of ages, and demonstrates a serviceable wind up and pitch in those very few scenes in which he was actually allowed to play baseball. But Gossett fights a losing battle with the pedestrian script and the by-the-numbers direction of Richard Colla. It's open to conjecture whether or not the film would have fared better under the guiding hand of its first director, George C. Scott; Scott walked away from the project while on location in Mississippi after making several pointed and obscene comments about working conditions and script deficiencies.

The best moment in *Don't Look Back* is the appearance in the prologue of the real Satchel Paige. Although he's confined to a rocking chair, there was a spark and authenticity in Satchel's brief scene that was noticeably lacking in the film that followed. And, as things turned out, the appearance had an element of poignancy; by 1982, one year after the film's telecast, Satchel Paige was dead at the reported age of 76.

Ed

Longview Entertainment/Universal; released March 15, 1996

Executive producers: Bill Finnegan, Bill Couturié, Brad Epstein. Produced by Rosalie Swedlin. Directed by Bill Couturié. Screenplay by David Mickey Evans. Story by Ken Richards and Janus Cercone. Photography: Alan Caso. Production designer: Curtis A. Schnell. Edited by Robert K. Lambert. Music composed and conducted by Stephen D. Endelman. Art Director: Michael L. Fox. Costume designer: Robin Lewis. Associate producers: Kathryn Couturié and Ned Gusick. Casting: Joseph Middleton, Shari Rhodes. Unit production manager: Richard Peter Schroer. First assistant director: Margaret E. Fannin. Second assistant director: Thomas Schellenberg. Second unit director/Visual effects supervisor: Robert H. Grasmere, Jr. Ed's special makeup created by Dave Nelson and Norman Tempia (of Animated Engineering). Set decorator: Crista Schneider. Storyboard artist: Tim Boxell. Camera operator: Rory Robert Knepp. Special effects coordinator: David Blitstein. Key costumer: Paul Carmen Viggiano. Key make-up artist: Dee Dee Altamura. Key hairstylist: Jill Crosby. Script supervisor: Martin Kitrosser. Stunt coordinator: Ernie Orsatti. Animated engineering staff: Dave Nelson, Norman Templa. Mechanical coordinator: Mecki Heussen. Hair department coordinator: Lynn Watson. Ed's tailor: James Hayes. Ed's contact lenses provided by Dr. Jonathan Gording. Baseball technical advisor/head baseball coach: Rod Dedeaux. Animal technical advisors: Dr. Roger S. Fouts, John Alexander. Animal trainers: Paul A. Calabria, Karen McElhatton, Sue Chipperton, Todd Forsberg. Foley artists: Margie O'Malley, Marne Moore. Special visual effects: VIFX. Digital effects coordinator: Gene Kozicki. Titles and opticals: Howard A. Anderson Co. Color by DeLuxe; Panavision. 94 minutes; DTS Stereo Sound. Rated PG.

Cast: Matt LeBlanc (Jack Cooper); Jayne Brook (Lydia); Jack Warden (Chubb); Bill Cobbs (Tipton); Patrick Kerr (Kirby "The Rug" Woods); Doren Fein (Liz); Charlie Schlatter (Buddy Halsten); Carl Anthony Payne II (Stats); James Caviezel (Dizzy Anderson); Mike McGlone (Barnett); Zacharias Ward (Dusty Richards); Philip Bruns (Clarence); Curt Kaplan (Randall "Zonk" Cszonka); Valente Rodriguez (Jesus Rodriguez); Jay Caputo, Denise Cheshire (Ed Sullivan); Gary Hecker (Voice of Ed Sullivan); Gene Ross (Red); Paul Hewitt (Bucky); Sage Allen (Cooper's Mother); Stan Ivar (Cooper's Father); Jim O'Heir (Art); Rick Johnson (Kurt "Crush" Binyon); Leonard Kelly-Young (Customer Joe); Troy Evans (Bus Driver); Mike McGlone (Oliver Barnett); Richard Gant (Umpire, Sharks Game); Bill Capizzi (Farley); Steve Eastin (Sharks' Manager); K.C. Corkery (Little Boy—banana toss); Jacquita Green (Little Girl); Ken Zavayna (Peanut Man); Kevin Kraft (Shortstop); Brad Hunt (Carnie); Mark Cassella (Security Guard); Joe Bucaro (Goon no. 1); Noon Orsatti (Goon no. 2); John-Clay Scott (Banana Truck Driver); Jessica Pennington (Nurse Rosa Cays); Tommy Lasorda (Himself); Mitchell Ryan (Abe Woods); Macka Foley (Umpire, Championship Game); Michael Chieffo (Dr. Middleton); Dave Nelson, Norman Tempia, Mecki Heussen, Timothy Ralson ("Ed" Puppeteers); Danny Rust, Lynn Salvatori, Dennis R. Scott, Eddie Yansick (Stunts).

Fresh from a farm in Oregon, gangly Jack "Deuce" Cooper is recruited as a pitcher by the Class-A Santa Rosa Rockets. Though he has a dynamite curve ball (during tryouts, he's clocked at 125 mph), the timid Jack invariably chokes on the pitching mound, forcing team manager Chubb to concoct a bizarre strategy aimed at teaching the young player to loosen up and enjoy himself. Chubb sends Jack to the bus depot to pick up a "rookie" named Ed—who turns out to be a chimpanzee, formerly owned by Mickey Mantle and purchased by the Rockets as a team mascot. It is embarrassing enough for Jack to baby-sit the capricious chimp; but when Chubb insists that Jack and Ed become roommates—and bedmates—it is misery unto eternity for the human half of the combination. Back on the ball field, a pop fly knocks out the Rockets' third baseman Dizzy Anderson. As a gag, Chubb sends Ed in as a replacement—whereupon the saucy simian proves to be a born baseball player, and an even faster pitcher than Jack! After carefully confirming that no rule presently exists barring "non–homo sapiens" from playing minor league baseball, Chubb puts Ed in a Rockets uniform, christens him with the last name of Sullivan (ouch!), and adds him to the starting lineup. Not only does this prove to be an excellent publicity ploy, but it also spurs the non-monkeys on the Rocket roster to play at peak level, and as a result the team sails effortlessly to the championship play-offs. Meanwhile, Jack's private life takes a turn for the better via his relationship with waitress Lydia, a relationship heartily encouraged and helped along by Lydia's precocious daughter Liz—and especially by Ed, who reveals himself to have the soul of a romantic despite his habit of plastering the walls with junk food, his volcanic flatulence and his scattershot bathroom skills. On the very eve of the championship clincher, Kirby Woods, the unscrupulous (and badly toupeed) son of the team's owner, sells Ed to a crooked contingent represented by a pair of electric prod–wielding pluguglies. Egged by Lydia and Liz, Jack steals Ed away from his sadistic keepers, and the two roomies make a daring getaway in a stolen van. As a result of a forced journey in the back of a truck carrying a cargo of frozen chocolate-covered bananas, Ed comes down with a bad case of the chills and is rushed to the hospital emergency ward. Jack and the rest of the Rockets vow to win the pennant-clincher as a tribute to Ed—who, happily, rallies just in time to witness the team's victory and Jack's triumph over his "stage fright" on the mound. And we know this all is *really* happening because Tommy Lasorda is in the grandstands.

There are certain films which automatically evoke a strong and sometimes loud reaction. While viewing *The Grapes of Wrath*, one may be moved to shout, "A pox upon those greedy capitalists who brought such shame and degradation upon the simple farming folk of Oklahoma!" While watching *Saving Private Ryan*, one is inspired to proclaim, "God bless the Greatest Generation who put their lives on the line to save us all from plunging into the abyss of fascism!" And upon seeing *Ed* for the very first time, one is prompted to stand up and bellow, "What the *hell* were they *thinking* of?"

As in the case of the 1988 disaster *The Slugger's Wife* (q.v.), *Ed* seemed to have all the "right" ingredients in place long before the first camera turned. The excellent financial returns of 1994's *Angels in the Outfield* (q.v.) had proven that baseball fantasies were viable box-office commodities. Screenwriter David Mickey Evans already had a winning ballpark epic under his belt with *The Sandlot* (q.v.). Director Bill Couturié had previously specialized in documentaries, but his credits within that genre—including the celebrated HBO feature *Dear America: Letters Home from Vietnam* (1989) and the Oscar- and Peabody Award–winning *Common Threads: Stories from the Quilt* (1989)—were impeccable. And last but far from least, the "human" star of the film was Matt LeBlanc, then a cast member of TV's most popular sitcom, *Friends*. How could *Ed* go wrong?

Let me count the ways.

To begin with, a fantasy film of *any* kind needs a foundation of credibility. Without offering an annotated list of examples, we need only cite such other baseball fantasies as *Angels in the Outfield*, *Little Big League* and *Rookie of the Year*. Fanciful though these films may have been, the filmmakers were careful to build in a basic believability so that the audience would not only accept the "fantastic" elements, but also root for, and empathize with, the main characters. *Ed*, however, hasn't a credible bone in its body. The baseball scenes are so gimmicked up with Hanna-Barbera–style sound effects and corny visuals that it is impossible to accept that the team members could get through nine innings of a kindergarten T-ball game, much less a Class-A championship race. And though we are supposed to accept without question that Jack Cooper (and, by extension Matt LeBlanc) is a phenomenal ballplayer, he is invariably filmed in extreme longshot, or from the back, when delivering one of his rocket pitches, invoking derisive cries of

"STUNT MAN! STUNT MAN!" from the less impressionable among us.

The acting is even less believable than the ballplaying, if such a thing is possible. An almost infallible tip-off that the film-makers either have contempt for their material or a very low opinion of the viewers' intelligence (or both) is the extent to which they will allow their actors to overact—or not act at all. In *Ed*, the most extreme end of the performing spectrum is represented by Patrick Kerr, who, as Kirby Woods, lets his "comic" villainy get so far out of hand that he makes the Big Bad Wolf look like Tom Hanks. Conversely, leading man Matt LeBlanc is so low-key that he practically vanishes before our eyes; if LeBlanc had hoped that this film would be his ticket to Big Screen stardom, it was fortunate indeed that he kept his day job (commented LeBlanc's *Friends* costar Matthew Perry, "I can joke with [Matt] about it because I read for *Ed* and didn't get it"). Even an accomplished veteran like Jack Warden is left floundering; by comparison, Tommy Lasorda's halting delivery of his single line, "Where is Ed the Chimp?" is worthy of an AFI Lifetime Achievement award.

Then there's Ed himself. The publicity people at Universal knocked themselves out with praise for the "genius" behind the animatronic puppetry, costuming, makeup work and acting that went into creating the film's chimpanzee protagonist. Dave Nelson and Norman Tempia of Animated Engineering were engaged to perform the same miracles that had distinguished their puppet-animation work in such earlier films as *Alien 3* and *Beethoven* to bring Ed to life. And in the scenes where a human performer was needed for smoother fluidity of movement or to express the subtler nuances of Ed's emotions, world-class gymnasts Jay Caputo and Denise Cheshire, who alternated in the "role" of Ed in the same manner that they'd previously portrayed anthropoids in films like *Congo* and *Gorillas in the Mist*,

were carefully coached in the intricacies of chimp behavior by John Alexander, an actor-stuntman whose own impressive resume of simian impersonations included such films as *Greystoke: The Legend of Tarzan*.

Yet, after all this hard work and effort, what emerged on screen was not nearly as convincing as that guy in the zippered gorilla suit who used to chase the Bowery Boys around all those haunted houses. Ed locks Jack out of his car and laughs about it. Ed points to his crotch when it's bathroom time, then sprays the toilet with air freshener. Ed switches the TV remote with his foot, exulting over finding a channel running *King Kong*, expressing dismay when he happens upon a scene with Maurice the Monkey in the TV show *Friends* (Get it, folks? Matt LeBlanc is in *Friends* too! Ha-ha-ha!), and humming—yes, humming—along with the National Anthem. Ed cleans up the kitchen with scrub-brushes on his hands and feet, to the tune of "Yackety-Yack." Ed puts on funny costumes and imitates Jim Carrey and Madonna. Ed engages a human child in a "fart-noise" contest. And Ed plays baseball, not "clown" baseball but genuine baseball; his third-base prowess, noted critic Mike Clark, "suggests a greatest hits video of Brooks Robinson and Graig Nettles combined."

This we wouldn't be able to swallow even if the special effects were good. But all this artifice might have at least been more amusing if, somehow, the filmmakers had been able to use a *genuine* chimpanzee to play Ed. Like it or not, chimps are sure-fire laugh-getters, especially when behaving in a human fashion, and most especially in PG-rated films targeted primarily at nine- to thirteen-year-olds. Chances are, however, that the sizable roster of "primate behavior" experts hired by the producers would have turned their opposable thumbs down at the use of a real chimp. Particularly the film's principal technical advisor, Dr. Roger Fouts, director of the Chimpanzee and

Human Communication Institute, who neatly laid out his own personal agenda by stating, "Chimps are persons. Ed is a non-human being. We call ourselves human beings, but the important essence of us is our being-ness. It's not the human part, so much. That's just an adjective that describes the noun." Uh-oh.

But let's get back to the cardinal rule in any baseball fantasy: that is, to at the *very* least establish a semblance of logic within its own boundaries. The examples of how this rule is defiantly ignored in *Ed* would tax the memory banks of even the most sophisticated word processor, so we'll merely pass along the three most glaring:

Coach Chubb wants Jack Cooper to loosen up, have fun, and gain a bit more confidence in himself. So he insists that Jack shack up with a chimpanzee who can play baseball infinitely better than practically anyone on the team. Oh, absolutely! There's nothing that will build up an ego quicker than the realization that you're being outclassed by a monkey.

Kirby Woods sells Ed to another team. Legally. So why does Kirby feel the need to have Ed kidnapped under cover of darkness and bundled into a truck?

And in the final sequence, when Ed

Ed: No Comment.

the Chimp is suffering from severe frostbite after a bumpy ride in a freezer truck, why is he rushed to the intensive-care unit of a *human* hospital?

But is it funny? Yeah, it's funny, if you enjoy being told ten times over what you've just seen; screenwriter Evans' repetitious grasp of the obvious, a minor irritant in *The Sandlot*, graduates to Fatal Flaw status in *Ed*. One example among many: When the velocity of Ed's pitches is demonstrated by the time-honored slapstick gag of the burning catcher's mitt, the catcher holds his smoking glove up to the camera *twice*, in closeup and medium shot, then laboriously wanders amongst his fellow players to show them what Ed has done to his mitt—and what started out as a mere throwaway gag is bloated into a Stanley Kubrick production. If the brief "Gates of Oz" bit from *Rookie of the Year* (q.v.) had been used in *Ed*, we would have undoubtedly endured a full orchestral rendition of "Ding Dong the Witch Is Dead" and a longshot of someone skywriting "Surrender Dorothy."

And don't get us started on the film's overabundance of "product placement." We will merely note in passing that even the cap Jack Cooper wears while relaxing at home is emblazoned with a "John Deere" logo.

Critical response to *Ed* was overwhelmingly unanimous: The film reeked worse than Jack Cooper's bathroom after Ed got through with it. Here's Mike Clark of *USA Today*: "Put an infinite number of monkeys in front of an infinite number of word processors, and one of them may indeed write *War and Peace*.... But more likely, they'll come up with something like David Mickey Evans' screenplay for *Ed* (*½ out of four), which certainly pulls its weight in contributing to one of the dopiest baseball pics ever (with or without a simian co-star)." Marshall Fine of the *Detroit News*, grouping *Ed* together with several other misfire films featuring popular TV personalities, observed that, "Adam Sandler's *Happy Gilmore* keeps looking better and better in comparison." And freelance Internet critic Sean Means opined that, "*Ed* is the movie equivalent of lawn darts. It's not merely awful, but it could be hazardous to a child's mental health."

Reaping an embarrassing $6 million at the box office, *Ed* is not likely to inflict any further damage on the mental stability of children or the future of the motion picture industry. *Ed* has, however, become the bane of motion picture historians, who since the film's release have been forced to revise their heretofore cast-in-stone consensus that *The Babe Ruth Story* was the worst baseball film ever made.

Eight Men Out

Black Sox, Inc./Orion Pictures; released September 1988

Produced by Sarah Pillsbury and Midge Sanford. Executive producers: Barbara Boyle and Jerry Offsay. Written and directed by John Sayles. Screenplay adapted from the book by Eliot Asinof. Photography: Robert Richardson. Edited by John Tintori. Production design by Nora Chavooshian. Costumes by Synthia Flint. Art director: Dan Bishop. Set decoration by Lynn Wolverton. Production supervisor: Mary Feldbauer Janson. Production coordinator: Heidi Vogel. Production manager and coproducer: Peggy Rajski. Music by Marion Darling. Musical arrangements by Billy Novick and Martin Brody. Song "I Be Blue" by John Sayles and Marion Darling, sung by Leigh Harris. Other musical performers: Billy Novick, Peter Ecklund, Butch Thompson, Art Boron, Robert Verdier, Bill Reynolds, Stu Gunn, and Jim Mazzy. Soundtrack available on Varege Sarabande. Sound by David Brownlow. Baseball training by Ken Berry. Assistant director: Gerry Marcus. Casting by Barbara Shapiro, Carrie Frazier, Shari Gilbert, and Avy Kaufman. Color by Technicolor. 120 minutes; sound. Rated PG.

Cast: John Cusack (Buck Weaver); Clifton James (Charles Comiskey); Michael Lerner (Arnold Rothstein); Christopher Lloyd (Bill Burns); John Mahoney (Kid Gleason); Charlie Sheen (Happy Felsch); David Strathairn (Eddie Cicotte); D. B. Sweeney (Joe Jackson); Michael Rooker (Chick Gandil); Don Harvey (Swede Risberg); James Read (Lefty Williams); Perry Lang (Fred McMullin); Gordon Clapp (Ray Schalk); Jace Alexander (Dickie Kerr); Bill Irwin (Eddie Collins); Richard Edson (Billy Maharg); Kevin Tighe (Sport Sullivan); Michael Mantell (Abe Attell); Studs Terkel (Hugh Fullerton); John Anderson (Judge Kenesaw Mountain Landis); Maggie Renzi (Rose Cicotte); John Sayles (Ring Lardner); Barbara Garrick (Helen Weaver); Wendy Makkena (Kate Jackson); Nancy Travis

(Lyra Williams); Jim Desmond (Smitty); Eliot Asinof (John Heydler); Clyde Bassett (Ban Johnson); John D. Craig (Rothstein's Lawyer); Michael Laskin (Alfred Austrian); Randle Weil (Ahern); Robert Motz (District Attorney); Bill Raymond (Ben Short); Brad Garrett (Peewee); Tay Strathairn (Bucky); Jess Vincent (Scooter); Ken Berry (Heckler); Merritt Holzman (Grubner); Josh Thompson (Winslow); Leigh Harris (Blues Singer); Philip Murphy (Jimmy); Stephen Mendillo (Monk Eastman); Dick Cusack (Judge Friend); Jack George, Tom Surber, Tom Ledcke, David Carpenter, Bart Hatch (Fans); Jerry Brent, Bruce Schumacher, Robert Walsh, Matthew Harrington, Richard Lynch, Garry Williams, Michael Harris (Writers); David Rice (A Fan); Tom Marshall (Browns Umpire); Julie Whitney, Dana Roi (Girls in Bar); J. Dennis Newman (Reds Player); Charles Siebert, II (Ivy Wingo, Reds Catcher); Jim Martindale (Cincinnati Umpire); Bill Jennings (Chicago Umpire); David Hinman (Announcer); Dayton Stone (Hired Killer); Patrick Grant (Irish Tenor); Tim Laughter (Gambling Man); Brad Armacost (Attendant); Jim Stark, Brad Griffith, Steve Salge (Reporters at Trial); Eaton Randles (Court Clerk); Max Chiddester (Nash); Rick Komenich (Jury Foreman); Patrick Brown, John Greisemer, Charles Yankoglu, Michael Preston (New Jersey Fans).

The Chicago White Sox are heavily favored in the 1919 World Series between the Sox and the Cincinnati Redlegs, a fact that two gamblers, Bill Burns and Billy Maharg, hope to exploit. Burns and Maharg approach several Chicago players, offering them $10,000 apiece to throw the series. White Sox first baseman Chick Gandil acts as liaison for the gamblers, involving six other players in the conspiracy, many of these players disgruntled by the low salaries levied by team owner Charles Comiskey. Third baseman Buck Weaver knows about the plot and keeps mum about it, but refuses to cheat or to accept any money. Burns and Maharg arrange financing of the scheme with "king of the gamblers" Arnold Rothstein; and on October 1, at the beginning of Game One, pitcher Eddie Cicotte "accidentally" tosses a ball that hits the back of Redlegs batter Morrie Rath, the signal to Rothstein and company that the fix is on.

The Sox play is so appalling that it is apparent to several people—including team manager Kid Gleason and newspaper reporters Ring Lardner and Hugh Fullerton—that something is amiss. As the series progresses, a few of the conspirators seem be to playing to win—notably Joe Jackson, who'd been sucked into the scheme because he wanted to be on the good side of his buddies, and Fred McMullen, who had threatened to blow the whistle if he wasn't cut in on the deal, but who never promised to cheat. Meanwhile, Burns and Maharg realize that the promised $10,000 per player will not be forthcoming from Rothstein no matter who wins. By Game Six, insecurity has set in, with no one knowing precisely who's still in on the fix and who isn't; Sox pitcher Lefty Williams, at first happily a part of the deal, has to be forced virtually at gunpoint to go through with the plan. Cincinnati "wins" the series four games to two, but Hugh Fullerton, dissatisfied with the results, begins a press campaign to uncover what he's certain was a sellout.

Once it becomes inevitable that eight members of the White Sox (including Buck Weaver, whose presence at the conspirators' meetings is regarded as complicity) will be brought to trial, Charles Comiskey desperately tries to save himself and the lucrative baseball industry. The owner is convinced by his lawyers to go through the motions of conducting an internal investigation while a cover-up is arranged. To assure the outside world that everything is on the square, the baseball leagues appoint "hanging judge" Kenesaw Mountain Landis as commissioner for life; by having a non-baseball man with a spotless reputation as the official head of the Sox investigation, there can't be anything dishonest going on. What Landis doesn't know is that there is already another conspiracy in the making.

In order to bring gambler Bill Burns into court, the grand jury must obtain some ballplayers' confessions. Sox members Eddie Cicotte, Lefty Williams, and Joe Jackson are convinced to sign written confessions by being promised immunity during the trial. But once Burns has been subpoenaed, the confessions mysteriously vanish—the handiwork of Arnold Rothstein, who is acting in concert with "interested parties" to remove all hard evidence that might lead to the three confessing players pointing their fingers at any of the other conspirators in court. With no written proof of wrongdoing, the trial jury finds the eight Sox players not guilty. But Judge Landis issues a statement to the press that, regardless of the verdict, none of the "Black Sox" will ever play professional ball again. The judge keeps that promise, barring even Buck Weaver, who till the end of his days tries fruitlessly to arrange a hearing that will clear his name.

It can be said without exaggeration that the 1988 film version of *Eight Men Out* was nearly thirty years in the making. The project was born in 1959 when Eliot Asinof, a onetime farm club player with several novels and baseball poems to his credit, was engaged by TV producer David Susskind to dramatize the Black Sox scandal for a *DuPont Show of the Month* special. Asinof was aware of an earlier book on the subject by James T. Farrell (of *Studs Lonigan* fame); Farrell himself dismissed his book as "lousy" but was willing to let it be used as a principal source, further allowing Asinof access to Farrell's unpublished notes. David Susskind's *DuPont* special was never produced, due to the intervention of baseball commissioner Ford Frick, who felt that dredging up the old scandal wasn't in the best interests of the game. But Eliot Asinof was hooked, and resolved in 1960 to dig deeper into the Black Sox.

The writer decided to interview as many of the surviving participants and witnesses to the fix as possible. Of the eight disgraced players, Joe Jackson, Buck Weaver, Fred McMullen, and Lefty Williams were dead. This left Chick Gandil, who quit the game on his own before being banned and moved to California, where he went into several businesses; Happy Felsch, who'd opened a tavern bearing his name in Milwaukee, Wisconsin; Eddie Cicotte, who was a retired Michigan game warden; and Swede Risberg, who'd taken up farming in Minnesota and tavern keeping in Oregon. It was well known in journalism circles that these men had formed a wall of silence surrounding the scandal, though Happy Felsch was coddled and flattered into cooperating a bit for *Eight Men Out*. Asinof found just as many doors closed by the innocent survivors as by the culprits; Ray Schalk, one of the honest Sox players who in the early 1960s was head baseball coach at Purdue, kicked Asinof out of his office the very moment the subject of the fix was brought up. The writer learned that this no comment (or, at best, guarded comment) policy was borne of fear of repercussions from the gambling community as much as from shame or anger. "I was told by more than one ballplayer," Asinof noted, "that it was safer to keep one's mouth shut about this whole affair."

At least one witness was eager and willing to keep his mouth open. Asinof's most valuable source turned out to be Judge Hugo Friend, whose very first case on the bench had been the Black Sox trial. Friend greeted the writer by saying, "I've been waiting for you for forty years." The jurist had always been plagued by the "lost" written confessions, which through their absence allowed the eight players to be acquitted and which kept Comiskey's White Sox—and, by extension, the rest of baseball—from collapsing under the weight of corruption. It wasn't until Asinof was doing general research on a lawsuit brought in 1924 by Joe Jackson against Charles Comiskey over withheld salary payments that the writer found the clue to the cover-up. As a strategy to discredit Jackson's lawsuit, the player's missing confession magically reappeared and Jackson—who'd testified under oath during the 1924 litigation that he was innocent of game-fixing—was fined for perjury, ultimately receiving only a fraction of the money Comiskey owed him. As Judge Friend observed to Asinof concerning the lost grand jury papers, "There had to be a meeting." Asinof now had reasonable proof of that meeting, and from this he pieced together the collusion between the good-guy baseball owners and the bad-guy gamblers which resulted in the outcome of the Black Sox trial.

After *Eight Men Out* hit the stands, a few Hollywood producers evinced interest—albeit cautiously, since baseball was still considered sacrosanct (and unprofitable) as a movie subject. 20th Century–Fox's plans to film *Eight Men Out* were scotched by a $2 million lawsuit filed by the representatives of onetime Cincinnati player Dutch Ruether; Asinof had repeated in print Ring Lardner's allegation that Ruether had been drinking before the first game of the series. Other potential movie deals were warded off when David Susskind sued Eliot Asinof for not accepting $20,000 to give authorization for Susskind's own adaptation of Asinof's original 1959 teleplay, which the writer felt that Susskind had falsified in the rewriting process.

We now fly past the 1960s to land in 1977. John Sayles, a young actor, screenwriter and novelist with aspirations to direct films, has penned his own screenplay adaptation of the Asinof book (Sayles's first novel, *Pride of the Bimbos*, had been a baseball yarn). No rights have been given or implied by Asinof; Sayles has written the script simply to provide Hollywood higher-ups with a sample of his work. In 1980, Sayles learns that producers Sarah Pillsbury and Midge Sanford have optioned *Eight Men Out*. Rather than fight over the project, Sayles suggests to Pillsbury and Sanford that they pool their resources and work as partners on the proposed film. It would take several years for Sayles and Pillsbury/Sanford to sufficiently secure their reputations—Sayles for such critical successes as *Return of the Secaucus Seven* and *Brother from Another Planet*, the producers for their 1985 project *River's Edge*—before a major movie company would consider releasing *Eight Men Out*. That company was Orion, a relatively new firm with a record of backing "iffy" films and filmmakers.

Part of the Orion deal involved Sayles's casting choices. Previously, the director had relied on a solid stock company of old friends, such as David Strathairn and Maggie Renzi, who could do ensemble work without expecting star treatment, an important requirement for the multicharacter *Eight Men Out*. Orion agreed that the director's favorites could be cast in the new film, but that a few mutually agreed upon "box office" performers would also have to be selected. Sayles obligingly hired John Cusack, an audience pleaser since *The Sure Thing* (1984), as Buck Weaver, and D. B. Sweeney, who'd recently earned plaudits for his role as a gung ho Vietnam-era American soldier in Francis Ford Coppola's *Gardens of Stone* (1987), as "Shoeless Joe" Jackson. The casting of these two actors was beneficial to Sayles's love of authenticity; Cusack was pretty impressive around a softball field, while Sweeney had actually played minor-league ball with the Kenosha Twins before being benched by a knee injury.

Though John Cusack received top billing, the biggest "name" on the film was Charlie Sheen, fresh from his triumph in the Oscar-winning *Platoon* (1986). Oddly, Sheen got his crack at *Eight Men Out* not through the producers seeking him out but through his seeking them out. Sheen had run into D. B. Sweeney at a New York bar, learned about the film, and called Pillsbury/Sanford to offer his services. "It gave me two things that were important to me at that point," the actor explained later. "Being part of an ensemble and having the chance to play ball." Charlie Sheen had nurtured big-league aspirations since his days at the Mickey Owen baseball camp and at Santa Monica High School; he had even been seriously scouted by the majors, despite his comparatively short stature (for more on the actor's ballfield prowess, see the notes on *Major League*). Sheen could have demanded a starring part, but willingly took the smaller role of Happy Felsch just to be in on Sayles' project and to get a little baseball workout in the bargain.

The rest of the cast was a mixture of established players with audience recognition value, and those hired on the basis of their baseball skill, their physical resemblance to their real-life counterparts, or their knowledge of the actual events. Veteran character actors Christopher Lloyd, Kevin Tighe, Clifton James, John Mahoney, and John Anderson were enlisted to inhabit the bodies and psyches of Bill Burns, "Sport" Sullivan (a high-rolling gambler who was brought into the scheme to attract Arnold Rothstein), Charles Comiskey, Kid Gleason and Judge Landis. While there was the occasional scenery chewing (most notably from Tighe and Anderson), all of these old pros understood that their parts were mere cogs in the wheel of the action, rather than the wheel itself. John Sayles pulled David Strathairn, Gordon Clapp, and Jace Alexander from his pool of "regulars" to portray Sox members Eddie Cicotte, Ray Schalk, and Dickie Kerr respectively, because the director was already acquainted with the trio's above-average athletic abilities. Bill Irwin, a mime artist, had been spotted by Sayles in Irwin's one-man stage show *The Regard of Flight*, and was chosen on the basis of his remarkable body control for the part of second baseman Eddie

Collins (unfortunately, Irwin provided one of the film's few authenticity gaps by batting right-handed instead of left, as Collins had).

From the ranks of baseball-savvy non-actors, Sayles hired Chicago journalist-raconteur Studs Terkel to play disillusioned sports reporter Hugh Fullerton; Terkel welcomed the opportunity to appear in a film that portrayed baseball club owners as craven, covetous, and double-dealing, at a time when Studs felt that fans of the game were misdirecting their resentment for higher ticket prices to the salary demands of the players. The part of John Heydler, National League president in 1919, was essayed by none other than *Eight Men Out* author Eliot Asinof. And in keeping with his policy of reserving a plum part for himself in each of his films, John Sayles transformed himself before the cameras into the living image of the saturnine, sardonic Ring Lardner—a bit of self-indulgence that won the approval of Lardner's son John.

To achieve the proper balance of grandstanding and teamwork necessary to recreate the 1919 Series competitors, John Sayles hired Ken Berry, who in a fourteen-year career amassed a lifetime batting average of .255 and coached for the Yankees and the Royals, to act as drill instructor to the performers cast as ballplayers (Berry can be seen as the man heckling Joe Jackson in the film's opening sequence). The regimen established by Berry was so severe that Charlie Sheen had to sneak off to smoke cigarettes for fear of being caught breaking training. Ken Berry's ersatz White Sox and Redlegs performed admirably, though Eliot Asinof observed that the actors were all slower in their movements than actual big leaguers.

For all his experience, Ken Berry was still a child of the present. John Sayles wanted his team to play ball as if they were performing in 1919. To that end, he engaged a leather goods manufacturer in Indiana (where the film's game scenes were shot) to

Kid Gleason (John Mahoney, second from right) forgets his suspicions long enough to celebrate a deceptive White Sox victory during the 1919 series in *Eight Men Out*.

assemble the sort of stiff, uncomfortable gloves that were used during the 1919 Series. The bats were similarly built in the style of the period at Sayles' behest, a task made easier due to the fact that the Louisville Slugger company had kept specification charts on their 1919 product.

Sayles also had his actors watch videotapes of old sports newsreels, as well as several screenings of the 1941 James Cagney boxing picture, *City for Conquest*. The director wanted his performers to not only move and play like the ballplayers of old, but to emulate the staccato speech patterns and carefree word choices used by athletes in the days before TV and radio had made people self-conscious about their voices and wary of making promises to "murder" the opposition which might prove embarrassingly inaccurate when played back on the six o'clock news.

All World Series games were filmed at

Bush Stadium in Indianapolis, home of that city's Triple-A Indians, which was built in 1931 and had the proper old-time dimensions and ambience necessary for Sayles' period piece. To pass for Cincinnati's long-gone Redland Field, Bush Stadium's light poles were camouflaged and a crane was brought in to put up old-fashioned billboards advertising Cincinnati-based enterprises. These placards were later taken down and replaced with Chicago business ads when Bush was reconverted into Comiskey Park. (Although the original Comiskey Park was still standing in 1987 and '88, Chicago's show business unions are rather insistent upon being paid scale wages; Indianapolis is an "open shop" so far as moviemaking is concerned.) *Eight Men Out* represented the very first instance that Bush Stadium, owned by the city of Indianapolis, had ever featured commercial billboards in its backfield.

An appeal went out for Indianapolis citizens to fill the stadium as extras, but save for the high school girls who showed up to ogle John Cusack and Charlie Sheen, surprisingly few people were interested in becoming movie stars for the day. To compensate for the empty seats, several life-size cardboard likenesses of the movie's location manager Paul Marcus were provided by the property crew; whenever an assistant director happened upon an unoccupied chair, the call went out for "another Paul Marcus."

The filming did attract a number of interested onlookers. Carl Erskine of the old Brooklyn Dodgers, retired and living in the nearby Indiana town of Anderson, showed up to check the accuracy of the film with a facsimile of the 1919 Series scorecard. Paul Barley, a man in his eighties who was so rabid a Sox fan that he'd kept a detailed scrapbook of the 1919 team, was enlisted among the extras, appearing in every crowd scene in the film. And a representative of the baseball museum in Cooperstown flew in to claim the replica of Joe Jackson's bat (the "Black Betsy") for a new Cooperstown exhibit of baseball movie memorabilia, which—as writer Charles Siebert II (cast in the film as Reds catcher Ivy Wingo) noted in an article for *Esquire* magazine—may be the only way that Shoeless Joe will ever get anywhere near the Baseball Hall of Fame.

Another visitor to the set illustrated rather dolefully John Sayles's assessment of the Black Sox scandal as one that, through its proof that "America's game, which was supposed to be pure and white ... could be corrupted," tainted the lives of the innocent as well as the guilty. The Cincinnati Reds, robbed of a clear win, were understandably oversensitized by the event, and many Reds players would be compelled to spend the rest of their lives declaring that they would have won without the fix. One such player was Edd Roush, whose protes-

tations over the years had (correctly or incorrectly) given him the public image of a man grasping at straws. Roush came to watch the filming of *Eight Men Out* one day; he talked to John Sayles for a brief time, never leaving his car, then was driven away. He died six months after filming had ended, at the age of 94, still firm in his belief that Cincinnati had what it took to win the 1919 Series honestly.

Sayles would have preferred a lengthier shooting schedule and a $20 million budget, but by the time he called a wrap he'd finished the whole thing in near record time for about $6 million. That *Eight Men Out* is as meticulous in its period detail as a multimillion-dollar epic (maybe more so than most epics) can be attributed not only to Sayles's know-how in using camera setups that hid all traces of 1988, but to the excellent production design of Nora Chavooshian and the costume work by Synthia Flint who, after toiling on the director's previous historical film, a tale of the 1920s coal-mining labor troubles titled *Matewan* (1987), were well versed in the art of achieving an A-picture look with TV-movie resources. Mention must also be made of the cinematography; Robert Richardson's use of soft focus and muted color is as richly evocative of the post–World War I era as a hand-tinted family photograph.

From a baseball game standpoint, *Eight Men Out* cannot be faulted; even those plays that have to be enhanced with dexterous editing techniques are so thoroughly convincing that at times we're hoping one or two of the Sox will relent long enough to win the series and not toss their futures away. The only sequences that might raise skepticism in the casual viewer are those in which the conspirators lose with such amateurishness, yet these moments are staged almost exactly as they happened.

Eight Men Out scores equally well in the accuracy department outside the Series scenes. Occasionally, events have been rearranged, but it's all for the good of the narrative. When the illiterate Joe Jackson, invited by a heckler to spell "cat," responds by asking the wiseacre to spell "shit," it is acceptable dramatic license to move this true-life event, which occurred around 1910, into one of the pennant race games of 1919, since the sequence establishes that Jackson will be unable to read the confession he's asked to sign later in the story. Similarly, the 1917 incident of Eddie Cicotte being deliberately benched by Charles Comiskey so that Cicotte would not be able to play thirty games and thus be eligible for a promised bonus is transposed to 1919 to give Cicotte a more immediate motivation for agreeing to the fix.

Some elements of the story that a viewer unfamiliar with the scandal might take to be Sayles's invention actually *did* happen. For example, Ring Lardner really did voice his suspicions by publicly singing a drunken chorus of "I'm Forever Blowing Bubbles," substituting the word "ballgames" for "bubbles." And as for that little boy's plaintive, "Say it ain't so, Joe," delivered outside the courtroom to a chastened Joe Jackson; well, maybe the actual remark was, "It ain't true, is it, Joe?" And maybe the whole thing never happened at all. But John Ford once made a movie in which somebody said that when the legend becomes the fact, print the legend. In this instance the legend *has* to be there. The audience would probably have shouted rude things at the screen if it hadn't been there.

Most importantly, the film's veracity is strengthened by John Sayles' refusal to present the characters in terms of black and white. "Good" characters like Buck Weaver are painted with as much three-dimensionality as "bad" ones like Arnold Rothstein. We can't totally like the honest players like Dickie Kerr because they come across as sanctimonious, nor can we thoroughly hate people like Charles Comiskey because they are shown to be as full of human frailties

and weaknesses as anyone. Many viewers feel that *Eight Men Out* is a plea for exoneration of victims of circumstance, like Buck Weaver, and victims of gullibility, like Joe Jackson. It is more an illustration of how some people can become so trapped by their character shortcomings (Weaver's unwillingness to expose what he knows is a con, Jackson's taking the fix money to be "one of the guys") that they'd eventually be losers even if events hadn't caught up with them; and no amount of public exoneration would ever change that.

So much for the good stuff. Now we've got to find something to pick on.

John Sayles had wanted to emulate the style of Eliot Asinof's book—that of a mosaic, in which each player, each owner, each gambler, each fan is but a small particle in a larger picture. As a result, *Eight Men Out* is a complex, complicated film, with the story's focus hopping from person to person, event to event, city to city with such rapidity that many viewers are left exhausted—and unsatisfied. The problem has been pinpointed by several critics as a lack of focus, the complaint being that in trying to tell everyone's story, the viewer is left with no one story to hold on to, and ends up watching with detachment rather than empathy.

Actually, that isn't the real problem. Sayles is perfectly capable of evenly balancing the various events leading up to and following the fix by exercising his screenwriters' tools of story structure and economy. He establishes the relationship between the gamblers and the players early on by having the gamblers' expository dialogue during a Sox game "introduce" each player to the audience, letting us know which players are corruptible and which aren't. The familiar device of counterpointing Charles Comiskey's expansiveness with reporters and his stinginess with his players is dusted off and successfully staged. The Sox fans' reactions throughout the film are reflected through the Greek chorus–like presence of a group of kids who follow the games, carry on conversations with Buck Weaver on the street, and are more demonstrative than their elders in conveying first disbelief then disillusionment when confronted by the facts. The mechanics of the fix are confined for the most part to a single scene set in a nightclub, where gamblers and ballplayers would logically congregate after a pennant win. And the combination of cross-purposes and intertwining interests involving players, owners, and gamblers is conveyed by a superbly timed sequence set in a hotel lobby, with characters representing varying degrees of honesty and suspicion popping in and out of rooms, following each other around, avoiding one another, and abruptly ending conversations with angrily slammed doors. In this last sequence especially, Sayles is able to create a sense of everything happening at once, yet still manages to keep people and events clearly delineated.

Had this balance been maintained for the rest of the film, there wouldn't have been a problem. The difficulty arises whenever Sayles pauses to allow an individual story to dominate the action. For a while, Buck Weaver's bouts with his conscience seem to be carrying the ball. Just when we've gotten used to Weaver, however, we're asked to care about Eddie Cicotte and his family; and no sooner have we accepted Cicotte as the major figure than we've bounced over to another set of events. Ring Lardner and Hugh Fullerton are fun to watch whenever making their sideline quips about the players' blatant dishonesty, but as the story winds down, the pair of journalists have turned into Woodward and Bernstein, facing public scorn as they doggedly pursue the miscreants with their typewriters. Is the story to be told from the viewpoint of Lardner and Fullerton, then? No; just when we've established the writers as the heroes, they're shunted to the background and the trial takes over. As for following the film through the eyes of the gamblers (who,

after all, introduced the story in the opening scene), once it's established that they're off to various corners of America (and the world) to avoid arrest, they're summarily dropped. John Sayles would have been more successful maintaining balance by spending *less* time exploring some of these characters than by stopping and lavishing lopsided concentration upon them. Though Sayles may have been trying for an ensemble feel, it seems at times as though the director was casting about for a central character but never found one.

On the other hand, it can be just as lopsided not to spend *enough* time on certain people. Viewers who knew of the Black Sox scandal only in conjunction with the name of Shoeless Joe Jackson were surprised to discover that, except for a scene here and there, Jackson was little more than a supporting character in this film. This would have been easy to accept if Sayles hadn't decided to end the film with a scene of Jackson playing in a Hoboken sandlot team under an alias; and then freeze-framing on Jackson's exultant expression after he's scored a home run. Since we've never gotten to know this character, what are we supposed to feel when we see this final image? Sorrow for a career cut short, outrage that he's been reduced to sandlots through the machinations of others, happiness that at last he's playing baseball for fun rather than greed, or all of the above? Moviegoers who'd been led down several plot paths throughout the film weren't altogether pleased when the paths led to the house of a virtual stranger. Perhaps a more appropriate final image would have been a close-up of Buck Weaver, who is present at Jackson's Hoboken game as an anonymous spectator. Weaver's facial expression, combining admiration over Jackson's undiminished skill and disgust at the way things have turned out, would seem to sum up the tragedy of *Eight Men Out* far better than Jackson's silly grin.

Perhaps, however, this final shot was

another of John Sayles's indications that there weren't any clear-cut issues in the Black Sox case. The director could have performed the obvious by freeze-framing on Weaver, but by closing on Jackson he seemed to be reiterating that the story was bigger and more complex than any one major or minor character. Let's take this point further: Maybe the moments of imbalance in the story were Sayles' way of keeping the audience off balance, and thus aware that if one missed a single tiny element of the story, one might be missing everything. That's as clever a way as any of sustaining audience interest in a seventy-year-old story without a single hero for 120 minutes.

Of the four major-studio baseball pictures released in 1988 and 1989, *Eight Men Out* was the least successful financially, posting a domestic gross of only $5,680,000. This lessens its genuine artistic value not one iota, but at the time it tended to discourage filmmakers who might have wanted to buck tradition by exploring baseball's darker side. It's important to remember, however, that *Eight Men Out*, after a quarter of a century of setbacks and false starts, and despite a 1988 motion-picture economy geared to blockbusters, sequels, and aggressively happy endings, finally *did* get on the screen; and this is very encouraging information indeed for any *future* filmmaker.

Elmer the Great

First National [Warner Bros.]; released April 29, 1933

Produced by Raymond Griffith. Directed by Mervyn LeRoy. Screenplay by Tom Geraghty, from the play by Ring Lardner and George M. Cohan. Photography: Arthur Todd. Edited by Thomas Pratt. Art director: Thomas Haas. Musical director: Leo Forbstein. Gowns by Orry-Kelly. 72 minutes; black and white; sound.

Cast: Joe E. Brown (Elmer Kane); Patricia Ellis (Nellie); Frank McHugh (High Hips Healy); Claire Dodd (Evelyn Corey); Preston S. Foster (Walker); Russell Hopton (Whitey); Sterling Holloway (Nick Kane); Emma Dunn (Mrs. Kane); Charles Wilson (Bull Wade); Charles Delaney (Johnny Abbott); Berton Churchill (Colonel Moffett); J. Carrol Naish (Jerry); Gene Morgan (Noonan); Douglass Dumbrille (Stillman); Jessie Ralph (Sarah Crosby); Gale Gordon (Radio Announcer at End); George Chandler (Mooney); Robert E. Homans (Police Captain); Lloyd Neal (Pop); Roy Gordon (Dice-Table Operator); John "Beans" Reardon, Mike Donlin (Umpires); Gus Leonard (Old Man in Barber Shop); Babe Herman, Charles Root, Larry French, Bill Brubacker, Charlie Moncrief, Tut Steinback, Frank Shellenback, Wally Hood, George Burns, Truck Hannah (Ballplayers); Jane Wyman (extra).

Elmer Kane, the gifted but rather dense star batter for the minor-league Terre Haute team, is offered a job with the Chicago Cubs. Elmer turns down the offer and chooses to stay in his tiny Indiana hometown of Gentryville, not because he feels unworthy of the honor (humility is definitely not Elmer's strong suit), but because he is in love with his boss, young Nellie Poole, proprietor of the general store. Nellie is equally fond of Elmer, but she realizes that the Cubs offer is his chance to make something of his life, so she feigns disinterest in the ballplayer, fires him, and sends him on his way. Once established with the Cubs, Elmer becomes the butt of the team's practical jokes, including a phony "coast to coast" radio broadcast staged with the help of the team manager's girlfriend, actress Evelyn Corey. Elmer is also the victim of duplicity from the team executives, who hide Nellie's letters to him, lest the valuable Kane bolt the Cubs to rejoin his girl back home. When Nellie comes to visit Kane in Chicago, she sees him with Evelyn, misunderstands, and walks out. A disconsolate Elmer decides to go out on the town with his pal High Hips, running up an enormous gambling debt at the Gold Coast Grotto. The club's crooked owner, Stillman, offers Elmer a chance to square his losses: all the boy has to do is stay away from the deciding game in the Yankees-Cubs World Series so that the gambler can clean up with the bookmakers. Elmer responds by punching Stillman out, and lands in jail—where, upon learning that his pals had bamboozled him with that fake radio broadcast, he elects to stay and sit out the big game out of pique. Nellie shows up to pay Elmer's gambling losses, and Stillman takes advantage of this by telling Elmer that the only way Nellie will ever see her money again is if Elmer accepts $5,000 to avoid the series. Kane takes the money and signs a promissory note to Stillman, which almost gets him thrown off the Cubs. But when Kane reveals that he's double-crossed Stillman by betting the whole $5,000 on the Cubs to win, he's reinstated (Pete Rose was drummed out of baseball for less!). Kane goes on to win the game, despite a downpour that has turned the ballfield into a swamp, inexplicably manages to avoid getting planted in a cement overcoat by Stillman, marries Nellie, and earns his opportunity to speak on a *genuine* radio broadcast.

The genesis of *Elmer the Great* was "Hurry Kane," a 1927 short story by Ring Lardner. The hero is Elmer Kane, a native of Yuma, Arizona, whose skill on the diamond is matched by his oversized ego, his insatiable appetite at the dinner table, and his dimwittedness, the latter quality making him a prime candidate for practical jokes. Lardner's story is a leisurely series of anecdotes, with special attention given to Elmer's devoted hometown sweetheart Minnie, and to Elmer's fascination with chorus dancer and woman of the world Evelyn Corey. To keep Kane happy, his teammates (who belong to an unnamed New York City club) write phony mash notes "signed" by Evelyn. The plot takes shape when Evelyn begins pining for the finer things in life, leading Elmer to fall in with a couple of crooked team members to fix a few games. But when an honest teammate tells Elmer

that Evelyn is the girlfriend of a big-time gambler—who, not coincidentally, is the mastermind of the fix—Elmer wins anyway, keeping the gambler's money and dividing it with the pal who gave him the lowdown on Evelyn. This story tells the reader as much about Ring Lardner himself as it does about the fictional Elmer Kane. Soured by the World Series fix of 1919 (see notes on *Eight Men Out*), Lardner could nonetheless never shake his belief that the gamblers were the real villains and the ballplayers were slow-thinking dupes. Elmer becomes a potential cheat not out of mean-spiritedness or greed, but because he's too dumb to figure out he's being taken for a buggy ride.

Given this premise, it's possible to see Elmer as a thinly disguised Shoeless Joe Jackson. Actually, Lardner based the character on an honest White Sox player (who was nowhere near the 1919 Series), Big Ed Walsh. The writer drew his characterization mostly from Walsh's swelled head, monumental food intake, and basic good nature. This latter quality was demonstrated by the fact that Ed Walsh remained friends with Lardner even after figuring out that he was the model for "Hurry" Kane.

Ring Lardner collaborated with George M. Cohan on a play version of "Hurry Kane," which they retitled *Elmer the Great*. The play premiered at New York's Lyceum Theatre on September 24, 1928, and though it ran a brief forty performances, it did rather better in later years on the road and in summer stock. The casting of forty-nine-year-old Walter Huston as the twenty something Elmer Kane might seem ludicrous to people more familiar with Huston's character roles in such films as *The Devil and Daniel Webster* and *Treasure of the Sierra Madre*; it is less ludicrous when one is made aware that allowing for the distance between audience and actor in a stage production, Huston could pull off the illusion of extreme youth and athletic prowess, and that—though baseball is talked about a great deal in the play—not one ball is pitched nor one run batted in throughout the whole three acts.

The play retains the short story's basic depiction of Kane; the complication of the girl at home and the girl in the city; several secondary characters, like Bull Wade (a teammate in the original, the team scout in the play) and Dave Walker (the team's player-manager); and, most prominently, the fixed-game angle. This last element is, in fact, the principal plot motivator for the whole third act. After Elmer foolishly totes up a heavy gambling debt, Stillman and Grayson, two underhanded gamblers, show up at Nellie Moore's general store in Gentryville. Grayson poses as a policeman and convinces Nellie that, if she signs a vaguely worded note wherein Elmer is encouraged to go along with the plans of a "Mr. Crabtree," she'll be helping to expose Stillman as a crook and also clear up Elmer's debts in the bargain. Back in St. Louis, where Elmer's "New York Champions" are in a hot and heavy pennant race, Elmer is shown the note with Nellie's signature and led to believe that Nellie is giving him the okay to go along with a fix, or else she'll lose her store due to her buying off his IOUs. Nellie shows up at the last minute to expose the crooks' machinations, and Elmer uses his fix money to bet on himself to win. The final scene is a genteel parody of the sort of merchandising indulged in by players like Babe Ruth, with Elmer signing for vaudeville tours, endorsements for "Hurry Kane" bats, and appearances in Fox Movietone newsreels.

Other than tightening Lardner's story with a firmer plot structure, the play's most important alteration of the original "Hurry Kane" was in the character of Evelyn Corey. A mercenary villainess in the short story, Evelyn is transformed into a street-smart but essentially decent Broadway actress, whom Elmer trusts implicitly and who is encouraged by Dave Walker (Evelyn's beau)

to draw Elmer out and discover the basis of the player's third-act slump.

Given his devotion to baseball (see the notes on *Alibi Ike*), Joe E. Brown would have been the ideal choice to play Elmer Kane. Brown agreed and, during a break in filming at his home studio of Warner Bros. in 1931, the actor tackled the role in a Los Angeles staging of *Elmer the Great*. The response to this engagement prompted Warners to buy the rights to the play from Paramount Pictures, which had already filmed an early talkie version of *Elmer* titled *Fast Company* (q.v.).

The opening scenes of Warners' *Elmer the Great* are so slavishly faithful to the play that they're a bit of a drag; laughs are infrequent, and nearly three reels go by before we even see a baseball. We are, however, treated to Joe E. Brown's justly famous "eating scene," which he had performed each night with real food prepared by his own chef in the play version of *Elmer*, and would continue to perform in revivals of the play into the 1940s. Brown added a punch line to the filmed version of his nonstop food fest by bending the spoon in his coffee cup rather than taking the time to remove the spoon before downing the liquid. The actor later reported that this little shtick got him in dutch with the mothers of America, who complained that after their kids had seen the film, there wasn't an unbent spoon to be found anywhere.

Once Elmer has left Gentryville for spring training (he plays for Chicago rather than New York in the film, a politic move in that the ballgame scenes were shot in L.A.'s Wrigley Field, owned by the same Wrigley who controlled the Chicago Cubs), the film's pace picks up considerably, and the plot, as indicated by the synopsis for the film at the beginning of this entry, takes several detours from the theatrical original. Since it would never do for Joe E. Brown fans to suspect for a minute that he's really sold out to the gamblers (both the short

Elmer Kane (Joe E. Brown) justifies the nickname *Elmer the Great*.

story and the play suggest this possibility as a means of building up suspense), it must be firmly established that Elmer is staying away from the crucial series game for reasons other than easy money. This is done by harking back to the earlier scene in which Elmer is snookered by his pals into thinking he's making a radio broadcast. The jokesters pass off a standing thermalite (a floor lamp with a built-in shade) as a microphone, so that Elmer makes his "broadcast debut" speaking into an empty bulb socket. Later, when recuperating in jail from his fight with gambler Stillman, Elmer notices a thermalite standing in the police doctor's office; he puts two and two together (a considerable undertaking for him), realizes his buddies have tricked him, and resolves to get even by never playing ball again.

That phony broadcast sequence serves to illustrate the means by which screenwriter Tom Geraghty softened the rough edges of the other ballplayers, so that the only truly unlikable characters in the film are the gamblers. In the play, Elmer is allowed to prattle before the "microphone" as his chums rather cruelly goad him on, stifling their laughter all the while. In the movie, Elmer starts making a heartfelt speech to his Mom, commenting that a boy's best friend is his mother. Touched by his sincerity, the other ballplayers feel ashamed of their hoax, hang their heads, and quietly end the "broadcast" before Elmer has a chance to discover the ruse and get his feelings hurt.

Once the screenplay was completed, it was filmed virtually as written, except for an added scene here or deleted character there. Acknowledging Joe E. Brown's large following among children, producer Raymond Griffith and director Mervyn LeRoy excised a few of the script's more questionable lines; for example, we no longer hear one of the Cubs allude to Elmer Kane's "well-known" brother Coke Kane. One juicy slice of scatology made it into the film, however, justified by the euphoria that Elmer Kane is supposed to be feeling at the moment. After being benched under suspicion of cheating, Elmer is permitted to run onto the ballfield and possibly save the team from defeat. Asked if he first wants to warm up, Kane replies with delightful pre–Production Code candor, "Warm up? Hell, I ain't been cool since February!" The line still gets a gasp from modern viewers who've

assumed all their lives that no one ever swore in the movies until *Gone with the Wind.*

From the first draft onward, the climactic ballgame was given the added visual dynamism of being played in a driving rainstorm (the production crew had to wait two weeks until a series of genuine California cloudbursts had subsided before they could set up their rain machines to film the sequence!). This downpour made possible a routine in which the Yankees' pitcher and catcher conspire to strike Elmer out by utilizing the "hesitation pitch." Taking advantage of the lowered visibility caused by the weather, the pitcher pretends to throw and the catcher smacks his mitt to simulate the sound of the ball hitting leather. Two "strikes" go by before Elmer, his suspicions aroused, jumps in front of the final "pitch"— proving that, unless the ball has passed through his body, something is rotten in Chicago. Though it seems odd that the New York Yankees would permit a filmed dramatization of two of their team members cheating, the fact is that the hesitation pitch was not officially illegal in 1933; it wasn't until 1948, after Satchel Paige tried to pull off the stunt in his second game with the Cleveland Indians, that the pitch was declared a no-no in the rule book.

The World Series climax was as rousing as the similar finales in Joe E. Brown's other baseball films, aided immeasurably by Brown's own physical dexterity, especially evident in his mud-caked winning slide into home. The sequence is buttressed by a film clip or two from the actual Yankees-Cubs series of 1932 (it was reported in the film's pressbook that director Mervyn LeRoy had made a special trip to that series to shoot background scenes for *Elmer,* which is quite possible in that most Warners films began preparation six months to a year in advance), and by the presence of several honest to goodness pro ballplayers in bit roles. Among the real diamond vets in *Elmer the Great* were Frank Shellenback, the Pacific

Coast League mainstay who was featured in all three of Brown's ballpark efforts of the 1930s, and Charlie Root, the hapless Chicago Cubs pitcher who, during the third game of the 1932 Series, had thrown the ball that Babe Ruth homered just after Babe had allegedly pointed to the location where the ball would land. Root had no qualms about appearing in *Elmer*, which, after all, depicted a Cubs victory, but he would later turn down flat the opportunity of recreating the "called shot" for *The Babe Ruth Story.*

While Elmer Kane was Joe E. Brown's personal favorite of all his roles, *Elmer the Great* was not necessarily the best of Brown's "baseball trio." Though it is a decided improvement upon the patchwork plotting of *Fireman Save My Child* (q.v.), *Elmer the Great* is weakened by the lethargic pacing in its opening scenes, and must therefore take a back seat to Joe E.'s next baseball picture, the excellent, never-a-dull-moment *Alibi Ike* (q.v.).

The Fan

Mandalay Entertainment/Sony Pictures Entertainment/Tri-Star; released August 16, 1996

Executive producers: James W. Skotchdopole, Bill Unger. Produced by Wendy Finerman, Margaret French Isaac and Greg Mooradian. Directed by Tony Scott. Screenplay by Phoef Sutton and [uncredited] Frank Darabont, from the novel by Peter Abrahams. Photography: Dariusz Wolski. Edited by Claire Simpson, Christian Wagner. Original music by Hans Zimmer; additional music by Jeff Rona. Casting: Ellen Lewis. Production design: Ida Random. Art director: Mayne Berke. Set decorator: Claire Bowin. Costume design: Daniel Orlandi, Rita Ryack. Key hair stylist: Ron Scott. Key makeup artist: Richard Snell. Production managers: Roger Joseph Pugliese, James A. Westman. First assistant director: James W. Skotchdopole. Second assistant director: John Wildermuth, Jr. Set designer: Beverli Eagan. Supervising sound ed-itor: Robert G. Henderson. Supervising foley editor: Scott Burrow. Foley artists: Gary A. Hecker, Jeffrey Wilhoit. Special effects supervisor: Joe D. Ramsey. Visual effects editor: Dwight Raymond. Music supervisor: Sharon Boyle. Costume supervisor: Dan Bronson. Camera operator: Martin Schaer. Helicopter camera operator: David B. Nowell. Knife consultant: Larry Cisewski. Baseball consultant: Calvin Edwin Ripken, Jr. Baseball trainer: William Hughes. Stunt coordinators: Chuck Picerni, Jr., Steve Picerni. Technical advisor: James Wells. Stalking Consultant: Lt. John Lane. Technicolor; Panavision. 120 minutes; Dolby/SDDS Sound. Rated R.

Cast: Robert De Niro (Gil Renard); Wesley Snipes (Bobby Rayburn); Ellen Barkin (Jewel Stern); John Leguizamo (Manny); Benicio Del Toro (Juan Primo); Patti D'Arbanville-Quinn (Ellen Renard); Andrew J. Ferchland (Richie Renard); Brandon Hammond (Sean Rayburn); Charles Hallahan (Coop); Dan Butler (Garrity); Kurt Fuller (Bernie); Michael Jace (Scalper); Frank Medrano (Leon, bartender); Don S. Davis (Stook); John Kruk (Lanz); Stoney Jackson (Zamora); Brad Henke (Tjader); Drew Snyder (Burrows); Edith Diaz (Elvira); Walter Addison (Detective Lewis); Wayne Duvall (Detective Baker); Joe Pichler (Sick Sean); James G. MacDonald (Sick Sean's Dad); Tuesday Knight (Nurse); Marla Sucharetza (Angie); Nikki Lee (Dawna); Marjorie Lovett (Stanford Woman); Michael Andolini (Man Behind Gil); M.C. Gainey (Man Behind Man); Michael Bofshever (Little League Coach); Kirk Ward (The Giant Mascot); Eric Bruskotter (Catcher); Kirk D. Terry, Abraham Flores, Dennis Neil Henderson (Umpires); Aaron Neville (Opening Game Singer); Jerry Saslow, Michael P. Byrne, Bret Lewis, Roger Lodge, Ron Pitts (Reporters); Stanley DeSantis (Stoney); Jack Black (Broadcast Technician); Thomas Duffy (Figgy); Don Fischer, Vernon Guichard II (Cops); Kim Robillard (Jefferson Sporting Goods Clerk); Keith Leon Williams (Stadium Official); Chanté Moore (Primo Tribute Singer); Paul Herman (Seedy Suit Guy); Robert Louis Kempf (Baggage Attendant); Jesse Ibarra (Padres Pitcher); James Betzold (Padres Catcher); Chris Fick (Giants Left Fielder); Ben Hines (Giants First Baseman); Rick Magnante (Giants Third Base Coach); Carl Mergenthaler, Clayton Holt, Lennox Brown, Troy A. Cephers, Freeman White (Bobby's Teammates); Bruce Hines (Umpire, Final Game); Adam Druxman

(Paparazzi); Kathy Stewart, Carolyn Washington, Nikki Hart, Bo Daniels, Randal Salguero, Tracy Leanne Mandac (Fans); Gregg Tome (Detective Schmerg); Sonya Bertelson (Waitress); Brian Freifield (Art); Jennifer Stander, Roy Conrad, Richard Riehle, Earl Billings, John Carroll Lynch, Tim Monsion, Ralph Bertelle, Norm Compton (Shopkeepers); Bob Arnolds, Mike Cameron, John Cenatiemp, R. J. Chambers, Craig Davis, Danial Donai, Richard Epper, Kane Hodder, Scott Hubbell, Leslie Jones, Mark Lonsdale, Billy D. Lucas, John Lucasey, Joe Manuella, Johnny Martin, Eddie Perez, John Polce, John Rottger, Carlton Lee Russell, Tierre Turner, Gene Williams (Stunts); Larry Cisewski (Knife Thrower); Michael Graziano (Bobby's Teammate); Patti Tippo (Shopkeeper).

"Baseball is better than life—it's fair." This is the credo of Gil Renard, to whom life has dealt a cold deck of disillusionment and humiliation. Embroiled in an acrimonious divorce and faced with the possibility of a restraining order barring him from visiting his son Richie, Gil is also on the brink of losing his job as a salesman for the knife manufacturing company that was founded by his own father. All that keeps Gil from completely unraveling is his unquenchable love of baseball, which was inherited from his father and solidified (according to his own rose-colored recollections) when he himself was a championship ballplayer in his youth. Hardly a day goes by that Gil isn't on his cell phone, singing the praises of his beloved San Francisco Giants over the radio talk show hosted by "Sports Babe" Jewel Stern. At present, Gil's attentions are focused upon the Giants' new $40,000,000 acquisition, center fielder Bobby Rayburn. In contrast to Gil, Bobby would seem to have it all: talent (.310 lifetime batting average, three-time MVP), money, fame, adulation, and, most importantly, a solid relationship with his own son Sean. But Bobby also has a few crosses to bear, not least of which is the fact that his traditional "lucky" uniform number, Eleven, is being worn by arrogant teammate Juan

Primo, who refuses to relinquish the number at any price. Feeling jinxed by this, and suffering from a serious opening-day injury, the superstitious Bobby falls into an early-season slump which causes the Giants fans to wonder if he is truly worth his astronomical salary. The more the public razzes Bobby, the more Gil—who identifies like mad with the beleaguered ballplayer—rallies to his defense. His obsession with Rayburn eventually costs Gil not only his job but also any future contact with his son Richie. By now completely round the bend, Gil vows to "save" Bobby's faltering career by any means necessary, beginning with the fatal stabbing of Juan Primo. Later on, Gil insinuates himself into Bobby's beachfront home by happening to be on hand to rescue little Sean from drowning. Totally unaware that he is playing host to Juan's murderer, the grateful Bobby agrees to a friendly game of catch with Gil, during which he makes the fatal mistake of dissing his public: "Fans are like women. When you're hitting they love you, when you're not they'd just as soon spit on you.... The only person you should play for is yourself." Mumbling something about Rayburn's lack of gratitude and "caring," Gil disappears into the night, but not before stealing Bobby's car and kidnapping Sean—and leaving behind Juan Primo's severed "Number 11" tattoo to prove the sincerity of his dedication to Bobby Rayburn. The terrified Sean is squirreled away with Gil's former baseball mentor, Coop, who becomes the next murder victim when he forces Gil to face the truth about his cherished "memories" of youthful baseball stardom. Contacting Bobby, Gil orders him to hit a home run in the upcoming game—and to publicly acknowledge the homer as a tribute to his "biggest fan," Gil—if he ever hopes to see Sean alive again. As Bobby and his agent Manny desperately work hand in glove with the authorities and the sympathetic Jewel Stern to track down and rescue Sean, Gil Renard shows up at Candlestick Park for a final, bloody showdown with Bobby Rayburn.

Interviewed at the 1996 San Sebastian Film Festival screening of *The Fan*, director Tony Scott explained his motivation for optioning the 1995 novel upon which the picture was based: "I've always wanted to do a film about obsession. For me, that is the heart and soul of *The Fan*.... It's about the haves and have-nots, the little people who want to be big people. I think the media encourages this sort of character to come to the surface, because the media thrives on people and situations like this."

Written by suspense specialist Peter Abrahams, the novel *The Fan* bears a surface resemblance to the film: The character names and most of the major incidents are the same, the author's parallel-development treatment of the lives of Gil Renard and Bobby Rayburn was carried over to the film, and both book and movie climax with a violent confrontation between stalker and stalkee during a nighttime ballgame.

Abrahams was a resident of Cape Cod, Massachusetts, so it naturally follows that the novel takes place in the Boston area rather than the film's San Francisco; accordingly, Gil Renard's lifelong allegiance lies not with the Giants but with the Red Sox. In the book, flashbacks serve the purpose of establishing that Gil's fanatical devotion to baseball was inherited from his father; in the film, the same point is made more economically when Gil claims that his dad moved his entire family from New York to the Bay Area when the Giants relocated in 1958.

Unlike the film, in which Gil Renard begins to unravel fifteen minutes after the opening Tri-Star logo, it takes an awful lot of hard knocks for the novel's Gil to metamorphose from mild neurotic to cold-blooded killer. His early scenes establish Gil as a man nearing the end of his rope, unable to maintain his quota as a knife salesman and keeping his job only as a

figurehead because his father created the business. As a means of escaping reality, Gil becomes more and more obsessive in his love of baseball, eventually blowing an important account—and his job—because he insists upon attending opening day at Fenway Park with his son Richie. In his unsuccessful efforts to juggle his professional responsibilities with his leisure activities, Gil thoughtlessly (but not maliciously) abandons Richie at the ballpark, obliging a friendly stranger to bring the boy back home to his mother. Up to this point, Gil's relationship with his ex-wife Ellen has been strained but cordial; but the desertion of Richie forces the reluctant Ellen to revoke Gil's visitation rights.

After losing practically everything he holds dear, Gil pathetically tries to recapture the carefree ballplaying days of his youth, the only time he was truly happy and at peace with himself. As a ghoulish but still nonviolent hint of the carnage to come, Gil begins his "sentimental journey" by digging up his father's grave to retrieve his beloved baseball trophy! He then seeks out his old catcher and role model, Len "Co" Boucicaut, hoping that Co will help him cope with his most recent setbacks. But much to Gil's dismay, Co's life has also gone sour, and he is now a small-time poacher and burglar. Sizing up the vulnerable Gil as a perfect patsy, Co talks his old friend into helping him rob the home of the wealthy Bostonian to whom Gil had previously sold his father's prized collection of handmade knives. The burglary goes awry, and Co is mortally wounded while trying to escape. As he lies bleeding to death, the ever-cynical Co deals the final blow to Gil by reminding him that their "golden days" of baseball ended when both men were 12-year-old members of the Little League.

Only after his last self-delusion is shattered is Gil pushed over the edge, and only then does he embark upon a homicidal rampage, beginning with the murder of

Co's nasty, manipulative girlfriend Claudine, whom Gil holds responsible for Co's downfall. After also knocking off Claudine's mangy junkyard dog Nig, the now-irredeemable Gil vows to "avenge" his current idol Bobby Rayburn by confronting and ultimately stabbing Bobby's rival Juan Primo (the *first* murder victim in the film). Gil later expunges one more bitter reminder of his lost innocence by murdering another of his former Little League teammates, a police officer named Claybourne, who dies while attempting to rescue the kidnapped Sean Rayburn. Up until this time, Gil's killings were impulsive and borne of necessity (at least in his own twisted mind). It is only during the climactic ballgame that he commits premeditated murder, slitting the throat of Socko, the Boston Red Sox mascot—the better to don the dead man's costume so he can get close to his intended final victim, Bobby Rayburn, without arousing the suspicions of Fenway Park Security.

The film's depiction of Gil Renard as a man who resorts to murder so that he can at last be master of his own destiny (and the destinies of others) is subtly touched upon in the book. At one point, while responding to an umpire's unpopular call by throwing batteries onto the ballfield, Gil triumphantly says to himself, "I'm a player. I'm a player in this game." (In this, of course, he is speaking for *every* overzealous fan who has disrupted a game with destructive behavior.) But Gil's kidnapping of Sean is *not* motivated by this lust for power and control, as in the film. Having effectively lost his own son Richie, Gil snatches Sean as a temporary "replacement" for Richie, not as a bargaining chip to extort Bobby into scoring a homer for Gil's sake. In fact, Sean is rescued long before the final showdown between Bobby and Gil; it is Bobby's ultimate fate which drives the rest of the book.

In both book and film, Bobby Rayburn is shown to be as obsessive as Gil, though his obsession is manifested in his desire for perfection on the ballfield, something that he can't achieve due to early-season injuries, and *won't* achieve until he learns to stop being so hard on himself. In the book, this is conveyed via lengthy interior monologues, in the manner of Michael Shaara's *For Love of the Game* (q.v.). Built into these monologues, and the narrative itself, is the fact that Bobby has been hired by the Red Sox at an exorbitant salary mainly because of his record of spectacular homers and RBIs—though, in fact, his real talent lies in faking out the opposition, usually by merely bunting the ball. Though roundly criticized for this habit by the press and his fans (they paid for the fireworks, they want the fireworks!), Bobby ultimately saves his own life by holding his bat in a bunt position and deflecting Gil Renard's thrown knife.

Bobby also has an overdeveloped sense of guilt, kicking himself for craving lucrative commercial endorsements while at the same time welcoming them with open arms, brooding over the fact that he has lost his youthful enthusiasm for baseball, and allowing himself to be haunted by the memory of a young leukemia victim for whom he'd promised to hit two homers (sardonically described by another character as a "William Bendix" moment), but who died before Bobby was able to fulfill his promise. It happens that the dying child was named Sean, the same name as Bobby's own son. This fact triggers the ballplayer's self-flagellation over not being a better father to his son and husband to his wife Laura, on whom he cheats shamelessly throughout the early chapters of the book. Both the novel and the film contrast Bobby's ultimate redemption with the deterioration and destruction of his doppelganger Gil Renard, though the film's Bobby is more sympathetic in that he is no longer married and thus technically free to canoodle as much as he wants; as a bonus, his relationship with Sean is on much firmer ground.

A deleted scene from *The Fan*: In the finished film, Gil Renard (Robert DeNiro, standing, right-center) does not come face to face with Bobby Rayburn (Wesley Snipes, left foreground) until after rescuing Bobby's son from drowning, while Gil's own son Richie (Andrew J. Ferchland, upper right) never meets Bobby at all.

Of almost equal importance to Gil and Bobby in the novel is the character of female sports commentator Jewel Walker. She, too, is obsessed in her own way, anxious to graduate from her daily call-in show on Boston station WJOC by writing a prestigious *New York Times Magazine* piece on Bobby Rayburn. With a past habit of getting intimately involved in her interviews, Jewel has a one-night fling with Bobby, after which she is inclined to be more sympathetic than her fellow journalists in her coverage of Bobby's slump. Both the book and film use a men's-room confrontation between Bobby and Juan Primo over ownership of "Number 11" as a means of bringing Gil Renard (who happens to be in one of the toilet stalls) into the argument. The book takes things several steps farther:

While investigating the Bobby-Juan contretemps as part of her magazine piece, Jewel discovers that Gil Renard witnessed the fight, leading her to check out Gil's current residence—where she is knocked unconscious by an unseen assailant. Her suspicions aroused, Jewel figures out that Bobby's new handyman, who calls himself "Curly Onis" (the name of a ballplayer who, like Moonlight Graham in *Field of Dreams* [q.v.], is famous in baseball-trivia circles as a Minor Leaguer who had "one cup of coffee" in the Majors), is actually the elusive Gil Renard. Putting a few more pieces together, Jewel recalls that the most persistent caller on her radio program is named Gil—and with these wisps of evidence, she concludes that Gil was responsible for Juan's murder. Continuing to take an active hand in the investigation, Jewel manages to be on the premises when the kidnapped Sean is rescued. Jewel then helps the cops lay a trap for the killer by introducing a weekly radio feature in which her most frequent callers are given the opportunity to shoot their mouths off as long as they wish—an invitation which naturally flushes Gil out of hiding. Ironically, although her amateur sleuthing cracks the case, Jewel manages to botch her opportunity to write the *New York Times* piece on Bobby—who, as a "front page" figure in a spectacular murder case, is now too big a subject to be shunted off to the newspaper's Sunday supplement!

In print form, *The Fan* has all the makings of a dynamite feature film, and had it been handled by anyone other than Tony Scott, most of the elements which keep things crackling in the novel would probably have been retained for the movie. But Scott had built his reputation on grandiose actioners like *Top Gun* and *Crimson Tide*, in which such frills as characterization, motivation and plot development were largely disregarded in favor of explosions, ear-splitting rock music, ultra-stylized violence, spectacular special effects, techno-thrilling combat scenes, and protracted climactic confrontations between Hero and Villain. There can be no argument that Tony Scott's formula was a winning one—but only with the right material. *The Fan* was not that material, despite Scott's efforts to bend it to his needs.

All things considered, screenwriter Phoef Sutton (here miles away from her previous writing/coproducing duties on the hit sitcom *Cheers*) and uncredited contributor Frank Darabont did a remarkable job whittling Abrahams' novel down to its barest essentials. Since Robert De Niro was going to be playing Gil, it would be neither necessary nor desirable to clutter the screen with secondary villains; thus, all that burglar business with the corruptive "Co" Boucicaut and his bimbo Claudine was thrown out. The film's equivalent to Co is the benign middle-aged security guard Coop, who, after finding out what Bobby is up to, makes a vain attempt to rescue Sean, thereby also fulfilling the story function of another character cut from the film, the doomed policeman Claybourne. Coop's "betrayal" of Gil—and his subsequent demise—allowed the writers to reestablish Gil's homicidal streak without dragging in all the other murders in the book.

Eliminating the character of Bobby's wife Laura necessitated the removal of a subplot in which Laura was carrying on an affair with Bobby's mercenary agent Chaz (Manny in the film), the knowledge of which Gil Renard uses to prevent Chaz from putting up resistance when Bobby hires Gil as a handyman (thus effectively making Chaz an accessory before the fact). Similarly, Jewel's one-night stand with Bobby was written out, though she remains one of Bobby's few friends in the media. The result of these excisions enabled Chaz and Jewel, who come off as obnoxious and unappealing in the early reels, to gradually "humanize," along with Bobby, as the story progresses, offering an even stronger contrast to the progressive dehumanization of Gil.

But in shortening the novel, the writers and director dispensed with the subtler character shadings that enabled the reader to understand why a basically decent guy like Gil Renard would go so tragically off the deep end. Peter Abrahams manages to make us "pull" for poor Gil right up to the moment that he commits his first murder; conversely, the viewer is uncomfortable with Gil from the very first time he appears in the movie version of *The Fan*, and within a few minutes discomfort has turned into active dislike as Gil unleashes a barrage of profanities at an unresponsive business client. While in the novel there is a glimmer of hope that somehow Gil can be dissuaded from going down the wrong path, there is no doubt from the get-go of the film that the man is a certifiable Looney Tune.

A few tentative efforts are made in the film to "explain" that Gil's breakdown is brought about by the nastiness of those around him. His new boss cruelly mocks Gil's striving for product excellence, exhibiting a terrifyingly mean streak of his own by pulling out a detached car door and maniacally poking it full of holes with an army knife; as he prepares to take his son Richie to the ballgame, Gil is warned by his shrieking harpie of an ex-wife that if the boy is not brought back at 6:05 on the dot, she will call out the cops; and even a ratty-looking ticket scalper treats Gil like excrement on his shoe. Nor is this unbridled hostility confined to the people in closest contact with Gil Renard; in the Gospel According to Tony Scott, *everyone* in the Bay Area has a mad-on about something, everyone is trying to hustle a fast buck, everyone is primed to punch out his neighbor, and everyone bandies about four-letter expletives with such impunity that it seems as if the entire city of New York moved to California along with the Giants.

This piling of indignity upon indignity, humiliation upon humiliation, worked quite well in justifying Michael Douglas' explosion of violence in director Jeff Schumacher's *Falling Down* (1993), but that was because the audience cared about Douglas' character from the beginning of the film. The same device fails to register in *The Fan* because Gil Renard doesn't appear to deserve any better treatment. To take two examples from many: In the novel, Gil may be a trifle pushy when insisting that his son share his interest in baseball, but he is never abusive toward the boy; plus, he is capable of turning on the charm for people who pose no threat to him. In contrast, the film's Gil Renard thinks nothing of knocking down and stepping over his son while trying to catch a fly ball; nor does he hesitate to lash out at a sweet, matronly baseball fan (apparently the only nice person in all of San Francisco) simply for looking at him—and this is *before* he has gone on his murderous rampage. Never mind the professional and personal pressures brought to bear against Gil: this is one bad actor, and it is a wonder that someone hasn't already locked him in a rubber room on general principles.

The most blatant example of the film's telescoping of its source material occurs in the final half hour. In the book, Gil spends several days as a handyman at Bobby's beach house, ingratiating himself with his host and little Sean and putting himself in a position of trust. All this changes when, during an impromptu game of catch, Bobby offhandedly comments upon Gil's insufficient ballplaying skills ("No hard feelings, huh, Curly? I'm a pro. It would be like us having a lawn-mower race or something, I wouldn't stand a chance"), with each patronizing remark fueling Gil's anger. Once more feeling betrayed by a person he trusts, Gil leaves the premises, stealing both Bobby's son and his station wagon. He does this not so much to get even with Bobby as to *become* Bobby, as if by taking the prized possessions of a successful man he can compensate for his own lifetime of failures. And given the extended time-frame of the beachhouse scenes in the book, it makes sense that Bobby would let his guard down, never dreaming that his own son—who, after all, owes his life to Gil—could be in any sort of danger.

The film concentrates all of this into a single night's action, beginning with Gil's rescue of Sean and concluding with the boy's abduction. Bobby still pushes Gil's buttons, not by dismissing his ballplaying talents but by characterizing diehard baseball fans as "losers"—an understandable response to the nasty drubbing Bobby has been receiving all season from the Candlestick Park patrons who hold it against him personally that his injuries prevented him from "deserving" his $40,000,000 paycheck. Sensing from his reaction that Gil is not quite the affable fellow he appeared to be at first, Bobby backs away, suggesting that Gil should head on home. Gil takes up this suggestion, but also kidnaps Bobby and leaves behind Juan Primo's "Number 11" tattoo—which he'd bloodily peeled from the ballplayer's arm in the process of murdering him—neatly plastic-wrapped in Bobby's refrigerator.

On the plus side, Gil's reaction to Bobby's comments about fans is in keeping with his obsessive nature and his overwhelming desire to be a "Big Person" instead of one of those faceless nobodies whom Bobby so contemptuously dismisses; this falls into line with Tony Scott's avowed purpose in making *The Fan*. Otherwise, the scene as it plays in the film stretches logic well beyond the breaking point.

Gil's plan to wreak vengeance upon Bobby doesn't begin to take shape in his mind until a few minutes before his departure. Suddenly, as if by magic, Gil instantly changes from a highly individualized psycho acting on impulse into a typical *movie* psycho. He may not have the perspicacity to hold a job, a wife or a kid, yet he has the presence of mind after rescuing Bobby's son from drowning—a lucky break he could not possibly have foreseen—to leave a severed tattoo in the fridge (even if he'd been carrying it around with him, his own clothes were soaked, and he left the house wearing one of Bobby's uniforms) and mastermind an elaborate and meticulously planned kidnapping. As for Bobby, once he catches on that Gil is a few French fries short of a Happy Meal, would not his *first* impulse be to check up on the safety of Sean before Gil left? And even allowing for the fact that he was grateful to the man who saved his life, little Sean seems far too intelligent to accompany Gil or any other stranger on a wild ride through the night;

had the longer timeframe of the book been retained, one could more readily believe that Sean would have grown to trust Gil implicitly, but here the boy just seems slow-witted.

A daunting lack of logic runs rampant throughout all of the film's final sequences. Once he realizes that Gil intends to kill Sean if his demands are not met, what is preventing old Coop from cold-cocking the unarmed Gil with a baseball bat while the two men play a nocturnal ball game with Sean? Can anyone explain why Sean is not at all frightened when he and Gil, both brandishing sharp knives, grinningly pose for ransom pictures—but the kid is suddenly petrified with terror when Gil starts pitching baseballs? And although Sean's initial hiding place is near the San Francisco train yards, where presumably a few well-armed authority figures venture from time to time, why is the escaping Sean unable to avoid recapture by Gil, even though the boy has a good head start and manages to elude his captor for several hours?

Nor is the closing baseball sequence a monument to cinematic realism. Rumor has it that Tony Scott intended to stage the entire final ballgame in a driving rainstorm, and when informed that Major League games are not played under such conditions, Scott let loose a stream of free-association scatology indicating that he was the director and could do whatever he pleased, so there. If this is true, a compromise was obviously reached; the rain does not persist throughout the game, but the ever-present *threat* of heavy precipitation adds an extra layer of suspense (if the game is unduly delayed, Sean is likely to die). Even so, there is still far too much rain during Bobby's climactic home run—but in fairness, this is no more unbelievable than the suggestion, set forth at the beginning of the sequence, that the umpire would automatically call the game at the first signs of inclement weather, rather than merely postpone it.

There are other aspects of the final scene that sorely try one's patience. Yes, it is true Gil has warned Bobby that if he gets a home run off an "easy pitch" he will kill Sean; but it would certainly have behooved Bobby to tell the other team what was happening, so that at least they would not have tried to *walk* him. Gil makes his "surprise" appearance at the game disguised as an umpire, whereas in the novel he was made up as the murdered team mascot; it would be easier to accept this alteration if only the audience had been told what happened to the *real* umpire. Once Gil is unmasked, director Scott goes into full slasher-flick mode: Even with eighteen ballplayers and full complement of Security on hand, nobody is able to subdue the knife-wielding Gil. When he is inevitably pumped full of lead by the cops, Gil still has sufficient strength to make a poignant death speech (Tony Scott isn't about to let *this* Money Scene slip through his fingers). And while Bobby is facing down Gil for the last time, the police manage to locate Sean's hiding place; under normal circumstances, the authorities would simply close in and remove the kid. But that just isn't dramatic enough for Tony Scott, who contrives to have a battalion of flashlight-wielding cops mill aimlessly around the hiding place until Gil is safely dead and Bobby is able to leave Candlestick, drive across town and make the rescue himself—meaning, presumably, that a child placed in jeopardy has had his agony prolonged *by the authorities* just so his dad can be the hero of the hour.

In fact, as pointed out by critic Leonard Maltin, *The Fan* holds the distinction of placing two different kids (Sean Rayburn and Richie Renard) in lengthy, trauma-inducing states of verbal and psychological abuse. R rating or no R rating, this is totally inappropriate in a film about baseball—but is all too symptomatic of Tony Scott's apparent attitude towards the National Pastime. From start to finish, the film shows us a baseball world populated almost exclusively by mean-spirited and avaricious ballplayers, parasitic agents and journalists, and contemptuously fickle fans who seem utterly incapable of completing the simplest sentence without the "F," "S" or "C" word. In the first edition of this book, it was noted that the TV movie *The Comeback Kid* (1980) stood alone as an *anti*-baseball film. After *The Fan*, the earlier film was alone no longer.

Well, at least we know what Tony Scott doesn't like. And judging from this and other films, we know what he *does* like: He likes disturbingly tight close-ups, graphically dwelling upon every burst blood vessel and sweaty orifice; he likes repeating his favorite effects *ad nauseum* (the director's idea of filming a pitched ball is confined exclusively to a slo-mo delivery aimed directly at the camera, accompanied by the sound of a sawed-off shotgun); he likes wall-to-wall rock music, in this instance a maximum-volume medley of Rolling Stones, Nine Inch Nails and Santana (one musical passage sounds like the entire orchestra is rhythmically breaking wind); he likes to shoot his interior scenes in funereal darkness (does no one ever turn on a ceiling light in San Francisco?); he likes to employ chainsaw-style editing even during the straight exposition scenes; and he likes aerial shots and lots and lots of noisy helicopters (at times one is unsure whether we're in the Bay Area or the Gulf of Tonkin). It takes the self-discipline of a Spartan for the viewer to avoid shouting, "Cut the smoke and mirrors and just tell the damn story!"

And while you're at it, the viewer might add, get things right once in a while! We can allow for the dramatic license of having both Bobby Rayburn and Juan Primo covet the magic "Number 11" when in truth neither man would be allowed anywhere near that number, since the Giants had retired it after the departure of Carl Hubbell. And it is possible to overlook the fact that, outside of Jewel Stern, there are virtually no radio talk show hosts on the face of the earth that would ask a bonus-baby baseball player about his recent divorce, or permit a caller to remain on the air after issuing two profanities in a row. But it is hard to forgive the haphazard use of stock footage in the ballgame scenes, in which teams and uniforms miraculously change in mid-game and often in mid-scene, the Giants wear "away" uniforms for home games, Candlestick Park abruptly morphs into Colorado's Coors Field, and one overhead view of the stadium is obviously taking place during a San Francisco 49ers game. And for Gil to state empirically that the Rolling Stones' "Start Me Up" was recorded in 1978—some three years off the mark—is enough to turn any self-respecting music fan into the next Gil Renard!

Given that Tony Scott's directorial approach tends to turn even the most talented actors into mere puppets, the stars give surprisingly good performances. As always, Robert De Niro (whose last baseball-flick experience had been 1974's *Bang the Drum Slowly* [q.v.]) left no stone unturned in researching his role as Gil Renard. De Niro spent five days interviewing real-life knife salesmen, querying them about their lives, families, clothing, cars and aspirations. The actor then immersed himself in videotapes of genuine stalkers and murderers, notably John Lennon's assassin and the "biggest fan" who killed actress Rebecca Schaeffer (*The Fan* may be the only sports film ever to include a closing credit for "Stalking Consultant"). That De Niro's performance often plays like a retread of Travis Bickle from *Taxi Driver* (1975) and Max Cady from *Cape Fear* (1991) is not entirely his fault since, as noted, the slow and deliberate buildup to Gil's insanity which Peter Abrahams carefully and meticulously detailed in the novel *The Fan* was ruthlessly jettisoned from the movie. Veering dangerously close to self-parody (and, as he has since proven in films like *Analyze This* and *Rocky and Bullwinkle*, few actors are better equipped to poke fun at themselves), De Niro still manages a few golden moments of relative subtlety, notably his deadpan reading of the line, "A simple 'thank you' would have been nice," his bewildered reaction to Coop's "betrayal" even as he bludgeons the man to death, and the marvelously underplayed moment in which he pretends to mistake Bobby Rayburn for Barry Bonds (upon whom Bobby's character is obviously based!).

Incidentally, in sharp contrast to Gil Renard, Robert De Niro's own life was on a high roll during filming; he'd just become the father of a baby girl, courtesy of longtime companion Touckie Smith. This, however, did not prevent a smidgen of Gil Renard from spilling over into real life: Reportedly, during a break in filming on location in San Francisco, De Niro drove a jeep across a railroad track—and when warned by a trackman that a train was due any minute, the actor responded, "Fuck you, *I'm* in charge!"

Returning to the baseball-movie genre seven years after his comic turn in *Major League* (q.v.), Wesley Snipes manages to invest the character of Bobby Rayburn with all the self-awareness, inner turmoil and essential humanity of his counterpart in the novel (not that it matters, but the book's Bobby is not African American), even though the actor was left with precious little to work with once the screenwriters were finished slashing and hacking away at the source material. The film, in fact, provides Snipes with one of the best scenes in his career: The moment between Bobby and the terminally ill youngster, in which the actor brilliantly (and all but wordlessly) conveys the combination of celebrity glad-handing, false bravado, queasy discomfiture and profound guilt that would genuinely attend such a moment. But while he was better served dramatically in *The Fan* than in *Major League*, the earlier film afforded Snipes more opportunity to show off his baseball skills. Though Cal Ripken, Jr., fresh from breaking Lou Gehrig's consecutive-game record, served as *The Fan*'s technical consultant, Tony Scott's hopscotching directorial approach never permits the viewer to fully witness Bobby Rayburn (or any of the other actor/ballplayers) at peak playing form. Even Bobby's final, plot-resolving home run is obscured by Scott's Veg-o-Matic editing, vertigo-inducing camerawork and laser-show lighting effects.

Third-billed Ellen Barkin could not have been happy that the character of Jewel Stern, so active a participant in the proceedings of the original novel, was, in the film version of *The Fan*, reduced to a human punctuation mark between action highlights. Professional that she is, Barkin manages to breathe life into her severely limited screen time; if nothing else, she is to be congratulated for her sympathetic portrayal of a chain smoker in these days of restrictive political correctness. While Barkin is generally ill served by the deletions made in her character, the versatile John Leguizamo benefits from the film's streamlined version of Bobby's smarmy agent Manny. On film, Manny is basically the same opportunistic wheeler-dealer as the novel's Chaz, but with the removal of his most deleterious character traits (notably his clandestine affair with Bobby's wife) he comes across as almost lovable. Like his costar Wesley Snipes (with whom he had previously appeared in drag[!] in 1994's *To Wong Foo, Thanks for Everything, Julie Newmar*), John Leguizamo manages to create a fully-rounded character through understatement and economy of movement. Without ever altering his snide, abrasive, mercenary personality, Leguizamo's Manny thoroughly convinces us that he has, by the end of the film, come to regard Bobby as a sincere human being and true friend instead of just another celebrity "asshole" and meal ticket.

Other actors are not so lucky. The usually reliable Patty D'Arbanville-Quinn is defeated by the scripters' decision to transform the novel's Ellen Renard, a quite reasonable character despite the provocations of her unstable ex-husband Gil, into a shrill, one-note Bitch on Wheels. The actress plays the role as shallowly as it is written, as if in a hurry to get off the set and into some other picture. Cast as Bobby's preening antagonist Juan Primo is the gifted Benicio Del Toro, hovering between his breakthrough role in *The Usual Suspects* (1995) and his Oscar-winning performance in *Traffic* (2000). Obviously regarded by the director and the scripters as merely a necessary evil to propel the plot forward, Del Toro is given no opportunity to shine whatsoever, and even the actor's most dedicated fans may have trouble remembering what his Juan Primo looked or sounded like (for the record, he's the guy with the red goatee and thick accent).

The official theatrical release of *The Fan* was briefly held up by the Major League Baseball Corporation, who, after a few test screenings, insisted that the violence be toned down (we shudder to think how much blood was shed *before* the film went back to the editing room). After surveying the press response to the film, one can readily understand why the studio refused to stage a pre-release screening for the critics. "[Robert] De Niro seems to have perfected his routine from *Taxi Driver* and *Cape Fear*," wrote Dave Goodman of the Associated Press. "The now predictable repertoire of psycho moves are all here—the twitches, the cold stare, the curled-down lip, the crazy smile where the eyes crinkle sinisterly. The overly familiar performance is ... lessened by some annoying, intrusive camera work. There are a few too many jump-cuts and extreme close-ups used to create tension. It's like the camera is the star here. Considering the film's collection of talent, that's an odd choice." Steven Rea of Knight-Ridder Newspapers dismissed the film as "an A-list stalker flick that becomes numbingly incoherent and implausible as it runs around the bases...," further noting that De Niro's character "makes no sense beyond a Hollywood caricature of an adrenalized sociopath." And Kenneth Turan of the *Los Angeles Times* called *The Fan* "One of the more feeble and misguided pictures in recent memory," stating that it beggared several probing questions: "Does anyone in Hollywood know how to read? Does anyone think? Is the word 'plausibility' more than an entry in a neglected dictionary?"

The kinder critics allowed that the film starts well, but by and by it "turns into a horror cartoon" and "loses track of subsidiary characters who gave the early scenes a harsh satiric bite." (Stephen Holden, *New York Times*) Others chose to ignore the picture per se and concentrate on the performances: Jay Boyar of the *Orlando Sentinel* observed that Robert De Niro "has done this sort of thing before," but that the actor's "deep understanding of the obsessive mind helps some of his work to survive the film's machete-style editing and pushy, metallic soundtrack." Boyar also regarded Wesley Snipes as "terrific," citing his key scene with the dying child. "When the man realizes that the kid's name is the same as that of his own son, his reaction—just the slightest hesitation—brings the contrived situation to life."

Costing $55 million, *The Fan* grossed a little less than $19 million domestically—a major letdown for Tony Scott, whose movies usually prove to be a license to print money. The film performed better in Japan, where a ready market exists for baseball pictures, good or bad; still, it did not bring in enough to encourage Scott to use baseball as a backdrop for any of his subsequent films, and for that we can be grateful. Admittedly, the leading players are good, and action fans should get their fill; otherwise, the film is best avoided by baseball enthusiasts. While most ballpark pictures invoke the sensory and olfactory pleasures of peanuts, popcorn and Crackerjack, after watching *The Fan* one is likely to be in desperate need of a large, economy-sized bottle of Excedrin.

Fast Company

Paramount/Famous/Lasky; released September 14, 1929

Directed by A. Edward Sutherland. Screenplay by Florence Ryerson, Patrick Kearney and Walter Butterfield; adapted by Patrick Kearney and Walter Butterfield from the play *Elmer the Great* by Ring Lardner and George M. Cohan. Dialogue by Joseph L. Mankiewicz. Photography: Edward Cronjager. Film editor: Jane Loring. Recording engineer: Eugene Merritt. First assistant director: Charles Barton. Song "You Want Lovin', I Want Love" by Sam Coslow. 70 minutes; black and white; sound (silent version, 7 reels/6,459 feet).

Cast: Evelyn Brent (Evelyn Corey); Jack Oakie (Elmer "Hurry" Kane); Richard "Skeets" Gallegher (Bert Wade); Sam Hardy (Dave Walker); Arthur Housman (Barney Barlow); Gwen Lee (Rosie LaClerq); Chester Conklin (Chamber of Commerce President); Eugenie Besserer (Mrs. Kane); Bert Rome (Hank Gordon); Irish Meusel, Arnold "Jigger" Statz, Truck Hannah, Gus Sanberg, Ivy Olson, Wally Rehg, Jack Adams, George Boehler, Howard Barkett, Red Rollings, Frank Greene, Lez Smith (Actual Ballplayers).

Small-town baseball dynamo Elmer "Hurry" Kane heads to the big city for the first time in his life when signed as a rookie for the New York Yankees. He falls hard for gorgeous vaudeville actress Evelyn Corey, who thinks Elmer is a bumptious hick and ignores his overtures. The Yankees' manager, Bert Wade, figuring that Elmer might head back to Gentryville if there isn't something to keep him going, begins sending fake love notes to the big lunkhead, ostensibly signed by Evelyn. Kane's talent helps the Yanks make it to the World Series against the Pittsburgh Pirates, but a ring of gamblers sees a chance for a quick turnover by approaching Elmer and pressuring him to throw a few games. When Kane goes into a slump, Bert Wade assumes his star player has cast his lot with the gamblers, but it turns out that Elmer is playing badly because he's learned that Evelyn's love letters have been faked. Wade locates Evelyn and talks her into showing up for the deciding game to cheer Kane on, and as she does so, she discovers, to her own surprise, that's she's really in love with Kane. Spurred on by romance, Elmer scores the winning run.

Although *Elmer the Great* wasn't the Broadway hit that everyone had anticipated in 1928, the standard operating procedure in Hollywood was to secure the rights for as many literary properties as possible to keep the cameras grinding fifty-two weeks a year (that's how a similar theatrical flop, *Everybody Comes to Rick's*, ended up being filmed as *Casablanca*). In purchasing *Elmer* from Ring Lardner and George M. Cohan, Paramount also bought the rights to "Hurry Kane," Lardner's short story precursor to the play. The subsequent screen treatment by Patrick Kearney and Walter Butterfield pulled elements from both versions of Elmer Kane's saga. Retained was the character of Evelyn Corey, who'd already undergone a transformation from scheming gold digger to essentially nice person when Lardner was cowriting the play with George M. Cohan, and who, for the purposes of the Paramount screenplay, ended up as Elmer's sweetheart instead of the team manager's girl. The business with the phony love letters, an element not in the play, was revived from the short story. The evil designs of the gamblers were also kept, albeit streamlined into simplicity (see the notes on the 1933 movie version of *Elmer* for the play's original, labyrinthine gangster subplot). And as a comedy, the film version couldn't very well do without the predilection of Elmer's teammates to pull practical jokes at the expense of their vainglorious but dimbulbed rookie—including the play's second-act highlight of convincing Elmer that he's making a national radio broadcast.

Gone from the screenplay was Elmer's hometown girl (Minnie in "Hurry Kane," Nellie in the play), lest the ballplayer come off as a heartless lothario when ending up with Evelyn at fade-out time. The Paramount team created a new female second lead, Evelyn's roommate Rosie LaClerq, who existed not for romantic complications but for laughs: Rosie is so dumb, the script tells us, that she was fired from the Five and Dime because she couldn't remember the prices. Another addendum to the source material was having Elmer play not for some fictional team but for the New York Yankees, a timely move in that the real-life Yankees had won the series in both 1927 and 1928 and were riding the crest of their national popularity.

Hired to provide a steady stream of one-liners for what was to be Hollywood's first all-talking baseball picture was young Joseph M. Mankiewicz, light-years removed from his later writer-director triumphs *A Letter to Three Wives*, *All About Eve*, and *The Barefoot Contessa*. Encouraged to build up stars Jack Oakie (as Elmer Kane) and Skeets Gallegher (as Bert Wade) as a team, Mankiewicz at first did what was typical procedure in the stage musicals and revues of the time. "I wrote what I thought were the dramatic necessities," recalled the writer years later, "but when I got to do a scene between Oakie and Gallegher, I wrote quite simply, 'And now follows a comedy sequence between the two comics, at the pleasure of the comedians.' I didn't think anybody ever *wrote* that dialogue!" Mankiewicz soon learned otherwise; he was dragged from a

Sam Hardy (center) labors mightily to steal focus from Skeets Gallegher (left) and Jack Oakie in this promotional still from *Fast Company*.

social engagement by the film's assistant director Charles Barton, driven to the set, and ordered to write some comic dialogue on the spot; thereafter, he remained on the set to punch up the humor during dull stretches. Most of Mankiewicz's efforts consisted of creating malapropisms for Jack Oakie, a job the writer retained throughout six more Oakie vehicles in the next few years.

While the brief climactic game scenes of the film were shot on location at Wrigley Field in Los Angeles (with several real ballplayers in attendance, including Truck Hannah, who also appeared in the Joe E. Brown version of *Elmer the Great*), the inadequacies of the early sound equipment forced the production crew to film most of the picture indoors, and then only between 5 P.M. and 5 A.M. to avoid picking up traffic noises from outside the sound stage. Star Jack Oakie later recalled that the actors and director A. Edward Sutherland kept their spirits up between scenes by bending an elbow or two. The free flow of drinkables during production was reflected in the film's "phony broadcast" sequence; instead of substituting a floor lamp for a microphone to fool Elmer Kane as in the play, the other ballplayers suspend a phony mike from the ceiling by a rope and fill it with empty liquor bottles. Just so we don't miss this gratuitous Prohibition-era gag, Elmer is told that, "Millions are waiting to 'drink up' every word that you utter!" Yes, friends, a laugh a minute.

The film's release title was changed from *Elmer the Great* to *Fast Company*; not only did this entice non-baseball fans with the promise of a raciness that transcended the source material, but it reflected the fact that Evelyn Brent (Evelyn Corey) was given top billing, and obviously *she* wasn't playing Elmer the Great. Humorist Will Rogers reported in a letter to the *Los Angeles Times* that he very nearly didn't see the film on the basis of the new title, considering the change a "sacrilege" and doubting that it would be suitable entertainment for his family; but he ended the letter by saying, "It was the most enjoyable entertainment we ever had."

Whether this blurb was heartfelt or whether it was just a preplanned publicity ploy is unimportant; Rogers's recommendation was extremely beneficial to *Fast Company*'s box office. The film did great business for Paramount, remaining in circulation for several years after its 1929 release before Warners bought the rights to the property for their 1933 Joe E. Brown version of *Elmer the Great* (q.v.).

Fast Company served not only as a money spinner but as a major boost to the career of Jack Oakie, who, like Joe E. Brown, would later designate Elmer Kane his favorite role. For Oakie, the ultimate accolade was a statement made by Walter Huston, who'd originated the role of Kane on Broadway and who reportedly had dearly coveted the lead in the movie version. At the premiere, Huston took Oakie aside and said, "Kid, you *are* Elmer—and you're great."

Modern-day viewers will unfortunately have little opportunity to savor Jack Oakie's performance. As part of the *Elmer the Great* deal with Warner Bros., Paramount removed *Fast Company* completely from public view, even keeping it out of their MCA television package. At last report, the film was leading a lonely life in the vaults of the UCLA Film Library.

Fear Strikes Out

Paramount; released March 1957

Produced by Alan Pakula. Directed by Robert Mulligan. Screenplay by Ted Berkman and Raphael Blau, from the book by James A. Piersall and Albert S. Hirshberg. Photography: Haskell Boggs. Edited by Aaron Stell. Special photographic effects by John P. Fulton. Additional photography: Frank J. Calabria [uncredited]. Art direction by Hal Pereira and Hillyard Brown. Set decoration by Sam Comer and Grace Gregory. Costumes by Edith Head. Makeup by Wally Westmore. Music by Elmer Bernstein. Technical adviser: Thomas E. "Pep" Lee. Assistant director: Richard Cafrey. Filmed in Vista-Vision. 100 minutes; black and white; sound.

Cast: Anthony Perkins (Jimmy Piersall); Karl Malden (John Piersall); Norma Moore (Mary Teevan); Adam Williams (Dr. Brown); Peter J. Votrian (Young Jimmy); Perry Wilson (Mrs. Piersall); Bart Burns (Joe Cronin); Dennis McMullen (Phil); Gail Land (Alice); Brian Hutton (Bernie Sherwell); Rand Harper (Announcer); Howard Price (Bill Tracey); George Pembroke (Umpire); Morgan Jones (Sandy Allen); Edd Byrnes (Friend Who Helps Jimmy Upstairs); Bing Russell (High School Coach); Don Brodie (Ed Slade); and James McNally, Ralph Montgomery, Robert Victor Storm, June Jocelyn, Wade Cagle, Courtland Shepard, Heather Hopper, Mary Benoit, Richard Bull, Gene Craft, John Benson, Eric Alden, Don McGuire, and Marilyn Malloy.

Jimmy Piersall, a young boy growing up in Westport, Connecticut, in the 1940s, wants more than anything to be in Major League baseball. He is reminded that he wants it every day by his father John, himself a frustrated ballplayer. Jimmy and his dad practice pitching until the boy's arm aches, but Jimmy, remembering his father's edict that "Nothing comes easy," never lets John see the pain. The young Piersall works his way into high school baseball, his nerves becoming more strained the more he succeeds; yet still he perseveres, and upon graduation in 1950 he's made it to the Boston Red Sox's farm system. The first stop is Scranton, where Jimmy meets and eventually marries Mary Teevan, a local nurse. She provides Jimmy's only balm from his crippling feeling of inadequacy, which his father unwittingly exacerbates by constantly urging the boy to battle his way out of the minors. The much awaited offer from the Red Sox finally comes, but even here Jimmy isn't completely happy; he believes that Sox owner Joe Cronin is moving him from the outfield (for which Piersall has trained) to the infield as some insidious effort to get rid of him before he even starts. Jimmy wants to quit, but his dad calms him down in his usual understanding manner by replying that if the boy walks, Jimmy is no son of his. Once young Piersall starts playing, he earns a reputation for being hotheaded and stubborn, and his behavior becomes violently erratic. Inevitably, he suffers a breakdown and has to be committed to Westborough State Hospital. His therapist, Dr. Brown, tries every means within his grasp to break down the wall Jimmy has built around himself. Ultimately Jimmy realizes that he's been living his whole life to please his father, and that he has no idea what he really wants for himself. After a brutal confrontation with John Piersall, Jimmy comes to grips with the fact that deep down he really loves baseball, but that he has to stop worrying that he's "not good enough" for his father, and that Dad's got to stop trying to live vicariously through his son. Reconciled with his father, and bolstered by Mary's love, a healthier Jimmy Piersall returns to the Red Sox.

In his 1984 autobiography *The Truth Hurts*, ballplayer cum broadcaster Jimmy Piersall described the film version of his earlier book *Fear Strikes Out* as "a lot of bullshit." He then calmed down, modified his opinion, and admitted that he really thought the film was "horseshit."

The publication of *Fear Strikes Out* in 1955 made Piersall, hitherto known only as the fight-prone bantam cock of the Boston Red Sox (whom a sportswriter described as having potential for being the greatest Boston player ever "if he doesn't get hit by a pitched ball first"), into a national celebrity transcending the sports world. As Jimmy later admitted, the best thing that ever happened to him in terms of fame was his 1952 breakdown; he might otherwise have been just another flashy rookie sent down permanently to the minors for an attitude problem. *Fear Strikes Out* had "soon to be a major motion picture" plastered all over it, but the first dramatic adaptation was to be for television; Tab Hunter (see *Damn Yankees*) portrayed Piersall in the August 8, 1956, presentation of CBS' anthology *Climax*. As Piersall is known far and wide as a fellow who keeps no bad opinion to himself, we must assume that his silence concerning Tab Hunter can mean only that Jimmy approved of the performance, or that he was playing ball that night and didn't see it.

The Paramount Pictures version of *Fear* represented the film debut of the producer-director team of Alan J. Pakula and Robert Mulligan, whose later collaborations included *To Kill a Mockingbird, Love with the Proper Stranger* and *Up the Down Staircase* (Pakula, of course, eventually became a director in his own right, with such superior films as *The Sterile Cuckoo, The Parallax View, All the President's Men* and *Presumed Innocent* to his credit). Producer Pakula described *Fear Strikes Out* in a 1985 article for *American Film* magazine: "It was a work of personal passion on my part.... It interested me on several levels. There was the theme of a boy trying to find his own identity—his own life. A young man finds himself possessed, almost literally possessed, by his father, and finds out that two lives are being led through his life—his father's and his own. The breakaway into his own identity—the breaking out of that chrysalis—is the major part of the story and that character's return to health."

The real Jimmy Piersall had no argument with the basic search for identity premise, but was upset that the film suggested that all his problems stemmed from his relationship with his father. Jimmy never held the elder Piersall responsible for the breakdown, and was always careful to explain that his mother was the family member with the severest emotional difficulties; she spent most of Jimmy's formative years in and out of mental hospitals. The film barely features the mother at all, and then only as a shadowy figure who retreats into the kitchen whenever her husband goes on one of his tirades. Mrs. Piersall's "illnesses" are alluded to in passing, as though her hospital stays were due to physical rather than cerebral ailments.

It would be presumptuous to suggest that the depiction of the father in *Fear Strikes Out* tells us more about the attitudes of the filmmakers toward fatherhood than the real facts of Jimmy Piersall's feelings for his dad. But this presumption would seem to be backed up by Hollywood history. Except for a brief cycle of films with monster moms in the early 1930s (*The Silver Cord*, *Another Language*, *Stage Mother*, etc.), motherhood was generally held sacred. If there was ever a parental villain in an American movie made between 1935 and 1960, it would usually be the father: the drunken lout, the philanderer, the child-beater, the corporate bigwig with no time for his sensitive offspring, and, of course, the aging athlete whose kid had better measure up. The sort of father pictured in *Fear Strikes Out* was even a subject of a 1951 comedy (also made by Paramount!), *That's My Boy*, in which scrawny Jerry Lewis becomes a "real man" in the eyes of his pompous poppa only after excelling in football.

The approach to the elder Piersall in *Fear Strikes Out* was not the only thing that bugged Jimmy. He found it ridiculous that the moviemakers would presume to make a film about a baseball player and then virtually flaunt their ignorance of the game itself. Jimmy would recall in amusement the

fact that Paramount would hire left-handed Anthony Perkins to portray a right-handed ballplayer, then assign Perkins a trainer, former Boston Braves outfielder Tommy Holmes, who was likewise a southpaw! (This absurdity is doubled when one considers the number of right-handed actors Hollywood has been able to conjure up over the years to play such lefties as Lou Gehrig, Babe Ruth and Eddie Collins.) Piersall would also get a laugh and a half out of the fact that the studio sent director Robert Mulligan to Boston's Fenway Park in the hopes of getting some good background footage to match with the close shots (filmed, as ever, at Wrigley Field in L.A.). "See if you can hit a home run tonight, will you, Jimmy?" implored Mulligan. Jimmy did so—and in fact did it in the ninth with the score tied, just like in the movies—but Mulligan's footage was never used. All we see of Fenway Park in *Fear Strikes Out* is a long shot under the opening credits and a brief scene in which Anthony Perkins walks out on the field alone and *imagines* he's in a big game.

While Piersall admitted he could not honestly judge the scenes in which his screen counterpart underwent shock treatment (the ballplayer remembered none of this experience), he was dissatisfied with the recreation of his breakdown. The scene occurs during a ballgame, in which Jimmy, pressured by his father in the stands to knock one out of the park, hits his home run, then scurries around screaming maniacally, "Was it good enough? Was I good enough for you?" and finally climbs the wire screen behind the catcher's mound. This scene, with its inescapable allusion to a trapped animal clawing at his cage, is the one everyone who's seen the film remembers most vividly. Piersall's response was simply that he never climbed any screen. He could have gone further by saying that there wasn't any screen to climb. His breakdown actually occurred in a hotel room in

Fear Strikes Out: Jimmy Piersall (Anthony Perkins, left) once again falls short of the standards set by his demanding father (Karl Malden, right).

Sarasota, Florida, miles and miles away from any ballpark.

Jimmy's biggest beef about *Fear Strikes Out* was the casting of Anthony Perkins. Piersall griped that Perkins "threw like a girl" and danced around the outfield "like a ballerina." It should be noted in all fairness that Piersall personally liked Anthony Perkins, and that one of the ballplayer's favorite movies was *Psycho*, in which, of course, Perkins played another young man living under the thumb of an oppressive—albeit stone cold dead—parent. (There. That's the only allusion to *Psycho* you're going to see in this essay. Aren't you glad I didn't comment on the scene in *Fear Strikes Out* when Anthony Perkins sticks his head under a shower?)

This dissatisfaction with Anthony Perkins has carried over to less intimately in-

volved observers of the film. Ron Shelton, the writer-director of *Bull Durham* (q.v.), commented in 1988 that the moment in which Perkins catches a fly ball with his wrists together was "probably the low point in sports movies." Shelton, like Piersall, was basing this reminiscence on impressions gleaned by a first viewing (in Piersall's case the *only* viewing) of *Fear Strikes Out*. Though it is obvious that Perkins was cast on the basis of his histrionic range instead of his athletic know-how, he never catches a ball with his wrists together in the film, nor is his zigzag clodhopping around the outfield evocative of a ballerina. While it's true that Anthony Perkins is as much a baseball player as the girl playing Mary Piersall, director Robert Mulligan takes great pains to work around this. Most of Perkins's ballplaying is represented by quick "flash" shots, interrupted by crowd reactions or long shots of the ballfield. For a movie novice, Mulligan—with the aid of film editor Aaron Stell—displays a firm grip on the art of staging a sports event through piecemeal illusion rather than head-on factual documentation.

The one complaint about Anthony Perkins in this film that has direct relation to the Jimmy Piersall that fans have come to know and love is that, even after getting out of the mental institution, Perkins seems constitutionally incapable of having any *fun*. The Piersall in *Fear Strikes Out* may have been capable of leaving his glove at home before going off to spring training in 1951, subliminally hoping that this would get him sent back (a true story, curiously unused in the movie). But this Piersall could never have pulled the stunts that the real Jimmy has carried off: Perkins' Piersall could never run backward around the bases after his one hundredth homer, nor bow and flap like a seal after making a stellar play, nor carry a can of bug spray into the outfield, nor come on the field wearing a football helmet after being ordered to get some head protection. Anthony Perkins's performance is a fascinating glimpse of what passed for realistic acting in 1957 (an odd brew of equal parts Montgomery Clift and James Dean), and it certainly keeps within the grim, unrelenting mood of the film itself; but in showing us how heavily, somberly serious he can be, Anthony Perkins never truly becomes that curious combination of tempestuous temperament and goofy grandstanding that is the Jimmy Piersall we've witnessed for over forty years.

Come to think of it, there would probably be a good film in the years *after* the breakdown, especially in the love-hate relationship between Jimmy Piersall and White Sox owner Bill Veeck. Perhaps Piersall, who was reportedly once courted by Hollywood to act in a film version of Booth Tarkington's *Clarence*, could be induced to

play himself—if Kevin Kline or Kevin Spacey weren't available, that is.

While *Fear Strikes Out* is shaky both as a true to life biography and as a textbook example of proper psychiatric procedure—few contemporary mental hospitals go for the straitjacket and electroshock therapy as quickly or as frequently as the treatment center depicted in this film—it still works on the level of tense, taut melodrama. The film is kept from getting completely out of hand by the careful performance of Karl Malden who, as Jimmy's father, is never a mustache-twirling villain but a troubled man driven by his own thwarted ambitions, a man who we never doubt for a moment dearly loves his son despite the unintended harm he inflicts upon him. In his 1997 autobiography *When Do I Start?*, Malden claimed that he based his characterization of John Piersall on his *own* father—something that he was not even consciously aware of until he saw the completed film!

Perhaps the passage of time will minimize the inaccuracies of *Fear Strikes Out* and allow it to stand on its own as a well-crafted character study. As for now, with the memories of Jimmy Piersall's playing days and his broadcast booth career still fresh in the minds of many baseball fans, the temptation is great to amend the introductory title of *Fear Strikes Out*, which tells us that the film is "taken from the account of [Piersall's] own life," by yelling back at the screen, "Yeah. Taken as far as possible."

Field of Dreams

Gordon Productions/Universal; released April 21, 1989

Produced by Lawrence and Charles Gordon. Directed by Phil Alden Robinson. Screenplay by Phil Alden Robinson, based on the novel *Shoeless Joe* by W. P. Kinsella. Executive producer and unit manager: Brian Frankish. Associate producer: Lloyd Levin. Photography:

John Lindley. Edited by Ian Crawford. Music by James Horner; popular songs heard on soundtrack performed by the original artists. Production design by Dennis Gasiner. Costumes by Linda Bass. Casting by Margery Simkin. Sound by Russell Williams, III. Makeup by Richard Arlington. Assistant director: William M. Elvin. Color by Deluxe. 106 minutes; Dolby Sound. Rated PG.

Cast: Kevin Costner (Ray Kinsella); Amy Madigan (Annie Kinsella); Ray Liotta (Shoeless Joe Jackson); James Earl Jones (Terence Mann); Burt Lancaster (Dr. "Moonlight" Graham); Timothy Busfield (Mark); Gabby Hoffman (Karin Kinsella); Dwier Brown (John Kinsella); Frank Whaley (Archie Graham); James Andelin (Feed Store Farmer); Mary Ann Kean (Feed Store Lady); Fern Persons (Annie's Mother); Kelly Coffield (Dee, Mark's Wife); Michael Milhoan (Buck Weaver); Steve Eastin (Eddie Cicotte); Charles Hoyes (Swede Risberg); Art LaFleur (Chick Gandil); Lee Garlington (Beulah, the Angry PTA Mother); Mike Nussbaum (Principal); Larry Brandenberg, Mary McDonald Gershon, Robert Kurcz (PTA Hecklers); Don John Ross (Boston Butcher); Bea Fredman (Boston Yenta); Geoffrey Nauffts (Boston Pump Jockey); Anne Seymour (Chisholm Newspaper Publisher); C. George Blasi (First Man in Bar); Howard Sherf (Second Man in Bar); Joseph Ryan (Third Man in Bar); Joe Glasberg (Customer); Mark Danker, Frank Dardis, Jim Doty, Mike Gold, Jay Hemond, Mike Hodge, Steve Jenkins, Terry Kelleher, Ron Lucas, Fred Martin, Curt McWilliams, Jude Milbert, Steve Olbering, Gene Potts, James Rogh, Paul Scherrman, Dale Till, Tom Vogel (Additional Ballplayers), Brian Frankish (Clean-Shaven Umpire); Jeffrey Neal Silverman (Clean-Shaven Center Fielder); The Voice (Himself).

"If you build it, he will come." This is the message that thirty-six-year-old neophyte farmer Ray Kinsella hears as he walks through the cornfield of his Iowa farm. Thrown off balance by the disembodied voice, Ray then sees flash images of a baseball field and of Shoeless Joe Jackson, the great ballplayer banned from the game for life in the wake of the 1919 Black Sox scandal. Jackson had been the idol of Ray's father, a man "worn down by age" who lived

a life of frustration after abandoning an incipient baseball career. Ray explains to his wife Annie that the message of the Voice has compelled him to avoid becoming like his father, who never did an impulsive, spontaneous thing in his life—which is why Ray proceeds to plow down his cornfield and build a baseball park! Ray somehow feels that the "he will come" part of the Voice's prediction means that the spirit of Shoeless Joe Jackson will appear in the ballfield, and appear he does. "Is this heaven?" asks Jackson, thrilled at the prospect of playing ball again. "No," replies Ray. "It's Iowa."

It's also real life outside that ballpark, and Ray is being pressured by his pragmatic brother-in-law Mark to sell his land or face bankruptcy. Mark is no romantic; he sees no Shoeless Joe, nor the ghostly White Sox teammates that Joe brings with him to play ball; but Ray, Annie, and their daughter Karin not only see the "visitors" but converse with them and kibitz their games. It isn't long before the Voice offers a second message to Ray: "Ease his pain." After attending a PTA meeting in which a debate is under way to ban from the local school the works of 1960s radical writer Terence Mann, Ray determines that it is the now-reclusive Mann's pain that must be eased— the pain of a man who once said in an interview that he'd always regretted never playing a ballgame at New York's old Polo Grounds. Further strengthening Ray's resolve is the fact that in his last short story, Mann named one of his characters John Kinsella, just like Ray's dad. Ray drives all the way to Boston where he abducts an unwilling Terence Mann at gunpoint (actually at finger point, since Ray carries no weapon) and compels the Pulitzer Prize–winning author to attend a baseball game at Fenway Park. Here the two men hear the Voice's next message—"Go the distance"—and see the name and statistics of a "Dr. Archibald `Moonlight' Graham" on the scoreboard.

Graham had been a New York Giants team member and had played one half of one inning in 1922, after which he left the big city to become a beloved, selfless doctor in Chisholm, Minnesota.

Following the logic that has dictated the rest of this story, Ray and Terence Mann set out for Minnesota in Ray's beat-up van to "collect" Moonlight Graham. It doesn't matter that Moonlight died sixteen years earlier, in 1972; Ray meets and talks with Graham all the same. The white-haired doctor has no regrets about becoming a general practitioner, but allows that he's always wished he had played one whole ballgame through and scored a hit. Graham refuses to join Ray for the trip back to Iowa, but on the road home Ray and Mann pick up a teenager who prattles on in the manner of a 1920s youth about becoming a Minor League ballplayer. The boy's name is Archie Graham, and once he's in the Iowa ballpark he suits up and plays with Shoeless Joe's White Sox and the specters of several other baseball greats, eventually achieving his home run.

By now, Terence Mann is able to see the ghosts along with the Kinsella family, but he doesn't understand why *he's* been called to the ballfield. Brother-in-law Mark, still blind to the whimsy that everyone else accepts, shows up to tell Ray that the Kinsellas are broke and to urge him to sell the farm. Even an impassioned speech by Terence Mann about baseball being the one good thing that has been constant in a changing America—and Mann's assertion that Ray can keep his farm if he allows visitors to come and share the past and their past dreams in the ballfield for only $20 per person—fails to dissuade Mark from trying to wrest the farm away. Suddenly, the Kinsellas' daughter Karin falls from the bleachers and gets a hot dog lodged in her throat. That's when young Archie Graham steps away from the diamond and becomes elderly Dr. Graham, here to save Karin

from choking. Dr. Graham cannot go back to the ballplayers, but he now has realized both his dream about playing and the fact that he'd been washed out of the game to become a doctor for a divine purpose. Mark relents, telling Ray that he's *got* to keep his farm! Dr. Moonlight Graham disappears into the cornfield surrounding the ballpark, and as the other players follow him, Shoeless Joe turns to invite Terence Mann to join them. Mann now knows that if he heads into that cornfield he'll have one great story to write—and realizes further that he's been called to Iowa to overcome his disillusionment that the 1960s hadn't turned out as well as he'd hoped and to reactivate his long-abandoned writing skills.

After Terence Mann vanishes, Shoeless Joe has one more surprise for Ray: the new player standing near the batter's box is Ray's own father. Now the younger Kinsella knows who "will come," whose pain will be eased, and why Ray has "gone the distance"—it's to be reunited with the father whom he'd never forgiven for growing old and never fulfilling his dreams. As Ray and his once more youthful father play a game of catch, we see that Terence Mann's prediction that people from all over would be inexorably drawn to the Field of Dreams was true: thousands upon thousands of motorists choke the highway, lined up to relive their own dreams in a cornfield in Iowa.

As anyone who's watched any of the cable–TV sports services in the past fifteen years can tell you, the Field of Dreams really exists, just four miles outside the teeming metropolis of Dyersville, Iowa, off Highway 136. Neighboring farmers Don Lansing and Al Ameskamp willingly permitted the filmmakers to plow down their crops, erect the ballfield, and lay the diamond. Lansing decided to let his portion of the ballfield stand as a memento of his fifteen minutes of fame, while Ameskamp replanted his corn, observing sardonically that, "the

Field of Dreams: Ray Kinsella (Kevin Costner, left) journeys back to 1972 to invite the long-departed "Moonlight Graham" (Burt Lancaster) to Ray's cornfield diamond in Iowa.

only voices I've been hearing out there are saying, 'Al, it's dry.'" Ameskamp eventually relented as hundreds of movie fans drove to Iowa in search of the phantom ballpark. The whole field was reconstructed as a tourist attraction, a place where anyone—no matter what degree of athletic talent—could show up with bat and glove and play baseball to his heart's content. In 1990 some 14,000 visitors were drawn to the site, a number which would increase dramatically (tenfold in 1991 alone!) with each passing year.

There might have been no such attraction, nor even any such movie as *Field of Dreams*, had producers Lawrence and Charles Gordon gone along with the Hollywood consensus that the proposed film, in Charles Gordon's words, "contained three elements that you should never make movies about: fantasy, baseball, and farming."

This "unsaleable" fantasy first appeared as *Shoeless Joe*, a 1982 novel expanded by author W. P. Kinsella from his own short story, "Shoeless Joe Jackson Comes to Iowa." Kinsella drew upon his love of baseball and the various elements surrounding the sport that had always intrigued him, adopting a "what if...?" approach. What if Shoeless Joe Jackson were given an opportunity in the next world to redeem himself for the sins committed in the first? What if "Moonlight" Graham, who actually existed and who really did play only half an inning in a single game in 1905, could be brought back from beyond and asked his feelings on the way his life turned out? And what if there was a real, perhaps cosmic, significance in the fact that the surname "Kinsella" appeared in two fictional works by J. D. Salinger—who appears under his own name in *Shoeless Joe*, rather than in the thinly disguised person of the film's Terence Mann—and who, in keeping with the baseball motif, actually once wrote a piece about missing the great days of Ebbets Field?

Three years or so after its publication, the novel was shaped into a screenplay by Phil Alden Robinson, who would ultimately direct the filmization of *Shoeless Joe* (the film bore that title almost until its April 1989 release; the change to *Field of Dreams* was made so that the film would not be confused with *Eight Men Out* [q.v.], a dramatization of the Black Sox affair which, of course, also featured Shoeless Joe Jackson). Robinson's treatment drew upon the novel's use of baseball as a metaphor for the game of life, and Ray Kinsella's ballfield as a four-cornered Land of Oz, where people are granted their heart's desire or learn that they've had their heart's desire all along but didn't realize it; the script also follows the novel's basic plotline. But there are significant differences between the Kinsella original and Robinson's screen version that are worth touching upon.

The first difference is in approach. Kinsella treats the story as a sort of adult daydream (though it's clear that everyone is wide awake), wherein people accept the unexplainable in stride, and once these people decide they're going to do something bizarre, they're able to do it with a minimum of resistance and a cheerful disregard for the realities of time and logic. As in a daydream, all of one's various icons congregate in a single place, and they're all agreeable people who interact and who carry on casual conversations using the sort of words that one had always imagined or wished they'd use. *Shoeless Joe* is in fact the "perfect" dream, wherein the protagonist calls all the shots and provides a happy ending within the framework of something that he dearly loves—in this case, baseball.

Sustaining a movie "dream sequence" is difficult enough for a few minutes, and well-nigh impossible for nearly two hours. In adapting Kinsella's book, Phil Alden Robinson opted for a head-on "This is really happening, folks!" approach. Anticipating audience resistance toward the fantasy angle, Robinson transferred that resistance to the two characters for whom "suspension of disbelief" was most crucial in the film: Ray Kinsella and Terence Mann. Initially, neither character can bring himself to accept that a "Field of Dreams" is possible (in Mann's case, skepticism takes the form of physical violence); but once their resistance is broken down by the course of events, it becomes easier for the audience to "go the distance" to the final scene. Robinson's use of Ray Kinsella and Terence Mann as bellwethers for the viewers makes the fantasy work on-screen. Think of how hard it would have been to swallow *Close Encounters of the Third Kind* and *Ghost* if the scripts hadn't provided, respectively, Richard Dreyfuss and Whoopi Goldberg to act as the audience's eyes, hearts, and minds, transmitting their gradual acceptance of fantasy as fact into *our* acceptance.

Several fascinating characters who provide twists and sidebars to the plot of *Shoeless Joe* are dispensed with in the screenplay. In the novel, Ray Kinsella has an identical twin brother named Richard, who earlier had stormed out of the family after harsh words with his father, while "good boy" Ray had stayed home. The Yin and Yang quality of nice and nasty mirror-image twins has its fascinations, but would have cluttered up *Field of Dreams'* relatively clean through-line, so out it went, and the screen character of Ray Kinsella became a combination of the positive and negative qualities of the book's twins. Another casualty from *Shoeless Joe* was Eddie Scissons, who claims he's the world's oldest living Chicago Cub. Scissons, who owns the mortgage to the Kinsella farm, is blackmailed into selling out to Ray's brother-in-law Mark when threatened with exposure as a fraud who never even made it to the Major leagues. A repentant Eddie Scissons ultimately has his own dream fulfilled on the ballfield, rallies the players together with an evangelical speech about "the Word of baseball," then dies and is buried in his Cubs uniform in Ray's cornfield. Screenwriter Robinson decided that, given Moonlight Graham's second crack at bat and J. D. Salinger/Terence Mann's rapturous speech on behalf of baseball and his courageous journey into the unknown beyond the cornfield, Eddie Scissons was rather extraneous to the script of *Field of Dreams*.

Even if Eddie had been retained, he wouldn't have worked because of the film's demonization of brother-in-law Mark. In the novel this character is likened by narrator Ray Kinsella to a top-hatted, mustachioed villain in an old-time melodrama. Mark and his equally odious business partners exist as The Menace, devoted to smashing dreams—literally, by taking a bulldozer to Ray's grandstands—rather than fulfilling them. While Phil Alden Robinson cannot be accused of subtlety—when, for example, Ray Kinsella steps back in time to 1972, he sees a "Re-Elect Nixon" poster, a movie marquee advertising *The Godfather*, and, in case we've missed the point up to now, a license plate dated 1972—it's to his credit that he humanizes the stock "evil land grabber" character of Mark into a businesslike young fellow whose stuffiness cannot conceal his genuine concern for his sister and brother-in-law, and whose only crime is a lack of imagination and faith.

The softening of Mark is emblematic of an overall improvement made by Robinson on Kinsella's source material. After watching *Field of Dreams*, it comes as a shock to find how petty and mean-spirited Ray Kinsella can be in *Shoeless Joe*, particularly when describing anyone who doesn't hold to his viewpoints, and most especially when trashing such major league towns as

Chicago and Cleveland. At the end of the story Ray uses a gun to ward off the bulldozers on his land; a justified act, perhaps, but one that smacks of those camouflage covered "survivalists" who plan to kill any neighbor invading their turf during a national emergency. Since it's very hard to completely like the book's Ray Kinsella, scenarist Robinson makes Ray more ingenuous and not at all vindictive. The benefits of this transformation can be found in Ray's first scene with Terence Mann, where Kinsella bends over backward to explain that he's not crazy nor is he demanding anything more of Mann but three hours' company at a ballgame. Had Robinson not removed the nasty streak which Ray Kinsella exhibits in the book, this sequence would have lost all its appealing sincerity and turned into the manipulative act of a very small person.

A few of Robinson's "improvements" are done to make the story accessible to viewers more familiar with their past movie-going experiences than with baseball history. It may seem like reaching for an easy laugh when one of the ghostly ballplayers dissolves into the cornfield while screeching a Margaret Hamilton–like "I'm melting! I'm mellllting!" or when Annie Kinsella kiddingly suggests that Terence Mann's fondness for baseball stems from his once owning a bat named "Rosebud." In all fairness, however, these lines do get laughs, they provide a frame of reference for the viewer, and they bring the story down to earth whenever it threatens to get too ethereal for its own good.

Only one of Robinson's alterations from the book can be considered a misfire, though its intentions were honorable. Robinson was faced with the problem of making the character of Annie Kinsella—who in the book is hardly a character at all—something that a decent actress would consider worth playing; he also had to make clear that Terence Mann was based upon

J. D. Salinger without incurring the wrath of Salinger himself, who was already annoyed at being made a character in someone else's novel. The solution to the Annie Kinsella quagmire was to take a cue from the fact that the screenplay establishes Annie and Ray as "children of the 1960s," so that Annie is naturally incensed that there's going to be a PTA meeting to possibly ban "obscene" literature from Iowa's schools. This plot device is drawn from several well-publicized real instances of communities trying to protect youngsters from thinking for themselves, wherein J. D. Salinger's *Catcher in the Rye* has frequently headed the "forbidden" list. As Annie vehemently defends Terence Mann against censorship at the PTA meeting, her words leave little doubt who Mann is supposed to be, and at the same time the scene gives Annie Kinsella a lot more to do in the film than her counterpart in the novel—who spends most of her time blandly agreeing to everything her husband says.

Alas, the PTA meeting is by far the worst sequence in *Field of Dreams*. The principal instigator of the censorship movement is an "establishment pig" stereotype straight out of the strident agit-prop "youth movies" of two decades earlier. This suppression-prone lady loses all credibility by defending her position with words like "masturbation" and "horse's ass"—a ham-handed effort to show the hypocrisy of self-styled censors. To make matters worse, we're supposed to root for Annie when she calls the PTA lady a "Nazi cow" and "Eva Braun"—phrases that reduce Annie to the same yahoo level as her opponent. As she leaves the meeting Annie says exultantly, "It was just like the sixties again." Unfortunately, she's right.

This misbegotten scene aside, Robinson's screenplay was a marvel to behold, and the producers—the Gordon brothers—were behind it wholeheartedly. The problem remained in pitching a baseball picture to an interested distributor, of which there were precisely none until MCA Motion Pictures Group executive Tom Pollock decided he liked the story so much he was willing to make it with an unknown as a star. "This is the kind of movie you make only if a voice tells you to," said Pollock, to which Phil Alden Robinson responded, "If you make it, they will come."

As it turned out, the star was no unknown but was instead rising young leading man Kevin Costner. When asked if he felt comfortable starting a baseball film so soon after completing *Bull Durham* (q.v.), Costner replied that he found Robinson's script "magical," and that he'd do five films in a row on a single subject if the material was that good (Costner's name was not yet quite as "magical" to Universal's publicists, who in their press releases frequently intimated that Burt Lancaster, cast in the six-minute cameo of Dr. Moonlight Graham, was the film's real star).

The trick was to make Kevin Costner, whose ballfield expertise in *Bull Durham* was becoming legendary in sports film circles, look like a rank amateur when playing against Shoeless Joe Jackson. It was up to the film's Jackson, Ray Liotta, to train for hours on end perfecting his pitching and batting technique to come within shouting distance of the great Shoeless Joe; indeed, Liotta became so accomplished in his newfound talent that he caused Kevin Costner to nearly drop character in surprise at the speed of Liotta's batted balls (the scene is in the film; watch for Costner's self-conscious giggle).

The filming was not an easy one, requiring sixty-four grueling shooting days in the sweltering summer of 1988; in fact, a lengthy Iowa drought forced the filmmakers to provide their own water—gallons of it—so that the cornstalks would grow tall enough to enable the actors to "vanish" into the cornfield. But the extra effort shows on screen; *Field of Dreams* comes as close to an ideal grown-up fantasy as one could ask for. The performances of Costner, James Earl Jones, Ray Liotta, and Burt Lancaster maintain the level of matter-of-fact acceptance of the hairiest events that is established from the first scene to the last by Phil Alden Robinson. Only Amy Madigan as Annie Kinsella seems a bit over the top, but her wacked-out performance is forgivable when one considers that she is the sort of woman an esoteric type like Kevin Costner's Ray Kinsella would probably end up marrying—someone who'd do all the shouting for both of them.

Director Robinson's comments on *Field of Dreams* in *Time* magazine provide a clue as to why he was able to achieve such superb, clearheaded results with a maximum of believability and a minimum of treacle: "It's a longing for a more innocent time, for easy connections that grew complicated with the years. We live in cynical times. We're all jaded. A lot of our heroes have turned out to have clay feet. I don't believe in astrology, crystals, reincarnations, heaven, hell. I don't believe dreams come true. But it's a primal emotion to want to make the bad good—to hope things will turn out in the end."

At one point in filming, something *did* turn out well in an almost mystical manner. The celestial fog that appears on the ballfield just before Joe Jackson asks if Iowa is heaven was no preplanned special effect courtesy of Industrial Light and Magic; it was a genuine mist, one that touched ground for a mere five minutes—and the *only* fog seen in that area throughout the entire summer of 1988!

Baseball buffs were as well served as fantasy fans. *Field of Dreams'* ballpark scenes transcend any and all plot absurdities with their energy, credibility, and cunning use of camera angles that put us in the thick of the action when the occasion dictates. The one glaring inaccuracy of these scenes, that of having Shoeless Joe bat right and pitch

left instead of the other way around, was forgiven once the baseball historians accepted the film's basic thesis: baseball is more than a game; it's an idea to love and an ideal to strive for. In this respect, *Field of Dreams* cannot be faulted. (And besides, reasoned the baseball aficionados, how many other films have had the decency to explain to non-baseball fans the reason why a southpaw is called a southpaw?)

It always helps to punch the right emotional buttons at the right time, and the spring of 1989 was precisely that time for *Field of Dreams*. Millions of male baby-boomers were waking up to find themselves on the fringes of middle age with most of their youthful aspirations and hopes of creating a better world either compromised or forgotten. Stories of men aged thirty-five to forty-five who sat with reddened, runny eyes as the "end" credits rolled on *Field* were legion; even movie idol Arnold Schwarzenegger admitted to having himself a good cry. This was the audience—above and beyond the female viewers who came to drool over Kevin Costner—that made *Field of Dreams* a box office hit to the tune of over $62 million, and a perennial "Opening Day" attraction on cable television ever afterward.

Finding Buck McHenry

Showtime Networks Inc.; limited theatrical release, January 1, 2000. Cable-TV premiere: April 16, 2000

Executive producers: Robert Halmi, Jr., Robert M. Heller, Lin Oliver. Line producer: Stephen J. Turnbull. Directed by Charles Burnett. Written by Alfred Sloate and David Field, based on the novel by Alfred Sloate. Photography: John L. Demps, Jr. Original music: Stephen James Taylor. Edited by Dorian Harris. Casting: Claire Hewitt, Pat McCorkle. Production design: Kathleen Climie. Art direction: Marilyn Kiewiet. Set decoration: Erica Milo. Costume design: Tamara Winston. Hair stylist: George Aywaz. Key makeup artist: Marysue

Heron. Production manager: Stephen J. Turnbull. First assistant director: Kim MacLachlan. Second assistant director: Allison Winn. Supervising sound editor: Andrew DeCristofaro. Sound effects editor: Rebecca Hanck. Production sound mixer: Michael LaCroix. Foley artists: Laura Macias, Sean Rowe. Color. 93 minutes; Dolby Surround Sound. Rated PG.

Cast: Ossie Davis (Mac Henry); Ruby Dee (Mrs. Henry); Ernie Banks (Ollie Johnson); Michael Schiffman (Jason Ross); Duane McLaughlin (Aaron Henry); Megan Bower (Kim Axelrod); Kevin Jubinville (Chuck Axelrod); Michael Rhoades (Jim Davis); Karl Pruner (Mr. Ross); Catherine Blythe (Mrs. Ross); Don Dickinson (Coach Barker); Marcello Meleca (Tug); Jim Millington (Brad); Anthony Antonacci (Joey Kovich); J. J. Gallo (Carl Diaz); Brad Borbridge (Camera Man); Conrad Coates (Hartford Cole); Michael Cranston (Franklin); Alex Crockard-Villa (Tyler); Tait Rowsel, Donovan Palma (Kids on Bikes); Lynn Vogt (Mrs. Baker); Sonia Dhillon (Channel 4 Anchorwoman).

Suburban youngster Jason Ross has a huge collection of rare baseball cards and an enormous poster of Mark McGwire in his bedroom, but simply loving the game and memorizing minutiae prove to be inadequate substitutes for genuine baseball talent. "It's hard when your skills don't measure up to your dreams," sighs Coach Barker as he cuts Jason from the Lasers, a team in the local Twelve-Year-Old League. As compensation, Barker suggests that Jason join the Stadium Sluggers, a new expansion team which is being formed by TV sportscaster Chuck Axelrod, who has gotten involved in the League so that his daughter Kim, a talented shortstop, can play ball. Jim Davis, owner of the sports-memorabilia shop where Jason spends virtually all his leisure hours, offers to sponsor the new team, provided that Jason can find an adult coach. After being given some savvy ball-playing tips by elderly grade-school custodian Mac Henry, Jason asks the old man to serve as coach. Reluctant at first, Mr. Henry finally accepts the job, hoping that participation in the team will shake his grandson

Aaron—who'd been a champion junior-league pitcher in his native Memphis—out of the deep depression that has weighed heavily upon the boy since the deaths of his parents. After a few days' drilling by Mr. Henry, whose baseball expertise is nothing short of amazing, Jason happens to drop by Jim Davis' shop, where he peruses a set of baseball cards celebrating the stars of the old Negro Leagues. Among these unsung heroes is right-handed pitcher Buck McHenry, who, during a meteoric three-year career in the late 1940s, chalked up ninety wins, but who sudden dropped out of baseball—and apparently off the face of the earth—after a skirmish with the Law. Scrutinizing the card, Jason becomes obsessed with the notion that Buck McHenry and coach Mac Henry are one and the same. Despite Mr. Henry's adamant denials that he is the long-lost Buck, Jason doggedly pursues the matter, ultimately convincing Chuck Axelrod to put together a TV tribute to the "rediscovered" McHenry. Worried that Jason's insistence upon transferring his own baseball fantasies to old Mr. Henry will cause nothing but trouble and embarrassment, both Jason's father and Jim Davis do some detective work on their own, arriving at the conclusion that the real Buck McHenry died in 1950. This is apparently confirmed beyond doubt when, during a visit to the Negro League Museum in Kansas City, Jason is informed by McHenry's best friend, retired baseball promoter Ollie Johnson, that Buck is not only dead but buried in the local cemetery. The disappointed Jason is on the verge of apologizing to Mr. Henry when a stroke of fate forces the old gentleman to make a startling confession—one which totally flummoxes Mac's wife of forty years, who up until this moment was convinced that she knew all she had to know about her husband.

Finding Buck McHenry came into being as a 1991 novel by Alfred Sloate, a writer who specialized in using baseball as a backdrop for such sensitive topics as divorce and terminal illness. The original novel is that rare thing, a children's book capable of entertaining and enthralling adult readers, and Sloate manages to capture most of its charm and appeal in his script (cowritten with David Field) for the TV-movie adaptation of *Finding Buck McHenry*.

Carried over to the film version is protagonist Jason Ross' encyclopedic knowledge of baseball statistics, gleaned from his vast collection of bubble-gum cards. Jason even identifies individual players by their original card numbers: Satchel Paige is "Ace 129," for example. As in the novel, the film's Jason assumes that just because he loves baseball and has committed reams of stats to memory, this will automatically make him a top ballplayer—and he is just as wrong in the film as in the novel.

In both the book and the film, Jason's interest in the Negro Leagues is piqued when Mac Henry challenges the boy to find out the reason why a Mickey Mantle rookie card commands a higher marketplace price than a first-year card for Willie Mays, especially since Mays was the better player. In the film, it seems odd that an inquisitive youngster like Jason, who knows baseball history inside and out, would never have heard of the Negro Leagues. The book addresses this matter by having first-person narrator Jason introspectively kick himself for his ignorance: "How could I know so much about baseball and all of a sudden know so little?" Once Jason *does* learn about the Negro Leagues, both the novel and the movie become post-graduate courses on the subject, with player names like Josh Gibson, Cool Papa Bell and Judy Johnson, and team names like the Pittsburgh Crawfords, the Indianapolis Clowns, the Cleveland Buckeyes, the Homestead Grays, the Kansas City Monarchs and the Baltimore Elite Giants bandied about with breezy abandon, encouraging readers and viewers alike to seek out even more information on the history of black baseball.

Most of the characters in the novel are faithfully transferred to the script, with a few improvements. Kim Axelrod, the sole female player on the Stadium Sluggers, is transformed from a standard tomboy into the film's resident 12-year-old curmudgeon, casting a disdainful eye upon ballplayers whose talents are inferior to hers, and making sardonic under-the-breath comments whenever circumstances are beyond her control. Nostalgia-shop owner Jim Davis, a likable if nondescript character in the book, is fleshed out in the film as the sort of ebullient overgrown adolescent who generally ends up running a comic-book store or trading-card emporium in real life. Delightfully played by Michael Rhoades (an actor previously typecast in villainous roles), Jim Davis has one of the best lines in the film: After warning Jason to be careful while delving into the past of Buck McHenry, Jim stops short and asks himself, "Since when did *I* become an adult?"

Where the book and the film radically part company is in the resolution of the Mac Henry/Buck McHenry dichotomy—and for those who have neither read nor seen *Finding Buck McHenry*, be warned that there are several "spoilers" ahead.

Jason stumbles upon the possibility that Mac Henry is really Buck McHenry relatively early in the novel—whereupon Mac, after token resistance, breaks down and admits that he is Buck McHenry, then launches into a stream of behind-the-scenes anecdotes about the pleasures and disadvantages of life in the Negro Leagues. But when sportscaster Chuck Axelrod, ever in pursuit of higher ratings, proposes a half-hour TV interview with Mac, the old man suddenly becomes reluctant to talk about himself. His back to the wall, Mac makes a jaw-dropping confession: *He isn't Buck McHenry at all!* True, Mac did briefly play baseball, but only on an obscure semipro team. His "eyewitness" knowledge of the Negro Leagues was based upon the fact that he saw the real Buck McHenry and his colleagues in action, and was picked up second-hand from black ballplayers who'd roomed with Mac's family in Georgia after being denied admission in the local white hotels and boarding houses. Mac is saved from further embarrassment when Kim Axelrod persuades her father to go ahead with the TV interview, albeit with an explanation as to why Mac Henry felt the need to lie about himself.

That explanation is threefold. First of all, Mac wanted to attract players to Jason's expansion team, and he felt that the kids would rather be coached by a "celebrity" than an obscure school custodian. Mac also felt obligated to apprise the general public about the sacrifices made by the original black ballplayers in blazing the trail for such later superstars as Reggie Jackson and Barry Bonds: the lousy pay, the poor accommodations, the lack of status, and above all, the humiliation endured by barnstorming Negro League players when forced to allow local white semipro teams to win against them in exhibition games. It wasn't that the African American players threw these games for money; rather, it was a matter of simply not winning so that they'd be invited back to play the same white teams the following season. As Mac explains, "You could [say] we earned our pay, because it was a lot harder to lose to those teams than to beat them." The scrape with the law that forced Buck McHenry to go into hiding occurred the day he refused to allow an inferior white player to strike him out, culminating in a free-for-all in which the angry Buck beat his white opponent senseless— virtually a hanging offense in the South of the 1940s. Since Buck McHenry was no longer around to tell his story—which in a sense was the story of *every* black ballplayer in the pre–Jackie Robinson era—Mac Henry took it upon himself to enlighten the world

about the "other" side of baseball that had so long been swept under the rug. One could describe Mac Henry as the Boswell for Buck McHenry's Samuel Johnson, except that Boswell never felt the urge to *become* Johnson to get his story out.

The most important catalyst for Mac Henry's lie was his grandson Aaron, a 12-year-old champion ballplayer who'd crawled into a hole of self-pity the day his parents were killed in a car accident (the book reveals something that the film doesn't go into; because his parents were en route to watch him play, Aaron feels responsible for their deaths). Realizing that Jason's expansion team would enable Aaron to come out of his shell, and all too aware that Aaron would not join that team unless there was sufficient motivation, Mac decided to take on the identity of Buck McHenry, thereby prodding Aaron to pick up the torch that Buck had dropped over forty years earlier. The strategy works, and thanks to his grandfather's prevarication Aaron pulls out of his funk, reverting to the same happy, athletically gifted youngster he'd been before tragedy struck.

By the end of the original novel, whether or not Mac Henry really is Buck McHenry is unimportant: He has succeeded in giving some enthusiastic kids an opportunity to play organized baseball; he has awakened public interest in a heretofore ignored but important aspect of baseball history; and he has brought his beloved grandson back to the world of the living.

A falsehood born of noble motivations is a device that works better on paper than on film—especially if that film was among the first projects in the Showtime Cable Network's new manifest of family-oriented features. The movie version of *Finding Buck McHenry* would have to scrupulously adhere to the standards set down by the many TV-watchdog groups monitoring the project. It simply would not do to present a story that sanctioned a bald-faced lie, even a "justifiable" one. Showtime's adaptation of *Finding Buck McHenry* would have to find a way to reach the same conclusion as the novel without Mac Henry pretending to be someone he is not.

In the film, 35 minutes go by before the "Buck McHenry" angle is even introduced. During the buildup period, Mac agrees to coach the new expansion team after seeing Aaron enjoy himself during a game of catch with Jason—thus, it is not necessary for him to pose as Buck McHenry to shake Aaron out of his doldrums. Once Jason latches onto the possibility that Mac Henry is hiding his true identity, the film takes on the trappings of a psychological mystery, with the focus on Jason. Is he right in his assertions that Buck McHenry is coaching the team, or is he merely fantasizing again, just as he'd previously fantasized about being the next Mark McGwire? Certainly Mr. Henry is of no help, hotly denying that he is now, or ever has been, Buck McHenry. Mrs. Henry backs up her husband, asking incredulously when Mr. Henry would ever have found the time to play baseball when he was busy supporting his whole family. Told by his father that Buck McHenry is dead, Jason lashes out in anger, accusing his dad of spending a lifetime saying "I told you so" without ever lifting a finger to help his son face reality. Suggesting that he and his father fly to Kansas City to verify the story of Buck's death with the Negro League Museum, Jason is told that such a trip would cost too much—at which point the boy offers to sell his precious baseball-card collection to finance the journey. Touched by his son's willingness to learn the truth even at a great personal price, Mr. Ross bankrolls the plane trip to K.C. himself. The mystery of Buck McHenry has brought father and son closer together, a touching story aspect that never enters into the novel.

The Kansas City scenes introduce another story element that exists only in the film version: The testimony of Buck McHenry's best friend Ollie Johnson, a retired businessman who'd spent his younger days booking games for Buck and his fellow black players. Johnson's eloquent reminiscences of days gone by serve much the same purpose as Mac Henry's long-winded recollections of Negro League barnstorming in the novel, but in a more cinematic and less pedantic manner. During this sequence, Johnson recalls the ballpark fight that prompted Buck to quit baseball, adding an additional detail: The white ballplayer who picked the fight had earlier spiked Buck, leaving a jagged scar on his leg. At last convinced that Buck McHenry is dead, Jason heads home to apologize to the truculent Mr. Henry—who inadvertently reveals that his leg bears that selfsame jagged scar! Forced to confess that he is indeed Buck McHenry, the old man explains that he nearly killed the white man who gave him that scar—and, fearful of ever letting his anger get the better of him again, he quit baseball cold, allowing those capable of turning the other cheek, like Jackie Robinson, to bring racial equality to the game. And no, he wasn't really lying when he insisted that he was not Buck McHenry. So far as he was concerned, Buck McHenry no longer existed—and with the complicity of Ollie Johnson, he had literally "buried" Buck in an empty grave.

With the cat out of the bag, Mr. Henry agrees to appear on Chuck Axelrod's TV show, there to tell the inside story of black baseball to the uninformed viewers. As a result of Henry's appearance, the team roster of the Stadium Sluggers swells to six times its normal size (no great feat, since the team previously had only three members). In rapid succession, the Sluggers score victory after victory, then celebrate their first season with an awards dinner—where Ollie Johnson makes a surprise appearance to honor his old pal and colleague Buck McHenry.

Presto! Unlike the novel-to-film adaptation of Bernard Malamud's *The Natural*, in which the altered ending completely changed the point of the original work, the book-to-screen transfer of *Finding Buck McHenry* manages to have its cake and eat it too: Mac Henry successfully keeps Jason's team afloat, imparts the history of the Negro Leagues to a huge TV audience, and helps his grandson overcome his depression—but instead of taking on someone else's identity, he accepts who he really is, and the only lies told are the ones he has told to himself.

Finding Buck McHenry was directed by Charles Burnett, one of the most highly respected black filmmakers in Hollywood. Born in Mississippi and raised in the Watts district of Los Angeles, he was among the first African American directors to emerge from the UCLA Film School in the early 1970s—"The LA Rebellion," as it was known at the time. His breakthrough picture was 1977's *Killer of Sheep*, the story of a disenfranchised black slaughterhouse worker; showered with film-festival honors, the picture has also been designated a "National Treasure" by the Library of Congress (unfortunately a buried treasure, since it is seldom seen today outside of classrooms and museums). Burnett's later works—*The Glass Shield, To Sleep with Anger, Selma Lord Selma*—focused on the African American family/community experience, realistically and without the standard stereotypes. Though more conventional than most of Burnett's films, *Finding Buck McHenry* has much in common with his earlier works, notably the relaxed, naturalistic handling of the scenes between the elder Henrys and their grieving grandson Aaron, and especially the climactic interview sequence when Mac Henry recalls the indignities heaped upon him during his Negro League days. The matter-of-fact restraint displayed by both Charles Burnett and actor Ossie Davis in this final scene is infinitely more powerful than if it

had been staged in the clichéd manner of a political-rally rant.

On a purely cinematic and non-sociological level, Burnett's biggest challenge was the staging of the baseball game between the three-member Stadium Sluggers and the champion-level Lasers. Somehow the audience had to be convinced that a trio of ambitious youngsters would be able to defeat a fully staffed and equipped team with a long track record of victories. The script helps out considerably by establishing that the game is unofficial, played for the benefit of a video camera crew to provide "atmosphere" shots for Chuck Axelrod's TV sports show. Also boosting believability is the opposing team's prideful refusal to go for a win by simply loading the bases and overwhelming the understaffed Sluggers. For all this, the scene would have fallen flat if the director hadn't been able to pull it off. Charles Burnett succeeded beyond anyone's wildest dreams, using unusual camera angles, rapid-fire editing and just a *soupcon* of strategically placed slow-motion to lend credibility to one of the most incredible moments in the entire canon of baseball films.

Finding Buck McHenry has so much going for it that one is reluctant to itemize its flaws. Though, as mentioned, most of the characters are improved in their transfer from book to screen, others are diminished, particularly sportscaster Chuck Axelrod, who, as played by Kevin Jubinville, is almost as dense and self-absorbed as *The Mary Tyler Moore Show*'s Ted Baxter. Also, for a film that prides itself on its exhaustive baseball expertise, some of the training sequences are incredibly disingenuous: it is hard to believe that second-stringer Jason is instantly transformed into a power hitter simply by changing his batting stance. And even though the Buck McHenry/Mac Henry resemblance is established much later in the film than in the novel, once the subject *has* been brought up, the script all but beats it to death. We hear the characters mumbling variations on "Hmmm ... Mack Henry ... Buck McHenry" so often that we soon become heartily sick of the whole matter; and when, during the final awards-banquet scene, Ollie Johnson pays tribute to his old friend by leading the gathered assembly in a chant of "Buck! Mack! Buck! Mack!," what was intended as a heartwarming finale comes off as ludicrously as David Letterman's "Oprah! Uma!" mantra during the 1996 Academy Awards show.

The film's shortcomings can be forgiven if only because of the towering presence of Ossie Davis. Bringing literally half a century of acting experience to the part of Mac Henry, the 83-year-old Davis displays that curious blend of wide emotional range *and* economy of speech and movement that only the greatest actors are capable of carrying off. And while it is clear from his body language that his actual baseball experience is limited, Davis manages to convince the viewer that he is a baseball man from head to toe by sheer attitude and force of will. Matching Davis' performance every step of the way is his real-life wife and frequent acting partner Ruby Dee, in her fourth baseball-film appearance (Dee previously played the title character's wife in 1950's *The Jackie Robinson Story*, the same character's mother in 1990's *The Court-Martial of Jackie Robinson* and Mrs. Roy Campanella in 1974's *It's Good to be Alive*). In the original novel of *Finding Buck McHenry*, Jason perceptively describes the relationship between Mr. and Mrs. Henry: "It was funny the way they talked to each other. Like they were onstage in front of me. Which, in a way, they were." Much the same can be said of the marvelous scenes between Ossie Davis and Ruby Dee in the film version of *Finding Buck McHenry*, but with one qualification: Staged though their scenes may have been, the couple's spontaneous respect and affection for one another is a joy to behold.

There were those prepared to tear down *Finding Buck McHenry* as being somehow beneath the talents of Davis and Dee, a mere triviality compared to their previous stage and screen triumphs and extensive political activism. One of these potential nay-sayers was John Leonard, who reviewed the film in the April 17, 2000, issue of *New York* magazine: "Halfway through *Finding Buck McHenry* ... I wanted to write a letter to someone complaining that Ossie Davis, that fine old radical, had been turned by television once too often into a Great Uncle Feel-Good. But then, of course, the school janitor who undertakes to coach a Little League 'expansion team' rises to the polemical occasion to explain what it was like playing ball in the bad old days, in the Jim Crow South, in the Negro Leagues, and why he quit the game not because he was afraid of the violence that might be done to him but, instead, because of the violence he might do. Watching him on television, his hitherto innocent wife is filled with admiration. Since she, of course, is Ruby Dee, I, of course, am mollified...."

But one *expects* Ossie Davis and Ruby Dee to be brilliant, which is all the more reason that the supporting performance of baseball great Ernie Banks comes as such a pleasant surprise. It is perhaps unnecessary at this late date to synopsize the career of "Mr. Cub"—18 years with the same Chicago ballclub, lifetime home-run record of 512, MVP two years in a row—to explain why he is one of the best-loved and most widely admired figures in recent baseball history. Many fans would have been satisfied if the 69-year-old Banks had merely shown up as himself for a moment or two. Instead, he is afforded generous screen time in the third-billed role of Ollie Johnson, a role especially written for him. He was essentially still "himself"—a former Negro League barnstormer who matriculated to the Majors and ultimately the Hall of Fame, long and contentedly retired from baseball, actively pursuing a variety of profitable business ventures—but with enough character coloring to confirm that Banks had natural acting ability and was not just another professional celebrity. Director Burnett gets maximum value from Banks by helping him avoid the two major failings exhibited by most athletes-turned-actors: the inability to convincingly exchange dialogue with more experienced performers, and the tendency to over-gesticulate. As Ollie Johnson, Banks dispenses fluent exposition in two lengthy monologues, only occasionally requiring him to respond to comments made by the other characters on screen. And as a means of keeping his hands busy, Banks is given a cane, which he puts to effective use as he points out the many photographs of past Negro League greats adorning the walls of his den.

The three principal youngsters in the film—Michael Schiffman as Jason, Duane McLaughlin as Aaron, Megan Bower as Kim—deliver refreshingly natural performances, all the more remarkable in that each actor was making his or her first starring appearance. The other child performers are equally convincing, though in the main ballgame scene one of the kids inadvertently says "aboot" instead of "about," betraying the fact that the film, ostensibly set in a suburb of Ann Arbor Michigan, was shot in its entirety in Toronto.

After several preview screenings at a number of regional film festivals, *Finding Buck McHenry* made its "official" premiere over the Showtime Network on April 16, 2000. Though shown in a Sunday evening Prime Time slot, the film earned Ossie Davis a *daytime* Emmy for "Best Performer in a Children's Special."

Fireman Save My Child

First National [Warner Bros.]; released February 1932

Directed by Lloyd Bacon. Story and screen adaptation by Ray Enright, Robert Lord, Arthur Caesar, and (uncredited) Lloyd Bacon. Photography: Sol Polito. Edited by Richard Marks. Art direction by Esdras Hartley. Musical direction by Leo Forbstein. Baseball sequences supervised by Spalding. 67 minutes; black and white; sound.

Cast: Joe E. Brown ("Smokey" Joe Grant); Evalyn Knapp (Sally Toby); Lillian Bond (June Farnum [this role was originally slated for actress Noel Francis]); George Meeker (Stevens); Guy Kibbee (Pop Devlin); George Ernest (Mascot for Roseville); Ben Hendricks, Jr. (Larkin [this role was originally slated for Andy Devine]); Virginia Sale (Miss Gallop); Frank Shellenback (Pitcher); Richard Carle (Dan Toby); Louis Robinson (Trainer); Curtis Benson (Radio Announcer); George MacFarlane (St. Louis Fire Chief); Dickie Moore (Herbie); Frank Coghlan, Jr. (Kid); Walter Walker (Mr. Platt); Mike Donlin (Umpire); Jim Crandall, Ernie Orsatti (Ballplayers).

Joe Grant of Roseville, Kansas, is known as "Smokey Joe" for two reasons; he's the town's most enthusiastic volunteer fireman, and he's the Roseville baseball team's star pitcher. Truly a man of two worlds, Joe frequently bolts from a ballgame whenever he hears a fire siren, forcing the other players and the spectators to wait patiently until he returns to complete the game. He's also an erstwhile inventor, working on a "fire extinguisher bomb" shaped like a baseball. When offered $7500 to play for the St. Louis Cardinals, Joe is none too eager to leave Roseville, but his girlfriend Sally Toby urges him to go to St. Louis, use his baseball earnings to finance his invention, and ultimately sell the extinguisher so Joe and Sally can get married. The Cardinals sail into the pennant race on the strength of Smokey Joe's pitching arm, but there's trouble afoot. Two of Joe's fellow players smuggle goodtime-girl June Farnum on the team train, and rather than get caught breaking training, they foist June off on Joe. He's quite taken by her, and she's quite willing to take him for all he's got. June gets Joe to spend all his money on her, keeping him on the leash with vague promises that she'll introduce him to an important patent lawyer. A dunking in a park lagoon results in a bad cold for Joe, and while he's being nursed back to health by June, who should come calling but Sally Toby; she is broken-hearted and walks out. Suddenly the plot goes off on a new tangent: Joe has been invited by the president of the Zenith Fire Extinguishing Company to demonstrate his invention. On the day when St. Louis and the Yankees have three apiece in the series, Joe heads to the Zenith company, and while newspaper headlines announce his disappearance, he's busy merrily setting fire to the curtains of the Zenith executive office in order to show the efficiency of his extinguisher bomb. A mix-up in briefcases results in Joe's temporarily misplacing his invention, but he manages to put the blaze out just as the St. Louis fire department crashes in. Zenith offers Joe a contract, the local fire chief rushes Joe to the big game, Joe wins the series (though he's almost lured off the field by a faraway siren), and he returns to Roseville just before the "End" title to marry Sally.

The first and weakest of Joe E. Brown's "baseball trilogy" (see also *Alibi Ike* and *Elmer the Great*), *Fireman Save My Child* is hampered by a script that can't make up its mind whether it wants to be a baseball story, a firefighting farce, a "crazy inventions" yarn or a romantic comedy—and as a result, it falls short in all its potential categories. The film opening is strong, with Smokey Joe Grant (Brown) juggling a fire at a sauerkraut factory with an important July 4 ballgame, but after this promising start, the story emulates the proverbial knight who jumps on his horse and dashes off madly in all directions at once. Further weakening the film are the numerous plot points left dangling or unexplained. Where, for example, did the offer from the Zenith Fire Extinguisher Company come from?

Why is such a big deal made about Smokey Joe refusing to sign up for a second season with the Cardinals if a relief pitcher is sent in for him, when the final scene seems to suggest that, after all that fuss, Joe has returned to his home town for good to settle down with Sally anyway? And what in the world happens to gold digging June Farnum after she disappears from the proceedings in reel four?

This last question is answered by a glimpse at the original story treatment for *Fireman Save My Child*, composed by the film's director Lloyd Bacon and by Ray Enright (who'd later direct Joe E. Brown's *Alibi Ike*). June Farnum, described in the pressbook for this film as an "adventuress," and in the Bacon-Enright treatment as a "hooker," was to have had a scene in which she makes fun of Joe Grant and details her plans for leaving him flat once she's taken him to the cleaners. Unbeknownst to June, Joe is standing behind her, soaking in every word; he tells her off and heads back to Sally. The final version of the film throws all this out without ever explaining why June Farnum has been so arbitrarily dropped; evidently the filmmakers were hoping that the slam-bang climactic race through the streets to the Big Game would keep viewers from noticing the holes in the story.

Perhaps the de-emphasize of June was due to the realization that Brown's biggest audience, the kids, would be confused or made unduly curious about the nature of June's station in life (team manager Pop Devlin growls that she should be banned at the beginning of every season, spelling out plainly that June is what we'd now call a "baseball groupie"). This concern for the preteen audience can be the only reason that many of the script's more pungent lines, which might otherwise have passed muster within the rather lax censorship guidelines of 1932, were cut before shooting started: we no longer are treated to Pop Devlin's designation of Joe Grant as a "fire-eating

Small-town pitcher Joe Grant (Joe E. Brown) discusses his future in pro baseball with ever-lovin' sweetie Sally Toby (Evalyn Knapp) in *Fireman Save My Child*.

E. Brown saves the day with his usual aplomb, utilizing another one of his eccentric wind ups at the pitcher's mound, showing off for the fans as he steals bases, and engaging in some delightful ad-libbed chatter with the opposing catcher.

Many of the spring training sequences have built-in credibility by virtue of being filmed at Hollywood's favorite ballpark, Wrigley Field. The level of authenticity is heightened by the prominent presence of Frank Shellenback, cast in the role of a pitcher. The role required no acting whatsoever: Shellenback, who began with the White Sox in 1918, spent much of the rest of his career in the high minors, toting up 295 wins in the Pacific Coast League alone—the most ever scored in a single minor league by any pitcher. Though the remainder of his life had fewer ups than downs, Shellenback gained a measure of fame in the 1940s as the pitching coach of Leo Durocher. Frank Shellenback was cast in all three of Joe E. Brown's baseball pictures of the 1930s, but *Fireman Save My Child* is the only one in which he earns on-screen billing (a mixed blessing, in that his last name is misspelled!).

The pressbook for *Fireman, Save My Child* reveals the prevalent 1930s attitude of

son of a bench-warmer," nor do we hear the offhand remark that Joe would need his "fire hose" to handle June.

The moment the audience is waiting for in *Fireman Save My Child*, Joe's winning of the Series, is somewhat mitigated by the wild slapstick of the previous scene in which the demonstration of his extinguisher bomb nearly destroys the offices of the Zenith company. The final baseball sequence is also weakened by the interspersing of very obvious, very out of focus silent stock shots of real ballgames. Nonetheless, Joe

most Hollywood studios toward baseball films. This publicity guide for potential exhibitors makes much of the fact that the small-town set seen in *Fireman* was patterned by designer Anton Grot after Joe E. Brown's own hometown of Holgate, Ohio. There is a story of how Brown's character's fondness for bananas and peanuts resulted in an off-camera bellyache for the actor. Additionally, we discover that one of the horses drawing the fire wagon in the opening scene is "Old Dan," who had performed the same function at the cataclysmic San Francisco conflagration of 1906. But except for a short sentence in which legendary centerfielder Tris Speaker offers an endorsement for the film, we have virtually no clue that *Fireman Save My Child* is a baseball picture. The selling angle, both in the newspaper-ad layouts and in the lobby posters, is a picture of Joe E. Brown in a fireman's helmet, flanked by two caricatured fire horses. And the cleverest of the advertising blurbs goes like this: "The Eternal Question is Answered at Last: Why Do Fireman Wear Red Suspenders?" Evidently terrified at the "box office poison" onus on baseball movies, Warner Bros. does its best to de-emphasize the one thing that Joe E. Brown does best. And we never do find out why firemen wear red suspenders.

Fireman Save My Child turned out to be a moneymaker for Warners, the result being that it would serve as something of a model for the two Joe E. Brown baseball vehicles that followed. In general, both *Elmer the Great* and *Alibi Ike* followed the formula established in *Fireman Save My Child*: the self-enamored small-town baseball whiz who heads for the big leagues, becomes a target for ridicule and practical jokery, disappears just before the Big Game, and wins in the clinch in a climax earmarked by a combination of silly slapstick and remarkable baseball know-how. And, in particular, the plot complication in *Fireman* involving Joe's girl at home and a girl in the city

would be revived in *Elmer the Great*, while its dunking-in-the-lagoon routine would resurface in *Alibi Ike*.

Saving Joe E. Brown's baseball trio from ending up as carbon copies of one another was the fact that each one of the three films was better than the last, with *Alibi Ike* emerging as the best of the batch. And by the time *Alibi Ike* was released in 1935, Warner Bros. wasn't worried about "box office poison": *Alibi* was advertised as a baseball film, pure and simple. Whenever Joe E. Brown popped up on screen in the company of a ball, a bat, and a uniform, there was plenty of box office, but not a trace of poison.

For Love of the Game

Beacon Pictures/Mirage Enterprises/Tig Productions/Universal; released September 15, 1999 (national release, September 17, 1999)

Executive producers: Marc Abraham, Ronald M. Bozman. Produced by Armyan Bernstein and Amy Robinson. Directed by Sam Raimi. Screenplay by Dana Stevens, from the novel by Michael Shaara. Original Music: Basil Poledouris. Photography: John Bailey. Edited by Eric L. Beason, Arthur Coburn and Daniel Craven. Casting: Lynn Kressel. Production design: Neil Spisak. Art direction: Steve Arnold, James C. Feng. Set decoration: Carolyn Cartwright, Karen O'Hara. Costume design: Judianna Makovsky. Makeup supervisors: Kris Evans, Bernadette Mazur. Production manager: Harvey Waldman. First assistant director: Eric Heffron. Second assistant director: Richard Oswald. Second unit director: David Stephan. Set Designers: Andrew Menzies, Sally Thornton. Storyboard artist: P.K. MacCarthy. Supervising sound editor: Wylie Statemen. Special effects: CFC/MVFX, LA. Visual effects: Cinesite Hollywood. Special effects coordinators: Mark Bero, Al Di Sarro. Special effects technician: Thomas Rasada. Digital effects supervisor: Rob Hodgson. Technical advisor: Audie Garrido. Stunt coordinator: Christopher Doyle. Stunt driver: John Escobar. Director of photography, second unit: Phil Abraham. Titles: Pacific Title. Main title designer: Pablo Ferro. Color by Deluxe; Panavision. 137 minutes; Dolby Digital/DTS/SDDS Sound. Rated PG-13.

Cast: Kevin Costner (Billy Chapel); Kelly Preston (Jane Aubrey); John C. Reilly (Gus Sinski); Jena Malone (Heather Aubrey); Brian Cox (Gary Wheeler); J.K. Simmons (Frank Perry); Vin Scully (Himself); Steve Lyons (Himself); Carmine Giovinazzo (Ken Strout); Bill E. Rogers (Davis Birch); Hugh Ross (Mike Udall); Domenick Lombardozzi (Tow Truck Driver); Arnetia Walker (Airport Bartender); Larry Joshua (Yankee Fan in Bar); Greer Barnes (Mickey Hart); Scott Bream (Brian Whitt); Jose Mota (Jose Garcia); Earl Johnson (Marcus Random); Chris Lemonis (Lee Giordano); Jesse Ibara (Dennis Skinner); Pedro Swann (Juan Vasquez); Michael Rivera (Jimmy Pena); Dave Eiland (Relief Pitcher/Kevin Costner's Pitching Double), Joe Lisi (Pete); Jim Colborn (Third Base Coach); Michael Borzello (Catcher Double); Paul Bradshaw (Tiger Pitching Coach); Gene Kirley (Tiger Bench Coach); Chris Fischer, Jonathan Marc McDonnell, Barry Bradford, Kevin Craig West, Wes Said Drake (Detroit Tigers); Michael Papajohn (Sam Tuttle); John Darjean, Jr. (Jonathan Warble); Donzell McDonald (Lenny Howell); Scott Pose (Matt Crane); Jesus Cabrillo (Vick Brown); Chris Ashby (Nardini); Bill Masse (Mike Robinson); Mike Buddie (Jack Spellman); Eric Knowles (Ted Franklin); Ricky Ledee (Ruiz); Juan Nieves (Francisco Delgado); Augie Garrido (Yankee Manager); Rick Reed (Home Plate Umpire); Rich Garcia (First Base Umpire); Jerry Crawford (Second Base Umpire); Robert Leo Sheppard (Yankee Stadium Announcer); Eddie Layton (Yankee Stadium Organist); Robinson Frank Adu (Locker Room Attendant); T. Sean Ferguson, Victor Colicchio, David Mucci (Hecklers); Jacob Reynolds (Wheeler's Nephew); Maurice Shrog (Yankee Stadium Usher); Karen Williams (Kisha Birch); Tracy Middendorf (Blonde Player's Wife); William Newman (Fitch); P.J. Barry (Waldorf Doorman); Frank Girardeau (Waldorf Bellhop); Caterina Zapponi (Waldorf Singer); Monty Alexander (Waldorf Pianist); Daniel Dae Kim (E.R. Doctor); Judith Drake (E.R. Nurse); Bill Vincent (X-Ray Technician); Bill Costner (Mr. Chapel); Sharon Rae Costner (Mrs. Chapel); Mark Thompson (Billy's Father, early years); Laura Cayouette (Masseuse); Christopher Cousins (Ian); Ted Raimi,

Michael Emerson (Gallery Doormen); Shelly Desai (Taxi Driver); Lucinda Faraldo (Airline Ticket Agent); Ed Morgan (Man at Café); Brian Donald Hickey, Tracy Perry (Autograph Seekers); Michael Neeley (Horseback Cop); Al Thompson (Pete); Tracy Howe (Cabbie—cut from final print); David Mitchell Evans (Airport Bar Patron—cut from final print); Spice Williams (Kelly Preston's stunt double); and Tom Bezas, Maureen Bothe, Phil Hawn, Sheila Lussier, Eric Lykins and Seth William Meyer.

Having spent half his life and his entire baseball career with the Detroit Tigers, 40-year-old star pitcher Billy Chapel is shocked to learn that the Tigers have been sold and the new owners intend to trade him. Former owner Gary Wheeler, Chapel's longtime mentor and friend, advises Billy to avoid humiliation by retiring—even though, with a season record of eight wins and eleven losses, he would hardly be calling it quits at the top of his game. In another devastating blow, Jane Aubrey, Billy's girlfriend of five years, has decided to call off their relationship and accept a job in London: "You don't need me," Jane explains. "You're perfect with you and the baseball and the diamond." Adding to the ignominy of the situation is Billy's upcoming game at Yankee stadium—the last of the season, and one that has absolutely no significance to the flagging Tigers, though it may cinch the Yankees' entrée into the Pennant race. While this is very likely his swan song on the mound, and despite the 4000-game accumulation of aches and pains in his once-powerful pitching arm, Billy is determined to give it his best shot, doing his utmost to "clear the mechanism" and concentrate exclusively on the job at hand. As the game drags on, Billy's mind constantly wanders to the past, specifically his rocky, ever-vacillating relationship with Jane. Snapping back to attention in the seventh inning, Billy suddenly realizes that he is on the verge of pitching a perfect game—a feat comparable to Yankee Don Larsen's celebrated World Series shutout way back in 1956. What was previously just another "job of work" to Billy is now a matter of survival. By defeating the Yankees, he intends to prove that even if he does opt for retirement, he isn't anywhere near as washed up as his fans and colleagues think. And just maybe, Billy will be able to finesse this victory by putting the shattered pieces of his "real" life back together again.

The third of Kevin Costner's baseball films, *For Love of the Game* was based on a short novel by Michael Shaara, whose 1974 volume *Killer Angels* won a Pulitzer Prize and served as the inspiration for the 1993 film *Gettysburg*. Despite this honor, Shaara was never in the best-seller category, and even after winning the Pulitzer he encountered difficulty getting his works in print. One of his pet projects was a baseball story, written in the early 1980s, which he finally gave up for lost after it was rejected by every major New York publisher. After Shaara's death in May of 1988, the manuscript for *For Love of the Game* was found among his effects by his son Jeff. Three years later, the book was published posthumously by Carroll & Graf.

Though it reads like a rough draft (one critic dismissed the prose as "awkward" and "downright embarrassing"), the 152-page *For Love of the Game* is a generally effective stream-of-consciousness effort, divided into six sections: "The Hotel," "The Park," "The Stadium," "The Game, Part One" (which occurs almost exactly halfway through the book), "The Game, Part Two" and "Goin' Home." The protagonist, aging pitcher Billy Chapel, mentally reviews his entire life before, during and after what will be his final game with the fictional Hawks ballclub. As he comes closer and closer to pitching a no-hitter, Billy's mental processes simultaneously channel themselves into six or seven different ribbons of thought, all interconnected by his lifelong love affair with baseball and his relationships with the people closest to him: his sweetheart, a

book editor named Carol Grey; his longtime teammate and catcher Gus; "The Old Man," the recently deceased owner of the Hawks; and Billy's mother and father, both of whom were killed years earlier in a car accident. Also weaving in and out of his subconscious are several elements not directly related to baseball or Billy's loved ones: Cary Grant movies, a fascination with flying (Billy owns a private plane), pop music of the 1970s and 1980s, even the philosophical musings of Immanuel Kant!

None of this excess baggage ever clutters Billy's primary objective, that of pitching the perfect game. Shaara is at his best with interior monologues, as Billy assesses the weakness and strengths of each player who steps up to bat, revels in the adrenalin which freely flows whenever he pitches, agonizingly endures two decades' accumulation of pains in his arms and shoulders, and alternates between euphoria and disappointment over the realization that this is truly his last moment in the sun. He even finds time to pray twice, once to win the game and once to *re*-win his estranged lady love Carol.

Many of Billy's brainwaves are conveyed by fragmentary single-sentence paragraphs and single-word sentences, as if the thoughts were occurring to both Billy and author Shaara at precisely the same moment. Shaara also fluctuates between first- and third-person, enabling him to ingrain the basic storyline with a wealth of colorful baseball lore, notably the refusal by the rest of the team to jinx Billy by ever mentioning the phrase "no-hitter." Though *For Love of the Game* seems at first to be loosely basted, it is actually quite intricately knitted together, in the grand manner of another single-situation, stream-of-consciousness novelette, Ernest Hemingway's *The Old Man and the Sea* (Shaara's obvious *homage* is addressed in his book by a direct reference to Hemingway, in the unlikely event that the reader has any doubts).

For all that, it *is* a very slight piece, and one can understand why so many New York editors took a pass on publishing the novel. Nor did *For Love of the Game* crack the *Times'* Top Ten list when it was belatedly published in 1991. It took the popularity of the Michael Shaara–inspired film *Gettysburg* to bring the late author's baseball book to the forefront—and to the attention of actor Kevin Costner, who first encountered the novel in 1996. "Loosely committed" to the project from the outset, Costner was firmly signed (through his own Tig Enterprises production firm) in the spring of 1998, agreeing to begin production upon completion of his romantic comedy *Message in a Bottle*—and, in the process, shelving *Thirteen Days*, based on Robert Kennedy's memoir of the Cuban Missile Crisis, until 1999.

It isn't hard to figure out what attracted Costner to the project. For one thing, it was a baseball story, a genre that had bolstered and affirmed his star power in the late 1980s via *Bull Durham* and *Field of Dreams* (see individual entries). For another, Shaara's novel was intensely character-driven, with one single prominent character in the driver's seat, and was also a deeply introspective work: It was the sort of material which had won Costner multiple Academy Awards in 1990 with the release of his "first-person" western epic *Dances with Wolves*. Above all, the concept of building an entire feature film around a single baseball game posed a creative challenge to Costner—and, as proven by *Dances with Wolves* and his post-apocalyptic films *Waterworld* and *The Postman*, if there was one thing Costner could not resist, it was a creative challenge, especially the kind that would have the usual Hollywood skeptics clucking their tongues and wailing, "Can't be done! Can't be done!"

The job of adapting the novel to the screen was assigned to Dana Stevens, a former actress who'd begun writing for films in 1994, and who had recently become bankable thanks to *City of Angels*, her 1998 adaptation of Wim Wenders' urban fantasy *Der Himmel uber Berlin* (*Wings of Desire*, 1987). First item on Stevens' agenda was to reshape Billy Chapel in the image of Kevin Costner. 37 years old in the novel, Billy became 40 in the film, only three years shy of Costner's actual age. Though Michael Shaara's Billy is relatively easygoing, with a few isolated moments of truculence and terrified confusion, Stevens saw to it that the character's film counterpart would run the gamut from boyish charm to sullen petulance, from levelheaded self-control to "deer in the headlights" anguish—in other words, the typical Kevin Costner emotional range. Finally, Billy's interior monologues in the book were spoken out loud by Costner in the film; as Dana Stevens and the entire moviegoing public well knew, there were few actors who could converse with themselves on screen as convincingly and un-selfconsciously as Kevin Costner.

Stevens' next task was to streamline the multitude of Billy Chapel's thought-streams in the novel into a workable two or three; while a novelist can get away with having an abundance of thoughts dance through the head of a protagonist on each page, this sort of sensory overload does not always translate successfully on film. It was decided to focus almost exclusively on the two "loves" in Billy Chapel's life: baseball and his longtime girlfriend, whose name was Carol Grey in the novel but who (presumably for legal reasons) was rechristened Jane Aubrey in the film. Much of the backstory of Billy's life before entering the majors at age 17 (18 in the film), his two-decade tenure with the same baseball team (altered from the mythical Hawks to the real-life Tigers), and his ascendancy to MVP stardom as a combination Bob Feller, Warren Spahn, Sandy Koufax and Christy Matthewson (or so Michael Shaara would have us believe), was neatly compressed into a montage of newspaper headlines and 8-millimeter home movies—some faked, others from Kevin Costner's own family archives—seen during the film's opening credits. A few of the novel's supporting characters, notably Billy's catcher and best friend Gus Sinski, were retained and expanded upon in the film; others, like Billy's mother and father, were diminished. In at least one case, two characters were merged: Dooby Ross, a sportswriter who in the novel informs Billy that the Hawks have been sold in hopes of getting an exclusive interview, was eliminated; the information about the sale was dispensed by former owner Gary Wheeler, who is identified as "The Old Man" in the original—and who, though having died before the main action of Shaara's novel got under way, was restored to life for expositional purposes by Dana Stevens.

Knowing what Costner's female fans had come to expect, the romantic angle, which takes up a little less than a third of the novel, was given equal footing with the baseball angle in the film. As conceived by Michael Shaara, Billy Chapel's girlfriend Carol Grey was something of a sexual predator. Meeting Billy at a Manhattan party, she aggressively comes on to him, forcing him to adopt an ingenuous "country boy" pose to keep her at arm's length; even so, they end up in bed within a few hours after exchanging introductions. Carol has apparently hit upon Billy as a means to overcome the pain of a failed marriage, and she also has a serious drinking problem; these factors as much as anything else lead to Carol's decision to end the affair.

Screenwriter Stevens did more than change the name of Billy Chapel's girlfriend from Carol Grey to Jane Aubrey: She gave the character a complete overhaul, with an oil change and brake realignment thrown in. The two characters' introduction is transformed into a "meet-cute" moment in which Billy, en route to Yankee Stadium

in his shiny new car, gallantly offers to jumpstart Jane's broken-down rental auto, even though what he knows about internal combustion engines would probably not fill a thimble. Both amused and bemused by the fact that a tow-truck driver was willing to soak her for an expensive haul-in until he found out that she was in the company of the Great Billy Chapel—whereupon the driver insisted that his services were free of charge—Jane, more out of curiosity than anything else, agrees to be Billy's guest at the upcoming ballgame. As in the book, the two wind up in the sack on their first date, but Jane is embarrassed by her sexual impulsiveness and spends the next several reels trying to talk herself out of any future contact with Billy, even though he behaves in a gentlemanly manner and goes to great lengths not to treat her as just another "baseball groupie."

As the relationship deepens, the audience learns why Jane was at first reluctant to build a lasting romance on the foundation of a one-night stand: An earlier, similar experience in her teen years had resulted in an out-of-wedlock pregnancy, forcing her to take on the responsibilities of adulthood before she was psychologically prepared to do so. Thus is introduced a character that appears nowhere in the novel: Jane's troubled teenaged daughter Heather. Worried that Billy would have deserted her had he been informed from the start that she had a daughter, Jane is gratified to discover that Billy accepts the situation and is even willing to act as surrogate father when the need arises. Gradually, however, Billy begins to feel penned in by new domestic responsibilities and seeks out other romantic partners with fewer strings attached. Though she'd previously assured Billy that she was not going to demand total fidelity from him, Jane admits she was lying when she finds that Billy has had a quickie fling with a sexy masseuse. Like Carol Grey in the novel, the film's Jane Aubrey is emotionally "needy," though the friction in her romance with Billy is due as much to his misbehavior as hers.

Later on, when Billy's pitching hand is seriously damaged during a wood-sawing mishap (another incident invented for the film), Jane rushes Billy to the local hospital and angrily demands that the blasé and inattentive staff give her sweetheart immediate and preferential medical attention. But if she hoped that Billy would appreciate the extent of her devotion, she was mistaken; as he is being helicoptered to a special clinic, Billy asks her to contact the Tigers' staff physician: "The most important person in the world to me right now." Billy's brooding self-pity during the recuperation process—stubbornly determined to stage a baseball comeback, he persuades himself that everyone who suggests that he think about retiring, including Jane, is "against" him—convinces Jane that no matter how much Billy professes his love for her, she will always run a distant second to his love for baseball. Plus, she cannot reconcile herself to the fact that he refuses to accept his accident as the stepping stone to a new beginning in life, just as he has shown her that being a single mother was not the end of *her* world. Thus, when Jane shows up in New York to tell Billy that it's all over between them, the reason is not the heroine's boozing or emotional immaturity as in the novel, but Billy's obsessive, muleheaded selfishness (Kevin Costner was never afraid to appear unsympathetic on screen, but he had a healthy enough ego to insist that key plot developments be dictated by the behavior of *his* character, rather than anyone else's).

In the novel, the resolution of Billy and Carol's romance, like most of the other secondary plot strands, is given less weight than the outcome of his final baseball game. While this works on paper, it would have seemed a cheat to throw away Billy and Jane's climactic reunion on film, especially since screenwriter Stevens has drawn out the suspense by having the London-bound Jane stranded at Kennedy International due to a delayed flight, compelling her to watch Billy's no-hitter over the airport's ubiquitous TV screens (at times, there seem to be more TVs than passengers!). The minute we see Billy, alone in his hotel room after pitching his perfect game, weeping copiously over the fact that he has apparently lost Jane, we know that an equally tearful reunion with his true love is but a few minutes away. As mentioned, the novel's Billy prays twice. The film's Billy prays once, on the ballfield; the second prayer is replaced by Billy's sincere promise to devote his whole heart to Jane if only she'll agree to remain with him in America. That this request is as selfish as any of Billy's previous gestures (after all, the London job carries both prestige and an enormous weekly paycheck) is forgotten in the ecstasy of the moment: Given all that has gone before, the female portion of the audience would probably have demanded their money back had the Billy/Jane romance not been given as spectacularly joyous a denouement as his baseball career.

The fleshing out of the feminine lead meant that Kevin Costner's costar in *For Love of the Game* would have to be a "name." Both Helen Hunt and Natasha Richardson were offered the role of Jane Aubrey, and both turned it down. Finally, less than a month before filming was to begin, Kelly Preston was cast as Jane. For many years best known as the wife of superstar John Travolta, Preston had of late emerged as a stellar attraction in her own right in such films as *Addicted to Love*, *Nothing to Lose* and *Holy Man*; of more significance to the film at hand, Preston had also appeared in the biggest moneymaking sports movie of all time, *Jerry Maguire* (1997). Intriguingly, Kelly Preston's performance in *For Love of the Game*, with her breathless, sometimes scatterbrained monologues and unpredictable crying jags, tends to remind one of another actress, Meg Ryan—suggesting that Dana Stevens, who had previously collaborated with Ryan in *City of Angels*, may have penned the role of Jane Aubrey with Meg in mind.

Though this is conjecture, it is known that *For Love of the Game* was conceived with a different director in mind. Around the same time that Costner was expressing interest in the Shaara novel, the property was being developed for the screen by Sydney Pollack and Amy Robinson of Mirage Productions, with Pollack planning to double as producer and director. Though both Robinson and Mirage remained with the film, Pollack dropped out of the project. Not long afterward, coproducer Armyan Bernstein had a meeting with director Sam Raimi, ostensibly to discuss an upcoming horror film—a subject on which Raimi was an acknowledged expert, given such credits as *The Evil Dead* and its sequels. Accidentally on purpose, Raimi let slip that he "loved" baseball, then proceeded to impress the producer with his thorough knowledge of the game, and also with his ideas of how best to bring *For Love of the Game* to the screen. This roundabout strategy worked magnificently, and Sam Raimi was signed to direct the picture in June of 1998.

Unlike so many other New York–based films which ended up being shot in Vancouver or Toronto, *For Love of the Game* began production in the genuine, unadulterated Big Apple in late October of 1998, with cast and crew on hand in Manhattan, Brooklyn, Long Island and Yankee Stadium. Securing permission to shoot at the last-named location did not come easily, as producer Amy Robinson explained in the film's pressbook: "When we started developing the project, baseball was really in the doldrums and people weren't liking the sport. Then, they had this glorious year with the home run race and the New York Yankees. We called George Steinbrenner, and when he heard that Kevin Costner was

involved, he became very interested. He's a big Costner fan." (See the entry on 1994's *The Scout* for a slightly different perspective on the "cooperative" Mr. Steinbrenner!) Dealing with Mother Nature proved much simpler than negotiating with Steinbrenner: An unseasonably warm snap of autumnal weather enabled the moviemakers to shoot the ballpark scenes in relative comfort, despite the usual logistics problems of filming on location with nonprofessional extras.

Though the film's Big Game is supposedly being played before a crowd of some 56,000 fans, no more than 800 to 1200 ballpark extras were used at any time; the empty seats were filled through the miracle of computer graphics. While the crowds were small, their enthusiasm was not—if heckling can be considered enthusiasm. John C. Reilly, the actor playing catcher Gus Sinski, would later claim that he was mercilessly razzed by the genuine Yankee fans in the stadium. "We … encouraged that, because that's what happens at games," Reilly recalled to interviewer Eric S. Arnold. "They told me to try not to listen, and I figured, oh yeah, I'll just tune 'em out. The impression you get is that it's just this low roar on the field, and that is so not true. It's a rude awakening." Especially disturbing were those moments when the extras insulted Reilly as *himself* and not his character. "And then you realize that they're Yankee fans, and it's their job to demoralize the visiting team, and that's what they're gonna do."

As was his custom in his previous baseball films, Kevin Costner underwent a demanding training process, working 10 hours per day, six days per week for four weeks. Like *Bull Durham*'s Ron Shelton before him, director Sam Raimi was bowled over by Costner's ballpark performance: "Had he not spent these ten past years not in movies but working on his baseball, I would extrapolate that he could be a major

For Love of the Game: **Twenty years' worth of hard knocks in the Major Leagues has transformed the face of Tigers pitcher Billy Chapel (Kevin Costner) into a "Field of Nightmares."**

league player." The film's technical advisor, University of Texas baseball coach Audie Garrido, echoed Raimi's remarks: "Kevin is a great athlete. He cannot only play baseball, but he can ski, golf and play basketball. And he has this fabulous mind that allows him to get focused like a true athlete or exceptional person in any field when he is performing." Exceptional though he was, Costner was not a twenty-year Major League veteran, so it was not expected that his playing would always be up to the fictional Billy Chapel's lofty standards. In some of the longshots, Costner was doubled by Dave Eiland, a former Yankee pitcher who at the time of filming was with the Tampa Bay Devil Rays; Eiland also acted in the film, as the relief pitcher who is briefly considered as Billy's replacement in the bottom of the Ninth.

Dave Eiland was one of several authentic baseball players in *For Love of the Game.* Before granting permission to display their uniforms and logos on-screen, the Detroit Tigers and the New York Yankees insisted that all the men portraying their team members be professional actors and/or current or former ballplayers; no mere dress extras or "civilian" stand-ins would suffice. Featured in the film were four members of the 1998 Yankees lineup: center fielder Donzell McDonald, outfielders Scott Pose and Ricky Ledee, and pitcher Mike Buddie. Also on hand were retired Milwaukee Brewer Juan Nieves, who, like Billy Chapel, had entered the record books for pitching a no-hitter against the Baltimore Orioles in 1987; and onetime Louisiana State College athletic star Michael Papajohn (see notes for *Little Big League*), here cast as Billy Chapel's longtime Yankee antagonist Sam Tuttle. Other big-leaguers on site were San Francisco Giants catcher Brent Mayne and Yankee catcher Mike Borzello, who, though they did not act in the film, served as coaches for the actors during the training sessions. Additionally, the film was honored by the presence of a trio of real umpires: Rick Reed, Jerry Crawford and Richie Garcia.

After leaving New York, the production team filmed additional scenes in Aspen, Colorado (where Billy Chapel suffers his career-threatening hand injury), and Los Angeles from December 1998 to January 1999. Once production wrapped, Costner met with the press to comment on his decision to make a third trip to the baseball-movie trough: "I could see that other people say, 'Oh God, another third movie.' I wouldn't want to do 'another third movie.' I was excited how this movie separated itself and what it was about." Of the character of Billy Chapel, Costner enthused, "I liked his journey as a man. I liked how the movie spun. I thought it was as realistic as you can make it in the movies."

Jeff Shaara, son of the original novel's author, claimed that Costner told him personally, "the role of Billy Chapel is one he has been waiting for all his career." (Incidentally, both Shaara and his wife Lynne appear in the film, he as a "disgruntled" Yankee Stadium patron, she as one of the player's wives in the scene where Jane attends her first ballgame as Billy's guest.)

One aspect of the film paralleled a frequent experience in Costner's own life as a big-time movie star: During the early stages of his romance with Jane Aubrey, Billy Chapel is constantly interrupted by insistent and borderline threatening autograph seekers and admirers. Noted Costner, "There are a lot of things that can threaten a relationship, and when you [add] the outside forces that come with celebrity and fame, you almost have to walk between the raindrops of your own relationship to avoid the kind of attention I and other people get."

Though Costner welcomed the opportunity to convey the burdens of celebrity to his fans, he was displeased with another pitfall of life in the Hollywood fast lane: the tendency on the part of major studios to re-edit completed films to conform with their own notions of what appealed to the public, rather than honoring the artistic vision of the filmmakers. No sooner had *For Love of the Game* reached the final-cut stage than Costner was making public statements complaining that the film had not been edited in accordance with his wishes— a tune that had been sung several times before by the actor regarding his previous efforts *Dances with Wolves*, *Waterworld* and *Wyatt Earp*. As reported by Marshall Fine of the Gannett News Service: "According to interviews, Costner maintains that scenes crucial to the tone and character development have been cut in the interest of speeding up the film." Judging by the evidence at hand, the trimmed sequences were mainly flashbacks, most of them filmed at C.W.

Post School in Long Island, involving Billy Chapel's parents (played by actors in most scenes, and by Costner's actual mother and father in a brief sequence set during the 1984 World Series). Also whittled down was a subplot concerning Billy's friendship with fellow Detroit Tiger Dave Birch (Bill E. Rogers), who, after being traded to the Yankees, ended up "facing down" Billy during his final game; and a poignant vignette in which Billy offered words of encouragement to an opposing batter who'd made the sort of "bonehead play" which his detractors would never let him forget. But to hear the newspapers tell it, what *really* pulled Costner's chain was the removal of a scene in which he appeared in the nude, an excision deemed necessary by Universal to soften the film's rating from an "R" to a "PG-13." (Without commenting further, one wonders what sort of character development could have been conveyed by a quickie shot of Kevin Costner's privates.)

Originally announced for an August release date, *For Love of the Game* was moved to mid–September of 1999 due to Universal's eleventh-hour editing decisions. If the studio had hoped to "speed up" the film by making cuts, they were in for a disappointment: At two hours and seventeen minutes, *For Love of the Game* takes longer to watch than it takes to read the original novel. While this in itself is not necessarily a bad thing, the problem lies not in the fact that the film runs 137 minutes, but in how much of that time is used—or, rather, squandered.

Off the ballfield, it is the tiny, personal moments that work best. Two vignettes that immediately come to mind are the moment in which Billy Chapel awakens from his troubled slumbers in his New York hotel room, mildly irritated that the complimentary pillow mint is stuck to his cheek; and, while prepping in the Yankee Stadium locker room, Billy takes a good long look at himself in the mirror, disdainfully pinching the "love handles" which have developed around his midriff—only to stop short when he realizes that someone other than a fellow team member is watching him. Jane Aubrey also has a nice moment when, suspecting that Billy is sizing her up as a potential bedmate, she launches into her philosophy that men and women should carry signs around their necks indicating their true personalities. And it is hard to top the opening scene in which, en route to New York by plane, Billy replies to his pal Gus' cautionary advice about his eating, drinking and sleeping habits by muttering, "I have the ugliest wife in baseball." (This scene also contains a neat inside joke: the book that Billy is reading on the plane is Michael Shaara's *Killer Angels*). Otherwise, the scenes outside the ballpark are overwritten, overacted, overdirected, and mired in sentimental drivel.

Even so, the decision to give the film's romance story as much screen time as the baseball story might have worked had not the screenwriter so quickly run out of things to say. Some of the scenes between Billy and Jane are not so much extended as padded and redundant; typical is a dialogue exchange in which Billy apologizes for losing his temper by reminding Jane exactly when and where the incident occurred ("I'm sorry what I said to you that day in the condo"), even though we've just seen what happened a few moments before. And even more gratuitously, Billy approaches the sniveling, puffy-eyed Jane and asks, "Are you crying?" Similarly, while Jane's rambling monologues, bittersweet witticisms, soggy sobfests and unexpected flashes of temperament are appealing the first time we see them, this appeal progressively diminishes the more often they're trotted out; as a result, the scenes in which these character traits *should* work in the film's favor—as when Jane bullies a regulation-bound hospital staff into immediately treating Billy's injury with the hysterical ad-

monition, "This is America!"—lose much of their effectiveness. Even the portions of the non-baseball scenes which directly relate to the Big Game are played far beyond their worth, notably that obnoxiously stereotyped Yankees fan with whom Jane verbally spars as they both watch Billy pitch his heart out on TV.

Curiously, for all of this tiresome and unnecessary protraction, certain elements of the Billy/Jane relationship are disappointingly underdeveloped. This is particular true in the case of Jane's daughter Heather (Jena Malone), who seems to exist only to propel the plot forward, rather than as a fully formed individual. Also given short shrift is the heartbroken Jane's rebound relationship with her handsome employer Ian (Christopher Cousins), who, as both a baseball fan and a connoisseur of Modern Art, has the makings of an interesting character before he abruptly vanishes from sight.

In the film's pressbook, co-producer Armyan Bernstein insisted, "I don't think of it as a baseball movie. Baseball is the action of our hero—it's what he's doing. I think of it as a schematic for him to reflect on his life." With all due respect to Bernstein, the film would have been better off had the producers thought of it *exclusively* as a baseball movie; like the novel, *For Love of the Game* truly comes to life only when Billy Chapel steps up to the pitcher's mound. To be sure, there is a certain degree of repetition here as well, but it is the sort of repetition one expects from the "typical" baseball game, and is handled throughout with nuance and freshness by star Kevin Costner and director Sam Raimi; indeed, it is difficult to believe that this was Raimi's first sports film, much less his first big-budget, mainstream effort. Commendably, screenwriter Dana Stevens holds back the saccharine with which she has smothered much of the rest of the film, allowing Michael Shaara's original prose and chain of events to carry the day. (And yes, this statement is made even though the entire premise of Billy's "last stand" is built upon a glaring inaccuracy: no baseball player with ten years in the Major Leagues and five years with the same ballclub can be traded against his wishes.)

Worthy of particular praise is the method in which director Raimi and film editors Eric L. Beason, Arthur Coburn and Daniel Craven assist the audience in charting the progress of the game. "Filmed" shots of Billy on the ballfield are intercut with "televised" shots of the game, as carried by the Fox Network, with superimposed box scores and statistics. Unlike many another baseball film (*The Slugger's Wife* in particular), there is never any confusion as to what inning we're in, which team is up, or the identity of Billy's latest batting challenge.

Especially well handled is Billy's mantra, "Clear the mechanism," which he repeats to himself whenever he needs to shut out the roars of the crowd and concentrate on his work. Used but once in the book, the phrase is repeated three times at three crucial junctures in the film. In the first two such instances, Billy's concentration is superbly conveyed cinematically, with everything but the batter at home plate melting into smeary soft focus, and the soundtrack fading into utter silence. By the time the third "clear the mechanism" rolls around, the audience, knowing what to expect, gets a bit edgy, worried that the baseball scenes will suffer from the same repetitious overkill as the romantic scenes. But surprise! Billy's efforts at focusing his attention *don't* work; the crowd noises persist, and the entire picture remains in sharp focus. With a jolting suddenness, predictability has been dashed to bits and suspense holds sway; two hours into the film, the audience has been dealt a wakeup call with as much startling impact as Billy's realization, several scenes earlier, that he is on the brink of a perfect game.

Because the audience's emotional investment is entirely in Billy's ballgame, one can forgive the occasional lapses into corniness. The moment that apple-cheeked rookie Yankee Ken Strout approaches Billy Chapel, expresses admiration, and introduces himself as the son of one of Billy's longtime teammates, we know that the last batter whom Billy will face at the end of the game will be that selfsame Ken Strout, and yet the viewer is willing to go along with this Dickensian coincidence because the suspense level is so high in the film's final moments (though some observers could not help but notice that Ken Strout's jersey number miraculously changed from 60 to 61 in the course of nine innings). Also, the hyperbolic play-by-play of booth announcers Vin Scully and Steve Lyons, which might under any other circumstances seem hopelessly contrived and stilted, comes across beautifully, not only because Scully has spent his entire career mouthing such purple prose as, "Chapel makes his fateful walk to the loneliest spot in the world—the pitcher's mound at Yankee Stadium," but also because *For Love of the Game* was filmed just after the Sammy Sosa/Mark McGwire home-run race, a golden era when sportscasters really *did* talk like that! Additionally, Scully's presence is supremely appropriate: It was he who, on October 8, 1956, called the play by play for the World Series match in which Don Larsen pitched his legendary perfect game against the Brooklyn Dodgers. (On July 18, 1999, as *For Love of the Game* was nearing the end of the preview-and-recut process, Yankee pitcher David Cone repeated Don Larsen's spectacular feat—during a Yankee Stadium game honoring Yogi Berra, for which Larsen himself threw out the ceremonial first pitch!)

The only ingredient in the ballgame scenes that falls short of perfection is the oppressively lush musical score by Basil Poledouris. With such credits as *The Blue Lagoon, Free Willy, Conan the Barbarian, Hunt* for *Red October, Starship Troopers* and the *RoboCop* films, Poledouris fully deserves his place in the Pantheon of film composers. Unfortunately, his 90 minutes' worth of symphonic music in *For Love of the Game* is almost entirely inappropriate to the film; when we hear Japanese ceremonial drums in one sequence, we half expect to see an army of Samurai Warriors march out of the bullpen. It is as if Bernard Herrmann were to score a Woody Woodpecker cartoon, or Erich Wolfgang Korngold were to provide themes for an Adam Sandler comedy: brilliant music, wrong picture.

Critical response to *For Love of the Game* indicated that the film was likely to appeal more to baseball fans than to romance-film devotees. Melanie McFarland of the *Seattle Times* observed that the film "is strongest as a baseball movie.... The true love story here is between Chapel and his teammates, particularly his catcher and right-hand man Gus.... Chapel and Jane are, by comparison, syrupy goo." Only a few reviewers, such as Bob Graham of the *San Francisco Chronicle*, felt that both baseball and romance were equally well served: "Movies like this express big, real emotions that we may be reluctant to put into words. That's one thing Hollywood movies are supposed to do for us." Others wanted no part of either aspect of the film: In the words of the anonymous *Toronto Sun* scrivener, "For love of the game, read the book."

For Love of the Game managed to achieve the Number Nine slot on the list of ten biggest moneymaking baseball films, though its $35,200,000 take was sparse compared to the $64,400,000 and $50,900,000 respectively raked in by Costner's earlier *Field of Dreams* and *Bull Durham*—especially since the budget for the 1999 film was bigger than that of the other two combined. It is perhaps too early to fully determine the film's success, financially or aesthetically; as these words are being written, two years after the picture's release, *For Love of*

the Game is slowly being "rediscovered" on the VHS and DVD circuit, and there is every likelihood that Kevin Costner will one day be able to restore the picture to its original pre-release length, as he has done with *Dances with Wolves*. In the meantime, the general critical consensus still stands: *For Love of the Game* excels on a pure baseball level, but the filmmakers would have been better off "clearing the mechanism" in the romance department.

Girls Can Play

Columbia; released June 1937

Produced by Ralph Cohn. Written and directed by Lambert Hillyer, based on the original story "Miss Casey at Bat" by Albert De-Mond. Photography: Lucien Ballard. Edited by Byron Robinson. Art director: Stephen Gooson. Costumes by Kolloch. 59 minutes; black and white; sound. [Also released as *Fielder's Field*.]

Cast: Jacqueline Wells [Julie Bishop] (Ann Casey); Charles Quigley (Jimmy Jones); Rita Hayworth (Sue Collins); John Gallaudet (Foy Harris); George McKay (Sluggy); Gene Morgan (Pete); Patricia Farr (Peanuts); Guinn "Big Boy" Williams (Lieutenant Flannagan); Richard Terry (Cisto); James Flavin (Bill O'Malley); Beatrice Curtis, Ruth Hilliard (Infielders); Lee Prather (Coroner); Harry Tyler (Dugan); Beatrice Blinn (Mae); George Lloyd (Blater); Michael Breen (Bit); Fern Emmett (Anna); Richard Kipling (Mr. Raymond); Bruce Sidney (Doctor); Lucille Lund (Jane Harmon); Evelyn Sclove (Fortune Teller); Lee Shumway (Captain Curtis); Ann Doran (Secretary).

Foy Harris, a seemingly honest drugstore proprietor who owns a girl's softball team, is actually a crook who oversees several shady enterprises. When a former partner comes to town and threatens to blow the whistle on Harris's watered-down liquor racket, Harris murders him. Also eliminated for knowing too much is Harris's moll Sue Collins, who is catcher on the ball team; Sue is done in by a poisoned catcher's mitt. Reporter Jimmy Jones suspects that some-

More *zaftig* than exotic at this point in her career, Rita Hayworth (right) prepares for batting practice as the top-billed star of *Girls Can Play*, Jacqueline Wells, awaits her turn.

thing is amiss, and with the help of the team's ace pitcher, Ann Casey (Casey! Get it?), and the lead-footed assistance of the police's Lieutenant Flannigan, Jones manages to collar Foy Harris before he skips town.

At the start of each production year, the Columbia "B" picture unit's executives would post a list of suggested titles for the studio's second-feature product. Columbia's writers were then invited to choose the titles that appealed to them most, and then write up a few story treatments. Albert DeMond, the lucky fellow who selected "Miss Casey at Bat"—which emerged on film as *Girls Can Play*—fashioned a gimmick-laden murder mystery which owed more than a little to MGM's 1934 programmer *Death on the Diamond* (q.v.), a similarity that did not go unnoticed by the review-

ers. Lambert Hillyer, a director more closely associated with Westerns, typed up the screenplay from DeMond's story and guided *Girls Can Play* through its two-week production with his usual barebones efficiency. The film was shipped out on the lower half of double bills, pleased the crowds, made a little coin, and then was forgotten.

Well, not completely. Future film historians would be compelled to dig up *Girls Can Play* when writing their career articles on Rita Hayworth, who had the small but flashy role of a shapely ballplayer who was murdered before the film was half over. The June 23, 1937, *Variety* review of *Girls Can Play* allowed that Hayworth "showed potentialities"—proving that the film had fulfilled its ultimate purpose, to allow Columbia president Harry Cohn to witness most of his studio's aspiring starlets in action all at once, then to separate wheat from chaff. It would take a couple more years of secondary roles in second-rate films for Rita's "potentialities" to really pay off with starring parts in "A" pictures—none of which had anything to do with spiked baseball gloves.

Something to ponder: The villain of this piece (played by John Gallaudet, who had quite an offscreen reputation as an athlete, albeit on the golf course rather than the baseball field) is a druggist who runs a girls' softball team. Buck Weaver, the real-life ballplayer whose career was destroyed by the Black Sox scandal (see *Eight Men Out*), had by the mid–1930s bought himself a drug store, and was himself a girls' softball team manager. While it's remotely possible that the filmmakers were aware of this when putting together *Girls Can Play*, it is safe to say that Buck Weaver never saw the picture—or else he would have used its coincidental tie-in with his own life to get into the newspapers and make another of his pleas for a chance to clear himself of all guilt in the 1919 Series fix.

Goodbye, Franklin High

Cal-Am Arts Productions; released in 1978.

Executive producers: Joseph R Laird, Jr., Kenneth J. Fisher. Produced and directed by Mike McFarland. Written by Stu Krieger. Associate producers: Kenneth A. Yates, Kool Lusby. Photography: Dean Cundey. Edited by Peter Parasheles. Production manager: Michael O'Donnell. Production assistant: Daniel Dusek. First assistant director: David Kahler. Second assistant director: Michael Bourne. Music editor: Ted Roberts. Script supervisor: Debra Hill. Camera operator: Ray Stella. Sound effects: Echo Film Services. Sound mixer: Art Names. Makeup supervisor: Dodie Warren. Wardrobe supervisor: Julene McKinney. Songs written and performed by Lane Caudell. Titles and opticals: Modern Film Effects. Color. 93 minutes; sound. Rated PG.

Cast: Lane Caudell (Will Armer); William Windom (Clifford Armer); Julie Adams (Janice Armer); Darby Hinton (Mark Jeffries); Ann Dusenberry (Sharon Bradley); Ron Lombard (Greg Lombardi); Stu Krieger (Kurt Moriarty); Myron Healey (Walter Craig, guidance counselor); Virginia Gregg (Nurse); Kenneth Tobey (Police Captain); Mary Treen (Miss Atwater, teacher); Hillary Horan (Mary Burton); Loren Ewing (Sgt. Raleigh, Marine recruiting officer); Joe Carlo (Skip Munson); Bary Paul Silver (Joby); Paulette Breen (Photo Shop Girl); Michelle Patrick (Nancy Bell); Steven Mond (Little Boy); Robert Bartlett (Gary Howard); Robin Green (Mark's Girlfriend).

Will Armer, star pitcher for the Franklin High School baseball team, is approached by major-league scout Skip Munson and offered a tryout with the California Angels' farm team. Though tempted to jump at the opportunity, Will must also weigh the feelings of his parents and his guidance counselor, who want him to accept a full scholarship at Stanford University. In the weeks before his graduation, Will weighs several other options, including a career with the Marine Corps and a chance to prove his "involvement" in the world by doing charity work in Guatemala. Will's final decision—should he chart his own course in life, or do what is expected of him?—is delayed by a multitude of outside issues, among them his unwillingness to make a lasting commitment to his girlfriend Sharon, his father Clifford's life-threatening emphysema, and the unsettling possibility that his mother Janice is having an extramarital affair. Though not all of these issues are resolved by the end of the film, Will has at least made a definite decision regarding professional baseball—and he has made it entirely on his own.

In the first edition of this book, I was unable to include a writeup of *Goodbye, Franklin High* for two compelling reasons: I could not locate a copy of the film, and very little information existed about it save for a tantalizingly positive review in *Leonard*

Franklin High's star pitcher Will Armer (Lane Caudell, right) reveals to teammates Mark (Darby Hinton, left) and Gregg (Ron Lombard) that he's been "in talks" with a Major League scout (*Goodbye, Franklin High*).

Maltin's TV Movies and Video Guide. Though I invited readers to submit any information concerning the picture, for all intents and purposes, *Goodbye Franklin High* was a "lost" film back in 1992.

That lost is now found, thanks to the kindness and generosity of Stu Krieger, who wrote the screenplay for *Goodbye Franklin High* and also appeared in the film as Will Armer's Harvard-bound buddy Kurt Moriarty (Krieger's wife, actress Hillary Horan, likewise showed up in the film as Mary Burton). Mr. Krieger not only offered background information on this fascinating project, but also provided a videotaped copy of the film, taken from a Los Angeles TV showing in 1983. Though slightly edited for content (we are no longer treated to the closing vignette in which Will's best friend Mark gives him a crotch protector as a gag going-away gift), the print was substantially

the same as the version of *Goodbye Franklin High* which was released theatrically in the Spring of 1978.

One of scores of small, independent movie projects to be afforded limited big-screen play in the waning days of drive-ins and double features, *Goodbye Franklin High* was a seminal experience for several of the people involved. It was the first screenwriting credit for 25-year-old Stu Krieger, who later specialized in such family-oriented fantasy films as *The Land Before Time, A Troll in Central Park, Zenon: Girl of the 21st Century* and the 1995 TV remake of Disney's *Freaky Friday*. And several of the film's production personnel would soon become associated with horrormeister John Carpenter, then poised to make his big directorial breakthrough with another low-budgeted, teen-oriented feature, *Halloween*. Those future John Carpenter colleagues included cinematographer Dean Cundey, who, after his tenure with Carpenter, went on to such A-budget projects as *Who Framed Roger Rabbit?*, *Jurassic Park*, *Apollo 13* and *What Women Want*; Debra Hill, who, upon serving her apprenticeship as *Goodbye, Franklin High's* script supervisor, signed on as Carpenter's producer for *Halloween, The Fog, Escape from New York* and other hits; and co-producer Kool Lusby, later the associate producer for *Halloween* and production coordinator for such star-studded endeavors as *Down and Out in Beverly Hills* and *The Big Easy*.

Beyond the older, more seasoned members of the cast (whom we'll discuss in due time), the film offers a talented array of twenty-somethings, of which the best known at the time was Darby Hinton, who a decade or so earlier had appeared as Fess Parker's preteen son in the TV series *Daniel Boone*. As obligatory "wisecracking best friend" Mark Jeffries, Hinton proved that he was more than just another overgrown child star, and was able to parlay this appearance into some worthwhile character parts over the next two decades, as well as the regular role of Ian Griffith during the 1985-86 season of the NBC soaper *Days of Our Lives*. As Will Armer's 16-year-old sweetheart Sharon Bradley, 24-year-old leading lady Ann Dusenberry, who'd already amassed some respectable film and television credits, here displays the ingratiating personality and casual poise that would later vault her to semistardom in such made-for–TV features as *Elvis and the Beauty Queen* (1981) and *He's Not Your Son* (1984).

Curiously, the two people who seem to have benefited least from *Goodbye, Franklin High* are the film's star and director. Singer/songwriter Lane Caudell made his second starring appearance in this film, pulling off the assignment admirably despite a tendency to overplay his hand in the emotional scenes, and the fact that he was far too old to convincingly portray a high school senior (though, in fairness, the same can be said for most of the other principals in the cast). While *Goodbye, Franklin High* could be regarded as merely an excuse for Caudell to showcase his own singing and compositions as often as possible, the musical interludes are logically (and not *too* obviously) fitted into the storyline: During an early school-dance sequence, for example, the hired deejay announces that his next record selection will be "Let's Have a Party"—written and performed by Lane Caudell! Had *Goodbye, Franklin High* been given wider distribution, it is possible that Caudell's name would now be more than an answer to a rock-music trivia question; instead, his film career petered out rather quickly, though like his costar Darby Hinton, he would briefly enjoy some prominence on NBC's *Days of Our Lives*, playing Woody King during the 1982-83 season.

Producer-director Mike McFarland had previously worked with Lane Caudell on the latter's first starring effort, *Hanging on a Star* (1978), which also featured legendary radio personality Wolfman Jack, star-to-be Deborah Raffin and former "Captain Kool and the Kongs" member Mickey McMeel. McFarland's confident melding of the variegated cast members and multiple subplots in *Goodbye, Franklin High*—and his remarkable facility for getting a millionaire's value out of a beggar's budget—should have opened innumerable professional doors for him. Alas, Mike McFarland's directorial career went down in flames after 1983's *Pink Motel*, an abysmal sex comedy starring Phyllis Diller and Slim Pickens. (Bet you'll all want to see *that* one now, won't you?)

Like so many independent baseball films covered in this book (*Finding Buck McHenry, The Last Home Run, Perfect Game*), *Goodbye, Franklin High* benefits immeasurably from the presence of several veteran character actors in the cast. Especially praiseworthy are William Windom and Julie Adams as Will's parents, Cliff and Janice Armer. Though Windom could have thrown the picture off balance by exploiting the bravura opportunities afforded him in his role—the hacking cough brought about by his respiratory ailment, his kidding-on-the-square relationship with son Will, his unexpected burst into song during Will's 18th birthday party—the actor generously avoids the temptation to dominate the action, and is all the more effective because of his restraint. Similarly, Julie Adams invests her character with those infinitesimal little touches that elevate a mere performance to the level of total credibility. Particularly memorable is Adams' struggle to keep her emotions in check when her husband is rushed to the emergency hospital, her nervous efforts to calmly go about her domestic chores while Will confronts her with evidence of her infidelity, and her final scene, in which she tearfully accepts the fact that Will is not yet capable of forgiving her, even though he wants to.

An unexpected treat for B-movie buffs is the presence in the cast of four familiar supporting players, each given his or her moment of glory in a brief but sparkling scene. As the gruff police captain who issues a stern warning to Will after the boy has gotten involved in a brawl, Kenneth Tobey is every bit as virile and commanding as he'd been in such cult classics as *The Thing* (1951) and *It Came from Beneath the Sea* (1955) (and could that be a trace of an understanding smile as Tobey curtly sends Will on his way?). Myron Healey, the sharkish villain of many a low-budget western, is here effectively cast against type as Will's bespectacled, bookish guidance counselor Mr. Craig, who, after reprimanding the boy for even considering a baseball career over a full Stanford scholarship, neatly avoids the standard "clueless authority figure" cliché by wearily agreeing that Will must be allowed to make up his own mind. Virginia Gregg, a former radio actress best

known for her countless appearances on the late–1960s revival of Jack Webb's TV series *Dragnet* (and as the uncredited voice of "mother" in Hitchcock's *Psycho*) likewise sidesteps the obvious in the role of an officious hospital admitting nurse, nullifying the audience's expectation that she will play the "rules are rules" game when the consumptive Cliff Armer shows up late one night by calmly explaining that she would be happy to summon a doctor—if only the Armer family will shut up and relax a second. And Mary Treen, whose other credits include the role of Cousin Tilly in the imperishable *It's a Wonderful Life*, succinctly offers an amusing apotheosis of every flustered study-hall teacher on Earth in her one-scene role as Miss Atwater.

Except for the embarrassingly bad and tiresomely prolonged scene in which Will confronts a goonishly gung-ho Marine recruiting officer (we know we're in for a dull ride when we see the slogan on the officer's desk: "Join the Marines, Travel to New Lands, Meet New People ... and Kill Them"), *Goodbye, Franklin High* has a firm grasp on the reality of what it was like to be a teenager in the late 1970s. Though a superb athlete, a bright and popular student, and a reasonably obedient son, Will Armer is a seething mass of believable imperfections: Warned to stay out of trouble by the cops, he cannot pass up the opportunity to stage a beer-and-pot party in a deserted house for the amusement of his friends; with plenty of money in his pocket, he is unable to resist stealing a couple of carrots at the local grocery store; after persuading his girlfriend (who's gone on the pill in honor of his birthday) to "do it" in a canvas-covered canoe, he balks at admitting that he's truly in love with her, and even blatantly flirts with another tootsie on the dance floor; and though his GPA is high enough to warrant him a scholarship, he considers the day wasted if he isn't able to cheat on an exam. Any one of these faults might have qualified Will as the villain in a high-school film made before 1965, but in the wake of the let-it-all-hang-out hippie era and the civil disobedience attending Vietnam, Will's furtive little acts of deviltry and defiance are almost endearingly innocent—and more importantly, all of them feed into the film's basic storyline, in which Will, confused over which direction to take in life, continues to seek out alternatives to the inevitability of thinking and acting like an adult.

Unlike such "bigger" films as *Saturday Night Fever* and *Annie Hall*, which offer a romanticized and exaggerated perspective of the 1970s, *Goodbye, Franklin High* defines its era with pinpoint accuracy. Much as we recall that time period as a dizzying kaleidoscope of BeeGees music, polyester, shag rugs, lava lamps, mood rings and Farah Fawcett posters, the fact remains that most people lived and behaved pretty much the way they lived and behaved in any other era, with the trappings and sensibilities of the decade acting as icing on the cake, rather than the whole cake itself. Also, the film's miniscule budget left the director no choice but to stage his highlights as they would actually happen in real life, minus the standard Hollywood glossiness and artifice of the era. Thus, when Will and his friends attend a "month before graduation" dance, we are not confronted with a bunch of over-rehearsed, gorgeous-looking, impeccably-garbed John Travolta wannabes strutting their stuff in a neon paradise, but instead a collection of normal, healthy, economically dressed high schoolers, amateurishly but enthusiastically swaying to the rhythm of the music in a low-rent auditorium adorned with dime-store decorations. And when in the same scene Will gets into a brief scuffle with a pugnacious fellow student, we don't see a corps of stuntmen engaged in a series of carefully choreographed falls and explosive body blows, but instead a minor row which looks as clumsy and ill-

timed as any real fight between a couple of hotheaded kids.

The film's most refreshing aspect is scriptwriter Stu Krieger's steadfast avoidance of predictability. Quite often we are led down the garden path of formula, only to be taken completely unawares by a startling and unexpected twist. When Will is threatened with an arrest if he ever gets into trouble again, we fully expect that his wild party later in the film will get him into real hot water—but when the dust settles, everyone *except* Will and his girlfriend is hauled off to the pokey. After being repeatedly reminded that Will's father is slowly dying of emphysema, we brace ourselves for the inevitable death scene; but by film's end, despite one or two false alarms, dear old Dad is still alive and kicking. And when Will suspects that his mother is seeing another man, conventional plot development dictates that his suspicions will be unfounded; but not in *Goodbye, Franklin High*, in which Mom not only confesses to having an affair, but also reveals that she is doing so with the full knowledge and permission of her ailing husband!

While all of this helps make *Goodbye, Franklin High* a better than usual "B" effort, it does not necessarily qualify the film as a baseball picture—and, admittedly, when this writer began viewing Stu Krieger's personal copy, it looked for a while as if the film would have to be disqualified on the grounds of insufficient baseball action, save for a brief spurt of diamond activity during the opening credits sequence. Halfway through the film, however, director Mike McFarland stages an eight-minute ballpark sequence which stands as one of the best of its kind from any film. The central baseball game in *Goodbye, Franklin High* works as well as it does because of its unadorned simplicity. Using only traditional camera setups, fast-paced but elemental editing, and the "natural" sounds of the crowd and the PA system, the scene conveys the excitement and enthusiasm attending a high-school championship game far more persuasively than if McFarland had gimmicked up the sequence with slick steadicam shots, zoom-ins, screen-filling closeups of eyes and hands, overamplified sound effects, pseudo-symphonic music and a surfeit of slow motion. Even more impressively, the scene sustains its excitement and comes to a thrilling climax without the artifice of a sudden-death play or a spectacular catch; a few foul balls, a couple of boggles and recoveries, a quick infield play or two, one last strikeout, and the game is over. The thrills are inherent in the staging of the game itself, not in how it is "improved" by script contrivances, directorial trickery or the post-production crew. So willing is the audience to be swept up by the exaltation of the moment that only on repeated viewings are we aware that the pitcher and the batter are never shown on screen at the same time, indicating that film editor Peter Parasheles was probably more responsible for Franklin High's victory than Will Armer.

For this single baseball sequence alone, *Goodbye, Franklin High* deserves to be rescued from obscurity. If a home-video market exists for such high-budget dreck as *The Slugger's Wife*, *Ed* and *The Fan*, surely some enterprising VHS or DVD distributor could see his way clear to bring this undiscovered little gem back into general circulation.

The Great American Pastime

MGM; released November 1956

Produced by Henry Berman. Directed by Herman Hoffman. Screenplay by Nathaniel Benchley. Photography: Arthur E. Arling. Music by Jeff Alexander. Edited by Gene Ruggiero. Art directors: William A. Horning and Randall Ovell. Set decoration by Edwin B. Willis and Edward G. Boyle. Special photographic effects by A. Arnold Gillespie. Makeup by William Tuttle. 89 minutes; black and white; sound.

Cast: Tom Ewell (Bruce Hallerton); Anne Francis (Betty Hallerton); Ann Miller (Mrs. Doris Patterson); Dean Jones (Buck River); Rudy Lee (Dennis Hallerton); Judson Pratt (Ed Ryder); Raymond Bailey (George Carruthers); Winifred Knapp (Mrs. Dawson); Bob Jellison (Mr. O'Keefe); Raymond Winston (Herbie Patterson); Tod Ferrell (Man Mountain O'Keefe); Paul Engle (Foster Carruthers); Gene O'Donnell (Samuel G. Garway); Smidgeon the Dog (Himself)*; and Nathaniel Benchley.

In an effort to be closer to his son Dennis, lawyer Bruce Hallerton agrees to coach the boy's Little League team, the Panthers. Bruce runs into interference from the parents of the other team members, who in typical suburban adult fashion expect their boys to be star players and offer unsolicited advice as to how Hallerton can best run the team. One of the boys' mothers, the widowed Doris Patterson, wants Hallerton to give her son a chance to pitch, but her excessive attention to Bruce is appraised by his wife Betty as a romantic overture. Despite pressure from the parents, Hallerton sticks to his guns so far as telling his boys that they're playing for the love of the sport and not for victory at all costs; but his team wins the championship all the same. At the end, Betty Hallerton joins the ball club as team secretary—not out of any love for baseball (she can't stand the game) but to keep Doris Patterson's hands off Bruce.

Though the Little League had been formed in Williamsport, Pennsylvania, in 1939, and had spread to all forty-eight continental United States, the Canadian province of Quebec, and Mexico by 1955, *The Great American Pastime* was the first full-length screen treatment of this particular aspect of baseball. The film was made with the cooperation of the Little League organization (*Variety*, in fact, suggested that local

*Smidgeon, named for actor Walter Pidgeon, belonged to actress Anne Francis, one of the film's two leading ladies.

Tom Ewell (center, back row) and his Little League charges doff their caps for the national anthem in *The Great American Pastime*.

screenings of the film be tied in with the league's promotional activities), so the more trenchant view of adult-sponsored kid's sports events depicted in *The Bad News Bears* (1977) (q.v.)—wherein the Little League is not mentioned by name, nor is it suggested that the film's teams are in any way associated with the league—is not to be found in *Pastime*. There is the expected comedy inherent in the concept of flabby, middle-aged adults living their dreams of glory through their children, but the satiric thrust is gentle to the point of being antiseptic. The young ballplayers perform vigorously in the film's sporadic game sequences, exhibiting more pep and enthusiasm than is found in 90 percent of the films about adult baseball.

However, *The Great American Pastime* attaches more importance to the subplot

of Bruce Hallerton being enticed by Doris Patterson to give her son a break (and of Betty Hallerton's jealousy in this matter) than on the Little League itself. Since Mrs. Patterson and Mrs. Hallerton are played by two extraordinarily attractive women, Ann Miller (whose last starring film this was) and Anne Francis, modern audiences are dumbfounded that either lady can see anything in Bruce Hallerton, who, as played by Tom Ewell, is such a ploddingly unromantic fellow, with so pronounced a tendency to comport himself like a TV sitcom "idiot father," that he makes Hugh Beaumont look like Cary Grant.

Like most major-studio programmers of the mid–1950s, the production costs of *The Great American Pastime* exceeded its profits. As a result, the Little League would rarely be used as the main subject matter in subsequent films of the 1950s and 1960s, though it would do service as a peripheral ingredient of such "suburbia" comedies as *Boys' Night Out* and *Critic's Choice*.

Hardball

Fireworks Pictures/Nides-McCormick/Tollin-Robbins/Paramount; released September 14, 2001

Executive Producers: Kevin McCormick, Herbert W. Gains and Erwin Stoff. Produced by Tina Nides, Mike Tollin and Brian Robbins. Directed by Brian Robbins. Written by John Gatins and [uncredited] Carl Franklin; based upon *Hardball: A Season in the Projects* by Daniel Coyle. Photography: Tom Richmond. Edited by Ned Bastille. Original music by Mark Isham. Music supervisor: Michael McQuarn. Production designer: Jaymes Hinkle. Production coordinator: Jennifer Corey. Supervising sound editor: George Simpson. Costume designer: Francine Jamison-Tanchucks. Baseball coordinator: Mark Ellis. Stunt coordinator: Rick Le Fevour. Acting coach: Bob Krakower. First assistant director: Benjamin Rosenberg. Second assistant director: Michael J. Moore. Casting: Marci Liroff, Claire Simon. Makeup: Aimee Lippert-Bastian, Jamie S. Weiss. Special effects: Tim Gibbons. Visual effects: Cinesite (producer, Mike Sullo). Foley editor: Chris Danielski. Panavision; Color by DeLuxe. 106 minutes; Dolby Digital/DTS Sound. Rated PG-13.

Cast: Keanu Reeves (Conor O'Neill); Diane Lane (Elizabeth Wilkes); John Hawkes (Ticky Tobin); D.B. Sweeney (Matt Hyland); Mike McGlone (Jimmy Fleming); Sterling Elijah Brim (Sterling); A. Delon Ellis, Jr. (Miles Pennfield, II); Julian Griffith (Jefferson Albert Tibbs); Bryan Hearne (Andre Ray Peetes); Michael B. Jordan (Jamal); Kristopher Lofton (Clarence); Michael Perkins (Kofi Evans); Brian Reed (Raymond "Ray-Ray" Bennet); Alexander Telles (Alex); DeWayne Warren (Janus "G-Baby" Evans); Graham Beckel (Duffy); Carol E. Hall (Pearla Evans); Jacqueline Williams (Lenora Tibbs); Freeman Coffey (Darryl Mackey); Mark Margolis (Fink); Greg Sandquist (Barber's Son); Stephen Cinabro (Gino); Aaron Evans (Aaron); Andre Morgan, Reginald McKinley (Umpires); Mark Ellis (Waatas Coach); Paul Turner (Bartender); Dawn Lewis (Ellen); Kwame Amoaku (Pizza Guy); Vince Green (Other Pizza Guy); Tom Milanovich (Ed); Michael B. Chait (Straight-Laced Kid); Father Donald M. Siple O.S.M. (Priest); Adam Tomei (Barfly); Sammy Sosa (Himself); Ronnel Taylor (Gang Member); Josefus Duanah, Jeffery Oatlin (Tough Kids); Carl Paoli (Keanu Reeves' stunt double). Cut from film: Trevor Morgan (role undetermined).

Two-bit ticket scalper, compulsive gambler and chronic drunkard Conor O'Neill has hit rock bottom—and few know it better than Conor himself. "No one can kick my ass better than me!" screams Conor when he is cornered by sports-bar owner Duffy, one of his many creditors. In desperate need of $12,000, Conor seeks out a loan from his stockbroker friend Jimmy Fleming. Rather than throw good money after bad, Jimmy offers to pay Conor $500 per week if he will agree to coach the Kekambas, a corporate-sponsored Little League team headquartered in one of Chicago's nastiest, most violent high-rise housing projects. While there are some talented players on the team, for the most part the Kekambas have locked themselves into the "born loser" mentality that unfortunately infects many ghetto children. Initially planning to chuck his coaching responsibilities as soon as he can square his debts, Conor instead develops a strong emotional bond with the Kekambas, and within a few weeks both Conor and the team have transformed themselves into winners—a metamorphosis that is especially gratifying to the kids' dedicated schoolteacher, Elizabeth Wilkes. Even when a devastating tragedy befalls one of the team members, the Kekambas will not be dissuaded from becoming true champions, both on and off the ballfield. As for Conor O'Neill, who has spent a lifetime running away from responsibility and commitment, he has finally learned that, "the most important thing in life is showing up."

Published in 1993, *Hardball: A Season*

in the Projects is journalist Daniel Coyle's eyewitness account of his experiences while coaching the First Chicago Near North Kikuyus, one of the twenty teams comprising a new Little League organization established at the infamous, gang-dominated Cabrini-Green housing project. Created in 1991, the organization, known dually as the Near North Little League and the African-American Youth League, was the brainchild of two dedicated activists: white insurance executive Bob Muzikowski and black community worker Al Carter. A former alcoholic and substance abuser, Muzikowski had several years earlier become a Born Again Christian, determined to spread the Good Word through good works. Carter, himself a product of Chicago's mean streets, had devoted his life to social and racial reform, and had returned from whence he came to use his considerable political clout to help provide the children of Cabrini-Green with the hope and incentive necessary to pull themselves out of the ghetto. As Coyle observes in his book, though Muzikowski and Carter often clashed violently over ideology and methods, the two men complemented each other perfectly: "Muzikowski provided the corporate sponsors and coaches [for the League]; Carter provided the players, the neighborhood expertise, and a focus on reinforcing the children's African-American heritage..." (it was Carter who suggested that each team be named after a specific African tribal group).

While the focus in Coyle's book was on the long upward climb of the "underdog" Kikuyus towards the 1992 League Championship, *Hardball: A Season in the Projects* also offered vivid thumbnail sketches of the history of the Chicago Housing Authority, the harrowing day-to-day perils of life in the Projects, and the ever-growing bonds of trust and mutual dependence between the poverty-stricken black ballplayers and their comparatively affluent white coaches. As published, the book all but cried out for a motion-picture adaptation, a cross between *The Bad News Bears* (q.v.) and the 1995 Michelle Pfeiffer vehicle *Dangerous Minds*, the fact-based story of how a first-year teacher—and ex-marine—managed to reach a group of "unreachable" inner-city schoolkids.

Tackling the assignment of transferring Coyle's prose to the Big Screen was the production team of Mike Tollin and Brian Robbins, of *Varsity Blues* fame, who were already deep into development of a radically different baseball picture, *Summer Catch* (q.v.). Carried over from both *Varsity Blues* and *Summer Catch* was screenwriter John Gatins, who elected to divide the script's focus between the wise-beyond-their-years ballplayers and their white coach, a fictional yuppie stockbroker whose company sponsored one of the teams. Idealistically driven by the desire to "give something back to the community," the hero would be in for a rude awakening once he actually took over the coaching responsibilities. As originally conceived, it would take nearly the entire running time of the film before the streetwise kids would stop regarding the well-meaning stockbroker as just another Limousine Liberal and accept him as being sincerely driven and dedicated—just as the hero himself would not be truly committed to his new responsibilities until he realized that the kids came first, rather than his own feelings of self-fulfillment. Unfortunately, Gatins' first few drafts didn't jell, so it was decided to make the stockbroker a secondary character, and reconceive the film's adult protagonist as a scuzzy gambler and ticket-hustler, a "lost soul" whose redemption would come about only when he learned to overcome his petty selfishness by giving of himself to others. Cast in this plum role was the versatile Keanu Reeves, a surefire box-office draw since his starring turn in the phenomenally popular *The Matrix* (1998).

Once Reeves was firmly in place,

producer Michael Tollin set about finding the youngsters to play the members of the Near North Little League. "The casting is complicated, you're finding mostly unknown young kids, eight, nine, ten years old, and you have to find kids who can both act and play a little ball," explained Tollin. "It's a real tricky one." Though an open casting call was posted throughout the nation, most of the kids were recruited from Chicago, where the bulk of the film was to be shot. Of the 600 children interviewed, 350 finalists were whittled down to forty during an exacting three-week training camp, overseen by the film's baseball coordinator Mark Ellis (who'd also worked on Tollin-Robbins' *Summer Catch*) and acting coach Bob Krakower. Only two of the principal child performers had previously acted on film: Brian Hearne, who played the cocky, athletically gifted Andre Ray Peetes, and Michael B. Jordan, cast as the ever-so-slightly underaged Jamal Evans. Of the other kids, A. Delon Ellis, who played the Walkman-toting pitcher Miles Pennfield II, could lay claim to being a celebrity by lineage, inasmuch as his father was former Chicago Bears defensive back Allan Ellis. The remaining members of the Kekamba team—Michael Perkins as Jamal's fatalistic cousin Kofi Evans, DeWayne Warren as Kofi's pint-sized, trash-talking younger brother Janus (aka "G-Baby"), Julian Griffith as chubby, asthmatic Jefferson Alan Tibbs, Brian Reed as Raymond "Ray Ray" Bennett, Sterling Elijah Brim as Sterling, Kristofer Lofton as Clarence, Alexander Telles as Alex—were all making their first movie appearances. And, it should be added, all the kids delivered uniformly excellent performances.

Apparently because the real Cabrini-Green was deemed too unwieldy and dangerous to serve as a filming location, the smaller, "safer" ALBA housing project was used for most of the ballgame scenes and exterior atmosphere shots. The producers bankrolled the construction of a new ballpark and playground, providing much-needed employment for several local residents. Both structures remained standing after production ended, as gifts to the community.

Filmed between August and October 2000, *Hardball* was supposed to have been released by Paramount Pictures in April of 2001. As it turned out, the producers could consider themselves lucky that the film was released at all. From the very beginning, filming of *Hardball* was staunchly opposed by several prominent Chicago functionaries, chief among them Mayor Richard J. Daley, Jr. and Chief of Schools Paul Vallas. Among the major complaints were that the film painted an "overly negative" picture of Chicago, that the youngsters cast as extras were being pulled out of school, and that the black characters were essentially stereotypes. Joining the chorus of protests were a number of coaches of the real Near North Little League. "We are kind of broken-hearted," observed one coach. "They have come to our town and taken a wonderful story about kids wanting to play baseball and dirtied it up because they think this is how black kids act. They are wrong." Fanning the flames of controversy was star Keanu Reeves, who reportedly defended the film's use of R-rated dialogue on the grounds that the producers wanted total authenticity.

Responding to the avalanche of adverse criticism, the producers trimmed *Hardball* from 112 to 106 minutes, removing a handful of the more volatile scenes. They also softened the film's rating from "R" to "PG-13" by slicing out or overdubbing several of the stronger epithets (though in the finished film, the kids still say "Bitch" and "Shit" to excess). Having already changed the names of all characters and teams, and careful not to refer to either Cabrini-Green or the Near North Little League by name, the producers added a disclaimer to the closing credits, noting that though the story was inspired by actual events, the film was a work of fiction.

These alterations and safeguards were still not sufficient as far as League founders Bob Muzikowski and Al Carter were concerned. Though they seldom, if ever, agreed over matters pertaining to the League, the two men were united in their fierce opposition to *Hardball*'s release. Speaking through an attorney, Muzikowski and Carter continued to protest that the children in the film were "racist caricatures" and that the script contained "more than a dozen" parallels to their own lives. A last-ditch effort to legally block the film's release was overturned in court on the grounds that such an action would be a violation of free speech. Echoing the sentiments of the producers and star Keanu Reeves, the judge proclaimed that moviegoers should be allowed to judge the film for themselves.

Sidestepping further comment on the controversies and legal imbroglios surrounding the film, it can be observed that the movie version of *Hardball* resembles the book version of *Hardball* only in that both take place in Chicago and both feature an inner-city Little League team. Whereas the book was primarily about the tribulations and triumphs of the enthusiastic young ballplayers and their hardworking coaches, the film is essentially a star vehicle, focusing on the redemption of Conor O'Neill, the character played by Keanu Reeves. The baseball angle is only sporadically addressed throughout the first two-thirds of the film; the lion's share of the footage is devoted to Conor's various strategies to raise enough cash to pay off his creditors, his dangerously close encounters with a wide variety of broken-nosed thugs and hulking henchmen (during one frantic nocturnal chase through a forbidding tenement neighborhood, the viewer is tempted to shout, "Yeah, Keanu, we know you were in *The Matrix*, now stop running and get back to the plot!"), and

his casual pursuit of romance with attractive schoolteacher Elizabeth Wilkes (Diane Lane, struggling valiantly to make something of her thankless role).

Somewhere around *Hardball*'s seventy-five minute mark, Conor's financial difficulties miraculously evaporate when he cinches the necessary $12,000 by betting on the Michael Jordan–less Chicago Bulls (inarguably the most unbelievable moment in the picture!). As if to transmit the message that Money Solves Everything, the film finally deigns to focus almost exclusively on the Kekamba team. Throughout the early portions of the film it has been established that though the kids already possess a respectable degree of baseball knowhow (in fact, the ballpark scenes *before* Conor's windfall, albeit frustratingly brief, are more excitingly staged than those that occur afterwards), what they have been lacking is a strong male parental figure to pull them together as a team. Freed from his monetary shackles, Conor can now devote all his time to becoming that figure. In an all-too-symbolic gesture, he decides to show the kids how a *real* baseball team operates by taking them all to their first-ever major league game at Wrigley Field, a sequence drenched with gushy symphonic background music and luminescent Spielbergesque cinematography. Once the kids' presence is graciously acknowledged by the Cubs' Sammy Sosa (who, in near–Papal fashion, waves and blows kisses at the beaming youngsters), we know that both Conor and the Kekambas have found salvation.

Beyond the garish Hollywood phoniness of this magic moment—made even more phony by the fact that the scene was not even filmed at Wrigley, but instead at Detroit's old Tiger Stadium—the film completely misses the point of the original book: the resilience of children even in the direst of circumstances. *Hardball* author Danny Coyle makes it clear that, while strong male authority figures are vital to

Hardball: Coach Conor O'Neill (Keanu Reeves) and youngest Kekamba member G-Baby (DeWayne Warren) are lost in their own thoughts as they watch a practice session.

the success of the ballplayers, the kids' *potential* to succeed is already in place. If we are to believe what we see in the film, however, the Kekambas become winners *only* because of Conor O'Neill. Though director Brian Robbins insisted that, "I didn't want to do the white-guy-saves-the-ghetto movie," this is exactly what comes across in *Hardball*, especially since the script contrives to set up the post-redemption Conor O'Neill as the sole positive adult male character in the film. This is not simply because we never see any of the kids' fathers (the ballgames are attended exclusively by mothers, grandmothers and aunts). Looking around at the other male grownups in the picture, we find a flaccid, noncommittal yuppie (Conor's stockbroker friend Jimmy, played by Mark McGlone), a mercenary comical sidekick (John Hawkes as Conor's best pal Ticky Tobin), a craven covey of small-time gamblers and bookies, an intransigent, rule-bound League president (Darryl Mackey, played by Freeman Coffey) and the arrogant, condescending coach of the League's best team (Matt Hyland, portrayed by D.B. Sweeney with none of the warmth and fellow-feeling the actor conveyed as Shoeless Joe Jackson in *Eight Men Out* [q.v.]).

The script's depiction of the two last-named characters is particularly offensive. One of the dilemmas facing anyone who tackles a film on Life in the Ghetto is the lack of any single identifiable villain: The menace is the Ghetto itself. (Nothing in the film is as palpably chilling as the moment in Coyle's book wherein one of the coaches is warned not to use certain hand signals with his players, lest they be misinterpreted as gang signs.) *Hardball* "solves" this dilemma by transforming League president Darryl Mackey and coach Matt Hyland into stock, mustache-twirling bad guys, cruelly refusing to allow star Kekambas' player Jamal to participate in an important game because he is a mere two months short of the minimum age requirement, and dis-

dainfully forbidding pitcher Miles Pennfield from wearing the Walkman which helps him concentrate on his throwing by shutting out the detrimental sounds of the Projects. It is even suggested that Mackey and Hyland are behaving in this obstreperous manner to prevent the Kekambas from succeeding, which would seem to defeat the entire purpose of the League. Small wonder that Robert Muzikowski and Al Carter cried "foul" when they read the script of *Hardball*.

In his review of the film, the Chicago *Sun-Times'* Roger Ebert noted that *Hardball* "drifts above its natural subjects, content to be a genre picture. We're always aware of the formula—and in a picture based on real life, we shouldn't be." An example of what Ebert is talking about can be found in the film's recreation of a moment in the original book, in which an asthmatic young ballplayer heads home after dark, only to be beaten up by a brace of gang members, leading to the threat of a lawsuit from the kid's mother, who had been assured that her boy would be protected from harm while practicing baseball. In the book, it is recorded that the coaches warned the youngster several times to go home before sundown, but he ignored their warnings and suffered the consequences. In the film, the boy's fictional counterpart, Jefferson (Julian Griffith), is *forced* to practice well past the daylight hours by the insensitive Conor O'Neill. Upon visiting the battered Jefferson in his hospital room, Conor suffers the first twinges of conscience that will ultimately lead to his conversion from lowlife to Human Being. Thus, Truth is distorted to adhere to Formula—and thus again, the focus of the story is artificially shifted from the kids to Conor.

Admittedly, the film often works quite well in its own button-pushing fashion. While the viewer can regret the omission of the amusing and heartwarming episode in the book wherein the ghetto ballplayers express wonder and amazement at the "outside world" when invited to play a game in Dubuque, Iowa (seeing mile after mile of identical red barns, one of the more cynical youngsters begins to suspect that he's being driven around in circles!), at least one of the movie's formulaic contrivances is quite effective. Denied permission to wear his Walkman during a crucial championship playoff game, pitcher Miles is inspired to excellence by his teammates, who, in unison, begin singing and dancing an *a capella* rendition of Miles' favorite rap song, Notorious B.I.G.'s "Big Poppa." Though clearly a ripoff of similar moments in *Major League* (the "Wild Thing" mantra) and the 1994 version of *Angels in the Outfield* (the *en masse* arm-waving gesture), this choice vignette manages to be both touching and hilarious at the same time. And while one is disappointed that the Kekambas' copping of the League championship is not shown, but only referred to in passing during the closing credits, the handling of the team's win just *before* the championship game is both original and novel. At the funeral of one of the Kekambas, who was killed in a drive-by shooting an hour or so after the team's victory, a tearful Conor O'Neil delivers a eulogy in which he recalls the dead boy's last moments of ballpark glory, which are then depicted in flashback fashion. This delicate and effective mixture of triumph and tragedy would have worked even better had it not been obvious from the outset of the picture that the kid in question was all but predestined to be killed. (Had *Hardball* been filmed in 1939, the team's sacrificial lamb would have been played by the diminutive, lachrymose Bobs Watson.) The moment we see the first screen-filling closeup of the unfortunate youngster, we realize that he is as foredoomed as any fresh-faced G.I. who wrote a letter home to his sweetheart in a World War II picture.

In observing that critical reaction to *Hardball* was mixed, it must be noted that the reasons were not necessarily a matter of personal taste. By a macabre stroke of fate, the film was released on Friday, September 14, 2001—the first major-studio release to hit the nation's movie screens after the cataclysmic terrorist assault on the World Trade Center, three days earlier. In general, the negative reviews appeared *before* the tragic events of September 11, while the positive critiques were published after that date. The evidence suggests that many of America's critics, numbed and disillusioned by breaking news events, and desperate to latch onto something even remotely inspirational, optimistic and life-affirming, embraced *Hardball* as the "feel good" movie of the year, lavishing praise on the film far beyond its actual value. The moviegoers of America, clearly yearning for a temporary respite from the appalling images of destruction and devastation on their TV screens, likewise took *Hardball* to their hearts. The film posted a first-weekend gross of $9.4 million, the first baseball picture since *A League of Their Own* to hit the Number One spot in the top twenty moneymaking films of the week. "It's fitting, really," observed *Entertainment Weekly*. "At a time of unprecedented national distress, baseball comes to the rescue."

Headin' Home

Kessel and Baumann/Cine-Vintage/Yankee; released September 19, 1920

Supervised by R. A. Walsh (some sources list Walsh as director, some as writer). Produced by William Shea and Herbert H. Yudkin. Directed by Lawrence Windom. Titles by Arthur "Bugs" Baer. 5 reels; black and white; silent.

Cast: Babe Ruth (George Ruth); Ruth Taylor (Mildred Tobin); William Sheer (Harry Knight); Margaret Seddon (Babe's Mother); Frances Victory (Pigtails); James A. Marcus (Cyrus Tobin); George Halman (Dog Catcher); Ralph Harolds (John Tobin, team owner); Charles Hurt (David Talmadge); George Halpin (Doc Hedges, Constable); William J. Gross (Ebeneezer); Walter

Lawrence (Tony Marino); Ann Brody [Brodie] (Mrs. Tony Marino); Ricca Allen (Almira Worters); Sam Blum (Jimbo Jones); Ethel Kerwin (Kitty Wilson); Thomas Cameron (Deacon Flack).

George Ruth, erstwhile iceman of the little town of Haverlock, frequently leaves his wares to melt in the afternoon sun whenever distracted by a local ballgame. Most of the time, George concentrates on his hobby of whittling baseball bats out of wood blocks. Despite his devotion to baseball, the Haverlock team won't let George play, regarding the big clod as something of the local joke—an opinion unfortunately shared by the girl of George's dreams, Mildred Tobin. George gets a chance at bat when the rival team is short a member during one game, and it is here that young Ruth learns that he plays best when he's riled—a hard lesson, since his batted ball smashes through the town church's brand new stained glass window. Only the intervention of the deacon keeps the crowd from rending George asunder; the hapless young man is banished from the ballfield and is compelled to leave Haverlock. But George manages to get on another team in another town, and here he excels. Meanwhile, Mildred falls for Haverlock's star player, Harry Knight, a city slicker who turns out to be a cad, a bounder, and incidentally an embezzler. Just as "curses on you" Harry Knight is about to have his way with Mildred, George pops up to vanquish the scoundrel. Redeemed in everyone's eyes, George gets to play for Haverlock again, but can't make the crucial play because all of his bats vanish. George's kid sister Pigtails comes to the rescue by running home and returning with one of George's whittled bats. He hits the time-honored winning homer, which leads to his almost instantly being signed for the New York Yankees. And you thought *Field of Dreams* was hard to believe.

Already a media celebrity by 1920, Babe Ruth was but a year into his New York Yankees contract (after several stellar seasons in Boston) when he was approached by producers William Shea and Herbert H. Yudkin to star in a feature film. Babe was promised $50,000 for his participation: $15,000 up front and a check for the rest. Filming of *Headin' Home*, which was financed by Kessel and Baumann—the somewhat shady entrepreneurs who'd helped Mack Sennett set up his Keystone studio—began in August in Haverstraw, New York, and Fort Lee, New Jersey. Ruth would drive up to location each morning, wrap up his movie work, then leave without removing his makeup for batting practice at the Polo Grounds, where his teammates would find a source of endless amusement in the heavy pancake adorning the Babe's countenance. During shooting, Babe fell ill, reportedly contracting malaria from an insect bite. Despite having to work around a sick star who had to spend most of his time either in bed or at the ballfield, director Lawrence Windom had *Headin' Home* in the can in less than four weeks.

Though the film was well photographed, especially in the long shots of the small-town ballfield and a pastoral sequence set on a riverbank, the *Headin' Home* plotline was a hodgepodge, ambling unevenly from one incident to another. To create a semblance of coherence, most of the story took the form of a flashback related by the film's narrator, an old geezer watching George Ruth play. The silent film's titles, composed by newspaper humorist Arthur "Bugs" Baer, took on a self-mocking tone, inviting the audience to laugh at Ruth's clumsiness both as his misfit screen character and as an actor. Actually, Babe isn't all that bad; while hampered by his chalky facial makeup, he appears to be far more natural and relaxed than his over gesticulating "professional" supporting cast. One saving grace of Ruth's performance is his easy, boyish grin, something lacking for the most part in his later screen appearances, by which time hard living had caught up with him and the best he could manage for the cameras was a cynical half-smile. It is also refreshing to see how thin and agile Babe was in 1920, before the added weight made him resemble a potato standing on two toothpicks. He looks terrific in the ballfield scenes, faltering only when the script calls upon him to lose confidence in himself when his bat breaks; that lack of confidence was never part of Babe's real-life repertoire.

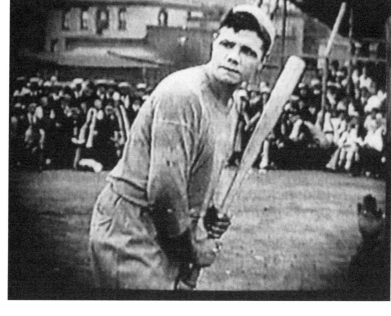

Babe Ruth stares at the pitcher through mountains of facial makeup in *Headin' Home.*

Headin' Home opened at New York's old Madison Square Garden on October 20, 1920. Predictably, the critics made mincemeat of the film; the *New York Times*'s reviewer noted rather haughtily that no one should expect quality from movies featuring such ephemeral celebrities as sports figures or persons made famous by spectacular divorce cases. *Variety* was a tad kinder, allowing that, "[Ruth], and he alone, makes it worth five minutes of anyone's time." Since the film cost almost nothing to make (the expensive looking climactic scenes showing Babe playing and signing autographs at the Polo Grounds were culled from inexpensive newsreel footage), it was a financial success, and prints remained in circulation throughout the 1920s. *Headin' Home* was still being offered by various sixteen-millimeter rental services into the sound era, and later showed up in prints of varying quality on the home video market. An abbreviated version was seen in episode number 12 of the 1963 syndicated TV series

Fractured Flickers, wherein we were told that Babe Ruth was in reality "Fungo Foster," champion bat whittler.

One person who failed to profit from *Headin' Home* was Babe Ruth himself. He was advised to wait until the film was finished to cash his $35,000 check, but after having a high old time showing off the slip of paper to his teammates, he discovered that the check was worthless. Although financial backers Kessel and Baumann had provided the money to producers Shea and Yudkin, the latter pair had headed for parts unknown when Babe came to collect. Ruth sued the producers but never saw another penny beyond the $15,000 he'd gotten when shooting started—a principal reason that, when Babe made his next starring feature, *Babe Comes Home* (q.v.), the ballplayer demanded he be paid a full $50,000 in advance. Still, Babe Ruth could look back on *Headin' Home* with a modicum of humor; it is said that he kept the producers' rubber check in his home for years as a conversation piece.

Here Come the Tigers

Filmways/American-International; released May 1978

Produced by Sean S. Cunningham and Stephen Miner. Directed by Sean S. Cunningham. Screenplay by Arch McCoy. Photography: Barry Abrams. Edited by Stephen Miner. Music by Harry Manfredi. Art direction by Susan E. Cunningham. Color by Movielab. 90 minutes; sound. Rated PG.

Cast: Richard Lincoln (Coach Eddie Burke); James Zvanut (Burt Homeger); Samantha Gray (Betty Burke); William Caldwell (Kreeger); Manny Lieberman (Felix the Umpire); Fred Lincoln (Aesop); Xavier Rodrigo (Buster Rivers); Kathy Bell (Patty O'Malley); Noel John Cunningham (Noel Cady); Sean P. Griffin (Art Bullfinch); Max McClellan (Mike "The Bod" Karpell); Kevin Moore ("Eaglescout" Terwilliger); Lance Norwood (Ralphy); Ted Oyama (Umecki); Michael Pastore (Fingers); Phillip Studeri (Danny); David Schmalholz (Bionic Mouth); Nancy Willis (Sharyn); Andy Weeks (Scoop); Todd Weeks (Timmy).

Rookie cop Eddie Burke takes it upon himself to whip a kids' baseball team full of misfits and malcontents into champions. He succeeds with the help of two star players: a deaf boy and a young karate champ.

Need we go any further? Add to the above synopsis the fact that the kids devote most of their time to spewing four-letter words and jokes about flatulence, plus the observance that the musical score employs quasi-classical themes in the style of Bizet's *Carmen*, and the purely noncoincidental resemblance to *The Bad News Bears* (q.v.) is complete.

There is a pleasant scene in which star Richard Lincoln has a heart to heart talk

The team ogles their lone cheerleader (Kathy Bell) in *Here Come the Tigers.*

with one of the lonelier kids. And the photography is serviceable. But otherwise, *Here Come the Tigers*, filmed on a smile and a shoeshine in Westport, Connecticut, is a compendium of bad acting and worse direction (by former documentary filmmaker Sean S. Cunnningham, who rebounded from this fiasco by launching the seemingly endless *Friday the 13th* horror series two years later). Most reviewers noted that the film was nothing more than the latest in an interminable parade of rip-off films released by American-International in the 1970s to capitalize on the success of such megahits as *The Exorcist* and *Jaws*. Janet Maslin of the *New York Times* wondered why the studio persisted in churning out its rank imitations, given the fact that when *Here Come the Tigers* opened in Manhattan, Ms. Maslin was the only person in the theater.

Hit and Run

Universal; released August 10, 1924

Written and directed by Edward Sedgwick. Story by Edward Sedgwick and Raymond L. Schrock. Photography: Virgil Miller. 6 reels/ 5,508 feet; black and white; silent.

Cast: Hoot Gibson (Swat Anderson); Marion Harlan (Joan McCarthy); Cyril Ring (George Collins); Harold Goodwin (Tex Adams); DeWitt Jennings (Joe Burns); Mike Donlin (Red McCarthy); William A. Steele (The Gopher).

Though as an outfielder he "couldn't catch the measles," cowpoke Swat Anderson is the star hitter for his desert-town ball team. With the help of scout Red McCarthy, Swat goes on to even greater success as a member of the big-league Blue Sox. Crooked gamblers conspire to fix the Big Game by hiring a thug to break Anderson's arm during a carefully framed brawl. When this fails, the crooks kidnap both Swat and Red McCarthy's daughter Joan, spiriting their captives away in a fast-moving train. But after foiling the villains with some

fancy lasso work, Swat escapes and wins the crucial game with—(pick one: [1] a home run; [2] a bunt; [3] a field goal).

Universal's cowboy star Hoot Gibson emulated his contemporary Tom Mix in *Hit and Run* by combining a standard Western story with a modern-day "hook," in this case baseball. In characteristic Gibson fashion, the film offers a generous supply of comedy, and also an exciting climax in which "The Hooter" manages to extricate himself and his sweetheart from danger without resorting to gunplay.

This pleasant if unremarkable six-reeler is distinguished by the presence in the cast of "Turkey" Mike Donlin (see *Right Off the Bat*), who settled in Hollywood after his baseball career was kaput to show up in roles both prominent and microscopic in ballfield yarns; and by the screenplay and direction of baseball buff Edward Sedgwick, who'd previously handled the very brief ballgame scenes in another western, Tom Mix's *Stepping Fast* (1923). Sedgwick would bring a breezy knowledgeability to future baseball sequences in such pictures as *The Cameraman* (1928), *Death on the Diamond* (1934), and most especially *Slide, Kelly, Slide* (1927).

Long unavailable for reappraisal, a worn but watchable print of *Hit and Run* showed up on the home-video market in the mid–1990s. In a 1997 article for the online magazine *Silents Majority*, film historian John DeBartolo quoted a contemporary review of the film, from the August 16, 1924, edition of *Harrison's Reports*: "This is a first-class comedy dealing with the national sport—baseball. So pleasingly entertaining is it and such a wealth of wholesome comedy does it contain that it should find favor with all picture patrons. Edward Sedgwick deserves praise for its direction. Hoot Gibson, impersonating a 'bush leaguer' from the 'tall and uncut,' has never done anything better.... It should well satisfy all classes of picture goers."

Hot Curves

Tiffany; reviewed in June 1930; released July 6, 1930

Directed by Norman Taurog. Screenplay by Earle Snell. Dialogue by Frank Mortimer and Benny Rubin. Photography: Max Dupont. Edited by Clarence Kolster. Music and lyrics by Violinsky and Silverstein. Recording engineer: Buddy Myers. 71 minutes (previewed at 87 minutes); black and white; sound.

Cast: Benny Rubin (Benny Goldberg); Rex Lease (Jim Dolan); Alice Day (Elaine McGrew); Pert Kelton (Cookie); John Ince (Manager McGrew); Mary Carr (Grandma Dolan); Mike Donlin (Scout); Natalie Morehead (Margie); Paul Hurst (Slug).

Jim Dolan, a cocksure young pitcher en route to the Pittsburgh Cougars' training camp, persuades soda jerk Benny Goldberg to convince the Cougar management that Dolan has been signed with another team so that Jim can negotiate a better salary. Benny's antics result in his getting himself signed by Pittsburgh as well. During training, Jim performs badly, until his silver-haired grandma encourages him to stop being so full of himself and to play better. While Benny works himself up into star player status and acquires practical joker Cookie as his girlfriend, Jim juggles his affections between his true love Elaine McGrew (the standard-issue daughter of the Cougars manager) and gold digging Margie. When his extracurricular affairs seriously compromise his playing skills, Jim is suspended, but he's called back to the team at series time. Benny is reported killed in a plane crash, but at the last minute shows up at the deciding game to catch for Jim. Dolan's home run exercises its usual Series-win prerogative.

Hot Curves was produced by Tiffany Studios, a minor-league outfit with major-league aspirations. After its first big talkie hit, *Journey's End* (1930), Tiffany determined that the straightest line to box office success

was to turn out lugubriously sentimental dramas with flashes of comedy relief. This resulted in an oversupply of long, dull exercises in turgidity that had the effect of chasing movie fans over to the theater across the street. (You don't know what "maudlin" is until you've seen Tiffany's *The Medicine Man*, a 1930 masterpiece in which a remarkably unfunny Jack Benny rescues the leading lady from what Leonard Maltin has described as "the most abusive father in screen history.")

Tiffany's *Hot Curves* was so bogged down with the molasses-like progress of Jim Dolan's love life that it was easy to forget that the film was supposed to have something to do with baseball—and easier still to forget that the film was ostensibly a vehicle for Benny Rubin, who, in addition to portraying comic ballplayer Benny Goldberg, also cowrote the script. A vaudeville headliner, Rubin was, according to director Frank Capra, barred from film stardom because he looked "too Jewish," thus making his films difficult to sell in neighborhoods—and countries—where anti–Semitism was the order of the day. Rubin himself later claimed, however, that his descent from top billing was due not to his appearance but to his own nasty temper and his addiction to gambling. Whatever the case, Tiffany's *Hot Curves* and another 1930 release, *Sunny Skies*, were the only talkie features in which Benny Rubin was awarded starring roles; thereafter, his career was confined to comedy bits, most notably (and rewardingly) a rich array of characterizations on Jack Benny's radio and television programs.

If Frank Capra's assessment of Benny Rubin's failure to become a movie star is true, it's ironic that he was hired for *Hot Curves* precisely *because* he looked "too Jewish." Filmgoers and reviewers in 1930 were quick to realize that the film was a spoof of New York Giants manager John McGraw's efforts to obtain a star player of the Jewish faith for his team. The critics noted that

McGraw's 1923 hiring of Moses Solomon, nicknamed the "Rabbi of Swat," and his more recent acquisition of player Abe Cohen, were moves made to attract what *Variety* so delicately described as the "Hebe followers" of baseball.

Hot Curves capitalized not only on this but on a then popular trend of depicting Catholic-Jewish romances on screen á la *Abie's Irish Rose*. Cast as Benny Rubin's aggressively Irish girlfriend Cookie was musical comedy star Pert Kelton—three years before her "official" screen debut in RKO's *Bed of Roses*, and nearly three decades before her Broadway triumph as Mrs. Paroo in Meredith Willson's *The Music Man*.

It Happened in Flatbush

20th Century–Fox; released May 28, 1942

Produced by Walter Morosco. Directed by Ray McCarey. Screenplay by Harold Buchman and Lee Loeb. Photography: Charles Clarke. Edited by J. Watson Webb. Art direction by Richard Day and Lewis Creber. Musical direction by Emil Newman. 80 minutes; black and white; sound.

Cast: Lloyd Nolan (Frank Maguire); Carole Landis (Kathryn Baker); Sara Allgood (Mrs. McAvoy); William Frawley (Sam Sloan); Robert Armstrong (Danny Mitchell); Jane Darwell (Mrs. Maguire); George Holmes (Ray Anderson); Scotty Beckett (Squint); Joseph Allen, Jr. (Walter Rogers); James Burke (Shaughnessy); Roger Imhof (McGuire); Matt McHugh (O'Doul); Leroy Mason (Scott); Pat Flaherty (O'Hara); Dale Van Sickel (Stevenson); John Burger (Harding); Jed Prouty (Judge); Robert E. Homans (Collins); Mary Gordon (Mrs. Collins); Vivian Blaine (Bit).

Frank Maguire, unjustly discredited after bungling an important game, rechannels his career and becomes a ball club manager. Maguire is working for the luckless Brooklyn team when ownership of the club is inherited by beauteous Kathryn Baker. Frank's interest in Kathryn coincides with his determination to bear down on the team and make them sweat their way to a pennant. The disgruntled ballplayers sign a petition to oust Frank on the basis of his relationship with Kathryn, but he ignores the petition and takes the team straight through to a pennant victory—and along the way he gives rookie pitcher Ray Anderson the second chance that Maguire was himself denied years earlier.

The sole raison d'être for 20th Century–Fox's "B Plus" production of *It Happened in Flatbush* was the Brooklyn Dodgers' National League pennant win of 1941, after nearly two decades of "bum" status. The character played by Lloyd Nolan in *Flatbush* had a lot in common with Dodgers president Larry McPhail who, after his installation in 1938, got the team on the right track, modernized the stadium, and cleaned up the Dodgers' image in the eyes of the news media. There was also a bit of Dodgers manager Leo Durocher in Nolan's portrayal, especially the fact that he becomes a winner without worrying about being a nice guy.

The tie-in between the unnamed Brooklyn team in *It Happened in Flatbush* and the real Dodgers was strengthened by the film's generous use of newsreel footage shot at Ebbets Field, notably a true-life vignette involving a fan charging out of the stands and punching out an umpire. This last episode was reenacted for the opening scene of Frank Capra's *Arsenic and Old Lace*—a somewhat incongruous addition to that famous "murder comedy" (as well as an anachronistic one—since *Arsenic* was supposed to be taking place on Halloween, a day that seldom accommodated any pro baseball activity in the 1940s).

With the Dodgers' victory fresh in the minds of moviegoers, and with the reassuring presence of old baseball movie "regulars" like William Frawley and Pat Flaherty in the cast, *It Happened in Flatbush* was a generally satisfying second-echelon effort. It might have been a classic of its kind, had not the screenwriters (or the film editors?) pulled the boner of having Brooklyn win the pennant with only half a game.

It Happens Every Spring

20th Century–Fox; released June 1949

Produced by William Perlberg. Directed by Lloyd Bacon. Screenplay by Valentine Davies. Story by Shirley W. Smith and Valentine Davies, from an unpublished novel by Davies. Photography: Joe MacDonald. Edited by Bruce Pierce. Special photographic effects by Fred Sersen. Art direction by Lyle Wheeler and J. Rossell Spencer. Set decoration by Thomas Little. Music by Leigh Harline, Mack Gordon and Joseph Myrow. Musical direction by Lionel Newman. Title song by Mack Gordon and Joseph Myrow. Costumes by Bonnie Cashin. 87 minutes; black and white; sound.

Cast: Ray Milland (Vernon Simpson, alias King Kelly); Jean Peters (Debbie Greenleaf); Paul Douglas (Monk Lannigan); Ed Begley (Stone); Ted de Corsia (Jimmy Dolan); Ray Collins (Professor Greenleaf); Jessie Royce Landis (Mrs. Greenleaf); Alan Hale, Jr. (Schmidt); Bill Murphy (Isbell); William A. Greene (Professor Forsythe); Edward Keane (Mr. Bell); Gene Evans (Mueller); Al Eben (Parker, Team Doctor); Ruth Lee (Miss Collins); John Butler (Fan); Jane van Duser (Miss Mengalstein); Ray Teal (Mac); Don Hicks (Assistant to St. Louis Announcer); Mickey Simpson (Cop at Gate); Johnny Calkins (Boy); Harry Cheshire (Doctor); Ward Brands, John McKee (Ballplayers); Debra Paget (Alice); Kathleen Hughes (Sarah); Mae Marsh (The Greenleaf Maid); Tom Hanlon (St. Louis Announcer); Sam Hayes (New York Announcer); Robert Adler (Reporter); Harry Seymour (Clerk); George Melford, Douglas Spencer (Conductors); Pat Combs (Messenger Boy); Lee MacGregor (Student); Robert Patten (Cabbie); Charles R. Moore (Workman); Bea Benaderet (Voice of Mabel Lanigan).

Vernon Simpson, chemistry professor at Norworth University and confirmed baseball addict, won't get married to Debbie Greenleaf, the university president's daughter, until he's financially solvent. Vernon hopes that his new formula, an insect repellant for tree bark, will lead to his getting a grant from a major chemical company. Alas, a stray baseball from a kids' sandlot game crashes through the laboratory window, and Simpson's formula ends up a mass of mixed-up reagents in the sink. But when Vernon takes the chemical-covered baseball out of the sink, he discovers that it has been rendered completely impervious to wood! The ball swerves around and hops over chunks of lumber—such as baseball bats—as if by magic. This accidental synthesis gives Simpson a brilliant idea; one that will not only net him the money he needs, but will satiate his love of baseball. Vernon bolts Norworth College on a mysterious "leave of absence," showing up the next day at the offices of the St. Louis ballteam. Knowing that St. Louis is deficient in the pitching department, Simpson cajoles his way into a tryout with the team. Secretly utilizing his "loaded" baseball, he tallies up strikeout after strikeout, earning himself a job as pitcher. Monk Lanigan, the St. Louis catcher, is assigned to keep an eye on Simpson, who is considered a "crackpot" because he refuses to be photographed and insists that he be paid only for the games he wins. Under the alias of "King Kelly," Vernon pitches St. Louis toward the pennant race. Back at Norworth, Debbie Greenleaf is convinced by Vernon's vaguely worded letters and by his gift of a diamond ring that her boyfriend has become a criminal. When she heads for St. Louis, Debbie learns from Monk just what has really been keeping Vernon away from home, and soon all of Norworth is eagerly following the World Series progress of "King Kelly." Unfortunately, Vernon spills all of his wood repellant before the deciding game, and it looks as though he won't be able to pitch a victory for St. Louis. But when the New York batter hits the crucial ball, Vernon desperately catches it with his bare hand—winning the series but sustaining an injury that will bench him permanently. Vernon is relieved that his ruse is over and that he's accumulated the necessary funds, but he's certain that his long absence has cost him both his job and his girl. Upon returning to Norworth, however, Simpson is lauded as a hero—with Debbie leading the cheers—and it develops that Mr. Stone, the owner of the St. Louis team, has provided a large endowment to the college's chemistry department, on the condition that Vernon Simpson be put in full charge of the research lab.

Before we go any farther: yes, the hero of *It Happens Every Spring* is cheating. No, *It Happens Every Spring* does not advocate cheating; it does not suggest that the St. Louis team itself is cheating; nor does it state flat out that the team could not have won *without* cheating. The script very carefully underlines several plot points that take the curse off the loaded-ball gimmick. Vernon Simpson is the only person who knows the secret of his miracle pitch; no one is in the lab with him when he discovers the effectiveness of his formula, and everyone on the ball club is convinced that the little vial full of liquid that Simpson carries with him is hair tonic. While greed and star-crossed romance seem at first glance to be Vernon's motivations, it has been established in the opening scene that Vernon's brief baseball career is funding research that will in the long run be beneficial to forest preservationists. Though he is brashness personified when he first offers his services to the team, Vernon goes through the torments of the damned throughout the rest of the film, wondering aloud in long, comically convoluted sentences whether or not the course of action he has taken is the right one. The film makes clear time and time again that the St. Louis team's "pre-Vernon" weakness is *only* in the pitching department; the club has an excellent infield and a full cotillion of power hitters.

St. Louis wins the decisive pennant game not on the basis of Vernon's pitch but on the strength of Monk Lanigan's tie-breaking home run. The series is won not by a doctored ball but through Vernon's own strength of will. At the end, Vernon is "punished" for his subterfuge by suffering a fractured hand (though the barely stifled smile on his face over the fact that he can finally shed his false identity indicates that this is hardly an earth-shattering tragedy). And since the formula came about by accident, there is little chance at fade-out time that St. Louis will ever again coast to victory on the jet-streams of chemical research—unless somebody on the team discovers steroids in the 1970s.

Enough said. Now that we have the rules and regulations purists off our backs, we can assess *It Happens Every Spring* as one of the most delightful baseball comedies ever made, and one of the few in which baseball itself is almost continually "in play," rather than functioning as an on-again, off-again backdrop for the laughs. The fantasy angle, which could have been cloyingly cute, pays off because it is given a solid framework of recognizable reality; beyond the "magic formula" gimmick, there is nothing in the film that is so far from real life that we'd be inclined to groan, "Aw, c'mon!" And as with a similar bit of ballpark whimsy, *Damn Yankees* (q.v.), the viewer experiences a vicarious enjoyment in seeing a mild "everyman" become a star player for at least one summer in his life.

Ray Milland (loaned to 20th Century–Fox by Paramount Pictures) is the key to the story's believability. He manages to capture the razzle-dazzle dimensions of "King Kelly" without ever completely stepping out of the bookish character of Vernon Simpson; it is a credit to Milland's consummate skill as a performer that he can remain "himself" (Simpson, that is) while putting on two different faces for two different sets of people. Given this circumstance, Paul

Douglas manages the nearly impossible task of stealing the picture away from Milland. His interpretation of Monk Lanigan as a rather dense ballplayer who has the instinctive talent of doing and saying the right thing at the right time is a masterful piece of work.

Even though they're obviously being doubled in a few long shots, the fact that the two male stars behave as though they know their way around a ballfield adds to the fun and the credibility of *It Happens Every Spring*. Ray Milland, an accomplished athlete since his days with the King's Royal Guards in England, was coached for his role in this film by onetime major leaguer Ike Danning. Milland worked so hard at his pitch on the first day of shooting that he suffered a sore arm, and then twisted his knee while sliding into first base; but he

stayed at it, even making an appearance on opening day with the Los Angeles Angels, whose Wrigley Field stadium was used for the film's ballgame sequences. Paul Douglas had also excelled in sports as a youth, and had even played pro football (see *Angels in the Outfield* for more on this). Like Milland, Douglas gave his all to his art in this picture. He twisted his sacroiliac while swinging at a pitched ball, forcing him to sleep on a board for a week; later, while playing catch at home with a neighbor's kid, Douglas injured his index finger—a disability that was worked into the script of *It Happens Every Spring*.

The real "star" of *Spring* was 20th Century–Fox's special effects maven Fred Sersen. A past master at applying matte and process work with an intelligence and showmanship that overcame frequently

Ray Milland (right) warily launches his season-long pitching career in *It Happens Every Spring*, while Paul Douglas looks on.

skintight budgets, Sersen had been with the studio since the early 1930s, tackling cinema problems both sublime (the Great Fire in *In Old Chicago*, the flood in *The Rains Came*) and ridiculous (turning Laurel and Hardy into "living skeletons" for the closing gag of *The Bullfighters*). In *It Happens Every Spring*, Sersen used cartoon animation to create Professor Simpson's fabulous "hop" ball, combining the effect with a rocket-like whizzing sound. Sersen also neatly camouflaged the fact that L.A.'s Wrigley Field was used for all the game scenes by matting in a different skyline around the park for each big-league city, a technique he would deploy with even greater success four years later in Fox's *The Pride of St. Louis* (q.v.). It's not for nothing that the huge man-made body of water on the 20th Century–Fox backlot was called Sersen Lake.

The Fox property crew was also on its toes in *It Happens Every Spring*. To maintain the illusion that the film was taking place during baseball season (it was actually filmed in late winter), the studio technicians coated Wrigley's grass with 500 gallons of green paint. And the prop crew rigged up a compressed-air tube for the famous gag in which Paul Douglas, dousing his scalp with wood repellant under the misapprehension that the stuff is hair tonic, discovers that his hair frizzes and flies whenever he comes near anything made of wood. As with Fred Sersen's hop ball, the trick is heightened by a sound effect, this time a cacophony of crackling static.

Valentine Davies, who was responsible for a similar combination of fantasy and feasibility titled *Miracle on 34th Street*, deftly fashioned a screenplay for *It Happens Every Spring* that works so well on a comic and audience involvement level that we scarcely notice the compromises with reality taken in the plot. Only after the film is over do we realize that none of the ball clubs depicted in the story are given names, but are merely referred to as the St. Louis team,

the Pittsburgh team, the New York team, and so forth; Fox's legal department just didn't have the time to obtain permission from all the major-league teams to use their actual names, so the film went on its merry way without mentioning any real-life club other than a gag reference to the House of David. Valentine Davies' story, written in collaboration with Shirley W. Smith—who, incidentally, was a seventy-four-year-old male—was so adroitly and persuasively constructed that we're even willing to believe that none of the newspaper photographers covering the pennant race would even surreptitiously take a forbidden picture of the reclusive "King Kelly," and that the notoriously thorough Baseball Commission would not bother to start its own investigation of Kelly and his offbeat pitching style.

Valentine Davies and Shirley W. Smith's labors were appreciated not only by the moviegoers but by their fellow screenwriters; *It Happens Every Spring* was nominated at Academy Award time for "best motion picture story." In an amazing turn of events that could only happen in Hollywood, the Oscar ultimately went to Douglas Morrow, the author of *another* baseball picture, *The Stratton Story*.

There are, however, some elements outside the screenplay that tend to lessen the overall effectiveness of *It Happens Every Spring*. It's hard not to notice that, despite the special effects wizardry of Fred Sersen, every ballpark depicted in the film is distinguished by Wrigley's huge left-field light tower; nor can we ignore the shadow that Ray Milland casts over the backdrop representing Norworth University in his first pitching scene. And a routine wherein Paul Douglas has wooden splints on his fingers and is thus incapable of picking up Milland's loaded baseball is rather clumsily handled, especially in comparison to Douglas's earlier "dancing hair" vignette. These shortcomings can be chalked up to the customary haste of director Lloyd Bacon, who was known for being so schedule conscious that he tended to pay more attention to the clock than to detail.

The fact that the ballplayers in *It Happens Every Spring* all seem to be well past retirement age, which on the surface appears to be another example of carelessness, was a deliberate production decision. Surrounding Ray Milland and Paul Douglas with middle-aged teammates and opponents modifies the fact that Milland and Douglas were forty-four and forty-two years old, respectively. The stock newsreel clips used for the World Series scenes were likewise chosen with the leading players' "maturity" in mind; most of these shots were culled from footage of the 1945 Tigers-Cubs Series, a match so depleted of young manpower by the war that it has been described by one witness as "the fat men against the tall men at the office picnic."

Minor carping aside, *It Happens Every Spring* is a film that is virtually impossible to dislike; it can be described without too much fear of contradiction as everyone's favorite baseball comedy until *The Bad News Bears* came along. Additionally, *It Happens Every Spring* owns the distinction of being the first baseball picture to be exhibited coast to coast in prime time on a national TV network. NBC televised the film on April 7, 1962, as one of thirty 20th Century–Fox pictures broadcast during the inaugural season of *Saturday Night at the Movies*; and after the film was over the network offered as a bonus attraction a brief, irreverent history of the Brooklyn Dodgers, narrated by Joe E. Brown.

It's Good to Be Alive: The Story of Roy Campanella

Larry Harmon Pictures/Metromedia; originally telecast February 22, 1974

Executive producers: Charles Fries and Larry Harmon. Produced by Gerald I. Isenberg. Directed by Michael Landon. Teleplay by Steven Gethers, based on the book by Roy Campanella. Photography: Ted Voigtlander. Edited by John A. Martinelli. Music by Michel LeGrand. Art direction by Roger Maus. Associate producer: Richard Marx. Production manager: Joe Wonder. Casting by Eddie Foy, III. 100 minutes; color; sound.

Cast: Paul Winfield (Roy Campanella); Lou Gossett, Jr. (Sam Brockington); Ruby Dee (Ruthie Campanella); Ramon Bieri (Walter O'Malley); Joe DeSantis (Roy's Father); Ty Henderson (David Campanella); Joe E. Tata (Pee Wee Reese)*; Julian Burton (Dr. Rusk); Lloyd Gough (Surgeon); Eric Woods (Young Roy); Ketty Lester (Roy's Mother); Len Lesser (Man at Accident); Stymie Beard (Preacher); Paul Savior (Attendant); Stanley Clay (Boy); Roy Campanella, Roxie Campanella, Joni Campanella, Tony Campanella, Routh Campanella (Themselves); and Nina Roman, Stuart Nisbet, Buck Young, Richard Hurst, Gene Tyburn, Willie McIntyre, Jr., Benny Nickleberry, Byron Nickleberry, and Azalie Nickleberry.

Roy Campanella, a nine-year veteran of the Brooklyn Dodgers, leaves his liquor store on the rainy evening of January 26, 1958, hops in his rented car, and heads toward his home in Long Island. He never makes it home; the car slides off the road and crashes. In the hospital, Roy discovers that his fifth cervical vertebra has been fractured, and that he will be permanently paralyzed. Were it not for the diligence of his physical therapist Sam Brockington, Roy would be willing to simply lie back and die. After months of grueling therapy, Campanella is able to move about a tiny bit, but he must face the fact that he'll need an attendant to take care of him for the rest of his life. The accident takes its toll on Roy's family as well, driving his already estranged wife Ruthie farther away from him and breaking the heart of his son David, who'd been raised on Roy's motto that one should

Evidently because of legal complications, the character of Pee Wee Reese has been eliminated from the home video version.

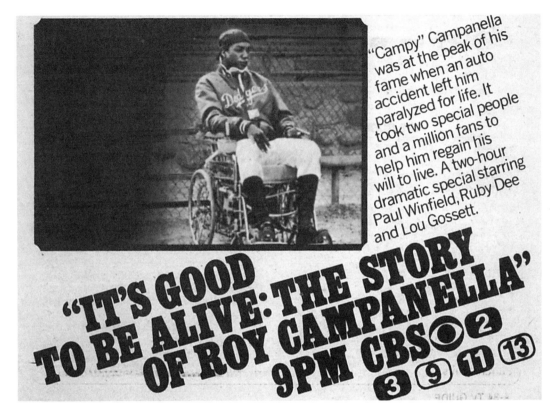

"Campy" Campanella was at the peak of his fame when an auto accident left him paralyzed for life. It took two special people and a million fans to help him regain his will to live. A two-hour dramatic special starring Paul Winfield, Ruby Dee and Lou Gossett.

"IT'S GOOD TO BE ALIVE: THE STORY OF ROY CAMPANELLA" 9PM CBS◉② ③ ⑨ ⑪ ⑬

TV Guide ad for *It's Good to be Alive: The Story of Roy Campanella* (1974).

never give up the fight. It isn't until a harrowing confrontation with David over a theft committed by the boy that Campanella realizes how much he's letting his loved ones down. With a new lease on life, Roy accepts an offer from Dodgers owner Walter O'Malley to coach the team during spring training. Although Campanella is still bound to his wheelchair, and although his marriage finally disintegrates, the exballplayer determines to get on with his life and live it to the fullest; and when he is honored with a standing room only "Roy Campanella Night" at the Los Angeles Coliseum in 1959, Roy is able to say with utmost sincerity that, "It's good to be alive."

Although Roy Campanella's 1959 autobiography *It's Good to Be Alive* chronicled his entire life up to the year of the book's publication, Stephen Gethers's script covers only the year following Roy's 1958 ac-

cident; as a result, we don't see very much baseball, except for a seconds-long flashback here and there and a three-minute sequence set at the Dodgers' Florida training camp. The film version of *Alive* is devoted to Campanella's convalescence (filmed at the VA Hospital in Long Beach, California, with several real-life patients in attendance), his domestic travails, and his long bouts of melancholia and self-pity before he's able to get his act together; in fact, the teleplay probes far deeper into the dark side of Campanella's psyche and his marital problems than the ballplayer's own published memoirs. Its lack of baseball action aside, this "GE Theatre" presentation is one of the better examples of the "Disease of the Week" TV movie genre, boasting excellent performances by Paul Winfield (who is compelled to do most of his acting from the neck up) as Campanella, Lou Gossett,

Jr., as his ceaselessly cheerful physical therapist, and Ruby Dee as Roy's embittered, near-alcoholic second wife. The acting is complemented by the superbly textured, Emmy-nominated camerawork of Ted Voigtlander.

That *It's Good to Be Alive* falls short of perfection is due partly to its smarmy *Love Story*–style musical score by Michel Le-Grand, and partly because director Michael Landon, who does a subtle, sensitive job during the first hour or so of the film, starts heaping on pathos with a trowel in the later scenes. The L.A. Coliseum finale is particularly overbaked, coming across like a B-picture ripoff of the climactic Lou Gehrig speech in *The Pride of the Yankees* (q.v.)—right down to Roy Campanella's voice echoing through the public-address system.

The real Roy Campanella appears in the prologue of the film and is joined by his third wife Roxie and most of his children in the epilogue. By the time *It's Good to Be Alive* first aired over CBS on February 22, 1974, Campanella had proven himself to be an engaging TV personality through his sporadic guest appearances and his own syndicated interview program, *Campy's Corner* (1960); thus, one genuinely regrets the fact that his cameo in *Alive* is so very brief.

The Jackie Robinson Story

Jewel Productions/Eagle-Lion; released May 1950

Produced by Mort Briskin. Associate producer: Joseph H. Nadel. Directed by Alfred E. Green. Screenplay by Lawrence Taylor and Arthur Mann; story by Lawrence Taylor and [uncredited] Louis Pollock. Photography: Ernest Laszlo. Edited by Arthur Nadel. Musical score by Herschel Burke Gilbert. Musical supervision by David Chudnow. Orchestral arrangements by Joseph Mullendore. Production design by Boris Leven. Dialogue director: Ross Hunter. Assistant director: Maurie M. Suess. Set decoration by Jack Mapes. Costumes by Maria Donovan. Makeup by Dave Grayson. Sound recording by Ben Winkler and Mac Dalgleish. Technical supervision by Arthur Mann. 76 minutes; black and white; sound.

Cast: Jackie Robinson (Himself); Ruby Dee (Rae Robinson); Minor Watson (Branch Rickey); Louise Beavers (Mrs. Robinson); Richard Lane (Clay Hopper); Harry Shannon (Charlie); Ben Lessey (Shorty); Billy Wayne (Clyde Sukeforth); Joel Fluellen (Mack Robinson); Bernie Hamilton (Ernie); Kenny Washington (Tigers' Manager); Pat Flaherty (Karpen); Larry McGrath (Umpire); Emmet Smith (Catcher); Howard Louis MacNeeley (Jackie as a Boy); George Dockstader (Bill); Bill Spaulding (Himself); Jimmy Dodd (Man in Spaulding's Office); Bill Baldwin (Announcer); Roy Glenn, Sr. (Gaines); Dewey Robinson (Brooklyn Bigot); Patsy Moran (Bigot's Wife); Dick Wessel (Spike); Ben Welden, Joe Devlin (Spike's Friends).

Jackie Roosevelt Robinson, a black California youth growing up in the 1930s and 1940s, distinguishes himself as a track star at Pasadena Junior College and as the All-Sports record holder at UCLA. When Jackie tries to get a coaching job after graduation, however, most doors are closed to him; career opportunities for African Americans in the "Jim Crow" era are typified by the street-sweeper job held by Jackie's brother Mack, who had likewise excelled in college athletics. Following a stint in the Army, Jackie gets a job in the Negro baseball leagues but, despite his expertise as batter and second baseman, his chances of getting into the white majors seem less than zero. Fortunately, Branch Rickey, general manager of the Brooklyn Dodgers, is eager to break down the color line in major-league baseball (his motives are only partly altruistic; many black and Hispanic players have proven to be league leaders in the minors). Jackie Robinson is chosen in 1946 to play for the Brooklyn farm system on the basis of his youth, his talent, his education, and his solid family values. Most importantly, Rickey selects Robinson because he wants a ballplayer "with guts enough not to fight back" in the face of racial hostility; he wants a man who will take the false "troublemaker" onus off black athletes. Jackie agrees to turn the other cheek for the first two years of his Brooklyn contract. Robinson's first season with the Dodgers' Montreal farm team is sheer hell: Other clubs refuse to play him by shutting down their stadiums on the slimmest of premises; opposing ballplayers go out of their way to inflict injury on Jackie; fans shout racial epithets from the stands; and even Montreal manager Clay Hopper, an old-fashioned Southerner, expresses the opinion that Jackie isn't "human." But thanks to Robinson, Montreal leads its league, and when option time comes around, Clay Hopper is Jackie's biggest booster. Robinson gets his chance to play for the Dodgers in 1947, despite a petition circulating among a handful of his teammates to remove Robinson from the roster. Jackie starts slowly with the Dodgers (he doesn't score a single hit in his first nineteen times at bat), but he and his team improve both on the diamond and in the personal-relations department. Brooklyn wins the pennant race, and the walls barring men of color from the major leagues at long last begin to tumble—though Jackie Robinson is well aware that the struggle is far from finished.

This film has no stars, no budget, no production values. Much of the background music seems to be drawn from stock themes that have been played to death in countless animated cartoons and cheap TV series. The script utilizes every old trick of fighting against all odds in the book. In short, *The Jackie Robinson Story* has no business being as good as it is. The film is an often brutally honest assessment of the inbred prejudices which afflicted (and which still afflict) race relations in America; it is also an immensely entertaining work, and one of the few baseball films of its era to offer a generous supply of enthralling and authentic diamond action.

The film may not have worked as well

had it stuck to its original concept. The first script, written late in 1949, was in flashback form, framed by Jackie Robinson's appearance at the House Un-American Activities Committee. Robinson had been invited by the HUAC to express his opposition to singer Paul Robeson's opinion that blacks would not fight for America in any war against a Communist nation. While Jackie was utterly against Robeson's political beliefs, he would later regret his HUAC appearance, since it had been concocted by certain politicians to "prove" that "good Negroes" were 100 percent American and against any form of social upheaval, including—it was implied—the civil rights movement. Robinson was made aware in retrospect how he had been used, and vowed never to let this happen again. Unfortunately, the first script of his life story was also "using" Robinson to slap the face of Paul Robeson rather than simply outlining Jackie's own battle against racism. It was typical knee-jerk anti-communist material, and thankfully was jettisoned before shooting started. The final version of *The Jackie Robinson Story* still ended with Jackie's carefully worded pro–America speech at the HUAC, but the subliminal reason he'd been called to the committee in the first place is left unexplored. (Ironic in this context is the fact that one of the scenarists of *The Jackie Robinson Story*, Louis Pollock, would later be blacklisted in Hollywood merely because he had the same name—actually, *almost* the same name—as a businessman who had refused to testify before the HUAC!)

A much modified screenplay, with less verbosity and a whole lot less condescension (in the original, for example, Jackie's mother was supposed to be confused by his use of three-syllable "college words"), was made ready for potential producers. Most major studios, worried that a film about a black man's fight against prejudice would die a dog's death in certain regions of

America, weren't interested; this was, after all, a period in which a big-time producer once rejected a script because, as he put it, "We don't want to offend the bigots." The two big studios that were attracted to *The Jackie Robinson Story* wanted to have the story doctored so it would appear that Jackie learned his baseball prowess exclusively from a white coach. In these instances, the promoters of the *Robinson Story* screenplay turned down the majors.

Finally, Eagle-Lion, a small studio that had previously been the even smaller Producers' Releasing Corporation, agreed to release *The Jackie Robinson Story*. Now it was the real-life Branch Rickey who began imposing conditions. Rickey would only permit Jackie Robinson to play himself if his film work didn't interfere with spring training. The Brooklyn manager also insisted that more of the hardships and opposition that had plagued Robinson both before and during his Dodgers career be included in the script. It was additionally agreed that five percent of the film's profits would be donated to the National League players' fund. (Jackie himself would receive 15 percent of the profits, as well as a salary of $30,000—only $5000 less than his annual income as a ballplayer.)

Robinson later claimed that during the film's no-slack shooting schedule, "I never had any spring training in which I worked any harder." There are scenes aplenty of Jackie running around and stealing bases, as well as numerous displays of Jackie's talents as a first and second baseman; he makes catches that range from "all in a day's work" to the spectacular. Since the movie avoids Hollywood's standard obsession with tie-breaking home runs in favor of parading Robinson's other ballfield accomplishments, one can overlook the fact that Robinson was compelled to alter his familiar batting stance in order to accommodate the camera's limited field of vision.

Denied the niceties of a second unit, stunt doubles, or process work, director Alfred E. Green exerted himself just as much as his star by seeking out fresh new camera angles that put the spectator in the thick of the game. Working in collaboration with cinematographer Ernest Laszlo, Green heightened the film's excitement and spontaneity with his newsreel-like rapid panning from one player to another.

The acting likewise transcends the miniscule budget of *The Jackie Robinson Story*. Contrary to the *New York Times* reviewer's statement that Robinson did a "minimum of acting," Jackie is quite adept at playing himself on screen. The stiffness and stoicism he exhibits in some scenes actually enhance his portrayal of a man forced to mask his inner turmoil and his instinct to strike out at injustice. It's also a pleasure to hear a genuine sports celebrity deliver lines with Robinson's conviction and articulation. The effectiveness of Jackie's film work is all the more obvious when one compares his performance to that of former UCLA sports director Bill Spaulding, also cast as himself in *The Jackie Robinson Story*, who performs with all the realism of a Disney World audio-animatronics exhibit.

While it goes without saying that most of the other cast members are far more experienced than Robinson, they go out of their way to use their gifts to make the star look better, rather than drawing the spotlight away from him. Jackie enjoys a marvelous on-screen rapport with Ruby Dee, who plays his wife Rae; in fact, they got along so famously that when Jackie brought his family to Hollywood, Dee watched over and played with the Robinsons' infant daughter Sharon between scenes (the actress was herself three months pregnant at the time). In Dee's 1999 autobiography *With Ossie and Ruby* (jointly written with her husband Ossie Davis), she recalled that the only problem she ever had with Robinson arose from a scripted bit of business in which she was supposed to massage Jackie's neck. At the touch of her hands, Robinson suddenly bristled, which Dee at first interpreted as being an implicit "Keep away!" warning from her somewhat reclusive costar. As it turned out, Jackie was upset merely because Ruby's hands were ice-cold, a problem that was quickly remedied without further incident.

Equally generous in providing give and take with Robinson are Joel Fluellen who, as Jackie's brother Mack, brilliantly combines the bitterness of a man trapped in a job beneath his talents with the pride of being able to support himself; and Louise Beavers, whose role as Jackie's mother must have been infinitely more rewarding than the maids and housekeepers she was usually obliged to portray. Interviewed by movie historian Jim Neibaur in 1978, actor Richard Lane (cast as Clay Hopper in the film) recalled that Louise Beavers was largely responsible for helping Robinson overcome his self-consciousness before the cameras. "Louise really took Jackie under her wing," noted Lane. "He was marvelous on the ball field, but he wasn't used to a movie set. It is pretty hard for a newcomer to deal with all those lights and cameras staring him in the face, and then to remember his lines and say them with conviction and all that. Louise was a real schoolteacher, though, and she helped Jackie along. They studied his lines together, and went over their scenes until Jackie got it right. He's still a little stiff, but believe me he would have been much worse without Louise's help."

That shameless old barnstormer Minor Watson could easily have pilfered the entire picture away from Robinson with his foxy grandpa portrayal of Branch Rickey. But even with all the surreptitious chuckling, knowing glances, expansive gestures, and the rest of the tricks of the trade at his command, Watson acts *with* Jackie rather than at him in their scenes together—particularly the key sequence in which Rickey out-

lines just what sort of humiliation Jackie will have to undergo while turning the other cheek—and is kind enough to make Robinson a full participant in those scenes rather than a sidelines observer to Watson's dispensation of ham. Less colorful but even more effective within the framework of the film is Richard Lane, normally a specialist in fast-talking wiseguy roles, cast against type in *The Jackie Robinson Story* as the laconic, slow-moving Clay Hopper. We're conditioned to like Branch Rickey because he's on Jackie's side all the way; Clay Hopper is a more difficult role because he is a man whose prejudices against blacks have been drummed into him since childhood, and the actor playing him must convince us that he has radically altered a lifelong attitude during his single season with Robinson without resorting to an overly obvious "seeing the light" approach. Richard Lane manages to pull this off, and in so doing makes Clay Hopper an encapsulation of all those white ballplayers, managers and fans who were willing to confront the pointlessness of their race hatred and to accept Jackie Robinson and the black players who followed him on the basis of talent rather than a compatability in skin color.

The only false note struck by the acting occurs in a scene wherein four small-town bigots try to scare Jackie out of town during a road game. The problem is one of audience preconditioning; the four actors cast as these rednecks—Dewey Robinson, Dick Wessel, Joe Devlin and Ben Welden—had by 1950 so often appeared as comic hoodlums that it was hard for the viewer to believe that they posed a genuine threat to Jackie. This is particularly true in the case of Ben Welden, who has become so familiar to modern audiences for his frequent funny-crook appearances on the *Superman* TV series that one half expects Jackie Robinson to respond to Welden's threats by running into a phone booth and changing into a cape and tights.

This poster for *The Jackie Robinson Story* (1950) emphasizes action and star appeal while deftly avoiding mention of the racial issues which motivate much of the storyline.

The weakness inherent in this sort of low-budget casting points out the fact that, despite its overall excellence, *The Jackie Robinson Story* is still a "B" picture, and as such tends to rely on the traditional economies and film grammar of Hollywood's cheaper product. The inexpensive locations chosen for the ballpark scenes, notably Anaheim's La Palma Park, never completely convince us that Jackie and his teammates are playing in big-league stadiums. Passages of time are conveyed via such tired old devices as newspaper headlines and pages falling from a calendar. The script props up its duller stretches with a wholly unnecessary "comic relief" character, a too-short rookie player portrayed by Ben Lessey. The tenseness of the confrontation with the quartet of bigots is mitigated by the strains of "My Country 'Tis of Thee" on the soundtrack; and as Jackie makes his HUAC speech, an image of the Statue of Liberty is superimposed.

Yet somehow, the seediness and overfamiliarity of these trappings work in favor of the film. It's true that the locations are unimpressive, but the cast and crew put as much effort and enthusiasm in the outdoor scenes as they would in a big-bucks, major-studio production, and this willingness to "work with what we've got" is oddly endearing. And while it's also true that the "passage of time" montage representing Jackie's first year with Montreal is unimaginative in terms of execution, the disturbing images within this montage—such as Jackie being racially harassed by an opposing team member who derisively slobbers over a watermelon—create so jarring a contrast between the banality of technique and the realism of content that the viewer is inexorably drawn into the story and the issues it raises.

This sort of audience involvement even saves the aforementioned gratuitous comedy relief, sledgehammer musical cues, and flag-waving imagery from being embarrassing or excruciating. One is willing to forgive a little bit of heavy handedness if the film as a whole makes its points with honesty and sincerity; and never for a minute is there any doubt that the filmmakers are honest and sincere, not merely a bunch of cynical Hollywood hacks slapping together a quickie to exploit its subject's rise to fame. And this statement is made even with full acknowledgment that *The Jackie Robinson Story* glosses over Robinson's childhood street-gang experience, Branch Rickey's notorious tightness with a dollar, and the resentment of the Negro League's Kansas City Monarchs over not getting a financial settlement when Jackie defected to the Dodgers. (The Monarchs aren't mentioned in the film; Jackie's first pro baseball stint is with a fictional team, the Black Panthers!)

Shortly before his death in 1972, Jackie Robinson would note that it was "exciting to participate" in the making of his life story, but that, "later I realized it had been made too quickly, that it was budgeted too low, and that, if it had been made much later in my career, it could have been done much better." He may have been right. A later, more thorough film could have delineated Robinson's stand against racism while in the Armed Services (which served as the basis for a 1990 cable TV movie, *The Court-Martial of Jackie Robinson*, starring Andre Braugher); it might have explored his personality clashes with Branch Rickey's successor, Walter O'Malley; it would likely have detailed Robinson's participation in the Republican Party, capped by his disillusionment with the Nixon-Agnew regime; and it definitely would have given space to the tragedy of Jackie Robinson, Jr., who died in a 1971 car accident just after he successfully kicked a debilitating drug habit. But even with its limited scope and parsimonious budget, *The Jackie Robinson Story* is a film well worth having, and—considering that a whole generation has grown up to whom the name "Jackie Robinson" has very little significance (as evidenced by a sobering poll conducted by *Sport* magazine in 1989)—it might be wise for all of us to take a second look at the fundamentally honest biopic of a man who almost single-handedly obliterated the color barrier in major league baseball.

Joe Torre: Curveballs Along the Way

British-American Entertainment/Norman Twain Productions/Showtime Networks; first telecast October 17, 1997

Executive producers: Bernard F. Conners, Thomas F. Leahy, Steven Hewitt. Produced by Norman Twain. Directed by Sturla Gunnarsson. Written by Philip Rosenberg. Photography: Mark Irwin. Edited by Ronald Sanders. Original music: John Welsman. Production designer: Ed Hanna. Art director: Ann Bromley. Set decorator: Peter Razmofsky. Costumer Designer: Suzette Daigle. Casting: Pat McCorkle. Makeup: Kathleen Graham. Hair stylist: Moira Verwijk. Production manager: Tina Grewal. First assistant director: Wendy Ord. Second assistant director: Filomena Guarasci. Script supervisor: Oliver Olsen. Baseball consultant: Billy Sample. Stunt Coordinator: Matt Birman. Storyboard artist: Keith Hamilton. Sound mixer: Henry Embry. Second unit director (New York): Peter Pastorelli. Foley mixer: Steve Copley. Foley artist: John Sievert. Color. 95 minutes; sound.

Cast: Paul Sorvino (Joe Torre); Robert Loggia (Frank Torre); Barbara Williams (Ali Torre); Isaiah Washington (Dwight Gooden); Gailard Sartain (Don Zimmer); Barry Flatman (Mel Stottlemyre); Marilyn Chris (Rae Torre); Eugene A. Clark (Bob Watson); Dean McDermott (David Cone); Diego Fuentes (Mariano Duncan); Aidan Devine (Wade Boggs); Kenneth Welsh (George Steinbrenner); Rummy Bishop (Rocco Torre); Victoria Mitchell (Sister Marguerite Torre); Howard Dell (Darryl Strawberry); Andrew Jackson (Paul O'Neill); Anthony Romano (Young Joe); Trent McMullen (Young Frank); William S. Taylor (Reggie Jackson); Diane Fabian (Buxom Neighbor); Jimmy Leone, A. Frank Ruffo, Tony Perri (Neighbors); Roz Michaels (Woman at Party); Michael Rhoades, Frank Pellegrino,

Demo Cates, Kathryn Winslow (Reporters); Sandra O'Neill (Soot Zimmer); Michael Filipowich, Rich Leitch (Ball Players); Ray Negron (Trainer); James Kidnie (Al Post); Matt Birman (Seattle Catcher); Julia Paton (New Jersey Nurse); Michael Fletcher (Ted Turner/Opposing Catcher); Walter Alza (Hector the Orderly); Vivian Reis (Rose Torre); Arlene Meadows (Anne Torre); Darlene Mignacco (Joey's Mom); Dick Callahan (Ticket Guy); Marvin Ishmael (Doctor); William Corno (Michael Torre); Christine Donato (Tina Torre); Vito Marchese (Kid Ballplayer); Matthew Morris (Program Vendor); Robert Collins (Frank Cashen); Wayne Robert McNamara (Young Tycoon).

The amazing story of the New York Yankees' "resurrection" as World Series champs during the 1996 season is shown through the eyes of team manager Joe Torre. The Brooklyn-born younger brother of legendary Milwaukee Braves star Frank Torre, and no mean ballplayer in his own right, Joe has just come off a debilitating personal and professional slump—two failed marriages, three quick-succession firings from the Mets, Braves and Cardinals—when, in 1995, he is hired by George Steinbrenner to captain the Yanks. A firm believer in hunches and second chances, Joe goes out on a limb by retaining such mercurial players as Dwight Gooden, David Cone and Darryl Strawberry. But all his gambles pay off, and after a shaky start (21 losses!) the Yankees are virtually guaranteed the Pennant, if not the Series itself—which, in addition to restoring the team to its former glories, will be a career first for Torre. Off the field, Joe's personal life is likewise scaling the heights with a happy third marriage and a new baby. Suddenly, however, the dark clouds gather over Joe's success, beginning with the death of his brother Rocco and the rapidly deteriorating health of his other sibling Frank. The home-stretch of the Yanks' series race coincides with Joe's desperate efforts to find a donor for Frank's heart transplant. Happily, by season's end, both the Torre family and the New York

Yankees emerge triumphant from their individual ordeals.

Not since 1962's *Safe at Home* has a "topical" baseball film been assembled with such haste as the made-for–TV *Joe Torre: Curveballs All the Way*; filmed in mid–1997, it debuted on October 17, a little less than a year after the Yankees' phoenixlike World Series comeback. And not since 1950's *The Jackie Robinson Story* has a low-budget baseball biopic been quite so good.

Like the previous season's cable–TV effort *Soul of the Game* (q.v.), *Joe Torre* crystallizes the life and work of its protagonist within the boundaries of a single baseball season. Except for the opening sepia-toned sequence in which the 17-year-old Joe Torre luxuriates in the triumph of his brother Frank's Milwaukee Braves in the 1957 Series—a scene necessary to establish the Torre brothers' devotion to one another and Joe's lifelong idolatry of his older sibling—and a shorthand montage of Joe's three pre–Yankee dismissals, everything in the film takes place within the period between Torres' hiring as Yanks manager in the fall of 1995 and the decisive Series game in the last week of October 1996.

The film can be regarded as the flip side of 1994's *Cobb*; whereas the earlier film wore its audience down by painting a relentlessly negative and unsympathetic portrayal of a thoroughly reprehensible man, *Joe Torre*'s overwhelmingly positive and sympathetic spin on its real-life characters and events might strike the more jaded viewer as being far too good to be true—except, astonishingly, most of it *is* true. In a *TV Guide* interview, the film's star, Paul Sorvino, insisted, "It's improbable fiction. The fact that it's true is the only reason you can make the movie."

By limiting the scope of the film, screenwriter Philip Rosenberg was justified in skimming through Joe Torre's earlier professional setbacks and checkered marital record—though perhaps to deflect potential criticism of this apparent glossover, Rosenberg inserted a near–Brechtian scene in which Torre speaks directly and candidly to the camera about his past failures and emphasizes the importance of making a success of both his third marriage and his new position with the Yankees. There was very little whitewashing required; married to Ali Torre since 1987, Joe had indeed finally found the domestic tranquility that had previously eluded him, and had also managed to strike a happy medium between his personal and professional life, devoting ample "quality time" to both.

Admittedly, there are times when the film's dialogue comes perilously close to merely parroting press releases and TV sound bites rather than reflecting the genuine give-and-take between Torre and his associates. Fortunately, this problem is addressed by scenarist Rosenberg in the same "two faces of mankind" manner that David Himmelstein used in his teleplay for *Soul of the Game*. Rosenberg expertly contrasts the "public" Torre with the man inside. The Joe Torre that everyone sees keeps his emotions in check, exercises diplomacy in all things, treats his players like human beings rather than high-priced cattle, blows his top only when absolutely necessary, and, above all, manages to keep his head in place while all those around him are losing theirs. The private Joe Torre, torn up over the serious health problems of his brother Frank and the strong likelihood that he won't be able to pull the Yankees out of the mire, lets his guard down and allows his actual emotions to flow freely. In these off-the-record moments, Joe's dialogue has the unquestionable ring of accuracy, amply compensating for the occasional stiltedness of the "Joe on the Job" scenes. Rosenberg's technique carries over to practically every other character in the film as well, most amusingly in the scene wherein George Steinbrenner, after expansively assuring Torre via telephone that the Yanks' poor start was an aberration and that he has complete confidence in his new manager's abilities, puts down the receiver and, without skipping a beat, angrily expresses his *real* feelings to the unfortunate subordinate standing beside him.

The robust, aggressive, sometimes smothering warmth and camaraderie exuded in the domestic scenes with Joe and his extended Italian-American family may strike some viewers as being a bit thick with *Godfather*-like zeitgeist (minus the *Godfather* menace, of course), but there is no reason to doubt that these scenes are drawn from life. These are, after all, born-and-bred Brooklynites, and everyone knows that Baseball is God in Brooklyn, so it only makes sense that Joe's family would bombard him with unsolicited advice regarding his handling of the Yankees—and, being a loyal Italian family man, Joe would indulgently listen to that advice, whether he intended to heed it or not. Because the film had too many things to cover in too little time, however, one real-life aspect of Joe's relationship with his family is left unexplored: the fact that all Torres, brothers Frank and Rocco especially, were unreconstructed Brooklyn Dodgers fans, and as such had been conditioned from infancy to despise the Yankees—until Joe's ascendancy to manager of that team forced them to change their lifelong tune.

The scenes between Torre and his ballplayers perfectly illustrate actor Paul Sorvino's assertion that the film made "improbable fiction." Under any other circumstances, would the viewer be able to accept without question the image of a tough, streetwise manager who speaks soothingly and noncondescendingly to his players, diligently avoids personal attacks on their intelligence, age or lack of hustle, steadfastly forsakes any finger-pointing or blame-spreading (even when such things are warranted), runs interference between indiscreet players and muckraking reporters by attacking the reporters and forgiving the players, and calmly assures his dispirited team

that "We will win this thing" when all evidence points to the contrary? And unless the facts were at hand, would it not seem the height of phony Hollywood sentimentality when Joe consoles a weeping Dwight Gooden over the terminal illness of Gooden's father, or solicitously informs Daryl Strawberry that his past problems with drugs are inconsequential so long as Daryl keeps his nose clean (literally) for the remainder of the season? Yet the record speaks for itself: To a man, the members of the 1996 New York Yankees swore *by* Torre rather than *at* him, all through the season. The image of Joe Torre as combination mentor, psychologist, surrogate parent and father confessor may to the uninitiated seem like a scriptwriter's lazy contrivance— but even the most virulent of Yankee haters will have to admit that Torre is one of the best-liked managers in the Major Leagues.

Since there was no real suspense in the film (even inhabitants of other galaxies are likely to know the outcome), and allowing for the fact that not everyone in the viewing audience was enamored of the Yankees—definitely not the followers of the Baltimore Orioles, who, after the infamous "fan in the stands" catch during the Pennant race, were not altogether unjustified in claiming "We wuz robbed"—the filmmakers made certain that the audience's interest was kept piqued, and its sympathies remained in the right place, by using Frank Torre's life-threatening illness as a dramatic thrust. Again, the Pearl White–style race to the rescue as Joe desperately seeks out a suitable heart donor for his rapidly fading brother while simultaneously embroiled in a Series race would probably never have passed the Smell Test in a fictional story—but it is an irrefutable fact that Frank Torre's heart-transplant surgery occurred on the very day before the Yankee's 3–2 series victory over Atlanta. Echoing Paul Sorvino, the real Frank Torre chuckled to reporters that, "If you had

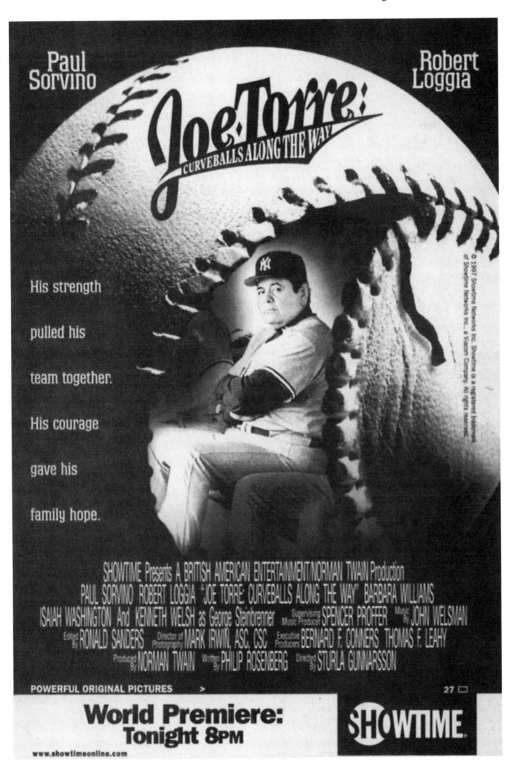

Near-surrealistic magazine ad for *Joe Torre: Curveballs Along the Way* (1997), spotlighting Paul Sorvino as Torre.

taken the book or movie to some producer they'd have thrown you out. They would have said it was too much of a fantasy."

Joe Torre: Curveballs Along the Way was directed by Sturla Gunnarson, a native of Iceland who was raised in Vancouver and began his career as a documentary film-maker in Toronto, eventually earning an Emmy Award for his 1997 television documentary *Gerrie and Louise*. Perhaps because of his grounding in "reality" films, Gunnarson seems more comfortable recreating actual events than handling the speculative scenes involving Joe Torre's private life. The fact that the film was made for television enabled Gunnarson and his editing staff to employ an ingenious, and relatively original, method of combining restaged scenes with TV footage of the actual baseball games. Though most of *Joe Torre* was shot on film, the game sequences were lensed on videotape, then seamlessly combined with clips from the genuine article. Thus, when we see a distance shot of the real Dwight Gooden making a crucial strikeout, Gunnarson quickly cuts to a perfectly matched close-up of the actor playing Gooden (Isaiah Washington), then cuts back to the actual footage. The deception does not, of course, go unnoticed, but the end result is a lot smoother and more satisfying than the clumsy insertion of grainy stock shots in such previous baseball films as *The Kid from Cleveland* and *The Babe Ruth Story* (see individual entries for both).

Characteristically, Paul Sorvino so immerses himself in the role of Joe Torre that at times it is impossible to separate character from actor. Likewise, Kenneth Welsh, Gailard Sartain, Barry Flatman, Dean McDermott, and the aforementioned Isaiah Washington (previously cast as Willie Mays in *Soul of the Game*) offer well-rounded impersonations of George Steinbrenner, Mel Stotlemyre, Don Zimmer, David Cone and Dwight Gooden. If Robert Loggia's portrayal of Frank Torre does not quite come

up to the actor's usual high standards, it may be because Loggia has played this sort of role once too often.

Although most reviewers and TV fans were pleased with *Joe Torre: Curveballs Along the Way*, the film ran into a great deal of critical resistance in the one town where it should have been welcomed with open arms: New York City. Eric Mink of the *New York Times* carped that, "It could not have been easy to turn the remarkable elements of this true story into such a flat and ordinary movie. The team behind *Joe Torre: Curveballs Along the Way* ... managed to do it." Mink also attacked one of the most successful devices in the film, the meshing of actual ballgame tapes with dramatic re-enactments, as "awkward" and "poorly timed," complaining that the mixture of real and fictional served only to underline the fact that the actors playing the Yankees were "infinitely better at delivering a convincing line reading than at throwing a baseball in a way that resembles pitching."

With all due respect, the critical drubbing received by the film in the Big Apple may have been a byproduct of sour grapes. According to Jim Slotek of the *Toronto Sun*, New York mayor Rudy Giuliani had expressed the hope that Hollywood producers would step up film production in the Five Boroughs once the area was made "safer" for such creative pursuits. But the exorbitant cost of technical talent in New York, coupled with the usual union and logistics problems, prompted producers Bernard F. Connors, Steven Hewitt, Thomas F. Leahy and Norman Twain to film most of *Joe Torre: Curveballs Along the Way* in Toronto, with that city's Skydome doubling as Yankee Stadium. This resulted in widespread protests throughout New York, mostly stirred up by the city's politically-connected film technician's unions—who, in Slotek's words, "went postal" over this and other recent cinematic examples of Canadian locations substituting for Manhattan and vicinity (remember the vast mountain ranges looming over the urban skyline in Jackie Chan's *Rumble in the Bronx*?). The Joe Torre biopic, concluded Slotek, was the last straw, worthy of a "suggested tagline" for all future films of this nature: "There are three million Torontonians pretending to be New Yorkers in the Naked City."

The Kid from Cleveland
Republic; released September 3, 1949

Produced by Walter Colmes. Directed by Herbert Kline. Screenplay by John Bright; story by Herbert Kline and John Bright. Photography: Jack Marta. Edited by Jason M. Bernie. Special effects by Consolidated Film Labs. Music by Nathan Scott. Makeup by Bob Mark and Louis Hipple. 89 minutes; black and white; sound.

Cast: George Brent (Mike Jackson); Lynn Bari (Katherine Jackson); Rusty Tamblyn (Johnny Barrows); Tommy Cook (Dan Hudson); Louis-Jean Heydt (Carl Novak); Ann Doran (Emily Novak); K. Elmo Lowe (Dave Joyce); John Berardino (Mac); Bill Veeck, Lou Boudreau, Tris Speaker, Hank Greenberg (Themselves); Bob Feller, Gene Bearden, Satchel Paige, Bob Lemon, Steve Gromek, Joe Gordon, Mickey Vernon, Ken Kettner, Ray Boone, Dale Mitchell, Larry Doby, Bob Kennedy, Jim Hegan (the 1949 Cleveland Indians); Franklin Lewis, Gordon Cobbledock, Ed MacAuley (Themselves, sports announcers); Bill Summers, Bill Grieve (Themselves, umpires); Lefty Weisman (Himself, team trainer).

Desperately unhappy since his widowed mother's remarriage, young Johnny Barrows runs away from home, seemingly the first step toward a career of juvenile delinquency. Johnny is befriended by sportscaster Mike Jackson, who tries to straighten out the kid by getting him a position as batboy for the world-champion Cleveland Indians. The regeneration of Johnny is paralleled with the progress of the Indians from a bad start at the beginning of the 1949 season to a brief but joyous return to their old form. At the end, Johnny is set on the straight and narrow with the help of Jackson and the team, and is reconciled with his mother and stepfather. As for the Indians, the film subtly intimates that the team is headed for their second consecutive World Series win; one can only hope that Johnny's new lease on life had more permanence than Cleveland's all-too-temporary midseason rally.

Filmed almost entirely on location in the titular Ohio metropolis, *The Kid from Cleveland* coasted into theaters on the coattails of the Indians' 1948 World Series win, but coasted out just as quickly when word got around that it was nine reels' worth of sentimental drivel and fatuous psychobabble, and that virtually the only baseball action in the film consisted of newsreel clips. The Cleveland Indians spent less on-screen time tossing the ball around than they did trying to rehabilitate Johnny Barrows, leading more than one critic to suggest that this was the reason that the team's post-series record was so pathetic. Fourteen-year-old Rusty Tamblyn, "introduced" in this film (though he'd been playing small movie parts since 1947), was described by *New York Times* critic Bosley Crowther as "attractive but unimpressive"; but Tamblyn managed to survive in pictures into young adulthood, turning in some attractive *and* impressive work in such musical films as *Seven Brides for Seven Brothers*, *tom thumb* and *West Side Story*. Another acting career launched by *The Kid from Cleveland* was that of real-life Indians player John Berardino, whose matinee-idol looks were so pronounced that team general manager Bill Veeck, ever pursuing an angle that would draw more publicity to his club, announced that he'd had Berardino's handsome features insured. Perhaps because he hadn't played in the 1948 Series, Berardino was the only Indian to appear on-screen as a character other than himself (and a surprisingly unsympathetic character at that!).

The critics singled out Bill Veeck as giving the best performance in the picture.

From the left: Rusty Tamblyn and Satchel Paige contemplate horsehides, while Bob Feller and Steve Gromek are evidently posing for a grecian urn in this shot from *The Kid from Cleveland*.

Though a recent viewing of the film does not entirely bear this out, the critical praise back in 1949 was not surprising, in that Veeck was universally regarded as a natural-born showman; he'd also previously gleaned some "legit" acting experience by playing Sheridan Whiteside in a professional production of *The Man Who Came to Dinner*. The play's requirement that Whiteside spend most of his time in a wheelchair amply compensated for the fact that Veeck had lost part of a leg in the war. Veeck might easily have been repeating one of his lines as the curmudgeonly Sheridan Whiteside when making his own assessment of *The Kid from Cleveland*: "I have one unwritten law at home that I adhere to: I never allow my kids to mention or see that abortion."

To a man, the rest of the Cleveland In-dians shared Bill Veeck's sentiments. Some, like Bob Feller, couched their opinions in softened tones: Referring to the movie's ad-campaign designation of the team as "Thirty Godfathers," Feller commented, "Those 'Thirty Godfathers' must have been the only people who ever saw it. At least that's what we hope." Others, like Lou Boudreau, kept their critiques of the film short and pointed: "I would like to buy every print of it and burn it."

Unfortunately for Boudreau, *The Kid from Cleveland*, for many years mercifully absent from television circulation, "enjoyed" a renaissance in the 1990s thanks to such cable–TV services as American Movie Classics. (Note to cable programmers: Please look up the definition of the word "classic.").

The Kid from Left Field

20th Century–Fox; released September 1953

Produced by Leonard Goldstein. Directed by Harmon Jones. Screenplay by Jack Sher. Photography: Harry Jackson. Edited by William Reynolds. Music by Lionel Newman. Art direction by Lyle Wheeler and Addison Behr. 80 minutes; black and white; sound.

Cast: Dan Dailey (Larry "Pop" Cooper); Anne Bancroft (Marian Foley); Billy Chapin (Christy Mathewson Cooper); Lloyd Bridges (Pete Haines); Ray Collins (Whacker); Richard Egan (Billy Lorant); Bob Hopkins (Bobo Noonan); Alex Gerry (J. R. Johnson); Walter Sande (Barnes); Fess Parker (Lefty MacDougal); George Phelps (Tony): John Gallaudet (Hyams); Paul Salata (Larson); John Berardino (Hank Dreiser); Gene Thompson (Jim Casey); Malcolm Cassell (Jimmy); Ike Jones (John Grout); Ron Hargrave (Craig); John Goddard (Riordan); John McKee (Hunchy Harrison); Claude Olin Wurman (Bermudez); Sammy Ogg (Herman); Robert Winans (Skeets); Jonathan Hole (Truant Officer); John Call (Ticket Taker); Al Green (Spectator); George Gomes, Rush Williams (Yankees); Leo Cleary (Yankees Manager); John "Beans" Reardon (Umpire); James Griffith (Proprietor); King Donovan (Bartender); Kathryn Givney (Judge); James F. Stone (Mac); Richard Shackleton (Newsboy); Larry Thor, Robert Kelly, Mark Scott (Announcers); Ruth Warren (Welfare Worker); Camillo Guerero (Principal); Ken Christy, Charles Tannen, Anthony DeMario (Fans).

Former big-league ballplayer Larry Cooper has been reduced to selling peanuts in the ballpark of the Bisons, a cellar-dweller team managed by the nasty and neurotic Billy Lorant. Cooper's son Christy (named for Christy Mathewson) tries to help his father's financial situation by getting a job as a Bison batboy. Larry is pretty hep as to why the team is losing, and he gives Christy pointers on how the Bisons can pull themselves out of their slump. Christy casually passes this advice on to third baseman Pete Haines, who is so impressed by the kid's apparent baseball savvy

that he shares Christy's second-hand "coaching" with his teammates. The Bisons start winning, and Pete tells his girlfriend, Marion Foley, that it's all because of Christy—information that Marion conveys to her boss, team owner Whacker. A Bill Veeck type who never passes up an opportunity for splashy publicity, Whacker concurs when his team insists that little Christy be made manager, replacing the infuriated Billy Lorant. As the team continues its winning streak, Christy wants to tell them that it's really his father who is the baseball expert; but the elder Cooper, who considers himself a worthless has-been, insists that Christy not reveal the truth. Christy takes his managing chores very seriously, and it looks as though his position is secured until a truant officer scoops him up and takes him back to school. During a brief illness, Christy reveals it was his father who was responsible for the tips that turned the Bisons into champs, the upshot of this revelation being that Larry Cooper is made the new manager of the Bisons.

Twentieth Century–Fox was well known for its habit of recycling successful film formulas until the audience cried "uncle"; as proof of this, one need only look at the studio's endless parade of musicals and comedies about three girls on the prowl for millionaire husbands. With *The Kid from Left Field*, Fox revived its winning actor-director combination of Dan Dailey and Harmon Jones from the studio's 1952 success, *The Pride of St. Louis* (q.v.), and threw in some of the whimsical ambience of Fox's 1949 ballpark comedy *It Happens Every Spring* (q.v.) for good measure.

Curiously, however, though *The Kid from Left Field* was advertised, reviewed and generally accepted as a comedy, it yielded precious few laughs. As *Sport* magazine noted in a 1989 article on baseball movies, the picture has the brooding quality of a film noir, with the baseball stadium itself (L.A.'s Wrigley Field again) looming over

A location shot at Wrigley Field, Los Angeles, from *The Kid from Left Field* (1953): Ex–big leaguer Pop Cooper (Dan Dailey, left) is given what-for by his concessionaire boss (Alex Gerry) while Pop's son Christy (Billy Chapin) looks on.

the action like some sort of shadowy, all-encompassing prison. The normally ebullient Dan Dailey's portrayal of Pop Cooper is a study in chronic self-loathing, while Richard Egan's characterization of the arrogant and vindictive Billy Lorant makes one worry that little Christy Cooper will be strangled in his sleep before the fade-out. Perhaps it was felt that the fanciful nature of the "kid becomes manager" story line would work best if everyone concerned played the whole story in deadly earnest; or perhaps director Harmon Jones, who'd previously managed to squeeze *The Pride of St. Louis* dry of most of its inherent humor, wouldn't have known a funny situation if it stood up and bit him. Whatever the case, *The Kid from Left Field* is more compelling

than comic; it's not the best baseball film ever made by a long shot, but it's certainly one of the strangest.

Except for an opening scene in which he rattles off baseball statistics in a stilted, unconvincing fashion, nine-year-old Billy Chapin successfully conveys a wisdom (and sadness) beyond his years as Christy Cooper; Chapin would use this child-man quality to even greater effect two years later as one of the children imperiled by mad preacher Robert Mitchum in *Night of the Hunter*. The young actor had been working in pictures since the age of twenty-two months, meaning that he was more a "veteran" than the leading lady in *The Kid from Left Field*, Anne Bancroft, who is decorous but rather forgettable in this, her fourth film.

The supporting cast is a feast of nostalgia for longtime sports fans. John "Beans" Reardon, a real-life umpire, appears in this capacity in *The Kid from Left Field* (he'd essayed similar "roles" years earlier in the silent film *Slide, Kelly, Slide* and Joe E. Brown's *Elmer the Great*). Reardon is given one brief, shining moment wherein he settles an umpire-manager dispute by literally carrying Billy Chapin off the ballfield. Also visible among the bit actors is sports announcer Mark Scott, who was recently spotlighted on the ESPN cable network via reruns of Scott's 1959-60 TV series *Home Run Derby*. Essaying the larger part of Hank Dreiser was ex–Cleveland Indian John Berardino (see *The Kid from Cleveland*), who by 1953 had renounced professional baseball for an acting career, though he would have to drop one of the R's from his last name and sign on as Dr. Steve Hardy on the ABC daytime drama *General Hospital* before becoming a full-fledged star. And of particular interest to film historians (if not baseball fans) is the appearance of Fess Parker, who plays the small part of a pitcher in *The Kid from Left Field* two years before attaining international fame in Disney's *Davy Crockett* series.

The Kid from Left Field

Gary Coleman Productions/Deena Silver-Kramer's Movie Company; originally telecast September 30, 1979

Executive producer: Deena Silver-Kramer. Produced by Russell Vreeland. Associate producer: Steven Freeman. Directed by Adell Aldrich. Teleplay by Kathryn Powers and Jack Sher, from a story by Jack Sher. Photography: Frank Thackery. Edited by Robert Hernandez and Peter Kirby. Music by David Frank. Art director: Allen Jones. Assistant directors: Roger Carlson and Brad Gross. Music by David Rapp. Music recorded and engineered by Garry Ulmer. Executive in charge of production: Paul Rapp. Color by CFI. 97 minutes; sound.

Cast: Gary Coleman (J. R. Cooper); Robert Guillaume (Larry Cooper); Gary Collins (Pete Sloane); Ed McMahon (Walker); Tricia O'Neal (Marion Fowler); Tab Hunter (Bill Lorant); Rick Podell (Leonard Hyams); Alberto Velasquez (Juan Telles); Steve Tannen (Orlando); Ken Medlock (Grosso); Stu Nahan (Sportscaster); Stanley Brock (Carl Hagen); Weldon Bleiler (Bill); Peggy Browne (Secretary); Jerry Coleman (Padres Announcer); Sonny Carver (Mr. Brown); Don Draper (Process Server); Dick Gjonola (Disgruntled Fan); Gordon W. Grant (Rydell); Bill Henderson (Brad Lindquist); Rance Howard (Bartender); Angelo Lamonea (Vreeland); Nancy Leonard (Mrs. Kruger); Dion Myal (Bryan); Justin Randi (Herman); Hank Robinson (Umpire); Owen Sullivan (Bob Holden).

The plot is substantially the same as that of the 1953 version of *The Kid from Left Field* (see previous entry). Significant differences include several character names. The kid is now named J. R. Cooper, after Jackie Robinson; the leading lady is now Marion Fowler, not Foley, and she has been transformed into a social worker concerned with J. R.'s welfare, rather than being merely the sweetheart of third baseman Pete Sloane (Pete Haines in the original); and the club owner is now named Fred Walker instead of "Whacker." One plot twist is added toward the end, when J. R. Cooper is taken away from his single father and placed in a foster home. And finally, the ball club in the story is no longer the fictional "Bisons," but the real-life (or very nearly real-life) San Diego Padres.

This remake, first telecast over NBC on September 30, 1979, has an advantage or two over the original. The credibility of the story is strengthened by the extensive location shooting in and around the San Diego Padres' stadium (the visual dynamics of the park's circular concourse is exploited to the hilt), and by several swiftly paced, albeit rather conventionally photographed, ballgame scenes. Changing the leading lady from a standard romantic foil to a social worker

A Ten-Year-Old Kid Becomes A Major League Manager.

Ed McMahon

Robert Guillaume

Tab Hunter

Gary Collins

7:00PM Gary Coleman in "The Kid From Left Field"
The world's cleverest kid is appointed Manager of the San Diego Padres. He outsmarts the pros... saves his Dad's career... and the entire team... in this heartwarming story that hits home. Gary Collins Robert Guillaume Ed McMahon, Tab Hunter **WORLD PREMIERE MOVIE**

NBC PROUD AS A PEACOCK

4, 5, 15, 17

TV Guide ad for *The Kid from Left Field* (1979).

brought into the story through her concern with J. R. Cooper's welfare may have been a "politically correct" move in 1979, but at least it also gave actress Tricia O'Neal a far more substantial role than was played by Anne Bancroft in 1953. And finally, Ed McMahon is a joy to behold in the old Ray Collins role of the publicity-hungry team owner, one of the few times that a TV movie "special guest appearance" offered value for money rather than a one-scene celebrity cameo.

Other elements of the 1979 *Kid from Left Field* aren't quite as successful. Tab Hunter is far too affable a screen presence to represent genuine menace as the mean Padres manager Billy Lorant, especially in

comparison to the venomous portrayal of the same character by Richard Egan in 1953. Robert Guillaume might be a more sensitive dramatic actor than Dan Dailey, but Guillaume's portrayal of Larry Cooper is bogged down with too many 1970s-style weeping scenes; after the third or fourth tear-drenched close-up of Guillaume, one gets the impression that this guy cries over card tricks. And in stretching the running time from the original's compact eighty minutes to the requisite TV-movie two hours (actually ninety-seven minutes plus commercials), the climax seems to go on for eons, especially during a pointless race by J. R. Cooper through the streets of San Diego to watch his dad's comeback, capped by the kid's arrival at the stadium just in time to witness a wearisome slow-motion winning play.

The 1979 *Kid from Left Field* is something of an endurance test for those who aren't overly fond of Gary Coleman—for this is, after all, a "Gary Coleman Production," and its principal reason for being was ten-year-old Coleman's popularity vis-à-vis his NBC sitcom *Diff'rent Strokes*. While Gary is tolerable in his father-son scenes with Robert Guillaume (these actors would later costar in what threatened to be a series of TV movies, *The Kid with the Broken Halo* and *The Kid with the 200 I.Q.*), he is no more successful in the "rattling off baseball stats" routine than Billy Chapin had been in 1953. And when it comes to the scene in which Coleman gives his team a fists-on-hips pep talk before a big game, it is all too clear that cuteness is an inadequate substitute for talent. The final image of the film is an animated scoreboard rendition of Gary Coleman winking at the audience. Do not watch this moment if you are the sort who hurls heavy objects at the TV set.

Production sidelight: Vincent Edwards, of *Ben Casey*, fame was slated to direct *The Kid from Left Field*, but he pulled out just before shooting. His replacement was Adell Aldrich, daughter of Robert Aldrich, whose own first feature film was likewise a baseball story, *Big Leaguer* (q.v.).

Kill the Umpire

Columbia; released May 1950

Produced by John Beck. Directed by Lloyd Bacon. Screenplay by Frank Tashlin. Photography: Charles Lawton, Jr. Edited by Charles Nelson. Musical direction by Morris Stoloff. Art direction by Perry Smith. Chase scene directed by Edward Bernds. 78 minutes; black and white; sound.

Cast: William Bendix (Bill Johnson); Una Merkel (Betty Johnson); Ray Collins (Jonah Evans); Gloria Henry (Lucy Johnson); Richard Taylor [Jeff Richards] (Bob London); Connie Marshall (Susan Johnson); William Frawley (Jimmy O'Brien); Tom D'Andrea (Roscoe Snooker); Luther Crockett (Sam Austin); Jeff York (Panhandle Jones); Glenn Thompson (Lanky); Bob Wilke (Cactus); Jim Bannon (Dusty); Alan Hale, Jr. (Harry Shay); Almira Sessions, Emil Sitka (Angry Fans); Vernon Dent (Businessman); Dick Wessel (Workman); Harry Hayden (Desk Clerk).

Bill Johnson of St. Petersburg, Florida, is a baseball fanatic—so much so that every time spring rolls around he spends so much time in the stands that he loses his latest job. Like most of his breed, Bill hates umpires with a purple passion, which doesn't sit too well with his ex-umpire father-in-law Jonah Evans. Partly out of concern for his daughter Betty and granddaughters Lucy and Susan, and partly out of sweet vengeance, Evans forces the unemployed Johnson to enroll in a nearby school for umpires. After a period of slovenly disregard for rules and regulations, Bill begins to take his ump chores seriously under the tutelage of coach Jimmy O'Brien, and before long our hero is given a tryout with the Texas Interstate League. As a result of his being the unwitting recipient of a bottle of eye drops which induce brief periods of double vision, Bill gains notoriety on the baseball circuit as "Two Call Johnson." Inevitably, crooked gamblers try to get Johnson to fix a few games. Bill refuses their bribes, but when he makes a call against popular local player Harry Shay during a crucial game, it looks as though "Two Call" has succumbed to easy money. The injured Shay has been hospitalized, and is thus unable to let the public know whether or not Johnson is on the square, the result being that Bill has to hide out from both the gamblers and the bloodthirsty fans. But Johnson is determined to umpire the Big Game, and after a wild race through town he makes it to the ballpark. Just when it looks as though Johnson is going to be deluged by debris from the grandstands, Harry Shay

Five points to anyone who can guess what William Bendix is saying in this scene from *Kill the Umpire*. (That's right. You win.)

makes an announcement over the P.A. system that the aforementioned unpopular call was a fair one, and that Bill is a prince of a guy. "Two Call Johnson" becomes the hero of the day—at least until making *another* unpopular call about thirty seconds later.

The Fuller Brush Man, a Red Skelton comedy, was a major moneyspinner for Columbia in 1948, prompting the film's screenwriter, Frank Tashlin, to cook up several more laugh riots wherein a "working stiff" protagonist ends up in a situation calling for a zany sight-gag denouement. Three such pictures were churned out in 1950 alone, each written by Tashlin and directed by Lloyd Bacon: *The Fuller Brush Girl, The Good Humor Man* and *Kill the Umpire*. *Umpire* was the only one of the trilogy that didn't use

a murder plot as the foundation for its comedy—unless one takes into consideration the killer instincts of the fans as they call for the speedy demise of umpire Bill Johnson.

Despite his poor showing in *The Babe Ruth Story* (q.v.) two years earlier, William Bendix was ideally suited for the baseball atmosphere of *Umpire*. Like Bill Johnson, Bendix was a lifelong devotee of the game (he'd once been a batboy for the New York Giants), and was known to amaze his costars with his encyclopedic knowledge of ballgame stats—though he must have had a run for his money from *Umpire* supporting actor William Frawley. Frawley was so enamored of the National Pastime that, despite his notorious tight-fistedness, he was one of the principal financial backers of the Pacific Coast League's Hollywood Stars; he also had a clause in his *I Love Lucy* contract that excused him from the program's shooting schedule during the World Series.

While the scenes involving the umpire training school are amusing and not so far removed from the real thing (rookie umps really do practice calling "Yer out!" and performing their hand gestures, though not always in unison), the actual baseball scenes are rather skimpy. What sticks in the mind most clearly after the last reel of *Kill the Umpire* has tumbled over the spool is the film's slapstick climax. One of Frank Tashlin's signatures as both writer and director was to end his films with looney, extended chase sequences involving as many exaggerated sound effects, near misses, broken props, and hair-raising stunts as the footage would allow. Tashlin also had a fondness for including the sort of "impossible" gags that were better suited to animated cartoons than to live action films (he was, after all, an alumnus of Warner Bros. Cartoons' "Termite Terrace"). Edward Bernds, assigned to direct the chase scene in *Kill the Umpire*, recalled years later that the first reaction from Columbia production manager Jack Fier to Tashlin's storyboard was, "That son of a bitch has written a cartoon sequence. You gonna get somebody to draw it? We gotta photograph it!"

As with most good comedies (and this little programmer is a notch better than good), the moments that work best in *Kill the Umpire* are those closest to truth. The final scene is a gem. Less than one minute after basking in the cheers of the fans for proving his honesty, Bill Johnson calls an out. Instantly the fans turn on him, with one sweet little old lady speaking for the throng by shouting, "Johnson, you stink!" As the scene fades to a chorus of boos and an orchestral rendition of "Three Blind Mice," we see Two Call Johnson scanning the grandstands with a look of disdain stamped two miles deep on his face; and although

actor Bill Bendix doesn't give out with his famous *Life of Riley* tag line "What a revoltin' development this is," we can hear it all the same.

Ladies' Day

RKO Radio; released April 9, 1943

Produced by Bert Gilroy. Directed by Leslie Goodwins. Screenplay by Charles E. Roberts and Dale Lussier, based on a play by Robert Considine, Edward Clark Lilley and Bertrand Robinson. Photography: Jack McKenzie. Edited by Harry Marker. Music by Roy Webb. Art direction by Albert D'Agostino and Feild Gray. 62 minutes: black and white; sound.

Cast: Lupe Velez (Pepita Zorita); Eddie Albert (Wacky Waters); Patsy Kelly (Hazel Jones); Max Baer, Sr. (Hippo Jones); Jerome Cowan (Updike); Iris Adrian (Kitty McGowan); Joan Barclay (Joan); Cliff Clark (Dan Hannigan); Carmen Morales (Mariana DiAngelo); George Cleveland (Doc); Jack Briggs (Marty); Russ Clark (Smokey); Nedrick Young (Tony DiAngelo); Eddie Dew (Spike McGowan); Tom Kennedy (Dugan, the House Detective); Ralph Sanford, Frank Mills, Bud Geary, Kernan Cripps (Umpires); Richard Martin, Russell Wade, Wayne McCoy, Malcolm McTaggart, Mal Marihugh, Charles Russell, Jack Shea, Jack Gargan, Cy Malis (Ballplayers); Rube Schaeffer (Runner); Jack Carrington (Field Announcer); Sally Wadsworth (Blonde); Mary Stuart, Ariel Heath, Mary Halsey, Anne Summers (Wives); Eddie Borden (Spectator); Don Kerry (Pepita's Assistant); George O'Hanlon (Young Rube); Earle Hodgins (Old Man Customer); Russell Hoyt (Assistant Director); Henry Hall (Dr. Adams); Wesley Barry (Reporter); Allen Wood (Locker Boy); Norman Mayes (Pullman Porter); Teddy Mangean (Upstairs Bellhop); Barrie Milman (The DiAngelo Baby); Jack O'Connor (Cab Driver); Jack Stewart (Doorman); George Noisan (Airport Messenger); Freddie Carpenter (Bellhop); Ted O'Shea (Airport Attendant); John Sheehan (Producer); Vinton Hayworth [Jack Arnold] (Director).

The Sox are pinning their World Series hopes on pitcher Wacky Waters; the ballplayers' wives have a stake in Wacky as well, since all of them need that series bonus money for a multitude of reasons (one of the wives is pregnant, another wants to open a restaurant, and so forth). Unfortunately, Wacky's game suffers whenever he falls in love—and currently he's head over heels thanks to vivacious movie star Pepita Zorita. The publicity-minded owners of the Sox encourage the romance and even orchestrate Wacky's marriage to Pepita, much to the detriment of his on-field performance and the discomfort of his teammates. Finally, the ballplayers' wives take matters in their own hands by kidnapping Pepita, but the flamboyant actress manages to escape just before the crucial series game. A last-ditch effort to convince Pepita that she's got a rare and contagious disease forestalls her appearance at the ballpark, but not for long. Happily, Pepita turns out to be Wacky's best motivation for winning the series, and there are smiles all around for the fade-out.

Watching some of the dull, ineptly staged ballpark scenes in *Ladies' Day* (rendered doubly unconvincing by alternating those scenes with jittery stock footage of real games), it's hard to believe that sports expert Robert Considine had anything to do with its creation. The only actor who looks like he has a clue about diamond deportment is Eddie Albert, who, after all, came to Hollywood on the strength of his performance as a collegiate ballplayer in the stage play *Brother Rat*.

Evidently, the filmmakers couldn't have cared less about the baseball angle; *Ladies' Day* was designed merely as a "B" vehicle for RKO's Latin Bombshell Lupe Velez, here playing a variation of her title character in the studio's "Mexican Spitfire" series. In this respect the film succeeds in filling an hour's worth of screen time with wheezy two-reel comedy gags.

In an apparent casting strategy to keep Lupe Velez from being the most irritating character on screen, two of the team wives were played by a brace of Hollywood's loudest and brassiest actresses: Patsy Kelly and Iris Adrian. Even allowing for their desperation in coveting their husbands' bonus checks, the ladies of *Ladies' Day* are a ferocious bunch as they repeatedly clobber Lupe with a baseball bat and bind and gag her with hotel towels.

While the leather-lunged female supporting players certainly kept the audience from falling asleep, they weren't enough to keep the critics from going after Lupe's performance with both barrels. One reviewer opined that the star was offering a feature length imitation of Donald Duck. But what more could one expect from a film wherein the comic high point is Lupe Velez disguising herself as a male bellhop—or a film in which professional baseball players are given nicknames like "Wacky" and "Hippo"?

The Last Home Run

Horizon Productions/The Shooting Gallery/Showcase Entertainment; Canadian TV and film-festival release date: 1996.

Executive producer: Roger Flax. Produced and directed by Bob Gosse. Coproduced by Larry Meistrich and Jeff Pullman. Associate producer: Tom Razzano. Screenplay by Ed Apfel and Roger Flax; story by Roger Flax. Original music: Jeffrey M. Taylor. Photography: Peter Fernberger. Edited by Rachel Warden. Production designer: Andras Kanegson. Costume designer: Laura Jean Shannon. Sound designer: Jeff Kushner. Production sound mixer: Ron Scelza. First assistant director: Tommy "T-Bone" Barone. Second assistant director: Brandon Rosser. Production coordinator: Diane Wheeler-Nicholson. Special effects: Rick Jones, Rick LaCoste. Hair stylist: Carol Raskin-Smaling. Makeup: Angela Johnson. Script supervisor: Diana Liebert. Opticals: Film Effects. Color. 95 minutes; Dolby Stereo Sound. Rated PG.

Cast: Tom Guiry (Young Jonathan Lyle); Seymour Cassel (Older Jonathan Lyle); Danielle Comerford (Jenny Neal); Jonathan Flax (Geo); Jordi Vilasuso (Tommy); Todd Logan (Reed); Clay Smalls (Rashid); Riley Gelwicks (Victor);

Ryan Hopkins (Donald); Vinnette Carroll (Emma); Manuel Arteaga (Jose); Frankie Man (Maxie); Mal Jones (Dugan); Badri Prasad Adhikari (Annand); Florence McGee (Frances); Gary Carter (Jeff Neal); Liza Harris (Judy Neal); Kenny Flax (Kenny Neal); Dave Winfield (Himself); Roger Flax (Umpire); Ed Pang (Koseo); Charlie Flax (Nutty Bellhop); Tommy Barone (EMS Worker); Lauren Razzano (Lauren); John B. Sterling (Baseball Announcer).

While growing up during the Depression, Jonathan Lyle wanted to play baseball so much that he could taste the horsehide, but his family was too poor to indulge in such frivolous activities. Now a retired gynecologist, the septuagenarian Jonathan spends his days gazing wistfully at the Little League ballpark across the street from the dreary Florida nursing home where he lives. Occasionally breaking the monotony by organizing his fellow seniors into impromptu sandlot ballgames, Jonathan is ultimately denied even this pleasure when he is diagnosed with a serious, perhaps fatal, heart condition. Having heard Jonathan say that he'd give anything for just one more chance to be a ballplaying kid again, fellow nursing-home resident Emma—who claims to be the aunt of Cleveland Indians outfielder Dave Winfield—arranges for the old man to get that chance. Emma sets up a meeting between Jonathan and a curious character named Mr. Kazio, who through mystical "Eastern" methods all his own, transforms Jonathan into a 12-year-old boy, with no memory of his adult existence. Thanks to a series of fortuitous coincidences, the younger Jonathan lands a slot on the Lake Worth Giants, the Little League team coached by Jeff Neal, an essentially nice guy who turns into a snarling Mr. Hyde on the ballfield. Befriended by Jeff's daughter (and team member) Jenny, Jonathan has an easier time adjusting to his new surroundings—and healthy new body—than might otherwise have been the case. Except for enduring the envious antagonism of troubled

teammate Tommy, and despite sporadic and unsettling reminders of his "older" self, Jonathan is at last able to relax and enjoy himself, and to fully appreciate that life is too short and precious a commodity *not* to be enjoyed. As a bonus, the boy is able to calm down the hypertense Jeff Neal, persuading the coach to let the kids have fun on the ballfield, rather than treat every game as a life-or-death ordeal. But as is often the case in baseball-fantasy films, there is a catch: Unbeknownst to Jonathan, he will remain a youngster only for five days—and at precisely 6:00 P.M. on the fifth day, Mr. Kazio makes preparations to reverse the magical aging process, restoring Jonathan to his old, pain-wracked, worn-out self.

Founded in 1990, the Bronx-based Shooting Gallery Productions was dedicated to producing inexpensive independent films for a broad-based audience. The company represented a collaboration between producer Larry Meistrich and filmmaker Bob Gosse, whose cousin was acclaimed independent director-screenwriter Hal Hartley (*The Unbelievable Truth, Simple Men, Amateur*). Before firmly entrenching itself in the movie mainstream with the Oscar-nominated Billy Bob Thornton effort *Sling Blade*, Shooting Gallery earned its spurs with modest but entertaining efforts like *The Last Home Run*.

Shot on location in Lakewood Florida, the film was executive-produced and cowritten by Roger Flax, a motivational psychologist. Given Flax' chosen profession, it should come as no surprise that *Last Home Run* bubbles over with New Age philosophy, with a pinch of Zen ("Time is like a horse," etc.) thrown in for flavor. Nor will it surprise anyone that the film's basic message is the old saw "It isn't whether you win or lose, but how you play the game"— though the filmmakers were wise enough to see that the game was won anyway so that the audience would go home happy and fulfilled. And given the fact that the executive producer is the fellow who puts up the money, we should not be shocked that the name "Flax" pops up with such regularity in the supporting cast—Jonathan Flax as ballplayer Geo, Kenny Flax as Jenny Neal's obnoxious kid brother Kenny, Charlie Flax as the "Nutty Bellhop" (a character who is about as funny as his name), Roger Flax himself as a bespectacled dentist-cum-umpire—nor that the songs heard in the background were penned by Roger Flax, with Roger himself providing vocals. To paraphrase the 1922 Buster Keaton comedy *The Playhouse*, "This fellow Flax seems to be the whole show."

Its occasional pretensions and excesses aside, *Last Home Run* is one of the better entries from the baseball-fantasy cycle of the mid–1990s. Bob Gosse never ceases to amaze with his ability to come up with fresh and often unique approaches to filming the many baseball games which dominate the film's midsection. Director King Vidor once boasted that he never used the same camera angle twice in his 1931 filmization of the stage play *Street Scene*. Well, Vidor had nothing on Bob Gosse, who in the course of the film's 95 minutes pulls out virtually the entire lexicon of ballpark visuals: close-ups of hands, feet and eyes, steadicam tracking shots of kids rounding the bases, dust-enshrouded base slides, handheld point-of-view shots, elliptical editing, quick Truffaut-like fades on game highlights, into-the-sun tilt pans on pop flies, judicious use of slow motion, and even one traveling "zoom" from the viewpoint of the baseball. While one might have wished that Gosse and cinematographer Peter Fernberger were not quite so enamored of the 360-degree circular shots which threaten to become wearisome as the film progresses, they are to be commended for making a baseball movie that really *moves*, effectively placing the viewer in the thick of things without inducing the vertigo or nausea that often accompanies the MTV-influenced action movies of recent years.

One of the more felicitous directorial touches is built around a simple sound effect: the distinctive hollow "ping" of an aluminum bat connecting with a baseball. Gosse and sound designer Jeff Kushner brilliantly harness this sound as a recurring motif, not only in the baseball scenes, but also whenever a sound of *any* kind is heard. The imitation "pings" emanating from video games, TV remote controls, cameras, revolving doors, elevators, and even the film's background music never let us forget the importance that baseball has in the life of the protagonist.

The film's fantasy angle leans towards verbosity and empty symbolism in its early stages, with one "crossover" prop, a sort of Rubik's Sphere called The Interceptor, given heavy emphasis as old Jonathan becomes young Jonathan, only to be abruptly dropped from the story as soon as it has served its purpose. Even so, during the key transitional sequence, director Gosse manages to pull off a "Steven Spielberg" on a budget roughly equivalent to Spielberg's weekly haircut.

The older Jonathan walks into a run-down video arcade managed by a scruffy-looking oriental chap wearing an eye patch. Once he has made his way past the flashing lights and flickering videogame screens, Jonathan steps into a sunny Japanese garden, whereupon the manager, minus the eye patch and dressed in flowing robes, reveals himself to be Mr. Kazio. After a stretch of *Kung Fu*–like dialogue about the relativity of time, Kazio dresses Jonathan in robes similar to his own; the old man then drinks a foul-tasting potion and obediently sits still while Kazio takes his picture. There follows a series of blinding flashes (hiding a succession of jump-cuts), during which Old Jonathan morphs into Young Jonathan, his "shrinking" represented by a subtle, almost imperceptible upward camera tilt. In his 12-year-old form, Jonathan wanders dreamily out of the arcade and into a nearby luxury hotel, where everyone, from the guests to the concierge on down, addresses the boy by his first name (a benign quote from a more ominous scene in Stanley Kubrick's *The Shining*). Escorted to his lavish suite, Jonathan isn't at all sure what has happened, or even who he is; but before any questions can be raised, his attention is drawn to a brace of photographs on his dresser, showing the most important people in the "old" Jonathan's life: his fellow nursing-home residents and his deceased daughter. Still a bit disoriented, Jonathan wanders out of the hotel, then just happens to stroll past the Little League park where he will spend the bulk of the next five days. In just a few minutes' screen time, and with a handful of deft directorial strokes, Jonathan has confronted his Past, Present and Future, as foretold by Mr. Kazio—and virtually the entire sequence was pulled off "in the camera," eschewing expensive computerized special effects in favor of sheer hands-on virtuosity.

As in the case of *Rookie of the Year* (q.v.), *The Last Home Run* is treated realistically until the fantasy angle is introduced: After that, all bets are off. Happily, director Gosse manages to sustain total credibility in even the most incredible sequence, wherein young Jonathan, instinctively summoning up the obstetric skills of his older alter-ego, expertly assists in the birthing when Jenny Neal's mother suddenly goes into labor.

The most gratifying aspect of the film is its absence of a clichéd villain. In any other baseball picture, the bullying perfectionism of coach Jeff Neal would automatically type him as the heavy of the piece. But Jeff is shown to be a loving husband and father, and genuinely concerned for the well-being of his team, especially when one of the players is injured on the field. His only "crime" as coach is his inability to

loosen up and enjoy the game, and thanks to the young Jonathan he ultimately learns to do just that. Similarly, one of the team members, a sullen boy named Tommy, resents Jonathan's baseball prowess, his encyclopedic knowledge of statistics and his "moving in" on Jenny. Accordingly, Tommy goes out of his way to pick a fight with Jonathan, even spitting in the boy's face. That this nominal bully is never totally reprehensible is because we are allowed to understand the motivation for his behavior: Tommy's parents have been divorced, and he resents anyone who might be remotely happy or secure. In the end, when Jonathan has been restored to his "real" age, a mellower Tommy renews his quasi-romantic relationship with Jenny, who has herself been emotionally cast adrift by young Jonathan's sudden disappearance. Wisely, this closing reconciliation is not milked, and in fact is filmed in extreme long-shot, sparing viewers the phony pathos of the usual "I'm sorry for everything" monologue.

Only in the inconsistency of the acting performances does *The Last Home Run* resemble a "typical" independent production. Overall, the younger players are more consistently believable than the adult performers (the actors playing the senior-center residents are so stereotyped that one expects them to carry ear horns and exclaim "By cracky!"). Fourteen-year-old Tom Guiry, previously the youthful star of *The Sandlot*, captures precisely the wide-eyed wonderment of being a stranger in a strange land in the role of young Jonathan; and in the bargain, Guiry's baseball skills (only minimally exploited in *Sandlot*) are first-rate.

Of the grownups, Seymour Cassel, an art-house favorite since his days as a member of filmmaker John Cassavetes' "stock company" (he was Moskowitz in 1971's *Minnie and Moskowitz*), is a joy to behold in one of his rare latter-day leading roles, making all his scenes as the older Jonathan count, no matter how brief they may be (Cassel later brought the same venerable vigor to his supporting role of waspish sports reporter Sam Simon in the baseball biopic *61** [q.v.]). Also registering well on screen are two real-life baseball players: 1981 All-Star Game MVP Gary "The Kid" Carter, formerly a catcher with the Montreal Expos; and recently retired outfielder Dave Winfield, who in 1992 achieved immortality by cinching the World Series for the Toronto Blue Jays with a game-winning double. Intriguingly, since Winfield plays himself, he is given "Special Guest Appearance" billing; but since Carter makes his acting debut in the role of coach Jeff Neal, his screen credit reads "Introducing Gary Carter."

Given a few rounds on the film-festival circuit before its relatively early home-video release, *The Last Home Run* has been surprisingly ignored by critics and is virtually unknown to baseball-movie fans. Some *cineastes*, turned off by director Bob Gosse's subsequent *Bonnie and Clyde/Badlands* wannabe *Niagara, Niagara* (1998), have expressed their disappointment with Gosse by summarily rejecting his other films sight unseen. If this book serves any purpose, it will be to elevate such neglected little gems as *The Last Home Run* and *Finding Buck McHenry* (q.v.) to the prominence they deserve—and, simultaneously, to consign such "bigger" baseball pictures as *Ed* and *The Fan* to the obscurity *they* deserve.

A League of Their Own

Parkway Productions/Columbia; released July 1, 1992

Executive Producer/Director: Penny Marshall. Produced by Robert Greenhut and Elliot Abbott. Co-producers: Bill Pace, Ronnie D. Clemmer. Associate producer: Amy Lemisch. Screenplay by Lowell Ganz and Babaloo Mandel; story by Kim Wilson and Kelly Candaele (based on their 1986 Public TV documentary). Photography: Miroslav Ondrícek. Original music by Madonna (theme song: "This Used to Be My Playground"), Hans Zimmer and [uncredited] Billy Joel. Edited by Adam Bernardi and George Bowers. Casting: Ellen Lewis, Amanda Mackey. Production design: Bill Groom. Art direction: Tim Galvin. Set decoration: George DeTitta, Jr. Costume design: Synthia Flint. Production manager: Timothy M. Bourne. Technical advisors: Pepper Paire Davis, Terry Donahue. Baseball coach: William E. Hughes. Key makeup artist: Bernadette Mazur. Key hair stylist: Francesca Paris. First assistant director: Michael Haley. Second assistant director: John Rusk. Storyboard artist: Jane Clark. Graphic designer: Ted Haigh. Sound editor: Wayne Griffin. Sound mixer: Les Lazarowitz. Foley editors: Pamela Bentkowski, Sukey Fontelieu. Script supervisor: Mary Bailey. Production coordinator: Alexis Alexanian. Optical effects by Pacific Title. Technicolor; Panavision. 128 minutes; Dolby SR Sound. Rated PG.

Cast: Tom Hanks (Jimmy Dugan, manager); Geena Davis (Dottie Keller Hinson, catcher); Madonna (Mae "All-the-Way" Mordabito, center field); Lori Petty (Kit Keller, pitcher); Jon Lovitz (Ernie Capadino); David Strathairn (Ira Lowenstein); Garry Marshall (Walter Harvey); Bill Pullman (Bob Hinson); Megan Cavanagh (Marla Hooch, second base); Rosie O'Donnell (Doris Murphy, third base); Tracy Reiner (Betty "Spaghetti" Horn, left field); Bitty Schram (Evelyn Gardner, right field); Don Davis (Racine Coach Charlie Collins); Renée Coleman (Alice Gaspers, left field/catcher); Ann Cusack (Shirley Baker, left field); Eddie Jones (Dave Hooch); Freddie Simpson (Ellen Sue Gotlander, shortstop/pitcher); Anne Elizabeth Ramsay (Helen Haley, first base); Robin Knight ("Beans" Babbitt, shortstop); Patti Pelton (Marbleann Wilkenson, second base); Kelli Simpkins (Beverly Dixon, outfield); Neezer Tarleton (Neezer Dalton, outfielder); Connie Pounds-Taylor (Connie Calhoun, outfield); Kathleen Marshall ("Mumbles" Brockman, outfield); Sharon Szmidt (Vivian Ernst, second base); Pauline Brailsford (Miss Cuthbert); Justin Scheller (Stilwell "Angel" Gardner); Alan Wilder (Nelson); R. M. Haley (Empathetic Umpire); Janet Jones (Racine Pitcher); Brenda Ferrari (Racine Catcher); Téa Leoni (Racine first base); Laurel Cronin (Maida Gillespie); Robert Stanton (Western Union Man);

Wantland L. Sandel, Jr. (Doctor); Joe Krowka (Heckler); Harry Shearer (Newsreel Announcer); Blaire Baron (Margaret); Ryan Howell (Jeffrey); Brian Boru (Bobby); David Franks (Vacuum Salesman); Ryan Olsen ("Dollbody" Kid); Ellie Weingardt (Charm School Instructor); Larissa Collins (Charm School Assistant); Douglas Blakeslee, Joey Slotnick (Doris' Fans); Brian Flannery, Stephen Feagley (Autograph Kids); Rae Allen (Ma Keller); Gregory Sporleder (Mitch Swaley); Eddie Mekka (Mae's Guy in Bar); Stephen Mailer (Kit's Date in Bar); Ray Chapman (Ticket Scalper); Joette Hodgen (Opera Singer); Lynn Cartwright (Older Dottie); Kathleen Butler (Older Kit); Eunice Anderson (Older Mae); Vera Johnson (Older Doris); Patricia Wilson (Older Marla); Mark Holton (Older Stilwell); Barbara Erwin (Older Shirley); Betty Miller (Older Betty); Eugenia McLin (Older Ellen Sue); Barbara Pilavin (Older Helen); Marvin Einhorn (Older Ira); Shirley Bukovich (Older Alice); Dolores "Pickles" Dries (Lady in Bleachers); Shelly Adlard, Vickie Buse, K. C. Carr, Julie Croteau, Tonya Gilles Koch, Kirsten Gretick, Stacey Gustaferro, Lisa Hand, Cheryl Jones, Shelly Niemeyer, Sally Rutherford, Lita Schmitt, Amanda Walker, Brenda Watson (Additional Players); David L. Lander (Radio Announcer); Eddie Quin (Doris' Father); Tom Rupert (Coach, Kenosha Comets); Ray Toler (Loudmouth from Lukash).

October, 1988: The recently widowed Dottie Keller Hinson prepares to fly to Cooperstown, New York, to participate in an induction ceremony at the National Baseball Hall of Fame. Forty-five years earlier, Dottie had been among the first women ballplayers to sign up for the All-American Girls Professional Baseball League, created by millionaire candy manufacturer and Chicago ballclub owner Walter Harvey as a means of keeping The Game alive while many of the top male Major Leaguers were fighting in the Second World War. Now Dottie is among the surviving All-American Girls who have been invited to be honored as the Cooperstown museum dedicates a special wing to "Women in Baseball." If she had her druthers, however, Dottie would remain at home; dismissing her single season in baseball, she claims that, "It was never that important to me. It was something I did." But her daughter and grandchildren are insistent, so she reluctantly packs her flight bags. As Dottie is driven to the airport, her mind drifts back to the Spring of 1943...

...when she and her younger sister Kit are the star players of the amateur women's fast-pitch softball team in Wilamette, Oregon. Impressed by Dottie's hitting and catching skills—not to mention her drop-dead-gorgeous looks—Ernie Capadino, a scout for the All-American Girls, offers Dottie a contract with the newly formed Rockford (Illinois) Peaches. Dottie turns him down; she doesn't want to play ball for a living, and besides, she is a married woman, anxiously awaiting the return of her soldier husband Bob. But kid sister Kit, who, though possessed of a raw pitching and batting talent, is not anywhere near Dottie's caliber, would give her eye teeth to get out of Oregon and become a professional ballplayer. Kit strikes a deal with Ernie: If she can persuade Dottie to sign up, she too will be given a berth with the Peaches. During the grueling tryout sessions in Chicago, Dottie forges a number of lasting friendships with her fellow teammates: former taxi dancer Mae Mordabito, nicknamed "All-the-Way Mae" for reasons that go beyond her talents as a center fielder; Mae's wisecracking best pal, third baseman Doris Murphy, who has joined the team to prove that her life is not going to be defined by her "loser" boyfriends; shy, withdrawn second baseman and power hitter Marla Hooch, signed by the team despite Ernie's opinion that Marla bears a close resemblance to General Omar Bradley; left fielder Betty Horn, nicknamed "Betty Spaghetti" because of her cooking skills; mousy right fielder Evelyn Gardner, who is forced to drag her bellicose young son "Stilwell Angel" along on road trips; illiterate left fielder Shirley Baker, whom Mae teaches to read with the help of her vast collection of pornographic paperbacks; and onetime beauty contestant Ellen Sue Gotlander, who, when not serving as shortstop, pursues the hobby of songwriting. During their first few games, the Peaches are forced to endure the patronizing jeers of the men in the crowd, not to mention the wolf whistles engendered by the girls' demeaningly short-skirted uniforms. The situation is relieved not at all by the Peaches' manager, embittered ex–Major League star slugger Jimmy Dugan. Knowing all too well that he has been hired just for his celebrity appeal, Jimmy drinks himself into oblivion before the start of every game, forcing Dottie to effectively take charge of the team.

By mid-season, owner Walter Harvey has decided to pull the plug on the League, arguing that the enterprise just isn't bringing in the bucks, and that soon the male ballplayers will be marching home from the War anyway. Refusing to have the rug pulled from under them, the Rockford Peaches vow to drag in crowds by exploiting their sex appeal and novelty value. Eventually, the girls win over the doubting male fans with good, solid ballplaying, and even Jimmy Dugan rallies to the League's cause, becoming their biggest booster and most enthusiastic athletic mentor. Still, Walter Harvey is reluctant to bankroll the League past its first season, prompting his promotional advisor Ira Lowenstein to take over the organization. All this boardroom intrigue means little to Dottie, who, upon the return of her war-wounded husband Bob, elects to give up baseball in favor of domesticity—a decision largely driven by the fact that the Game has driven a wedge between herself and her envious sister Kit, who has been traded to the Racine Belles in order to lessen the family friction. Even so, when the Peaches find themselves in a tight World Series race against the Belles, Dottie shows up at the deciding game in

full catcher's regalia; she may be many things, she explains, but she's not a quitter, even if it means facing down her own sister at the bottom of the Ninth.

Her reminiscences over, the elderly Dottie Keller Hinson arrives at the induction ceremony in Cooperstown, where she is joyously reunited with many of her former teammates. Caught up in the elation of the festivities, Dottie now admits that her year with the Rockford Peaches was among the greatest highlights of her life—and that despite all the tears and setbacks, she basks in the pride of being a true pioneer in the realm of women's professional sports.

The real All-American Girls Professional Baseball League (hereafter known as AAGPBL) came into being in late 1942 as the brainchild of chewing-gum manufacturer Philip K. Wrigley, the owner of the Chicago Cubs, and Wrigley's close friend and aide Arthur Meyerhoff, a Chicago advertising executive. With most of the top male baseball stars off fighting World War II, there was serious talk that the National Pastime would be closed for the duration. A potential alternative to the manpower shortage were the many professional women's ballclubs that existed in North America; unfortunately, these teams suffered from lack of funds and a centralized organizational structure. Wrigley and Meyerhoff established a unified female league, not only to keep baseball alive but also as a home-front morale booster, in much the same manner that the "Rosie the Riveter" image assured the public that women were keeping the assembly lines running while the men were making the world Safe for Democracy. Once his new league was up and running, Wrigley built up an aggressive and often ruthless network of recruiters, who wooed away the best female ballplayers from dozens of American and Canadian teams with promises of salaries as high as $75 per week (an extremely attractive stipend at the time). At least two of the smaller women's

A League of Their Own: Team shot of the fabulous Rockford Peaches. Top, left to right: "Beans" Babbitt (Robin Knight), Alice Gaspers (Renée Coleman), Doris Murphy (Rosie O'Donnell), Mae "All-the Way" Mordabito (Madonna), Evelyn Gardner (Bitty Schram), Helen Haley (Anne Elizabeth Ramsey), Shirley Baker (Ann Cusack). Bottom, left to right: Team chaperone Miss Cuthbert (Pauline Brailsford), Neezer Dalton (Neezer Tarleton), Marbleann Wilkenson (Patti Pelton), Connie Calhoun (Connie Pounds-Taylor), Beverly Dixon (Kelli Simpkins), Marla Hooch (Megan Cavanagh), Dottie Hinson (Geena Davis), Kit Keller (Lori Petty), Ellen Sue Gotlander (Freddie Simpson), "Betty Spaghetti" Horn (Tracy Reiner) and manager Jimmy Dugan (Tom Hanks).

baseball franchises, both headquartered in Chicago, were forced to disband once the AAGPBL had plundered their talent pool.

Though Wrigley was prepared to spend what was necessary to get the best (and prettiest) players available, he worried that there might be resistance to having baseball overrun by "a bunch of dames." Thus, Wrigley hired several famous managers, among them Dave Bancroft, Bill Wambsganss and Max Carey, to lend masculine star appeal to the AAGPBL, figuring that these baseball greats would be the new league's strongest drawing card. And to make certain that the major media of the era (newspapers, magazines, newsreels, radio) would

shower attention upon the League, Wrigley and Meyerhoff decreed that the ladies' uniforms—actually modified culottes— would show as much leg as possible. "In the beginning, a lot of people came to laugh and the guys to look at the legs," recalled AAGPBL veteran Lavone "Pepper" Paire Davis forty years later.

Though extremely modest by today's standards, the players' abbreviated uniforms ran the risk of condemnation from the local moral arbiters in the midwestern cities where the teams were located. To deflect this, Wrigley's publicity flacks made much over the fact that the female ballplayers were carefully instructed in matters of conduct, personal appearance and etiquette. As former AAGPBL outfielder Helen "Gig" Smith recalled in 1997, Wrigley "wanted the girls to conduct themselves as ladies at all times, but to play like men." It was the old double standard: Male athletes could pretty much comport themselves in any way they chose fit so long as they showed up to work on time, but women were expected to be Above Suspicion twenty-four hours a day. A number of rigid rules were established from the outset of the League: no smoking or drinking in public places; chaperones at all social engagements; a curfew of no later than two hours after the finish of the last game of the evening; a ban on jewelry of any kind; uniforms no shorter than six inches above the kneecap, and modest feminine attire when off the field (nix on slacks and shorts!); long well-groomed hair in lieu of "boyish bobs"; lipstick always in place but never too much; and on and on. In addition, it was mandatory for each team member, no matter what her social background, to attend one of the League's "charm schools," where the ladies were drilled in the proprieties of sportsmanship, posture, eye-contact, dealing with obstreperous male fans, and even choice of deodorant.

Once the women actually began playing, it was obvious that AAGPBL's most powerful selling angle was neither the stellar lineup of male managers nor the mildly provocative uniforms, but the players themselves. "We made believers out of [the fans] by playing great, hard-nosed baseball," remembered Pepper Paire Davis. "Then they fell in love with us and we became part of their towns. Whole family entertainment." Despite strong fan and media support, by the end of the 1944 season P.K. Wrigley had concluded that there was no pressing need to remain in the women's baseball business; Major League Baseball was still as popular as ever, and public morale had never been higher. He sold the AAGPBL to the league's co-creator Arthur Meyerhoff,

who, even more so than Wrigley, appreciated the value of the "Big Sell." It was during Meyerhoff's regime that the League truly hit its stride; expanding the number of teams and spearheading a huge all-out publicity blitz, the new owner increased average attendance nearly 200 percent. The League's best year was 1948, when it attracted close to one million fans.

While it might be politically expedient to suggest that professional women's baseball ultimately faded away because those Evil Male Chauvinist Pigs lost interest once the big Major League names returned from the war, according to most historians the AAGPBL began losing money because several of its teams reverted to local rather than League control in 1951. Also, fewer and fewer women were going out for professional baseball in the postwar years, with many potential players opting for marriage, college, or year-round jobs which afforded better pay. In 1954, with dwindling attendance and a roster of aging and secondstring talent, the AAGPBL was dissolved.

Within a few years, the League had been all but forgotten by most baseball fans. The team members themselves regarded their years in uniform in much the same way that male veterans looked back upon World War II: many chose to treat their ballplaying careers as a closed book, discussing the matter as little as possible; while many others considered the experience as one of the greatest and most significant in their lives, and enthusiastically passed along their fondest memories to their children and grandchildren.

In this latter category was Canadianborn Helen Callaghan, who played with the Minneapolis Millerettes in 1944, and with the Fort Wayne Daisies from 1945 to 1948, alongside her older sister Marge. Helen, who also played under her married name Candaele, was known as "The Ted Williams of Women's Baseball"—a durable, consistent player who racked up a lifetime batting average of .257 (.299 in 1945 alone) and stole 354 bases in 388 games. (Sister Marge was likewise an excellent player, leading the league in fielding percentage on second and third base in 1944 and 1945.) After ending her career, Helen concentrated on raising her five sons, one of whom grew up to be Casey Candaele of the Houston Astros.

Another son, Kelly Candaele, became a professor of history and political science with the Los Angeles College Community District. In 1986, Kelly told his mother that her life story would make a fascinating TV documentary. In collaboration with Kim Wilson, Kelly put together an hour-long montage of newsreel clips and interviews with his mother and other AAGPBL veterans; the end result, *A League of Their Own*, was distributed by Community Television of Southern California, ultimately achieving national viewership when it was picked up by PBS in 1987. This documentary led to a widespread resurgence of interest in the long-defunct League. In October of 1988, with scores of surviving ballplayers and their families in attendance, a special "Women in Baseball" exhibit was dedicated at the Baseball Hall of Fame in Cooperstown.

Among those who had been enthralled by *A League of Their Own* during its PBS go-round was onetime *Laverne and Shirley* star Penny Marshall, who had recently put her acting career on hold to become a film director. The outstanding box office performance of her first major release, *Big*, in June 1988 had given Marshall enough clout to pick and choose her future film projects—and she was determined that one of those projects would serve as a paean to the AAGPBL. If nothing else, the filmed saga of the League would vividly dramatize the triumphs and heartaches of courageous women struggling to succeed in a man's business, something with which Marshall, one of a mere handful of successful women directors, could empathize with 100 percent.

Attending the Women in Baseball induction at Cooperstown, Marshall interviewed a number of the former players, gleaning many of the ideas and anecdotes that would eventually work their way into her film. She also singled out two women who would serve as her technical advisors: the aforementioned Pepper Davis, and Terry Donahue, who had played for the League's team in Melavel, Saskatchewan. "It's a subject nobody knew about. A baseball league existed, but *nobody knew about it*," Marshall later remarked. "I felt I owed it to the league's real players to get this movie done. And because of my situation, I'm the only person who could do it." At the time, however, Marshall was deep into preparation for her next film directorial assignment, *Awakenings*. While this project was taking shape, a pair of young TV producers, Bill Pace and Ronnie Clemmer, had formed their own company, Longbow Productions. Like Marshall, Pace and Clemmer had been attracted to the story of the AAGPBL. Attending a players' reunion in mid–1989, the two producers successfully negotiated the screen rights for a dramatized version of Candaele and Wilson's *League of Their Own* documentary. By the time Marshall was finally able to redirect her attention to her own AAGPBL proposal, she was compelled to strike a deal with Longbow, which included affording Pace and Clemmer a co-producer screen credit.

Judging from Longbow's later made-for–TV efforts—notably 1992's *A Private Matter*, the story of abortion-rights pioneer Sherry Finkbine—Pace and Clemmer had had a serious "message" film in mind. Marshall opted instead to fashion a sentimental comedy with dramatic undertones in the manner of her earlier hit *Big*. She engaged the services of screenwriters Lowell Ganz and Babaloo Mandel, a team with a successful track record in the realm of quirky, offbeat comedies, primarily their collaborations with director Ron Howard (*Nightshift*,

Splash, Parenthood et al.). The fact that the project had its roots in the Kelly Candaele-Kim Wilson documentary was acknowledged by giving Candaele and Wilson an "original story" credit, though their actual creative input in the Marshall film would be minimal.

Too busy with *Awakenings* to do anything more than executive-produce *A League of Their Own*, Marshall chose TV-series veteran David Anspaugh to direct the film. Anspaugh had already demonstrated a gift for parlaying sports and nostalgia into big box-office profits with his theatrical feature debut *Hoosiers* (1986), the story of a 1950s-era high school basketball coach. *League* was pitched to 20th Century–Fox, who agreed to bankroll and release the picture provided that Marshall line up major stars for the leading roles. Though Marshall had originally wanted to use unknowns, she agreed to Fox's selection of Demi Moore and Daryl Hannah to play the characters based on Helen and Marge Callaghan. But when Moore and Hannah became tied up with other movie commitments, Fox relegated the film to "development hell," finally canceling the project and writing off its initial $5 million investment as a loss.

By now as doggedly determined to get the film off the ground as the ladies of the AAGPBL had been to prove their worth to skeptical male baseball fans, Marshall shopped *League of Their Own* to Columbia Pictures, which was already committed to distribute *Awakenings*. Marshall still felt she was too busy to direct as well as produce, so the megaphone was handed over to Alan J. Pakula, whose only previous foray into baseball films had been as producer of the 1957 Jimmy Piersall biopic *Fear Strikes Out* (q.v.). Like Fox, Columbia wanted big names in the leads, so the producers lined up Debra Winger, a two-time Academy Award nominee (*An Officer and a Gentleman* and *Terms of Endearment*) to play the Helen Callaghan counterpart, Dottie Keller Hinson—

a character name obviously chosen as a tribute to champion AAGPBL first baseman Dottie Kamenshek, who, during her nine seasons with the Rockford Peaches, accumulated a lifetime batting average of .292. For the part of Dottie's sister and teammate Kit (who, unlike Marge Callaghan, was for plot purposes the *younger* sister), Marshall had initially intended to honor her original concept of hiring unknowns by casting Moira Kelly, a 22-year-old TV actress who had never before appeared in a theatrical film. Unfortunately, Kelly was injured while shooting the made-for–TV movie *The Edge*, so the role of Kit went to Lori Petty, who was likewise a relatively unfamiliar face (her first actual starring appearance in *Point Break* would not hit the screens until 1991).

While the female characters were to be the focal point of the story, there was an unspoken agreement that the film would require a bankable male actor in the principal role of boorish, bibulous team manager Jimmy Dugan. Originally written to be played by a man in his late forties, Dugan was "younged up" to attract a potential star name. When the film was first being considered by 20th Century–Fox, the role of Dugan had been slated for Jim Belushi, who, since the death of his brother John, had all but cornered the market in lovable-slob roles. By the time *League of Their Own* had been optioned by Columbia, Belushi was no longer available, and several potential replacements let it be known that they had no interest in playing a character who didn't show up until 30 minutes into the film, and who, despite receiving top billing and several showcase scenes, would end up subordinate to the female leads. Happily, there was one actor in Hollywood secure enough in his talent and star appeal to tackle the part of Jimmy Dugan without fretting over the character's comparatively limited amount of screen time. That actor was Tom Hanks, who in a sense "owed" his starring career to the *League of Their Own* team: One of Hanks' earliest film successes had been 1984's *Splash*, written by Lowell Ganz and Babaloo Mandel; and the actor's breakthrough film had been 1988's *Big*, directed by Penny Marshall.

Welcoming the opportunity to show off his own baseball skills (albeit briefly), Hanks was also pleased that the character of Jimmy Dugan would provide him with a refreshing break from his established nice-guy image. "It's the kind of role they never, ever give me," he explained at the time. "They just want me to be charming and youthful and naïve. I don't want to go to the charm bank too many times." He also joked that he would have been crazy not to jump at the opportunity to spend his summer working with dozens of attractive actresses—the sort of quip that only an actor with a famously secure and solid marital relationship could make without prompting the gossipmongers to rush to their fax machines. Finally, there was a more pragmatic reason that Hanks agreed to play Jimmy Dugan; except for an uncredited cameo in *Radio Flyer*, he had been in a self-imposed exile from the screen ever since that disaster of disasters, *Bonfire of the Vanities* (1990), and was in dire need of a hit film to re-establish himself.

But would *A League of Their Own* indeed *be* a hit? While Tom Hanks seemed confident, Columbia was trepidatious. As noted so often in this book, baseball films were not guaranteed audience magnets. Though the triple-play combination of *Bull Durham*, *Field of Dreams* and *Major League* had reaped enormous profits a few years earlier, all three of those films had been produced on modest budgets. There had not been a big-budget baseball picture since 1984's *The Natural*, which, though a money-maker, was not a spectacular success. With a starting price tag of $40 million, *A League of Their Own* was going to be the most expensive baseball film ever made; thus the nervous Columbia execs could only cross their fingers, grit their teeth and pray that Penny Marshall knew what she was doing.

Just before rehearsals began in May of 1991, extensive tryouts were held for the actresses who would play the ballplayers in the film. "You couldn't get into a batting cage in L.A. for two weeks," remembered Lori Petty. "Famous, famous women were out there putting their quarters in." Soon the Hollywood media was abuzz with mostly apocryphal stories about auditioning actresses who'd been sent home in disgrace after grabbing the wrong end of the bat or bitching because they'd ruined their nails while trading pitches. Eventually, some 200 finalists were recruited from Los Angeles, New York City and Chicago, then put through their paces by USC and Olympic athletics coach Rod Dedeaux. Though he knew that the female leads would have to be cut some slack, Dedeaux let it be known that he would be extremely demanding with the candidates for the supporting, bit and extra roles: "I have a passion against faking baseball movies and the producers assured me they wanted realism."

One of the few auditionees who survived the first cut was comedienne Rosie O'Donnell, who, though she had not yet appeared in a film, had been playing baseball for nearly all of her 29 years. Director Marshall was so impressed by O'Donnell's ballfield performance that she immediately cast her in the role of third baseman Doris Murphy, who as originally written was a curvaceous hot-to-trot sexpot. Though undeniably appealing, the charmingly chubby O'Donnell was not exactly the temptress type, so the character was rewritten to accommodate Rosie's appearance, effusive personality and acerbic comic edge. When Rosie O'Donnell's Doris Murphy dices the League's short skirted uniforms by grousing, "We're ballplayers—not ballerinas!" the fusing of actress and character is total and inextricable.

In contrast to O'Donnell, two of the

other supporting actresses were not natural athletes, though their ballplaying skills showed promise. Even if this hadn't been the case, their casting was a done deal: Left fielder "Betty Spaghetti" Horn would be played by Penny Marshall's daughter Tracy Reiner, and outfielder "Mumbles" Brockleman would be essayed by Marshall's sister Kathleen. Marshall had no qualms about nepotism, inasmuch as her own early acting career had been helped along by the industry pull of her older brother, producer-writer Garry Marshall—who *also* appeared in *A League of Their Own*, in the P.K. Wrigleyesque role of "candy king" Walter Harvey. Once on the set, Penny Marshall treated her family members the same as the other actors, expecting no less a degree of hard work and dedication. Tracy Reiner and the two "other" Marshalls responded by delivering faultless performances, with Reiner a standout in a role which spanned the spectrum from wide-eyed ingenuousness to heartrending emotionalism.

By mid–May, most of the cast was in place and baseball workouts had begun, using the smaller gloves, wooden bats and flannel uniforms indigenous to the 1940s (in one respect, however, accuracy gave way to practicality: sponge baseballs were used to avoid concussions). All signs indicated that filming would commence the second week in June, as scheduled. Then on May 18 a central pivot slipped out of the mechanism when actress Debra Winger walked off the project. Several reasons have been postulated for Winger's exit, but the popular consensus is that she left upon learning that Columbia wanted to hype the film's box-office appeal by hiring pop-music phenomenon Madonna, fresh from her well-received star turn in *Dick Tracy* (1990), to play the secondary role of center fielder Mae "All-the-Way" Mordalino. Apparently, Debra Winger felt that there was room for only one diva on the set of *A League of Their Own*, so she removed herself from the running—

and when Winger exited, so did director Alan J. Pakula.

The Pakula predicament was quickly solved when a reluctant but resigned Penny Marshall placed herself in the director's chair. Finding someone to fill Debra Winger's cleats would be more difficult, since whoever was chosen as replacement would have to undergo a crash course in baseball to keep apace with the rest of the cast, who'd already been working and playing ball together six days a week for three weeks—and principal photography was less than a month away. The producers put in a call to statuesque leading lady Geena Davis, who, like Debra Winger, was a certified "name," and who, like Winger, had previously been nominated for an Academy Award (*The Accidental Tourist*, 1988)—the difference being that Davis had won the prize. As Davis remembered it, "I got this call, 'Can you come like *tomorrow* to Chicago and do this movie?'" At first, she admitted, the assignment was "daunting," because the other actresses were not only miles ahead of her in baseball know-how but had already bonded into a closely-knit ensemble; "but I think I thrive on challenge, on seemingly impossible tasks." With no time for fun and games, Davis squirreled herself away in her dressing room to study the script, and spent all her "outside" hours training on the ballfield. The other cast members and the crew personnel tried to be supportive, offering baseball tips whenever Davis took a breather. Soon, however, she found that this well-meaning but unsolicited input was spoiling her concentration, so she erected a sign outside her dressing room door: NO ONE MAY TELL GEENA HOW TO PLAY ANYMORE.

By the time filming began, Geena Davis had pulled herself up to everyone's playing level, and then some: "The others had an advantage over me, but in the end I *slaughtered* them." So confident was the actress of her ballplaying capabilities that,

Geena Davis in full regalia as Dottie Hinson, "Queen of Diamonds."

when her stunt double proved unable to execute a tricky behind-the-back catch in one scene, Davis pulled off the feat herself—in a single take. Beyond her total immersion into the role of Dottie, Davis brought along an unexpected bonus when she signed for the film: One week after her arrival in Chicago, the actress' most recent film, *Thelma and Louise*, opened nationwide; its subsequent spectacular success increased Davis' bankability—and, by extension, the potential bankability of *A League of Their Own*—ten times over.

Just before Geena Davis joined the cast, her costar Madonna arrived in Chicago to undergo her basic ballfield training. At first noncommittal to the project, the singer was persuaded to accept the role of Mae by supporting actress Rosie O'Donnell, who had approached Madonna at the behest of Penny Marshall (like many others in the industry, Marshall tended to be weak-kneed and tongue-tied in the commanding presence of the Material Girl; remember Kevin Costner's bashful hemming and hawing in the 1991 documentary *Truth or Dare?*). Madonna tackled her new assignment with the same ferocious intensity and concentration that she applied to her music; indeed, she worked so hard in batting practice that her hands blistered and bled. The film's baseball coach, William E. Hughes, was so impressed by Madonna's stick-to-itiveness that he rushed out a statement to the press: "She has a burning desire to excel at the job. Nobody, *nobody* works like she does. Wore me out."

The training-and-coaching process continued as filming commenced in early June, with a few establishing and atmosphere sequences staged at USC's Dedeaux Field. One of the first location stops for the production crew was Chicago's Wrigley Field, for the tryout scenes in which the aspiring ballplayers were whittled down to 64 finalists and organized into the first four AAGPBL teams: the Rockford Peaches, the

Racine Belles, the Kenosha Comets and the South Bend Blue Sox. Every person involved in these scenes has recalled her feelings of awe and reverence while playing baseball within the hallowed walls of Wrigley. Some of the participants, notably actress Robin Knight (cast as shortstop "Beans" Babbitt), brought along plastic bags for the purpose of scooping up souvenir dirt from the Wrigley diamond.

Also filmed in the Chicago area was the "jitterbug" sequence, with FitzGerald's Pub in Berwyn, Illinois, substituting for the Suds Bucket roadhouse where "All-the-Way" Mae energetically cuts a rug with several overheated dance partners, and where woebegone second baseman Marla Hooch (Megan Cavanagh), her inhibitions shed with the help of a few good stiff drinks, belts out a deathless rendition of "It Had to Be You," winning the heart of her future husband Nelson (Alan Wilder). FitzGerald's was closed down three weeks to shoot a sequence that lasted only five minutes or so on screen; but the owners didn't complain, since the 1940s-style stage backdrop painted for the film turned out to be a lucrative tourist attraction for several years to come.

Elsewhere in the same general vicinity, the train-depot sequences involving Dottie, Kit, Marla Hooch and team recruiter Ernie Capadino (Jon Lovitz) were lensed at the Illinois Railway Museum in the town of Union (see notes on the use of the same location in *The Babe* [q.v.]). The old Nebraska Zephyr, standing in for the Oregon Zephyr, which transports Dottie and Kit to the Windy City, was shown chugging down a lengthy expanse of the I.R.M.'s private tracks. Also, the museum's main building doubled for the high school in Fort Collins, Colorado, where Marla Hooch is first seen demonstrating her switch-hitting talents—indoors!

Since most of the characters in the film were associated with the Rockford

Peaches, some consideration was given early on to using the Peaches' actual stamping grounds, Rockford, Illinois', Beyer Field. Unfortunately, the structure was dilapidated beyond repair, so the crew set up shop in Evansville, Indiana, home of Bosse Field. Built in 1915, and with a seating capacity of 5,000, Bosse was not only in excellent condition, but it could pass as a genuine 1940s ballpark with only a minimum of redressing. The owners of Bosse agreed upon a daily rental fee and a few other considerations, including a $20,000 grant and a brand-new scoreboard. Used for some of the "away" games was League Field in Huntingburg, Indiana, while a Victorian-style residence in nearby Henderson, Kentucky, was pressed into service as the Rockford boarding house where the Peaches were billeted during the baseball season.

The ballgame sequences at Bosse Field were shot in July during a devastating heat wave, with temperatures hovering between 106 and 110 degrees. At first it was no problem to gather local citizens to impersonate the fans in the stands (though, in lieu of the huge crowds required for the final play-off scenes, the prop department placed dummies and cardboard cutouts in the empty seats, á la *Eight Men Out* [q.v.]), but after a few days of wearisome stop-and-start filmmaking, coupled with the oppressive humidity, many of the ersatz extras lost their enthusiasm for being in the movies. To keep up morale, Tom Hanks joked with the crowd, put on impromptu puppet shows, and led cheers with megaphone in hand. Rosie O'Donnell participated in these pep rallies by singing show tunes and songs popularized by her costar Madonna, while even the relatively reclusive Geena Davis pitched in with her own peculiar renditions of Queen's "Bohemian Rhapsody" and highlights from *Jesus Christ Superstar*.

The locals weren't the only ones who needed to have their spirits uplifted. By mid–July, the film was already several days behind schedule, and the budget had bloated well beyond the original limit. Many of the costly delays can be attributed to on-set injuries: Megan Cavanagh and Tracy Reiner suffered concussions during sliding practice, Rosie O'Donnell stumbled over a sound cable, another actress nearly broke her nose, and so on. In an odd turn of events, these war wounds added to the overall realism of *A League of Their Own*. Whenever one of the film's characters is shown with an injury of any kind, it is invariably a real-life injury sustained during the filming process. Thus, when "Betty Spaghetti" is shown nursing a nasty bruise on her leg, and when Kit Keller casually reveals that every finger on her right hand is individually bandaged, be assured that these little touches of authenticity were *not* created by the makeup department.

Another contributor to the schedule overrun was director Penny Marshall, who, in the tradition of the late great Sam Wood (see individual entries for Wood's *Pride of the Yankees* and *The Stratton Story*), insisted upon shooting every scene—even the shortest of inserts—a minimum of ten to twenty times. Marshall herself adamantly defended her obsession with multiple retakes, proclaiming, "I don't do retakes! I do coverage, coverage!" ("Coverage" refers to shooting a scene from every conceivable angle, so that the editing department won't come up short when assembling that scene for the work print.) Whatever the terminology, Marshall's repetitious technique tended to push her more sensitive actors to the boiling point, as did her apparent indecisiveness when staging difficult scenes and her reluctance to provide actors with character motivation. Virtually everyone from the cast of *A League of Their Own* can still perform a devastatingly accurate imitation of Penny Marshall, perfectly duplicating her singsong nasal whine and her tendency to mumble when she wasn't entirely certain of the thought she was trying to convey.

To her credit, Marshall has always been the first to admit that she is not keen on working under pressure, and has been known to cheerfully refer to herself as "the antidirector." Miraculously, her technique has nearly always brought out the best in her performers. Tom Hanks has attempted to explain this phenomenon: "She can drive me crazy, making you do things one-hundred thousand times. But Penny's passive personality gives a collective feeling on the set instead of the idea that the director is God." Elaborating on this, both Geena Davis and Rosie O'Donnell have observed that there were certain problematic scenes that worked only because the actresses were allowed to arrive at the solutions themselves, without Marshall interfering with their creative processes. A collective spirit, the pride inherent in solving one's own problems: Wasn't that what Professional Women's Baseball was all about?

Except for a few minor temper flare-ups and the anticipated mood swings, the cast and crew of A *League of Their Own* got along splendidly, an important consideration when several high-strung people are obliged to work together in close proximity six days per week. Tom Hanks in particular thrived on the experience, even showing up on days that he wasn't needed to participate in the baseball practice sessions and to serve as unofficial second-unit director for the crowd scenes. In a later TV interview, Hanks insisted that the thrill of wearing his uniform and walking out onto the ballfield was "electrifying," claiming that sometimes he forgot he was play-acting: "I'm out here, I'm not *really* one of the guys—but I'm out here, and I *am* one of the guys!" Upon hearing this, costar Lori Petty quipped that Hanks was more like "one of the girls"—a remark that in any other circumstances might have been misconstrued as an insult, but which here underlined the team spirit which pervaded the film.

The actors' relationship with the peo-ple of Evansville, however, was not always so harmonious. Upon their arrival in the Indiana metropolis, the performers were impressed by the generosity and hospitality of the locals; but as production dragged on through the summer, the moviemakers and the "civilians" tended to get on each other's nerves. Mostly, the Evansville people were miffed that not everyone in the cast was as friendly as Tom Hanks, who remained courteous and outgoing even when gawkers gathered around while he was busy devouring hot dogs and ice cream at a local Dairy Queen so that he would gain the extra 20 to 40 pounds necessary to play the bloated Jimmy Dugan (many of the actresses were envious of Hanks in this respect, since they'd been ordered to shed their excess baggage). In contrast, Madonna exhibited her usual Garboesque desire for total privacy; making a point of avoiding fans and ignoring requests for autographs and pictures, she further distanced herself from the public by declining invitations from her fellow cast members to congregate at their favorite Evansville nightspots. The locals tolerated Madonna's aloofness until that fateful day when, in a *TV Guide* interview, she compared filming a movie in Evansville to working "in Prague" (among her biggest complaints was that her hotel room had not been wired for the MTV cable service). The citizenry was outraged at this disparaging remark, and before long certain locals were taking out their displeasure with Madonna upon the rest of the cast in the form of cold shoulders, catcalls and veiled threats. Even the affable Tom Hanks was forced to hire bodyguards after one Evansville resident took loud and profane umbrage at an imagined slight.

Once the Evansville scenes were finished, Penny Marshall filmed the epilogue, set during the 1988 Women in Baseball induction ceremony, on location in Cooperstown, New York. Nine weeks over schedule and $10 million over budget, A *League of Their Own* was finally in the can on October 30, 1991. The sneak-preview cycle began in early 1992, in anticipation of the announced midsummer release date. Following the advice of her older brother Gary, Penny Marshall clocked the number of laughs at each preview, periodically juicing up the film's comedy content by dubbing in new lines of dialogue—especially in the early scenes with Jon Lovitz as the caustic Ernie Capadino, which always seemed to go over particularly well with the crowds.

The final sequence in the prerelease version of *A League of Their Own* showed the elderly Dottie Hinson and her former baseball-playing buddies enjoying an emotional reunion at Cooperstown, followed by an impromptu game of baseball featuring actual veterans of the AAGPBL. By rights, every hankie in the theater should have been drenched with tears at this point, but for some reason the finale left the preview audiences cold. Again it was Gary Marshall who came to sister Penny's aid, pointing out that the audience was less interested in seeing a bunch of old ladies in baseball caps than in finding out whether or not Dottie Hinson had ever resolved her differences with her younger sister Kit. Promptly acting upon her brother's advice, Penny Marshall went back and shot an additional locker-room sequence with the younger Dottie and Kit, set immediately after the tie-breaking World Series game, in which the girls patched up their quarrel and embraced each other. The director then reengaged the services of the actresses playing the older Dottie and Kit, and lensed an additional "Cooperstown" scene which clarified the point that the two siblings were still on the best of terms after 45 years. These emendations made all the difference: Once audiences were assured that the sisters' relationship had mended, they were able to focus on the Cooperstown finale without any distractions—and there was nary a dry eye in the house.

Of course, these additions meant that other scenes in the film would have to be trimmed to keep the running time down to a manageable length. Among the casualties were a handful of scenes involving Jon Lovitz, which is why the character of Ernie Capadino disappears 25 minutes into the story.

One proposed sequence was excised before it ever went before the cameras. During the early scripting stages, it was planned for the married Dottie Hinson to have a quickie sexual relationship with randy manager Jimmy Dugan. Ultimately, the filmmakers decided that the film worked better without Dottie's extramarital fling, and it was written out of the picture—thankfully so, since otherwise Dottie's tender reunion with her wounded war-hero husband Bob (Bill Pullman, in one of his many "Ralph Bellamy" roles of the 1990s) would have been cast in a somewhat unsavory light. Tom Hanks for one was happy that the Dottie/Jimmy fling was dispensed with: "I thought it was great that [the film] did nothing to adhere to the usual formulaic relationship between a guy and a woman.... The story of my guy's side was that he respected Geena Davis' character, who proved she was a ballplayer. I thought that to stick to that was a cool thing."

Ushered in with a huge pre-release publicity juggernaut on such TV cable services as HBO, VH-1 and QVC (where Penny Marshall auctioned off tie-in merchandise from the film), *A League of Their Own* opened nationwide on July 1, 1992. Before discussing the finished film, it might be worth our while to analyze its overall accuracy. For starters, did the women in the film play baseball anywhere near as well as their real-life counterparts?

In the early stages of filming, *Entertainment Weekly* interviewed David Strathairn, who played Ira Lowenstein, the character based on AAGPBL cofounder Arthur Meyerhoff. Having previously portrayed

Eddie Cicotte in John Sayles' painstakingly authentic historical baseball drama *Eight Men Out* (q.v.), Strathairn was as good a judge as any of the ladies' ballplaying skills. A true diplomat, the actor said merely, "From the evidence I've seen, some of the women in this film are playing very good baseball." After filming wrapped, however, Tom Hanks offered a somewhat different perspective: Asked if the women could *really* play ball, Hanks bluntly replied, "No more than Superman could really fly. This absolutely required the magic of motion-picture making." He then chuckled, indicating that he was having a bit of fun at the girls' expense, and allowed that Rosie O'Donnell was an "excellent player," Lori Petty a "fierce pitcher," Robin Knight "a baseball player, pure and simple," and Freddie Simpson (cast as beauty queen-cum-shortstop Ellen Sue Gotlander) was "so authentic a player that she dipped Skoal." Technical advisor Pepper Paire Davis concurred with Hanks, giving the highest marks to O'Donnell, Knight and Simpson. The film itself reveals that Hanks was not far wrong in stating that motion-picture magic saw many of the actresses through the tougher ballplaying scenes; on the other hand, all of the performers look so good and so confident on the diamond that the viewer is willing to accept the cinematic manipulations of director Penny Marshall and editors Adam Bernardi and George Bowers in the key sequences.

And how about the film's *historical* accuracy? Again, Pepper Paire Davis: "[The film] was 70–80 percent of the truth—manipulated truth because of a money and time element. But Penny listened to a lot I had to say. They read my scrapbooks, heard my stories and songs—and the young girls became All Americans.... They realized it was a true story and the truth came through." And here's another AAGPBL alumnus, Helen "Gig" Smith: "*A League of Their Own* had a little of Hollywood in it.... Still, the movie was basically on target."

Although the names of the actual teams were retained in the film (the Rockford Peaches, the Racine Belles et. al.), the names of the players, managers and team owners were all changed to allow for a certain degree of dramatic license. Some of the actual accomplishments of the genuine League participants were attributed to others in the film: "The All-American Girls Professional Baseball League Song," the stirring anthem written and performed on screen by fictional Rockford Peaches shortstop Ellen Sue Gotlander, was actually composed by the ubiquitous Pepper Paire Davis. And several episodes in the film had indeed occurred, but not in the same timeframe as the story. For example, the characters of Evelyn Gardner (Bitty Schram) and her obnoxious offspring "Stilwell Angel" (Justin Scheller) were based upon center fielder Pat Keagle of the Grand Rapids Chicks and the noisy, red-haired son whom she was forced to drag along with her from game to game. But Keagle did this in 1948, some five years after the events in *A League of Their Own*.

The most liberties were taken with the real-life Major Leaguer upon whom the character of Jimmy Dugan was based: Jimmie Foxx, catcher/first baseman for the Philadelphia Athletics from 1925 to 1935 and the Boston Red Sox from 1936 to 1941. A three-time MVP, Foxx played on ten All-Star teams, and in 1932 slugged out 58 home runs, falling short of Ruth's record only because of a wrist injury in August of that year. Ranking ninth on the list of home-run sluggers (534), sixth in RBIs (1,921) and fourth in batting percentage (.609), Foxx might have done even better were it not for his love affair with the bottle. Retiring after a disappointing 1942 season with the Chicago Cubs, he was brought out of mothballs in 1944 due to the wartime shortage of seasoned players. After brief stints with the Cubs and the Philadelphia Phillies, he ended his playing days in 1945. Spending his final years in a variety of baseball-related pursuits, from coaching minor league teams to serving as radio sportscaster for the Red Sox, Foxx nonetheless ended up penniless due to his excessive drinking, his bad business ventures and his boundless generosity towards his fellow players. But though he was broke, he was never bitter: In the words of sportswriter Al Hirshberg, "Foxx hated no one and no one hated him." He died in 1967 (twenty years before the demise of the fictional Jimmy Dugan) after choking on his food at a restaurant.

Asked if *A League of Their Own* offered an accurate portrayal of Jimmie Foxx, Pepper Paire Davis replied, "Yes and no." Yes, he did manage the Fort Wayne Daisies for a single season; yes, he did spend most of the summer in a drunken stupor, obliviously snoozing away while the players ran the ballclub; and yes, the team won the Pennant that year all the same. But Foxx was not (as Tom Hanks was apparently led to believe) among the first of the Major League greats to manage an AAGPBL team; in fact, he wasn't even signed by the Daisies until 1952. And, unlike Jimmy Dugan, Foxx was anything but an obnoxious, sexist, short-tempered, self-pitying vulgarian. According to all the women who worked with him, he was kind, generous, exceedingly patient—and in the words of Pepper Davis, "he was a gentleman!"

Acknowledging that it was dramatically necessary to alter the character of Jimmy Dugan—it would have been pretty dull for the ballplayers to prove their salt to someone who already liked them and treated them respectfully—makes it easier to accept another, more blatant historical distortion in the film. Most of the surviving AAGPBL members insist that they managed to win over the doubting fans by playing serious, top-dollar baseball. In *A League of Their Own*, however, it is flatly stated that the crowds began to respond only when the ladies began indulging in razzle-dazzle showmanship: ostentatiously seeking out "cheesecake" photo ops, performing spectacular splits and cartwheels on the diamond, showering kisses on any man lucky enough to catch a pop fly, practicing their pitching skills by knocking over cardboard caricatures of Hitler, Mussolini and Tojo, and so on. While this minimizes the genuine accomplishments of the League members, the film nonetheless arrives at a basic, fundamental truth: Stuck in a male-conceived, male-controlled and male-dominated professional situation, the girls of the AAGPBL only began to flourish when they themselves took full charge of the ballfield.

Outside of the baseball scenes, the film maintained an acceptable degree of historical verisimilitude, from the "A" gas-ration sticker on Bob Hinson's old Ford to the roadside Burma Shave signs. Happily, the filmmakers by and large avoided the temptation to impose 1990s sensibilities on a 1940s story. Ira Lowenstein's impassioned speech to Walter Harvey, urging his boss not to abruptly rob the AAGPBL players of their chance to play professionally just because the male ballplayers would soon be coming home, could be construed as an example of premature feminism, but Lowenstein says nothing that wasn't actually being said in the more enlightened magazine and newspaper editorials of the era. And the wonderful moment in which a black female spectator exhibits a dynamite pitching arm when she returns a foul ball to Dottie Hinson, nodding her head knowingly as if to say "Our time is coming, sister!," is well in line with the blossoming civil rights movement of the War years. Admittedly, most of the male characters fall into the two standard 1990s-movie categories, Crass Clod or Sensitive Soul; only Jimmy Dugan truly develops as a human being, though he demonstrates that he hasn't *completely* seen the light by evoking memories of his latest sexual conquest while leading the team in prayer just before the deciding Series game! And Harry Shearer's offscreen newsreel narrator is a lot more mocking and sarcastic when describing the aspirations of the female players than was customary in actual newsreels of the era, though the film was right on target when pointing out that the media of 1940s was more concerned with "leg art" than with treating women seriously. (Film buffs must have gotten a hearty chuckle out of the "Columbia Moviescope" vignettes, amused by the presumption that parsimonious Columbia Pictures boss Harry Cohn would ever have bankrolled a newsreel department.)

The only glaring inaccuracy occurs in the scene where "Betty Spaghetti" finds out that her husband has been killed in the War. Granted, the scene serves an important narrative purpose by providing an additional emotional layer to the subsequent reunion between Bob and Dottie Hinson—which in turn leads into Dottie's temporary decision to give up baseball in favor of domesticity, and culminates in her eleventh hour return to the Peaches during the World Series. Well and good, but the staging of the scene is ludicrous. An insolent, insensitive Western Union boy barges into the Peaches' locker room, and in full view of the entire team gripes about having to deliver "We Deeply Regret" wires from the War Department. Unable to remember which of the women is to receive the wire, he abruptly elects to scoot back to the telegraph office for further instructions. Angrily grabbing all the telegrams from the protesting messenger, Jimmy Dugan slowly walks over to Dottie and Betty, who happen to be sitting side by side, while both women—and the audience—agonize over which of the two has become a war widow. Anyone who was alive in the early 1940s will remember that a death-notice telegram was *never* delivered in this fashion. First off, no delivery boy worthy of his uniform would have behaved in so callous a fashion; all

Western Union employees were painstakingly drilled in the proper manner of imparting bad news, especially to women, and were advised to deliver this news when the recipient was alone or surrounded by her immediate family, preferably at her place of residence. Even when the messenger was obliged to show up at the woman's workplace, her boss would compassionately take her into his office, shut the door and hand over the telegram in private, respecting the woman's right to be alone in her hour of grief. The scene in *A League of Their Own* may have packed a powerful dramatic punch—but it was wrong, wrong, wrong!

As with any box-office success, *A League of Their Own* remained "alive" in the hearts and minds of its fans with an abundance of "Money Scenes" and blockbuster lines of dialogue. Even those who'd only seen the film once harbored fond and rosy memories of former *Saturday Night Live* regular Jon Lovitz making a meal of the role of cigar-smoking, sarcasm-spouting baseball scout Ernie Capadino, a character especially written for him (we prefer to believe that the actor was ad-libbing when, while trying to persuade Dottie Hinson to try out for the League, he turns sharply to a mooing cow in the background and bellows "Will you SHUDDUP?"); Dottie Hinson's unflinching one-handed catch during her first training session, "answered" later on when Doris Murphy manages to grab a hot dog in her teeth while recovering a fly ball; the besotted Jimmy Dugan stumbling into the girls' locker room, making his way to the toilet stalls and uninterruptedly relieving himself while the dumbstruck ladies clock the duration of his golden shower (though amused by this gag, AAGPBL veteran Helen Smith observed, "if the manager had come into our locker room and urinated for fifteen minutes, we would have thrown him out bodily"); Dottie and Jimmy's "dueling signals" during an important game; "All-the-Way" Mae's uninhibited jitterbugging at the Suds Bucket (irrefutable proof that Madonna is capable of exuding sex appeal even while wearing an unbecoming black wig, a shapeless print dress and bobby socks); Mae's later offer to pump up ticket sales by "accidentally" exposing her bosoms to the men in the grandstands, to which Doris Murphy harrumphs, "Ya think there are men in this country who ain't seen your bosoms?"; the caterpillar-to-butterfly evolution of gormless Marla Hooch, followed by her wedding ceremony where Marla's teammates hold their bats aloft in the manner of military swords; the prepubescent rampages of Evelyn's demonic son "Stilwell Angel," and Jimmy's immensely satisfying retribution against the little monster; and the climactic display of mutual respect and admiration between the rejuvenated Jimmy Dugan and the Women of Baseball.

Garnering a sizeable amount of audience and critical attention were the framing sequences at the beginning and end of the film, in which the sexagenarian Dottie Hinson nervously girds herself for the induction ceremony at Cooperstown, then has a thoroughly wonderful time catching up with her old friends and teammates, pausing for the occasional moment of dewy-eyed wistfulness when informed that at least two of her beloved former colleagues have passed away. Although it was well publicized that the elderly actresses cast as the 1988 versions of Kit, Mae, Doris, Marla, Betty et al., had had their dialogue dubbed by the film's stars (whose voices were electronically "aged"), a few impressionable critics could not be dissuaded of the notion that Geena Davis had somehow been cosmetically altered so that she could portray the older Dottie. Beyond that, it was rumored that the older versions of the younger ballplayers were actually nonprofessionals, chosen exclusively because of their facial and physical resemblance to their youthful counterparts; some observers even chose to believe that *all* of the older women had

been members of the AAGPBL, rather than just those seen during the closing credits.

A little research might have dispelled these misconceptions. Many of the older females were portrayed by veteran character actresses who, though not familiar by name, had been extremely active over the previous several decades. The older Dottie was enacted by Lynn Cartwright, aka Danielle Carver, who had prominently appeared in such 1950s drive-in fodder as *Cry Baby Killer* (Jack Nicholson's film debut), *Queen of Outer Space* and *The Wasp Woman*; Cartwright was also the wife of B-picture actor, writer, director and cult figure Leo Gordon. Other familiar faces in the closing scenes included Kathleen Butler (the Older Kit), a New York–based actress whose credits included several episodes of TV's *Law & Order*; Betty Miller (the Older Betty), who was seen in such art-house perennials as *The Pope of Greenwich Village* (1984) and *The Wizard of Loneliness* (1988); and Patricia Wilson (the Older Marla), who in 1959 appeared opposite Tom Bosley in the Pulitzer Prize–winning Broadway musical *Fiorello!*, and also played Trixie Norton in a 1962 revival of "The Honeymooners" on Jackie Gleason's *American Scene Magazine*. (Keep an eye peeled for another seasoned character actress in the early scenes on the Keller farm: cast as Dottie and Kit's mother is musical comedy star Rae Allen, the irrepressible Gloria Thorpe in the stage and film versions of *Damn Yankees* [q.v.].)

By far, the single most famous moment in *A League of Their Own* occurs when Jimmy Dugan, outraged that rightfielder Evelyn Gardner responds to his merciless browbeating by bursting into tears, shouts incredulously, "There's no *crying*! There's no crying in *baseball*!" This would become the film's signature line, embossed upon millions of souvenir T-shirts and baseball caps, endlessly replayed as a sound bite on thousands of local radio sports call-in shows, and repeated *ad infinitum* by sportscasters and play-by-play announcers throughout the English-speaking world. In the tradition of such previous trademark lines as *To Be or Not to Be*'s "So they call me Concentration Camp Ehrhardt!" and anticipating such future bon mots as *Jerry Maguire*'s "Show me the money!" it is the artful and multifaceted repetition of the "no crying in baseball" line *within* the film that gives it special permanence. Jimmy Dugan says the line five times, in five different ways, within the course of 60 seconds; and since this moment is the turning point in Jimmy's relationship with his all-girl team, we are literally witnessing the death throes of a confirmed Male Chauvinist, each successive line reading reflecting the traditional stages of Anger, Denial and Resignation. As performed by Tom Hanks, "There's no crying in baseball!" has as many layers of meanings as Othello's obsessive repetition of the phrase "The handkerchief!" And the line still gets laughs when heard today for an entirely different reason: The unabashed public boohooing of such athletes as Sammy Sosa and Mark McGwire has proven conclusively that, let us face it, there *is* crying in baseball.

For my money, however, the *best* line in the film takes place just before Dottie Hinson is about to leave the Peaches high and dry to go on her second honeymoon. By now having achieved a renewed purpose in his own life, Jimmy Dugan chastizes Dottie for her lack of dedication. When Dottie replies wearily that baseball has just gotten "too hard," Jimmy responds, in a faraway voice suggesting that he is speaking as much to himself as to Dottie, "It's supposed to be hard. If it wasn't hard everyone could do it. The hard is what makes it great."

Not since *Pride of the Yankees* had a baseball film contained as many of the established "popular" elements as *A League of Their Own*. And not since *Pride of the Yankees* had a big-budget baseball film performed so far beyond its expectations. Perhaps hoping to temper its popularity with pragmatism and perspective, several critics chose to dwell on the film's handful of shortcomings. Todd McCarthy of *Variety* wrote that the movie "hits about .250 with a few RBI's but more than its share of strikeouts.... Downside includes contrived plotting, obvious comedy and heart-tugging, some hammy thesping and a general hokiness...." Richard Schickel of *Time* magazine allowed that the film was "energetic, full of goodwill and good feelings," but complained that the production went far afield of reality and lacked "the graceful nonchalance and self-confidence with which finely tuned athletes—and comedies—move to enchant us." Schickel also took the film to task for its apparent hypocrisy in insisting that the female characters be accepted for their abilities rather than their looks, only to poke cruel fun at the expense of ugly-duckling Marla Hooch.

For the most part, critical response was positive, if somewhat guarded. Roger Ebert of the *Chicago Sun-Times* observed, "The movie has a real bittersweet charm. The baseball sequences, we've seen before. What's fresh are the personalities of the players, the gradual unfolding of their coach and the way this early chapter of women's liberation fit into the hidebound traditions of professional baseball. By the end, when the women get together again for the reunion, it's touching, the way they have to admit that, whaddaya know, they were pioneers." Peter Travers of *Rolling Stone* magazine wasn't all that crazy over the film's sentimental moments, but noted, "At her best, [Penny] Marshall captures the camaraderie of these women in ways that rip the film out of its clichéd roots. [Geena] Davis, who is terrific, subtly shows us the conflicting emotions of a Forties woman torn between ambition and duty, without patronizing Dottie or her choices." And Rita Kempley of *The Washington Post* wrote, "A

League of Their Own isn't a perfect picture, but it is irresistibly ebullient with not one, but nine Babes on base…. Graced by Davis and enlivened by [Jon] Lovitz and the ensemble cast, it sends us home feeling a little higher, with visions of peanuts and Cracker Jack floating in our heads." All things considered, however, the most gratifying accolade was served up by *Sports Illustrated*: "Nobody in *A League of Their Own* throws like a girl. In fact, everybody throws better than John Goodman did in *The Babe*."

The film posted a domestic gross of $107,458,000, taking its place in the record books as the most profitable baseball movie of all time. Virtually the only aspect of *A League of Their Own* that was not a spectacular success was the inevitable TV-series spin off. Debuting April 10, 1993, on CBS, the weekly half-hour series version of *A League of Their Own* recycled most of the film's characters and settings. Tracy Reiner, Megan Cavanagh and Gary Marshall repeated their screen roles of Betty "Spaghetti" Horn, Marla Hooch and Walter Harvey, while the roles originally played by Tom Hanks, Geena Davis, Lori Petty, Madonna, Rosie O'Donnell and Bitty Schram were filled respectively by Sam McMurray, Carey Lowell, Christine Elise, Wendy Makkena, Katie Rich and Tracy Nelson. Though the opening-night reviews were surprisingly laudatory, and the series benefited from the creative input of executive producer Penny Marshall—who directed one of the episodes, as did Tom Hanks—this *League of Their Own* suffered the same ignominious fate as so many other movie-to-TV transformations. The series was yanked by the network after three showings, its remaining two episodes consigned to the Ratings Siberia of mid–August 1993.

Life's Greatest Game

Emory Johnson Productions/Film Booking Offices; released September 28, 1924

Produced and directed by Emory Johnson. Screenplay by Emilie Johnson. Photography: Paul Perry. Assistant directors: Charles West and Jerry Callahan. 7 reels/7,010 feet; black and white; silent.

Cast: Tom Santschi (Jack Donovan); Jane Thomas (Mary Donovan); Dickie Brandon (Jackie Donovan, Jr., age 3); Johnnie Walker (Jackie Donovan, Jr., age 20); David Kirby (Mike Moran); Gertrude Olmstead (Nora Malone).

Jack Donovan, a player for the 1906 Chicago Cubs, won't throw a big game at the behest of gambler Moran, so Moran retaliates by breaking up Donovan's happy marriage. Mary Donovan and her little son Jackie, Jr., take an ocean voyage and are reported as being lost at sea. Eighteen years later, Jack Donovan is managing for the New York Giants. Jackie, Jr., who, along with his mother, hadn't really drowned after all, leaves college to join the Giants as a pitcher. When he learns that his old man is manager, Jackie, Jr., is incensed, since he has long believed that the elder Donovan had deserted his mother. Spurred by revenge, Jackie, Jr., deliberately loses an important series game—but when he learns that his father still loves him, the boy wins the next game, reuniting his parents in the process.

Life's Greatest Game was cited by Jack Spears in his 1968 *Films in Review* article on baseball movies as one of the first films of its kind to take a realistic look at the game, authentically depicting the rigors of practice and concentrating on the team as a unit rather than eight men led by one star. Critics in 1924 were less enthused; although *Life's Greatest Game* won plaudits for its opening scene, in which 600 extras were convincingly garbed as vintage 1906 ballpark patrons, *Variety* groused about the film's unconvincing splicing together of staged action with newsreel footage of real ballgames. Most New York City reviewers could not understand why this modestly assembled picture was being shown at premium prices in a Broadway movie house, nor why its hackneyed plot was allowed to poke along for a full eighty-two minutes.

Director Emory Johnson was not a baseball buff per se; *Life's Greatest Game* was simply the latest in Johnson's series of "common man" films, dramatizing the lives of those who lived from paycheck to paycheck (which most ballplayers certainly did in 1924). Other films in Emory Johnson's working stiff *oeuvre* included *The Third Alarm, The Westbound Limited, In the Name of the Law,* and an epic that must have resulted in SRO business at the box office, *The Mailman.*

Little Big League

Lobell-Bergman Productions/Castle Rock Entertainment/Columbia; released June 29, 1994

Executive producers: Steve Nicolaides and Andre Bergman. Produced by Mike Lobell. Directed by Andrew Scheinman. Screenplay by Gregory K. Pincus and Adam Scheinman; story by Gregory K. Pincus. Photography: Donald E. Thorin. Production designer: Jeffrey Howard. Edited by Michael Jablow. Casting: Mary Gail Artz, Barbara Cohen. Costume designer: Erica Edell Phillips. Original music: Stanley Clarke. Additional music: Steve Cropper, Booker T. Jones and Jeff Beck. Associate producer: Adam Merins. Production manager: Donna E. Bloom. First assistant director: Mark McGann. Second assistant director: Philip A. Patterson. Music supervisor: Peter Afterman. Set decorator: Ethel Robins Richards. Camera operator: Frederic Smith. Script supervisor: Karen Golden. Production coordinator: Ellen Hillers. Sound mixer: Bob Eber. Key makeup artist: Pamela Westmore. Key hairstylist: Chari Ruff. Storyboard artist: Chris Buchinsky. Special effects coordinator: Danny Gill. Baseball coordinator: Steve Levine. Technical advisor: Ed Farmer. Visual effects coordinator: Walter Hart. Visual effects by Dream-Quest Images. Visual effects producer: Robert Staad. Matte Artists: Karen DeJong. Matte Painter: Bob Scifo. Head of Digital Imagery: Howard Burdick. Supervising sound editor: George

Simpson. Foley Editor: John Carr. Music editor: Lise Richardson. Second unit producer: Bill Pohlad. Second unit director: Barry Zelickson. Second unit photography: John Stephens, Scott Browner. Aerial photography: Bill Hedenberg. Technicolor; Panavision. 119 minutes; DTS/ Dolby/SDDS Sound. Rated PG.

Cast: Luke Edwards (Billy Heywood); Timothy Busfield (Lou Collins); John Ashton (Mac Macnally); Ashley Crow (Jenny Heywood); Kevin Dunn (Arthur Goslin); Billy L. Sullivan (Chuck Lobert); Miles Feulner (Joey Smith); Jonathan Silverman (Jim Bowers); Dennis Farina (George O'Farrell); Jason Robards (Thomas Heywood); Wolfgang Bodison (Spencer Hamilton); Duane Davis (Jerry Johnson); Leon "Bull" Durham (Leon Alexander); Kevin Elster (Pat Corning); Joseph Latimore (Lonnie Ritter); Bradley Jay Lesley (John "Blackout" Gatling); John Minch (Mark Hodges); Michael Papajohn (Tucker Kain); Scott Patterson (Mike McGrevey); Troy Startoni (Larry Hilbert); Antonio Lewis Todd (Mickey Scales); David Arnott (Little League Manager); Jeff Garlin (Opposing Little League Manager); Allan Wasserman (Little League Umpire); Teddy Bergman (Lowell); Cammy Kerrison (Shelly Hogeboom); Allen Hamilton (Mr. Patterson); Lavin Erickson (Margaret Sullivan); John Beasley (Roberts); Joe Johnson (Whitey); John Gordon (Wally Holland, WCCO Announcer); Jason Wolf (Wally's Stat Guy); O'Neil Compton (Major League Umpire), Steve Cochran (Reporter No. 1); Tim Russell (Reporter No. 2); Mark McGann (Agent), Peter Syvertsen (Hotel Manager); Jodie Fisher (Night Nurse No. 1), Jodi Russell (Night Nurse No. 2); Kristen Fontaine (Night Nurse No. 3); Gary Groomes (Doctor in "Night Nurses from Jersey"); Charlie Owens (Patient in "Night Nurses from Jersey"); Tony Denham, Vinnie Kartheiser, Brock Pierce (Stickball Kids: Phil, James, and Sidney); Chris Berman, Ken Griffey, Jr., Mickey Tettleton, Sandy Alomar, Jr., Carlos Baerga, Randy Johnson, Dave Magadan, Paul O'Neill, Dean Palmer, Lou Piniella, Ivan Rodriguez, Eric Anthony, Alex Fernandez, Wally Joyner, Lenny Webster, Rafael Palmeiro, Tim Raines (Cameo appearances); Kevin Burns, Jessie Elies, Scott Meadows, Richard Petterson, James Roth, Edward Stryker, Patrick Wright, Steve Eiswirth, Mike Knight, Kent Paulson, Patrick Pohl, Daniel Smith, Jay Wange (Twins Team); Robert Schiel, Dean Wittenberg (Trainers); Ronald J. Wojcik (Doctor);

Ryan Anderson, Marc Gittleman, Clint Parnell, Eric Jeffrey (Batboys).

As far as Thomas Heywood, the crusty millionaire owner of the Minnesota Twins, is concerned, the only person who knows—and cares—more about baseball than he does is his 12-year-old grandson Billy. Thus, after Heywood's sudden death, an astonished Billy inherits the Twins, lock, stock and jockstrap. When surly Minnesota manager George O'Ferrall flatly refuses to take orders from a punk kid, Billy fires O'Ferrall and becomes the first owner/manager in Major League baseball since Connie Mack. Everyone, from the team members on down, predicts disastrous consequences from Billy's bold and precocious move. Meanwhile, Billy learns the hard way that simply loving baseball isn't quite enough: He must also hack his way through the treacherous jungles of free-agentry, labor negotiations, media marketing and executive backstabbing. Making the boy's job all the more vexing is the growing jealousy and antagonism of his two best friends, Chuck and Joey. Twins first baseman Lou Collins, who happens to be sweet on Billy's widowed mom Jenny, tries to help the youngster survive his ordeal. Ever so gradually, Lou's formerly hostile teammates also rally around their new coach and perform like they've never performed before, taking to heart Billy's locker-room admonition: "Maybe the problem is, you guys forgot how much fun this is. You're major leaguers. You're on baseball cards. What could be better? Don't worry about winning and losing. Just go out and play, have fun." But will Billy *himself* be able to live by those words as he continues to wrestle with the challenge of being a small boy in a big man's world?

The essence of *Little Big League* can be summed up in three quotes. One, mentioned in the film, is from Bob Lemon: "Baseball was made for kids; grownups only screw it up."

The second is from the film's director Andrew Scheinman, quoted in the pressbook for the film: "...In a way this is a metaphor for any kid who wants to do something that is primarily in the realm of adults. There's excitement, but there's also a big penalty to pay."

And the third, likewise recorded in the studio pressbook, came from producer Steve Nicolaides: "When the film begins, Billy [Heywood] thinks he's walking into Camelot. He soon realizes it's IBM."

Released almost exactly one year after the similarly themed baseball fantasy *Rookie of the Year* (1993), *Little Big League* was inevitably compared to the earlier picture. Both films deal with a preteen baseball addict who is unexpectedly thrust into the adult world of Major League ball. In both cases, the kid has to overcome the hostility and/or avariciousness of his adult colleagues. Each of the young protagonists is the product of a single-parent home, with that parent (the mother) eventually falling in love with the most sympathetic member of the baseball team. Both films feature honest-to-goodness Big League players in cameo roles. And in both *Rookie of the Year* and *Little Big League* the hero does an awful lot of growing up in a short space of time, but still manages to remain the same likeable, spunky youngster he'd been when the film began.

A key difference between the two films is that *Rookie of the Year* was basically a fantasy, while *Little Big League* crossed over into the realm of probability. Allowing for the usual comic and dramatic exaggeration, there is nothing in *Little Big League* that could not conceivably happen in Real Life.

Film executive Adam Scheinman claimed that he chose *Little Big League* as his directorial debut because, "[I have] always been a sports fan and this story has baseball and a lot more. It operates on many levels physically, emotionally and comedically." His decision may have also been a

Twins first baseman Lou Collins (Timothy Busfield) and preteen manager/owner Billy Heywood (Luke Edwards) mull over the new starting line-up in *Little Big League*.

bit of *droit du seigneur*: As one of the five partners in Castle Rock Entertainment, the production company responsible for the film, Scheinman could do pretty much what he darn well pleased, and it pleased him at this particular moment to be a director. This was certainly the case several years later when Scheinman very nearly appointed himself to direct the Ben Affleck-Matt Damon project *Good Will Hunting*; fortunately, he finally acquiesced to the more experienced Gus Van Sant.

Another Scheinman, Adam, co-scripted *Little Big League* with movie newcomer Gregory K. Pincus, who dreamed up the story in the first place and had managed to get it to the development stage as early as 1991. In Pincus' original treatment, the story took place in Kansas City, and the team taken over by Bill Heywood was the K.C. Royals. The decision to move the action to Minneapolis was based on the availability of the Twins' domed stadium, which would allow the filmmakers to shoot their ballpark scenes any time of the year, in any kind of weather. Also, as a member of the production team rather tactlessly pointed out, Minneapolis was regarded as a "safer" town in which to shoot.

Other locations included Minnesota's Minnehaha Falls (of "Hiawatha" fame), seen in a recurring sequence wherein Billy and his Little League buddies go fishing. One sequence, in which Billy nostalgically participates in a sandlot stickball game between more important professional engagements, was filmed in Chicago in the dead of winter, requiring the production team to break out the snow shovels and heated dressing trailers. A second unit went around the country filming highlights of actual games, to be spliced into the action when needed. As for the non-game scenes, actual locations were given preference over studio mockups. One noteworthy exception was the Twins' locker room, which was recreated in a studio in order to provide the actors and the crew with more playing space and better lighting. Even so, the producers made certain that the ballplayer/actors felt "at home" in their artificial surroundings by allowing them to decorate their individual lockers with their own collections of keepsakes and memorabilia.

This was but one of several production touches which provided *Little Big League* with a modicum of authenticity. It was director Scheinman's philosophy that if the people on camera believed what was happening, so would the audience—a theory that has been disastrously ignored by other fantasy or quasi-fantasy films, in which the actors mug horrendously and bellow their lines as if to say, "We don't buy this for a minute, folks, and neither should you!" As observed by critic Roger Ebert in his Chicago *Sun-Times* review of the film, Scheinman was careful to have the adult characters react in as plausible a manner as possible to the potentially nonsensical situation of taking their marching orders from a 12-year-old kid. "[Scheinman] is aware that his material is a minefield of hazards, and that a mistake in tone could take a serious moment and make it ludicrous. He doesn't step wrong." This is never truer than in the director's handling of the team's ultimate acceptance of Billy as their spiritual guide. Notes Ebert, "In the case of Billy's inspirational locker-room speech, they listen impassively and do not respond much at all. In other situations, they ignore the kid, disregard his advice. But Billy really does know a lot about baseball, and by the end of the season he has won their grudging respect. It does not come easily..." This was in sharp contrast to *Rookie of the Year*, in which the grownup ballplayers are really Big Kids at heart, and behave accordingly.

Scheinman also avoided the old base-ball-film pitfall of having actors who couldn't really play the game, or actual ballplayers who couldn't act their way out of the proverbial paper bag. The director insisted upon casting actors who had extensive prior experience on the ballfield, and also hired only those professional athletes who could speak lines, or at the very least react to other actors' lines, in a credible manner.

At first glance, Timothy Busfield, best known as the whine-and-cheese yuppie adman Elliot Weston on the TV series *thirtysomething*, seemed be a curious choice for the film's nominal adult male lead, first baseman Lou Collins—especially since the actor's previous foray into the world of baseball films was as Kevin Costner's obstreperous brother-in-law in *Field of Dreams* (q.v.). But Scheinman was well aware that Busfield had played semipro ball for the San Diego Smokeys before becoming a full-time actor, and it was this fact as much as his acting ability which landed him one of the few sympathetic starring roles in his career. As for Jonathan Silverman, the talented young star of Neil Simon's *Brighton Beach Memoirs* and *Broadway Bound* could in any other situation have coasted through the role of off-kilter ballclub philosopher Jim Bowers on the strength of his comic abilities alone. Instead, Silverman was cast in *Little Big League* primarily on the strength of his baseball-playing prowess; he was, in fact, recommended to director Scheinman by Billy Crystal, one of Tinseltown's most talented ballplayers (see notes on *61**), with whom Silverman had participated in the Hollywood All Stars charity games at Dodger Stadium.

Busfield and Silverman joined the other actors cast as ballplayers in a series of intense pre-film training sessions with the actual Minnesota Twins, under the supervision of such real-life team members as outfielder Kirby Puckett and first baseman Kent Hrbek. In addition to this athletic conditioning and toning, Busfield and Silverman harked back to their acting-class training by basing their characterizations on existing baseball stars: Busfield's Lou Collins was inspired by left-handed Twins hitter Chip Hale (the actor wore Hale's Number 4 on his uniform, and even shifted from "rightie" to "leftie" to authenticate his characterization), while Silverman's Jim Bowers was an affectionate caricature of former Boston Red Sox player Bill "Space Man" Lee.

As noted, the bona fide ballplayers seen in the film were largely selected on the basis of their ability to play "themselves" without stinking up the place (no small task, as witness so many other films covered in this book). Of course, the very fact that the film's supporting cast was filled to overflowing with genuine players further sustained the aura of realism that Scheinman was striving for. The on-camera roster included three-time All Star First Baseman Leon "Bull" Durham; Ken Griffey, Jr., Lou Piniella and Randy Johnson of the Seattle Mariners (as one wag noted, you knew the Twins wouldn't win when Johnson showed up no matter *what* the script said); the Texas Rangers' Rafael Palmeiro, Dean Palmer and Ivan Rodriguez; Sandy Alomar, Jr. and Carlos Baerga of the Cleveland Indians; Mets shortstop Kevin Elster; Cincinnati Reds relief pitcher Brad "The Animal" Lesley; Mickey Tettleton of the Detroit Tigers; and the New York Yankees' Paul O'Neill. In addition, the film featured top minor-leaguers Scott Patterson, Troy Startoni, Tony Todd, John Minch, as well as Louisiana State college star Michael Papajohn (who also appeared in *Mr. Baseball*, *The Fan* and *For Love of the Game*) and, in a sizeable supporting role, the University of Virginia's Wolfgang Bodison. All of these worthies are better served here than the genuine ballplayers in *Rookie of the Year*, who, despite a big publicity buildup, ended up as little more than window dressing.

An extra dash of flavoring is provided by real-life Minnesota Twins sportscaster John Gordon. Identified in the film as "Wally Holland," Gordon, like Bob Uecker in the *Major League* films, delivers a sly self-parody of his standard broadcast delivery, right down to his familiar catchphrase "Touch 'em all."

Essential to the film's overall verisimilitude is the casting of the youthful leading role. Billy Heywood is played by 13-year-old Luke Edwards, a journeyman child actor who'd previously been seen in such major releases as *Newsies* and *Guilty by Suspicion*. Perhaps because he so closely identified with his screen character—"Like Billy, I live with a single parent, my mom, work in a world of adults, and sometimes don't see my friends for months"—Edwards' performance is one of the most convincing of its kind, so much so that we're willing to go along for the ride even when the diminutive Luke is forced to take out a surly pitcher who is nearly three times his size.

Like *Rookie of the Year*, *Little Big League* has moments of extraneous humor that the film could easily have done without, but by and large these gratuitous bits of business succeed because they don't stray too far from the basic premise. Particularly amusing is the scene where Billy's mom "benches" her son for swearing at the umpire, and a climactic sequence in which the other team members try to help the boy solve a weighty math-homework problem. Less successful is a prolonged running gag involving a softcore porno film called *Night Nurses from Jersey*, the viewing of which is evidently a rite of passage for all new members of the ballclub, Billy included. Even here, however, the gag is felicitously linked to the film's premise: Secure in the belief that he has gotten away with watching an R-rated movie without his mother's knowledge, Billy is appalled to discover that every single premium-channel telecast of *Night Nurses from Jersey* has been carefully itemized on his mom's credit card bill—and once again, our hero learns the hard way that the piper must always be paid in the Real World.

If the film has any serious shortcomings, they are in the realm of baseball accuracy. It is hard to forgive the fact that the Twins wear their "away" uniforms while attending a team meeting, then a few seconds later take the field in their "home" uniforms. And without giving away too much of the ending, it can be noted that the "Little League" trick used by Billy to score a crucial out against Ken Griffey, Jr., is technically a balk, which in an actual game would have allowed Griffey to advance an additional base.

A trifle too long for its own good, *Little Big League* nonetheless satisfies on the strength of its well-filmed baseball scenes, its ability to tell a fanciful story without straining credulity, and its refusal to condescend to either its characters or the audience. Had the film not been released a scant two weeks before the box-office bonanza *Angels in the Outfield* (q.v.), *Little Big League* might have earned a lot more than its meager $12,211,000 domestic gross.

Little Sunset

Bosworth Inc./Oliver Morosco Photoplay Company/Paramount; released May 6, 1915 (copyrighted 1914)

Director unknown, but was probably Hobart Bosworth. Screenplay based on a short story by Charles Emmett Van Loan. Four reels; black and white; silent.

Cast: Gordon Griffith ("Little Sunset" Jones); Hobart Bosworth (Gus Bergstrom); Joseph Ray (Jones); Rhea Haines (Mrs. Jones); Marshall Stedman (Apache manager).

Little Sunset is the demon-tempered son of Jones, a ballplayer in the minor-league Apaches. The boy hero-worships star outfielder Gus Bergstrom, "The Terrible Swede." After Little Sunset's mother dies, he's made the Apaches' mascot, and Gus

becomes his closest confidant. When the lad falls ill, Gus falls into a slump, and upon being chewed out by the manager for making a bonehead play in an important game, the Terrible Swede uses the incident as an excuse to quit the team and go into another business. But Gus returns to win the pennant for the Apaches, thereby cementing his friendship with Little Sunset, who was disillusioned and angry when Gus had walked out.

At four reels, *Little Sunset* was the longest dramatic baseball movie made up to 1914, and since it secured better States' Rights bookings on the basis of its length than it would have as a short subject, the picture can be regarded as the very first baseball feature film. The plotline was based on a 1912 short story by Charles Emmett Van Loan, who in his time was the foremost writer of baseball fiction in America. Van Loan was given credit in *Little Sunset* as "associate supervisor," an empty title most likely bestowed upon the writer in lieu of royalties. Featured in *Little Sunset* as the "Apaches" were members of the Pacific Coast League's Venice team—California's finest pro ballplayers in 1914.

Long Gone

Landsburg Productions/HBO Pictures; first telecast May 23, 1987

Executive producers: Alan Landsburg and Joan Barnett. Produced by Joan Barnett. Supervising producers: Arthur Fellows and Terry Keegan. Directed by Martin Davidson. Teleplay by Michael Norell, based on a novel by Paul Hemphill. Photography: Robert Elswit. Edited by Gib Jaffee. Production design by Glenn Ganis. Costume design by Sandy Davidson. Music by Kenny Vance. Original score by Kenny Vance and Philip Namanworth. Music performed by Peter Himmelman and the Good Ole Boys from Memphis, Tennessee, with Hugh McCracken and Elliot Randall. "The Stogie Stomp" written and performed by Larry Riley. Vintage country-western songs performed by the original artists. Assistant directors: Deborah Love and Rod Corn. Casting: Randy Stone (Los Angeles); Julie Hughes and Barry Moss (New York); Independent Castings: Lillian Gordon Barnitt and Kathryn Laughlin (Tampa), Unique Castings and Yonit Hamer (Miami). Technical advisers: Hal Smeltzky and Dean Rodriguez. Baseball coach: Ken Dominguez. Associate producer and unit production manager: Paul Kurta. Executive for production: Kay Hoffman. Executive in charge of production: Howard Lipstone. Color. 110 minutes; sound. Not Rated: strong language, nudity, adult themes.

Cast: William L. Petersen (Cecil "Stud" Cantrell); Virginia Madsen (Dixie Lee Boxx); Dermot Mulroney (Jamie Don Weeks); Larry Riley (Joe Louis Brown); Katy Boyer (Esther Wrenn); Henry Gibson (Hale Buchman); Teller (Hale Buchman, Jr.); Robert Easton (Cletis Ramey); Panchito Gomez (Paco Izquierado); David Langston Smyrl (Monroe Wright); Guich Koock (Bump Klein); Arthur Rosenberg (Peaches Cluff). As the Tampico Stogies: Will Zahrn (Knuckles Chapell); Edward Blatchford (Will Whitenant); Joel Murray (Bart Polanski); Kenneth Eriksen (Bubba Bean); Neil P. DeGroot (Poky Smathers); Steve Groot (Buster Smergalia); Ken Dominguez (Corky Lucadello); Mike McKown (Scooter Cagle); Nardi Contreras (Hose Harrigan); John Bauldrey (Tommy Tatum); and Ken Krannick (Rock Robb). And Hazen Gifford (J. Harrell Smythe); Kathryn Hasty (Bonnie); Monica Moran (Mrs. Wrenn); Ronn Allen (Mr. Wrenn); Tracy Roberts (Redhead); William Wohrman (Whitey Connarly); Dave Emrheim (Virgil Hawkins); Coleman Male (Minister); Debbie Maples (Midge); Ed Montgomery (Stumpy); Kip Radigan (Policeman); Carmen Alexander (Bartender); David Carlisle (Baseball Announcer); Bob Donahay (Umpire 1); Stan Babicz (Umpire 2); Lynn Adams (Umpire 3). And the Lakeland High School Marching Band and the Santa Monica High School Marching Band.

The time is 1957; the place, Tampico, Florida. Stud Cantrell, a one time big leaguer whose career never recovered after he was wounded in World War II, is player-manager of the Tampico Stogies, a Class D minor-league team which plays so poorly that the Alabama-Texas League may be forced to invent "Class F" baseball. The Stogies need a stronger defense and at least one more power hitter to survive. Stud finds a superb fielder in second baseman Jamie Don Weeks, a squeaky clean young fellow with strong religious convictions; and he finds his star slugger in Joe Louis Brown, a strong-limbed black man compelled by the segregation-ridden Southern society of the 1950s to pose as a Venezuelan. The Stogies take off like a rocket, with a pennant win all but in the bag. Meanwhile, Stud's ever ready libido is satisfied by beauty contest winner Dixie Lee Boxx, a seemingly empty-headed baseball groupie who actually has a steel-trap mind and a strong hankering to get Cantrell to the altar. Jamie Weeks also finds the love of his life, a proper Southern belle named Esther Wren, who sheds all her inhibitions (and Jamie's) in the back seat of Jamie's car. Complications ensue when Cantrell, who yearns for a major-league position, is given an opportunity to take a step toward "The Show" by managing the top-level Dothan Cardinals after the 1957 season is over—all he has to do is make sure that the Stogies lose the 1957 pennant race to Dothan. It's a rock and a hard place situation: If Cantrell loses to the Cardinals, he'll lose the respect of his team and the love of Dixie Lee Boxx; if he wins for the Stogies, he'll not only blow his chance at the majors, but he'll be banned from baseball thanks to the machinations of the crooked Dothan owner J. Harrell Smythe, who also happens to hold the mortgage on the Stogies. Neither Cantrell nor Joe Louis Brown—who has also been bought off by Smythe—shows up at the park for the Big Game. Eventually, however, both Cantrell and Brown succumb to integrity, making their long-awaited appearance in the seventh inning. Despite the efforts by J. Harrell Smythe to manipulate the outcome of the game from the stands, the Stogies win the pennant; and while Cantrell's future in baseball is uncertain, he's been inspired by all this "nobility shit" to propose to Dixie Lee Boxx. Stud and Dixie Lee join Jamie Weeks and the wee-bit-pregnant Esther Wrenn for a double wedding ceremony, held at home plate with a full turnout of Tampico Stogies in attendance and the park announcer calling the "play by play."

At first glance, *Long Gone* might be regarded as cable television's "answer" to such theatrical features as *Bull Durham* and *Major League*—except that in this case, the "answer" appeared a year or two before the "question." Home Box Office (HBO), the first and, for many seasons, foremost of the pay cable services, was riding high in 1987 with several home-grown feature films and specials (including Barbra Streisand's long-awaited return to TV). One of HBO's solid hits was the raunchy sitcom *First and Ten*, which told in very graphic language of the misadventures of a professional football team. The success of this venture led HBO to believe that baseball could undergo the same funny/scatological treatment, and the result was *Long Gone*, adapted from a novel by Paul Hemphill and produced for cable by Alan Landsburg Productions.

Paul Hemphill, who specialized in essays about life in the Deep South, and who himself had once played on a Class D ball-team for five whole days, wrote *Long Gone* in 1979. It was the short and not too sweet saga of Stud Cantrell, hard-drinking manager of the rock-bottom Graceville (Florida) Oilers. In the novel Cantrell marries Dixie Lee Box (one "x") at the halfway point, so the film's joyous double ceremony conclusion is nonexistent. Jamie Weeks is no babe in the woods, and in fact turns into a rather scabrous carbon copy of Stud Cantrell; he adopts Stud's "love 'em and leave 'em" policy with the pregnant Esther Wrenn and refuses to marry the girl. J. Harrell Smythe explains away his plan to fix the pennant race with a cock-and-bull story about avoiding a scandal with the compromised wife of the Dothan Cardinals manager; Stud is not

promised a managerial job with Dothan, but is still threatened with banishment from baseball. Cantrell goes along with Smythe's plan principally because he's fed up with chasing rainbows, and the only "noble" gesture he's capable of making is to urinate in the swimming pool at Smythe's country club.

From this engrossing but fairly bleak material, scenarist Michael Norell fashioned a "feel good" movie, completely faithful to the novel only in its overabundance of four-letter words and in its aggressively positive portrayal of Joe Louis Brown. The name of the team is changed to the "Tampico Stogies" due to the onetime actual existence of a "Graceville Oilers" club. One of the novel's principal characters, a homosexual hellfire and brimstone radio preacher named Q. Talmadge Ramey who owns the ball club, is softened and reshaped for the film into a loquacious Colonel Sanders–type restaurateur who places a confidence-building wager on the team. Another important character, an Air Force widow named Selma Myrick who tries in vain to keep Jamie Weeks from losing his soul, is dispensed with entirely in the film, allowing Jamie to choose the right path on his own. And as in the screen adaptation of Bernard Malamud's *The Natural* (q.v.), the hero's pre-arranged last-game loss in the book version of *Long Gone* is altered into a crowd-pleasing victory for the film.

Unlike most TV movies, *Long Gone* was no rush job. A full eight weeks were invested in its production, which isn't much for a theatrical film but is unusually generous for a two-hour picture aimed at the small tube. Care was taken to make the baseball element as authentic as possible. During those eight weeks the actors cast as ballplayers lived together, played together, drilled together, traveled together and even (no surprise here) caroused together. And while HBO's casting of William L. Petersen as Stud Cantrell may have been principally motivated by Petersen's recent star turn in the adventure film *To Live and Die in L.A.*, it is clear that the actor's own athletic excellence had a lot to do with his being selected.

The main playing ground for the film's Tampico Stogies was Tampa's William Field, which was dolled up to resemble a minor-league ballpark of the 1950s, complete with period billboards (though a few 1980s–style logos for such companies as Frito-Lay managed to sneak in). The rest of the locations, from a modest clapboard Baptist church to a neon-laden fleabag hotel, were also chosen with both eyes on period credibility. Little touches—such as including the sort of comic strips found in the Sunday newspapers of the time—bolster the late 1950s zeitgeist of the film, as do the vintage country-western songs (notably Hank Williams's "Long Gone Lonesome Blues") which grace the soundtrack. Even the actors' haircuts were in keeping with the style of the era—and if you think this isn't important, take a look at how the believability of other baseball pictures of days gone by have been compromised by the shaggy manes and long sideburns adorning the heads of the male performers.

The one aspect of the script (and the novel) that may not have been precise period detail was the excess of profanity. Granted, ballplayers have never been saints in the dugout, bullpen, or shower room, but the nonstop barrage of obscenities was simply not an everyday public occurrence in 1957—especially in that region of the country known as "The Bible Belt." The salty dialogue in *Long* Gone was symptomatic of the efforts by HBO to offer viewers something they wouldn't find on free TV. In the excitement of getting to use words that had previously been verboten on television, the characters in *Long Gone* sounded less like pillars of maturity and more like grade school kids swapping dirty jokes on the playground.

Its overemphasis on blue language isn't really that annoying, since *Long Gone* is one of the most thoroughly enjoyable baseball comedies made in the last two decades. It's a tribute to the exuberance of the players and the superior staging of the baseball sequences (especially the climactic twenty-minute pennant game) by director Martin Davidson and camera virtuoso Robert Elswit that the script successfully gets away with being an anthology of the obvious. We know from the beginning that the Tampico Stogies will pull themselves into the pennant race. We fully anticipate that the supposedly sluttish Dixie Lee Boxx will wed self-styled maverick Stud Cantrell, despite the puerile nature of their character names. We can predict the moment that the virginal Jamie Weeks and Esther Wrenn will wind up in the sack. We have every confidence that Joe Louis Brown will at first endure the racially motivated "silent treatment" of his fellow players, only to be wholeheartedly accepted and defended by those players in due time. And when an old-time ballplayer confesses that his oft-told story of the time he struck out Ted Williams was mere fabrication, we can practically recite that confession along with the actor.

All clichés, true enough. But clichés fail to work only when the basic material isn't entertaining enough to sustain them (1983's *Blue Skies Again* [q.v.] is a prime example of a cliché festival that falls apart due to lackluster production trappings and dull performances). It was once said that there were really only six basic plotlines; if the talent is there, along with the willingness to please, any old bromide or plot twist can be made to seem fresh and innovative. Watching *Long Gone* is like viewing your favorite old 1940s picture for the fifteenth time, knowing what is going to happen but still basking in the sheer professionalism of it all.

In fact, *Long Gone* uses its familiarity

Leading lady Virginia Madsen is the center of attention in this *TV Guide* ad for *Long Gone* (1987).

to lure us into a surprise or two. When Joe Louis Brown has sold out to the scheming J. Harrell Smythe, we discover that Brown's "price" was a brand spanking new Cadillac, and our first thought is "a black man and a Caddy—here's another cheap laugh based on an old racial stereotype." That's when Brown demonstrates that he wants no part of Smythe's scheme by smashing the Cadillac to a pulp with his baseball bat—the sort of moment that brings cheers of delight from the audience in a theatrical film simply by exploiting a cliché and then playing away from it.

Similarly, we fully expect Stud Cantrell to do his movie hero duty of smacking out a home run to prove to Smythe that he can't be compromised either. But the manner in which Stud brings in the winning run is so against the grain of the usual last-minute homer that has standardized too many other baseball films that we hesitate here to reveal Cantrell's strategy. Let's just repeat the observation made in the book *The Whole Baseball Catalog* that Stud Cantrell wins the game with his head.

As a footnote, we observe that one minor bit of casting in *Long Gone* is such a reversal of audience expectation that we're willing to go along with some of the more predictable moments to follow. In the film the Stogies are financed by a father-son pair of hardware store managers, known affectionately as "Asshole and Asshole Junior." The senior anal accoutrement is played by Henry Gibson; the son is played by Teller, the nonspeaking member of the popular "gonzo" magic act known as Penn and

Teller. In *Long Gone* the normally silent Teller unexpectedly has so much dialogue that he not only lulls the viewer into thinking that similar surprises will distinguish the rest of the film, but he puts to rest for good and all the notion held by some of Penn and Teller's more impressionable fans that the actor-prestidigitator is a genuine mute.

Long Gone might have been a classic were it not for the fixed-game contrivance at the end—the sort of cliché that virtually never works, simply because it's all but impossible to believe that a post-"Black Sox" World Series (even a minor-league one) can be dishonestly "bought." The notion that a team owner could, with impunity, manipulate a player to throw a game is even less credible in *Long Gone* than it had been in *The Natural* (q.v.), due to the outrageous overplaying of Hazen Gifford as J. Harrell Smythe. Gifford/Smythe is so blatant in his efforts to pull the strings of the pennant race from the grandstands that it's astonishing the Baseball Commission has let him get this far without an emergency hearing. After ten minutes of J. Harrell Smythe's smirking nefariousness, we're a little disappointed that he doesn't turn to one of his coconspirators and growl, "Don't waste a bullet on him. I have a better plan."

While the unconvincing nature of its finale relegates the film to second-string status, there is still much to enjoy in *Long Gone* for lovers of both comedy and baseball; spotters of "stars in the making" can also revel in *Long Gone* as a big step in the right direction for the then blossoming careers of William L. Petersen and Virginia Madsen. Though HBO gave the film a big publicity send-off when it premiered on May 23, 1987, repeating the film several times throughout the month of June, *Long Gone* has gained its greatest reputation and widest viewership on the videocassette rental circuit. The creased, glitch-filled VHS copy of the film witnessed by this writer should be proof enough of this last assessment.

A Love Affair: The Eleanor and Lou Gehrig Story

Stonehenge/Charles Fries Productions; first telecast January 15, 1978

Executive producer: Malcolm Stuart. Produced by David Manson. Directed by Fielder Cook. Teleplay by Blanche Hanalis, adapted from the book *My Luke and I* by Eleanor Gehrig and Joseph Durso. Photography: Michael Hugo. Edited by David Newhouse. Music by Eddy Lawrence Manson. Art director: Herman Zimmerman. Production manager: Art Levinson. Assistant director/unit production manager: Ron Wright. 97 minutes; color; sound.

Cast: Blythe Danner (Eleanor Twitchell Gehrig); Edward Herrmann (Lou Gehrig); Gerald S. O'Loughlin (Joe McCarthy); Ramon Bieri (Babe Ruth); Jane Wyatt (Mrs. Twitchell); Patricia Neal (Ma Gehrig); Georgia Engel (Claire Ruth); Michael Lerner (Dr. Canlan); David Ogden Stiers (Dr. Mayo); Gail Strickland (Dorothy); Valerie Curtin (Kitty); Jennifer Penny (Jennifer); Lainie Kazan (Sophie Tucker); James Luisi (Tony Lazzeri); Joe E. Tata (Lefty Gomez); William Wellman, Jr. (Bill Dickey); Charles E. Gray (Kenderly); Fred Downs (Papa Gehrig); James Greene (John Kieran); Robert Burr (Joseph Durso); Wynn Irwin (Barrows); Scott Mulhern (Bud); Norman Bartold (Grabiner); George Cooper (Twitchell); Ellen Blake (Nurse 1); Jan Jordan (Fanny Barrows); Jonathan Segal (Draftsman); Michael Yama (Purser); Milton Parsons (Driver); Victoria Carver (Nurse 2).

Eleanor Gehrig relates the story of her life with the New York Yankees' "Iron Man" Lou Gehrig to her biographer, Joseph Durso. Mrs. Gehrig tells of her formative days in Chicago of the 1920s, how she met the chronically shy Lou on a blind date in 1933, her conflicts with Lou's insufferably possessive mother, and her 1934 elopement with Gehrig, whom she nicknames "Luke" ("Lou Gehrig belongs to the Yankees—Luke belongs to me"). Along the way, Eleanor relates her experiences with Lou and Mr. and Mrs. Babe Ruth during the Yankees' 1936 trip to Japan, and also Lou's determination to play in 2,000 consecutive games. The story draws to a close when Lou contracts amyotrophic lateral sclerosis in 1939, prompting his emotional farewell to the Yankees that same year. After Eleanor Gehrig concludes her reminiscences with Lou's death in 1941, she insists that, despite its tragic denouement, she wouldn't have traded the few years with her "Luke" for anything.

A Love Affair: The Eleanor and Lou Gehrig Story was based on Eleanor Gehrig's 1976 autobiography, and thus naturally told the story from her point of view. This was in keeping with the policy of popular entertainment in the 1970s to exploit the cause of feminism (though usually this exploitation took the form of satirical comedy), and of the tendency in that era to offer "revisionist" histories. The pre-telecast publicity for *A Love Affair* suggested something radically different from the Valentine-like sentiment of the 1942 Gehrig biopic, *The Pride of the Yankees* (q.v.); in fact, one of Eleanor's first lines before the flashbacks take over is, "I've waited a long time to tell this story."

Why she's waited this long we couldn't tell you. Except for the less than shocking revelation that Lou Gehrig and Babe Ruth were far from close buddies at the time of Gehrig's retirement (due to a silly misunderstanding while shipbound to Japan in 1934, which *Love Affair* delineates), and except for stating honestly that Eleanor had learned of Lou's fatal illness before her husband and insisted that he not be told that he was doomed, rather than repeating *The Pride of the Yankees'* assertion that Lou bravely kept the truth from Eleanor, there was very little in this TV movie to suggest that America had been sheltered from the truth since 1941. To be sure, there is a lot more made of Ma Gehrig's oppressive de-

votion to Lou, and the resultant hostility between Ma and Eleanor, but this was fairly common knowledge by 1978. And we do learn that Lou was fond of opera, which was considered a faintly nonmasculine trait back when the first Gehrig film was made; but again, this is hardly a matter of earth-shattering dimensions.

In point of fact, Blanche Hanalis's well-crafted teleplay (which earned an Emmy nomination) manages to avoid a few of the truths laid out in Mrs. Gehrig's autobiography. We don't see any of Eleanor's father's extramarital affairs, which soured the girl on indulging in hero worship—hence her "so what?" attitude upon first meeting Lou. We also aren't made aware that Lou's "you and me against the world" bond with his mother was actually brought about by the casual cruelties of Lou's father; in the film, Mr. Gehrig is a henpecked walk-on, allowing the mother to embody The Menace in the plot all by herself.

And what a plot! There are so many flashbacks within flashbacks that you can't keep the years straight without a scorecard. The film is also burdened with anachronisms, from the "dry look" 1970s haircuts on the men to such dialogue as the line spoken to get the attention of a distracted Mrs. Gehrig: "Planet Earth to Eleanor!" Conversely, some of the "throwaway" efforts to indicate that the story is taking place in the 1930s are about as casual as a midair collision—notably the needless "special appearance" by Lainie Kazan as an undernourished Sophie Tucker.

There is, however, much to recommend in *A Love Affair*. Particularly effective is Lou Gehrig's farewell speech at Yankee Stadium. Anxious not to invite comparison to the legendary reenactment of this moment in *The Pride of the Yankees,* nor to exceed the telefilm's budget, *A Love Affair* director Fielder Cook harked back to his shorthand days of live television and came up with an impressionistic interpretation of the event. We hear Lou deliver the speech in toto, and see his face double exposed on a series of sepia-toned still photographs taken of Gehrig's actual final appearance at Yankee Stadium in 1939.

A Love Affair was also distinguished by uniformly fine acting, though both Blythe Danner (as Eleanor) and Patricia Neal (as Ma) do fall prey to affectation now and again, Danner with a distracting "smoker's rasp" as she narrates the story and Neal with a bizarre old-country dialect that defies any attempt to determine its national origin. Otherwise, both actresses are excellent, as are the performances of Ramon Bieri as a lovable Babe Ruth and Georgia Engel as a self-protectively aloof Mrs. Ruth.

Edward Herrmann was worried before shooting started that he would breathe very little life into the role of Lou Gehrig. "What made it so tough was that I could find no 'key' to his character," Herrmann explained in 1990. "There was no strangeness, there was nothing spectacular about him. As Eleanor Gehrig told me, he was just a square, honest guy." Herrmann never would be happy with his portrayal of Gehrig, though it is precisely the character's unspectacular quality which makes the actor's low-key performance work so well—in fact, he comes across far more credibly than Blythe Danner's somewhat mannered Eleanor. The real Mrs. Gehrig was delighted with Edward Herrmann; she sent the actor a letter saying that his Gehrig was miles ahead of Gary Cooper's portrayal in *The Pride of the Yankees*. Herrmann may not have completely concurred, but he was proud of the fact that he had learned to bat southpaw for his role, a skill that had completely flummoxed Cooper.

If only we could have seen Edward Herrmann play. If only we could have seen *anyone* play! *A Love Affair* is a baseball story almost completely stripped bare of baseball. We're an hour into the film before we get to spring training camp, where most of the action takes place off screen. The only time Lou Gehrig even picks up a ball is when he's playing catch with Eleanor at home. *A Love Affair* thus appears in these pages purely by association; it may be the story of the Iron Man of Baseball, but it has about as much ballpark activity as *The Birdman of Alcatraz*.

This hardly matters, though, since the film's premiere showing was seen by practically no one. *A Love Affair* was originally scheduled to air over NBC on October 9, 1977, but was preempted by, of all things, a World Series playoff game. When it finally was shown on January 15, 1978, it was scheduled opposite the first nighttime Super Bowl—meaning that the only people watching were the guys in the NBC control room.

THE "MAJOR LEAGUE" FILMS

The trio of films constituting the *Major League* "series" are best analyzed chronologically rather than alphabetically; thus, they will be discussed under the above umbrella heading.

1. *Major League*
Morgan Creek/Mirage Productions/Paramount; released April 7, 1989

Produced by Chris Chesser and Irby Smith. Executive producer: Mark Rosenberg. Coproducer: Julie Bergman. Written and directed by David S. Ward. Photography: Reynaldo Villalobes. Edited by Dennis M. Hill. Production designer: Jeffrey Howard. Art director: John Krenz Reinhart, Jr. Music by James Newton Howard. Song "Most of All You" by James Newton Howard and Marilyn and Alan Bergman; performed by Bill Medley. Sound recording by Susumu Tokunow. Assistant directors: Jerry Graney and Louis D'Esposito. Unit production managers: Irby Smith and Edward Markley. Costumer designer: Erica Edell Phillips. Casting by Joanne Zaluski. Stunt coordinator: Rick

LeFevour. Technical adviser: Steve Yeager. Trainers: Bill Lemke, Greg Goodwin, Mike Malzak, and Marty Caldwell. Color by Technicolor. 105 minutes; Dolby Stereo Sound. Rated R.

Cast: Tom Berenger (Jake Taylor); Charlie Sheen (Ricky Vaughn, aka "Wild Thing"); Corbin Bernsen (Roger Dorn); Margaret Whitton (Rachel Phelps); James Gammon (Lou Brown); Rene Russo (Lynn Wells); Wesley Snipes (Willie Mays Hayes); Charles Cyphers (Charlie Donovan); Charlie Ross (Eddie Harris); Dennis Haysbert (Pedro Cerrano); Andy Romano (Pepper Leach); Bob Uecker (Harry Doyle); Steve Yeager (Duke Temple); Peter Vuckovich (Haywood); Stacy Carroll (Suzanne Dorn); Richard Pickren (Tom); Kevin Crowley (Vic Bolito); Mary Siebel (Thelma); Bill Leff (Bobby James); Mike Bacarella (Johnny Wynn); Skip Griparis (Monty, the Colorman); Gary Houston (Ross Farmer); Ward Ohrman (Arthur Holloway); Marge Kolitlisky (Claire Holloway); Tony Mockus, Jr. (Brent Bowden); Deborah Wakeham (Janice Bowden); Neil Flynn (Longshoreman); Keith Uchima (First Groundskeeper); Kurt Uchima (Second Groundskeeper); Richard Baird (Hal Charles); Julia Milaris (Arlene); Roger Unice (Reaman); Michael Thoma (Gentry); Patrick Dollymore (French Waiter); Joseph Liss (Guy in Bar); Gregory Alan Williams (Bullpen Guard); Peter Ruskin (Gateman); Michael Hart (Burton); James Deuter (Phil Butler); Jack McLaughlin-Grey (Jerry Simmons); Tim Bell (Body Building Assistant); Joe Soto (Security); Ted Noose (Lyle Mathews); Lenny Rubin (Clubhouse Man); Thomas P. Purdoff (First Umpire); Jeffrey J. Edwards (Second Umpire); Alexandra Villa (Hostess); Michelle Minyon (Working Class Bar Patron); Rick LeFevour, George Aguilar, Stacey Logan (Stunts); Alex Flores, Michael F. Twarog, Ted White (Stuntmen/Spring Training Players); Gregory Ashburn, Mark Cibraric, Jeff Dickert, Larry Duncan, Luke Fera, Mark Gaynor, Dave Globig, David Huff, Steve Janacek, Roy Jeske, Todd Johnson, Paul Keltner, Michael Koster, John Liberger, John Meier, Bill Mosser, Jim Pandl, Pascual Rodriguez, David Roscoe, Brian Sienke, John Silbernagel, Slade Smith, Timothy Sweeney, Peter Whalen (Cleveland Indians); Jerry Augustine, Scott Brooks, Jim Burian, Chris Chesser, Sean Cooney, Charles Crook, Con Geary, Philip Higgins, Jeff Hirschenseiger, Jay Jaster, Steve Kosrowski, Randy Little, John Nedset, Earl Niebaur, George Prince, Art Rink, Bob Sanders, Dave Schariat, Todd Schneider, Ken Senfi, Paul Sikorski, Chris Stander Dan Wnuk, Dale Wnuk, Dave Wnuk, Jim Wolff, Steve Zimmerman (New York Yankees); Tim Brunenkant, Mike Chandler, Sean Christian, Luis Graterol, Billy Ireland, Andre Linsey, David Markzon, Jim Minor, Rusty Pennoc, Rick Rupkey, Roger Sands, Dan Seidenholz, Dale Summer, Mike Thorell, Manny Valencia, Gene Whitney, Kevin Williamson (Spring Training Players); Ray Bellican, Phil Brabant, Shawn Carlson, Jerry Colver, Jeff Edwards, Hector Garcia, Carlos Guerra, Alan Hayves, Michael Hughes, Bill Krohn, Ray Norvell, Tom Purdoff, Dewey Schiele, Ron Tourtillot, Bob Hoskins, Bill Huggin, Bill McQuerry, Frank Mera, John Schwab (Umpires); Tim Cole, Terry Gearhardt, Ramon Guzman, Bill Lund, Ted Schmitz, Leonard Williams (Stand-ins).

Donald Phelps, owner of the Cleveland Indians, is dead, leaving the fate of the team in the hands of his widow, ex-showgirl Rachel Phelps. Rachel despises Cleveland and is anxious to move the franchise to Miami, where she's been promised a number of perks. The problem is that the city will not yield its lease on the team unless yearly attendance falls below 800,000—something that may happen any day now, since the Indians haven't won a pennant since the dawn of recorded time. Rachel figures the only way to empty the grandstands is to get the team to play even worse than it already does, and to that end her 1988 roster is made up of has-beens, never-weres and probably-never-will-bes. The new Indian lineup includes Jake Taylor, one-time member of the club who banged up his knees once too often and has been relegated to Mexican baseball; Ricky Vaughn, a spike-haired recent reformatory graduate whose amazing lightning pitch is tempered by his lousy aim; Roger Dorn, a well-heeled free agent with both eyes on a lucrative business career who has no intention of getting injured exerting himself in the infield; Pedro Cerrano, a disciple of voodoo incapable of hitting anything slower than a fastball; and Willie Mays Hayes, who shows up uninvited at spring training and astounds one and all with his running skills, but who can't hit straight to save his life. New manager Lou Brown hopes he can mold something from this feckless material, but on opening day in a practically deserted Municipal Stadium, Cleveland loses 9–0 to the Yankees, forcing Indians' announcer Harry Doyle to start his drinking earlier each morning. Oddly enough, the Indians start winning a few, mostly due to the enthusiasm of Jake Taylor, for whom this represents a last chance. The disgruntled Rachel Phelps decides to break the Indians' spirit by not "coddling" them; she alters their transportation from luxury jet to war-vintage prop planes, and finally consigns them to a rickety bus. As a last insult, she refuses to repair the team's whirlpool bath, compelling the boys to rig a jerry-built whirlpool with an old outboard motor. Still, the team gets better and better, especially after Ricky Vaughn dons a pair of glasses and is finally able to see what he's pitching at. As ballpark attendance grows, Jake Taylor tries to patch up his personal life along with his career by reuniting with his ex-fiancée Lynn, who is about to tie the knot with a more "dependable" type. The pace accelerates when the team discovers Rachel's plan to dump them all and move to Florida. Adopting an attitude of "us versus the bitch," the Indians really begin to pull together; even Roger Dorn allows himself to play wholeheartedly rather than constantly protecting himself against pain, though this is due less to a love of his teammates than to Jake's threat to eviscerate Dorn's private parts if he ever tanks another ball. Wonder of wonders, Cleveland makes it to the pennant playoff against the Yankees. Despite a last-minute complication in which Dorn's wife gets even for her husband's infidelity by sleeping with Ricky Vaughn, the Indians play together beautifully. The pennant is theirs, thanks in particular to "has-been" Jake Taylor and "never-will-bes" Ricky Vaughn, Pedro Cerrano, and Willie Mays Hayes; and Jake's "ex," Lynn, is right there in the jam-packed grandstands, her engagement ring conspicuously absent from her finger.

After the enormous, Oscar-winning success of his screenplay for *The Sting* in 1974, writer David S. Ward was beset with over a decade's worth of bad luck. Major disappointments in Ward's portfolio included the notorious money eater *Cannery Row* (1982), which represented the writer's directorial debut, and the ill-advised *The Sting II* (1983). A planned epic on California in the 1880s in which Ward invested two years of effort never made it to the cameras thanks to the industry "ban" on western-type pictures after that mother of all fiascoes, *Heaven's Gate* (1980). Ward finally got back on the track with his script for the film directed by Robert Redford, *The Milagro Beanfield War*, in early 1988, prompting Morgan Creek and Mirage Productions to have enough faith in the writer-director to evince interest in *Major League*, which Ward had written in 1982 but had been unable to sell for over five years.

David S. Ward wasn't quite sure why *Major League* suddenly became so salable; "I guess it was time for baseball again" was the writer's pithy comment. Baseball was indeed in the air in the Hollywood of 1988, thanks to the recent *Bull Durham* (q.v.) and the still in the offing *Eight Men Out* (q.v.) and *Shoeless Joe* (released as *Field of Dreams* [q.v.] in 1989). The possibility of a profitable new trend has always got the blood circulating in the movie colony, and Morgan Creek/Mirage had no intention of missing out on the ground floor of a baseball flick craze. Still, producers moved cautiously when approaching a genre that had not exactly been a record-breaking success in the past; David Ward was allotted a budget of $10 million for *Major League*, which may seem like all the money in the world to you and me, but was peanuts within the parameters of the megabucks mentality of late 1980s Hollywood.

As David Ward himself has admitted, *Major League* was unabashedly an entertainment, with no deeper meaning, no desire to better the world, and certainly no aspirations to originality. The film was deliberately designed to reap laughs by pressing the right buttons and pulling the correct strings. We are encouraged to cheer the heroes, hiss at the villain (we never see Rachel Phelps kicking dogs or stealing candy from babies, but the script doesn't stop short of anything else), revel in the thrill of thoroughly anticipated victory after the opening reels' agonies of defeat, and roar with merriment at a parade of some of the most timeworn jokes since the days of Abbott and Costello. David Ward pulls this off not by presenting his clichés in the wimpy, apologetic manner of *Blue Skies Again* (1983) (q.v.); not with the artsy-craftsy posturings of *The Natural* (1984) (q.v.); not by adopting the cynical "they'll swallow anything Neil Simon writes" attitude of *The Slugger's Wife* (1985) (q.v.); nor within the artificial "crooked game" angle of *Long Gone* (1987) (q.v.). Ward makes *Major League* work by exuberantly playing each situation with all the stops out—and with a shamelessness that is positively admirable. If Jake Taylor is going to win his girlfriend Lynn back, he's going to do it in the most boyishly charming manner possible; lacking a regular automobile to drive to Lynn's apartment, Taylor putt-putts through the streets of Cleveland in the Indians' pint-sized bullpen car. Ricky Vaughn isn't just a tough kid; he shows up for training fresh from the slammer, declaring his presence by hitching a ride on the back of a cycle and sporting the most flamboyant of punk haircuts. Pedro Cerrano is no mere dabbler in voodoo; he sets up a shrine to his personal god Jovo right there in the locker room, with burning incense and flash pots aplenty,

causing the sprinkler system to drench his teammates. And sportscaster Harry Doyle isn't just mildly disappointed with the performance of the home team; he chugalugs from an open whisky bottle during each game and curses a blue streak into an open microphone. The script for *Major League* is David Ward declaring, "If this is hoke, let's give it the full treatment—and full speed ahead!"

Film comedy is best digested when built upon a realistic foundation. Ward is unerringly accurate in conveying the sort of fever that grips a big-league town during a winning season, especially a town that has been in the basement too long. The writer-director personalizes the populace of Cleveland by concentrating on the ongoing observations of three sets of people: a pair of longshoremen, two Japanese ballpark groundskeepers, and the patrons of a blue-collar bar. As their enthusiasm grows over the Indians' success, the audience's enthusiasm likewise grows. The best illustration of this burgeoning civic pride is manifested in the old rock song "Wild Thing," which is used in *Major League* as a signature for pitcher Ricky Vaughn. We first hear the tune in association with the tempestuous Vaughn when it is warbled during the dismal opening game by Cleveland's ragtag, six-person band of volunteer cheerleaders. As Vaughn's reputation grows, the strains of "Wild Thing" follow him everywhere, particularly in the jukeboxes of the bars he frequents. When it looks as though Cleveland has a chance at the pennant, we see that the "Wild Thing" tag has been picked up by everything from T-shirts to national magazine covers. And finally, when Ricky Vaughn makes his overdue appearance at the deciding Indians-Yankees game, the 25,000 fans in Municipal Stadium greet him with so boisterous a chorus of "Wild Thing" that the average moviegoer is hard pressed not to stand up and start singing along. This is very basic, Frank Capra–style

Corbin Bernsen and Charlie Sheen settle their differences during the pennant race in *Major League*, as Milwaukee's County Stadium doubles for Cleveland's Municipal Stadium in the background.

predecessors Gary Cooper and Anthony Perkins ever did. Charlie Sheen made the best showing of all, but he had a leg up thanks to his previous extensive baseball experience (outlined in the notes on *Eight Men Out*). While he himself was uncharacteristically modest about his skills, noting that he'd always been the sort of player for whom they'd send in a pinch hitter if the game was in trouble, Sheen was able to pitch a ball at a full 85 m.p.h.—some 16 miles short of the standard set by his screen character Ricky Vaughn, but remarkable all the same.

"montage" technique—and we'll be damned if it doesn't work magnificently.

In keeping with his policy of constructing the comedy on a realistic base, David Ward hoped to correct a problem that had plagued many an earlier serious baseball film. "Today's audiences are so sophisticated that you can't fake athletic ability," Ward noted. "There's so much confusion in football and basketball scenes that actors don't have to be decent athletes. But baseball is mostly isolated action. An actor can mimic body language, but he has to catch the ball. You can't be filmed throwing off the wrong foot." To that end, the director whipped his cast into playing shape by having ex–Dodger Steve Yeager put them through a rigorous training program (Yeager appears in the film as a mean Yankee pitcher who is described as having beaned his own kid in a father-son game). Actors Tom Berenger, Corbin Bernsen, Wesley Snipes et al. consequently look far more convincing out on the field than their movie

At least 25 percent of the running time in *Major League* is devoted to playing the game, meaning that Ward had to go still farther in his quest for fundamental realism by shooting in a genuine, regulation-size major-league ballpark. Ward's obvious first choice was Municipal Stadium, in his own home town of Cleveland. This proved to be impractical in that the stadium was being used on the weekends Ward had planned to shoot by the Cleveland Browns for a series of exhibition football games. Ward then discovered that Milwaukee's County Stadium, which served as the home of that city's Brewers from 1969 until its demolition in 2000, had been designed by the same architect who'd worked on Municipal, and looked enough like the Cleveland park to pass in the long shots. Milwaukee's mayor picked up on this; anxious to establish his city as a desirable filming site in the manner of its "sister to the south," Chicago, the mayor wooed Ward to the Wisconsin metropolis, reminding the director that union restrictions in Milwaukee did not prohibit moviemakers from filling the stands with thousands of extras free of charge. Thus it followed that, except for a few establishing shots set in Cleveland and an extended sequence shot at the Indians' spring training camp in Tucson, Arizona, the *Major League* crew spent July, August, and September 1988 aiming its Panaflex lenses at Milwaukee.

There were twenty-three days devoted to shooting at County Stadium alone, and Ward's method of "crowd control" in dealing with his volunteer extras (which numbered from 3,000 for the opening-day scenes to 25,000 for the pennant-win finale) might be of academic interest to any budding filmmakers planning to shoot a baseball movie in their own town. To keep the ersatz fans happy during the long stretches between camera setups, comedian Bill Leff (cast in the film as one of the Indians' besotted cheerleaders) bombarded the assemblage with a parade of jokes; contests were held with prizes awarded; FM radio music was piped through the P.A. system; and popular TV programs were shown on the stadium's giant screen scoreboard. That scoreboard was also used as an electronic assistant director, flashing such messages to the fans as "Everybody Stand Up" and "Cheer." Bill Leff likewise functioned as an "A.D.," telling the crowd the degree of affection with which they should greet the individual "Indians," and advising the loyal Brewers fans that ex–Milwaukee player Pete Vuckovich had been cast as a New York Yankee, and thus wasn't supposed to be wildly applauded when he sauntered to the plate.

In getting County Stadium, Ward was also able to secure the services of Brewers' radio announcer Bob Uecker to portray long-suffering Cleveland sportscaster Harry Doyle. Uecker's ongoing commentary, peppered with snide throwaway comments and his desperate efforts in the earlier scenes to convince the listeners at home that something worth shouting about was happening in the stadium, is easily the highlight of the whole film, expertly blending the contrivances of Ward's gag-filled script with the smooth, spontaneous credibility of Uecker's performing style.

The resultant on-location footage is so thoroughly realistic that it surpasses all the comic exaggerations of Ward's screenplay. As for the director's necessary pilgrimage to Wisconsin, only the residents of Cleveland or Milwaukee could possibly suspect that the whole film hadn't been shot on the shores of Lake Erie instead of Lake Michigan. The single exclusive-to–Milwaukee element is the logo for that city's WTMJ-TV on the scoreboard, and even this is taken care of by changing the call letters of Cleveland's NBC affiliate from WKYC to WTMJ in the film's sportscast scenes. (The one noticeable "blooper" in the film is something that could have happened in any city; the scoreboard clock has been stopped at 10:20, meaning that not only are all day games seemingly played before noon, but that the climactic pennant game takes place in a sort of baseball Twilight Zone where time stands still.)

Judging by the critical hostility directed towards *Major League*, most of the newspaper and magazine reviewers apparently could not abide seeing audiences respond so positively to a film with so few surprises. It was beyond these critics' comprehension that, in some instances, people don't *want* surprises. This point was driven home while the film was being sneak-previewed before its official release date. At one juncture, a different ending was used, wherein it was revealed that the heretofore despicable club owner Rachel Phelps did not want to move the Indians to Miami at all! She was merely putting her team through Hell to test their mettle, and to bully them into becoming world-class winners if for no other reason than to prove that no mere woman could run them into the ground. Under this setup, the film's climax included a sequence in which a smiling and grateful Rachel came into the locker room to deliver a curtain speech along the lines of "I knew you guys had it in you all along." This undeniably surprising but thoroughly unbelievable last-minute conversion of Rachel Taylor from bitch to benefactress was all but booed out of the theater, and was abandoned in favor of the more conventional "Curses! Foiled again!" denouement.

While a workable device within the framework of the film, the demonization of Rachel Phelps underlines the one major criticism that might legitimately be held against *Major League*: its undercurrent of misogyny. This is a "male bonding" picture through and through, and the female characterizations suffer for it. Rachel is not only an unrelenting *chienne*, but she throws her power around by walking unannounced into the locker room and playing touchie-feelie with the players' family jewels (subliminal message: girls can get away with this; men get their faces smacked and are called pigs). Jake Taylor's ex-fiancée Lynn can't see beyond his irresponsibility to realize what a swell fellow he is, preferring instead the security of a marriage to a snotty-nosed attorney (message: girls all marry for money). And Roger Dorn's sweet little wife Suzanne, presented with one single instance of her husband's fooling around, immediately disguises herself as a seductive barhopper and beds Roger's least favorite person, Ricky Vaughn (message: Scratch a housewife and you'll find a harlot). At the end, when Dorn first knocks Ricky down and then, beaming broadly, helps his teammate to his feet and embraces him, we are reminded of all those "buddy" movies in the 1930s where the heroes stop slugging it

out because those dames just aren't worth it.

So much for social consciousness. *Major League* was a solid smash at the box office, racking up a domestic gross of $49,800,000; and while it didn't immediately lead to an overload of baseball movies, it enabled David Ward to finance his next project, *King Ralph* (1991), a comedy that wallowed in its obviousness and its glorious exploitation of every reluctant monarch movie cliché in the book—resulting in yet another box office bonanza.

And, oh yes: *Major League* ultimately spawned a brace of sequels. Read on...

2. Major League II

Morgan Creek/Warner Bros.; Released March 4, 1994

Executive producer: Gary Barber. Produced by James G. Robinson and David S. Ward. Directed by David S. Ward. Screenplay by R. J. Stewart. Story by R. J. Stewart, Tom S. Parker and Jim Jennewein. Production designer: Stephen Hendrickson. Photography: Victor Hammer. Edited by Paul Seydor, Donn Cambern, Kimberly Ray, Frederick Wardell. Original Music: Michel Colombier. Additional music: James Newton Howard. Costume designer: Bobbie Read. Makeup: Allan A. Apone, Jeanne Van Phue. Production manager: Edward D. Markley. Assistant director: Jerram A. Swartz. Storyboard artist: Raymond Prado. Special effects: Bruno van Zeebroeck. Script supervisor: Susan Bierbaum. Second unit director of photography: Tom Houghton. Technical advisor: Steve Yeager. Technicolor. 104 minutes; Dolby Stereo sound. Rated PG.

Cast: Charlie Sheen (Rick "Wild Thing" Vaughn); Tom Berenger (Jake Taylor); Corbin Bernsen (Roger Dorn); Dennis Haysbert (Pedro Cerrano); Margaret Whitton (Rachel Phelps); James Gammon (Lou Brown); Omar Epps (Willie Mays Hayes); Eric Bruskotter (Rube Baker); Bob Uecker (Harry Doyle); David Keith (Jack Parkman); Alison Doody (Flannery); Michelle Burke (Nikki Reese); Takaaki Ishibashi (Isuro Tanaka); Steve Yeager (Coach "Duke" Temple);

Kevin Hickey (Schoup); Skip Griparis (Monte); Kevin Crowley (Vic); Bill Leff (Bobby); Michael Mundra (Frankie); Courtney Pee (Steve); Farajii Rasulallah (Tommy); Edward Woodson (Tim); Ted Duncan (Ron); Mary-Louise White (Lisa); Saige Ophelia Spinney (Big Woman); Michael Willis (Airport Photographer); Jason Kravits (Accountant); Alan Wade (Psychiatrist); Keith Johnson (Vaughn's Valet); Jay Leno (Himself); Susan Duvall (Lou's Nurse); Ron Meadows, Jr. (Orderly); Jesse Ventura (White Lightning); Keith Uchima, Kurt Uchima (Groundskeepers), Richard Salamanca, Harold Surratt (Reporters); Daniel O'Donnell (Suit No. 1), Richard Schiff (Director); Louis Turenne (Distinguished Gentleman); Patrick Robert Smith (Clapper Boy); Dan Kilday (Slider); Barry Cochran, William Reuter, Ken Medlock, Michael Forrest, David Boswell, Skip Apple, Bob Roesner, Stefan Aleksander (Umpires); Dick Stilwell (Cleveland Trainer); David Sherrill (White Sox Center Fielder); J. Michael Sarbaugh (Pirate Shortstop); Jeff Sheaffer (Pirate on Second Base); Tom Quinn (Red Sox Manager), Jim Milisitz (Red Sox Catcher); Jim Dedrick (White Sox Pitcher); Bob Hopkins (Toronto Shortstop); Bobby Joe Brown (Ballplayer Playing Cards); Wayne Crist (Vendor), Julia Miller (Stadium Control Room Operator); Ashton Smith (*Black Hammer/White Lightning* Announcer); Randy Quaid (Johnny, obnoxious Indians "fan"); Rene Russo (Lynn); Paul M. Clary, Big Ben Kennedy (Fans in the Stands); Daniel S. Markham (Trainer).

Although the "new" Cleveland Indians introduced in 1989's *Major League* were able to exceed all expectations and win the American League East playoffs, we learn at the beginning of this 1994 sequel that they were ultimately knocked out of the Series race by the Chicago White Sox (oh, the humanity!). Nonetheless, the Indians are still the heroes of the hour when spring training rolls around—and with former third baseman Roger Dorn having assumed ownership of the team from the despicable Rachel Phelps, it looks like the boys will be even bigger winners than before. Aaaand ... maybe not, judging by the collateral damage that fame and fortune has done to last year's Cinderella team. Punkish relief pitcher

Ricky "Wild Thing" Vaughn has been given a radical image overhaul by his attractive new agent Flannery, and is currently being touted as a man of urbanity and sophistication, thereby eroding his raw athletic talent and incurring the scorn of Nikki Reese, an inner-city schoolteacher who "knew him when." Fleet-footed center fielder Willie Mays Hayes has become the star of empty-headed action flicks and now spends more time entertaining his sycophantic hangers-on than he does exerting himself on the job. And power hitter Pedro Cerrano has forsaken voodoo in favor of Buddhism, acquiring so much "inner peace" that he cannot bring himself to even consider beating the opposing team. It is up to catcher Jake Taylor, who, after being invalided out of the starting lineup, has reluctantly agreed to stay on as assistant coach, to whip the Indians back into shape. The club's newest members include corn-bred catcher Rube Baker, who habitually misses the pitcher's mound when he returns the ball because he thinks too much; and Japanese baseball hero Isuro "Taka" Tanaka, whose chauvinistic obsession with the Samurai Code is almost as detrimental as his inability to speak coherent English and his cute habit of (literally) knocking himself out on the field. After a bad start, owner Dorn finds himself in such a financial hole that he is forced to sell the Indians back to the hated Rachel Phelps, a demoralizing move which only accelerates the team's descent to the cellar. Worse still, veteran coach Lou Brown suffers a heart attack, forcing Jake to half-heartedly take over Lou's duties. Just when things seem bleakest, an impassioned locker-room speech by an unexpectedly eloquent Rube Baker galvanizes the team into their old fighting form. With Cleveland radio announcer Harry Doyle calling the play-by-play throughout the season (and going back on the wagon from which he'd fallen back in the spring!), the Indians make it all the way to the Division playoffs again. With

Major League II: **Relief pitcher Ricky "Wild Thing" Vaughn (Charlie Sheen) psyches out the competition with his custom-made "specs."**

the playoffs tied 3–3, it all depends upon a "reformed" Ricky Vaughn to bring home the bacon—and, incidentally, to settle accounts with an old enemy, surly White Sox batter Jack Parkman.

There are several different methods filmmakers employ when making a movie sequel. The three most popular seem to be: (1) Remake the original film scene for scene, highlight for highlight, as in *Home Alone II*; (2) Postulate a number of detrimental changes in the personalities or career goals of the main characters which must be "corrected" so that those characters can revert to their old lovable selves by fadeout time, as in *Ghostbusters II*; or (3) use the first film as merely the groundwork for an entirely new set of supporting characters, story tangents and stylistic choices, in the fine tradition of Steven Spielberg and George Lucas.

Instead of choosing from among these tried-and-true methods, *Major League II* jumbles all three together—and, as a result, never completely succeeds with any of them.

Before delving further, we must address the question of why it took five years to come up with a sequel to the 1989 surprise hit *Major League*. In the *Major League II* pressbook, director/coproducer David S. Ward, *auteur* of the original film, explains: "Basically, I wasn't sure I wanted to do it again, for a lot of reasons. It took a while to come up with a story that I thought would be a worthy successor to the first one. It had to be fresh enough to be different, while still giving audiences the characters they'd gotten to know and love."

While Ward was primed to direct the sequel, he was hesitant to work on the script. That assignment went to R. J. Stewart, who, as one of the writers of the tongue-in-cheek TV detective series *Remington Steele*, was well versed in the art of fashioning new material for characters created by other hands. Stewart was also a skilled rewrite man, having previously worked on the 1988 remake of Roger Vadim's *And God Created Woman*; as such, he was eminently qualified to refashion the patented *Major League* formula into something "fresh enough to be different." In passing, it should be noted that R. J. Stewart's professional future did not hinge upon the success or failure of *Major League II*. Highly respected in industry circles for fashioning the uncredited rewrite which "saved" the troubled Kevin Costner vehicle *Waterworld* (1995), he went on to develop, produce and cowrite the internationally popular "sword and sorcery" TV series *Xena: Warrior Princess*. Though he has never publicly itemized any difficulties he may have encountered on *Major League II*, it is understandable that Stewart tends to downplay the film on his resume, favoring instead his later triumphs in a wholly different genre.

Though he received sole screenplay credit for *Major League II*, Stewart collaborated on the story with the writing team of Tom S. Parker and Jim Jennewein, fresh from the scattershot cable–TV spoof *Stay Tuned* (1992), and who also trafficked in live-action versions of such cartoon properties as *Richie Rich* and *The Flintstones* (both 1994). The clash of styles between the story- and character-driven R. J. Stewart and the "anything for a quick laugh" Parker/Jennewein combination goes a long way in explaining the schizophrenic nature of the *Major League* sequel (of which more later).

Even with one baseball picture under his belt, director David S. Ward still wrestled with many of the production difficulties that had plagued *Major League*. Though he did not mention it during the making of the first film, this time around the director noted the recurrence of an acute logistics problem: Mainly, that the distance between bases forced Ward, cinematographer Victor Hammer and editor Donn Cambern (who'd also worked on 1993's *Rookie of the Year* [q.v.]) to "telescope" much of the action, "although on big hits we always try to have the pitcher and hitter in the same frame. We don't cheat our hits. It's difficult and definitely time-consuming..."

Once again, Ward was obliged to find a substitute for Cleveland's Municipal Stadium, which in *Major League* was "impersonated" by Milwaukee's County Stadium. The 62-year-old Municipal was slated for demolition (though it would not fall to the wrecker's ball until 1996 due to money problems), and the city's new Jacob's Field was not yet completed. Also, since the film would be shot in mid-to-late Autumn, chilly Milwaukee was out of the question. The producers settled upon Camden Yards in Baltimore, Maryland, principally because executive producer James G. Robinson lived in Baltimore and was chummy with the local politicians. Ironically, the choice of Camden almost proved to be a drawback

when the Baltimore Orioles made it to the American League pennant race, meaning that their extended season had the potential of spilling over into Ward's production schedule—placing James G. Robinson in the paradoxical position of publicly cheering on the Orioles and silently rooting for the team to lose.

Once filming was able to get under way, the stadium's familiar "Camden green" was changed to blue to conform to the film's Cleveland setting, the advertising signs and scoreboard were altered, and the special-effects department matted in the Cleveland skyline (though in several scenes they neglected to remove the huge red-brick building next to Camden, virtually a landmark in itself). To keep the unpaid local extras pumped up during the lulls between scenes, several professional entertainers were brought in, including a carryover from the original *Major League*, comedian Bill Leff (who, as before, also appeared in the film). No extra incentive was needed, however, to summon up audience response for the final pitcher's-mound appearance of Charlie Sheen as Ricky Vaughn: All 20,000 spectators lustily cheered and sang in unison the moment Vaughn's signature tune "Wild Thing" was piped through the Camden PA system. One might suspect that these folks had seen the earlier picture.

The film's "away" games were also lensed in Baltimore, with Memorial Stadium standing in for Chicago's Comiskey Park, Oakland's Alameda County Stadium and Boston's Fenway. Riverside Stadium in nearby Harrisburg, Pennsylvania, the home of the Triple-A Harrisburg Senators (many of whose members appeared in the film), was used for the early scenes set in the Indians' Winter Haven, Florida, spring training headquarters—with actual palm trees brought in to complete the illusion! (During most of the shooting the temperature hovered just above or below freezing, which is why some of the players wear long-sleeved shirts in Florida, and why we can see everyone's breath during those "balmy summer evenings" in Cleveland). A second unit was dispatched to Chicago and Cleveland for the atmosphere and actual-game shots that were interspersed throughout the film.

Brought back from the first *Major League* to serve as technical advisor and to shepherd the actors and real-life ballplayer extras through a gruelingly genuine training session was former LA Dodger catcher Steve Yeager, who also reprised his role of Duke Temple, now "Coach" Temple and a considerably nicer fellow than he'd been in the earlier picture. Though some of the actual ballplayers didn't survive the "final cut," it was a foregone conclusion that the principal actors would make it through the training, and that Yeager would issue official proclamations concerning their excellence on the ballfield. "Charlie [Sheen] is a terrific pitcher and has great mechanics. Dennis [Haysbert] plays in the entertainment league and knows the game.... We could give the real Cleveland Indians a run for their money."

In addition to Yeager, the producers were able to secure the services of most of the original *Major League* stars—the aforementioned Charlie Sheen and Dennis Haysbert (who, since the first film, had portrayed another ballplayer in *Mr. Baseball* [q.v.]), and Tom Berenger, Corbin Bernsen, Margaret Whitton, James Gammon and Bob Uecker. Conspicuous by his absence was Wesley Snipes, who in the first *Major League* had made a vivid impression as base-stealer supreme Willie Mays Hayes. Catapulted to full stardom in Spike Lee's *New Jack City* (1991), Snipes had kept the momentum going with such films as *White Men Can't Jump* (1992), *Passenger 57* (1992) and *Demolition Man* (1993), and had neither the time, the need nor the desire to reprise his colorful but admittedly secondary *Major League* role (though he would eventually return to the baseball-film genre with 1996's *The Fan* [q.v.]).

Rather than eliminate the popular Hayes character, David Ward simply recast the part with Omar Epps, whom Ward had directed in the 1993 football drama *The Program*. "I loved the first film, and the character of Willie had been my favorite," declared Epps for the benefit of the Warner Bros. publicity department. "I loved Wesley Snipes in the part, and the opportunity to take over was something I couldn't pass up." Unfortunately, in the intervening years Epps has had incredibly bad luck in choosing film properties, reaching rock bottom with the 1999 movie version of the old TV series *The Mod Squad*. This is no way a reflection on Epps' talent: Though not yet in the Wesley Snipes league, he handles himself with smooth assurance in both the comedy and action highlights of *Major League II*.

In many ways, the second *Major League* is slavish in its fidelity to the formula of the original film: the basic characters, the chaotic spring training session, the "nutty" newcomers who learn to harness their eccentricities for the benefit of the team, the club's mediocre showing at the start of the season, the midseason pulling together of the highly individualistic players for the Greater Good, the omnipresence of a manipulative and menacing team owner, the showers of praise and deluges of damnation alternating from the lips of the team's long-suffering radio announcer, the cliff-hanging Division playoff, the last-minute race to the rescue by Ricky "Wild Thing" Vaughn. Some of the repeated bits of business work quite well within the new framework, including the "red tag" sequence in which the aspiring Indians find out who has been retained and who has been cut during spring training, and the "second time's the charm" confrontation between Ricky Vaughn and his beastly nemesis, mean-spirited batter Jack Parkman. Other recycled bits tend to fall flat this time around: Lacking the first *Major League*'s carefully coordinated buildup of the "Wild Thing" cult, the final entrance of Ricky Vaughn in *Major League II*, accompanied by a recorded rendition of his signature tune and the orgiastic screams of the crowd, is enjoyable enough, but fails to arouse and excite the viewer as it had in the original film.

The sequel's efforts to show that the characters have undergone changes that have done them no good, the better to joyously restore the original film's status quo at the end, are fitfully successful. Although Willie Mays Hayes' matriculation into a self-enamored movie star may have been intended as a petulant jab at Wesley Snipes' refusal to appear in the sequel, the gags surrounding Willie's bloated ego are very funny, as is the preview clip from his latest movie epic, *Black Hammer: White Lightning.* (Come to think of it, I'd pay good coin to see a shoot-'em-up costarring Willie Mays Hayes and the pre-gubernatorial Jesse "The Body" Ventura, if only to revel in the sequence in which "Black Hammer" seeks revenge for the murder of his pet boa constrictor.) Less effective are the scenes in which Ricky Vaughn attempts to obliterate his street-punk image by abandoning his crop-circle haircut, leather jacket and motorcycle in favor of custom-tailored suits, dinner engagements with the "right" people and upscale television ads (when was the last time *you* saw a deodorant commercial populated by old-money croquet players?), though some laughs are to be had when Ricky tries to market his new image by naming his pitches, á la Nolan Ryan: "The Terminator," "The Eliminator" and so on.

The film's broad lampooning of the relentless overcommercialization of baseball and its players, using Ricky Vaughn as an example of how corruptive a force this can be, indicate that the screenwriters were casting about for a new story tangent that would allow the film to stand as a separate entity, rather than merely an appendage of the earlier *Major League.* There is also the suggestion that the filmmakers intended to go off in yet another direction by spoofing the vexing Hollywood practice of Product Placement. This occurs when the financially strapped Roger Dorn resorts to plastering the walls of Municipal Stadium with low-cost advertising billboards for bowling alleys and bail-bond services. In this respect, *Major League II* may well have been poking fun at itself; nary a scene in the film goes by without a strategically planted plug for Pepsi Cola, Dunkin' Donuts or Seven-Eleven.

Unfortunately, these satirical elements are never allowed to reach their full potential; it was apparently deemed easier and more desirable to go for the cheap laugh whenever possible. This is most glaringly obvious in the performances of at least two actors who should have known better. Margaret Whitton's portrayal of superbitch Rachel Phelps, not exactly a paragon of subtlety in the original *Major League* (and hardly representative of the actress' excellent work in such films as *Ironweed* and *The Man Without a Face*), is grotesquely beyond control here; one would not be surprised if she was shown stealing and skinning Dalmatian puppies. Her performance is helped not at all by the writers' contemptuous habit of having Rachel explain her every action to us poor dumb yokels in the audience. We don't really need lines like, "*That* oughta shrink their sphincters!" to understand what she is up to; to quote another character in the film, "Don't insult their intelligence."

And while Bob Uecker, repeating his role of besotted play-by-play announcer Harry Doyle, does a masterful job delivering the film's opening expository monologue, recapping the events of the first *Major League* while setting the stage for what is to come, the remainder of Uecker's performance descends to the depths as often as it scales the heights. In fairness, while Margaret Whitton must shoulder most of the blame for her performance in *Major League II*, Bob Uecker is sabotaged not so much by his line delivery as by the costume department, which insisted upon dressing him in outfits that Liberace would have rejected as being too gaudy. It is a sure sign that the filmmakers have lost confidence in the script when they have to resort to funny costumes.

On the other hand, the formerly voodoo-obsessed Pedro Cerrano's conversion to Buddhist philosophy, which on paper doesn't seem too promising and which also relies extensively on silly costuming, works beautifully, thanks to the evenly measured performance of Dennis Haysbert—and by the surprising restraint exercised by the writers once the "new" Cerrano has been established. As idiotic as it may sound, the early scene in which Pedro slugs out a four-bagger, only to stop short as he rounds the bases to compassionately retrieve a wounded pigeon which he has accidentally knocked from the sky, is one of the best bits in the movie. It wouldn't have been quite so effective, however, if the writers had hammered the joke to death with a plethora of examples of Cerrano's newfound pacifism. Instead, this character trait is carefully held in check until its payoff in the final game between the Indians and the White Sox, when Cerrano serenely demonstrates that he has struck a happy medium between Inner Contentment and the Will to Win.

Also successfully handling the broader comedy in the film is another *Major League* alumnus, James Gammon as bullfrog-voiced coach Lou Brown. Not only does Gammon manage to extract laughs while having an on-screen heart attack, but he also hams it up deliciously in the scenes where, confined to a hospital bed and ordered to watch nothing but PBS reruns of *Upstairs Downstairs* so as not to overexcite himself,

he secretly monitors the Indians-Sox Division race by way of a hidden transistor radio. "I *love* this English shit!" he proclaims when his nurse expresses bewilderment over his shouts of exultation.

The "newer" characters, created by the writers in the hope of sustaining freshness while simultaneously paying homage to the established *Major League* formula, are a mixed bag. Erik Bruskotter, heretofore and afterward essentially a TV-series actor—his previous credits included a supporting role in *Tour of Duty* and a guest spot on Bob Uecker's *Mr. Belvedere*—is for the most part enjoyable as the terminally unfocused Rube Baker. While Rube's "Forrest Gump" persona sometimes allows the writers to lapse into gratuitous bad taste ("My mama always said it's better to eat shit than not eat at all"), Bruskotter invests the character with a lot more believability than the script affords him. Also good for a few loose chuckles are Rube's efforts to focus his concentration on the ballfield by reciting, from memory, the vapid "biographies" of the *Playboy* Playmates of the Month—and when this strategy loses its effectiveness, he begins committing to memory the "Frederick's of Hollywood" catalog. Only the fact that the comic value of both *Playboy* and Frederick's was pretty much tapped out by 1994 prevents this recurring gag from bringing down the house.

Cast as combative Tokyo Giants alumnus Isuro Tanaka is Takaaki Ishibashi, one of Japan's most beloved comic actors and recording artists, and the host of the highly-rated radio talk show "All Night Nippon." While some American viewers may find Ishibashi's *Major League II* antics to be even more annoying over-the-top than those of Margaret Whitton's Rachel Phelps, it should be observed that the Japanese sense of humor does not always translate well to non–Japanese audiences (take a look at the comedy-relief reporter in *Mothra* sometime). Besides, Ishibashi isn't given much of a chance to shine, thanks to the clichéd "funny foreigner" gags mercilessly forced upon him by the writers; for example, no opportunity is missed to translate the actor's Japanese rantings into scatological English subtitles, a routine that was already showing signs of senility in the first *Major League*. Happily, Ishibashi is given the privilege of introducing one of the more agreeable running gags in the picture: Frustrated over Pedro Cerrano's placidity, Isuro Tanaka, whose grasp of English slang is at best tenuous, challenges Cerrano's manhood by shouting "You have no marbles!" After a moment's befuddlement, Pedro gets the drift of Tanaka's insult, thereby setting up an amusing punchline in which, during the decisive Division game, the entire Indians lineup tries to provoke Cerrano into blasting out a home run by waving huge bags full of marbles.

Of the other newcomers to the *Major League* franchise, David Keith is obviously having a jolly good time cast against type as the repulsively arrogant free-agent catcher Jack Parkman. "The chance to play the bad guy is always great fun, and to act with this great cast is icing on the cake," commented Keith at the time of shooting. One wishes that he'd been the film's *only* bad guy so that it would not have been necessary to resurrect the tiresome Rachel Phelps, but the writers didn't see things this way. True, Parkman is an unpleasant individual, but principally because he has the talent to back up his brag and the nasty habit of speaking the truth about his "inferiors." Normally, this would be sufficient to qualify Parkman as Villain Supreme in a "root for the underdog" picture like *Major League II*, but apparently the scripters felt that he wasn't menacing enough, thus Rachel is arbitrarily shoehorned into the proceedings.

Except for a brief uncredited appearance by Rene Russo, repeating her *Major League* role as Jake Taylor's understanding helpmate Lynn (we'd just as soon not discuss the dishearteningly boring performance by the film's *other* uncredited A-list actor, Randy Quaid), the love interest in *Major League II* is evenly divided between the two women in Ricky Vaughn's life: Alison Doody as his gorgeous fashion-plate agent and lover Flannery, and Michelle Burke as his former flame, inner-city schoolmarm Nikki Reese. Either by accident or design, the writers subversively played havoc with audience expectation by making Flannery the more sympathetic of the two characters. Though she has clearly latched onto Ricky for his earning and marketing potential, and while at one point she expresses a crushingly condescending attitude towards her client/sweetheart, one is never in doubt that Flannery genuinely cares for Ricky as both a person and a romantic partner: Their ultimate parting of the ways comes about simply because she isn't the right woman for him. In contrast, Nikki Reese comes off as an incredible nag, showing up at Indians games apparently for the sole purpose of haranguing Ricky for forgetting his roots, and to demand that he drop his pretensions and go back to his "old self" (what, does she want him to become a carjacking jailbird again?). Even when Ricky moves heaven and earth to find time for both Nikki and Flannery, it isn't enough for Nikki, who has to be coerced into forgiving Ricky by one of her more sensible and less judgmental young students. The unexpected role-reversal treatment of Flannery and Vicki is easily the most original and intriguing aspect of *Major League II*.

Intriguing in a less positive way are the film's lapses in its own self-imposed logic. As mentioned, the premise of *Major League II* is carefully set out at the beginning of the film with an uninterrupted stream of fluent exposition delivered by Harry Doyle. If, as Doyle claims, the entire city of Cleveland—and, one supposes, the entire American League—is aware that former Indians owner Rachel Phelps deliberately undermined her team so that she would be able to sell the franchise to Miami, why would anyone tolerate her repurchase of the team in mid-film? And why, if she professes to despise Cleveland, would she even *want* the Indians back?

Also, we are to assume that the action takes place the year following the Indians' miraculous turnaround in the first *Major League*, which was released in 1989. Okay, that means the story takes place in 1990, so we can ignore the comments made by some observers that neither the Indians nor the White Sox were still in the American League's East Division in 1994, the year *Major League II* was released. Yet how can one explain Ricky Vaughn's appearance on Jay Leno's *Tonight Show*, since Leno did not take over from Johnny Carson until 1992?

Finally, since it has been established that Ricky Vaughn has been pulled from the rotation for the decisive Division game, it makes perfect sense that the young lady in the stadium control room has to conduct a frenzied search to find the tape cartridge containing Ricky's theme song "Wild Thing" when he makes his hitherto unannounced appearance. It makes less sense, however, that the fans in the stands would have their own "Wild Thing" signs at the ready in their hot little hands on a night that Vaughn wasn't supposed to be playing.

For all its faults and inconsistencies, *Major League II* is still great audience material, and the main credit for this should be attributed to director David S. Ward. Even with the weakest material, Ward knows how to stage a comedy scene for all it is worth, and then some. Particularly memorable are the silent reaction shots whenever a character looks askance or dumbfounded at a particularly appalling turn of events, or when confronted with a stream of verbal gobbledygook from Rube Baker or Isuro Tanaka (some of Tom Berenger's "takes" are worthy of an Oliver Hardy!).

Even better in the context of the film, Ward demonstrates the same confidence and expertise in staging the baseball scenes that he did in the first *Major League*—and, as before, these scenes are all the more satisfying because the actors are obviously doing their own ballplaying.

Nowhere near the cash cow that *Major League* proved to be, *Major League II* still posted a comfortable domestic gross of $30,626,000. That's the good news. The fact that the film's profits encouraged production of a another sequel, *Major League: Back to the Minors*, is something else again.

3. Major League: Back to the Minors

Morgan Creek Productions/Warner Bros.; released April 17, 1998

Executive producers: Michael Rachmil, Gary Barber, Bill Todman, Jr. Produced by James G. Robinson. Written and directed by John Warren; based on characters created by David S. Ward. Photography: Tim Suhrstedt. Edited by O. Nicholas Brown and Bryan H. Carroll. Original Music: Robert Folk. Casting: Pam Dixon Mickelson. Production design: David Crank. Set decoration: Frank Galline. Costume design: Mary E. McLeod. Key makeup artist: Vivian Baker. First assistant director: Christine Larson. Second assistant director: Kristin Killey. Supervising sound editor: Larry Kemp. Camera operator/"A" camera steadicam operator: Charles Papert. Set designers: Michael W. Devine, Colleen Balance. Illustrator: Scott Ritchie. Script supervisor: Thom Rainey. Foley editors: Kelly Oxford, Mark LaPointe. Foley artists: Dan O'-Connell, John Cucci. Japanese translations: Mariko Nagai. Digital visual effects: Perpetual Motion Pictures. Visual effects supervisor: Richard Malzahn; coordinator: Kimberly Sylvester. Technical adviser: Steve Yeager. Technicolor. 100 minutes; DTS/Dolby Digital/SDDS Sound. Rated PG-13.

Cast: Scott Bakula (Gus Cantrell); Corbin Bernsen (Roger Dorn); Dennis Haysbert (Pedro Cerrano); Takaaki Ishibashi (Taka Tanaka);

Jensen Daggett (Maggie Reynolds); Eric Bruskotter (Rube Baker); Ted McGinley (Leonard Huff); Bob Uecker (Harry Doyle); Walton Goggins (Downtown Anderson); Kenneth Johnson (Lance Peré); Judson Mills (Hog Ellis); Lobo Sebastian (Carlos Liston); Thom Barry (Pops Morgan); Peter MacKenzie (Doc Windgate); Tim and Tom DiFilippo (Juan No. 1); Ted DiFilippo (Juan No. 2); Steve Yeager (Coach Duke Temple); Larry Brandenberg (Chuck Swartski); Jack Baun (Chuck Ledbetter); Mike Schatz (Renegades Batter); Joe Kelly (Miracles Catcher); J. Don Ferguson (Umpire); Brian Beegle (Young Player); Ted Manson (Miracles Manager); Ronald "Buzz" Bowman (Miracles Announcer); Alex Van (Billy [Mascot]); Tim Ware (Hot Dog Vendor); Robert M. Egan (Rockcats Announcer); Michael A. Lynch (Chief Umpire); Richard Bruce Doughty (Boll Weevils Announcers); Al Hamacher (Diner Cook); Natalie Hendrix, Stephen Hardig, Leroy Myers, Gary P. Pozsik (Reporters); Andre Tardieu (Maitre D'); Brien Straw (Waiter); R. J. Kackley (First Base Umpire); Bradley Cable (Twins Runner); Ken Medlock (Twins Assistant Coach); Lucinda Whitaker (Bar Girl No. 1); Kimberly Herndon (Bar Girl No. 2); Elizabeth Diane Wells (Diner Waitress); Gary Murphy (Home Umpire); Scott Foxhall (Second Base Umpire); Warren Pepper (TV Reporter); Dee Thompson (Head Umpire); Raymond Sterling (First Base Umpire); Ron Clinton Smith, Richie Dye, Dolan Wilson (Tutu Men); Laura-Shay Griffin (Stewardess); Mark Storm (Mr. Buzz); Bayani Ison (Ishibashi Photo Double); T. J. White, Lonnie Smith, Kevin Ball, Gerard Williams, David Paul Lord, Rex Reddick, Danny Downey, Larry Rippenkroeger (Stunts); Cal Johnson (Stunt Coordinator); Eric Corps, Josh Fauske, Kawri Brown, Darren McClellan, Sean McClellan, James Nichols, Luke Owens-Bragg, Tyler Bain, Justin Lopez (Buzz Players); B. J. Dowdy, Max Sterling (Taka Doubles); Tim Cossins, Andy Barkett, Frank Charles, Daniel Fagley, Jason Lakeman, Greg Shephard, Skip Shipp, Allen Ritter, Robert White, Darrick Williams, Mark Kanapo, Marcus Hugee (Twins Players); Dan Frarracio, Jason Berry, Bradley Oates, Matt Toms, Kenneth Nelson, Scott Peek, Warren Lewis, Jimmy Eby, Greg Martin (Boll Weevils); Brian Vandell, Craig Halter, Ryan Butler, David Huss, Austin Alexander, Thomas Ragan, Damon Shabeldeen, George Huckabee, Tony Noviello, Sean McClellan, Joel Fenske (River Dogs); Scott Wease, Dennis Carpin, Bobby Hayward, Steve Conte, Jeff Patterson, Steve Deal, Brian Batson, Donald Morillo, Frank Charles, Andy Barkett, Brett Fallow (Crawdads); Ed Hill, Avery Fields, Jim Lynch (Umpires); Garry Weeks (Buzz Player); David Bowles (Spectator); Shawn Lerner (Hog Fan).

The career of burned-out Minor League pitcher Gus Cantrell is given a jumpstart when his old pal Roger Dorn, former Cleveland Indian and current owner of the Minnesota Twins, offers Gus the opportunity to manage the Twins' Triple-A South Carolina farm team, the Littletown Buzz. Gus certainly has his work cut out for him: Though one can detect faint glimmers of talent amongst the Buzz players, for the most part the team is a motley crew of misfits, foul-ups and knuckleheads. Among the players are first baseman Pops Morgan, who has been languishing in the Minors for 20 years; Lance Peré, a ballet-dancing outfielder; bespectacled intellectual pitcher Doc Windgate, whose "fast" ball sometimes actually reaches a velocity of 50 m.p.h.; another pitcher named Hog Ellis, who speaks in monosyllables and is terrified of anyone even slightly taller than he; the Gomez brothers, a pair of identical twins (with identical names!) who can't stand each other; and power hitter Downtown Anderson, an undeniably talented hotdog who feels he is slumming in the Minors and may jump ship before he is genuinely ready for the Big Show. Miraculously, Gus molds this unpromising material into a real team, and before long the Buzz is enjoying its first winning streak in years. Impressed with these results, Dorn invites Cantrell's team to the Metrodome, where, sparked by the smoldering feud between Gus and the stupidly arrogant Minnesota manager Leonard Huff, the Buzz plays the Twins in a well-publicized exhibition game. Thanks to Huff's underhanded tactics (including short-circuiting the stadium's lighting system), the game ends in a draw. Though at first uncertain as to whether or not the Buzz can *really* beat their major-league counterparts, Gus challenges Huff to a rematch—this time on the Buzz' home field. Aiding and abetting the Buzz in cleaning the Twins' clock are a trio of holdovers from the two earlier *Major League* films: the towering Pedro Cerrano (who's a Born-Again Christian this season), the feckless Rube Baker, and the incomprehensible Isuro "Taka" Tanaka.

Most of the participants in the first two *Major League* films were willing to stick the proverbial fork in the franchise before a third film could be made. Not even David S. Ward, who started it all with the original *Major League* in 1989, wanted anything to do with the third and final series entry, *Major League: Back to the Minors*. Ward's "contribution" this time out is confined to the contractually-dictated "based on characters created by" screen credit, leaving only producer and Morgan Creek CEO James G. Robinson, along with a mere four of the original film's cast members, to valiantly soldier forward.

Judging from the evidence at hand, it is likely that the third film was conceived in hopes of luring back a fifth cast member from the first *Major League*. Though the character played by former *Quantum Leap* star Scott Bakula may be called Gus Cantrell, he is clearly meant to be Jake Taylor, the aging "team leader" so vividly portrayed by Tom Berenger in the two earlier films. The fact that Gus is on old-buddy terms with *Major League* carryovers Roger Dorn and Pedro Cerrano, and *Major League II* alumni Rube Baker and Isuro Tanaka, would seem to confirm that Cantrell is Taylor in everything but name. And although Gus Cantrell is a pitcher while Jake Taylor was a catcher, both characters are suffering from the same sort of career-threatening aches and pains in the joints—and both Gus (in this film) and Jake (in the previous film) deliver quickie monologues in which they muse over the likelihood of pursuing careers outside of baseball.

Whether or not Tom Berenger was approached to appear in *Major League: Back to the Minors* is a moot point: The only returnees from the two earlier pictures were Corbin Bernsen as Dorn, Dennis Haysbert as Cerrano, Erik Bruskotter as Rube, Takaaki Ishibashi as Tanaka, Bob Uecker as play-by-play announcer Harry Doyle and former LA Dodger Steve Yeager, doubling as an actor in the role of Coach Duke Temple and as the film's technical advisor/baseball coach.

As was the case with the final installment of the *Bad News Bears* series (see notes for *The Bad New Bears Go to Japan*), the decision was made to forsake most of the familiar story elements and surroundings of the earlier *Major League* pictures and pursue an entirely different direction—and that direction was downward, into the Triple-A Minors (the Cleveland Indians, who "starred" in the earlier films, are here not mentioned at all). Chosen to lead the franchise down a brand-new path was writer/director John Warren, a 1986 recipient of the AFI screenwriting fellowship who, prior to *Back to the Minors*, had filmed several independent projects, a number of episodes for such TV series as *Nightmare Café* and *The Adventures of Brisco County Jr.*, and the Pauly Shore/Janine Turner direct-to-video starrer *The Curse of Inferno* (1997). John Warren's non-showbiz credentials would seem to have made him the ideal choice for the assignment. "Baseball is in my blood," he explained in the film's pressbook. "I was a pitcher in high school and at Ohio University. In the summers I played semi-pro ball. But much like the character of [Doc Windgate] in the movie, I couldn't throw a fast ball to save my life."

Warren had also learned to "work cheap" in the Indy-film and TV-series mills, an important qualification inasmuch as the budget of *Back to the Minors* was radically

Major League: Back to the Minors: The Littletown Buzz, all together for a change. Front row, left to right: Downtown Anderson (Walton Goggins), Lance Peré (Kenneth Johnson), manager Gus Cantrell (Scott Bakula), coach Duke Temple (Steve Yeager), Juan No. 1 and Juan No. 2 Gomez (Tim and Ted DeFilippo). Back row, left to right: Hog Ellis (Judson Mills), Dock Windgate (Peter MacKenzie), Pedro Cerrano (Dennis Haysbert), Rube Baker (Eric Bruskotter), Thom Barry (Pops Morgan). Missing: Taka Tanaka (Takaaki Ishibashi).

scaled down from the first two films (which were themselves hardly in the *Titanic* category). If we are to believe the studio press releases, Warren welcomed the chance to explore the world of low-maintenance baseball: "It's hard to care about the tribulations of millionaires. So I came up with this group of eccentric, misfit minor league players who are underdogs that people can root for. These characters have humor and heart and an endless passion and love for the game. What's endearing about these guys is they are really trying."

In place of the standard audition process, Warren played baseball with the actors reading for the supporting roles: The more enthusiasm displayed on the field, the better chance the actor stood of being cast (in a way, it was a fond hark back to the days when Buster Keaton selected his gag-

men and technicians primarily on the basis of whether or not they were willing to play on Keaton's studio ball team). Steve Yeager coached the actors whom Warren ultimately chose for the film, and also worked with the hundred or so real-life Minor League ballplayers who were recruited for the game scenes. "I think baseball players and a lot of sports athletes and personalities kind of act as they play," noted Yeager. "They play for the crowd; the actors act for the audience. It's very similar. They took what I passed on to them and applied their own personalities to the characters."

Taking a page from the gamebook of his predecessor David S. Ward, Warren strove to instill a genuine sense of team spirit in the cast by having them train from four to five hours a day for two weeks, no matter what the weather, and by keeping up the training sessions during actual filming. While this process may have been exhausting to the actors, it was second nature to the real ballplayers, who were recruited from such honest-to-goodness Minor League teams as North Carolina's Hickory Crawdads and Piedmont Boll Weevils, the Charleston (South Carolina) River Dogs, and the *real* Buzz—which, unlike its *Back to the Minors* counterpart, was a Pacific Coast League team located in Salt Lake City. In exchange for their cooperation, and in lieu of huge salaries, these teams were allowed to retain their names and wear their uniforms on-camera.

To keep the budget under control, *Major League: Back to the Minors* was filmed virtually in its entirety in and around Charleston, South Carolina, except for the four days spent shooting the Buzz-Minnesota game in the Twins' Metrodome. Advantageously, Charleston boasted no fewer than six minor-league parks; seventeen days were devoted to filming the Buzz "home games" at College Park (then the headquarters of the Single-A Charleston Rainbows), while other locations included the American Legion's Collins Park, the College of Charleston's Remley's Point, the ballfield at Summerville High School, Joe Riley Stadium—home of the aforementioned River Dogs and here doubling for Roger Dorn's Metrodome skybox—and Charleston Coliseum, which stood in for Metrodome's locker rooms and tunnelways. A seventh ballpark, picturesque Mirmow Field in nearby Orangeburg, South Carolina, accommodated two days' filming of selected "away" games. And rather than expensively shuttle cast and crew to an out-of-state soundstage for interior scenes, a temporary studio was constructed at the former Charleston Naval Base, with additional makeshift sets built in the grand ballroom of the city's luxurious Francis Marion Hotel.

Making excellent use of the authentic locations and genuine baseball talent at hand, director Warren exhibits a sure and steady hand in his staging of the ballgame scenes, this despite a bit of obvious post-production trickery in "improving" a couple of pitched balls so they'd appear faster and more accurate on screen. Warren also has a firm grasp on the warm, almost familial relationship between the players of the Minor Leagues and their enthusiastic middle-income fans—not quite as well realized here as in the definitive "Minors" film *Bull Durham* (q.v.), but almost as satisfying. And as in most "little" baseball pictures (see notes for *The Last Home Run* and *Perfect Game*), it is the tiny atmospheric touches in *Back to the Minors* that come across best: the concession-stand operator returning four dollars' change from a ten-dollar bill for the purchase of three hot dogs and three sodas (try swinging a deal like *that* in a Big League stadium), the economy-conscious nocturnal bus rides from game to game, and a delightful vignette in which Gus Cantrell is picked up from the Littletown airport in a jeep driven by team mascot "Mr. Buzz" (Mark Storm), who, running a bit late, is already dressed in his requisite bee costume—all except the bee's head, with which an uncomfortable Gus is forced to share the back seat. In many ways, the pinchpenny budget of *Major League: Back to the Minors* works in its favor, creating a pleasantly nostalgic small-town, small-market ambience that a more expensive and ambitious film might not have been able to sustain.

Perhaps because the pressures of a huge budget and high expectations were off their backs, the two principal returnees from the first *Major League* deliver what are probably their best and most amiable performances in the entire trilogy. As Roger Dorn, Corbin Bernsen has totally purged himself of the character's least attractive qualities, his preening egomania and selfish reluctance to put himself out for his other players. Modest, ingratiating, unassuming, willing to poke fun at himself for occasionally taking on airs, Bernsen might as well be playing another character entirely, and it is only the fact that the script has established that the action is taking place several years after the first two films that we are able to reconcile this kinder, humbler Roger Dorn with the selfish narcissist whom we have come to expect. Remarkably, Bernsen manages to get just as many laughs playing a down-to-earth nice guy as he did in his previous swell-head guise.

In a similar fashion, Dennis Haysbert's Pedro Cerrano has ceased to be the caricatured cult follower of the two earlier *Major Leagues* and has evolved into a full, multifaceted human being. True, Pedro has embraced Christianity with the same fanatical fervor with which he previously practiced voodoo and Buddhism; this time, however, he is no mindless disciple, but is fully aware that his behavior may seem odd to others and is willing to accept this rather than expect everyone else to march to his drummer. And while he is occasionally compromised by the silliness of the script (one of his new concentration tactics is to wear a black hood while pitching!), one always gets the feeling that Pedro is much smarter than his behavior would suggest, whereas the earlier films tended to buffoonize his character. Pedro's best scene finds him good-naturedly "ordering" his statue of the voodoo god Jovo (a prominent feature of the original *Major League*) to keep itself scarce so that the Buzz can defeat the Twins without any outside help.

Despite all that is going for it—or should have been going for it—*Major League: Back to the Minors* is a failure, easily one of the weakest and most disappointing "second sequels" ever made. For all his expertise in staging the baseball highlights, John Warren cannot seem to maintain any sort of variety or pace; each successive ballgame looks exactly like the one which preceded it, and none is particularly thrilling or suspenseful. Save for a few lively moments in the opening scenes, the film has all the excitement of a three-hour rain delay.

As for the performers, while the aforementioned Corbin Bernsen and Dennis Haysbert manage to survive the film without egg on their faces, the other *Major League* carryovers are not so fortunate. Again cast as play-by-play sportscaster Harry Doyle (who, judging by the script, seems to have been demoted to a Minor League radio network for the crime of giving up drinking), Bob Uecker comes off a bit better than he did in *Major League II*, investing his larger than usual role with his razor-sharp comic timing and delivery; unfortunately, the material he has to deliver is downright dreadful at times, and only gets worse the longer he remains on screen.

In the same vein, Japanese comedian Takaaki Ishibashi, already a bit of a pill in small doses in *Major League II*, is utterly indigestible in his extended encore appearance as Taka Tanaka. For starters, Ishibashi does virtually none of his own ballplaying; all of his best diamond stunts are performed by a brace of doubles who look nothing like him. Secondly, there is just so much humor that can be extracted from the premise of a Japanese ballplayer who is so incomprehensible that he needs to have English subtitles even when speaking English. In one pathetically botched sequence, Ishibashi carries on a conversation with Gus Cantrell and Pedro Cerrano; after laboriously establishing the aforementioned subtitled–English bit, the scene goes straight into the toilet by having Cantrell and Cerrano's words translated into Japanese at the bottom of the screen—and then repeating this "joke" for nearly *two minutes*.

Reprising his *Major League II* role as Rube Baker, the hayseed Cleveland Indians catcher with a serious control-and-concentration problem, Eric Bruskotter is even more lamentably mishandled than Takaaki Ishibashi, and not only because Rube's endearingly pointless "Forrest Gump" aphorisms are totally absent here. If we are to take *Back to the Minors* at face value, Rube Baker's demotion to the Triple-A Buzz will not be enough to whip him back into Big League condition; he seems to have totally lost whatever talent he once might have had, and would be well advised to listen when coach Gus Cantrell half-seriously suggests that Rube find some other line of work. Even worse, the viewer never finds out if Rube pulls himself out of his slump; the character gradually fades away as the story progresses, and it is difficult to remember if he even shows up in the climactic ballgame. There seems to have been no real reason to include Rube Baker in *Back to the Minors* at all, unless it was a favor granted by star Scott Bakula, with whom Erik Bruskotter had previously appeared in several *Quantum Leap* episodes. (Fortunately, Bruskotter was able to survive this career setback, and within a year or so he was safely ensconced in a recurring role on the popular NBC TV weekly drama *Providence*.)

Most of the film's "new" characters run the gamut from tedious to bloody awful. The various members of the Buzz certainly conform to John Warren's description of a bunch of "eccentric misfits" who love the game, but at times they are so irritatingly inept that one wonders how they could have survived a backyard whiffleball tournament, much less a season in the Minors. And unlike their counterparts in the original *Major League*, this new batch of misfits lacks even the veneer of credibility. The former ballet dancer who pirouettes his way across the field, the overanalytical pitcher with the slowest arm in the south, the nervous rookie whose vocabulary is limited to pithy phrases like "'S cool," the combative identical twins who have to be tethered during training to keep them from crashing into one another.... These are comic-strip caricatures, not living, breathing human beings; punchlines, rather than

people. As a result, it is impossible to truly care about what happens to them.

Two of the newer characters are more substantial, but both suffer from a structural defect in the script. Conceited pitching phenomenon Downtown Anderson (Walton Goggins) has some worthwhile scenes when he angrily accuses Gus Cantrell of holding him back from the Majors out of jealousy when the real reason is because the boy isn't quite ready yet, then subsequently returns to the Buzz to sheepishly admit that Cantrell was right and to solicit Gus' help in improving his game. And Gus' fiancée Maggie Reynolds (Jensen Daggett) is extremely appealing as she provides moral support and confidence to her man when he needs it most. The problem here is that these two characters are completely defined by, and exist only within, their relationship to Gus Cantrell. The ensemble approach of the first two *Major Leagues*, in which the characters remained distinct, separate individuals no matter how much interaction occurred between them, is infinitely more preferable to the direction taken by *Back to the Minors*, in which Downtown's sincere humility and Maggie's selfless encouragement are merely convenient devices to make Gus Cantrell look good.

The film's two villains also fall flat, for entirely different reasons. On a purely farcical level, Warren's instincts were right on target when he chose to revive a plot device that had served the earlier *Major League* films quite well: The nasty, egotistical, intimidatingly talented opposing batter who, after making a fool of "our" pitcher, must himself be humiliated by that same pitcher in the final scene. In *Back to the Minors*, the beastly batter is the Minnesota Twins' Carlos Liston, whose reputation is so fearsome that he is able to send a gaggle of TV reporters scurrying for their lives after a disastrous locker-room interview. Normally, this is a "can't miss" comic set-up, but miss it does by a mile. In the role of Carlos Liston, improvisational comedian Lobo Sebastian—who only one year earlier was chillingly effective as a homicidal high school bully in director Kevin Reynolds' *187*—conveys about as much menace as a plate of tapioca pudding. Nor is Sebastian helped along by the incredibly clumsy staging of his key scenes; especially painful is his final showdown with pitcher Hog Ellis (Judson Mills), who overcomes his fear of Carlos Liston—and of speaking complete sentences—by reciting a long and stupefyingly unfunny parody of Clint Eastwood's "Do ya feel lucky, punk?" speech from *Dirty Harry*.

If Lobo Sebastian is not enough, Ted McGinley as the brayingly braggadocio Twins manager Leonard Huff is too, too much. While we should be thankful that *Major League: Back to the Minors* is not burdened with the arm-flapping excesses of Margaret Whitton as Rachel Phelps, Ted McGinley (an otherwise gifted comic actor, as witnessed by his work as Jefferson D'Arcy on the long-running TV sitcom *Married ... with Children*) can hardly be regarded as a fair trade. Evidently, McGinley was operating on the theory that if you yell loud enough and grimace incessantly, no one will notice that nothing really funny is happening. We notice.

In fairness, McGinley received some of the film's best reviews, with many critics expressing gratitude that at least one of the actors was able to inject some energy in the otherwise dull and plodding proceedings. It should also be observed that the ultimate failure of the Leonard Huff character can be traced back to the script. As tiresomely repetitious as she eventually became in the earlier *Major League* entries, Rachel Phelps was a plausible villain because she owned the Cleveland Indians, and as such she had the power to behave as obnoxiously as she wanted because she called all the shots. Similarly, the fractious Jack Parkman in *Major League II* was able to get away with his

antisocial behavior because of his unquestioned batting skills. But in *Back to the Minors* it is established time and again that Leonard Huff is a lousy manager, plunging the Twins into a debilitating losing streak because he is incapable of reining in the players' prima donna behavior. Indeed, at one point in the film he actually expresses pride over his inability to bring the team together! With no justification for Huff's strident egomania, there is no logical reason that Roger Dorn, who as owner of the Twins wields far more clout than any manager, does not fire Huff on the spot, yet it takes Dorn the entire movie to realize what the viewer has known all along, that Gus Cantrell should be the man guiding the destiny of the Twins. There is nothing wrong in creating an insufferably arrogant villain like Leonard Huff—but the character can't work unless he actually has something to be insufferably arrogant about.

It might border on sacrilege to suggest within the pages of this book that simply knowing how to successfully stage a baseball scene is not enough to make a successful baseball picture. This, however, was the unfortunate case with *Major League: Back to the Minors*. Though John Warren brought a wealth of actual ballpark experience and insight to the game scenes, he was totally out of his element when it came to staging the comedy sequences. David S. Ward, the man behind the first two *Major Leagues*, was equally adept at both baseball and comedy, and his input is sorely missed the third time out. Apparently, Warner Bros. also sensed that Ward's absence was a portent of failure, inasmuch as the studio refused to allow critics to view the film before its release. Premiering at 2322 theaters in mid–April of 1998, *Major League: Back to the Minors* posted a first-weekend gross of $2,057,000, steadily losing ground thereafter. If you're wondering why the film almost immediately dropped out of theatrical release and retreated to home video, do the math.

The Man from Left Field

Burt Reynolds Productions Inc./CBS; originally telecast October 15, 1993

Executive Producers: Burt Reynolds, Lamar Jackson, Renée Valente. Directed by Burt Reynolds. Written and coproduced by Wayne Allan Rice. Original music: Bobby Goldsboro. Photography: Nick McLean. Edited by Tony Hayman. Casting: Shay Griffin. Production design: Beala Neel. Set decoration: Bobby Amor. Costume supervisor: Howard Sussman. Key makeup artists: Brian McManus, Sandy Spika. Sound: Joe Foglia. Production manager: Don Gold. First assistant director: James Van Wyck. Second assistant director: Dave Stern. Special effects: John Patteson, J. B. Jones. Color. 97 minutes; sound.

Cast: Burt Reynolds ("Jack Robinson"); Reba McEntire (Nancy Lee Prinzi); Kauwela Acocella (Beau Prinzi); Derek Baxter (Malcolm); Adam Cronan (Bama Block); Sean Dunne (Peanut); Billy Gardner, III (J.C.); Adam Ohren (Hooksy); Tino Taylor (Tino); Joe Theismann (Phil Corey); Bradley Barfield (Eddie Corey); Jonathan Bouck (Jackie Denard); Suzanne Dodd (Personnel Receptionist); Clarence Goss (Papa Charlie); Danny Greene (Mr. Block); Brian Iannitti (Albert); Ken Kay (Bill Garrett); Tom Kouchalakos (Mr. Hookstratten); Richard LePore (Personnel Manager); Marc Macaulay (Mr. O'Connor); Michael O'Smith (Mr. Bates); Avert Sommers (Mrs. Carver); David Berardi (Darryl); Gene Deckerhoff, Vic Prinzi (Announcers); Jennifer Kays (Jennifer, secretary); C. James Lewis (Officer Lewis); Aaron Vaughn (Aaron Corey).

The baseball-happy youngsters of Indiantown, Florida, may be dirt poor, but what they lack in material things they make up for in team spirit. Unfortunately, the Indiantown Indians will be unable to join the ritzy Walker Key Junior Baseball League unless they can come up with an adult coach by 11 A.M. on the registration-deadline date. As the kids sneak a practice session on the league's fancy ballpark diamond, Indians pitcher Beau Prinzi notices a dark, phantomlike figure lurking somewhere in left field. On closer examination, the figure turns out to be a shabby, amnesiac derelict who has been sleeping in the bullpen for the past few days. Beau persuades the taciturn drifter to act as coach for the Indians; when league manager O'Connor demands to know the new coach's name, Beau's black teammate J.C. quickly comes up with "Jackie Robinson"—which is just as quickly modified as Jack Robinson. The youngsters pay for a shave and new wardrobe for "Jack," then find him a paying job as a woodcutter and a place to stay in the stable loft of a nearby horse farm. Though Jack still has no idea who he really is, nor where he comes from, it is obvious that his baseball skills, and his A-to-Z knowledge of the game, are second to none. As Jack and the boys get to know each other better, and as the team's baseball prowess improves by leaps and bounds, several curiously contradictory facts come to light. While he can be gentle and sagacious in dispensing advice concerning the boys' behavior on and off the field—among other things, he convinces the team's sensitive catcher Hooksy that there's nothing shameful in having a father who is a "mere" gardener—Jack also has an extremely violent temper, as proven when he breaks the hand of the belligerent boyfriend of Beau's single mother, Nancy Lee; when he deploys martial-arts skills to dispose of a trio of punks who've been extorting money from the Indiantown youngsters; and when he beats the living hell out of the abusive, alcoholic father of team member Bama Block. Though for the most part she finds him personable and charming, Nancy Lee senses that Jack is carrying a lot of rage inside him. But only after he rescues J.C. from drowning—an event that triggers a flood of painful memories—does Jack reveal the full extent of, and reason for, that rage. And only then do we learn that Jack Robinson is really Buddy Lee Howser, a former major-league ballplayer and, more recently, a prominent New York sports physician who, having been traumatized by a devastating series of personal tragedies, simply "checked out" of life.

Had *The Man from Left Field* been telecast fifteen or even ten years earlier than its October 15, 1993, playdate, it would have fostered a media blitz commensurate to live CNN coverage of the Second Coming. Here was Burt Reynolds, for many years the number one movie box-office attraction in the nation, deigning to return to his television roots—not only to star in and direct a humble made-for–TV movie, but also to give one more major boost to the community of Jupiter, Florida, where the local economy and tourist trade had been booming ever since the actor had established the celebrity-magnet Burt Reynolds Dinner Theatre in 1979.

By the time *The Man from Left Field* hit the airwaves, however, Reynolds' movie career had pretty much fizzled as a result of such D.O.A. film projects as *Rent-a-Cop*, *Switching Channels* and *Physical Evidence*. And there was no novelty to his appearing on television, inasmuch as his weekly CBS sitcom *Evening Shade*, for which the actor earned an Emmy, had been playing to respectable ratings since 1990. This last fact alone might have been sufficient reason for CBS to give *Man from Left Field* a big publicity send-off; Reynolds still had a strong fan base, even though they weren't attending his movies as often as before. Unfortunately, the air was thick in the fall of 1993 with negative publicity surrounding the breakup of Reynolds' marriage to actress Loni Anderson, which even by Hollywood-gossip standards was a nasty, messy business.

Evidently not wishing to provide any more ammunition to Reynolds' detractors, CBS virtually threw *Man from Left Field* away in a sacrificial Friday night slot opposite ABC's highly-rated sitcom block *Step by Step* and *Hangin' with Mr. Cooper*, and the popular newsmagazine *20/20*. Even CBS' print ads seemed calculated to downplay Burt Reynolds' participation, offering a lovely backlit medium portrait of costar Reba McEntire while consigning Reynolds to a blurry, back-to-camera distance shot. All of which was quite unfair, since the film, while not without its flaws, had much to offer for Burt Reynolds devotees and baseball fans alike.

Despite the star/director's personal problems, he managed to maintain a happy set on location in Jupiter, unfailingly exhibiting the warmth, generosity and fellow-feeling that characterized his best days. On her official website, country singer Reba McEntire, who'd previously guest-starred on Reynolds' TV series *Evening Shade*, has nothing but glowing words for the filming experience and her costar: "It was a fun shoot, with friends and family taking turns to go with me. The weather was beautiful there on the coast of Florida. I also loved working with Burt Reynolds.... Burt has given back a tremendous amount of love and support to the town of Jupiter, Florida."

The youngsters and teenagers in the cast were all recruited from the Burt Reynolds Dinner Theater acting classes. Under Reynolds' patient tutelage, the kids delivered wonderful, naturalistic performances, and also acquitted themselves quite nicely on the baseball field. While there was the occasional danger of lapsing into stereotype—especially in the case of Adam Ohren, who, as "Hooksy," was required to play the obligatory team intellectual, speaking more like a Thesaurus than a real kid—overall the youngsters were thoroughly credible and appealing (Ohren's brief and touching scene with Reynolds as they discussed what was truly important in life more than made up for the youthful actor's stilted dialogue delivery in the earlier reels). It is all the more puzzling, then, that none of the child actors in *Man from Left Field* graduated to full-scale stardom, or even had much of a film career after 1993.

Generally speaking, the younger actors come off better than the older ones; some of the performances by the supporting and bit players are so overripe that one wouldn't be surprised if the name of Mack Sennett, Hal Roach or Jules White appeared in the opening credits. These hammy excesses are, however, amply compensated for by the refreshingly relaxed and down-to-earth performance of Reba McEntire as "baseball mom" Nancy Lee Prinzi. Characteristically, McEntire—who is confident enough in her singing talents that she can afford to be modest about other things— has credited Burt Reynolds with putting her at ease on the set and allowing the naturalism to flow freely without any sort of "actorish" tricks. With or without Reynolds' input, however, McEntire has that rare gift, shared only with such pantheon actresses as Carole Lombard and Jean Arthur, of being able to realistically play scenes with whomever she is appearing, and to make that other person seem to be every bit as good as she is. Five minutes into Reba's first scene with her screen "son" Kauwela Acocella, and the audience is absolutely convinced that the actress is the boy's real mother.

Perhaps because he was preoccupied with extracting good performances from his actors, and in dreaming up the richly evocative location shots which permeate the film, Burt Reynolds the director outshines Burt Reynolds the actor on this occasion. It is taking nothing away from the man to observe that Reynolds' portrayal of the mysterious "Jack Robinson" is at its most fascinating in his early, largely nonverbal scenes, in which he is more a presence than a character. Once Jack Robinson cleans himself up and begins talking in complete sentences, he has morphed into the old familiar Burt Reynolds, and as such offers little that we haven't seen before: The effortless charisma, the all-knowing sideways glances, the laconic wit, the ubiqui-

tous toothpick tucked in the corner of his mouth. It is nice to have an old friend back in near-peak form, even if Reynolds' line delivery is a bit off the mark (according to Reba McEntire, he had some trouble learning lines and had to have his dialogue piped in via a tiny, well-hidden earphone). Still, one rather misses the inscrutable pre-regeneration Jack Robinson, if only because the character proved that Reynolds' true acting range extended well beyond his patented screen persona.

Reynolds' most challenging scene occurs shortly before the end, when, in a long, rambling stream-of-consciousness monologue, he sobbingly recaps his entire life, from his salad days as a college athlete to his present sorry condition as a man running away from himself. Samuel Beckett–like soliloquies of this nature are difficult for even the most versatile of actors, and in this case Reynolds may have bitten off more than he could chew. Perhaps out of self-consciousness, the actor hides his face from the camera throughout most of his harangue, while Reba McEntire, in medium shot, reacts sympathetically to her costar's past woes—and again, McEntire's unaffected performance (coupled with Reynolds' direction) makes the scene far more riveting than it really is.

The Man from Left Field falls short of classic status in several respects. By rights, the tribulations and triumphs of the youthful Indiantown Indians should be the main focal point throughout, but halfway through the proceedings the film becomes a Burt Reynolds Picture, with Reynolds' Jack Robinson singlehandedly solving everyone's problems and determining the story's outcome. Far too often, Robinson's solution to a crisis is to resort to brute strength, and while in each instance the person on the receiving end of Jack's fists is eminently deserving of a good trouncing, the overabundance of violence in the last half hour of the film tends to wear down the viewer.

And after so much preaching to his team that a man should not be measured by wealth or material possession but instead by what he is inside, the hero's conspicuous consumption at the end of the picture—posh New York offices, custom-made suits, a private helicopter descending upon the team's final championship game—is hard to reconcile with the messages conveyed in the rest of the film. (Also, Jack's last-minute arrival at the game is such a "grabber" that we never find out who wins!)

The film's nadir occurs when, as a means of bonding with his youthful charges, Jack Robinson accompanies them to a "dirty" movie. Even allowing for the fact that the team members are from the wrong side of the tracks and not entirely up to date as to what is considered "hip" in the world of mass entertainment, it is impossible to believe that anyone in AD 1993—young or old alike—would regard a fuzzy, splicey public-domain copy of Jane Russell's 1943 starrer *The Outlaw* as the *ne plus ultra* in raw, unadulterated R-rated steaminess. (If Jack had *really* wanted to give his boys a rush, he should have taken them to see Hedy Lamarr's *Ecstacy* [1933], which, like *The Outlaw*, has lapsed into public domain and wouldn't have stretched the film's budget one extra bit.) At that, this bonding sequence is more tolerable than the thematically similar scene in Burt Reynolds' subsequent theatrical feature *Cop & ½* (1993), in which Reynolds and his new little buddy (Sammy Hernandez) "make swords" while standing at a urinal.

It must, however, be noted that the good moments in *Man from Left Field* far outnumber the bad. Highlights include the impromptu batting-cage competition between Jack Robinson and swellheaded rival coach Phil Corey, played by former Washington Redskins quarterback Joe Theismann. Adding to his list of accomplishments as the NFL's Most Valuable Player of 1983, his many thriving business and charitable enterprises, and his lengthy hitch as color analyst for ESPN, Theismann, like Reba McEntire, proves to be an accomplished "natural" actor; his depiction of Corey as an arrogant jerk who imagines himself the soul of humility could not have been bettered even by a more experienced performer. Also worth the admission price (if indeed admission were charged for a free–TV presentation) is the third-act montage in which the Indiantown Indians matriculate from awkward amateurs to seasoned players during Jack's exhaustive practice sessions. Bobby Goldsboro's musical score perfectly complements the action, beginning with a faltering, single-finger rendition of "Chopsticks" as the team struggles to get their bearings, then gradually evolving into a full-orchestra rhapsody as the players slowly but surely improve with each passing day.

With more time devoted to the kids and less to Burt Reynolds, especially in the overly rushed climactic sequences, *The Man from Left Field* might have been one of the best made-for–TV baseball films of the 1990s. But considering the many small pleasures the film offers us, we are willing in this case to accept second best.

*The Marksmen**

One Body Productions/Shoreline Entertainment/Promotional Management Group/ Bouquet Pictures Distribution. World premiere, 1997; limited theatrical release, 1998; video premiere, April 1999.

Executive Producer: Van Horneff. Produced by Jay Schillinger, Branden Miller, Timothy Harsh, Peter B. Mulroy and Christopher Newton. Directed by Steve Kanaly. Written by Jay Schillinger. Color. 88 minutes; sound.

*Re-released as Sliding Home on October 6, 2000.

Cast: Jay Schillinger (Tommy Madden); Martha Byrne (Alison Wells); Steve Kanaly (Hank Madden); Martin Kove (Samuel J. Weber); Christopher Burgard (Eddie Fletcher); Timothy Harsh (Jim "Cheeze" Cheezowski); E. J. Dougher (Max Danielson); Bekki Vallin (Kelly Marks); Joe Nienow (Joe Watson); Kimberly A. Osborne (Amy Winters); Michael T. Dorski (Hans Lachner); Pastor Ray Connor (Himself); Paul LaPree (TV Reporter); Jim Vercimac (Police Officer); Craig Beilky (Umpire 1); Shawn Lee (Rob "Pig Pen" Shorey); Peter B. Mulroy (Chad "Muskrat" Shultz); Zaque Meyers (Paul Marz); Clinton A. Copps (Mike "Moose" Mathies); Mike Mathies (Mike Dorski); Cris Newton (Art Hickman); Lisbeth Schara (Clarise Wilson); Scott Gruening (Scott Thompson); Debbie Kazinski (Doris Favre); Robert Bruss (Reporter 1); Joy Marquardt (Reporter 2); Dan Erdman (Photographer); Jeff Binder, Carl Brown, Kingsley Forbes (Bar Regulars); John Copps (Umpire 2); Matt Copps (Umpire 3); Brent Kanaly (Sara Madden); Dean Michael Kovalski (Dean Morton).

Four years after leaving his home town of Wausau, Wisconsin, to join the New York Yankees, local baseball hero Tommy Madden returns in disgrace, having been unceremoniously banished from the Major Leagues for allegedly accepting a bribe. Brought back to Wausau by the death of his mother, Tommy has a lot of fences to mend, especially with his long-estranged father Hank, and with his high school sweetheart Alison, whom he'd previously dumped without even the courtesy of a letter or a telephone call. In addition, he is wrestling with a deep, dark secret, one that compelled him to cut all ties with his friends and loved ones in the first place. Weary of running away from adversity (and himself), Tommy decides to remain in Wausau— where, bolstered by the love and encouragement of the ever-loyal Alison, he organizes his old ballplaying pals into a fastpitch softball team, the Marksmen. Despite the omnipresence of disreputable high school coach Sam Weber, who shares our hero's sinister secret, Tommy coaches the Marksmen to a string of victories, ulti-

mately guiding the team all the way to the National Softball Fastpitch Tournament.

Filmed in July and August of 1996, *The Marksmen* was produced on a $500,000 budget by two Hollywood marketing executives: Branden Miller of 20th Century–Fox, and Jay Schillinger, formerly of Disney. The idea originated with Schillinger, who in his youth had been a Wisconsin state wrestling champion. Though his sport of preference was baseball, Schillinger admitted that his game was never up to professional standards. "So," he explained to Jan Uebelherr of the Milwaukee *Journal-Sentinel*, "I though I'd make a movie of it. It's in the vein of *Rocky*. It's fun."

While the film concentrated on fastpitch softball, Schillinger considered it "a universal story, in the sense that if anyone's ever left town in pursuit of their dreams, there's always a lingering fear of, 'What if I came back with my tail between my legs?'... I wanted to write a story that I knew I could film in Wisconsin." Specifically, *The Marksmen* was filmed in the cities of Mosinee, Rothschild, and Schillinger's home town of Wausau; he himself played the lead role of Tommy Madden, with several local actors and nonprofessionals filling out the supporting parts, bits and extra assignments.

Drawing upon his Hollywood connections, Schillinger enlisted the services of actor Steven Kanaly, previously a costar of the long-running Prime Time soap *Dallas*. In addition to playing Tommy's father, Kanaly also directed, having served his apprenticeship in this capacity with several *Dallas* episodes. The film's nominal villain, Sam Weber, was played by another Hollywoodite, Martin Kove, basically reprising his role as nasty martial-arts instructor John Kreese in the first two *Karate Kid* films— which, along with *Rocky*, would seem to have formed the bulk of the inspiration for *The Marksmen*. The other "name" actor in the film was Martha Byrne, familiar to viewers for her Emmy-winning work as Lily Walsh on the daytime drama *As the World Turns*, and here cast as Tommy's childhood heartthrob Alison.

After its theatrical premiere in Wausau, the film enjoyed a limited (10 theater) release in 1998. It also made the film festival rounds, notably in Hermosa Beach, California, where Steve Kanaly copped a "best director" prize; the Pennsylvania Film Festival, where its screening was hosted by Scranton-based actor E. J. Dougher, who appeared in the film as Max Danielson; and, of course, Cannes. Though audience reaction was generally warm and appreciative—all reports indicate that the cinematography was first-rate, especially in the dust-flecked baseball scenes—Schillinger was unable to find a national distributor for *The Marksmen*. The "special edition" video release of the film in 1999 failed to rack up significant sales, perhaps because the list price was too exorbitant for the casual fan.

The Marksmen then showed up fitfully on cable TV before vanishing altogether in early 2000. On October 6 of that year, the film resurfaced under the new, more baseball-evocative title *Sliding Home*, and in this form was given what was described as a "world premiere" in Milwaukee, Wisconsin. Though local journalists had little to say about the film, the premiere itself was given extensive coverage as the last public event to be staged in County Stadium, longtime home of the Milwaukee Brewers, which would soon be demolished and replaced by the mammoth, retractable-dome Miller Park. As both a sendoff to County Stadium and the "official" unveiling of *Sliding Home*, the show was an impressive one, replete with a spectacular fireworks display and performances by local rockabilly bands.

After this auspicious rebirth, the film again hit the festival trail, winning a Bronze medal at the 2001 Worldfest Houston, among other honors. The videotape version, still titled *The Marksmen*, became an increasingly rare—and still excessively overpriced—commodity. As of this writing, the film has yet to receive a nationwide theatrical release, a fact that obviously cannot be attributed to any lack of quality. Perhaps as a result of its general inaccessibility, *Sliding Home* may someday achieve cult status, the baseball-movie equivalent of *Let It Be* or the uncut version of *Re-Animator*.

Million Dollar Infield

CBS Entertainment; first telecast February 2, 1982

Produced by Rob Reiner and Peter Katz. Directed by Hal Cooper. Teleplay by Rob Reiner, Phillip Mishkin, and Richard S. Wimmer. Story by Richard S. Wimmer. Photography: Thomas Del Ruth. Edited by Jim Benson. Music by Artie Kane. Art director: Bill Ross. 100 minutes; color; sound.

Cast: Bonnie Bedelia (Marcia Miller); Robert Costanzo (Artie Levitas); Rob Reiner (Monte Miller); Christopher Guest (Bucky Frische); Bruno Kirby (Lou Buonomato); Candy Azzara (Rochelle Levitas); Gretchen Corbett (Carole Frische); Elizabeth Wilson (Sally Ephron); Philip Sterling (Henry Ephron); Meeno Peluce (Joshua Miller); Oliver Robins (Aaron Miller); Shera Danese (Bunny Wahl); Jack Dodson (Chuck); Elsa Raven (Dr. Isabel Armen); Neil Billingsley (Jay Frische); Keith Mitchell (Vance Levitas); Mel Allen (Himself); Bonnie Campbell-Britton (Marlene); Cis Rundle (Shari); Harry Shearer (Jack Savage); Jack Banister, Harold Franklin, Neal Kaz, Ken Lerner, Pat Paccinelli (Long Island Bucks).

Four wealthy Long Islanders, lifelong pals who play for an amateur softball team, are undergoing midlife crises. Artie Levitas can't seem to keep his waistline from expanding nor his bank account from shrinking; Monte Miller wakes one morning to find his marriage tottering; Bucky Frische is kicked out of his house by his wife; and Lou Buonomato, also married, is looking for love in all the wrong places. The hapless

IT'S THE GRAND SLAM COMEDY OF THE YEAR!
Monte and his buddies play softball for laughs. But what it's doing
to their lives is no joke!

NEW! FIRST TIME ON TELEVISION!

CBS TUESDAY NIGHT MOVIES

MONTE
He's hitting
.450 at bat–
and .000 at home!

BUCKY
The umpire said,
"You're safe." His wife
said, "You're out!"

ARTIE
His checks are like
baseballs–always
bouncing!

LOU
He does his
best pitching in
singles bars!

MILLION DOLLAR INFIELD
Starring Rob Reiner, Bonnie Bedelia and Christopher Guest.
8PM CBS 2, 3, 6, 23

FEBRUARY FIREWORKS!

TV Guide ad for *Million Dollar Infield* (1982).

foursome try to forget their problems by channeling all their pent-up frustrations into their weekend ballgames. The result is a burst of energy that propels their team, the Long Island Bucks, toward its first league championship. As victory approaches, all four men come to realize that they've achieved their material and athletic gains at the expense of their own happiness and maturity. Although the Bucks lose the deciding game, Artie, Monty, Bucky, and Lou are able to achieve a measure of joy and fulfillment off the ballfield.

The baseball scenes are entertaining and directed with verve by Hal Cooper, but otherwise *Million Dollar Infield* is only mildly diverting, though it deserves a place in social history as one of the earliest "yuppie angst" comedy dramas which would encroach upon television like an overgrowth of kudzu in the 1980s. The film hasn't been seen much since its CBS debut on February 2, 1982, but if *Million Dollar Infield* does enjoy a latter day revival, it won't be because of the baseball scenes nor the token appearance by sportscaster Mel Allen, but by virtue of its leading players. This was one of Rob Reiner's first post–*All in the Family* projects, and as such represented a formative example of Reiner's skills behind the camera that would culminate in such superior theatrical films as *This Is Spinal Tap* (which featured *Infield* co-stars Christopher Guest and Harry Shearer), *The Princess Bride* (with Christopher Guest again), and *Misery*. Reiner's *Infield* leading lady, Bonnie Bedelia, was in 1982 just beginning to recover from a lengthy career slump; the recovery was complete, as witnessed by Bedelia's subsequent star turns in *Presumed Innocent* and the *Die Hard* pictures. And given a good early showcase in *Million Dollar Infield* was Bruno Kirby, who in 1991 would be riding high on the box-office hog thanks to another, far better "middle-age crazy" male bonding film, *City Slickers*.

Mr. Baseball

Outlaw Productions/Pacific Artists/Universal, in association with Dentsu Productions; released October 1992

Executive producers: Jeffrey Silver, John Kao. Produced by Fred Schepisi, Doug Claybourne and Robert F. Newmyer. Directed by Fred Schepisi. Written by Gary Ross, Kevin Wade, Monty Merrick; story by Theo Pelletier and John Junkerman. Original music: Jerry Goldsmith. Photography: Ian Baker. Edited by Peter Honess. Casting: Dianne Crittenden. Production design: Ted Haworth. Art direction: Russell J. Smith. Set Decoration: Cloudia. Costume design: Bruce Finlayson. Casting: Dianne Crittenden. Makeup artist: Lon Bentley. Set designer: Sean Haworth. Production manager: D.

Howard Grigsby. Assistant Directors: Cellin Gluck, Bruce Moriarty. Supervising sound editor: Terry Rodman. Sound mixer: David Kelson. Foley mixer: Paul Pirola. Visual Effects: Michael J. McAllister. Location managers: Andrew M. Comins (US), Ed Licht (Japan). Team Trainer: Richard Lougee (Shinwa Medical of Japan). Color by DeLuxe; Panavision. 113 minutes; Dolby Stereo Sound. Rated PG-13.

Cast: Tom Selleck (Jack Elliot); Ken Takakura (Uchiyama); Aya Takanashi (Hiroko Uchiyama); Dennis Haysbert (Max "Hammer" Dubois); Toshi Shioya (Yoji Nishimura); Art LaFleur (Skip); Nicholas Cascone (Doc); Larry Pennell (Howie Gold); Kosuke Toyohara (Toshi Yamashita); Toshizo Fujiwara (Ryoh Mukai); Mak Takano (Shinji Igarashi); Kenji Morinaga (Hiroshi Kurosawa); Joh Nishimura (Tomophiko Ohmie); Norihide Goto (Issei Itoi); Kensuke Toita (Akito Yagi); Naoki Fuji (Takuya Nishikawa); Takanobu Hozumi (Hiroshi Nakamura); Leon Lee (Lyle Massey); Jun Hamamura (Hiroko's Grandfather); Mineko Yorozuyo (Hiroko's Grandmother); Shôji Ohoki (Coach Hori); Tomoko Fujita (Hiroko's Assistant); Kinzoh Sakura (Umpire No. 1); Ikuko Saiton (Morita-san); Hikari Takano (Commercial Director); Tim McCarver, Sean McDonough (Themselves); Greg Goossen (Trey); Scott Plank (Ryan Ward); Charles Fick (Billy Stevens); Michael McGrady (Duane); Frank Thomas (Davis, the Promising Rookie); Michael Papajohn (Rick); Rolando Rodriquez (Manuel); Todd A. Provence (Tom Selleck's Baseball Double/Young Ball Player); Frank Mendoza (Player–New York); Ken Medlock (Umpire); Carrie Jean Yazel (Coed in Bed); Mary Kohnert (Player's Wife); Makoto Kuno, Michiyo Washizuka (Japanese Sportscasters); Shinsuke Aoki (Nikawa, Dragons owner); Rinzoh Suzuki (Sato, Dragons owner); Dragons players: Shintarô Mizushima (Sugita), Nobuyuki Kariya (Uemoto), Satoshi Jinbo (Tsuboi), Masanao Matsuzaki (Koboyshika), Shôtarô Kusumi (Takahashi), Katsushi Yamaguchi (Kobayshi), Hiro Nagae (Mutsui) and Yoshimi Imai (Ishimara); Cin Chi Cheng (Itami, coach); Makoto Kaketa (Umpire No. 2); Shogo Nakajima (Umpire No. 3); Bradley Jay "Animal" Lesley (Niven); James Corey Kaufman (Fan).

New York Yankees power hitter Jack Elliot, the MVP of four years ago, has of late been unable to improve upon his previous season's batting average of .235; the only time he gets into the newspapers these days is when he is arrested for drunken driving. Even so, the undisciplined, swaggeringly arrogant Elliot doesn't realize how precarious his position is with the Yankees until his manager Doc turns over Jack's commercial endorsements to an up-and-coming rookie—who promptly supplants Jack in the team's batting order. The Yanks decide to trade Elliot, but the only taker turns out to be the Chuinichi Dragons of Nagoya, Japan. Resentful over the trade, Jack goes out of his way to insult his "adopted" country and his new teammates, and stubbornly resists adjusting to the strange and (to him) often illogical rules, traditions and basic etiquette of Japanese baseball. Jack also balks at taking orders from dictatorial Dragons manager Uchiyama, to whom saving face and displaying respect for opponents is equally as important as winning pennants. What Jack doesn't know is that Uchiyama, Japan's most revered baseball hero, has put his own career on the line by hiring the contrary but undeniably talented Mr. Elliot. Gradually, Jack learns to appreciate and respect his new country and colleagues, while Jack's girlfriend, attractive business executive Hiroko, struggles to establish a common ground between the headstrong Jack and the taciturn Uchiyama—who happens to be Hiroko's father. The professional futures of both men ultimately hinge upon a crucial game between the Dragons and the much-feared "national team" of Japan, the Giants.

Taking into consideration Japan's fanatical devotion to baseball, it is surprising that up until the early 1990s only one American film had been made about the "divided by a common game" relationship between Japanese and American baseball players: 1978's *The Bad News Bears Go to Japan* (q.v.). On the other hand, considering the mediocre box-office performance of that picture, it is equally surprising that anyone would ever attempt to make a film on the subject again.

But with the success of *Major League, Bull Durham* and *Field of Dreams,* coupled with recent news reports of how "washed-up" American ballplayers had gained a new lease on life—and popularity beyond their wildest dreams—in Japan, Universal Pictures gave the go-ahead to *Tokyo Diamond,* which the studio intended as its major Summer release for 1991. Slated to be filmed on location in the Japanese cities of Nagoya and Okaski, with additional sequences in Los Angeles and at Detroit's Tiger Stadium, the project, produced in association with Dentsu Productions, began shooting in mid 1990.

The script was written by Gary Ross, who'd previously contributed to Penny Marshall's *Big* (1988), and Monty Merrick, late of *Memphis Belle* (1990), from a story by Theo Pelletier and John Junkerman. Pelletier was a movie newcomer, while Junkerman, a student of Japanese history and culture, had produced the 1987 documentary *Hellfire: A Journey from Hiroshima.* Assigned to direct the film was Peter Markle, who, as the guiding creative force behind *Hot Dog ... the Movie* (1984) and other such lowbrow efforts, was regarded as just the right man to bring to life a script in which the culture clash between East and West was going to be played for full bellylaugh value.

Cast as Jack Elliot was Tom Selleck, who, though a longtime TV favorite thanks to several seasons on the weekly actioner *Magnum PI,* had only recently emerged as a bankable film property in *Three Men and a Baby* (1987) and *Three Men and a Little Lady* (1990). To insure that the film would play as well in Japan as in the US, the role of "legendary" Chuinchi Dragons manager Ushiyama was filled by Ken Takakura. Properly billed as Takakura Ken in his own country, the actor was an even bigger legend than his screen character—and internationally a more recognizable name than Tom Selleck. Having ascended to stardom as leading man opposite Toei Studios' reigning screen queen Hibari Misora, Takakura

Mr. Baseball (1992): Tom Selleck as Jack Elliot, just before the Yankees trade him to the Chuinichi Dragons. (Interestingly, this production photo bears the film's working title *Tokyo Diamond* and a copyright date of 1990.)

went on to headline some 200 films, including such dual-market Japanese/American efforts as *Too Late the Hero* and *The Yakuza*. At the time of *Tokyo Diamond*, the actor was best known to American filmgoers as Michael Douglas' costar in *Black Rain* (1989). Rounding out the main roles were 27-year-old leading lady Aya Takanashi, whose first (and last) screen appearance this was; Dennis Haysbert, the fearsome voodoo-practicing slugger Pedro Cerrano in *Major League* (q.v.), here essaying the more sedate role of transplanted American ballplayer Max "Hammer" Dubois; and, cast as wily team translator Yoji, Toshi Shioya, a recent AFI award nominee for his portrayal of Lieutenant Tanaka, the conscience-stricken Japanese communications officer in the Australian POW drama *Prisoners of the Sun* (1990).

Beset with unforeseen production setbacks, filming on *Tokyo Diamond* went over schedule and over budget, but the film's problems were only beginning. Reportedly, the representatives of Matushita, the parent company of MCA (which in turn controlled Universal), attended screenings of the film's rushes and expressed displeasure over the derisive humor made at the expense of Japan and its traditions; they were also unhappy that the first few drafts of the script contained some questionable jokes about American-Japanese hostilities during World War II. Director Peter Markle was removed from the project and replaced by Australian filmmaker Fred Schepisi, an odd choice in that his only previous comedy had been the 1987 Steve Martin vehicle *Roxanne*; otherwise, his forte was intense drama, as witness *The Chant of Jimmie Blacksmith* (1978) and *A Cry in the Dark* (1988). Though the reason was not articulated at the time, perhaps it was felt that Schepisi would be sensitive to the more serious and poignant aspects of being a stranger in a strange land; the aboriginal protagonist of *Chant of Jimmie Blacksmith* and the thawed-out Neanderthal Man in *Iceman* (1984) were just as much fish out of water as the displaced Jack Elliot in *Tokyo Diamond*, though, of course, not in as comedic a fashion.

Signed up along with Schepisi was his longtime cinematographer, Ian Baker. At the same time, screenwriter Kevin Wade, most recently associated with the 1988 corporate comedy *Working Girl*, was hired to help retool the script. While it cannot be stated for certain that Wade was responsible for excising the potentially offensive material, one can safely assume on the basis of *Working Girl* that it was he who fleshed out the character of the film's aggressively independent heroine, Hiroko Uchiyama.

The title *Tokyo Diamond* was discarded, replaced by *Mr. Baseball*, which in the film is the designation (spelled phonetically as "Mr. Bēsubōru") bestowed upon Jack Elliot by the Japanese media. This was not necessarily done to stroke the ego of Tom Selleck. For one thing, "Mr. Baseball" had a slightly sarcastic edge to it, since it is used mockingly by the Japanese newspapers when Jack goes into another slump. For another, the nickname is equally applicable to Dragons manager Uchiyama, who is established in the film as a national idol and four-time MVP; as such, "Mr. Baseball" could just as easily refer to actor Ken Takakura, who would receive top billing on screen and in all the print ads upon the film's release in Japan.

Mr. Baseball was in the can by the end of 1991, but its release would have to be delayed until Universal had distributed another baseball picture (and intended "blockbuster"), *The Babe*, in April of 1992. The disappointing financial returns from that film, coupled with fears that *Mr. Baseball* would be compared unfavorably to the similarly-themed 1992 TV movie *Comrades of Summer* (q.v.)—in which an ageing American ballplayer was hired to coach the first Russian Olympic baseball team—led Universal to wonder if the long-delayed Tom Selleck film should ever be put into general release. But the success of Columbia's *A League of Their Own* in July of 1992 convinced Universal that *Mr. Baseball* might have some box-office potential after all—though, hedging its bets, the studio sent the film out during the first week of October, traditionally one of the slower business periods in the movie industry.

Whenever there is an inordinately long period between the completion of a film and its release, the veteran moviegoer is conditioned to hunker down and prepare for the worst. The telltale signs of a troubled production include gaping holes in the continuity, go-nowhere subplots, characters that suddenly appear out of nowhere and disappear just as suddenly and pointlessly, uneven acting performances, inconsistent camerawork, choppy editing, hoked-up sound effects or inappropriate music, and that hideously deformed spawn of the sneak-preview process: the tacked-on ending that has little relation to what has gone before. None of these flaws are present in *Mr. Baseball*; in fact, few films, baseball-oriented or otherwise, have flowed so smoothly from first frame to last. Beginning with the opening sequence, in which a hung-over Jack Elliot awakens from a surreal ballpark nightmare to find himself in bed with a giggly coed whom he doesn't recognize, and straight on to the perfect finish, in which the renewed and renovated Jack, now a coach for the Boston Red Sox, displays admiration for his Japanese "skipper" Uchiyama by effectively *becoming* Uchiyama (and wedding the boss' daughter to boot!), this is a film that knows exactly what it is about and where it is going, with only a few draggy patches and absolutely no waste footage.

In virtually any other comedy of the era, the fact that the main character's last name is Elliot would have thrown open the gates for a flood of tasteless dialect jokes focusing on the Japanese tendency to invert the "L" and "R" sounds. There would also have been gags aplenty about the quaint Japanese habit of misinterpreting or misapplying American slang phrases, the presumed myopia and short stature of the average Japanese male, the country's fondness for exotic and (to Occidental palates) inedible food, the baffling tastes in native entertainment and leisure activities, the overenthusiastic emulations of Western pop culture, the rigid adherence to ancient rituals and frantic avoidance of centuries-old taboos, and so on *ad infinitum*. And in all these instances, the joke would be on the Japanese characters.

While admittedly there is lot of standard "oriental" humor in *Mr. Baseball*, the scripters carefully contrive to make Jack Elliot the butt of the jokes. Arriving in Japan under protest, armed with preconceived notions and prejudices, Jack behaves wretchedly at first, making offensive wisecracks about his hosts and fellow players, bitching and moaning about the "inconveniences" of life in the Far East, and imperiously refusing to follow orders or behave like the team leader he is supposed to be. According to standard storytelling procedure, Jack must be shown up for his wrongheadedness—thus, the script relentlessly pokes fun at Jack, rather than ridiculing the "eccentricities" of Japan and its people.

An example of the film's refreshingly novel approach is in its use of the timeworn (and worn-out) "funny English subtitles" gag. Standard operating procedure is to have one of the Japanese characters rattle off a long stream of unintelligible phrases, whereupon the subtitled translation would be "You suck!" or something more profane. In *Mr. Baseball*, Jack Elliot makes insulting comments during his first few Japanese press conferences and his early run-ins with Uchiyama—whereupon the team's quick-witted translator Yoji defuses potentially embarrassing situations by "re-interpreting" Jack, so that he seems to be speaking reverentially and respectfully to the reporters, and agreeing with every order issued by his new manager. Rather than recycle the old dirty subtitles bit, the script finds humor in the fact that the superimposed words are completely harmless. And the joke is not at the expense of the Japanese for failing to understand Jack; rather, it is Jack who appears the fool for smugly thinking that he can control a situation by indulging in his usual petulant behavior.

Clearly, Jack is going to have to learn to accommodate Japan, rather than expect the country to accommodate *him*; "Ac-cept!" is the pithy advice given him by his girlfriend Hiroko. And once he finds out that Uchiyama is not his enemy, and in fact had personally requested that he be signed for the Dragons, Jack gratefully (if painfully) submits to the grueling physical regimen demanded by Uchiyama to rid him of the "hole" in his swing. Throughout the first hour of the film, Tom Selleck strenuously works against his established nice-guy image by portraying Jack as a complete and utter *gaijin* (obnoxious outsider). Risking the possibility that the audience will turn against Jack, Selleck and the scriptwriters instead succeed in making totally believable the scene in which the chastened Jack humbly and sincerely apologizes to the other Dragons for his past misdeeds, even going so far as to offer his apology in Japanese. Though the scene works beautifully on a dramatic level, the writers have not forgotten that *Mr. Baseball* is comedy and that Jack must continue to be the fall guy: In attempting to express his hope to "build a bridge" between himself and his colleagues, Jack chooses the wrong Japanese phrase and offers instead to "build a chopstick."

To make sure that Selleck's costar Ken Takakura would have equal importance in the film, the scriptwriters allowed plenty of room for the character of Uchiyama to grow and develop as well. On a professional level, Uchiyama must realize that he will get better results from his players if he treats them like talented individuals rather than (in his words) "the lowliest dogs"— and also if he backs off from terrifying them into performing at peak level. Put simply, while Jack learns from Uchiyama that baseball is hard work, Uchiyama learns from Jack that baseball is also a game, "and a game should be fun." The climactic coming to terms between the two biggest egos in the film is as gratifying as any of the comic set pieces.

On a personal level, Uchiyama must resign himself to the fact that his feisty daughter Hiroko is not going to conform to his image of the "traditional" obedient and subservient Japanese female. Just as Jack Elliot is obliged to shed his stubbornness and apologize to his fellow ballplayers, so too must Uchiyama stop acting like a domineering parent and beg Hiroko's pardon for *his* bullheadedness—and, to show the level of his acceptance that she will makes choices with which he does not entirely agree, he even implores Hiroko to patch up her briefly shattered romance with Jack (this scene is likewise performed entirely in Japanese—with *no* jokes this time around!).

Early in the film, Hiroko explains to Jack that, "Japan takes the best from all over the world. And makes it her own." This pretty much sums up the game of baseball as played in *Mr. Baseball*: superficially the same as the American version, but with a wealth of fascinating differences both big and small—differences that might have proven overwhelming or confusing to American viewers had not director Fred Schepisi handled the ballpark scenes with what

reviewer Stu Kobek described as "the savvy of the outsider." The Melbourne-born Schepisi saw no need to emphasize the "strangeness" of Japanese baseball, since the rules, regulations and traditions probably made just as much sense to him as those in American baseball! In a disarmingly casual and nonjudgmental manner, Schepisi successfully demystifies the Japanese version for American audiences. Before long, the viewer takes for granted the fact that the strike zone in Japan is considerably wider than that in the States; that a base hit to first does not necessarily result in an RBI even with men on second and third; that the pitcher can get away with beaning the batter so long as he tips his hat in apology; that it is considered disrespectful for the man with the ball to take a runner out with a "slide"; and that a tied game must be called after 15 innings—and *remain* on the books as a tie, without the opportunity for a make-up game. The "fans in the stands" scenes, most of them filmed during real games in Tokyo, Nagoya, Okazaki, Yokohama, Hiroshima and elsewhere, provide even more revelations about Japanese baseball traditions, with noodle-soup vendors working the crowd, brass bands in the bleachers, and pretty young girls handing bouquets of flowers to the winning runners. Once again, all of this is presented respectfully and without comment, minus the "Look how weird the rest of the world is!" attitude prevalent in many of the lesser comedies of the 1980s and 1990s.

For a man who had never previously directed a sports film of any kind, Schepisi handles the baseball highlights with remarkable assurance. Much of the field action is conveyed through clever editing and seamlessly smooth tracking shots, while the pitcher-to-batter scenes are frequently shot in single takes, lending authenticity to the home runs, base hits and bunts. Though Tom Selleck is doubled in some scenes by Todd A. Provence (who also appears in the small role of a young player), Schepisi frames Selleck's scenes is such a way that the deception goes by completely unnoticed. And in the role of Jack Elliot's American teammate Max Dubois, Dennis Haysbert is an even more impressive diamond presence than he'd been in *Major League*—so much so that the audience would probably have stormed the projection room in protest had not a scene been added near the end of the film showing that Dubois had finally gotten a ticket back to the American Majors after five years' faithful service in Japan.

Dubois' personal triumph occurs during the film's climactic game, which is thrilling enough to compensate for some of the slower-paced romantic scenes in the earlier reels. Transcending its "stock" setup—the score is 6–5; the Dragons are two runs away from defeating their traditional rivals, the Giants, and cinching the pennant; there are two outs with the bases loaded—the climax of *Mr. Baseball* is fueled by a truly unique situation. If Jack Elliot knocks out a home run, the Dragons will win; but in so doing, he will break the seven-consecutive-homer record set years before by manager Uchiyama—and if *that* happens, Uchiyama will "lose face" and be fired by the Dragons management so that he will not bring disgrace to the team!

Incredibly, several American critics chastised *Mr. Baseball* for relying too heavily upon "clichéd" situations, with some observers taking the film to task for trotting out all the old "funny Japanese" jokes. Evidently these critics had entered the wrong theater, or had somehow projected themselves forward six years to the genuinely puerile ethnic humor in *Major League: Back to the Minors* (q.v.). Japanese reviewers were kinder, though a few took offense at the scene in which, having been told it is polite to loudly slurp one's noodles while dining at another family's house, Jack Elliot makes enough noise to wake up the family's ancestors. Some of the Japanese critics also looked askance at the interracial romance between Jack and Hiroko—which, though it quickly reaches the physical stage, is handled with commendable discretion for a PG-13 movie.

Opinions were divided as to the effectiveness of Jerry Goldsmith's synthesized music score. Those who liked the music reveled in Goldsmith's sly adaptation of the traditional six-note "Charge" tune heard in American ballparks. Those who didn't share this enthusiasm felt that Goldsmith's entirely appropriate use of the *shakuhachi*, or Japanese pan flute, was in some way imitative of James Horner's deployment of the same instrument in *Field of Dreams* (q.v.)—even though the image of a cornfield in Iowa has *never* entered the mind of anyone watching *Mr. Baseball*.

While the film performed well in Japan, *Mr. Baseball* earned only $20,883,406 domestically—a larger amount than that posted by Universal's previous baseball opus *The Babe*, but not enough to qualify as a hit. The film would not find the audience it truly deserved until the late 1990s, by which time it had become a cable–TV stalwart along with *The Natural*, *Field of Dreams* and *Major League*, eminently suitable for broadcast on Opening Day in March and during the October pennant sweepstakes.

Murder at the World Series

ABC Circle Films; first telecast March 19, 1977

Produced and written by Cy Chermak. Directed by Andrew V. McLaglen. Photography: Richard C. Glouner. Edited by Richard A. Harris and John F. Link, III. Music by John Cacavas. Art director: Elayne Cedar. 97 minutes; color; sound.

Cast: Michael Parks (Larry Marshall); Bruce Boxleitner (Cisco); Hugh O'Brien (Governor); Lynda Day George (Margot Mannering); Karen Valentine (Lois Marshall); Murray Hamilton

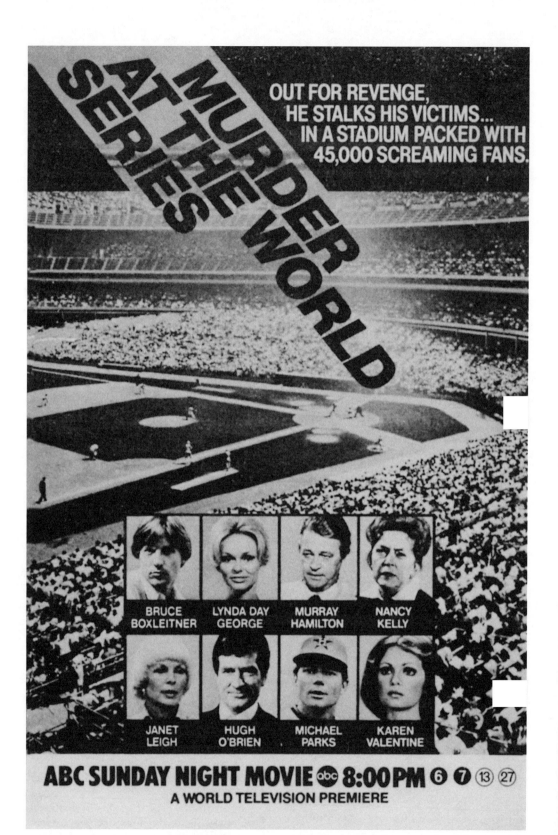

TV Guide ad for *Murder at the World Series* (1977).

(Harvey Murkison); Gerald S. O'Loughlin (Moe Gold); Janet Leigh (Karen Weese); Nancy Kelly (Alice Dekso); Johnny Seven (Severino); Tamara Dobson (Lisa); Joseph Wiseman (Sam Druckner); Larry Mahan (Gary Vawn); Cooper Huckabee (Frank Gresham); Maggie Wellman (Kathy); Cynthia Avila (Jane Torres); Monica Gayle (Barbara Gresham); Lisa Hartman (Stewardess).

Rejected by the Houston Astros, would-be ballplayer Cisco, who's a few bricks shy of a full load, plots to kidnap the wife of one of the Houston players during the Astros–Oakland A's World Series. As tension mounts in the Astrodome, Cisco's plan imperils four other women—who, thanks to the contortions of the script, have enough problems as it is.

On Saturday, March 19, 1977, millions of TV viewers were witness to the final first-run episode of *The Mary Tyler Moore Show*. Apparently sensing that the audience would be in a melancholy mood, ABC decided to schedule *Murder at the World Series*—a movie that was good for a limitless supply of laughs, none of them intentional—for March 20. *Murder* was originally titled *The Woman in Box 359*, but it might as well have been called *Just an Echo in the Ballpark*, since its plot owed so much to two other psycho-in-the-grandstand yarns, Thomas Harris's 1975 novel *Black Sunday* and the 1976 motion picture *Two-Minute Warning*, both set during the Super Bowl.

What passed for a plot might have been more palatable in a ninety-minute slot (with a commercial-free running time of 73 minutes), but in order to waste two hours of TV time, *Murder at the World Series*'s writer-producer, Cy Chermak, and director, Andrew V. McLaglen, pad the basic story out with a whole bunch of TV actors suffering through a whole bunch of TV-type deprivations, from sexual inadequacy to cancer. It hardly mattered; by 9:30 most people had switched over to the Bing Crosby special on CBS.

Before we move on to better things, a question: Just what is it about the Houston Astrodome that attracts crummy movies? The same year that *Murder at the World Series* appeared, we were treated to *The Bad News Bears in Breaking Training*, which was murder of a different sort. And in 1989 the Astrodome served as the setting for the opening and closing scenes of *Night Game*, wherein still another sicko commits his gruesome murders only on the nights that the Astros play at home; the fact that *Night Game* isn't really a baseball picture is all that's keeping us from boring you with its inane storyline in this book. One of these days, some astute filmmaker will take advantage of the genuine photogenic qualities of Houston's indoor stadium and make a real movie there. Let's hope it isn't titled *The Revenge of the Killer Astroturf!*

The Natural

Tri-Star; released May 11, 1984

Executive producers: Robert Towne and Phillip M. Breen. Produced by Mark Johnson. Associate producer: Robert F. Colesberry. Directed by Barry Levinson. Screenplay by Roger Towne and Phil Dusenberry, based on the novel by Bernard Malamud. Photography: Caleb Deschanel. Edited by Stu Linder. Music by Randy Newman. Production design by Angelo Graham and Mel Bourne. Art directors: James J. Murikami (L.A.) and Speed Hopkins (N.Y.). Set decoration by Bruce Weintraub. Costumes by Bernie Pollock and Gloria Gresham. Production managers: Robert F. Colesberry, Peter Burrell, and Thomas A. Razzano. Assistant directors: Chris Soldo, Patrick Crowley, Tom Davies, Carol Smetana. Casting by Ellen Chenoweth. Baseball trainers: Anthony J. Ferrara and Ken Hendler. Baseball consultants: Gene Kirby, Richard Cerrone. Color by Technicolor. 134 minutes; Dolby Sound. Rated PG.

Cast: Robert Redford (Roy Hobbs); Robert Duvall (Max Mercy); Glenn Close (Iris Gaines); Kim Basinger (Memo Paris); Wilford Brimley (Pop Fisher); Barbara Hershey (Harriet Bird); Robert Prosky (Judge Goodwill Banner); Richard Farnsworth (Red Blow); Joe Don Baker

(The Whammer); John Finnegan (Sam Simpson); Alan Fudge (Ed Hobbs); Paul Sullivan, Jr. (Young Roy); Rachel Hall (Young Iris); Robert Rich, III (Ted Hobbs). As the New York Knights: Michael Madsen (Bump Bailey), Jon Van Ness (Jon Olsen), Mickey Treanor (Doc Dizzy), George Wilkocz (Bobby Savoy), Anthony J. Ferrara (Coach Wilson), Philip Mankowski (Hank Benz), Danny Aiello, III (Emil LaJong), Joe Castellano (Allie Stubbs), Eddie Cipot (Gabby Laslow), Ken Grassano (Al Fowles), Robert Kalaf (Cal Baker), Barry Kivel (Pat McGee), Steven Kronovet (Tommy Hinkle), James Meyer (Dutch Schultz), Michael Starr (Boone), Sam Green (Murphy); Martin Grey, Joseph Mosso, Richard Oliveri, Lawrence Couzens, Duke Charboneau, Robert Rudnick, Ken Kamholz (Other Knights); Sibby Sisti (Pirate Manager); Philip D. Rosenberg (Pitcher Vogelman); Christopher B. Rehbaum (Pitcher Youngberry); Nicholas Koleff (Umpire Augie); Jerry Stockman (Umpire Babe); James Quamo (Memorial Camp Umpire); Joseph Strang (Final Home Game Umpire); James Mohr (Al); Ralph Tabakin (Al's Customer); Dennis Gould (Carnival Boy); Joshua Abbey (Home Plate Photographer); Gayle Vance (Maid); George Scheitinger (League Official); Peter Poth (Dr. Knobb); Bernie McInerney (Hospital Doctor); Elizabeth Ann Klein (Stern Nurse); Charles Sergis (Newsreel Narrator); Edward Walsh (Newsreel Presenter); The Buffalo Swing (Nightclub Band); Darren McGavin (Gus Sands).

Roy Hobbs, a nineteen-year-old pitcher fresh off the farm, aspires to the big leagues, and to that end Roy grabs his homemade bat "Wonderboy" and accompanies his newfound manager Sam Simpson on the eastbound train in the spring of 1923. While en route, Roy manages to beat legendary ballplayer "Whammer" Whambould in an impromptu pitching exhibition, arousing the interest of another passenger, the mysterious Harriet Bird. When this strange lady asks Roy what he wants out of life, his brash reply is that he wants to be "the best there is." Evidently this isn't the right answer; during a romantic rendezvous at a Chicago hotel room, Harriet pulls out a gun and shoots Roy down. Sixteen years pass

before Hobbs emerges from the bush leagues to try the majors again, this time as a thirty-five-year-old rookie for the troubled New York Knights. Roy excels at bat—indeed, at one juncture he literally tears the cover off the ball—and soon his teammates' uniforms bear the lightning-bolt insignia that adorns "Wonderboy." Again Roy stirs the emotions of an enigmatic lady; this time it's Memo Paris, the high-living niece of Knights manager Pop Fisher, who happens to be the mistress of big-time gambler Gus Sands. As the Knights win their way to the series, Hobbs again succumbs to false pride, his overindulgence in the rewards of fame resulting in a hospital stay. It is here that events conspire to "ruin" Roy for a second time: Knights owner Judge Goodwill Banner, in collusion with Gus Sands, tries to force Roy to take a bribe to throw the series, or else the judge will reveal the evidence uncovered by sportswriter Max Mercy that Hobbs had been the central figure of the Harriet Bird scandal back in 1923. But Roy doesn't intend to blow his second chance in life, especially not after being reunited with his childhood sweetheart Iris Gaines and meeting Iris' son, who may very well be Roy's flesh and blood. The New York Knights, bolstered by Roy's spectacular nightlight-smashing home runs, emerge victorious from the series, and the last image of the film is of Roy Hobbs back on the farm, blissfully playing catch with his "new" son.

Bernard Malamud sure made life easier for English literature teachers when he stated that, "The whole history of baseball has the quality of mythology." This renders even more obvious the purpose of Malamud's first novel, *The Natural*.

Written in 1952, the novel, which Malamud claimed was inspired by a *New York Times* column by Arthur Daley, is a mostly successful attempt to create a "mythos" for baseball. Using the tools of the great Golden Age mythmakers, Malamud takes many small truths about the Great

The Natural: Roy Hobbs (Robert Redford) and "Wonderboy" in action.

American Pastime and weaves them into a single, larger than life legend. *The Natural* invokes memories of "Merkle's Boner," the failure of Fred Merkle to touch second base which lost his team the 1908 World Series, by burdening Knights coach Pop Fisher with the curse of "Fisher's Folly." The on-field accidental death of Ray Chapman, killed by a pitched ball at the Polo Grounds in 1920, is recreated in *The Natural* through the demise of Roy Hobbs's rival, Bump Bailey, who meets his end by crashing through a fence in pursuit of a batted ball (Bailey also stirs recollections of St. Louis's Earl Combs and Brooklyn Dodger "Pistol Pete" Reiser, both of whom suffered concussions and fractures by making contact with outfield walls). "The Whammer" is obviously Babe Ruth—even though Ruth's crippling 1925 "bellyache" is transferred to Roy Hobbs—while various bleacher regulars who attend the Knights games are based upon such colorful real-life fans as clamorous Dodgers booster Hilda "The Bell" Chester. Throwaway lines in *The Natural* allude to the notorious three-man pileup on third base during a 1926 Brooklyn game, to Wilbert Robinson's attempt to catch a grapefruit thrown from a plane, and to Chuck Hostetler's fall between third and home during a tight series match.

The whole "throwing the game" angle was, of course, evocative of the 1919 Black Sox scandal, right down to the snooping of reporter Max Mercy (a rough-hewn amalgam of Hugh Fullerton and Ring Lardner) and to a little kid's plaintive "Say it ain't true, Roy." And the early near fatal shooting of Roy Hobbs by Harriet Bird was a re-creation of an incident still fresh in the minds of baseball fans in 1952. Phillies player Eddie Waitkus was invited to Chicago's Edgewater Beach Hotel in 1949 by his "biggest fan," Ruth Ann Steinhagen. What he didn't know was that Steinhagen, who'd built a shrine to Waitkus in her bedroom, had determined that, in her own words, "if I can't have him, nobody else can. And then I decided to kill him." She pulled out a .22 and plugged Waitkus, who had time only to gasp "Why did you do that?" before passing out. Fortunately, his was a fairly rapid recovery (he lived until 1972), though the shooting made Waitkus extremely paranoid in public, prompting a premature retirement from the game.

Bernard Malamud took all this raw material and gave it coherence by defining Roy Hobbs's rise and fall within the perimeters of baseball—and by borrowing heavily from the legend of King Arthur. In emulation of the Sword in the Stone, Roy Hobbs's bat "Wonderboy" is carved from a tree struck by lightning; and once he has greatness thrust upon him, Roy must learn the best and most responsible manner of using his heaven-sent talent. He defeats the ageing "monarchs" standing in his way (The Whammer, Bump Bailey) and rallies the New York Knights (that's right, knights) around him, only to fall prey to vain gloriousness, greed, and the pitfalls of romance (first Harriet Bird, then Memo Paris). Malamud imbues Hobbs with a "fatal flaw" reminiscent not only of Arthur but of the protagonists in Greek Tragedy: Roy fails to pass the various tests placed before him, including Harriet Bird's loaded questions about what he wants from life, Memo Paris's primrose path temptations, and a potential romance with the wholly good Iris Lemon (Iris Gaines in the film), whom Roy selfishly rejects when he learns she's a grandmother. At the end, Roy is "usurped" by opposing pitcher Herman Youngberry, who, in full-circle manner, is a young idealist who wishes to retire to his farm, just as Roy had once wanted to do. A too-late effort to redeem himself results in an injury from Roy's fly ball to Iris Lemon and to a series loss, which appears to have been brought about by Hobbs's cheating. Alone, disgraced, and exiled from the "Camelot" of baseball, Roy is condemned to suffer life's hard knocks all over again because he hasn't learned anything from his previous mistakes.

The Natural is hardly full of hidden meanings; Bernard Malamud's allusions are so out in the open that any halfway intelligent student can get the gist of the book without even bothering to highlight the important parts with yellow magic marker. The most obvious of Malamud's techniques was to underline the necessity of Roy Hobbs' learning to temper his talent with responsibility by having someone die or physically suffer whenever Hobbs exercises his skills. During his early victory over The Whammer, Roy pitches with such force that he inadvertently crushes the chest of his mentor, Sam Simpson, who expires as a result. Roy's excellent showing for the Knights compels the team's jealous star player Bump Bailey to play recklessly, resulting in Bailey's death. And during the final game, Roy not only beans Iris with a pop fly, but the fact that Roy is unable to win the game causes old Pop Fisher to suffer a heart attack.

This guilt-ridden throughline is in keeping with the later, more complex works of Bernard Malamud, all of which explored Jewish themes. Perhaps because *The Natural* is more accessible to the casual reader than Malamud's other novels, it has long been out of favor with the novelist's more fervent devotees. Ironically, many of these same Malamud disciples would condemn the 1984 film version of *The Natural* for not being faithful to its "classic" source!

The radical changes made in the film version did not come about abruptly during shooting. Star Robert Redford chose the property because he was anxious to play a baseball player before he was too old to get away with it (at forty-six he was cutting it close, though he looked awfully good when wielding a bat). But the actor was also anxious to succeed at the box office, since *The Natural* would be his first on-screen appearance in four years. One of the problems facing Redford throughout his career was that critics urged him to expand his acting range with more substantial material, while his fans insisted that he remain the handsome young lad who always wins out over adversity. In most of the actor's previous adaptations from book to movie (*Three Days of the Condor, All the President's Men*), he'd triumphed over his on-screen

foes and made money for his studio. The last film in which a Redford character was an ultimate "loser" had been *The Great Gatsby* (1974), a financial bust which was so faithful to Fitzgerald's novel that the effect was suffocating. Had *The Natural* adhered strictly to its source, "word of mouth" would have killed it in an instant: "It looks just like a book—bor-ing!"; "I wanted him to win the last game"; "Every time he hits a ball, somebody croaks!"; "Why doesn't he get the girl?"

Not this time. Robert Redford would bow to the intelligentsia by selecting a literary work as his next film—and to keep the fans happy, Roy Hobbs would no longer come a cropper within his limited baseball-dominated perspective on life, but would now win within that perspective and benefit from his experience. It's curious, then, that one of the executive producers for *The Natural* was Robert Towne, who'd demonstrated a flair for cynical defeatism in his script for *Chinatown* (1974) and thus would have been an ideal choice to adapt Malamud had a more faithful approach been called for; on the other hand, Towne had been an uncredited contributor to *Bonnie and Clyde* (1967), so he knew a little something about sustaining the sort of outsized legend that Roy Hobbs would become (Towne's brother Roger co-wrote the screenplay with Phil Dusenberry).

To avoid winding up with a four-hour movie, a lot of streamlining was necessary. First to go was the notion of Roy's abilities inadvertently causing disaster to those around him, since this would have cluttered the now simplified storyline; Sam Simpson doesn't die, Pop Fisher has no coronary, and the death of Bump Bailey, which had to be kept because it makes room for Hobbs' ascending stardom, is treated in a throwaway, slightly comic manner. Most of the novel's baseball history allusions are dropped, since what was "gospel" in 1952 was by and large forgotten by 1984; only the more immediately recognizable references to Babe Ruth and the Black Sox are retained for the film. Some of Malamud's quirkier character motivations were also dispensed with. Memo Paris no longer enmeshes Roy in the cheating subplot because she neurotically seeks vengeance for the death of her old boyfriend Bump Bailey; in the film she is motivated purely by greed, something that the screen version of Roy can understand and thus overcome.

The most gratifying aspect of the movie *The Natural* is that it changes the outcome of the original while still retaining the novel's spirit. The Arthurian trappings still dominate, though the script borrows the more upbeat finale of the musical adaptation of that legend titled *Camelot*: When Roy's bat "Wonderboy" breaks during the climactic game, a hero-worshiping batboy offers up his own homemade bat, "The Savoy Special." And the book's "what comes around, goes around" subtext, which condemns Roy Hobbs to tread a circuitous path to reduced circumstances, is adopted for the film as a leitmotif for Roy's triumph. Roy is "saved" from big-city evildoers by transforming Iris from the chance acquaintance in the novel to Roy's hometown girlfriend in the film, who beckons him back to the simpler, more wholesome existence of his youth; and the film ends as it begins, with a lyrical shot of a father and son playing catch.

To enhance the mythical qualities of *The Natural*, the plot was moved from its contemporary setting in the novel to the 1930s—that is, the idealized 1930s as envisioned in the Hollywood films of that era. Director Barry Levinson and production designer Mel Bourne then decided that the story should unfold stylistically and symbolically on a visual level, rather than through the acting or writing. Director of photography Caleb Deschanel evoked nostalgia in the early rural scenes by using an "Autochrome" color style, reminiscent of the

muted two-color system favored in Europe in the 1930s and '40s. The baseball scenes were always filmed in extremely bright sunlight or under the glare of electric illumination, and the same bright lighting crept into the locker rooms; this was to provide contrast between the purity of baseball and the conspiratorial darkness of the scenes in Judge Banner's office and Gus Sands's favorite nightclub. To emphasize the idea that baseball is Roy Hobbs's real life and everything else is slightly lifeless, the walls of War Memorial Stadium in Buffalo, New York, were freshly painted, and the ballfield grass was dyed solid green, while the extras in the stands were instructed to wear black, grey, or otherwise colorless costumes; even their chairs were dyed in dull hues. This color scheme was particularly striking when used to emphasize the angelic whiteness of Iris Gaines' dress in the closing scenes.

The Natural's excessive use of slow-motion photography was likewise a carefully deliberated choice; the slowing down of the action occurs only when something momentous is about to happen to Roy Hobbs. "Even if you make a mistake with [your choice of] point of view," Caleb Deschanel noted shortly after the film was completed, "you're much better off having a point of view than going out and shooting a bunch of shots." The slow motion may be a bit precious in *The Natural*, but in terms of the film's overall concept, it isn't a mistaken choice—although it unfortunately set the precedent of slow motion being used to tip off the fact that the hero is about to achieve victory, thus effectively robbing many a future sports film of any element of suspense.

In a few instances, Caleb Deschanel's camerawork was dictated by the actors' characterizations instead of the film's preconceived design. Robert Prosky's interpretation of Judge Goodwill Banner is almost exactly the same loquacious villain described in the novel: "It is a description that presents itself in visual terms, which is wonderful," observed Deschanel, and he took full advantage of this by providing Prosky with the sort of low-key lighting and film noir shading befitting his Sydney Greenstreet–style character. Conversely, Robert Duvall took Bernard Malamud's obtrusive but otherwise nonvillainous character of sportswriter Max Mercy and developed him into a truly sinister, serpentine presence; obligingly, Deschanel lit Duvall's scenes in an undergroundish, catacomb-like manner.

The result was a beautifully assembled film that is consistently pleasing to the eye, but a film that is ultimately unsatisfying. Because it is so obviously preplanned and rehearsed, *The Natural* lacks the spontaneity and promise of surprise that would be part and parcel of a real baseball season. Everything falls into place so perfectly and with such clockwork precision that by the middle of the film we'd like to have someone look momentarily flustered or blow a line—anything to convince us that these are living human beings rather than puppets being guided by some unseen hand through a maze of stylization. It's small wonder that Glenn Close, who played Iris, complained that she felt "manipulated" throughout the shoot, and that director Barry Levinson failed to provide *The Natural* with the same freewheeling personal touch he has demonstrated in his trilogy of films about life in Baltimore (*Diner, Tin Men* and *Avalon*)—although Levinson's hand was evident in the early scene in which Wilford Brimley (as Pop Fisher) and Richard Farnsworth (as team coach Red Blow) try to one-up each other with baseball trivia, bringing a smile to the lips of anyone who recalls the prenuptial "football quiz" in *Diner* and Jackie Gayle's obsession with minutiae of the TV series *Bonanza* in *Tin Men.*

Despite the confinement of the film's overall design, the cast of *The Natural* turns in excellent work, though it would have been nice to see Robert Redford play more of a person and less of an icon. With an embarrassment of riches in the talent department (the aforementioned Robert Redford, Robert Duvall, Glenn Close, Wilford Brimley, Robert Prosky and Richard Farnsworth, plus the formidable distaff villainy of Kim Basinger as Memo Paris and Barbara Hershey as Harriet Bird), Darren McGavin made absolutely certain that movie reviewers would mention his portrayal of Gus Sands, not only by giving a superb performance, but by having his name removed from the screen credits. (McGavin's lead would be followed by the equally unbilled—and likewise positively reviewed—John Candy in 1993's *Rookie of the Year* [q.v.]).

The Natural sold tickets by virtue of Robert Redford's overdue return to the screen; its domestic gross was $48,000,000, making it the seventh most profitable baseball film in history. Thanks to the film's excessive budget, however, business wasn't good enough to result in a baseball movie trend, though 1985's *The Slugger's Wife* (q.v.) might have never passed the planning stage had it not been for the anticipated success of the Redford picture.

The one major lasting cultural contribution of *The Natural* was its marvelous musical score by Randy Newman. In the years since 1984, Newman's pastoral main theme has been adopted by many a television news department for its human interest features, particularly those stories about people who've renounced the big city for an agrarian existence and have, like Roy Hobbs, "returned to the soil."

The New Klondike

Famous Players/Lasky/Paramount; released March 15, 1926

Presented by Adolph Zukor and Jesse Lasky. Directed by Lewis Milestone. Screenplay by Thomas J. Geraghty, from a story by Ring Lardner. Photography: Alvin Wyckoff. Art director:

Walter E. Keller. 8 reels/7,445 feet: black and white; silent.

Cast: Thomas Meighan (Tom Kelly); Lila Lee (Evelyn Curtis); Paul Kelly (Bing Allen); Hallie Manning (Flamingo Applegate); Robert Craig (Morgan West); George DeCarlton (Owen); J. W. Johnston (Dave Cooley); Brenda Lane (Peggy "Bird Dog" DeVoe); Tefft Johnson (Colonel Dwyer); Danny Hayes (The Speiler).

Minor-league pitcher Tom Kelly arrives in Florida for spring training, where he is promptly fired by manager Dave Cooley, who feels threatened by Kelly's superior knowledge of baseball. Casting about for some quick money, Kelly sells the use of his name to a Florida real estate developer, and soon all his teammates have become investors. Morgan West, a crook in league with Dave Cooley, sells Kelly some worthless swampland, which turns all his pals into paupers. Kelly gets the money back, Cooley is fired, and Kelly is appointed manager in his place.

Thomas Meighan, one of those "mature, dependable" movie stars popular in the years following World War I, was undergoing a slump in 1926 and needed a surefire hit to cinch the renewal of his Paramount contract. Meighan wanted a director willing to take a risk with him by coming up with a quickly assembled eight-reeler based on nothing more than a title, *The New Klondike*. This "Klondike" was the designation given by writer Ring Lardner to the then current Florida land boom—a blitz of speculation, overspending, and shady business deals in the sunshine state that also served as the subject of the Marx Brothers's *The Cocoanuts*. The director chosen by Meighan was Lewis Milestone, who, with his newspaperman friend Tom Geraghty in tow, took the star's forty-man crew to Miami, hoping that inspiration would strike and an acceptable screen story would result. Milestone and Geraghty strolled the streets of Miami soaking up what the director would later describe as "local flavor,"

retiring to a hotel each evening to trade ideas.

The resultant storyline concerned a ballplayer who, by virtue of spring training, would logically be ensconced in Florida from the first scene onward (thus justifying the location shooting), who was on the downgrade (just like Thomas Meighan), and who was saved from poverty by the real estate craze. *The New Klondike* was good enough to secure Thomas Meighan's studio contract, but the collapse of the land market in a hurricane-plagued Florida within a year of the film's release cut its potential salability in half.

Since the baseball element in *The New Klondike* was virtually a last-minute decision, the game naturally took a back seat to the film's satiric focus on the land boom. Thomas Meighan was a reliable performer—perhaps "sturdy" is a better word—but he was out of his league on the ballfield; though cast as a pitcher, he was never seen throwing a ball, and in fact his only activity in uniform consisted of a few halfhearted swings at bat. So ill suited was Meighan to the roughhousing indigenous to baseball stories of the period that even when he was engaged in a fistfight, the audience "saw" the battle mostly through the sideline reactions of others. *The New Klondike* did contain one piquant moment wherein the baseball theme and the main real estate plot intersected: During the first spate of land sales, one of Meighan's teammates slugs out a possible home run, then stops cold while rounding the bases to peruse a map of Florida.

One in a Million: The Ron LeFlore Story

Roger Gimbel Productions/EMI Television; first telecast September 26, 1978

Executive producers: Roger Gimbel and Tony Converse. Produced by William S. Gilmore. Associate producers: Michael and Carol

Raschella. Directed by William A. Graham. Teleplay by Stanford Whitmore; based on the book *Breakout* by Ron LeFlore and Jim Hawkins. Photography: Jordan Cronenweth. Edited by Aaron Stell. Music by Peter Matz. Art director: William Foster. Color by CFI. 97 minutes; sound.

Cast: LeVar Burton (Ron LeFlore); Madge Sinclair (Georgie LeFlore); James Luisi (James Karella); Larry B. Scott (Gerald LeFlore); Paul Benjamin (John LeFlore); Zakes Mokae (Pee Wee Parker*); John R. McKee (Ralph Houk); Billy Martin (Himself); Yaumilton Brown (Leroy); Walter King (Antoine); Jimmy Spinks (Umpire); James Butsicarus (Himself†); Matt Stephens (Mickey Stanley); Tony Mockus (Parole Board Chairman); Al Kaline, Norm Cash, Bill Freeman, and Jim Northrup (Themselves, Members of the Detroit Tigers); Tom Erhardt (Parole Officer); James Karella (Heckler).

Ron LeFlore, centerfielder for the Detroit Tigers, who in 1976 bats .316, steals fifty-eight bases, and scores hits in thirty consecutive games, makes a less than sentimental journey that same year to the tough Detroit neighborhood of his youth. There he recalls the hard, long road he climbed to get out of the streets. The younger LeFlore was an unregenerate punk whose life of petty crime culminated in 1970 with a five-to-fifteen stretch for armed robbery. Sent to the Michigan State Penitentiary at the age of nineteen, Ron at first did everything possible to buck the rules, ending up in solitary for his troubles. But when he learned that his younger brother Gerald, whom he'd tried to protect from the ravages of the street, was himself getting involved in the drug scene, LeFlore set about the task of getting out of prison early. Advised by fellow convict James Karella that the parole board went easy on prisoners ex-

hibiting unusual skill in athletics, Ron joined the baseball team, where his latent talents developed to the point that the other prisoners petitioned Tigers manager Billy Martin to give Ron a tryout. Allowed to show his stuff at Tiger Stadium during a one-day furlough, LeFlore impressed Martin enough for the manager to see to it that Ron was absorbed by Detroit's farm system upon LeFlore's parole in 1973. As Ron worked his way up the Tigers ladder, brother Gerald, who at first cleaned up his own life out of adulation of Ron, wound up back on the street with a severe drug problem. Ultimately, Gerald died during a shootout; as Ron observed tearfully to the new Tigers manager Ralph Houk, the streets had finally claimed his younger brother. Ron LeFlore's flashback draws to a close as he looks around his old neighborhood and realizes that, given the opportunities offered most of Detroit's ghetto kids, LeFlore's rise to baseball fame was truly a one in a million shot.

Unlike some baseball films like *Major League* and *Long Gone*, where the nonstop profanity seems self-consciously tacked on at times, *One in a Million: The Ron LeFlore Story* cries out for more graphic language and a grittier, more realistic approach. Alas, at the time the film was first telecast over CBS (September 26, 1978), television was undergoing one of its sporadic clean-up campaigns, purging itself of violence and rough language to appease those who saw television only in terms of *The Brady Bunch*. While the actors, particularly LeVar Burton (who one year earlier had exploded onto the scene with his brilliant Kunta Kinte in the ABC miniseries *Roots*), give credible performances, they seem straitjacketed by TV's

*In many sources, Zakes Mokae's character is listed as "Rabbit Spencer," the actual name of a "lifer" who befriended Ron LeFlore in prison. Evidently his name was changed in the film because of legal complications. On the other hand, James Karella, LeFlore's baseball mentor in prison, not only permitted use of his name, but actually appeared in One in a Million in the minor role of heckler.

†James Butsicarus was a tavern owner who acted as liaison between his good friend Billy Martin and the baseball-playing inmates of Michigan State Penitentiary.

censorial policies, forced to mouth such artificial epithets as "you son of a buck" and restrained from going all out in their portrayals of ghetto dwellers and prisoners.

This quality weakens the film to the point that what seemed uncompromisingly realistic within the TV terms of 1978 looks rather antiseptic today. Although the prison scenes were shot on location, the convicts are about as threatening as a bunch of kids on a boy scout retreat. And after Ron LeFlore and his buddies pull off a tavern robbery, the effect is softened by having them discover that they're driving away with their headlights off, whereupon one of the guys says he was confused by "the excitement of the moment." Yep, that's the brutal jargon of the streets, alright.

The most amusing compromise with reality is manifested in former Tigers manager Billy Martin's self-portrayal. In his very few scenes, Martin is smiling, convivial, soft-spoken, and given to spouting lines about how all the boys on the team are pulling for LeFlore. One suspects that it wasn't Billy Martin at all, but Alan Alda with a false nose.

None of this "Mickey Mouse" treatment of the source material detracts from the excellence of the baseball scenes in *One in a Million.* LeVar Burton was doubled (though not obviously so) during the more difficult plays, but he gives a magnificent account of himself as he runs and slides from base to base. The staged scenes in Tiger Stadium—together with a handful of long shots at Milwaukee's County Stadium, the site of LeFlore's major-league debut—are seamlessly matched with stock footage of actual games, and the level of energy is sustained by the use of rapid wipe-dissolves from one inning to another.

So effective are the ballgame sequences that the hamstrung approach to the rest of the plot is all the more glaring. The remarkable beating-the-odds story of Ron Le-

Flore's rise from dead-end loser to the top of the baseball heap was a story that deserved better treatment, and perhaps would have received such treatment had *One in a Million* been made ten years later for one of TV's pay cable services. Alas, any such film would have to include Ron LeFlore's arrest for possession of narcotics in 1982; unlike a movie, real life can't be tied up in a nice neat package.

One Touch of Nature

Edison/K.E.S.E.; released July 30, 1917

President of K.E.S.E.: George Kleine. Directed by Edward H. Griffith. Screenplay based on a *Saturday Evening Post* story by Peter B. Kyne, published March 1, 1913. Photography: Charles Gilson. 5 reels; silent.

Cast: John Drew Bennett (William Vandervort "Battling Bill" Cosgrove); Viola Cain (Madame de Montignon, nee Leonora O'Brien); John McGraw (Himself); Edward O'Connor (Shamus O'Brien); George Henry (E. P. Cosgrove); Helen Strickland (Mrs. Cosgrove); with Edward Lawrence and members of the New York Giants.

"Battling Bill" Cosgrove, star player for the Yale baseball team, is disowned by his wealthy meatpacker father when Bill marries vaudeville "artiste" Madame de Montignon, who's actually Leonora O'Brien, the daughter of plumber Shamus O'Brien. John McGraw, general manager of the New York Giants, offers Bill a contract with the team. It happens that Old Man Cosgrove is a baseball fan, and when he attends a Giants game, he not only sees his boy play but also becomes acquainted with O'Brien the plumber. The younger Cosgrove is forgiven and the two warring families bury the hatchet when Bill belts out a home run. (Remind us sometime to write a book about "Conditional Love in the Cinema.")

John McGraw, patriarch of the New York Giants, was well versed in the ways of show business by the time *One Touch of Nature* was filmed; McGraw had already sent many of his star players on a promotional vaudeville tour way back in 1902. Why neither John McGraw nor his wife mentioned *One Touch of Nature* in their separately published memoirs is anybody's guess, but chances are that the five-reeler's mediocre financial performance had blocked the McGraws' memories. The film was one of a handful produced by K.E.S.E., a conglomerate of four failing pioneer movie studios—Kalem, Edison, Selig, and Essanay—all of whom had been practically pushed off the map by such star-studded organizations as Universal, Fox, and Paramount. K.E.S.E. hoped to forestall bankruptcy with such pictures as *One Touch of Nature*, which had the supposed built-in appeal of being based on a story by the extremely popular Peter B. Kyne, who'd created the character of "Broncho Billy" that Essanay executive G. M. Anderson had parlayed into a long-running series of lucrative western films. But by 1918 K.E.S.E. was out of business—"proof" once more that baseball pictures were slow death at the box office. (In reality, it was proof that *bad* pictures were becoming less and less tolerable as more and more people joined the ranks of regular moviegoers.)

The marriage of ballplayer Bill Cosgrove and vaudeville performer "Madame de Montignon" which motivated the plot of *One Touch of Nature* had its basis in the brief real-life union of Giants player Rube Marquand and musical comedy star Blossom Seeley. Because neither baseball nor showbiz were totally "respectable" professions in 1917, the story concentrated less on the clash of careers than on the snooty reaction of Bill Cosgrove's millionaire father. By the time this ballplayer-marries-singer bit was recycled for *The Slugger's Wife* (1985) (q.v.), Mr. and Mrs. Cosgrove could easily have bought up his father's business and thrown the old man out on his ear.

Out of the West

Robertson-Cole/FBO; released September 1926

Presented by Joseph P. Kennedy. Directed by Robert De Lacy. Screenplay by Frederick Arthur Midlin. Photography: John Leezer. Assistant director: John Burke. 5 reels/4,609 feet; black and white; silent.

Cast: Tom Tyler (Tom Hanley); Bernice Welch (Bernice O'Connor); L. J. O'Connor (Jim Rollins); Ethan Laidlaw (Bide Goodrich); Alfred Hewston (John O'Connor); Frankie Darro (Frankie); Sitting Bull (O'Connor Mascot); Gertrude Claire (Granny Hanley); Barney Fusey (A Scout).

Two rival ranchers, John O'Connor and Jim Rollins, extend their enmity into their opposing amateur baseball teams. O'Connor ranch hand Tom Hanley becomes his team's star player, and thus also becomes the fly in the ointment to the plans of Bide Goodrich, who's been bribed by Rollins to throw the next game. Together with O'Connor's daughter Bernice, Tom is kidnapped and sequestered in a cave to keep him from playing. With the help of his young pal Frankie, Tom escapes to win the match, but when a major league scout offers him a contract, Tom elects to stay on the O'Connor ranch and settle down with Bernice.

Out of the West was a fifty-seven-minute sponge, soaking up plot elements from both Charles Ray's *The Busher* (q.v.) and Hoot Gibson's *Hit and Run* (q.v.), as well as virtually every other baseball picture—and western—made up to 1926. Star Tom Tyler was the sort of muscle bound, stolid, flint-eyed western actor that comedians were so fond of lampooning in the early days of television; even in his heyday, critics poked fun at Tyler's clichéd demeanor, referring to him in dime-novel fashion as "Our Tom." (Tyler would later mature into a dependable character player, contributing memorable villainous portrayals to such films as *Stagecoach* and *Talk of the Town.*) The *Variety* review for *Out of the West* joined the bandwagon of Tom Tyler bashers; the critique made much of the unsolicited laughs that accompanied the film's Manhattan release, particularly the moment in which Frankie Darro rescued Our Tom by bouncing a rubber-like rock off a bad guy's head.

Past the Bleachers

Signboard Hill Productions/Hallmark/ABC; first telecast June 22, 1995

Executive producers: Richard Welsh, Don Rhymer. Produced by Alan Jacobs. Directed by Michael Switzer. Teleplay by Don Rhymer, from the novel by Christopher A. Bohjalian. Co-producer: Brent Shields. Line producer: James T. Davis. Photography: William Wages. Edited by Mark W. Rosenbaum. Original Music: Stewart Levin. Production Design: Charles C. Bennett. Casting: Phyllis Huffman, Olivia Harris. Costume design: Tom McKinley. Set decorations: Frank Galline. Makeup: Harriette Landau. Key hairstylist: Taylor Knight. Script supervisor: Ira Hurvitz. Color. 90 minutes; sound.

Cast: Richard Dean Anderson (Bill Parrish); Barnard Hughes (Mr. Godfrey); Glynnis O'Connor (Harper Parrish); Ken Jenkins (Hilton Burberry); Grayson Fricke (Lucky Diamond); Noah Fleiss (Charlie); Jenny Krochmal (Melissa); Jennifer-Maria Thompson (Jill); Harvey Reaves (Jamie); Michael Martin (Dickie); Chad Linley (Josh); Trey Lineberger (Nathaniel); Gerry Valencia (Umpire); Helen Stenborg (Tilda).

The lives of Bill and Harper Parrish have never been the same since the death of their 11-year-old son Nathaniel. Though the Parrishes outwardly go through the motions of normalcy, the couple's marriage is slowly but surely being torn apart by their tragic loss. Evidently hoping that Bill will be able to let go of past sorrows if he is able to reach out to other children, local logging tycoon and former Boston Red Sox general manager Hilton Burberry persuades Bill to manage the town's junior-league baseball team. Among the newer team members is an odd young boy named Lucky Diamond, who was born mute—though he can hear and is able to communicate by writing pithy messages on a notepad. Quickly getting past Lucky's handicap, Bill is thrilled to learn that the boy is a natural-born ballplayer, perhaps the best in the league. Still, there is something not quite right about Lucky, nor the shadowy character who seems to be Lucky's father. Doing some quick checking in the state's school records, Bill is unable to find any trace of a "Lucky Diamond" or of Lucky's parents; it is as if the boy never really existed. Things get curiouser and curiouser after an accident on Hilton Burberry's property takes the life of logger Jeff Grout; according to Burberry, the only person who knows the facts behind the accident is Lucky's "father," who allegedly disappeared the moment Grout died. Not wishing to see Lucky turned over to an institution or foster family, Burberry prevails upon Bill and Harper to temporarily look after the youngster. Only when he is absolutely certain that Lucky is destined to fill the aching void in the Parishes' lives—and vice versa—does Burberry reveal the whole truth about the enigmatic Lucky Diamond.

Filmed in the fall of 1994, *Past the Bleachers* was first telecast as an ABC *Hallmark Hall of Fame* special on June 22, 1995. The film was based on the 1992 novel by Christopher A. Bohjalian, whose other works included the Oprah Book Club selection *Midwives*. Explaining his literary approach in an interview for National Public Radio, Bohjalian stated that his books are "about the sorts of happy people we see everyday on the street, who are suddenly thrown into crucibles that are not of their own making. How do these families circle the wagons and try to survive—and keep the bonds between parents and children (and husbands and wives) intact?"

The crisis facing Vermont resident

Bill Parrish in the original novel is the loss of his beloved son Nathaniel to leukemia a year or so before the story proper begins. As a means of survival and to maintain his mental well being, Bill volunteers to coach the baseball team for which Nathaniel had played. New to the team is the mysterious Lucky Diamond, who in addition to lacking the power of speech seems to have no family or background whatsoever. For reasons which he does not immediately explain, wealthy team owner Hilton Burberry seems to have a vested interested in Lucky, going far beyond the fact that the boy is the team's best player. When Lucky's father is apparently killed, Burberry urges Bill and his wife Harper to take the boy under their wing. Ultimately, Burberry reveals that he has been trying to "play God" by maneuvering the now-childless Parrishes into adopting Lucky. It seems that when Burberry was general manager of the Red Sox, rookie "phenom" Ben Slaughter had gotten a fifteen-year-old girl pregnant. After drinking himself blotto at a party held at Burberry's house, Slaughter was killed in a car accident. Feeling responsible for his lack of control over his star player, Burberry had raised Ben's son by proxy, leaving the boy in the care of various employees and making certain that no one would connect the kid with either Slaughter or the unwed mother by changing his name to Lucky Diamond. When Bill's son died, Burberry felt that the Harpers would be the ideal stepparents for Lucky—and, knowing that the grieving Bill would have rejected such a notion, Burberry concocted an elaborate charade to get Lucky on the baseball team and into the hearts of Bill and Harper. The unforeseen death of Lucky's guardian, logger Jeff Grout, conveniently expedited the process that Burberry had secretly set in motion. Though in retrospect it seems a bit callous that poor Jeff Grout had to kick the bucket to bring about a happy ending for the Parrishes and Lucky, the basic through-line of *Past the Bleachers* adheres to Christopher A. Bohjalian's literary checklist: Happy, Normal People; the Crucible; Events Not of Their Making; Circling the Wagons to Survive; the Strengthening of Family Bonds.

Bohjalian had given himself the challenge of writing a cohesive novel that incorporated elements of warmth, nostalgia, family values, baseball lore, mystery, intrigue and even the supernatural—and succeeded admirably. He also imbued the work with a sense of urgency and immediacy by writing in present tense, except for the occasional flashback sequence in which Bill recalled his son Nathaniel, or his own childhood baseball experiences.

To hype the "mystery" angle, Bohjalian plants all sorts of red-herring clues regarding Lucky's identity. At various junctures in the book, it is suggested that a symbiotic relationship exists between Lucky and the late Nathaniel, notably in the short scene where Bill's wife Harper discovers that Lucky shares Nathaniel's interest in reading—and many of the same books! No sooner has one digested the notion that Lucky might in fact be Nathaniel Parrish *redux* than Bohjalian introduces another, more sinister symbiosis: Lucky Diamond as the ballplaying equivalent of Damien from *The Omen*. It seems that wherever Lucky goes, someone else is incredibly *un*-lucky. While checking up on the trailer where Lucky and his supposed father live, Bill comes across a blood-soaked shirt. One of Lucky's youthful teammates suffers a heart attack, while another kid—the team bully who has been on everyone's case since the season began—nearly sustains a concussion when Lucky "accidentally" lobs a foul ball past the youngster's ear. Later, Lucky's presence seems to drive the Parrishes' pet cats into a violent frenzy, culminating in a bloody feline free-for-all. And during a visit to the local amusement park, Harper is almost crushed to death by a huge dinosaur statue!

In his script for the TV-movie version of *Past the Bleachers*, Don Rhymer (whose past credits included the CBS sitcoms *Hearts Afire* and *Evening Shade*) dispenses with most of the false clues planted by Bohjalian in the novel. There is one scene towards the end of the film in which, while watching Lucky round the bases, Bill Parrish briefly envisions Nathaniel in Lucky's place, but this serves primarily to set up the climax in which Lucky permanently replaces Nathaniel in the Parrish household. The only mysterious accident linked with Lucky in the film is the death of Jeff Grout; the moment in which Lucky deliberately throws a "wild" ball a scant few inches past a taunting kid's head is retained, but this is less a demonic portent than a matter of the nonverbal Lucky communicating the message "I'm mute, not dumb—so don't mess with *me* again!" While a substantial amount of the original novel makes its way into the movie—character names, progression of events, denouement—there were a number of significant changes, beginning with the story's locale. *Past the Bleachers* was filmed in the Georgia towns of Lithonia and Covington, communities that in no way resemble the New England setting of the novel: Thus, the film's actual location remains unidentified. Also, the cause of Nathaniel's death (leukemia) and the reason for Lucky's muteness (he was born without a larynx), carefully delineated in the novel, remain unexplained in the film.

Other alterations: In the book, Bill Parish becomes a baseball coach on his own volition; in the film, he has to be virtually strongarmed into taking the job by Hilton Burberry, making Burberry even more of a behind-the-scenes "puppeteer" than Bohjalian had intended. And despite their devastating loss, the relationship between Bill and Harper is rock-solid (and extremely sex-driven!) in the novel, their only arguments occurring when Harper disapproves of Bill's relentless grilling of Lucky to determine the boy's background. Conversely, the relationship between the Parrishes in the film is nearly strained to the breaking point, with Harper bitterly lashing out at Bill for obsessing over Nathaniel's abandoned model-train set and excluding her from the "secret guy stuff" that fathers and sons talk about.

The most pronounced novel-to-film changes are manifested in the character of old Mr. Godfrey, and in the depiction of the young players on Bill's junior-league team. In the novel, Godfrey, a resident of the retirement home which is subsidized by the university where Bill works, has, like the Parrishes, endured the tragedy of outliving his beloved son. Godfrey's philosophical acceptance of the situation serves as a contrast to Bill's wallowing, and as an example that Bill realizes he'd be better off striving for. But whereas the novel's Godfrey is merely a punctuation device, appearing only in a handful of episodes, the film's Godfrey is a major character: Not only does he always seem to be at hand to dispense advice, philosophy and exposition, but he also serves as Bill's assistant baseball coach. As played by Barnard Hughes, Godfrey also injects some much-needed levity in the proceedings, encouraging Bill to remember the upbeat and amusing things about Nathaniel by recalling the day that his own late wife impulsively donned a hat made out of balloons, and muttering curmudgeonly comments about the ineptitude of Bill's baseball players.

The characterization of Bill's team as a motley crew of foul-ups, nervous Nellies and overinflated egos is likewise found only in the film version of *Past the Bleachers*. The team members in the book are raw and inexperienced, but basically competent, and the ballgame sequences themselves are totally believable (it is clear that author Bohjalian has had extensive experience in small-town baseball). In the film, the kids are contemptuously caricatured along the lines of *The Bad News Bears in Breaking Training*: The players stupidly misunderstand signals and don't even know how to cheer in unison, one of the girl players performs cartwheels in the outfield and obstinately refuses to take instructions, the smallest of the boys (wearing thick glasses, of course) has a mortal fear of any sort of physical injury, and so on. Apparently, the filmmakers dumbed down the team so that Lucky Diamond's ballfield prowess would be all the more spectacular in contrast—and, perhaps, to provide a few more laughs in what otherwise might have been an exercise in relentless solemnity. Unfortunately, the klutziness of the children comes off as contrived and derivative, considerably weakening the film's overall effectiveness and rendering several of the baseball sequences ludicrous (how often are we going to be force-fed the old gag in which the dimwitted batter is so distracted that he—or, in this case, she—allows two strikes to go by unnoticed?).

Another weakness of the film is the performance of Richard Dean Anderson, who had recently wrapped up seven seasons as star of the TV action series *MacGyver*. Though a formidable physical presence, especially on the ballfield, Anderson may well be the most impassive screen actor since the days of Alan Ladd. It was apparently beyond his range to summon up the emotions required for the role of Bill Parrish, leaving it to the other characters to fill in the blanks by telling us what Bill is supposed to be feeling: "You're hurting, Bill—anyone can see it"; "Everyone in town could see the pain you're in"; etc.

Fortunately the other players are in fine fettle, especially Glynnis O'Connor as Harper and the aforementioned Barnard Hughes as Mr. Godfrey. The central character of Lucky Diamond is played by Grayson Fricke, whose previous screen roles included the younger brother of the Nick Nolte character in *Prince of Tides* (1991) and

Edward Furlong's character as a boy in *The Grass Harp* (1995). Even without the benefit of dialogue, Fricke captures all the nuances of his inscrutable character and handles himself admirably in the baseball scenes. After *Past the Bleachers* Fricke apparently took a sabbatical from acting, not to appear before the cameras again until 2000.

Outside of Grayson Fricke's ballpark scenes, *Past the Bleachers* is one of those baseball pictures that works best when *off* the diamond—which cannot be said of the novel, where the author's unabashed love of The Game is practically contagious. While the film version of *Past the Bleachers* is passable for a general audience, baseball purists are advised to seek out the book instead.

Pastime

Bullpen Productions/Open Road Ltd./Miramax; released September 1991

Produced by Eric Tynan Young and Robin B. Armstrong. Associate producer and unit production manager: Jonathan G. Chambers. Co-producer: Gerald R. Molen. Directed by Robin B. Armstrong. Screenplay by D. M. Eyre, Jr. Photography: Tom Richmond. Additional photography: Ralph Chandler. Edited by Mark S. Westmore. Music by Lee Holdridge. "Swing Low, Sweet Chariot" sung by Jubilant Skyes. Production designer: David W. Ford. Production coordinator: Ronald A. Morhoff. Assistant directors: Roberto Quezada and Michael Purcilly. Set decorator: Ellen Totleben. Costume designer: Kristine Brown. Makeup/Hairstyles designer: Steve Wanzell. Casting: Deborah Baryski, Camille Patton, and Superior Casting. Storyboard artist: Kristen Deem. Title design by George Bonaz. Special effects by Special Effects Unlimited. Sound mixer: Clark King. Baseball technical advisers: Pitching, Geoff Zahn; and On-field, Joey Banks (also stunt coordinator). Production executives: Robert Latham Brown and Jeffrey McCracken. Color by CFI. Dolby sound. 94 minutes. Rated PG.

Cast: William Russ (Roy Dean Bream); Glenn Plummer (Tyrone Debray); Noble Willingham (Clyde Bigby); Jeffrey Tambor (Peter LaPorte);

Dierdre O'Connell (Inez Brice); Scott Plank (Randy Keever); Reed Rudy (Spicer); Ricky Paull Goldin (Hahn); Peter Murnik (Simmons); John Jones (Colbeck); Pat O'Bryan (Walsh); Charles Tyner (Arnold); Kathryn Kates (Ethel); Troy Evans (Art); Joey Banks (Sliding Base Runner); Chuck Fick (First Base Umpire No. 1); Don Perry (Drunk old-timer); Brogan Roche (Bomber Pitcher); Craig Stark (Bomber Catcher); Tom Davidson (Beaned Bomber); Mary Pat Gleason (Woman at Bar); Charles Stranski (Elton); Susan Cash (Mrs. LaPorte); Meghan Geary, Sarah Zinsser (Catty Women at Party); Tom Pletts (Funeral Director); Sy Mogel (First Base Umpire No. 2); Aaron Albert, Chris Allen, Darin Burton, Greg Chizek, Tony Jaramillo, John Martin, Rick Slagle, Tony Solis, Darryl Allen, Richard Cavazos, Glen Gillespie, Lonnie Kalapp, David Lyons, Mike Main, Mike Neil, Vince McAllister, Larry Stalhaufer, Joe Szczepanski, Paul Visone, and Mike Wood (Baseball Players). And special appearances by Ernie Banks, Bob Feller, Harmon Killebrew, Bill Mazeroski, Don Newcombe and Duke Snider.

Central California, 1957: 41-year-old Roy Dean Bream, who'd once played in the majors for three weeks in the 1940s, is now a relief pitcher for the Class D Tri-City Steamers, a team so woebegone that it averages a nightly take of 75 dollars. Although Steamers manager Clyde Bigby won't admit it, Roy Dean remains on the team as a "charity case"; he's no great shakes as a player, and nearly always folds in the clinches despite his experience, but baseball is the only life Roy Dean knows, a life to which he has sacrificed everything, including his health and any possibility of romance. The younger team members can barely tolerate Bream's undauntable good cheer, ceaseless bullpen chatter and unsolicited advice, nor can they hide their giggles when Roy Dean demands that a recording of "Star Spangled Banner" be played before every game so that he can sing discordantly along. Manager Bigby sees Roy in a different light—as a man so overflowing with spirit and love of baseball that he actually serves as an inspiration to the team. When rookie Tyrone Debray, a 17-year-old black pitcher with a superior talent but no sense of self-worth, joins the Steamers, Roy Dean takes the boy under his wing and begins coaching him. This infuriates team gadfly Randy Keever, a so-so pitcher who viciously resents both the ongoing presence of Roy Dean and the threat to his job posed by Tyrone. The Steamers' new owner, Peter LaPorte, has no problem with Tyrone, who obviously has a great future ahead of him, but he insists to Bigby that Roy Dean is a has-been who should be let go. Bigby has no choice but to agree after Roy Dean loses an important game with an error that proves he's too far gone to be of any use as a player. At a team party, where Roy shows up in the company of warm-hearted bartender Inez Brice (his first date in years!), neither Bigby nor LaPorte can bring themselves to tell the ever ebullient pitcher that he's been fired, but a smirking Randy Keever "accidentally" lets the news slip. To save face, Roy Dean tells LaPorte that he's quitting for a coaching job, then dashes off into the night alone to confront the truth about himself that he's been purposely avoiding for years. As a last-ditch effort at self-consolation, Roy grimly enters the deserted ballpark, turns on the floodlights and desperately pitches a bagload of balls to an imaginary opponent. Tyrone, who has been sent by Inez to find Roy Dean, discovers the washed-up player sprawled on the pitcher's mound—the victim of a fatal heart attack. Roy Dean's teammates seem relieved that they'll no longer have to "carry" the aging pitcher, but Tyrone has not forgotten the inspirational legacy that his mentor has left him. Through Roy Dean Bream, Tyrone Debray has gained a sense of self-pride stronger than any taunt or career setback, a pride that will eventually elevate Tyrone out of the Class Ds and into the major leagues.

The working title for *Pastime* was *One Cup of Coffee*, a slang term used to describe

Roy Dean Bream (William Russ, left) passes on a little bullpen wisdom to rookie Tyrone DeBray (Glenn Plummer) in *Pastime*.

a minor leaguer's one chance (usually extremely brief) at playing in the majors. In addition to being less confusing to a general audience, the film's release title served a double-edged capacity: *Pastime* refers not only to the National Pastime, but to the fact that protagonist Roy Dean Bream's time is indeed past.

The influence of its hero pervaded both the title and the critical reception of this film. Just as manager Bigby seeks to protect Roy Dean because of the pitcher's unabashed and enthusiastic adoration of baseball, so too did critics bend over backward to find special value in *Pastime*, an obvious labor of love for its actors and production personnel. A recent Paramount baseball picture, *Talent for the Game* (q.v.), had been sent back to the shelf after a smattering of playdates due to lack of critical

support. Reviewers were determined that this would not happen to *Pastime*, especially since the film was distributed by Miramax, a new and comparatively small independent company that had attained "critics' darling" status after issuing a steady stream of such highly acclaimed films as *My Left Foot*, *The Thin Blue Line*, *sex, lies and videotape*, *Cinema Paradiso*, and *The Grifters*. There was additional pressure upon reviewers to sing the praises of *Pastime* in view of its winning the Audience Award for Best Dramatic Film at the 1991 Sundance Film Festival, an event organized in part by Robert Redford to support and encourage worthwhile low-budget movie projects.

To be sure, there is much to treasure in *Pastime*. As staged by debuting director Robin B. Armstrong, each ballgame scene expertly plants the viewer in the very thick of the action. We are alternately exhilarated by the exciting moments and made impatient by the dull stretches, just as in a real game. The seventeen-inning match in the middle of the film has enough comic, pathetic, thrilling and excruciating vignettes to fill ten baseball pictures. And the payoff of the scene, in which Roy Dean fails to deliver the goods at the crucial moment, is so well executed that one can almost *hear* the pain of the hapless pitcher as he realizes the fruitlessness of his labors.

The crowning glory of *Pastime* is the performance of star William Russ, a relatively unknown performer whose prior claim to fame was a recurring role on the TV series *Wiseguy*. Without benefit of the audience preconditioning that frequently greets big name actors, Russ has the moviegoer in the palm of his hand from his first scene to his last. There are few characters harder to play than those who remain cheerful when it's obvious they have nothing to be cheerful about; but Russ does it, and don't ask us how.

The actor's high point is his monologue about his minuscule career in "The Bigs." As Roy Dean, Russ describes in affectionate detail the thrill of standing in the middle of Wrigley Field and attempting to strike out Stan Musial with his "trick" pitch, which he calls "Bream's Dream." Never mind that Stan the Man knocked the ball into the stratosphere—what's important is that Roy Dean had his moment in the majors. As a coda to his monologue, Roy Dean proudly displays a yellowed newspaper clipping of his Big Game's box score; even the fact that his name was misspelled does not dampen Bream's thrill at actually having played in the same ballpark as Musial. It's a "test" scene: Had William Russ made one wrong acting choice, Roy Dean would have been just another pathetic rainbow-chaser or, worse, an idiotic clown. But Russ makes all the right moves, and we're in love with Roy Dean Bream from that moment forward.

Almost as good as Russ (and perhaps we should drop the "almost") is Glenn Plummer as the raw but gifted rookie Tyrone Debray. Like William Russ, Plummer has an unenviable acting task: To make believable an incredibly naive and painfully shy young man who in any other film might be an object of ridicule. And like Russ, Plummer passes his test with flying colors. Worth the price of admission in itself is the scene where the nonplussed Tyrone Debray is ordered by his manager to throw a ball directly at an opposing batter as retaliation for a similar beaning from the other team's pitcher. The look of pain, amazement, and incredulity on Glenn Plummer's face says more without words than any amount of well-written dialogue ever could.

A cogent point here. There is a lot of well-written dialogue in *Pastime*, but it's a tad too much of a good thing. Reportedly, screenwriter D. M. Eyre (who first attracted attention in 1980 for his script for another low budgeter, *Cattle Annie and Little Britches*) had written *Pastime* back in 1974, when he was still tending bar in Colorado. Eyre's screenplay definitely does have all the earmarks of a maiden project: Scenes go on too long, plot points are established and then hammered to death, and many characters talk about their thought processes at far greater length than they would in real life. Jeffrey Tambor, for example, establishes his interpretation of long-suffering team owner Peter LaPorte by elucidating on how baseball is a business that must purge itself dispassionately of "dead weight" like Roy Dean Bream—all the while qualifying this sangfroid by saying that he, LaPorte, isn't really a bad fellow, but that he's got to make a profit like anyone else. Surely Tambor is an accomplished enough performer to delineate LaPorte's contradictory nature without prattling on as if he was visiting his analyst.

Conversely, several other characters are underdeveloped stereotypes: the crusty

Roy Dean Bream (William Russ, right) explains the intricacies of his "Bream's Dream" pitch to Tyrone DeBray (Glenn Plummer) in *Pastime*.

but lovable manager, the tough but tender barmaid, the bullying but insecure rival pitcher, and so forth. Director Armstrong and actors Noble Willingham, Dierdre O'Connell and Scott Plank do their utmost to bring these people to life, but they aren't given much support by D. M. Eyre's script, which seems so proud of avoiding certain baseball movie clichés that it ignores the other clichés still lurking about.

All these shortcomings can be forgiven and forgotten in view of the excellence maintained by *Pastime*—up to the point that Roy Dean Bream suffers his nervous breakdown (a brilliantly handled vignette; we see Roy sitting alone inside his car, his anguished wails muted by the tightly closed doors). Once Roy Dean pitches himself to death on the deserted ballfield, however,

the whole project disintegrates. We are forced to endure a *Death of a Salesman*–like funeral, attended by no one but Tyrone, Bigby, Inez, and three elderly VFW members. This is supposed to be painfully poignant—poor, poor Roy Dean, who gave his life to his work but who can't even raise a crowd at his own funeral. The explanation of the sparse turnout is that the services are being held during a Steamers game; we're evidently expected to be outraged at the cruelty of Roy's teammates, who'd rather make a living than honor their fallen comrade. But the question that nags at us during this scene is not "How can life be so unfair?" but "Why didn't they hold the funeral at a more convenient time?" Strike One.

Then we go to the ballpark, where, for

the convenience of the screenplay, hot-headed pitcher Randy Keever transforms himself from a mere insensitive jerk to a double-dyed villain, screaming sarcastically to Tyrone that he should "win this one for Roy Dean." At this point, Tyrone's worm turns, and he beats Keever to a pulp while manager Bigby looks on approvingly. It's clear that this is intended to be an audience rousing sequence, where we're encouraged to hiss the bad guy and cheer the good guys. Perhaps such a response did indeed greet *Pastime* when it played the Sundance Film Festival. But the admittedly small audience in attendance when this writer saw the film, who'd been preconditioned by both the critics and the quality of the earlier scenes to expect something better, sat watching the climax in stone cold silence—the sort of disillusioned silence one would expect from a group of people who'd walked up a gangplank only to find out there wasn't any ship. Strike Two.

Strike Three? Take your choice. The final nail in the coffin is either the grindingly dull slow-motion photography in the final scene (accompanied by the equally boring musical score by Lee Holdridge) or the film's surprising lack of showmanship when showmanship was certainly called for. This last point refers to the fact that the makers of *Pastime* were the last "civilians" allowed to set up cameras within the walls of Chicago's old Comiskey Park before that venerable landmark was demolished in late 1990. They needn't have bothered: In the final scene, where Tyrone finally makes the "Bigs," we see so very little of Comiskey that the sequence could just as well have been filmed at the rundown San Fernando Valley ballpark utilized for the rest of the movie.

In addition, the pressbook of *Pastime* makes much of the fact that several veteran ballplayers were cast in minor roles. But since none of these players are given screen credit, you must rely on your own fading memory to recognize Ernie Banks of the Cubs and Duke Snider of the Dodgers, barely visible as Steamers fans in the opening scene; Don Newcombe, also a former Dodger, making a seconds-lasting appearance as a flag raiser; and Bob Feller of the Indians, Harmon Killebrew of the Twins, and Bill Mazeroski of the Pirates, all three sitting stock still and moving nary a muscle as the three VFW representatives attending Roy Dean's funeral. We're told in the *Pastime* pressbook that the fleeting appearances of these big-league legends were supposed to "add an extra layer of depth and richness to the picture." Strike three, and you're out.

But we're spending way too much time on the downside. *Pastime* is three-fourths of a great movie, and that's a good enough average in any man's league. And while it earned only a piddling $267,265 during its domestic theatrical release, the film has since performed well on the home-video circuit, where the reader can still find it today. For full enjoyment, it's best to fast forward past the more ponderous dialogue stretches and activate the "stop" button right before the lachrymose climax. Just savor the ballgame sequences and William Russ's flawless performance; then you'll see what all the film critics' shouting was about.

Perfect Game

Up to Bat Productions/Buena Vista; US video release: April 18, 2000

Executive producer/Writer/Director/Editor: Dan Guntzelman. Produced by Joseph Scott. Producer/Production Manager: James S. Bardellati. Photography: John Gunselman. Music composed and conducted by David Benoit. Production design: Melody [Lavigna]. Costume design: Judith Brewer Curtis. Production supervisor: Giampaolo Deboll. Sound mixer: William G. Flick. Special effects foreman: Bill Cochran.

Casting: Amy Lieberman. First assistant director: Peter Merwin. Second assistant director: Lincoln Myers. Script supervisor: Susan Straughnharris. Color. 97 minutes; Dolby Stereo Sound. Rated PG.

Cast: Edward Asner (Billy Hicks); Patrick Duffy (Bobby Geiser); Cameron Finley (Kanin Crosby); Tracy Nelson (Diane Crosby); Sam Anderson (Steven); Evan Arnold (Ed Spangler); Drake Bell (Bobby Geiser, Jr.); Mark Blankfield (Coach Ron); Orlando Brown (Marcel Williams); Joanna Daniels (Robin); Bill Kirchenbauer (Coach Hank); Paul Robert Langdon (Enrique); Christopher [Naoki] Lee (Satoshi Migake); Bryan Matsuura (Osamu Migake); Hayley Palmer (Kelly); Chelsea Parnell (Logan Crosby); Sara Paxton (Sydney); Martin Spanjers (Brian Cudahy); Jacqueline Steiger (Marsha); Gil Espinoza (Burly Coach); Rob Roy Fitzgerald (Kelly's Dad); Ruben Gonzalez (Jesus); Robert Harvey (Mayor Rice); Michael James Johnson (Tall Umpire); Antonia Jones (Store Babe); Benjamin Lum (Hayato Migake); Shelley Malil (Coach Ravi); Shannon McLaren (Suzette); Armando Molina (Coach Harvey); Beans Morocco (Clerk Librarian); Eduardo Rodriquez (Zapata); Yolanda Snowball (Lelani Williams); Jason Waters (Store Clerk); Nick Wechsler (State Umpire); Peter Acosta, Buchanan Britton, Zachary Britton, Jason Klein (Ball Players); Kimberly Anderson (Young Girl); Marvin Bos, Rodney Madsen, Jesse Murphy, Charles Van Rennselaer (Quartet); Martha Britton (Kelly's Mom); Tom Brumansky (Dream Pitcher); Giampaolo Deboll (Skinny Umpire); Adrian Felan (Coach Rich); Zachary Foster (Batter); Mark Grant (Dream Catcher); Kanin Guntzelman (Tall Kid); Logan Guntzelman (Scoreboard Girl); Chase Lunt (Pitcher); Linus Merwin (Snotty Kid), Trudy Mockenhaupt (Catcher); David Oredugba (Pitcher); Rai Oredugba (Taller Kid); Charles Spann (Catcher); Trent Teebken (Wolf Batter); Charles White (Umpire); Harry Wright (Catcher); Bill Wilson (Dream Umpire); Phil Hawn (Little League Dad); Polli Magaro (Woman in Audience).

For eight straight years the Park League baseball championship has been won by the Bulldogs, the adolescent team coached by the swaggering Bobby Geiser. This year, however, the playing field has been leveled: According to the new rules, all Park League teams must be "balanced and equal," meaning that Geiser can no longer snatch up all the best kids during tryouts, but must give the other teams an even break. Insisting that the rules have been changed only to keep him from taking home a ninth championship trophy, Bobby bets the other team coaches $1000 that he can sign up the worst players in the League and still sweep the season. Naturally, he doesn't tell these "losers" the real reason they've been chosen for the Bulldogs: So far as they're concerned, to be on "Bobby's Team" is the closest thing to Heaven on Earth. The happiest of the new Bulldogs is 11-year-old Kanin Crosby, who eagerly welcomes the chance to live up to the standards set by his late father, a college baseball star. After the team's first victory, Bobby magnanimously informs the new kids that henceforth, whenever the Bulldogs win there will be no practice. As the season progresses, Kanin cannot help but notice that even though the Bulldogs are tops in the League, his own game has not improved one iota; for that matter, neither he nor his fellow "rookies" have been allowed to do anything but bring up the rear for the established team members. Doing some detective work on his own, Kanin discovers that Bobby has been holding secret practice sessions for his best players, deliberately leaving the "losers" out in the cold. The parents of the Bulldog second-stringers are apprised of this deception, and also find out about the thousand-dollar bet. Led by Kanin's mom Diane, the team parents fire Bobby, who promptly accepts a job with the rival Scorpions, taking his finest players—including his own son, Bobby Jr.—along with him. Unwilling to reveal the details of the wager, the parents try to spare their kids' feelings by disbanding the Bulldogs. But the team, basking in the glow of being "Number One," insists upon staying together. A new coach is found in the corpulent, crusty form of retired high-school athletics teacher and town "character" Billy Hicks, who might have been a Major League baseballer had he not incurred a serious injury during World War II. Despite Billy's hard-driving tactics, the Bulldogs continue to wallow in mediocrity until Kanin accidentally learns the truth about Bobby's bet. Angry and humiliated, Kanin tosses all of his father's precious sports mementos out the window—whereupon Billy Hicks, impressed by the boy's unerring arm and muscle control, realizes that the best way to make his team excel is to get them good and mad and *keep* them that way! Initially opposed to this "motivational strategy," Diane and the other parents find themselves vicariously enjoying the Bulldogs' gonzo euphoria, especially if it means taking the wind out of the sails of the arrogant Bobby Geiser. The Bulldogs get that chance when, after clinching their division, the kids are pitted against Geisler's Scorpions in the championship playoff game. Bobby ends up forfeiting the game by completely losing his cool when the umpire makes a call against Bobby Jr. Refusing to accept victory on these unsatisfying terms, the Bulldogs challenge the Scorpions to a winner-take-all sandlot game—as far away from those meddling grownups as the kids can possibly get!

Perfect Game was filmed independently by Dan Guntzelman, a former Cincinnati-based TV news producer whose Hollywood writing and producing credits included the network sitcoms *WKRP in Cincinnati*, *Growing Pains* and *Just the Ten of Us*. Quoted on the Disney Studio website, Guntzelman described the film as "built around the turning point in the life of an 11-year-old boy who is struggling with the recent death of his father, harboring the resultant anger and anxiety, all of which is compounded by the fact that he's the worst baseball player in the league. However, through a sometimes harsh, poignant and often humorous turn of events, he summons the courage and the will to win and steps up to the plate on his own terms. It's a movie about growing up and kids learning to accept themselves and determining what they have to do in order to achieve something that's important to them. That happens to be a lifelong process from which adults are not immune, as [you] see in the picture."

Interviewed by the Cincinnati *Enquirer*, Guntzelman further revealed that he had more than a passing knowledge of his subject matter. His own son, who, like the film's protagonist, was named Kanin, had played baseball in a real-life California Park League, though one can only hope that his performance was at least a *little* better than that of his movie counterpart. And like the film's Kanin, Guntzelman lost his own father at a relatively early age.

With a beggarly $100,000 budget to work with, Dan Guntzelman was obliged to wear several hats: producer, director, writer, even film editor. The cinematographer was the director's brother, John Gunselman, who, like most everyone else on the picture, worked for union scale or thereabouts. Many of the bit players and extras were unpaid (or barely paid) members of the production crew's family, including Dan Guntzelman's son Kanin and daughter Kelly, the latter contributing a droll nonspeaking performance as the blasé scoreboard girl. Virtually all baseball scenes were filmed at the same municipal diamond in the Simi Valley, California, town of Santa Clarita, with the filmmakers creating the illusion of several different parks through the use of cunning camera angles and a variety of special lenses. The filming sessions ranged anywhere from twelve to twenty hours—explaining the preponderance of night scenes in what is essentially a "daytime" story—though by law the children had to be sent home at midnight. One day's shooting was devoted to the dream sequences, scattered throughout the film, in which Kanin imagines himself batting out homers in a big-league stadium, with his ghostly father acting as a one-man cheering section: These scenes were filmed at San Diego's Qualcomm Stadium.

"I set out to make *Perfect Game* a family movie that's funny and appealing to kids and grown-ups alike," observed Guntzelman in the Disney-website piece. In this he succeeded.

"We don't do funny little rock 'n' roll cues off the nervousness about the games," said Guntzelman to the Cincinnati *Enquirer*. "This is serious stuff for the kids.... They really respond to the challenge of batting a ball, of not looking foolish in front of your friends, of getting through with some dignity." So far so good.

Guntzelman has also claimed that the film was built around the kids, who "drove the action." Uhhhh, not quite, Dan. That may have been the intention going in, but what emerged on-screen was a new variation on the same question posed nearly a quarter century earlier by the thematically similar *The Bad News Bears*: Do adults organize their youngsters into sports teams for the sake of the kids, or to massage their own egos?

On any number of fronts, the action is driven by the adults: the insufferable A-list team coach who is willing to trample on everyone's emotions to win; the envious rival coaches who insensitively participate in a wager that might potentially rob a bunch of innocent youngsters of their dignity and pride; the misguided practitioners of Political Correctness who insist upon lowering standards of excellence in pursuit of that elusive and generally unattainable commodity called fairness, claiming that it's "for the children" when it's really for themselves; those same practitioners who are willing to fold their tents and concede defeat the minute things don't go *their* way, and never mind what the kids want; the self-absorbed sourpuss who exploits a young boy's hostility to achieve victory; the

Team Mom who, after bending over backward to shelter her son from the vicissitudes of life, does an about-face when given the opportunity to use the boy as a vessel of wrath against an adult whom she personally despises.

Granted, the young baseball wannabes learn to stop feeling sorry for themselves and to stop putting themselves down on their own volition; and it is the youngsters who resolve the storyline by shedding all those adult-imposed rules and restrictions and playing for the sheer love of the game. But what sticks in the viewer's memory is not the kids' eventual triumph as much as the backstage shenanigans of a bunch of grownups with their own set of agenda.

This might have been a nasty pill for the audience to swallow, but *Perfect Game* manages to undercut the vitriol by maintaining a light touch throughout, thanks largely to the smooth performances of three TV-series veterans: Ed Asner as the curmudgeonly Billy Hicks, Tracy Nelson as the well-meaning Diane Crosby, and Patrick Duffy as the vainglorious Bobby Geiser. The beauty of these characterizations is that, though each one is essentially a cliché, the actors themselves play *away* from the clichéd elements to come up with well-rounded, believable performances. Ed Asner never pulls out the wearisome "I'm really a swell guy underneath" gimmick, remaining just as contentious at the end of the film as the beginning, but withal investing the character with an innate likeability. It was probably second nature for the actor, who'd previously done this same sort of thing for nearly a dozen years on *The Mary Tyler Moore Show* and *Lou Grant*, but it is reassuring to see a master at work. In a less showy but no less important role, Tracy Nelson craftily adopts the soft, melodious whine of the "typical" overprotective suburban mom and makes all of her character transitions *within* that whine, avoiding the standard "lamb into lion" metamorphosis so common to films of this nature. The actress' finest moment occurs when, encouraged to trash-talk her son to spur him into playing better, the strongest insult she can come up with is "Your penmanship is sloppy!"

As obnoxious as Patrick Duffy's Bobby Geiser may be, his character is all the more irritating because he's *right*: The league rules have been changed for the express purpose of putting him at a disadvantage, and the only true way to have a consistently winning team is to pick consistently winning players. In fact, with a little bit of shuffling Bobby could have been the hero of the piece, and indeed he *is* a hero to his best ballplayers, whom he treats like royalty (none of that "bullying for success" nonsense here!). By avoiding the temptation of turning Bobby Geiser into a stock villain, Patrick Duffy is able to elicit a certain amount of sympathy from the audience when, during the final game, Bobby drops his mask of confidence and reveals himself to be an overgrown spoiled brat. Like Diane Crosby, the viewer has been eagerly anticipating the inevitable moment that Bobby's ego will be deflated; and, like Diane, the viewer is both startled and not a little embarrassed when that moment actually arrives.

Most of the younger actors maintain the level of credibility and conviction established by Asner, Nelson and Duffy. Cameron Finley, who'd previously essayed the title role in the 1997 film version of the vintage TV sitcom *Leave It to Beaver*, delivers a straightforward, unaffected performance as Kanin Crosby, with the other child performers following his lead. Like the grownups, the youngsters are forced to wrestle with clichéd characters straight from the *Bad News Bears* training camp: the wisecracking best friend, the geekish "brain" with the requisite computer-catalogue vocabulary, the pseudo-tough guy, the tomboy on the verge of womanhood, the neurotic asthmatic, the pugnacious "shrimp," the Japanese boy whose English is conveyed via jokey subtitles. Though the kids never completely transcend these stock character types, they remain believable within their limits.

While *Perfect Game* was in development, producer-director Dan Guntzelman pitched the project to Disney Studios, who agreed to distribute the film through their Buena Vista home-video division. The subsequent Disneyfication of Guntzelman's property proved to be a mixed blessing: While the film received wider exposure than might otherwise have been the case, the Disney folks imbued the picture with any number of supposedly surefire gimmicks, which tended to dumb the picture down to the usual "family comedy" level. *Perfect Game* does not really need a lengthy bicycle chase through sunny suburban streets, a messy food fight in a pizza parlor, a clumsy comedy-relief assistant coach, nor a painfully mechanical scene in which one of the kids imitates an adult over the phone with the help of a dubbed voiceover; but these extra ingredients where just what the doctor ordered so far as Disney was concerned. And in its pursuit of a "G" rating, Disney saw to it that the film was shorn of anything that might remotely be regarded as objectionable, which is why we see kids shouting "You stink" while their lips are forming the words "You suck," among other examples; whether this self-censorship was an improvement or a detriment is a matter of taste, but it made certain scenes look like highlights from an old Godzilla picture.

Additionally, the film is too long by at least ten minutes, suggesting that Disney was prepping the property for a commercial–TV sale, where a 97-minute length made the film easier to sell to potential sponsors for a "two hour" slot. The problem here was not so much the protraction of scenes that played better in a shorter and more succinct form, but in the overplugging of David Benoit's musical score, which was repetitious to begin with and became annoyingly redundant as the film wore on.

In one respect, however, Disney's apparent elongation of Guntzelman's screenplay was a distinct advantage. With more time to play with, the filmmakers were able to trace the progress of the Bulldogs via a series of lengthy montage sequences, which were among the film's most cinematically creative moments. In one noteworthy example, the "main" baseball action is stretch-framed in the background, while medium-shot images of the various ballplayers crawl horizontally across the screen, in the style of a superimposed graphic on a network sports telecast.

And if the decision to pad out the running time resulted in the piling on of extra baseball-game sequences, so much the better. There are few films, big budget or small, that have captured the familial atmosphere and across-the-board enthusiasm of Junior League baseball as well as *Perfect Game*. Equally admirable is the fact that the film's games are not always won or lost on the basis of athletic talent alone; as in any real game, team strategy and umpirical decisions are just as important as power or speed. As a result, when the "underdog" kids manage to come out on top from time to time, their victories flow naturally from the action and do not seem to be mere scripted contrivances to make the audience feel better.

While *Perfect Game* can be classified as a direct-to-video affair, the film has received limited theatrical exposure, and in 2001 it copped two awards—best director and best child actor (Cameron Finley)—at the Santa Clarita International Film Festival (it is mere coincidence, of course, that the ceremony was held in the town where the picture was made). This writer first saw the film via closed-circuit TV during a Caribbean ocean cruise, where it proved an enjoyable antidote for a brief bout with *mal-de-mer*. *Perfect Game* may not be the most original baseball film to come down the pike, and it may have strayed some distance from the director's original concept, but at least it has heart—something, the song tells us, ya just gotta have.

The Pinch Hitter

Triangle/Ince/Kay-Bee; released April 26, 1917

Produced by Thomas H. Ince. Directed by Victor L. Schertzinger. Screenplay and titles by C. Gardner Sullivan. 5 reels; black and white; silent.

Cast: Charles Ray (Joel Parker); Sylvia Beamer (Abby Nettleton); Joseph J. Downing (Obediah Parker); Jerome Storm (Jimmy Slater); Louis Durham (Coach Nolan); Darrel Foss (Alexis Thompson).

Obediah Parker has promised his wife on her deathbed that he'll see to it that their son Joel is enrolled in Williamson College. Unfortunately, Joel is probably the least prepossessing citizen of Turkey Creek, Vermont; he's described via subtitle as "orful bashful and sorta dummified," and he's also a total loss as an athlete. Once at Williamson, Joel is mercilessly hazed, finding solace only in the kindnesses of beauteous Abby Nettleton, who runs the campus confectionery store. Joel tries out for the Williamson baseball team, where by virtue of his school spirit he's made the team mascot—though tenderhearted Coach Nolan doesn't tell young Parker that he isn't a full-fledged team member. During a crucial game against Bensonhurst College, Williamson's star player is injured; having run out of substitutes, Nolan sends Joel in to pinch-hit. Inspired by Abby Nettleton, Joel wins the game and is redeemed in the eyes of his father, who by chance (and the machinations of the screenwriter) is attending the game.

The Pinch Hitter utilized the natural baseball skills of Charles Ray as the basis for one of the star's most popular "misfit makes good" stories. The film represented the first directorial assignment for songwriter Victor Schertzinger, launching a career that would extend to the Bob Hope-Bing Crosby "Road" pictures of the 1940s. Schertzinger would go on to guide Charles Ray through thirteen more films in the three years after the 1917 release of *The Pinch Hitter.* "I can't explain how it is between Vic and me," said Ray of his favorite director. "We so thoroughly understand each other we don't even have to talk when he directs. He looks at me, I look at him. It must be thought-transference or something, but I feel harmonious when he is around." If Vic only could have cooked....

Happy-go-lucky Charlie Ray offers moral support to his teammates in *The Pinch Hitter* (1917).

Victor Schertzinger's directorial approach to *The Pinch Hitter* was in keeping with the adroit crosscutting editorial style that was commonplace by 1917; it was also typical of the "pretty picture" era when filmmaking began to be regarded as an art form. When Joel Parker (Charlie Ray) hits his winning homer, its distance is indicated by a cutaway shot of the ball landing in the street outside the park; and just before scoring that hit, Parker is inspired by his girl Abby, whose face, framed by an iris effect in a tight closeup, dissolves languidly into view over a long shot of the grandstands. C. Gardner Sullivan's descriptive subtitle complements the visual hyperbole of this moment: "Two eyes, not entreating, despairing, or condemning, but spelling in vibrant letters one grand word—Confidence! Confidence in *him!*" C. Gardner Sullivan was at that time one of the highest priced title writers in movies. Evidently he was paid by the word.

Audience response to *The Pinch Hitter* was enough to prompt Charles Ray to appear in another pre–1920 baseball epic, *The Busher* (1919) (q.v.), which was directed by one of the supporting actors of *The Pinch Hitter,* Jerome Storm. The earlier film remained in distribution throughout the 1920s: It was reissued by United Pictures three years after its debut, then went the rounds again in a reedited 1923 version courtesy of Tri-Stone Pictures. *The Pinch Hitter's* most lasting effect was that it very likely inspired Harold Lloyd's *The Freshman* (1925), which, except for its switch from baseball to football, had virtually the same plot. Once word got out that *The Freshman* was in the works, Associated Exhibitors cooked up another variation on the same theme—a remake of *The Pinch Hitter* (see next entry).

The Pinch Hitter

Associated Exhibitors; released December 13, 1925

Directed by Joseph Henabery. Screenplay by C. Gardner Sullivan. Photography: Jules Cronjager. 7 reels/6,259 feet; black and white; silent.

Cast: Glenn Hunter (Joel Martin); Constance Bennett (Abby Nettleton); Jack Drumier (Obadiah Parker); Reginald Sheffield (Alex

Thompson); Antrim Short (Jimmy Slater); George Clive (Coach Nolan); Mary Foy (Aunt Martha); James E. Sullivan (College Dean); James Burke (Charlie).

This remake of the 1917 Charles Ray vehicle of the same name was the same mixture as before except for some slight alterations. Hero Joel Martin (Joel Parker in Ray's film) is now the nephew, rather than the son, of Obadiah Parker, and heroine Abby Nettleton has been demoted from sweet-shop owner to humble waitress in the Williamson College eatery.

The 1925 *Pinch Hitter* would probably have remained unproduced had it not been for the success of Harold Lloyd's July release of that year, *The Freshman*; but though *The Pinch Hitter* owed a lot to the Lloyd picture (which, as previously mentioned, was indebted to the 1917 *Pinch Hitter*), it took pains not to look too much like its inspiration. For example, while Harold Lloyd tried to buy his popularity in *The Freshman* by footing the bill for everything from shakes at the soda shop to a fancy dress ball, the hero of *The Pinch Hitter* was prohibited from spending any money at all by his tightwad uncle. Both films, however, ended with the feckless team mascot metamorphosing into Big Man on Campus during an important athletic match. (As a footnote without further comment: In October 2000, the granddaughter of Harold Lloyd filed a $50 million lawsuit against the distributors of Adam Sandler's football comedy *The Waterboy* [1998], claiming that Sandler had lifted the plot of his film from *The Freshman*.)

The ballgame scenes for *The Pinch Hitter* were shot at Rutgers Baseball Field in New Jersey. Years after the fact, writer Stephen Longstreet recalled that Babe Ruth himself showed up for filming at Rutgers one day, allegedly to teach actor Glenn Hunter how to hit. This, however, was mere press agent puffery; Ruth signed a few autographs,

shook a few hands, and then went home (or wherever), leaving Glenn Hunter just as much a baseball novice as before.

Those very few ticket buyers who attended *The Pinch Hitter* could not have known that the film's ingénue, Constance Bennett, would one day reach the pinnacle of screen stardom. In 1925 Bennett was just one of many starlets under contract to MGM, though thanks to the prestige of her father, Broadway star Richard Bennett, she'd managed to wangle a deal whereby she could work for outside studios whenever MGM had nothing lined up for her. Why Constance Bennett would elect to play a nondescript role in a forgettable programmer like *The Pinch Hitter* was just as much a mystery as her rationale for portraying a working-class hash slinger in the regal manner of Gloria Swanson.

Play Ball

Pathé; released July 1, 1925

Directed by Spencer Gordon Bennet. Screenplay based on stories suggested by John J. McGraw (though actually ghostwritten by Frank Leon Smith). Released as a ten-chapter serial, each chapter two reels in length; black and white; silent. Chapter Titles: *To the Rescue; The Flaming Float; Betrayed; The Decoy Wire; Face to Face; The Showdown; A Mission of Hate; Double Peril; Into Segundo's Hands; A Home Plate Wedding.*

Cast: Allene Ray (Doris Sutton); Walter Miller (Jack Rollins); J. Barney Sherry (Mr. Sutton); Harry Semels (Segundo); Mary Milnor (Maybelle Pratt); Wally Oettel (Rugger Farnsworth); and John McGraw and the New York Giants.

A rookie player for the Giants falls in love with the daughter of a wealthy businessman suspected of financing a deposed monarch's return to power. There's blackmail, death threats, explosions, danglings from skyscraper ledges, and other random acts of mischief before everything is set aright in chapter ten.

Play Ball was a ten-episode serial from Pathé Studios, which in 1925 was the league leader in weekly chapter plays. The Pathé product was distinguished by solid story values, better than average acting, and non-stop thrills. Director Spencer Gordon Bennet, who would make serials his life's work, and writer Frank Leon Smith were the principal instigators of this singular sort of entertainment, and Pathé's star team of Walter Miller and Allene Ray would soon become the Tracy and Hepburn of the cliffhangers. Add to these ingredients the never-ending publicity gimmicks perpetrated by New York Giants general manager John McGraw, and you have—or *had*, if you'd been around in 1925—*Play Ball*.

Some film historians have complained that the cockeyed combination of baseball and foreign intrigue in *Play Ball* was the *ne plus ultra* of contrivance—a complaint that would forever gall the serial's author, Frank Leon Smith.

In a letter to *Films in Review* in 1968, Smith revealed that he and director Spencer Gordon Bennet were hardly in any position to make the plot any more logical than it was, since the whole affair was forced upon them. Smith and Bennet had just completed a production in Florida when Pathé sent a certified check to John McGraw in care of the filmmakers, with instructions that they take the check to John McGraw at spring training in Sarasota. It was part of a prearranged deal whereby McGraw would give Pathé permission to film his Giants at the Polo Grounds in New York in exchange for "story credit" for *Play Ball*. Neither the studio nor McGraw had given a second thought to the possibility that Smith and Bennet might know absolutely nothing about baseball—which happened to be the case.

Smith noted that there wasn't time to become acquainted with the game—he was merely required to come up with a series of perilous situations in which to embroil his hero and heroine. "I didn't have to be told that Pathé wanted melodrama," Smith remembered, "but how do you get life and death motives into a serial involving a ball game? You can't unless you keep your melodrama well away from the baseball diamond." That they did; most of *Play Ball* took place as far from the Polo Grounds as the moviemakers could get, including a ledge-climbing sequence shot atop Manhattan's Algonquin Hotel.

Even if Smith and Bennet had wanted to film action sequences at the Polo Grounds, they were stymied by the National League's ban on cameras in the ballpark during the actual playing of games. Moreover, Pathé had only signed an agreement with John McGraw; none of the other seven National League teams had granted permission to use their players, uniforms or insignias in *Play Ball*.

All things considered, the serial turned out rather well, making a tidy profit for Pathé and even garnering a good review or two. Looking back on the whole affair, Frank Leon Smith felt he had nothing to be ashamed of. As for those come-lately critics who found *Play Ball* contrived, Smith issued a challenge: "Well, maybe one of these historians will try some day to evolve a film dramatizing a Big League team in action that is plausible and profitable."

"Maybe," Smith added, with the amazing 1969 World Series still in the future, "he will even try it with the Mets."

The Pride of St. Louis

20th Century–Fox; released May 1952

Produced by Jules Schermer. Directed by Harmon Jones. Screenplay by Herman J. Mankiewicz, from a story by Guy Trosper. Photography: Leo Tover. Edited by Robert Simpson. Music by Arthur Lange. Musical direction by Lionel Newman. Art direction by Lyle Wheeler and Addison Behr. Special photographic effects by Fred Sersen. Costumes by Travilla. Wardrobe direction by Charles LeMaire. 93 minutes; Black and white; sound.

Cast: Dan Dailey (Jerome Herman "Dizzy" Dean); Joanne Dru (Patricia Nash Dean); Richard Hylton (Johnny Kendall); Richard Crenna (Paul "Daffy" Dean); Hugh Sanders (Horst); James Brown (Moose); Leo T. Cleary (Ed Monroe); Kenny Williams (Castleman); John McKee (Delany); Stuart Randall (Frankie Frisch); William Frambes (Herbie); Damian O'Flynn (Johnny Bishop); Cliff Clark (Pittsburgh Coach); Fred Graham (Alexander); Billy Nelson (Chicago Manager); Pattee Chapman (Ella); Richard Reeves (Connelly); Bob Nichols (Eddie); John Duncan (Western Union Boy); Clyde Trumbull (Mike); John Butler (Waiter); Freeman Lusk (Doctor); Jack Rice (Voorhees); Al Green (Joe); Phil Van Zandt (Louie); Victor Sutherland (Kendall Sr.); Kathryn Card (Mrs. Martin); George McDonald (Roscoe); Joan Sudlow (Miss Johnson); Frank Scannell (Chicago Third Base Coach); Larry Thor, John Wald, Hank Weaver, William Forman, Jack Sherman, and Tom Hanlon (Various Radio Announcers); Chet Huntley (Tom Weaver); John Doucette (Benny); Harris Brown (Hotel Clerk).

Oklahoma-born Jerome Herman Dean is spotted by a scout for the St. Louis Cardinals while pitching for an amateur club in the Ozarks in 1928. Jerome starts out with the Texas League team in Houston, where he meets and falls for department-store employee Patricia Nash, whom he eventually marries. It is during an exhibition game versus the Chicago White Sox that an opposing coach bestows upon Jerome the nickname "Dizzy" to throw off Dean's game; but after the Houston team wins, the "Dizzy" label sticks as a sign of affection instead of derision. Dean makes it into the majors as a St. Louis pitcher, taking with him his younger brother Paul, likewise an ace pitcher, whom the newspapers designate "Daffy" Dean after the brothers distinguish themselves with the Cardinals, not only through their dazzling skills but through their wacky publicity stunts. The Dean boys go on strike against the Cards when they're fined for missing a game, but Dizzy is convinced to stop licking his wounds after befriending Johnny Kendall, a wealthy cripple who manages to keep a smile on his face no matter what the provocation. With the help of Dizzy and Daffy, St. Louis wins the 1934 World Series—after which things begin to go downhill for Dizzy. He sustains several injuries, and ultimately his pitching arm fails him. Following an unsatisfying 1938 stint with the Chicago Cubs, Dean is sent back to the minors from whence he came. Dizzy starts feeling sorry for himself again, and his subsequent descent into gambling and alcohol prompts his wife Pat, fed up with her husband's immaturity, to walk out on him. But old pal Johnny Kendall comes to Dean's rescue; Johnny convinces his father, who happens to operate a successful brewery, to sponsor Dizzy's entry into the broadcast field as a play by play announcer for the St. Louis Browns. In spite of a committee of St. Louis schoolteachers who try to get Dean taken off the air due to his faulty grammar, Dizzy's radio career is a success—and at the end Pat Dean comes home to her husband, who's at long last "found himself."

When Dizzy Dean was approached by 20th Century–Fox with an offer of $50,000 for the movie rights to his life story, Dean's response couldn't have been more characteristic: "Jeez, they're gonna give me fifty thousand smackers just fer *livin'*!" The studio was less generous to Paul "Daffy" Dean; when Paul balked at the pittance he was getting, Dizzy, ever looking after the best interests of his younger brother, gave Paul $5000 of his own money from Fox. Payments were made in small annual installments at the insistence of Dizzy's wife Patricia, who was well aware that a big chunk of money up front would wreak havoc on the Deans' income-tax situation. Satisfied by the financial end of the deal, Dizzy Dean never took *The Pride of St. Louis* to task for declaring itself in an introductory title to be a "true story." Had Dean ever been

The Pride of St. Louis: Dizzy (Dan Dailey, left) and Daffy (Richard Crenna) flank Mrs. Dean (Joanne Dru) in this *Singin' in the Rain*–style publicity still.

asked to comment on the film's occasional fabrications, he might have responded with the phrase he always used whenever he was caught stretching the truth in an interview: "Them ain't lies—them's scoops."

Beyond the similarity of its title, *The Pride of St. Louis* invites comparison with the 1942 Lou Gehrig biopic *The Pride of the Yankees* (q.v.) in that Herman J. Mankiewicz

worked on the screenplays for both pictures. The two films pretty much chart the same plot course: Young ballplayer moves into the big time, "meets cute" (his future wife), hits the pinnacle, then suffers a downslide due to health problems. Unlike the Lou Gehrig story, the saga of Dizzy Dean could not have ended with a tearful farewell to the fans with death just around the corner, so Mankiewicz and his collaborator Guy Trosper contrived another method to get Dean before a microphone for an emotional goodbye.

The scenarists pounced upon the true-life incident of several St. Louis school-teachers complaining to Dean's radio sponsor, Falstaff beer, that Dizzy's malaprops and colloquialisms ("The players are goin' back to their respectable places," "He slud into first base," and so forth) were detrimental to the grammatical development of their students. In real life both Dean and his sponsor laughed off the teachers' charges (when told he had no sense of syntax, Dean replied "Sin tax? Ya mean they got a tax for that, too?"). In the film, however, the teachers are a serious threat, prompting a chastened Dean to close one of his broadcasts by saying that he'll bow to pressure and leave the air, advising the kids at home to "talk educated" and adding, "I never wanted to hurt nobody." Had Dean conveniently expired after this incident in the manner of Lou Gehrig, the picture would have ended then and there; but, of course, Ol' Diz was still in the broadcast booth at the time *The Pride of St. Louis* was released in 1952, so Mankiewicz and Trosper serve up some more fresh-buttered corn by having the shamefaced schoolteachers relent, telling Dean that, "We'll keep teaching them English and you keep learnin' them baseball."

Disciples of Herman Mankiewicz, particularly those who have pressed the case that it was Mankiewicz's screenplay of *Citizen Kane* which gave that film its classic status rather than Orson Welles's direction, have pointed to Mank's last work, *The Pride of St. Louis*, as a pitiful example of how the writer's drinking and self-abuse had diminished his talents. Actually, the screenplay moves along smoothly and professionally, and in fact earned an Oscar nomination. What the script does reveal is that Mankiewicz, like most New York "wits" of the 1920s who'd sold out to Hollywood,

tended to treat screenwriting as a hack job, and as such aimed his film work at the lowest common denominator. *The Pride of St. Louis* blithely condescends to the "rabble" by using the most time-honored of clichés to propel the story forward—including one of Mankiewicz's favorite devices, the "severest critic" character who acts as the protagonist's conscience, á la Jed Leland in *Citizen Kane*. This character is represented in *The Pride of St. Louis* by the fictional Johnny Kendall, a crippled millionaire whose buoyancy and stick-to-itiveness inspires Dizzy Dean to stop moping over his own reversals of fortune. With typical audaciousness, Mankiewicz saw to it that Johnny Kendall regenerates Dizzy Dean not once but twice within the film's 93 minutes.

That *The Pride of St. Louis* seems more pedestrian than *The Pride of the Yankees* is less the fault of Herman Mankiewicz than of Hollywood's factorylike studio system. *The Pride of the Yankees* was the only 1942 release from independent producer Samuel Goldwyn; thus the Goldwyn studio gave the film the extra care and attention that its "special event" status warranted. *The Pride of St. Louis* was merely one of forty films released by 20th Century–Fox in 1952—and wasn't even one of Fox's "prestige" pictures of that year (which included *Les Misérables, O. Henry's Full House, The Snows of Kilimanjaro* and *Viva Zapata*). As a consequence, it has a soulless, assembly-line look, from the unprepossessing camerawork to the rubber-stamp design of the main credit titles. The Fox people knew they could rely on a healthy number of bookings for *St. Louis* due to the drawing power of star Dan Dailey, and that the film would earn a profit since it hadn't cost much to begin with, but Fox also knew that baseball pictures seldom generated really big business; so why bother to go the extra mile and make the film any better or more memorable than it was?

About the only functionary behind

the scenes who exhibited extra effort was special effects wizard Fred Sersen, who in *The Pride of St. Louis* improved immensely upon his technique, first seen in *It Happens Every Spring* (1949) (q.v.), of making it appear that Los Angeles's Wrigley Field was in fact several different ballparks in a multitude of different cities. This time around, Sersen even managed to de-emphasize Wrigley's distinctive light tower—though he was less successful in hiding the *shadow* of that tower, a major drawback in that the film was set in the mid to late 1930s, when most major-league ballfields had no lighting for night games.

One of the oddest aspects of *The Pride of St. Louis* was its overall lack of humor, despite the fact that the Dizzy Dean story was one with built-in surefire laughs. Such potentially amusing situations as Dizzy's attempts to elope with Pat Nash and then vainly trying to talk her into staging the wedding at home plate, or Dean's playful habit of changing the particulars of his life story whenever giving a newspaper interview, are handled in so perfunctory a manner by director Harmon Jones that hardly a snicker is raised. Many of the more famous laugh-inducing highlights of Dizzy's career—including the newspaper headline following Dean's head injury which declared "X-Ray of Dizzy's Head Shows Nothing"—are ignored completely. This makes the reaction of *New York Times* reviewer Bosley Crowther, who referred to *The Pride of St. Louis* as "howlingly humorous," virtually incomprehensible, unless Crowther went into the picture preconditioned by memories of Dean's antics in the announcer's booth.

Despite its faults, *The Pride of St. Louis* still entertains, particularly in its nicely mounted baseball sequences—that is, whenever the plot machinery stops long enough to give us a glimpse of a ballpark. Musical comedy performer Dan Dailey brings a professional dancer's dexterity

to the role of Dizzy Dean, most notably in his loose-limbed delivery at the pitcher's mound. Dailey is equally at home with the bucolic braggadocio of Dizzy's dialogue in his early scenes; the heavier dramatic moments following Dean's arm injury are also well handled, though they must have been personally taxing to Dailey, who at the time was recovering from a nervous disorder which had temporarily held up the production. "That figures," Dizzy Dean would later comment on the subject of Dan Dailey. "After this Danny feller found he was going to have to take my part he went nuts."

Richard Crenna, in his second film role, registers well as Paul "Daffy" Dean, emulating the more businesslike baseball comportment of Dizzy's younger brother. The real Paul Dean had no problem with the casting of Crenna, but he was pretty sore at the film's implication that Dizzy had all the talent in the family; while Paul may not have been as skillful or charismatic as his brother, he was more of an asset to the 1934 St. Louis lineup than the film suggests, winning 19 games to Diz's 30 during the Dean boys' first season together. Paul's displeasure might have been aggravated by the fact that his movie counterpart virtually vanishes from the proceedings during the film's last thirty minutes, and that the fictional "Daffy" spends the balance of his screen time being shooed out of the Dean living room whenever Dizzy and Patricia feel the urge to make love. Considerably less diplomatic than this on-screen acquiescence to romance was Paul Dean's assessment of *The Pride of St. Louis*: "Heck, it stunk."

There are other points of interest to consider while viewing *The Pride of St. Louis*: though several sports movie veterans dot the cast list, from actor-athletes Fred Graham and John McKee to radio announcer Tom Hanlon, the one cast member who could in later years lay claim to the strongest real-life ties to major league baseball was leading lady Joanne Dru. Dru was the sister of game show host Peter Marshall, who in turn was the father of onetime Kansas City Royals player Pete LaCock.

And no, your eyes aren't playing tricks on you: That really *is* NBC news anchorman Chet Huntley, of "Huntley and Brinkley" fame, enacting the role of Dizzy Dean's announcing booth cohort Tom Weaver in the closing scenes.

The Pride of the Yankees

Samuel Goldwyn Studios/RKO-Radio; released July 14, 1942

Produced by Samuel Goldwyn. Directed by Sam Wood. Production design by William Cameron Menzies. Screenplay by Jo Swerling, Herman J. Mankiewicz and (uncredited) Casey Robinson. Original story by Paul Gallico. Photography: Rudolph Maté. Edited by Daniel Mandell. Art director: Perry Ferguson. Associate art director: McClure Capps. Set decorations by Howard Bristol. Music by Leigh Harline. Song "Always" by Irving Berlin. Costumes by Rene Hubert. Special effects by Jack Cosgrove and R. O. Binger. Sound by Frank Maher. Assistant director: John Sherwood. Produced with the assistance of Mrs. Lou Gehrig by arrangement with Christy Walsh. 128 minutes; black and white; sound.

Cast: Gary Cooper (Lou Gehrig); Teresa Wright (Eleanor Twitchell Gehrig); Babe Ruth (Himself); Walter Brennan (Sam Blake); Dan Duryea (Hank Hammond); Elsa Janssen (Mom Gehrig); Ludwig Stossel (Pa Gehrig); Virginia Gilmore (Myra Tinsley); Bill Dickey (Himself); Ernie Adams (Miller Huggins); Pierre Watkin (Mr. Twitchell); Harry Harvey, Sr. (Joe McCarthy); Robert W. Meusel, Mark Koenig, Bill Stern (Themselves); Addison Richards (Columbia Coach); Hardie Albright (Van Tuyl); Edward Fielding (Scripps Clinic Doctor); George Lessey (Mayor of New Rochelle); Edgar Barrier (Hospital Doctor); Vaughan Glaser (Doctor in Gehrig Home); Douglas Croft (Lou as a Boy); Gene Collins (Billy); David Holt (Billy, Age 17); Veloz and Yolanda (Themselves, Dance Team); Ray Noble and His Orchestra (Themselves); Rip Russell (Laddie); Frank Faylen (Third Base Coach); Lane Chandler (Player in Locker Room); Jack Shea (Hammond); George McDonald (Wally Pipp); George Offernan, Jr. (Freshman); David Manley (Mayor LaGuardia); Max Willenz (Colletti); Jimmy Valentine (Sasha); Anita Bolster (Sasha's Mother); Robert Winkler (Murphy); Spencer Charters (Mr. Larsen); Rosina Galli (Mrs. Fabini); Billy Roy (Joe Fabini); Sarah Padden (Mrs. Robert); Janet Chapman (Tessie); Eva Dennison (Mrs. Worthington); Montague Shaw (Mr. Worthington); Jack Stewart (Ed Barrow)*; Fay Thomas (Christy Mathewson)*; Vinton Hayworth [Jack Arnold], Bernard Zanville [Dane Clark], John Kellogg, Tom Neal (Fraternity Members); Lorna Dunn (Nurse in Hospital); Patsy O'Byrne (Scrubwoman); Matt McHugh (Strength Machine Operator); Charley Williams (Strength Machine Player); William Chaney (Newsboy); Pat Flaherty (Baseball Player); Mary Gordon (Maid); Francis Sayles (Cab Driver); Gary Owen (Vendor); Walter Tetley (Delivery Boy); Harry Hayden (Furniture Store Clerk); Emory Parnell (Cop); George Lloyd (Paperhanger); Sam Lufkin (Man with Drill).

The son of European immigrants, young Lou Gehrig would love to become a baseball player, but his iron-willed mother has determined that he will become an engineer. To that end, Mom Gehrig cooks for a fraternity house at Columbia University to earn the money which will help Lou attend that New York City cathedral of learning. While at Columbia, Lou excels at sports, particularly baseball. Through the influence of sports reporter Sam Blake, Lou is offered a job with the New York Yankees, but he hesitates, fearing that taking such a job would break his mother's heart. When Mom Gehrig needs money for an operation, however, Lou signs up with the Yankees, though he tries to keep his source of income a secret from his mother—a ruse that works only until his skill earns Lou

---

*You try to find "Ed Barrow" and "Christy Mathewson" in this film. Except for their appearances on two of young Lou Gehrig's (unseen) baseball cards, I couldn't find them.

several sports-column headlines. After gaining experience in the minors, Lou is made a first baseman for the 1925 Yankees, which boasts such formidable talent as Babe Ruth, Bill Dickey, Bob Meusel, Mark Koenig, and Tony Lazzeri. Pinch-hitting for Wally Pipp during a game at Chicago, Lou makes his big-league entrée by tripping on a row of bats. This earns him the laughter—and, as it develops, the love—of young baseball fan Eleanor Twitchell, who marries Lou shortly after the 1926 Yankees-Cardinals World Series. Over the next few years Lou gains a national reputation as the "Iron Man of Baseball" who never misses a game, culminating in an outpouring of affection from fans and fellow ballplayers alike on the occasion of Gehrig's 2,000th consecutive game. Lou's world crashes in upon him in 1939 when he learns he has a terminal neurological disease called amyotrophic lateral sclerosis. On July 4, 1939, a little less than two years before his death, Lou stands before a crowd of 62,000 at Yankee Stadium to bid farewell to baseball. His voice choking with emotion, Lou Gehrig reveals that, though he's had a bad break, "Today, I consider myself the luckiest man on the face of the earth."

The Pride of the Yankees, the most financially successful film of its kind made up to 1942, was the mold from which virtually all future baseball biopics would be shaped. Every crucial plot element is defined in this one film: the humble, formative years of the hero; the early triumphs and tribulations; the mentor, friend, or relative who cheers the hero on; the rise to fame, generally reflected by newspaper headlines; the loving and supportive wife who keeps a scrapbook or collection of memorabilia of her husband's accomplishments; the crisis which topples the hero from his lofty perch; and the hero's courageous head-on confrontation with that crisis. All this, plus "Take Me Out to the Ballgame" woven into the musical score, along with a popular tune as leitmotif for the romantic subplot.

(In *The Pride of the Yankees*, Eleanor and Lou Gehrig's "special song" was Irving Berlin's "Always," for which Samuel Goldwyn paid Berlin $15,000 because it was *Goldwyn's* favorite ballad.)

To tell the background story of *The Pride of the Yankees* we must pause for the occasional legend. Practically all sources agree that producer Samuel Goldwyn was initially resistant when his story editor Niven Busch came up with the idea of a Lou Gehrig biography. "It's box office poison," Goldwyn reportedly responded. "If people want baseball, they go to the ballpark." (Some historians embellish this by having Goldwyn ask, "Who's Lou Gehrig?") Busch pressed his case by running a newsreel clip of Gehrig's farewell speech, and when the clip ended, the producer, with tears in his eyes, commanded the projectionist to run it again. At this point, Goldwyn either immediately bought up the rights to the Gehrig story or played the coquette with Mrs. Gehrig, feigning only a slight interest in the project in hopes of bringing her price down. Either way, Goldwyn obtained the rights for a price tag of $30,000, then engaged Paul Gallico, who'd written the recently published biography of Lou Gehrig, to fashion the screen story.

A story too good to be true originated when Goldwyn started hiring real-life ballplayers to play supporting roles. Everyone who's written on this, from first-hand witnesses to far removed film buffs of the 1980s, has insisted that Goldwyn, weaned on the studio hierarchy principle that a first assistant was more valuable than a second assistant, couldn't understand why he should pay a third baseman as much as a first baseman. This anecdote is often used to perpetuate the image of Sam Goldwyn as an uneducated lummox—though if the bulk of baseball pictures turned out by other Hollywood producers is any indication, Goldwyn was certainly not alone in his lack of baseball savvy. In fact, the producer was

Yankees manager Joe McCarthy (Harry Harvey, center) bids farewell to Lou Gehrig (Gary Cooper) in *Pride of the Yankees*.

more than aware that he'd have to hire a scenarist who knew more about the game than the average Hollywood writer; so he engaged sports buff Jo Swerling to fill the script with plenty of "baseball stuff." Goldwyn would acknowledge in 1942 that *The Pride of the Yankees* was his toughest project to date because, unlike the fictional characters who'd populated most of his other films, Lou Gehrig had actually existed and was still fresh in the public's memory, and any bloopers in the chronology of Gehrig's career or in the ballgame scenes would be fatal to the film's success.

One criticism that has been leveled against *The Pride of the Yankees* is that the personal story of Lou Gehrig commands more attention than the baseball element—and again, this complaint is often used to vilify Sam Goldwyn, as though he was some

sort of "fans be damned" mogul who cynically assumed that no one would sit still for an undistilled two-hour baseball story. This is exactly what he did assume, though this opinion grew not out of cynicism but out of the plain fact (backed up by records of box office receipts) that you weren't going to have a big hit in 1942 if your film didn't appeal to as wide a spectrum of moviegoers as possible. This meant that you had to attract the ladies, who in turn would get their husbands or boyfriends to take them to the movies. Goldwyn reported during filming that he had to be careful "to watch my baseball so that it didn't get the best of my personal story." He wanted a *well-balanced* film, one that would attract both the baseball fans and those filmgoers who didn't give a hoot for baseball. Perhaps Goldwyn overplayed his hand by including a glitzy nightclub sequence spotlighting a deadly dance team named Veloz and Yolanda; but if you look at the film carefully, you'll notice that the baseball scenes are just as lavishly and carefully produced as this musical interlude balm to the female viewers. Goldwyn may have cut down on the number of ballgame sequences, but he didn't sell them short.

The Pride of the Yankees contained an inherent story problem that might have stopped a producer less imaginative than Goldwyn dead in his tracks. The problem was that, outside of his record of 2,130 consecutive games, his baseball skill, and his fatal illness, Lou Gehrig was in private life a rather bland, unspectacular personality. This was amply compensated for when Goldwyn hired Herman Mankiewicz to co-write the screenplay with Jo Swerling. Mankiewicz's reputation was founded on his ability to take an otherwise commonplace, mundane scene or situation and pinpoint exactly what was needed to pep up the proceedings. (Some historians have claimed that Mankiewicz's uncredited collaborator, Casey Robinson, was the film's true "pepper-upper"; whoever it was, he certainly earned his money.) In one superb example of cinematic succinctness, the script of *The Pride of the Yankees* capitalized on Gehrig's well-known aversion to drinking, smoking, and womanizing by turning this recalcitrance into a "humiliation" sequence and then taking this sequence one step farther into a plot development. During a fraternity party, Gehrig's college frat brothers, amused by Lou's social clumsiness, set him up with a campus flirt. The next day they rag Lou mercilessly for naively succumbing to the girl's synthetic charms. An embarrassed Lou reacts by punching out the pranksters, and as they run from the room, reporter Sam Blake arrives at the frat house to tell Gehrig that he's being scouted by the Yankees. Lou thinks this is just another joke and cold-cocks Blake. In the next

scene, right on schedule, Lou is seen with a recovered Blake and a Yankee scout, discussing his future in baseball. It would have been a lot simpler to have Lou merely meet Sam Blake without the "humanizing" illustration of Gehrig's innocent gaucherie and the subsequent fisticuffs—a lot simpler and a lot duller.

A later scene takes into consideration the fact that Lou and Eleanor Gehrig's married life was a relatively contented one. How does one get any punch into this? The script solves the problem by having the Gehrigs fight over their *good* points. When Lou comes home wearing a horseshoe wreath commemorating his 2,000th game, Eleanor is so amused by the sight that she begins playfully removing flowers from the wreath and pelting them at her husband. Lou reciprocates, and a battle is on, with a flower being thrown each time one of the opponents recalls a kindness or act of unselfishness on the part of the other person. And as with the frat-house scene, this light-hearted vignette segues into the plotline. As Lou and Eleanor laughingly wrestle each other to the floor, Lou feels the first pangs of the neurological disease that will ultimately kill him.

Even before shooting started, Sam Goldwyn felt that only one film star could bring the right "average guy" touch to Lou Gehrig while still maintaining audience interest. That star was Gary Cooper, who had just won an Academy award for his portrayal of another common-man national hero in *Sergeant York*. Though the hiring of Cooper was a foregone conclusion, Goldwyn's publicity people stirred up prerelease interest in *The Pride of the Yankees* by going through the motions of a *Gone with the Wind*–style search for the right actor to play Gehrig; at one juncture, it was announced that such prominent performers as Eddie Albert, William Gargan, and Dennis Morgan had offered to play the part for free, just for "the love of it." For the record, Gary Cooper's salary totaled $150,000—an amount that would have taken Lou Gehrig nearly ten years to earn with the Yankees!

Though cinematographer Rudolph Maté had to work overtime to make the star look younger than his forty-one years, Gary Cooper had all the necessary physical and thespian attributes required to play Lou Gehrig, save two: Cooper couldn't play baseball, and he was right-handed. Lefty O'Doul, a onetime Yankee player who'd toured Japan with Gehrig in 1934, was engaged to train Cooper, and though O'Doul assessed the actor's skills by noting that he "threw the ball like an old woman tossing a hot biscuit," the end result was more than acceptable for the closeups. (In long shots, Cooper was doubled by former Dodger Babe Herman.)

The problem of making Cooper appear left-handed is yet another source of Hollywood legend. One story goes that director Sam Wood was thrilled to death at the progress made by Cooper thanks to Lefty O'Doul's training, only to be told by ex–Yankee Mark Koenig that Gehrig was a southpaw and Cooper was not. This was supposed to have come as a complete surprise to Wood, throwing him into a tizzy. While this story serves its purpose of making Sam Wood seem as big an ignoramus as Sam Goldwyn was supposed to have been (many professional writers can't shake the notion that all producers and directors were so cretinous that Hollywood could never have survived without—you guessed it—professional writers), it is hard to digest; not only was Wood an avid sports fan, but he also had read the script, which in one scene makes a big deal of Gehrig's left-handedness when a congratulatory cake is rejected by Lou's parents because the little ballplayer doll on the cake is batting rightie.

Another story that has made the rounds is that whenever we see Gary Cooper step up to bat, the postproduction lab has made the actor appear left-handed by reversing the picture—requiring Cooper to wear a uniform with the words "N Y Yankees" written backward. There is a kernel of truth in this. *The Pride of the Yankees'* Oscar-winning film editor Danny Mandell claimed in the early 1970s that he'd come up with the idea of "flipping" the picture of Cooper because he couldn't find any newsreel footage of Gehrig in training for the early montage scenes. This would mean that practically the only time a reverse image was necessary was when Gehrig was playing for the minor-league team in Hartford, Connecticut, and the "H" on his uniform would have looked the same backward and forward.

I've watched *The Pride of the Yankees* a number of times, and have come to the conclusion that the Hartford scenes are the only ones that could logically have been "flipped." Most of the shots of Cooper batting at Yankee Stadium (actually Los Angeles's Wrigley Field) were filmed outdoors, with the grandstands in full view and without benefit of back projection; and brilliant though he was, is would have been difficult for production designer William Cameron Menzies to reverse an entire ballpark just to make his star look good. There *is*, however, some obvious trickery in the batting scenes: Cooper's swings have been artificially sped up to make them look more powerful.

There was no necessity for the postproduction people to improve upon Gary Cooper's moving interpretation of Gehrig's 1939 farewell speech; even after six decades this moment still has the power to bring tears to the eyes of the most jaded viewer, and is all the more effective by being the very last speech in the very last scene of the film, minus a surfeit of hokey embellishments. During his tours with the USO in World War II, Cooper frequently repeated this farewell speech for servicemen stationed in the South Pacific, to whom Lou Gehrig's courage in the face of impending doom had special significance.

Supporting Gary Cooper was a cast

made up of such Goldwyn regulars as Walter Brennan and Dan Duryea, as well as such economical freelance character people as Ludwig Stossel and Elsa Janssen (as Lou's parents). For the larger role of Eleanor Gehrig, Niven Busch enthusiastically recommended Teresa Wright, whom Busch would eventually marry. Wright was nominated for an Academy award for her multifaceted performance as Eleanor, and though she lost in the Best Actress category, she managed to pick up a best *supporting* actress Oscar for her work in another 1942 release, *Mrs. Miniver*.

The real Mrs. Gehrig, who said at the time she was "completely happy" with the film (though she would retract this endorsement when it came time to film her own autobiography for television in 1977 [see *A Love Affair: The Eleanor and Lou Gehrig Story*]), enjoyed watching her screen counterpart but allowed, "I'm no Teresa Wright, that's for sure." One real-life personality who could not make a statement of this sort was Babe Ruth, who emerged from retirement to play himself—for $25,000—in *The Pride of the Yankees*. Ruth rose to the occasion with an enthusiasm that he hadn't exhibited publicly in years, and—sad to say—he paid dearly for that enthusiasm. In one Pullman-car scene, Ruth got so carried away that he smashed his hand through a glass window; and after shedding forty-seven pounds in an effort to photograph as he had in his prime, Babe landed in the hospital suffering the effects of over dieting. Even after recovering from these setbacks, Babe's troubles weren't over; in April 1942 he came down with a near fatal case of pneumonia which kept him off the set for two weeks.

You'd never know that Ruth spent most of his shooting time in extreme pain while watching his totally ingratiating performance in *The Pride of the Yankees*; Babe's full-faced smile, which hadn't been flashed on-screen since 1920 (see *Headin' Home*), gave every indication that this was the Babe Ruth we knew back when he was on top of the world. Moreover, this was by far the best *acting* performance ever given by Ruth; and much the same can be said for the relaxed, natural self-portrayals offered by Ruth's old compadres Bill Dickey, Bob Meusel, and Mark Koenig.

Which brings us to *another* Hollywood myth, that of director Sam Wood being merely a high-priced hack who covered up his inability to discern good work from bad by decreeing that every scene be filmed twenty times, whether it was necessary or not. To be sure, this technique infuriated many professional actors, who felt that the more often they had to repeat a scene the less "fresh" they became. But when dealing with nonperformers like Ruth, Dickey, et al., Wood's obsession with retakes performed miracles; with each new take, these amateur thespians became less stiff and self-conscious, until finally they were behaving like human beings rather than third-rate play actors. Nor were the ballplayers the only people to benefit from Wood's approach; such usually mannered performers as Walter Brennan and Dan Duryea likewise excel after being worn down and forced to act without "adornments." Sam Wood was, by most accounts, an unpleasant individual, a political reactionary, and a bigot. But Wood knew his profession inside and out, and his best films—including *A Night at the Opera*, *Goodbye Mr. Chips*, *Our Town*, and still another baseball biography, *The Stratton Story* (q.v.)—bear out this statement.

Looking at the previous paragraphs, one would think that there was nothing at all to carp about in *The Pride of the Yankees*. Not so; the film is very easy to pick apart in terms of accuracy. Though the baseball scenes are faithfully recreated (with the exception of those light-tower shadows which spill across the Yankee Stadium diamond several years before the actual introduction of night games), the screenplay takes any number of liberties with Lou Gehrig's private life. We see Lou's mother browbeating her husband into near invisibility, though it has since been documented that Mom Gehrig's overbearing demeanor was a defense mechanism against the blunt cruelties of Pa Gehrig (a fact likewise distorted in *A Love Affair: The Eleanor and Lou Gehrig Story*, 1977). Lou first meets Eleanor in 1925, nearly eight years before the fact; he meets her during his first major-league game (which he didn't) where she gives the impression of being a dyed-in-the-wool baseball fan (which she wasn't). The very serious personality clash between Eleanor and Mom Gehrig is minimized with a frivolous argument over a choice of wallpaper. Instead of accurately showing Lou and Eleanor eloping to avoid one of his mother's tantrums, the Gehrigs are married in a civil ceremony in Lou's New Rochelle home, with Mom in attendance. And after getting the bad news about his health at Scripps Clinic (the Mayo Clinic in real life), Lou nobly insists that Eleanor not be informed of the seriousness of his condition, which was slightly at odds with what really happened: Eleanor was told the full truth and kept it from Lou.

All right, so it isn't gospel. What *The Pride of the Yankees* is is a blue-ribbon example of pure storytelling, in which every individual component of the filmmaker's art converges into a totally satisfying whole. Nowhere is this better demonstrated than in the film's "Win one for Billy" sequence. This ten-minute episode is based on the true story of Johnny Sylvester, the young boy confined to a sickbed who was promised a home run in his honor from Babe Ruth during the 1926 Series. The first news report concerning this incident said simply that Johnny had an infection. As the story grew from retelling, Johnny got sicker and sicker, and the source of his debilitation ranged from a riding accident to a life-threatening respiratory ailment. By the

time the legend was recounted in *The Babe Ruth Story* (1948), Johnny was so far gone that he looked like he was about to join the Choir Invisible before Babe even entered his room. (Fear not: The real Johnny Sylvester recovered and lived into his seventies.)

The Pride of the Yankees uses this incident as the framework for a number of character revelations and the gathering of several climaxes. In this version Babe promises to hit a home run for a hospitalized Billy while in full view of a battery of reporters and photographers. Everyone then leaves, except for Lou, whom bright-eyed Billy inveigles into promising to hit *two* homers; Lou does so only after Billy agrees to not give up and to get well. During the game, rival reporters Sam Blake (Gehrig's pal) and Hank Hammond (a Ruth partisan) pass along different versions of the Billy story to play by play announcer Bill Stern (a bombastic radio personality whose unabashed "tall tale" approach to baseball lore made him very popular in the 1940s). Within seconds, the whole world knows about Little Billy—the world in this case including Eleanor, sitting alone in her home, and Mom and Dad Gehrig, huddled around their radio with their neighbors in attendance. Babe gets his homer, and Lou gets the first of his four-baggers; then tension mounts when it looks as though he'll be walked without fulfilling his promise to Billy. But Lou comes through, to the tumultuous cheers of the fans and the separate at-home hurrahs of Billy, Eleanor, and Lou's parents.

Here's what we see in this sequence beyond the excellence of its performances, its direction, and its split-second editing. We see the fundamental difference between Babe Ruth and Lou Gehrig, with Babe basking in the press coverage of his promise to Billy, while Lou waits until the press has left to make *his* promise to the boy. We see the clash between the "sincere" fans of the game (you and I) and the world-weary cynics (Them), as represented by the press booth rivalry between guileless Sam Blake and sarcastic Hank Hammond—with sincerity winning out. We see for the first time the full extent of Eleanor's love for Lou, as she practically goes into Saint Vitus's Dance over his second homer. We see that the initially resentful Mom Gehrig has been won over by her son's chosen profession, and that Lou's parents have totally abandoned their plans to make their son an engineer, as shown by the damage done by Pa Gehrig to a picture of Uncle Otto Gehrig, whose success had previously been thrown up to Lou. And we see how Lou Gehrig's reputation as a ballplayer of integrity has been secured in the eyes of everyone. And beyond that...

Yes, *beyond* that we have a perfect setup for the final scene in *The Pride of the Yankees*. For when Lou Gehrig is about to enter Yankee Stadium for the last time, who should step forward to greet him but Little Billy, grown up and completely cured—all because he took Lou's advice and never gave up—an ideal lead-in for Gehrig's own speech about being a lucky man despite his bad breaks. Call it as corny as Kansas in August, but the whole Billy business is so entertaining that it nearly lifts you out of your chair.

We close our discussion of this film by hopefully putting to rest a newly coined legend. An otherwise responsible baseball historian has suggested that, though *The Pride of the Yankees* was a better than average effort, it did disappointing business at the box office—proof once more that baseball films are never as satisfying as going to the ballpark for real. This just isn't true. Not only was *The Pride of the Yankees* the most profitable baseball film of its time, but it made more money than *any* of Samuel Goldwyn's previous productions. The picture earned $3 million—not to mention the wagers won by Goldwyn from his fellow moguls who had bet that the profits would never get past $2 million. If $3 million in 1942 is disappointing, cut me a slice of that heartache!

*Prisoner of Zenda Inc.**

Hallmark Entertainment/Showtime Networks/Sugar Entertainment Ltd.; first telecast September 29, 1996

Produced by Larry Sugar. Directed by Stefan Scaini. Written by Richard Clark and Rodman Gregg. Original music: John Welsman. Photography: Marie H. Jansons. Edited by Bill Goddard. Casting: Stuart Aikins, James Forsyth. Line producer/production manager: Laurie McLarty. Production design: Andrew Wilson. Art direction: Maya Ishiura. Set decoration: Ian Nothnagel. Costume design: Vicki Mulholland. Casting: Stuart Aikins, James Forsyth. Key makeup artist: Tone Rorvik. Key hairstylist: Danna Rutherford. First assistant director: Lydia Stante. Second assistant director: Gary Blair Smith. Third Assistant Director: Christine Dore. Sound mixer: Roger Stafeckis. Special effects coordinator: Rae Reedyk. Stunt coordinator: Rob Wilton. Script supervisor/offscreen voice: Beth Mercer. Visuals: Gajdecki Visual Effects; John Gajdecki, VFX director. Titles and Opticals: Film Effects Inc. Color by Deluxe. 101 minutes; Ultra Stereo Sound. Rated PG.

Cast: Jonathan Jackson (Rudy Gatewick/Oliver Gillis); Jay Brazeau (Professor John Wooley); Richard Lee Jackson (Douglas Gatewick); Don S. Davis (Colonel Zapf), Katherine Isobel (Fiona); John Tench (Leon); Jed Rees (Buddy); Mark Acheson (Frankie); William Shatner (Michael Gatewick); Howard Dell (Coach Wilson); Sean Amsing (Charlie Rosemerkel); Demetri Goritsas (Baxter); David Kaye (Mr. Gillis); Alan Robertson (Arthur); Stephen E. Miller (Coach Palmer); Sean Campbell (Cop 1), Mike Kopsa (Cop 2); Catherine Swing (Mrs. Gillis); Campbell Lane (Lawyer 1); Blair Slater (Ben); Jeff McLeod (Jock 1); Marcus Turner (Jock 2); Douglas Newell (Mr. Walston); Jane MacDougal

---

*American Home Video Title: Double Play, from Evergreen Entertainment.

(Ann Broder); Edward Allan Custer (Umpire 3); Danielle Fraser (Alice); Daniel D. Pratt (Umpire 1); James Sherry (Andy); Elan Ross Gibson (Board Member 1); Jesse Moss (Schoolmate); Jewel Staite (Theresa); Tyronne L'Hirondelle (Lawyer 2); Richard Yee (Maxwell); Wayne Daly (Pitcher); Bill Garrett (Umpire 2); Richard Sargent (Lawyer 3); Eric Hui (Boy); Michael Andaluz (Courier); Bobby Stewart (Gym Teacher); John R. Taylor (Janitor); Adam Paton (Player); Nick Misura (Programmer 1); Colin Warner Wallace (Programmer 2); Chris Lovick (Tommy Aiken); Georgina Hegedos (Mrs. Cochran); Simon Ouellette (Photo Double/Stand-In); Michael Sugar (Sports Announcer); Richard Lewis (Stand-In).

Upon the death of California computer mogul Thomas Gatewick, the chairmanship of Gatewick's multimillion-dollar company Zenda Inc. passes into the hands of Gatewick's mentor, Professor John Wooley, and the corporation's star programmer, Gatewick's 14-year-old son Rudy. Though a pleasant and unspoiled lad, Rudy is the quintessential computer geek—glasses, pocket-protector and all. A student at high-scale St. Matthews Academy, Rudy is subjected to endless harassment and ridicule from his cousin Douglas, the school's best baseball player. And though he doesn't know it at first, Rudy has also been targeted for persecution by another family member: his greedy uncle Michael Gatewick, who regards himself as the only person qualified to run Zenda. With chairman of the board Colonel Zapf firmly in Rudy's corner, Michael decides to place the matter in the hands of the stockholders, who in three days will gather for their annual meeting to hear their new CEO's plans for the future. Under Zenda bylaws, if Rudy is not present at this meeting, Michael will take charge of the company—and to make absolutely certain that this happens, Michael secretly hires a trio of cloddish crooks to kidnap Rudy and keep him under wraps until the meeting is over. The next morning, John Wooley receives a ransom note, warning him not to tell anyone about the kidnapping lest harm befall the boy. More concerned with Rudy's safety than the future of Zenda, Wooley and Colonel Zapf put up a brave public front so no one will suspect that the boy is missing. While dutifully attending a Zenda-sponsored high school baseball playoff, Wooley and Zapf discover to their astonishment that the star pitcher for the Los Angeles Tigers, teenager Oliver "Ollie" Gillis, is the spitting image of Rudy Gatewick! Quickly formulating a plan to save Zenda from Michael's clutches, the two men try to persuade young Ollie to impersonate Rudy until the boy can be located. Initially refusing to cooperate—for one thing, he is terrified of computer technology—Ollie agrees on condition that Zenda find a job for his long-unemployed father. After being given a crash course in computers, Ollie takes Rudy's place at St. Matthews, where he capriciously decides to give his athletically disinclined lookalike a "makeover" by joining the school's baseball team and by putting the obnoxious Douglas in his place—a feat that wins Ollie the admiration of fellow student Fiona, who has always harbored a bit of a crush on the shy Rudy. As fate would have it, Douglas' father is none other than the scheming Michael Gatewick, who, upon learning from his son that "Rudy" is still in school, figures out that Wooley and Zapf have found an impostor. Meanwhile, the real Rudy, lost in the woods with his clumsy captors, manages to escape from right under their noses, but not before discovering that Uncle Michael was behind his abduction. As Rudy races back to Zenda headquarters in a hot-wired van, Ollie finds himself on the horns of two devastating dilemmas: Not only does he face exposure and humiliation at the stockholder's meeting, but he also may be forced to pitch for the St. Matthews Giants against his *own* team in the final game of the playoffs!

It takes plenty of gall to use the oft-filmed Anthony Hope adventure novel *The*

Prisoner of Zenda as the springboard for a modern-day baseball picture. And it takes plenty of talent to actually pull it off. Fortunately, the folks responsible for *Prisoner of Zenda Inc.* had talent to spare—and though the film falls far short of perfection, it is an altogether agreeable way to spend 101 minutes on a rainy afternoon.

The film was cowritten by American Film Institute alumni Rodman Gregg and Richard Clark, both of whom made something of a cottage industry out of scripting updated versions of classic literary pieces. A prime example of Gregg's later work was a script titled "My Fair Lacy," in which two upper-class jocks tried to turn a klutzy 16-year-old girl into an ace gymnast. Clark, the more prolific of the team, went on to the Shakespeare-inspired *Ronnie and Julie*, the Victor Hugo derivation *The Halfback of Notre Dame*, and the self-explanatory *Dr. Hackenstein* and *Treasure of the Sierra Madre Mall*. Though subtlety is not the strong suit of *Prisoner of Zenda Inc.*, one cannot help but admire the audacious ingenuity with which the authors incorporated their source novel's key incidents and character names (Rudy, as in "Rudolph Rassendyl"; Michael Gatewick, as in "Black Michael"; Colonel Zapf as in "Colonel Zapt") into a palatable contemporary family film.

In addition to borrowing from Anthony Hope, Gregg and Clark also plundered popular culture in a manner that might have come off as oppressively cute or hopelessly contrived in lesser hands. Acknowledging the presence of William Shatner in the cast, the screenwriters contrived to have Rudy carry a *Star Trek* lunchbox to school and to wear Mr. Spock–like clothing while noodling with his computer at home. And when Shatner's character is seen perusing his favorite book, its turns out to be *Greed Is Good* by Gordon Gekko—the credo and character name of Michael Douglas in Oliver Stone's *Wall Street* (1987). That these "inside" jokes do not elicit groans from the audience is proof enough that the touch of Rodman Gregg and Richard Clark was, if not light, then certainly sure-handed.

Director Stefan Scaini had cut his teeth on such Canadian-based television series as *TekWar, Forever Knight, Avonlea, My Secret Identity* and *The Wind at My Back*. Like most other laborers in Canada's film and TV industry, Scaini knew how to supply a king's ransom of entertainment value on a peasant's budget. Reserving what little money he had for the special-effects sequences in which the two lookalikes circled one another, shook hands and high-fived (it is a tribute to the skill and resourcefulness of John Gajdecki and his SFX staff that the average viewer takes such sequences for granted), Scaini cannily cuts corners elsewhere but never lets us know it. The film's exhilarating baseball sequences—shot with straightforward and unadorned camera angles so we know exactly where we're supposed to be looking at all times, employing swift cuts to accelerate the action and hide the paucity of extras in the grandstands, and featuring a refreshingly sparing use of slow-motion during crucial plays—undoubtedly cost but a fraction of the budget for the pretentiously prolonged ballpark climax in *For Love of the Game* (q.v.), but they are arguably more entertaining and believable.

What really socks the material over is the virtuoso performance of 14-year-old star Jonathan Jackson, who'd previously proven his mettle with his Emmy-winning performance as Lucky Spencer on the ABC daytime drama *General Hospital*. Without employing any of the clichéd and obvious acting tricks that are often trotted out by adult actors in dual roles, Jackson is 100-percent convincing as both the bookish, withdrawn Rudy Gatewick and the robust, outgoing Ollie Gillis. Equally effective in a less colorful assignment is Jonathan's real-life older brother Richard Lee Jackson (of *Saved by the Bell* fame), here cast as the insufferable Douglas Gatewick (the older Jackson, a talented singer-composer, also supplied one of the tunes heard on the soundtrack, "Roof Top Talk"). The only quibble one can have about Richard Lee's performance is not the fault of the actor but of the scriptwriters. Since it is necessary for Michael Gatewick to stumble onto the fact that "Rudy" is really "Ollie," it was decided to establish Douglas as the son of Michael. While this plot peg works well within its own isolated context, it also diminishes Douglas' character in the final playoff-game sequence, which occurs shortly after Rudy has exposed Michael's evil machinations during the stockholder's meeting. Surely the fact that his father has just been publicly discredited and arrested (an event worthy of screaming newspaper headlines) would have had a deleterious effect on the boy; yet because the plot now requires the ballpark rivalry between Douglas and Ollie to take center stage, Douglas seems sublimely indifferent to his dad's fate—and even a creep like Douglas Gatewick is not *that* big a creep.

There are other problems with *Prisoner of Zenda Inc.* which lessen its overall effectiveness, notably the sudden and often jarring shifts of mood and tone. Most of the basic plot scenes with Ollie, Rudy and their respective friends and loved ones are played as straight as possible under the circumstances; but many of the comic scenes, especially those involving the three numbskull kidnappers, are so grotesquely overplayed that it appears the filmmakers were aspiring to the "anything for a cheap laugh" policy of the lesser Disney comedies of the 1970s (the bad guys are, in fact, at one point referred to as "Huey, Dewey and Louie"). Admittedly, these scenes *are* funny in a sophomoric sort of way, but they do considerable damage to the credibility of the film as a whole.

It is pointless to critique the performance of William Shatner; as always, he is a law unto himself. Shatner, who'd previously worked with director Scaini on the TV series *TekWar*, was so enamored of the script that he accepted only a third of his usual salary—amply compensating for this reduction by delivering three times the usual amount of ham. Fitted with steel-rimmed glasses and caterpillar-like moustache, and barking out his lines in the manner of John Huston with hemorrhoids, Shatner is never for one moment believable as the villain, but we defy you to take your eyes off him. One can never accuse William Shatner of merely phoning in a performance.

Its California setting notwithstanding, *Prisoner of Zenda Inc.* was filmed entirely in Vancouver, British Columbia. Originally telecast over the Showtime Cable Network on September 29, 1996 (with a surprising lack of print publicity or fanfare!), it has since been released to video. While we recommend that the reader give the film a try despite its faults, don't try looking for it under its original title. So as not to mislead viewers into thinking that they are renting a Ruritanian swashbuckler, the video version has been retitled *Double Play*.

Rhubarb

Paramount; released September 1951

Produced by William Perlberg and George Seaton. Directed by Arthur Lubin. Screenplay by Dorothy Reid and Francis Cockrell, based on the novel by H. Allen Smith. Additional dialogue by David Stern (uncredited). Photography: Lionel Lindon. Edited by Alma Macrorie. Music by Van Cleave. Song "It's a Privilege to Live in Brooklyn" by Jay Livingston and Ray Evans. Art direction by Hal Pereira and Henry Bumstead. Set decoration by Sam Comer and Ross Dowd. Special photographic effects by Gordon Jennings. Special optical effects by William Nolan. Costumes by Edith Head. Makeup by Wally Westmore. 95 minutes; Black and white; sound.

Cast: Ray Milland (Eric Yeager); Jan Sterling

(Polly Sickles); Gene Lockhart (Thaddeus J. Banner); William Frawley (Len Sickles); Elsie Holmes (Myra Banner); Taylor Holmes (P. Duncan Munk); Willard Waterman (Orlando Dill); Henry Slate (Dud Logan); James J. Griffith (Oggie Meadows); Jim Hayward (Doom); Donald MacBride (Pheeny); Hal K. Dawson (Mr. Fisher); Strother Martin (Shorty McGirk); Hilda Plowright (Katie); Adda Gleason (Maid); Richard Karlan (Pencil Louie); Edwin Max (Fish Eye); Anthony Radecki, Leonard Nimoy, Bill Thorpe, Frank Fiumara, Lee Miller, Mike Maloney (Ballplayers); Roy Gordon, Stuart Holmes, Eric Wilton, Wilbur Mack (Golfers); Harry Cheshire (Seegle); Douglas Wood (Carroll); Paul Maxey (Reese); Tristam Coffin (Dr. Stillman); John Breen (Western Union Boy); Ralph Sanford (Eddie, Brooklyn Police Captain); James Flavin (George, Manhattan Police Captain); Donald Kerr (Cabbie); Mack Grey (Detective); Oliver Blake (Cadaver Jones); Madge Blake (Mrs. Thompson); George Sherwood (Mr. Thompson); Edward Clark (Judge Loudermilk); Stanley Orr, Roberta Richards (Reporters); Harold Kennedy (Sporting Goods Salesman); Hans Herbert (Bit Doctor); Billy Wayne (St. Louis Manager); Al Ferguson (Cop in Garden); Rex Moore, Joe Terry (Caddies); Gail Bonney (Woman with Dog); H. Varteresian (Elbert); Ben Welden (Gabby Joe); Dorothy Vernon (Crying Woman); Sandra Gould (Bettor); Jack Stoney (Henchman); Paul Douglas (Man on Park Bench); "And introducing the newest addition to Hollywood's galaxy of stars: That dynamic, exciting, scintillating personality, Rhubarb (by special arrangement with the SPCA, AMA, YMCA, UCLA, BPOE, RFC)."

Fed up with humanity, multimillionaire Thaddeus J. Banner wills his $30 million estate and all his business holdings to his cat, whom Banner admires because the feline is a street-wise scrapper who takes guff from no one—that's why the cat was named "Rhubarb," a word coined by sportscaster Red Barber to describe a fracas during a baseball game. Upon Banner's death, the business mogul's press agent, Eric Yeager, discovers to his chagrin that he's been assigned to be Rhubarb's guardian and business manager. The members of the Brook-

lyn "Loons," an eighth-place ballteam owned by Banner, are likewise upset that they will now have to answer to new owner Rhubarb. Yeager manages to mollify the players by capitalizing on their superstitions and convincing them that by stroking the cat during each game the Loons will be showered with good luck. Surprise! Yeager turns out to be a prophet, and the Loons perform so brilliantly that the team is renamed the Brooklyn Rhubarbs. This is good news for Brooklyn but bad news for Yeager, who is compelled to attend every game because he's the only person who can properly handle Rhubarb—which effectively louses up Eric's romance with Polly Sickles, daughter of team manager Len Sickles, who discovers that she's highly allergic to the cat. The plot thickens once Brooklyn enters the World Series: Rhubarb is kidnapped, the victim of a conspiracy between T. J. Banner's neurotic daughter Myra—who was shafted in her Dad's will and thus has spent most of the film either in court or plotting to bump off the cat—and Pencil Louie, a bookie who's placed a number of bets against Brooklyn. Polly Sickles uses her allergy to sniff out Rhubarb, but before the cat can be recovered, he escapes his captors and scurries off to parts unknown. All seems lost until it is realized that Rhubarb has made a beeline to the ballpark in pursuit of his girlfriend, a pampered pussycat named Su-Lin who is attending the game with her owners. Inspired by Rhubarb's eleventh-hour appearance, Brooklyn wins, and there's also a happy denouement for Eric Yeager once Polly learns that her sneezing fits are due not to Rhubarb but to the vicuna lining of his cage. At fade-out time we see Eric and Polly walking contentedly through Central Park, followed by Rhubarb, Su-Lin, two more female cats, and a passel of kittens. Actor Paul Douglas, playing actor Paul Douglas, watches the pussy promenade from a nearby park bench and exclaims, "What a cat! A litter from three wives!"—providing not only a cute closing gag but a shameless plug for Douglas's own picture, *A Letter to Three Wives*.

Rhubarb first appeared in 1945 as a novel written by H. Allen Smith, a member of the California State Legislature, a baseball enthusiast, and a comic satirist of the first order. Smith used the notion of a millionaire cat as an excuse for a freewheeling lampoon on several aspects of society, extending beyond the obvious humor inherent in the international publicity given Rhubarb's sudden financial windfall. Radio advertising gets a good drubbing when the novel's T. J. Banner is soured on mankind because consumers have taken the "double your money back if not satisfied" offer bestowed upon Banner's line of hair-oil products far too literally. The book goes after people whose hobbies have become obsessions with its depiction of a take-no-prisoners war between two cat fancier societies. Smith uses his insider status to poke fun at the inanities of the American legal system: Myra Banner finds a lawyer who'll attest in court that Rhubarb is insane and thus unworthy of the inheritance, while the doddering judge on the case is preoccupied with his favorite pastime of translating the works of romance novelist Faith Baldwin into Greek. And, as was customary in satirical pieces of the mid–1940s, there's a quick jab at psychiatry: During the sanity hearing, a pair of dignified analysts come to blows over Rhubarb's prognosis.

The baseball angle was thus but one of many targets for H. Allen Smith's ridicule. Smith has fun with the fact that the dimwitted Loons are rather easily thrown off their game by such distractions as low-flying airplanes. Equal comic time is given to manager Len Sickles' disastrous marriage to an ex–chorus girl, as well as an uproarious "win one for the gipper" takeoff when, on the day of the Big Game, Rhubarb lands in the hospital with a huge hairball lodged in his stomach.

Heading the list of Smith's targets was the state of sexual mores in the postwar era. When *Rhubarb*'s "human" hero Eric Yeager resists the advances of beautiful bodybuilder Polly Pickney as heartily as he resists the suggestion that Rhubarb's foul temper could be cured by "fixing" the cat, it's clear that Yeager considers both Polly's athletic superiority and the cat's potential emasculation as implicit threats to Eric's own sexual accoutrements. Much is made of the fact that Rhubarb has the morals of—well, of an alley cat; this culminates in a riotous scene during a type of *Information Please* intellectual radio broadcast wherein Rhubarb, appearing at the insistence of the program's sponsor as a guest star, decides to express his adoration of the radio host's own pet—a female cat—and does so on the air, while the flustered host inadvertently describes the particulars of Rhubarb's courtship to a nationwide audience. In point of fact, the basic plotline of the novel has its foundation in sex: The outcome of the story is determined by a plan concocted between Myra Barker and a Benedict Arnold type on the Banner staff to pass off an addled middle-aged lady as Myra's real mother, whom Banner had purportedly agreed to make the sole beneficiary to his millions out of shame for his extramarital indiscretion.

Though these last elements would have to have been watered down, if not eliminated entirely, by the censorship standards of 1951 for the film version of *Rhubarb*, it wasn't the sex angle that kept moviemakers from filming the story immediately after its publication. The foremost problems involved the baseball angle and the depiction of Rhubarb himself. At one point it was suggested that the Loons be changed to a football team, on the theory that football was more beneficial to the box office than baseball; this change was rejected because it would have eliminated the very necessary tension-filled World Series climax.

All-encompassing ad campaign for *Rhubarb* (1951).

Another suggestion was to change Rhubarb from a cat to a dog, because everybody loves a dog story; again, this was given the thumbs down, simply because a pugnacious pooch isn't anywhere near as funny as a combative cat. Finally, in the wake of the popular talking mule picture *Francis* (1949), some genius had the notion to give Rhubarb the power of speech. There's no record of what happened to the fellow who made this suggestion, though there are rumors that he subsequently found a job at a taco stand.

The director of the aforementioned *Francis*, Arthur Lubin, was engaged to wield the megaphone on *Rhubarb*. Judging by the correspondence between Lubin and producers William Perlberg and George Seaton, the director had been under the impression that the film would adhere closely to the book, and Lubin was not happy with the changes made by scenarists Dorothy Reid and Francis Cockrell. H. Allen Smith was equally vocal in his objections to the filmization of *Rhubarb*, his principal complaint being that the cat had been made far too lovable for his taste.

While the subsequent roars of audience approval tended to drown out the protestations of Arthur Lubin and H. Allen Smith, it is quite true that the film version of *Rhubarb* bears only a passing resemblance to the novel, and that—in some instances—a great deal was lost in transition. The movie's Eric Yeager is given a new girlfriend, Polly Sickles, whose compulsion to sneeze whenever she comes in contact with Rhubarb provides the usual coitus interruptus complication indigenous to comedies of the early 1950s. Polly Pickney disappears, but her bodybuilding mania is transferred to Myra Barker, whose homicidal attitude toward Rhubarb is made doubly menacing by her athletic prowess. Also written out of the film was Myra's husband, a boobish Loons pitcher named Hannibal who, in the book, has his eyes on the team manager's job and thus joins Myra in her scheme to eliminate Rhubarb; in keeping with Hollywood's then standing gentleman's agreement with major league baseball, there's no room in this film for villainous ballplayers.

The novel's climactic courtroom sequence was originally a prime showcase for H. Allen Smith's singular brand of humor, which included making light of unusual occupations (one of the character witnesses is a burnisher in a putty knife factory) and toying with verbal clichés that we've used so often we aren't even aware that they *are* clichés (when Myra claims that even "the man on the street" knows that Banner wasn't in his right mind when he willed his estate to Rhubarb, the judge orders the bailiff to go out and find a man on the street—which he does). Besides changing the purpose of the hearing from determining whether or not Banner's "lost love" is worthy of his legacy to deciding whether or not the cat claiming to be Rhubarb really *is* Rhubarb, the film version removes the satirical tone of the original and replaces it with what Milton Berle used to call "lappy" humor—humor so easy to grasp that it can be dumped into the lap of the stupidest audience member and still raise a laugh. Thus the comic high point of the film's courtroom scene is Polly's positive identification of Rhubarb through her sneezing spasms. All that's left of H. Allen Smith is his *own* "lappy" habit of bestowing upon his characters such Dickensian monikers as Orlando Dill and P. Duncan Munk.

What passes for satire in the movie version of *Rhubarb* is of a similar easy variety. H. Allen Smith's clever swipes at radio are converted by the film into an attack on the motion picture industry's favorite early 1950s target—television. The resultant gags involving singing commercials and poor TV reception common to those pre-cable days were already old hat by 1951; additionally, these gags tell us more than we want to know about Hollywood's paranoia regarding the threat of free entertainment posed by television. (The jokes are particularly petty considering that *Rhubarb* was filmed at Paramount, one of the few studios that was actually making efforts to break into the TV business.)

Another example of flogging a dead horse in *Rhubarb* can be found in the film's ceaseless jokes about Brooklyn. One would have thought that the comic potential of this subject had been squeezed dry by all those World War II pictures featuring William Bendix waxing poetic about "dem beautiful Brooklyn bums." Evidently, however, this opinion was not shared by *Rhubarb*'s scenarists, who were even *more* enamored with Brooklynese in the picture's shooting script, which, mercifully, was pared down before filming started. And once again this source of humor is far afield of the original novel, which located the Loons in Manhattan.

The one aspect of the script that most irritated director Arthur Lubin was the decision to change the novel's ending by dragging in all that gangster-gambler business. *Rhubarb* was filmed at a time when the works of Damon Runyon were enjoying a renaissance thanks to the Broadway musical *Guys and Dolls*—resulting in an abundance of movie adaptations of Runyon, including *The Lemon Drop Kid, Bloodhounds of Broadway* and *Money from Home.* Anxious to jump on the bandwagon, the makers of *Rhubarb* overpopulated the climax with such freshly minted Runyonesque characters as Pencil Louie, Fish Eye, and Cadaver Jones—all so totally in contrast to the mood that the film had established that we suddenly seem to be watching another movie. (Incidentally, Arthur Lubin's objections to the stuff about crooks and bookies was based less on his reluctance to use worn-out material than on his concern that an undue emphasis on crime would give foreign filmgoers a distorted picture of America.)

In all honesty, however, we must admit that *Rhubarb* pleased the crowds in 1951 and still amuses when seen today; it's just that the film could have been even funnier had the filmmakers trusted the H. Allen Smith original more. Proof of this can be seen in the film's extended ballgame sequence, which is drawn almost verbatim from the novel. In this scene (shot at L.A.'s Wrigley Field, or have you guessed that by now?) Rhubarb chases after a dog owned by the St. Louis team, causing the opposing catcher to miss a batted ball and thus allowing the Loons, who've loaded the bases, to score four runs. Just when it seems that Brooklyn will be retired from the inning scoreless due to the confusion stirred up because the rulebook doesn't cover interference caused by a cat, the umpire declares that the Loons player had batted a foul ball and that everyone has to return to their bases so the whole event can be replayed. This superbly staged and edited sequence serves to develop the film's plot: The Loons player who fouled was the only member of the team who had resisted stroking Rhubarb for luck, but the interference business forces him to reconsider. The result is a home run, and this is followed by a demand from the Loons that Rhubarb attend all future games, with poor Eric Yeager in tow.

Some overacting from the gangster types aside, the performances in *Rhubarb* are attractive and believable, from the sure-handed contributions of baseball picture veterans Ray Milland and William Frawley to the eye-opening comic timing of leading lady Jan Sterling, who normally appeared in such heavy dramas as *The Big Carnival, The High and the Mighty* and *1984.* (It's likely that Sterling's impending marriage to actor Paul Douglas resulted in Douglas' gratis gag appearance at the end of the film.) Several familiar faces in the supporting cast make *Rhubarb* a special treat for film buffs, especially the presence of future Oscar-nominated character actor Strother Martin in a lengthy uncredited role as a country-boy ballplayer; you'll have to look fast, however, for Leonard Nimoy as another member of the Brooklyn Loons.

Rhubarb himself is honored with a silly, big-buildup introductory credit, though the two stunt cats used in the long shots receive nary a mention (reportedly, as many as fourteen different felines played Rhubarb at various junctures in the film; three of these lookalikes appeared in the trial scene, wherein Polly was ordered to choose among them). Rhubarb would remain in professional harness into the 1960s, his most notable appearance occurring in *A Comedy of Terrors* (1964). And in case you're wondering, Arthur Lubin's directorial technique in handling the cantankerous cat was to smear food all over someone or something in order to encourage Rhubarb to run, walk, or simply stare in the right direction. Hollywood should have tried that trick with Babe Ruth.

Right Off the Bat

Mike Donlin Productions/Arrow/All Feature Booking Agency; released September 1915

Directed by Hugh Reticker. Screenplay by Albert S. LeVino. Photography: Henry Bredeson and C. W. Van Ranst. Assistant director: Charles Mather. 5 reels; black and white; silent.

Cast: Roy Hauck (Young Mike Donlin); Henry Grady (Mike's Father); Fran Bourke (Mike's Mother); Doris Farrington (Little Viola Bradley); George Henry (Bradley); Mabel Wright (Mrs. Bradley); Harry Six (Archie); Peter Conroy (Tom Marshall); Mike Donlin (Himself, as an Adult); John McGraw (Himself); Claire Messereau (Viola Bradley); Rita Ross Donlin (Lucy, Viola's Friend)*; Charles Mather (Tom); Thornton Friel (Evans); George Sullivan (Jake Dunning); Frank Fayne, Jr. (Boy).

Young Mike Donlin of Winstead, Connecticut, first meets Viola Bradley when they're both children and Mike saves Viola from drowning. Years later Mike is gainfully employed as a mechanic in Viola's father's shop, but his heart is in baseball, and he satisfies that urge by pitching on the local bush-league team. Thanks to Mike, the Winstead club makes it to the championship, whereupon Donlin is approached by Oil-Can Harry—er, gambler Jake Dunning—with a bribe to throw the Big Game. True blue Mike disdains the offer, so Dunning has him kidnapped on the eve of the Big Game. Viola, who's invited a New York Giants scout to the Big Game, gets wind of Dunning's plan and effects Mike's rescue. Mike hits a home run during the Big Game, which not only secures him a position with the Giants, who play lots of Big Games, but enables Donlin to afford to marry Viola, which may turn out to be the Biggest Game of all.

This much is true: There really was a Mike Donlin, affectionately known as "Turkey Mike," who'd breezed into the record books by scoring five runs (two doubles, two triples) for Baltimore on a single day in 1901, and who had a lifetime batting average of .333. Mike Donlin really was born in Winstead, Connecticut (where *Right Off the Bat* was filmed), and he really did play for the New York Giants—for twelve seasons, in fact. Most of the rest of *Right Off the Bat* is a cautionary example of what happens to your brain when you read too many dime novels (cut to close-up of an egg frying in a skillet).

Mike Donlin was completely enchanted by the glamour of show business. He'd undertaken several vaudeville tours during his peak years, and after his retirement he headed to Hollywood in 1923, where he became a fixture in baseball films, playing everything from unbilled bits (*Elmer the Great*) to meaty supporting parts (*Hit and Run*, *Warming Up*, and *Hot Curves*). Occasionally

---

*Rita Ross Donlin was Mike Donlin's second wife.

he was given technical adviser credit, though in most cases the extent of his advice was to tell the star which end of the bat to hold. High living and excessive imbibing would hasten his death in 1933, but Donlin retained his matinee idol looks to the last, and was seen to good advantage in such non-baseball pictures as John Barrymore's *The Sea Beast* (the 1926 version of *Moby Dick*), Buster Keaton's *The General* (1927), William Wellman's *Beggars of Life* (1928), and John Ford's *Born Reckless* (1930). And though he didn't know it in 1915, Mike Donlin was making cinema history with *Right Off the Bat* by being the first-ever baseball star to play himself in a fictional feature film.

Roogie's Bump

John Bash Productions/Republic; released August 25, 1954

Produced by John Bash. Directed by Harold Young. Screenplay by Jack Hanley and Dan Totheroh, based on a story by Joyce Selznick and Frank Warren. Photography: Durgi J. Cortner. Music by Lehman Engels. 71 minutes; black and white; sound.

Cast: Robert Marriot (Roogie Rigsby); Ruth Warrick (Mrs. Rigsby); William Harrigan (Red O'Malley); Robert Simon (Boxey); Olive Blakeney (Mrs. Nora Andrews); David Winters (Andy); Michael Hann (Benji); Archie Robbins (P. A. Reikert); Louise Troy (Kate); Guy Rennie (Danny Doowinkle); Todd Lawrence (Announcer and Narrator of Film); Michael Keene (Barney Davis); Robbie the Dog (Himself); and members of the Brooklyn Dodgers, including Roy Campanella, Billy Loes, Russ Meyer and Carl Erskine.

Little Remington "Roogie" Rigsby is not a happy camper. A recent émigré from Ohio, Roogie is taunted by his new playmates in Brooklyn, who refuse to let him play baseball because he's so short. Roogie's father has recently died; his mother, who works in a dress shop, and his Aunt

Kate, an aspiring actress, have no time for him. The only one who seems to care is his grandmother, who keeps the boy going with stories of her old and long-departed flame, ballplayer Red O'Malley. After another kid tears his baseball card of O'Malley, Roogie goes off to a secluded spot at a nearby park to console himself. There he meets an elderly man in a baseball uniform who turns out to be the spirit of Red O'Malley, and who manifests all his pitching skill in a bump on Roogie's arm. Soon Roogie is throwing balls with such power that he's able to knock down smokestacks and bore holes through brick walls! No one in his household believes that the boy has become a pitching whiz, so Roogie writes a letter to Brooklyn Dodgers coach Boxey who, out of amusement, sends the boy a free pass. After an impromptu demonstration of Roogie's heaven-sent throwing skill at Ebbets Field, Boxey anxiously signs the boy up to play for the Dodgers—once Roogie grows up, of course. But the team's publicity agent, Reikert, sees a gold mine of merchandising and promotion in Roogie, so he pulls strings to get the kid into the Dodger lineup. Roogie becomes world famous, but he also falls victim to hucksters who want him to hawk their products. Upset at the boy's exploitation, Coach Boxey pulls Roogie off the team, which promptly goes into a slump. Pressured by fans and the baseball commissioner alike, Boxey returns Roogie to the field in the eighth inning of a pennant race game. Suddenly, Roogie's bump vanishes, and so does his pitching prowess. It seems that the ghost of Red O'Malley has overstepped his bounds by bestowing magical powers on the boy, plus O'Malley feels guilty that the kid is being forced to grow up too fast. No matter; the Dodgers immediately make Roogie their mascot, Roogie rubs the team's bats for luck, and Brooklyn wins the pennant. At the end, football season is upon us, and as a priest who closely resembles Red O'Malley looks on,

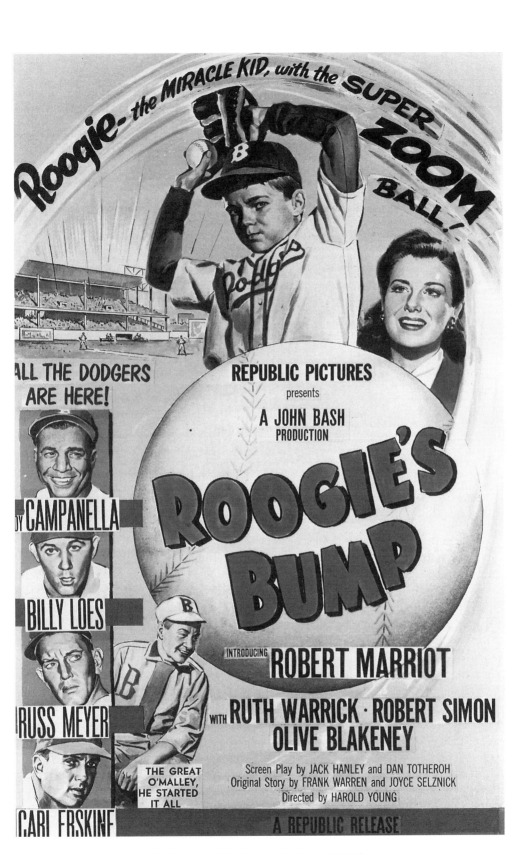

Lobby card for *Roogie's Bump* (1954).

Roogie Rigsby discovers that he's able to boot the pigskin right over the Brooklyn Bridge.

Roogie's Bump, the sort of movie that seems to have been destined from the start for church basement showings, may well become the *Plan Nine from Outer Space* of baseball films. We submit for your approval the following snatches of dialogue:

In the first scene narrator Todd Lawrence tells us that Brooklyn is "called the city of churches, because there are so many churches there." Later, the same Todd Lawrence, proving to us that he's a bona fide sportscaster, comments on a game in progress by saying, "This is a crucial time for the game, when decisions must be made."

When Coach Boxey asks Roogie if he'd like to play for the Dodgers, the lad replies, "Golly, Mr. Boxey, what kid wouldn't?" In a later scene Boxey advises Roogie that, "You'd better drink your milk tonight. You've got to pitch again tomorrow." Still later, Boxey is about to walk out on the Dodgers rather than force Roogie to play. He's stopped by the following impassioned speech by the commissioner: "The team needs you."

And at the end, just after Roogie kicks a football across the East River, narrator Todd Lawrence tells us, "It could only happen in Brooklyn."

The high standard set by the dialogue is matched by the visuals, particularly the utilization of newsreel footage. Right after we see the Dodgers hit one homer after another, the narrator tells us that Brooklyn's in trouble; and two seconds after Duke Snider is called out, Snider steps up to bat again. The method of demonstrating Roogie's pitching power is handled with equal care and credibility; the cartoon animation used to show the ball grinding its way into a brick wall makes *Clutch Cargo* look like the Night on Bald Mountain in *Fantasia*.

Then there's the matter of Product Placement. The film condemns the crass commercialization of Roogie Rigsby, yet everywhere we turn there's a paid endorsement. Roogie opens a can of dog food, making sure that we see the Ken'l Ration label; Aunt Kate goes for a cigarette, taking great care to flash an oversized Phillip Morris carton at the camera; and in the Ebbetts Field radio announcer's booth, which ostensibly can't be seen by the fans at home, there's a huge poster for TWA Airlines on the wall. *Roogie's Bump* indeed. Looks more like Roogie's Plug.

Okay, okay. You saw the film when you were seven years old and you had a ball (Evidently *someone* saw the movie; see separate entry on 1993's *Rookie of the Year*). It was, after all, deliberately aimed at the kiddie trade, and though there's a strain of condescension throughout the film, it can still entertain a group of undiscerning children. Maybe I was wrong; maybe *Roogie's Bump* isn't bad *enough* to reach the cult status of *Plan Nine*.

We must take into consideration the talent on both side of the cameras. Director Harold Young had once put Leslie Howard through his paces in *The Scarlet Pimpernel* (1934), while scenarist Joyce Selznick later forsook writing to become a top actors' agent. Roogie's mother is played by Ruth Warrick, who'd been cast as "Wife Number One" in *Citizen Kane* and who has more recently starred in the ABC daytime drama *All My Children*. And Red O'Malley—he with the faraway look in his eyes, brought about either by wistfulness or by an effort to see the cue cards—is enacted by William Harrigan, who was, according to all reports, brilliant as the Captain in the original stage production of *Mister Roberts*.

And let's not discount the bonus of seeing Brooklyn Dodgers members Roy Campanella, Billy Loes, Russ Meyer and Carl Erskine, none of whom can act but all of whom are seen in their considerable prime. It's of particular nostalgic value to watch Roy Campanella—whom many modern viewers have never seen outside his wheelchair—not only sprinting about the field but taking backward somersaults when he's purportedly bowled over by Roogie's pitches.

Roogie's Bump is what it is. It wasn't made for the critics; it wasn't made for the sophisticates; it wasn't even made for baseball buffs. It was made for an audience of youngsters who hadn't yet become jaded by *The Matrix* and Lara Croft. Let's leave it at that.

But before we forget: The British title for *Roogie's Bump* was *The Kid Colossus*—conjuring up irresistible images of a fifty-foot Roogie Rigsby straddling the Brooklyn Navy Yard.

Rookie of the Year

Featherstone/20th Century–Fox; released July 7, 1993

Executive producers: Jack Brodsky, Irby Smith. Produced by Robert Harper. Directed by Daniel Stern. Written by Sam Harper. Photography: Jack Green. Production designer: Steven Jordan. Costume designer: Jay Hurley. Edited by Donn Cambern and Raja Gosnell. Original music: Bill Conti. Associate producer: Joan Aguado. Casting: Linda Lowy. Production manager: Barry Berg. First assistant director: Henry Bronchtein. Second assistant director: Mathew Dunne. Art director: William Arnold. Set decorator: Leslie Bloom. Camera operator: George Kohut. Sound mixer: Scott Smith. Special effects coordinator: Dieter Sturm. Special effects foreman: Yvonne Sturm. Makeup artists: Rodger Jacobs, Linda Boykin Neuffer. Hair stylists: Gunnar Swanson, Donald Abbinati. Script supervisor: Sioux Richards. Foley editors: James Christophre, Baylis Glascock. Baseball advisor: Tim Stoddard. Visual effects coordinator: Erik Henry. Visual effects by Pacific Data Images and Metrolight Studios. Titles and opticals by Pacific Title. Color by DeLuxe; Panavision. 103 minutes; Dolby Stereo Sound. Rated PG.

Cast: Thomas Ian Nicholas (Henry Rowengartner); Gary Busey (Chet Steadman); Dan Hedaya (Larry "Fish" Fisher); Amy Morton (Mary Rowengartner); Bruce Altman (Jack Bradfield); Eddie Bracken (Bob Carson); Robert Gorman (Clark); Patrick LaBrecque (George); Albert Hall (Sal Martinella); Daniel Stern (Brickman); Colombe Jacobsen-Derstine (Becky); Kristie Davis (Tiffany); Tyler Ann Carroll (Edith); Tom Milanovich (Heddo); Ross Lehman (Dr. Kersten); John Gegenhuber (Derkin); James "Ike" Eichling (Little League Coach); Josh Wagner (Little League Fielder); Erik Vandersteuyf (Windemere); James Andelin (Wizard of Wrigley); Andrew Mark Berman (Ernie); Mark Doran (Richards, Cub Catcher); Neil Flynn (Okie, Cubs First Base); E. Milton Wheeler (Suarez, Cubs Second Base); Sam Sanders (Fern, shortstop); Neil Fiala (Mullens, Cubs Third baseman); W. Earl Brown (Frick, bullpen catcher); Frank L. Wiltse (Peyton, Cubs Pitcher); Barry L. Bonds, Bobby Bonilla, Pedro Guerrero (Three Big Whiffers); Jerry Saslow, Mike Bacarella (Bleacher Bums); Don Forston (Big Bum); Ken Earl (Pepsi Executive); Anthony Diaz-Perez (Rude Hot Dog Vendor); Mike Houlihan (Carson's Hot Dog Vendor); Tim Stoddard (Dodger Pitcher); B. J. Sanabria (Chicken Runner); Cristian Mendez (Other Mets Runner); Mike Daughtry (Mets Third Base Coach); Toney Howell (Surprised Expos Runner); Blake Hammond (Screaming Patient); Ian Gomez (Odd Bellman); R. A. Bauer (Bellman); Mathew Dunne (Commercial Director); Askia Bantu (Mr. Banks); Robert Harper (Confused Teacher); Peter Bankins (Flower Shop Customer); Cindy Becker (Receptionist); Dan Conway, Ron Beattie, Sunnie Hikawa, Al Joyner (Press Conference Reporters); Christopher Howe, Karen L. Stephens (Airport Reporters); Jon Hilario, Michael Keeney (Phys Ed Dweebs); Kimberly Dal Santo (Kid Autograph Seeker); Phillip J. Maxwell, Tom Brennan, Arnie Silberman, Larry Brelsford, Dave Slickenmeyer, George H. Drenth (Umpires); Rick LeFevour (Stunt Coordinator); Stephan Choiniere (Henry's Double); Paul Stevens (Chet's Double); John Candy (Cliff Murdock, Cubs Announcer).

Twelve-year-old Henry Rowengartner loves baseball, but baseball doesn't seem to love him; though he dreams of hitting, pitching and catching with the best of 'em, Henry suffers from an acute lack of skill and coordination. Hoping to impress a girl during an impromptu playground ballgame, Henry attempts to catch a pop fly but succeeds only in breaking his arm and shoulder.

When the cast comes off four months later, the doctor announces incredulously that "the tendons have fused with the humerus"—and as a result of this medical phenomenon, Henry is now capable of throwing a ball in excess of 100 miles per hour! The next logical turn of events is for young Henry to be signed by the Chicago Cubs—who, in their usual fashion, are perilously close to folding by August. Though he manages through sheer dumb luck to pitch a winning game his first time out, Henry obviously needs some serious coaching, so manager Sal Martinella appoints aging Cubs pitcher Chet "The Rocket" Steadman to show the boy the ropes. Resentful at first, Chet grows genuinely fond of Henry, and even more so of Henry's single mother Mary. As the youngster's game improves, so do the Cubbies' chances of winning the Division championship—and possibly the World Series, after lo these many eons. Meanwhile, Mary's avaricious boyfriend Jack Bradfield shamelessly exploits Henry's commercial value and enters into a conspiracy with Larry Fisher, nephew of Cubs owner Bob Carson, to sell Henry to the Yankees for a cool $25 million. As for Our Hero himself, he begins to grow dog-weary of his demanding new career, especially since his tight schedule has put a severe strain on his relationship with his best friends, Clark and George. Inevitably, Henry "loses" his miracle arm right in the middle of the Division playoff game with the New York Mets. But by drawing upon his inborn ingenuity—and banking on the fact that his fellow baseball players are really kids at heart—Henry cinches a happy ending for all the characters whom the audience cares about most.

Building upon an already established and popular baseball-film subgenre of the 1990s—the story told from a youngster's point of view, à la *The Sandlot* (q.v.)—*Rookie of the Year* gilded the lily by adding a wish-fulfillment angle seasoned by Fantasy. As

noted by writer Sam Harper and producer Robert Harper (no relation): "We thought, what better way to make a child's fantasy come true than to put him on a Major League baseball team—a fantasy, incidentally, which is shared by many adults. As a kid it's wonderful to feel that anything is possible, and as an adult it's important to be reminded about the days when you felt that way." A huge financial success, *Rookie of the Year* served as the launching pad for a veritable cycle of "fantastic" kid-oriented baseball pictures, including *Little Big League*, *Angels in the Outfield* and *Ed* (see separate entries).

At the time of *Rookie's* release, many observers compared it to such earlier baseball fantasies as the original *Angels in the Outfield*, *It Happens Every Spring* and *Damn Yankees* (Rita Kenney of the *Washington Post* in fact suggested that the film represented the "Disneyfication" of *Damn Yankees*, labeling it "*Those Darned Cubs*"). Only those reviewers with a thorough grounding in film history, notably *USA Today*'s Mike Clark and *The Great Baseball Films* author Rob Edelman, recognized the similarities between *Rookie of the Year* and the obscure 1954 ballpark flick *Roogie's Bump* (q.v.), which also offered a preteen baseball fanatic who landed a spot on a Major League club (the Brooklyn Dodgers) by virtue of a dynamite pitching arm brought about by an accident. *Roogie's Bump* is not mentioned at all in the official studio presskit for *Rookie of the Year*, nor are the screenwriters of the earlier film cited in the opening credits of *Rookie*, as Dorothy Kingsley and George Wells would be in the 1994 remake of 1951's *Angels in the Outfield*. This is not to suggest that the makers of *Rookie* were churlish in neglecting to mention a film that obviously served as an inspiration to their own work. Though it is true that *Roogie's Bump* and *Rookie of the Year* share the same basic premise, the earlier film only scratched the surface of that premise's potential, while the later film milked it for all it was worth.

Rookie of the Year's executive producer was Irby Smith, who'd previously struck a cinematic mother lode with the 1989 baseball opus *Major League* (q.v.). Not surprisingly, *Rookie* adhered faithfully to the *Major League* formula, minus the R-rated edge: The opening overhead shots of a major baseball-franchise metropolis (Cleveland in the earlier film, Chicago in this one); the establishing scenes of a big-time ballpark "coming to life" and opening its doors to the first fans of the season; the venerable ballclub threatened with a quick sale to another city because of a lousy season and flagging attendance; the greedy owner (or in this case, the owner's nephew) who intends to squeeze every last penny out of the franchise for his own benefit and at the expense of the players and loyal fans; the miraculous turnaround of the team in mid-season; the sardonic Greek Chorus–like radio sportscaster whose faith in humanity is restored when his team begins to show signs of life; the progress of the team charted by *Sports Illustrated* covers and high-profile TV commercials (this time it was Pepsi-Cola who grabbed up most of the product-placement opportunities); the brutish *bête noire* opposing batter—tobacco-stained beard, satanic eyes, subhuman growl—whom the pitcher protagonist must face down at the beginning and end of the story; the "wrong" boyfriend replaced in the heroine's heart by the unkempt-but-lovable veteran ballplayer; the excessive deployment of slow-motion photography during crucial plays; and the climactic Pennant race, won as much by strategy as by skill.

By exploiting the standard baseball-movie clichés as set down by *Major League* and other films of its ilk, the filmmakers were able to spring a few non-clichéd surprises on the unwary viewer. A good example: Early in the film, young Henry Rowengarter is publicly embarrassed when his mother Mary proves to have a better pitching arm than he does. The audience accepts this as a typical family-movie throwaway gag, capping a whole series of baseball-related humiliations endured by the hapless Henry, and the bit is forgotten for the time being. As the movie progresses, the notion is planted in the viewer's mind that Henry's long-departed father was a championship pitcher, and it was from dear old dad that the boy inherited his love of baseball: Again, no surprises here. But three-quarters of the way through the film, Mary's embittered ex-boyfriend reveals that Henry's dad not only never set foot on a ballfield but also deserted Mary when she announced she was pregnant. Now the audience braces itself for what seems to be the inevitable lachrymose "confession" scene between Henry and Mary. Instead, Henry casually informs Mary that he knew all along that his father was a deadbeat with no baseball talent, but that he allowed his mother to tell little white lies because it made *her* feel good. This cliché reversal is satisfying enough on its own, but the filmmakers aren't through with us yet. During the climactic playoff game, after Henry loses his miracle arm and is forced to rely upon his wits and inner strength to beat the other team, he is spurred on by the discovery that his pitcher's mitt had once belonged to his mother—and that *she* had been the youthful pitching whiz from whom Henry gleaned his devotion to baseball. Suddenly the audience's mind races back to that opening gag concerning Mary's pitching prowess—and just as suddenly, the realization dawns that this apparently minor gag actually served as the foundation for a crucial plot point, making the climactic scene not only logical but utterly believable.

Believability is, in fact, *Rookie of the Year*'s strongest suit; though our minds inform us that the story could never happen in a million years, our hearts tell us that it should happen, and that we *want* it to happen. This would not have come about without the sincerity of screenwriter Sam

Harper, who, born in the Chicago suburb of Winnetka, had grown up adoring the Cubs without ever having actually seen a game (his father, an inveterate White Sox fan, would not permit Harper to even come within proximity of Wrigley Field until he was an adult!). Having resigned himself to the seemingly cast-in-stone fact that the Cubbies would probably never again cinch a Pennant, much less a World Series, Harper decided that he would make his dream become reality through the magic of celluloid. For all the business surrounding Henry's amazing pitching arm, the notion that the Cubs would ever come close to a Pennant race is probably the film's most fantastic element—and the one most dearly coveted by the largest percentage of the film's fans.

As with *Major League*, *Rookie of the Year* was shot entirely on location—but unlike the earlier film, in which Milwaukee stood in for Cleveland, *Rookie* was lensed in the city where most of the action took place. Twenty days were devoted to filming the Wrigley Park scenes, while Comiskey Park stood in for Dodger Stadium in the Los Angeles sequences. According to the 20th Century–Fox publicity brigade, the filmmakers encountered very little difficulty in rounding up unpaid extras for the ballpark scenes; no Chicago baseball fan worth his salt would ever pass up the opportunity to see the Cubbies win a Pennant, even if it was only make-believe.

Wisely, the film's fantasy is grounded in reality. Nothing of an unbelievable nature happens until Henry breaks his arm and shoulder; and after he is "cured," thereby losing his pitching skills and, by extension, crash-landing back into Real Life, the psych-out strategies Henry and the other Cubs use to defeat the New York Mets are, if not entirely ethical, certainly within the realm of credibility. Even within the fantasy framework the film creates its own reality by remaining consistent to its convictions, chief among them that within every grown-up

baseball player is a small boy struggling to break free, and that a unique talent is truly effective only when it is used with wisdom and discipline. Also helping the viewer go with the flow is the warm and sincere relationship between young Henry and his mother Mary, creating an aura of audience empathy and identification that would be sorely lacking in the later baseball fantasy *Ed*, in which the characters existed only as soul-less puppets.

The film's litmus test so far as the viewer's willingness to suspend disbelief occurs in the scene where Henry enters the players' entrance of Wrigley Field for the first time. Director Daniel Stern has gone on record comparing *Rookie of the Year* to *The Wizard of Oz*, and Henry's pitching arm to the ruby slippers. "There's this magical element that drives the story, but in the end you learn a very down-to-earth lesson about having a heart and a brain." As if to literalize this comparison, the scene at the player's entrance is staged exactly in the manner of Dorothy's arrival at the gates of the Emerald City—complete with a mustachioed gatekeeper, identified in the credits as "The Wizard of Wrigley," welcoming Henry with a Frank Morganish "Wellll ... that's a horse of a different color!" In the tradition of Woody Allen's tumble over a giant banana peel in *Sleeper* (1973) and Marty Feldman's "Walk this way please!" in *Young Frankenstein* (1974), the sheer audacity of suddenly and without warning tossing a *Wizard of Oz* spoof into the middle of *Rookie of the Year* is enough to generate the audience's laughter. If the viewer is able to watch this scene without wincing and groaning, then the rest of the film will be just as easy to swallow.

Though *Rookie of the Year* has a lot to recommend it, the film also has more than its share of shortcomings. The film tends to lose focus halfway through, particularly in the protracted and easily disposable scenes showing Henry and his young pals Clark and George spending their spare time building and sailing their own boat. Twelve-year-old Thomas Ian Nicholas, whose previous screen credits included *Radio Flyer* and *Harry and the Hendersons*, is generally okay as Henry, especially when expressing slack-jawed fear and astonishment over the realization that he will be playing "real" baseball in front of 35,000 screaming fans; he is less effective in the scenes where he taunts the other players into committing bonehead blunders, if only because there are far too many such scenes. Even so, Nicholas' performance is more convincing than that of the film's principal villain Dan Hedaya, who seems to be laboring under the misapprehension that he is appearing in a tent-theater production of *Nixon: The Final Days*. But Hedaya is the epitome of subtlety compared to Daniel Stern, who as the film's director exercised his "it's my ball and my bat" prerogative by casting himself in the role of addlepated Cubs batting coach Brick-

man. Though Stern's direction is by and large commendable (he'd honed this particular aspect of his talent with ten episodes of the TV sitcom *The Wonder Years*), especially in the 20-minute closing ballgame sequence, his out-of-control portrayal of the blathering Brickman is about as funny as a full frontal lobotomy.

Other performances tend to be over the top as well, but are much easier to digest. Amy Morton hams it up as Henry's mom, but her scenes require that type of playing. Also fun to watch is John Candy (in what may turn out to be the largest uncredited role in movie history) as the Cubs' Harry Caray–like announcer; again, it is the type of role that all but demands top-of-the-lungs overkill, and Candy makes a meal of the opportunity (need we add that the actor was a rabid Cubs fan in real life?). On the less demonstrative side of the scale, Gary Busey is just fine as the over-the-hill Chet Steadman, proving that after all those years

Stop the presses! Barry Bonds actually smiles in this posed shot from *Rookie of the Year* (Thomas Ian Nicholas at left).

of eyeball-rolling bad guys, he was still capable of playing a "normal" character—and a romantic lead to boot. Best of all is Eddie Bracken as the Cubs' childlike septuagenarian owner Bob Carson, who timidly avoids setting foot in the Wrigley bleachers for fear of being lynched by angry fans. Definitely an acquired taste in his starring vehicles of the 1940s, Bracken here delivers what may be the most relaxed and likable performance of his screen career. Every one of his line deliveries is right on the money, and his nonplussed reaction upon being told the cost of a Wrigley hot dog is priceless.

Several genuine Major Leaguers make cameo appearances in *Rookie of the Year.* Pitcher Tim Stoddard, formerly of the Orioles, Cubs, Padres and Yankees, was seen as a Dodgers player, and pulled double duty as the film's technical adviser. Also on hand were the Cardinals' Pedro Guerrero, the Mets' Bobby Bonilla, and the Now and Future King of the Diamond, Barry Bonds. Somewhat disappointingly, these three powerhouses were dismissed in a single montage scene which lasted but a few seconds. The subsequent family-oriented baseball film *Little Big League* (q.v.) would exhibit a stronger sense of showmanship in its utilization of real-life ballplayers. (Incidentally, which one of the bonafide pitchers in the film was responsible for tossing the alleged "pop fly" during the climactic game? We know that the ball wasn't batted because we can see the thrower's hand at the bottom of the screen!)

Critical response to *Rookie of the Year* was mixed, to say the least. Some adored the film, others hated it, and a large majority regarded it as uneven. Chris Hicks of Salt Lake City's *Deseret News* summed up the consensus: "The first third or so of *Rookie of the Year* is hysterically funny, but then the film settles into a sentimental rut, only to pick up again here and there with amusing bits."

The biggest surprise among those who praised the film was Roger Ebert, for whom the word "curmudgeon" was apparently invented. While his *Chicago Sun-Times* critique of *Rookie of the Year* could not be called a rave, he was much kinder to the film than one might have expected. Additionally, Ebert let his celebrated guard down a bit by admitting that his opinion was colored by his own painful childhood experiences as an also-ran Little League ballplayer: "I am no longer a kid, and this movie is not likely to make my list of the year's best, but I can remember those miserable Little League games and so in a modest way I'm grateful for this film. It is pure wish-fulfillment, 40 years after I needed it."

No matter what the critics said, *Rookie of the Year* was a hit at the box office. Its domestic gross of $53,579,000 made it the third most profitable baseball film of all time, outdistanced only by *A League of Their Own* and *Field of Dreams* (see separate entries).

Safe at Home!

Naud-Hamilburg Productions/Columbia; released April 1962

Produced by Tom Naud. Directed by Walter Doniger. Screenplay by Robert Dillon, based on a story by Tom Naud and Steve Ritch. Photography: Irving Lippman. Edited by Frank P. Keller. Music by Van Alexander. Set decoration by James M. Crowe. Assistant director: Leonard Katzman. 83 minutes; black and white; sound.

Cast: Mickey Mantle (Himself); Roger Maris (Himself); William Frawley (Bill Turner); Patricia Barry (Johanna Price); Don Collier (Ken Lawton); Bryan Russell (Hutch Lawton); Ralph Houk, Whitey Ford (Themselves); Eugene Iglesias (Mr. Torres); Charles G. Martin (Henry's Father); Desiree Sumatta (Mrs. Torres); Joe Hickman (Joel); Chris Hughes (Phil); James R. Argyras (Jackie); Fred A. Schwarb (Coach Benton); Joe Morrison (Hank); and Mickey Mantle, Jr., and David Mantle.

Young Hutch Lawton fibs to his friends that he can get his "pals" Mickey Mantle and

Roger Maris demonstrates his acting range as he tackles the role of a baseball player in *Safe at Home!*

Roger Maris to show up at Hutch's Little League banquet. While his dad goes on a three-day fishing trip, Hutch hitches a ride to the Yankees' Florida spring training camp. There the boy is reprimanded by Mantle and Maris for telling tall tales and is sent packing. Hutch returns to his home town in disgrace—only to be hailed as a hero because Mickey and Roger have invited the whole little-league team to spring training!

It is perhaps superfluous to note that *Safe at Home* was rushed into production to capitalize on the New York Yankees' spectacular 1961 season, which included a World Series win, Mickey Mantle's fifty-four home runs, and, of course, Roger Maris' record-breaking sixty-first homer on October 1 (see notes on the made-for–TV biopic *61**). These events transpired a mere six months before *Safe at Home!* was released in the spring of 1962; in several cities the film was issued as part of a double bill with *Twist Around the Clock*, which was likewise hastily patched together to take advantage of a transient American fancy.

Frank Scott, agent for Mickey Mantle and Roger Maris, recalled in 1986 that *Safe at Home!* was the first glimpse most Americans had of the Yankees' new spring training headquarters in Fort Lauderdale, where the bulk of the film was shot. Scott noted that it was fun to participate, especially due to the presence of baseball-happy William Frawley in the cast (it was the last of Frawley's half-dozen ballpark epics; the actor died in 1966). The agent also remembered that Mantle and Maris got $5,000 each for their three days' work, though Mickey Mantle insisted in his autobiography that he and Roger both received $25,000. It's likely that Frank Scott's estimate was closer to the actual compensation, since one look at the finished film makes it hard to believe that its producers had $50,000 to spend on anything.

Mantle basked in any sort of publicity; Maris, on the other hand, hated the limelight but went along because it was expected of him. Roger Maris's discomfort was reflected in his performance, which was drolly summed up by film critic Leonard Maltin: "The stoic poetry of Jack Webb's acting pales beside that of Maris' in this kiddie time capsule." Also struggling to play themselves convincingly were Yankees manager Ralph Houk and teammate Whitey Ford. Ford had one single line—"Hey Rog, Mickey! Mr. Houk wants to see you right away!"—and was surprised to receive a residual check for that brief recitation. The $100 check was dropped in the mail following a telecast of *Safe at Home*—in 1984!

Among the many youngsters in the cast were Mickey Mantle's sons Mickey, Jr., and David. Mantle was amused that director Walter Doniger went to such great pains to give the boys "motivation" and "subtext" for their every movement—which is an awful lot more than Doniger did for their dad. One young boy who *wasn't* in the cast was eleven-year-old Kurt Russell, though more than one baseball historian has placed Russell, who as an adult became a top box office attraction, in the role of *Safe at Home!* protagonist Hutch Lawton. The error is understandable. When young Kurt discovered that his actor father Bing Russell (who'd once played minor-league baseball) was up for a part in the film, the boy begged his father to take him to the set for an audition, not so much to win a role as to meet his idols Mantle and Maris. As it happened, neither of the Russells was cast; the role of Hutch Lawton went to *Bryan* Russell, no relation to Bing or Kurt.

The Sandlot

Island World/20th Century–Fox; released in April 1993

Executive producers: Mark Burg, Cathleen Summers, Chris Zarpas. Produced by Dale De La Torre and William S. Gilmore. Associate Producer: Robert Gunter. Directed by David Mickey Evans. Written by David Mickey Evans and Robert Gunter. Photography: Anthony B. Richmond. Edited by Michael A. Stevenson. Original music: David Newman. Art director: Marc Dabe. Production designer: Chester Kaczenski. Set decorator: Judi Sandin. Costume design: Grania Preston. Key makeup artist: Karl Wessen. Key hair stylist: Leslie Ann Anderson. First assistant director: William M. Elvin. Second assistant directors: Alan Edmisten, Grant Gilmore. Production manager: Frederic W.

Brost. Production coordinator: Dennis Williams. Stunt coordinator: John Moio. Storyboard artist: Darrin Fletcher. Conceptual artist: Tom Southwell. Beast puppeteers: Brian Simpson, Mark N. Weatherbe, Cleve Hill. Special effects: Clifford Wenger, Rick Lazzarini's Character Shop. Visual effects animator/compositor: Adam Howard. Script supervisor: Becca Poulos. Color by DeLuxe; J-D-C Scope. 101 minutes; Dolby Stereo Sound. Rated PG.

Cast: Tom Guiry (Scotty Smalls); Mike Vitar (Benjamin Franklin Rodriguez); Patrick Renna (Hamilton "Ham" Porter); Chauncey Leopardi (Michael "Squints" Palledorus); Marty York (Alan "Yeah-Yeah" McClennan); Brandon Quintin Adams (Kenny DeNunez); Grant Gelt (Bertram Grover Weeks); Shane Obedzinski (Tommy "Repeater" Timmons); Victor DiMattia (Timmy Timmons); Denis Leary (Bill); Karen Allen (Scotty's Mom); James Earl Jones (Mr. Mertle); Marley Shelton (Wendy Peppercorn); Herb Muller (Young Mr. Mertle); Garret Pearson (Police Chief); Eddie Mathews, Keith Campbell (Thieves); Wil Horneff (Phillip); Tyson Jones (Little League Punk No. 2); Karl Simmons (Schoolyard Pitcher); Maury Wills (Coach); Robert Apisa (Home Plate Umpire); Pablo P. Vitar (Older Benny); Robbie T. Robinson (Third Base Umpire); Charles Fick (Giants Catcher); Tim Page (Giants Pitcher); Dennis Williams (Giants Third Baseman); Cynthia Windham (Mother at Pool); Shane LaVar Smith (Toddler); Art LaFleur ("The Babe"); Charlie Croughwell, Jack West, George Marshall Ruge, Brian Smrz, Orwin Harvey, Brian J. Williams, Bob Yerkes, Phil Minsky, Randy Fife, George Fisher, Bill Hart, Walt Robles, Lane Leavitt, John Robotham (Stunts); Arliss Howard (Adult Scotty); David Mickey Evans (Narrator); and Brooke Adams.

From the vantage point of the early 1990s, Scotty Smalls recalls the Summer of 1962 as the most wonderful time of his life—and the time that he got himself into "the biggest pickle I'd ever been in." Flashing back, we find 10-year-old Scotty, his mother and his stepfather moving into a suburban West Coast community. Happening across a sandlot, Scotty sees a group of enthusiastic youngsters playing what seems to be a perpetual baseball game, with no teams, rules or score. After an embarrass-

ingly bad start, Scotty is taken under the wing of the group's best player, Benjamin Franklin Rodriguez, and is soon fully accepted by the rest of the kids. As Summer stretches languidly onward, Scotty and his new friends have all sorts of marvelous adventures—none more exciting than the day they encounter "the Beast." Until Scotty's arrival, none of the kids had dared to climb over the fence separating the sandlot from the foreboding house of the mysterious Mr. Mertle, whose cluttered backyard is fiercely guarded by a vicious, gargantuan junkyard dog. According to neighborhood legend, the Beast has claimed 173 human victims and nearly as many stray baseballs. Then comes the fateful day that Scotty steps up to bat and socks out his first home run, which lands in the forbidden domain of the Beast. The homered baseball, surreptitiously "borrowed" from Scotty's stepfather, was autographed by Babe Ruth Himself, and therefore *must* be retrieved from Mr. Mertle's backyard despite the terrible danger involved. Using Scotty's trusty Erector Set, the boys construct a variety of Rube Goldberg–esque contraptions to reclaim the precious ball without disturbing or provoking the Beast, but all their best efforts fail. About to concede defeat, Benny Rodriguez has a dream in which the spirit of Babe Ruth urges him to strive for greatness: "Heroes get remembered, but legends never die." The next day, Benny dons a pair of P.F. Flyers—guaranteed to make him "run faster and jump higher"—and saunters alone into enemy territory for a final, decisive confrontation with the Beast. After a wild chase through the neighborhood, with Benny barely managing to keep one step ahead of the relentless canine, the boys end up back in the Mertle backyard—where they rescue the Beast from a falling fence, thereby earning the big mutt's undying, slobbery gratitude. Amused that the boys hadn't merely knocked on his front door and politely asked for their ball back, Mr.

Mertle invites them into his den, which is covered from stem to stern with baseball memorabilia. Revealing himself to be a former Major League player who retired after going blind, Mertle is unable to return the coveted "Babe Ruth" ball, but he manages to mollify Scotty's stepdad by presenting him with a baseball signed by *every member* of the 1927 Yankees! His recollection over, the adult Scotty Smalls returns to the present, and his job as play-by-play radio announcer for the Los Angeles Dodgers—pausing briefly to exchange a knowing smile with his lifelong friend, Dodgers power hitter "Benny the Jet" Rodriguez.

After six years of comparative obscurity in the Hollywood screenwriting mills, David Mickey Evans grabbed the brass ring with his script for *Radio Flyer* (1992). Directed by Richard Donner, this was a Spielbergesque yarn about a pair of 1950s youngsters who retreated from the harsh reality of a brutal, drunken stepfather by building a fantasy world around their beloved "Radio Flyer" wagon. An often unsettling blend of rosy nostalgia and gut-wrenching violence, the film was effusively overpraised in some quarters, mercilessly damned in others. Whatever its virtues or vices, it succeeded in putting its creator on the map, and as a result David Mickey Evans was permitted not only to write his next movie project (with Robert Gunter), but to direct as well.

Like *Radio Flyer*, *The Sandlot*—filmed on location in and around Ogden, Utah—is an extended flashback, mixing straighton reality with whimsical fantasy. But by studiously avoiding the grimness of *Radio Flyer* (the stepfather was a *much* nicer fellow this time around), and including a generous supply of broad comedy, *The Sandlot* appealed to a much wider audience than its predecessor, ending up the tenth highest-grossing baseball film of the 20th century ($32,400,000—not a bad return for an extremely modest investment). Even so, the film is an irritatingly mixed bag, its best

moments compromised by misfire gags and droning repetition.

The Sandlot suffers from a bad case of wanting to be *A Christmas Story* (1984)—that irresistible cult classic based on the writings of Jean Shepherd, which also combined a child's-eye view of a bygone world with heavy doses of slapstick exaggeration. Evidently, screenwriter Evans did not understand, or chose to ignore, one of the principle reasons that *Christmas Story* worked. The "adult" narration of the earlier film offered ironic counterpoint to the images at hand and never patronized the characters on screen. When narrator Jean Shepherd recalled the thrill of receiving an eagerly anticipated box-top premium or the embarrassment of putting on a hideous pair of pajamas given to him by a doting relative, he deftly combined the breathless present-tense emotions of a child going through the experience with the wry and affectionate knowledgability of an adult who could remember just how he felt before, during and after that experience. (Who can forget the adolescent excitement in Shepherd's voice as his younger counterpart slowly deciphered the Little Orphan Annie Decoder Badge—and the weary tone of middle-aged disillusionment when the secret message turned out to be a commercial for Ovaltine?)

In contrast, the narrator of *The Sandlot*, the adult Scotty Smalls (actually the unbilled voice of writer-director Evans), rarely utters a word that isn't dripping with condescension or contempt for the child he once was. With few exceptions, the older Scotty is relentlessly critical of the young Scotty and his friends, telling us *ad nauseum* what a "goofus" he was and how foolish they were. The narration is overloaded with such self-deprecating phrases as, "I had no idea what they were talking about ... so I lied"; "If I'd known what was going to happen, I never would have gone"; "The stupidest thing any of us had ever done"; and "The biggest pickle I'd *ever* been in!"

Benny (Mike Vitar, left) and Scotty (Tom Guiry) admire the vintage autographed baseball owned by Mr. Mertle (James Earl Jones) in *The Sandlot* (1993). (Alas, in the film itself we never get to see the fascinating model display in the foreground of this still.)

(which is tiresomely trotted out no fewer than three times). If it is true that a film's narrator is supposed to represent the viewer, it must follow that the viewer is supposed to be as harshly judgmental of the *Sandlot* kids as the older Scotty Smalls. For some observers, this line of thinking tends to build a wall between the audience and the characters.

Too, the narration is often totally superfluous, either telling us what we've already seen or tipping off what is about to happen—effectively undercutting the comic value of the worthwhile scenes and stretching the lesser moments far beyond their worth. A well-staged sequence in which team member "Squints" nearly drowns himself in the municipal swimming pool just so he can steal a kiss from sexy female lifeguard

Wendy Peppercorn would have gotten by just fine without the narrator's running commentary. Conversely, the vomitous vignette wherein the kids suffer the consequences of chewing tobacco just before boarding an amusement park tilt-a-whirl is rendered doubly disgusting and unfunny by the narrator's irritating interpolations.

The film's awkward structure also lessens its effectiveness. It could be argued that at base, *The Sandlot* is an "Our Gang" two-reeler about a group of inventive youngsters devising various mechanical methods to outwit a huge and snarling mastiff. Or maybe it's about the new kid on the block learning how to make friends with strangers. Or perhaps it's the story of a boy and his stepfather uncomfortably trying to bond with one another. Or, conceivably, the film is a "coming of age" opus. Or could it be about a precociously talented baseball player, obviously destined for the Majors, who in the autumn of his childhood would rather play ball with his friends for the sheer fun of it than tangle with the politics and prima donna egos of Little League competition?

Any one of these premises could have made a serviceable feature film. Put together, they *might* have blended smoothly with a bit more cohesion. As it stands, however, *The Sandlot* never entirely jells, moving in fits and starts from one episode to another without making up its mind which of its subplots is the most important until an hour into the proceedings.

Moreover, for a film which prides itself on its knowledge of All Things Baseball, *The Sandlot* contains two significant "boners." One of these occurs near the end, when the sandlot kids discover that their neighbor Mr. Mertle had in his youth been a professional ballplayer, and even stood shoulder to shoulder with Babe Ruth. Inasmuch as the action takes place in 1962 and Mertle is played by James Earl Jones, the believability factor is diminished; the chances of a black ballplayer ever having been on the same team with the Bambino, whose playing career ended in 1935, run the gamut from Slim to None.

And at the very beginning of the film the narrator carefully establishes that Babe Ruth will somehow be crucial to the outcome of the story by invoking Babe's celebrated "called shot" of October 1, 1932. Okay so far. But when Mr. Narrator Man states baldly that Ruth's subsequent home run took place at the bottom in the ninth inning, one can almost hear an anguished mass groan arise from the millions of baseball-savvy filmgoers who have committed to memory the fact that Babe's momentous feat occurred at the top of the Fifth. (As to the credibility of the plot point that young Scotty Smalls has never even heard of Babe

Ruth—hey, let's cut David Mickey Evans a *little* slack, okay?)

Still, *The Sandlot* works quite well on several levels. Particularly amusing are the many deliberate "quotes" from earlier films, a real treat for the dedicated movie buff. Some of these are blatant, but still enjoyable. Smacking out a home run, Benny Rodriguez tears the cover off the ball in a slo-mo spoof of *The Natural* (q.v.), replete with Randy Newman–style musical orchestrations courtesy of Randy's cousin David Newman. As Benny faces down the Beast, the film shifts into an extended takeoff of director Sergio Leone's spaghetti westerns, enhanced with ever-tightening close-ups and composer Newman's lampoon of Ennio Morricone's theme from *The Good, the Bad and the Ugly*. And when the Beast pursues Benny throughout the neighborhood, we're treated to an on-target parody of a typical Disney Movie climactic chase, right down to the disrupted outdoor party and the inevitable gooey, three-tiered cake. Other movie references in *The Sandlot* are somewhat subtler but no less fun. Benny's advice to Scotty, "Stop thinking and have fun," could just have easily been said by Kevin Costner to Tim Robbins in *Bull Durham* (q.v.). And while watching the lissome Wendy Peppercorn sensuously massage her fabulous legs with suntan lotion, one highly aroused youngster remarks, "She doesn't know what she's doing!" whereupon his more worldly companion replies, "She knows"—a dialogue exchange lifted bodily from *Cool Hand Luke*.

One of the funnier cinematic in-jokes occurs when the neighborhood kids tell Scotty Smalls the legend of the Beast. As the marrow-chilling story unfolds, we dissolve to a grainy, black-and-white parody of a "world's worst director" Ed Wood, Jr. film, with gloriously awful camera angles, mismatched shots, flimsy sets, pathetic special effects, comic-book "burglars" with domino masks and striped sweaters, and badly dressed cops scratching themselves and carelessly gesturing with their weapons in the tradition of the immortal "Officer Kelton" in *Plan 9 from Outer Space.*

Though many of the baseball scenes suffer from a preponderance of cartoonish sound effects and hoked-up opticals (we *know* that Scotty is slamming out the Babe Ruth–autographed baseball; we don't really need to see a process shot of the autograph sailing towards the camera), it is to the credit of both director Evans and his young actors that the kids are completely convincing as sandlot ballplayers—not so polished as to be of championship caliber, but accomplished enough that they could pass muster in a genuine game. Though never overtly stated, it is implicit from the action and dialogue that future major leaguer Benjamin Franklin Rodriguez has generously passed along his baseball knowhow to his boyhood pals in much the same way that he gently and calmly gives advice to newcomer Scotty Smalls. The idea of a natural-born leader sharing his expertise without boast or bravado is the film's most satisfying example of wish fulfillment: Who wouldn't have wanted a good buddy like Benny while growing up—and wouldn't it be wonderful if *all* kids with special talents would behave in this modest, unassuming manner?

Benny's presence on the neighborhood team and unspoken influence on his friends lends credibility to the scene in which the sandlot kids challenge a snotty, expensively-uniformed Little League team to an impromptu game on their own turf—and win! It would not have hurt, however, had this scene had a more substantial buildup, perhaps with the Little Leaguers behaving antagonistically throughout the early portions of the film so that their comeuppance would have been even sweeter. In its present form, the scene, enjoyable though it is, comes out of nowhere and goes back whence it came.

In contrast, another isolated episode, visually underlining the deep, unconditional love of baseball that permeates the film, works superbly on its own without a buildup—or even a follow-up. During a Fourth of July block party, while Ray Charles' rendition of "America the Beautiful" is heard on the soundtrack, the kids assemble on the sandlot for their only "night game" of the year, played under the luminescent glow of a spectacular fireworks display. It is a stirring and unforgettable image, conveying the notion of baseball as "America's Game" as profoundly as Terence Mann's curtain speech in *Field of Dreams.*

While David Mickey Evans lacks Steven Spielberg's flair for directing children, the younger players transcend the stereotypical characters allotted them to give worthwhile, full-rounded performances. As Scotty Smalls, 12-year-old Tom Guiry was convincing enough to land another baseball-oriented role in 1996's *The Last Home Run* (q.v.). Fourteen-year-old Tom Vitar, a.k.a. "Benjamin Franklin Rodriguez," clearly knew his way around the ballfield, just as he would later exhibit a talent for hockey as Luis Mendoza in Disney's *Mighty Ducks* films (Tom's older brother Pablo Vitar played the adult Ben Rodriguez in *The Sandlot*'s epilogue). Thirteen-year-old Patrick Renna, cast as the chubby, redheaded Babe Ruth wannabe Hamilton Porter, graduated to adulthood as a dependable character actor. And 11-year-old Chauncey Leopardi, the bespectacled wisenheimer "Squints," later costarred in the short-lived but critically acclaimed TV sitcom *Freaks and Geeks.*

On the whole, the younger troupers were better served than the big-name adult actors. It is rather dispiriting to see the underused (in films at least) Karen Allen in the thankless role of Scotty's mom; while briefly displaying some of her old *Raiders of the Lost Ark* spunk when she implores her reclusive son to go outside and "break some windows," the fact remains that her part could have been played by any competent actress. As Scotty's stepdad, Denis Leary is undeniably impressive in his ability to play a "normal" character minus the manic edginess he usually brings to his movie work; but like Karen Allen, Leary's unique talents are sorely wasted. James Earl Jones, an old hand at making a lot out of a little, clearly relishes his short scenes as Mr. Mertle: "I play the grandfather type and it's a great thrill," noted the actor shortly after the film was completed. But while Jones makes the most of a limited opportunity, it is frustrating to discover that a considerable chunk of his intended screen time wound up on the cutting room floor.

Though its individual components are more satisfying than the sum total, *The Sandlot* emerges as an enjoyable time filler. The same, however, cannot be said for screenwriter David Mickey Evans' *next* ballpark opus, the nauseating *Ed* (q.v.).

The Scout

Ruddy-Morgan/20th Century Fox; released September 30, 1994

Executive producers: Jack Cummins, Herbert S. Nanas. Produced by Albert S. Ruddy and Andre E. Morgan. Directed by Michael Ritchie. Screenplay by Andrew Bergman and Albert Brooks & Monica Johnson, based upon the *New Yorker* article by Roger Angell. Photography: Laszlo Kovacs. Production designer: Stephen Hendrickson. Edited by Don Zimmerman and Pembroke Herring. Original Music: Bill Conti. Costume designer: Luke Reichle. Casting: Richard Pagano, Sharon Bialy, Debi Manwiller. Associate producer: Thomas Mack. Production managers: Jack Cummins, Carol Cuddy (New York), Hector Lopez (Mexico). First assistant director: Thomas Mack. Second assistant director: David Kelley. Art director: Okowita. Set decorator: Merideth Boswell. Set designers: Thomas Betts, Gina B. Cranham. Camera operator: Wayne Shepard. Sound mixer: Kim Ornitz. Script supervisor: Pamela Alch. Key makeup: Robert Ryan. Key hairstylist: Barbara Lorenz.

Supervising music editor: Jeff Carson. Supervising sound editor: Don Hall. Foley editors: Catt H. LeBaigue, Stacy Saravo. Foley artists: John B. Roesch, Hilda Hodges. Foley mixer: Mary Jo Lang. Foley recordist: Carolyn Tapp. Production coordinator: Lisa A. Becker. Special effects: Carrol Lynn Enterprises. Stunt coordinators: Juan Manuel Vilchis, Glenn Randall, Jr., Mike Russo. Mexico Unit: Production chief, Efren Flores; First assistant director, Rene Villareal; Art director, Enrique Echeverria; Set decorator, Fernando Solorio; Script supervisor, Ana Rebuelta. New York Unit: Second assistant director, Joe Burns; Set decorator, Kevin McCarthy. Yankee Technical Advisors: Tim Hassett, Kirk Randazzo, Bob Wilkinson, John Franzone. Boss Films Unit: Visual effects supervisor, Neil Krepela; Visual effects producer, Jenny Fulle; Digital effects supervisor, Jim Rygiel; Digital imaging supervisor, Ariel Shaw; Digital editor, Scott Keppler; Digital matte supervisor, Michael Moen; Model shop supervisor, Dave Jones; Model maker, Monty Shook; Scoreboard animation, Karen Johnson Productions. Scoreboard fireworks: WCPO-TV. Main title design: Seiniger Advertising. Titles and opticals: Pacific Title. Panavision, Color by DeLuxe; Panavision. 101 minutes; Dolby Digital Stereo sound. Rated PG-13.

Cast: Albert Brooks (Al Percolo); Brendan Fraser (Steve Nebraska); Dianne Wiest (Doctor Aaron); Anne Twomey (Jennifer); Lane Smith (Ron Wilson); Michael Rapaport (Tommy Lacy); Tony Bennett (Himself); George M. Steinbrenner, III (Himself); Bob Costas (Himself); Barry Shabaka Henley (McDermott); John Capodice (Caruso); Garfield! (Stan); Louis Giovannetti (World Series Catcher); Stephen Demek (Yankee Catcher); Ralph Drischell (Charlie); Brett Rickaby (George's Assistant); Jack Rader (Mr. Lacy); Marcia Rodd (Mrs. Lacy); Steve Eastin (Clubhouse Manager); Lee Weaver (Ben); John LaMotta (Elevator Guard); Luis Cortes (Mexican Desk Clerk); Chuck Waters (Photographer); Antonio Lewis Todd (Yankee Player); Abel Woolridge (Nachito Fan); Gabriel Pingarron (Mexican Umpire); Lolo Navarro (Widow in Stands); Frank Slaten (College Umpire); Charlie Stavola (Umpire); Jimmy Raitt (World Series Umpire); Larry Loonin (Radar Gun Man); Harsh Nayyar (Cab Driver); J. K. Simmons (Assistant Coach); Bruce Wright, Steven M. Porter, Josh Clark, Jordan Lage, Chris Willman (Reporters); John

Sterling, Bobby Murcer, Keith Hernandez, Bret Saberhagen, Steve Garvey, Roy Firestone, Tim McCarver, Bob Tewksbury, Ozzie Smith, John Roland, Rosanna Scotto, Carl White, Tom Kelly, Ken Brett, Reggie Smith, Bob Sheppard, Phil Pote (Themselves). Appearing in footage from *King Kong*: Robert Armstrong (Carl Denham).

Al Percolo, peripatetic veteran scout for the New York Yankees, has not had much luck of late in recruiting hot prospects. Percolo's latest catch, a small-town high school "phenom" named Tommy Lacy, makes his Big League debut by locking himself in the clubhouse, upchucking on the pitcher's mound and finally bolting out of the stadium, never to be seen again. As punishment for all the "head cases" whom Percolo has dredged up from the hinterlands, his boss Ron Wilson exiles Al to the parched plains of South Central Mexico. "Why don't you just fire me?" asks the plaintive Percolo. "I thought of that," replies Wilson sharkishly, "but I like this better." While trolling Mexican ballparks where chickens are exchanged for bleacher seats and goats graze in the outfield, Percolo stumbles upon the greatest baseball player since Babe Ruth: Steve Nebraska, a transplanted American whose home runs scale astronomical heights and whose 110-mph pitches invariably flatten both the catcher and the umpire! Though he can't quite shake the premonition that the affable but mercurial Steve may yet turn out to be another of the off-balance wackos with whom he has recently been saddled, Al personally signs the kid up and brings him to the Big Apple, where, after an intense bidding war, Steve lands a record $55 million contract with the Yankees. Unfortunately, Al's worst fears are realized when, during his first press conference, a ticked-off Steve grabs a photographer and lifts the poor guy over his head. More disturbing is the fact that Steve, who was physically and psychologically abused by his father as a child, has

neurotically latched onto Al as a father substitute—and refuses to let go. Ordered to get written certification that Steve is *not* the loose cannon that he appears to be, Percolo enlists the aid of a lady psychiatrist whose main "qualification," so far as Al is concerned, is that her name is H. Aaron. Meanwhile, Steve's nervousness over making his Major League debut has been temporarily mollified by the agreement that he will not have to pitch for the Yankees until the next season—or until the Yanks get into the World Series, a contingency that seems as likely as Hell freezing over. But when the team actually makes it as far as the Pennant race, Steve's trepidations deepen into stark, raw terror—after all, Yankees owner George Steinbrenner has promised the media that Steve Nebraska will throw out the first pitch of the Series!

This one started out as "Scout," an essay written in June of 1976 for *The New Yorker* by that magazine's longtime fiction editor Roger Angell. Acclaimed by his devotees and disciples as the world's finest baseball writer, Angell possessed the rare gift of conveying his love for the Game while maintaining the objective detachment of a veteran reporter. In "Scout," Angell summed up the subject of the piece with clarity, honesty and eloquence: "Nobody knows his name, but everybody recognizes him, for he is a figure of profound, almost occult knowledge, with a great power over the future. He is a baseball scout."

The essay focused upon Ray Scarbrough, regional and special-assignment scout for the California Angels. Famous amongst his peers for having helped assemble the championship Baltimore Orioles teams of the 1960s and 1970s, Scarbrough was chronicled by Angell as he traveled throughout the country—Ohio, Michigan, Virginia and New Jersey—checking out high-school players who might have potential as members of the Angels organization. As a former pitcher for the Southern Class

A and B Minors, and for the old Washington Senators from 1943 to 1953, Scarbrough knew the business of baseball frontward and backward, applying a keen clinical mind to his player assessments and refusing to let any outside distractions— bad weather, poor roads, inadequate hotel accommodations—sway him from his appointed duties. Like Scarbrough himself, "Scout" concentrated on the nuts and bolts of the scouting business, but also found time to appreciate the camaraderie and friendly rivalry amongst his fellow scouts and the surging delight of locating a likely prospect. As competitive as the next man, Scarbrough often found himself trying to persuade a likely baseball star to postpone college in favor of an Angels tryout, but also scrupulously avoided bringing promising players along *too* fast, lest they burn out before reaching their full potential. On a more cerebral level, the essay detailed the mysterious, sometimes inexplicable methods used by professional scouts to judge their prospects; the image one comes away with is of a group of inscrutably silent, well-tailored gentlemen conspicuously seated amongst the cheering fans in the bleachers, diligently scribbling away on notepads and enigmatically nodding their heads.

Reading "Scout" some 25 years after its publication, one finds a picaresque character study that is warm, witty, and wise— but not in the least funny or even mildly amusing, intentionally or otherwise. With this in mind, one could describe screenwriter Andrew Bergman as a scout himself, capable of divining within Angell's article the potential for an uproarious comedy feature film where the average person would find nothing to laugh at whatsoever. A former academician whose history of Depression-era films, *We're in the Money* (1972), is still required reading in many a college cinema course, Bergman had been a novelist and a playwright before making his Hollywood breakthrough as author of the origi-

nal story for the Mel Brooks comedy smash *Blazing Saddles* (1974). Fashioning a screenplay from Angell's "Scout," Bergman was able to pitch it to Warner Bros. as a movie vehicle for Peter Falk, with Howard Zieff, who'd recently graduated from award-winning TV commercials to the critic's-darling feature films *Hearts of the West* (1975) and *Slither* (1976), lined up as director. For various reasons, chief among them the fact that Hollywood's studio bigwigs were still antsy about the salability of baseball pictures, despite the success of *The Bad News Bears* (1976), Andrew Bergman's *The Scout* was shelved; Bergman went on to work with Peter Falk on the popular screwball comedy *The In-Laws*, while Howard Zieff eventually made his sports-flick debut as director of the boxing comedy *The Main Event* (1979).

The spectacular success of *A League of Their Own* in the Summer of 1992 emboldened Alan Bergman to pull *The Scout* out of mothballs and place it into consideration once more. This time around, the property caught the eye of comedian Albert Brooks and his longtime writing partner Monica Johnson, whose prior collaborations included such gut-busters as *Real Life* (1979), *Modern Romance* (1981) and *Lost in America* (1985). Brooks quickly perceived that Bergman's protagonist Al Percolo would afford him another golden opportunity to indulge in the manic desperation that he'd established as his comic stock in trade. To insure that the film would emerge as a suitable Albert Brooks vehicle, Bergman's screenplay was extensively revised and updated by Brooks and Johnson.

Ruddy-Morgan Productions and 20th Century–Fox gave the green light to *The Scout* in late 1993. Reportedly, both production firms were attracted to the project because they had long wanted to make a film based on the career of LA Dodgers pitcher Fernando Valenzuela, who, after being recruited from Mexican baseball at age 20 in 1980, went on to win his first ten

Major League games in row, thereby becoming the first rookie to earn the Cy Young Award. While there was never an official Fernando Valenzuela biopic, certain aspects of his personality were adopted by various Fernando wannabes on film, notably his early dependence upon an English-Spanish interpreter when granting interviews or taking instructions on the field. The talented rookie in *The Scout* had no trouble speaking English, but, like Valenzuela, he emerged from the comparative obscurity of the Mexican leagues to bowl over fans and colleagues alike with his phenomenal pitching skills. (One can only hope that Valenzuela never endured the same demoralizing psychological problems suffered by the film's Steve Nebraska!)

Though Albert Brooks preferred to direct his starring film projects, this time he entrusted that responsibility to someone else. *The Scout*'s intended director, Howard Zieff, had worked harmoniously with Brooks on *Private Benjamin* (1981) and *Unfaithfully Yours* (1983), but was already committed to the 1994 sequel to his 1991 success *My Girl*. Producers Albert Ruddy and Andre E. Morgan approached Michael Ritchie, who had demonstrated his facility for using organized sports as a

The picture tells the story: Albert Brooks (on his knees) as Al Percolo and Brendan Fraser as Steve Nebraska in *The Scout*.

springboard for contemporary social satire in the aforementioned *The Bad News Bears*, as well as *Semi-Tough* (1977) and *Wildcats* (1986). While Ritchie had collaborated with screenwriter Andrew Bergman on *Fletch* (1985), he signed onto *The Scout* on the strength of the Albert Brooks-Monica Johnson rewrite.

In preparation for his portrayal of Al Percolo, Brooks worked extensively with the film's technical advisor, real-life Major League scout Phil Pote (who also appears on screen, appropriately cast as one of Al's rival scouts). A battle-scarred veteran of three decades in the field, Pote later commented, "I was impressed by Albert and [Michael Ritchie]'s total commitment to learning about scouting and their attention to detail in getting inside this world which is a mix of camaraderie and one-upsmanship. Albert was very believable, and he got the scouting look and persona down very quickly." Michael Ritchie echoed these sentiments, noting, "Albert threw himself into the part of the scout with enormous concern for authenticity. He gained over twenty pounds so he would have a gut that hung over his polyester pants just like any real scout." (I'll bet Phil Pote really appreciated *that*!) As to finding a hook upon which to hinge his characterization, Brooks said "I think one of the keys is the hat. It seems to be a tradition. You can look in the stands, which are filled with thousands of people, but the scouts will always sit together and always wear these hats." Indeed, there are very few scenes in *The Scout* in which Brooks is seen *without* a hat—which may be why the film contained no shower sequences.

Surprisingly, the film was shot more or less in sequence, starting with the Mexican scenes. Principal photography began in January of 1994 in the small Veracruz town of Zempoala, using a virtually all–Mexican production crew. Accompanying the unit to Mexico was Albert Brooks' 26-year-old costar Brendan Fraser, who, having played the thawed-out caveman title character in the 1992 comedy *Encino Man*, was the perfect choice to bring the proper balance of raw ego, naïveté, casual sex appeal, gaucherie and smoldering hostility to the similar fish-out-of-water role of Steve Nebraska.

Two weeks into production, the unit moved to Los Angeles, which was just digging itself out of a severe earthquake, though no evidence of the rubble appeared on-screen. Most of the New York interior scenes were filmed here, including the Empire Room nightclub sequence spotlighting singer Tony Bennett (then cashing in on his renewed popularity vis-à-vis his appearances on the MTV cable network). Finally, production moved to New York, where the Yankee Stadium scenes were to be filmed. Assuming a prominent place in the proceedings at this juncture was real-life Yankees owner George M. Steinbrenner, III, whose permission had to be secured to film within the stadium. Almost immediately, Steinbrenner went into his customary short-fuse routine, chewing out the crew for "ruining" his ballpark and trampling down the outfield. If the 20th Century–Fox publicity boys are to be believed, Steinbrenner immediately shut his pie-hole and became docile as a lamb when he began shooting his scenes as "himself."

The finished film version of *The Scout* had about as much to do with the original Roger Angell article as the Battle of Thermopylae. Angell's protagonist Ray Scarbrough and the film's leading character Al Percolo are both Major League scouts, beating the bushes for new baseball talent—and that is where the resemblance ends. Unlike the stoic and philosophical Scarbrough, Percolo is *always* grousing about the difficulties and discomforts attending his job. Whereas Scarbrough's fellow scouts were a generally convivial bunch despite all the competition, Percolo's mean-spirited rivals cannot wait to pounce upon and laugh derisively at his failures. And while Scarbrough is a success in his chosen profession, Percolo is on the verge of being sacked for a string of disastrous selections. Steve Nebraska is more than the Resurrection of Ruth; he is Al Percolo's last chance.

The vast difference between Roger Angell's vision and Albert Brooks' interpretation can best be demonstrated by the early scene in which Al Percolo sweats bullets in persuading tanktown phenom Tommy Lacy to sign with the Yankees. Though Angell's Ray Scarbrough is not above trying to spirit good players away from college teams and into the pros, he remains completely ethical, even backing off whenever he realizes that one of his prospects would be better off completing his academic career. But in the movie version of *The Scout*, the words "ethics" and "Al Percolo" are oxymoronic. Forewarned by the other scouts that Tommy Lacy not only intends to go to college but is also extremely religious, Al all too emphatically agrees that Tommy is off limits—only to corner the kid in a school parking lot thirty seconds later. Inviting himself to the Lacy home, he works overtime ingratiating himself with the boy's devoutly Catholic parents, wearing an ostentatious cross around his neck, complimenting them for the picture of Jesus on their wall ("Excellent likeness!"), even claiming that Yankee legend Mickey Mantle had a sister who was a nun—"Sister Micki Elizabeth Mantle." In his efforts to discourage Mr. and Mrs. Lacy from forcing their son into college, Al spins a masterful web of deceit, promising that the Yankees will provide the 15-year-old Tommy with a tutor, just as they'd done for Babe Ruth and Lou Gehrig. When Mrs. Lacy recalls that Gehrig died of a horrible disease, Al is quick to point out that Lou didn't catch his ailment from playing baseball: "He got it in college."

Not that there's anything wrong in transforming Roger Angell's soft-edged, character-driven prose into a jagged, gag-driven Albert Brooks vehicle. In fact, *The Scout* is at its most screamingly funny during the early Tommy Lacy scenes, and also

The Scout: Concealing his nervousness, Yankees scout Al Percolo (Albert Brooks, right) inroduces his latest discovery, the deceptively benign Steve Nebraska (Brendan Fraser).

during Al Percolo's *Apocalypse Now*–like odyssey into the bowels of rural Mexico. And while Brooks' slant on "Scout" is far afield of the spirit and tone of the original, it was not too distantly removed from Roger Angell's own trenchant refusal to sentimentalize the game of baseball. In an interview with Salon.com's Steve Kettman, Angell remarked: "The stuff about the connection between baseball and American life, the *Field of Dreams* thing, gives me a pain. I hated that movie. It's mostly fake…. In *Field of Dreams* there's a line at the end that says the game of baseball was good when America was good, and they're talking about the time of the biggest race riots in the country and Prohibition. What is that? That dreaminess, I really hated that."

These jaundiced comments are well in keeping with the overall cinematic output of Albert Brooks, who, despite such notable exceptions as his performances in *Broadcast News* (1985) and *Mother* (1996), may well be the most heartless comedian working in Hollywood today. Not "heartless" in the sense of cruel or nasty, but in the fact that his abrasively neurotic screen persona seems to work best when he completely eschews sentimentality and warmth, neither eliciting nor expecting the audience's sympathy. Grasping, conniving, wheedling, always out for Number One, the typical Albert Brooks character encourages the audience to laugh at his failures and comeuppance, not exult in his triumphs or changes of heart.

Had *The Scout* stuck to the anecdotal approach adopted in Roger Angell's article, with Al Percolo bouncing from town to town, rookie to rookie, the film's unsympathetic, slightly nasty edge might have registered better. But once Steve Nebraska is introduced to the narrative, it becomes imperative that we "pull" for Al, or Steve, or preferably both. But we can't. From what we've seen of Al Percolo, and what we are going to see as he tries to flimflam a scrupu-

lously honest psychiatrist into unequivocally endorsing Steve's Major League baseball career—which may well end up doing irreparable damage to the boy's psyche—there is no compelling reason for us to care what is going to become of him. Even in the climax, where a chastened Al appears to have seen the light and agrees to stop pressuring Steve into performing on the ballfield, there is the lingering suspicion that this epiphany is just another scam, and that Al will soon be off and running again, espousing phony religiosity in someone else's dining room or trying to pull the wool over the eyes of yet another therapist.

Nor is Steve Nebraska a satisfactory candidate for audience empathy, despite his miserable childhood and his shameless exploitation at the hands of Al Percolo. Brendan Fraser does a good job in underlining the broadly comic elements in Steve's makeup—his complete and utter lack of the simplest social graces, his ingenious acceptance of the fact that strange women keep giving him their phone numbers, his insatiable appetite for junk food, his obsessive fascination with scented magazine ads, and his vociferous habit of singing along with records, TV variety shows, Musak and live nightclub entertainers. Unfortunately, Fraser does *so* good a job that when time comes for him to show his darker side—his surly reluctance to discuss his past, his impulsively violent outbursts, his desperate and life-threatening efforts to avoid humiliation at Yankee Stadium—the audience, conditioned to laugh at him, continues to laugh even when the story dictates that Steve is sorely in need of the viewer's concern and support.

Judging from the slightly lampoonish handling of the "poignant" scenes—Steve's asinine interpretations of the sensory-association pictures shown him by psychiatrist Dr. Aaron (a drawing of a sobbing woman rushing from a room is, to Steve, a "sneezing lady standing at the door"), Al's

Harry Ritz–like double take when Steve begins having a nightmare about his brutish father, the climactic quibbling over contractual percentages as Al tries to coax Steve off the roof of Yankee Stadium—it may have been the intention of Brooks and director Michael Ritchie all along to undercut the pathos with laughter and discourage the viewer from becoming too emotionally involved in the story. If so, it was a courageous experiment, and sometimes it tentatively pays off; but in the final analysis, the experiment is a failure.

Within the framework of the film, only one character comes across as completely three-dimensional and worthy of the audience's respect: Dr. H. Aaron, played by Oscar winner Dianne Weist. Hesitantly agreeing to psychoanalyze Steve despite her perception that Al is striving to manipulate her into issuing a clean bill of health, genuinely worried about Steve's future well-being and advising him not to play baseball even though she herself is an enormous Yankees fan, unwilling to compromise her professional integrity even if it means making 99.9 percent of the New York population unhappy, Dr. Aaron is the only person in the picture who has no ulterior motive, hidden agenda or axes to grind. As such, the audience is totally on her side even when we *should* be rooting for Al Percolo to knock her off her ethical high horse so that he will be able to keep his job. On a pure performance level, Dianne Weist is also the only member of the cast who has stumbled onto the fact that, when playing comedy, sometimes less is more. Superbly capturing the soft, sterile, noncommittal cheeriness of the professional psychiatrist, conveying her thoughts with subtle nuances of expression while others are mugging to the heavens, the actress earns her laughs by playing for truth rather than the quick and easy "boffo."

In the film's pressbook, director Michael Ritchie stated emphatically that *The Scout* was not a sports film, adding, "I've directed a number of films that involved sports, and with each one it was suggested that I say that they were not sports films. Well, I can tell you now, they *were* sports films. But *The Scout* really isn't. This is a relationship story. Although the film's final is set at the World Series, the ultimate victory is a very personal one for the scout and the kid." Costar Brendan Fraser likewise refused to classify the film as a baseball picture pure and simple: "Baseball is the vehicle that brings Steve and Al together." This could explain why, despite Ritchie's adroit handling of the baseball highlights in his previous *The Bad News Bears*, the ballpark sequences in *The Scout* are so skimpy and unfulfilling. Faced with the challenge of convincing the viewer that Steve Nebraska is the most awesome all-around baseball player of the past half century, Ritchie realized that no amount of genuine ballplaying on Brendan Fraser's part could come close to what was expected of him. Thus the director literally does Fraser's work for him, creating the illusion of Steve's 100-mph-plus pitches by rapidly swish-panning from the pitcher's mound to home plate, then showing both catcher and umpire knocked off their pins by the velocity of the pitch. This directorial trickery is extremely effective the first time we see it; unfortunately, it is not the *last* time we see it, and familiarity quickly breeds contempt. Likewise, there are only so many ways that one can film a home run flying over the heads of a cheering crowd—and once Ritchie hits upon what he considers the best way, he falls hopelessly in love with it, an affection not necessarily shared by the viewer.

Beyond this, the most disappointing element of *The Scout* is the script's recurring *King Kong* analogy. Even before the credits have faded, we see Al Percolo, ever in search of new blood for the Yankees, sitting alone in a Midwestern motel room, preparing a spaghetti dinner on the elaborate hot plate he keeps in his attaché case (one of the film's nicer touches, by the way). Switching on the TV, he finds to his delight that his all-time favorite fantasy film, *King Kong*, is playing. As he becomes engrossed in the film, he begins reciting the lines along with the actors, and by the time Robert Armstrong as Carl Denham is seen introducing the captive Kong to a dumbstruck New York City theater audience, Al says aloud what we have been suspecting for several minutes: He'd give anything to enthrall the blasé Yankee fans by returning to Manhattan with his *own* King Kong—not a 50-foot ape, but a human "Eighth Wonder of the World" with pitching and hitting skills beyond the ken of any ordinary mortal. And at this point we are pretty certain that the *King Kong* comparisons are going to continue to be played for all they're worth.

Part of the fun in watching a modern-day adaptation of William Shakespeare—say, *Ten Things I Hate About You* (1999) or *O* (2001)—is not so much guessing how Shakespeare's iambic pentameter will be translated to contemporaneous dialogue, but how the Bard's most famous scenes will be restaged and reshaped to suit the purposes of the film. The same can be said of the *King Kong* allusions in *The Scout*, and we must admit that these were pulled off with considerable ingenuity. Like the mighty Kong, Steve Nebraska is regarded as a god in his adopted Mexican town; he is involuntarily brought to New York, where he is fêted as the biggest show in town; and he freaks out when flashbulbs pop in his face at the press conference, prompting him to react by tossing bodies about. Finally, when Steve feels that the world is closing in on him during the first World Series game, he seeks out "fresh air" by climbing to the loftiest height in his immediate vicinity—not the Empire State Building, but the roof of Yankee Stadium, where he is besieged not by World War One fighter planes but by a police helicopter.

Though none too witty, the *King Kong* parallels do manage to score some solid "shock of recognition" belly laughs. And had scriptwriters Albert Brooks and Monica Johnson left well enough alone, everything would have been hunky-dory. Instead, the entire *Kong* running gag is appallingly dumbed down by having Al Percolo persistently inform us of what we've just seen: "I found Kong!" "I took this Kong thing too far!" and other such spell-it-out exclamations. What makes this belaboring of the obvious all the more galling is that, once upon a time, there was a monologist named Albert Brooks who took great pleasure in skewering people who underestimated the intelligence of the American Public (who could forget the comedian's sidesplitting "Talking Mime" routine?). In *The Scout*, Brooks has apparently arrived at the conclusion that we clods in the audience are incapable of grasping the intricacies of his humor unless we are slavishly and repeatedly spoon-fed the jokes.

Still, the laughs *are* there, and in abundant supply throughout most of the film. And though the baseball sequences leave the viewer wanting—what's the point of being told that Steve Nebraska has pitched 81 strikes, 27 strikeouts and a perfect game if we barely see anything?—the film makes intelligent use of the genuine sports (and other) celebrities who appear as themselves on screen. Ballplayers Keith Hernandez and Brett Saberhagen are seen during Steve's unveiling before the assembled ballclub owners at Yankee Stadium, genially ribbing themselves by marching up to the redoubtable Al Percolo and demanding to be paid in advance for deigning to appear. This gag reaches a perfect climax during the Empire Room sequence in which singer Tony Bennett invites the audience to put their hands together for visiting luminary Steve Nebraska—at which point Al turns to his companion, Yankees executive secretary Jennifer (Anne Twomey), to confirm that Bennett has already received *his* payoff. In that same scene, Tony Bennett bemusedly walks off stage when the clueless Steve begins leading the assemblage in a singalong to "I left my heart in San Francisco"—a gag that has *its* punchline when Bennett shows up to sing the National Anthem at the first Series game, and without losing his jaunty stride or dropping his beaming smile he walks past Steve and threateningly mutters, "You gonna sing *this* one for me too?" The play-by-play commentary of such authentic sportscasters as Bob Costas and Roy Firestone is consistently amusing without resorting to the acidulous verbal barbs of Bob Uecker in the *Major League* films; the biggest laughs are generated when Costas and his colleagues struggle manfully to offer logical explanations for the outrageously embarrassing ballpark behavior of Al's various protégés.

Also used to excellent advantage are TV personalities John Sterling, Tim Mc-Carver and Rosanna Scotto, and sports stars Bobby Murcer, Steve Garvey, Bob Tewksbury, Ozzie Smith, Reggie Smith and Ken Brett. But the real "acting" honors go to Yankees owner George Steinbrenner, who, in a stroke of casting genius, has been assigned the colorful role of Yankees owner George Steinbrenner. It is he who utters the single funniest line in the picture. Celebrating the fact that the fans and the media are convinced that Steve Nebraska's surprise appearance on the stadium roof, and the boy's subsequent helicopter rescue, are all part of a brilliant publicity stunt masterminded by him, Steinbrenner shares his boyish enthusiasm with the assistant standing beside him. And when that assistant has the temerity to say, "I wonder whose idea it really was?" George cuts him dead with a stiletto-like stare and snarls, "It's mine *now*, stupid."

Critical response to *The Scout*'s September 1994 release was split right down the middle: Those who loved it did so fervently, and those who hated it did so with equal fervor. The positive reviews cited the fact that the film avoided the standard 1990s movie cliché of the losing ballclub being saved at the very last minute, and also found its lack of a sappy romantic subplot refreshing. Richard Schickel of *Time* magazine called the film "the best baseball comedy ever," and was especially enchanted by all that *King Kong* business. Hal Hinson of the *Washington Post*, noting that the film "resembles less the realistic jock style of *Bull Durham* or *Pride of the Yankees* than the fantastical tradition of *Field of Dreams* and *The Natural*," pegged the picture as "a genuine—and immensely enjoyable—curiosity." On the other hand, Roger Ebert of the *Chicago Sun Times* carped that, "Rarely does a movie start high and go downhill so fast. It's as if the filmmakers progressively lost their nerve with every additional scene." Internet reviewer James Bernadelli was even less impressed than Ebert: "It's been a long time since there's been a good baseball movie. *The Scout* makes you wonder if there's ever going to be one again."

Among the better bits of business in *The Scout* is the wave of mocking laughter which greets the Yankees executive staff when, during Steve Nebraska's first press conference, it is suggested that Steve be activated the moment the Yankees appear in the World Series—a notion that was always good for a few derisive snickers in the days before Joe Torre turned dreams into reality. As it happened, the laugh was on *every* team in Major League baseball; a long and acrimonious strike caused the cancellation of the 1994 World Series which is so lovingly hypothesized at the end of the film. It may have been the ill feelings harbored towards baseball by thousands upon thousands of disgruntled fans that caused moviegoers to stay away from *The Scout* in droves; the film grossed a pathetic $2,667,163, effectively putting the whammy on any future baseball films for nearly two years.

61*

Face Productions/61* Productions/HBO Pictures; first telecast April 28, 2001

Executive producers: Billy Crystal, Ross Greenberg. Produced by Robert F. Colesberry, Charles J. Lindsay, Nellie Nugiel and Samantha Sprecher. Directed by Billy Crystal. Written by Hank Steinberg. Photography: Haskell Wexler. Edited by Michael Jablow. Production design: Rusty Smith. Original music: Marc Shaiman. Casting: Mali Finn, Bradley Morris. Unit production manager: Robert F. Colesberry. Art directors: Denise Hudson, Rolfe Bergeman. First assistant director: Alan Edmisten. Second assistant director: Lisa J. Bloch. Costume designer: Dan Moore. Script supervisor: Joanie Blum. Makeup dept. head: Peter Montagna. Set dresser: Damian "Rocky" Polito. Sound recordist: Jeff Wexler. Sound designer: Scott M. Silvey. Music re-recording mixer: Gary Coppola. Storyboard artist: Chris Buchinsky. Special effects coordinator: Paul Lombardi. Special effects supervisors: Scott Blackwell, David Peterson. Baseball coaches: Reggie Smith, R. J. Smith, Paul Gallo. Consultants: Marlyn Mantle; Patricia Maris; David and Mickey Mantle, Jr.; Kein, Richard, Sandra and Roger Maris, Jr.; Yogi Berra; Whitey Ford; Bob Cerv; Andy Strassberg; Marty Appel; Jim Ogle; Julie Isaacson. Visual effects: Centropolis Effects; Aaron Dem, head of production. Matte painter: Laurent Pen-Mimoun. Color. 129 minutes; sound. Rated PG-13.

Cast: Barry Pepper (Roger Maris); Thomas Jane (Mickey Mantle); Richard Masur (Milt Kahn); Bruce McGill (Ralph Houk); Chris Bauer (Bob Cerv); Christopher McDonald (Mel Allen); Jennifer Crystal Foley (Pat Maris, 1961); Bob Gunton (Dan Topping); Donald Moffat (Ford Frick); Joe Grifasi (Phil Rizzuto); Peter Jacobson (Artie Green); Robert Joy (Bob Fischell); Michael Nouri (Joe DiMaggio); Seymour Cassel (Sam Simon); Anthony Michael Hall (Whitey Ford); Rene Taylor (Mrs. Claire Ruth); Pat Crowley (Pat Maris, 1998); Dominic Lombardozzi (Moose Skowron); Bobby Hosea (Elston Howard); Paul Borghese (Yogi Berra); Dane Northcuff (Randy Maris, 1998); Scott Connell (Roger Maris, Jr., 1998); Rebecca Klinger (Susan Maris, 1998); Joe Burk (McGwire's 60th and 62nd Home Run Announcer); Jon Miller (McGwire's 61st Home Run Announcer); Cameryn and Brynne McNab (Susan Maris, 1961); Richard Brown (Yankee Bat Boy); Bob Sheppard (Yankee Stadium Announcer); Shannah Laumeister (Pretty Young Woman); Randall Godwin (Fan No. 1); David Courtney (Tiger Stadium Announcer); Shiva Rose (Toot's Girl); Mitchell Edmonds (Hotel Manager); Scott Waara (Gus Mauch); Robert Hunter, Jr. (Angry Fan); Valentin Olteanu (Yelling Senators Fan); David Whalen (Anchorman); Dell Young (Writer No. 1); Connor Trineer (Writer No. 2); Mathew Kaminsky (Raytown Reporter No. 1); Kevin Kendrick (Raytown Reporter No. 2); Kevin Kelly (Raytown Reporter No. 3); J. D. Cullum (Gabe Pressman); Sean Marquette (Young Boy); Maile Flanagan (Housewife); David Dionisio (Reporter No. 2); Donald Elson (Older Man); Juliet Naulin (School Girl); J. R. Remick (Ball Hound); Reuben Yabuku (Roger Heckler); Robert Costanzo (Toots Shor); K. J. Steinberg (Picture Girl); Jerome Zieminski (Umpire); Tim Hammer (Angry Umpire); E. E. Bell ("The Babe"); Jeffrey Herman (Chair Umpire); Kiff Vanden Heuvel (Detroit Fan No. 2); Haynes Brooke (Bartender, Detroit); Scott Williamson (TV Reporter); Michael Gallagher (Frick's Assistant); Conor O'Farrell (Luman Harris); Dick Stilwell (Kansas City TV Station Manager); Mike Carlucci (Memorial Stadium Announcer); Al Kaplon (Memorial Stadium Umpire); Tom Candiotti (Hoyt Wilhelm); Andy Strassberg (61st Home Run Fan); James Intveld (Sal Durante); D. C. Ford (Bobby Hosea's stand-in); Chris Marquette (Angry Fan), Todd Bacile (Heckling Fan); Richard Alan Brown (Fred Bangis); Richard Goteri (Brooklyn); Gaston Wurth (Milt Pappas).

The year is 1961: John F. Kennedy is in the White House, *Gunsmoke* is TV's top-rated program, Alan Shepard is about to be the first American astronaut launched into space, and the New York Yankees' star slugger Mickey Mantle is back in uniform after a disappointing previous season. On Opening Day, however, all attention is focused on a newcomer to the Yanks: former Kansas City Athletics right fielder Roger Maris, who has just been voted 1960's Most Valuable Player. Ever in search of a hot scoop, the New York newspapers fabricate a feud between Mantle and Maris. Though the two men are actually fast friends, they could not be any more dissimilar if they'd been from different species: The swaggering, freewheeling Mickey is a boozer, carouser and shameless philanderer, while the taciturn, businesslike Maris is a stalwart family man who abstains from all vices except tobacco. As the season wears on, the two men find themselves locked in what the media trumpets as a "home run battle"—in fact, both Mantle and Maris are within hailing distance of beating the 60-homer record set by the immortal Babe Ruth. It is obvious that both press and public would prefer the more colorful, gregarious Mantle to break that record than the sober, tightlipped Maris, if for no other reason than Mickey has been a Yankee for eleven years, while Roger is regarded as a rank outsider and pretender to the throne. Though both men feign indifference to their rendezvous with destiny, both secretly yearn to topple "That Fat F__k" Ruth from his pedestal. Meanwhile, baseball commissioner Ford Frick, a longtime friend and worshipper of the late Babe, is determined that the record will remain sacrosanct. To that end, Frick declares on July 17 that, since the 1961 season will be eight games longer than the 1927 season in which Ruth knocked out the Celebrated Sixty, a "separate record" will be established should either Mickey or Roger hit that 61st home run any later than the 154th game of the season—and that the number 61 will forever be asterisked in the record books. Even with this proviso, pressure mounts on both Yankee batters, with Mickey drinking and womanizing more than ever. Sensing that the rest of the team looks up to the Mick, Roger takes it upon himself to keep Mantle in top condition throughout the season, going so far as to gently insist that Mickey move in with Roger and fellow Yankee Bob Cerv in a modest Queens apartment, where Mantle's behavior—and liquor intake—can be more closely monitored. But it is not

Mickey who needs the T.L.C.; instead, it is Roger who nearly goes off the deep end, taunted and tormented by unsympathetic reporters and booing fans who don't want him to either pass up Ruth or show up Mantle. Subjected to hate mail, death threats and physical assaults from thuggish ballpark patrons, the young Maris begins losing his hair and breaking out in ugly rashes. By now Roger's closest friend, Mickey advises him to ignore the shabby treatment, pointing out that he too was raked over the coals during his early years with the Yankees for such "crimes" as daring to challenge the supremacy of Joe DiMaggio; he also continues to proclaim that beating Ruth is not as crucial as winning the Pennant. But when Mantle insists upon continuing to play after a serious forearm injury, everyone realizes just how important this season is to him. Once Mickey reluctantly pulls himself out of the race after 54 homers, public hostility towards Maris intensifies—everywhere but within the New York team itself, where the "boys" are solidly united behind Roger. On the occasion of that fateful 154th game, symbolically held in Babe Ruth's home town of Baltimore, a capacity crowd watches as Maris, 58 homers to his credit, steps up to the plate. Determined to show his detractors that he can't be destroyed by their vitriol, Roger manages to knock out a 59th four-bagger; but any hopes that this will be the night that Maris will bypass Ruth are dashed when Roger fails to score either #60 or #61 off Baltimore's notorious knuckleballer Hoyt Wilhelm. Though eight more games remain in the season, the song is over so far as Ford Frick and most of the public is concerned. On October 1, 1961, the day Maris finally hits number sixty-one, there are only 23,000 people in the stands at Yankee Stadium. True, the fickle fans, and the members of both ballteams, cheer Maris madly, as does Mickey Mantle from the vantage point of his hospital bed. But thanks to the boardroom maneuvering of

Ford Frick, the asterisk would not be removed from Roger's "61" until new commissioner Fay Vincent elected to right past wrongs on September 3, 1991—by which time Roger Maris had been dead for over six years.

All too often nowadays, producers of baseball films, apparently worried that some demographic group or other will complain about being slighted, feel the need to issue public statements along the lines of "This isn't *really* a baseball film." No such obfuscation was practiced by comedian/ producer/director Billy Crystal regarding 61*. To say that this made-for-cable film was a labor of love for Crystal may well turn out to be the understatement of the 21st century.

Like Joe E. Brown before him, Crystal was just as comfortable on the baseball field as he was before the cameras, regularly playing in charity games for the Hollywood All-Stars and habitually shoehorning baseball references into his films (notably *City Slickers*) and his standup comedy routines (remember Billy's impression of Yul Brynner as Babe Ruth, promising to hit "One-two-three home runs, et cetera, et cetera, et cetera?"). Having forged a strong friendship with his long-retired childhood idol Mickey Mantle (the two met in 1982 while appearing as guest stars on Dinah Shore's syndicated talk show), Crystal wanted to produce, write and possibly direct a film about the fateful 1961 season from Mickey's point of view. Interviewed by sports novelist Tim Wendel, Crystal said, "I joke that I've been in preproduction for [61*] since 1956 when I first walked into Yankee Stadium as a kid. The more I worked on the script the more I felt it was going to be hard for me to give it to somebody. So, I carved out the time and decided I was going to do it myself."

The disappointing financial returns of such recent sports biopics as *The Babe* and *Cobb* rendered the Mantle project unsaleable, at least as a theatrical feature. Practically the only person who wanted to see the film come to fruition was Mickey Mantle himself; he even agreed that such a film would have to include his darker side—booze, broads and all—so long as his baseball accomplishments remained in the forefront. After Mantle's death in 1995, one would think that interest in Crystal's project would be running high (if nothing else, a lot of dramatic value could be milked from Mickey's eleventh-hour liver transplant), but both baseball and baseball movies had been in the doldrums since that accursed 1994 strike. The HBO pay-cable service evinced interest in the Mantle film, but advised Crystal to wait until the marketplace was more amenable to such a production.

While Crystal was formulating his Mickey Mantle project, young screenwriter Hank Steinberg, who hadn't even been born at the time of the Mantle/Maris home run race, had developed a fascination for the story of Roger Maris, who only recently, and posthumously, had been given his full due for smashing Babe Ruth's record. "What I had an interest in doing was vindicating a person who I thought was treated very unfairly. That was what attracted me to the story to begin with. I thought that he had been forgotten, and that he had not been given his due at the time he had achieved this remarkable thing. I'm a baseball fan, but that was what ultimately touched me about it." With theatrical baseball pictures on the outs, Steinberg pitched his Maris project to the HBO pay-cable service in 1997, but the network wasn't interested, presumably working on the philosophy that 1996's *Soul of the Game* (q.v.) had fulfilled HBO's quota of baseball biopics for the time being. But during the summer of 1998, with both Mark McGwire and Sammy Sosa bidding fair to break Roger Maris' 37-year-old home run record, HBO gave Steinberg's script a second look—then a *third* look when McGwire and Sosa not only broke the record

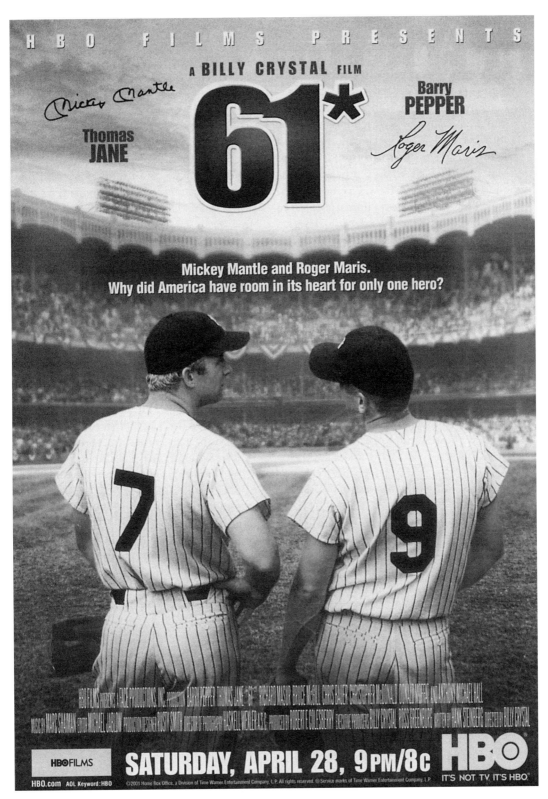

Magazine ad for *61** (2001). Even from the back, the two actors chosen to play Mantle and Maris look just like the genuine article!

but spectacularly surpassed it, with 70 and 66 homers respectively. Introducing David Steinberg to Billy Crystal, the HBO people suggested that both men collaborate on a film celebrating the Mantle-Maris traveling show of 1961. Crystal agreed, though it would mean shifting focus from Mantle to Maris. Though he knew and loved Mantle and had never met Maris, Crystal realized that there was far more dramatic value in concentrating on the underdog than on "fair-haired boy" Mickey (though the script makes clear that the fans were pretty rough on Mantle at the beginning of the '61 season).

In the course of his research, Steinberg read every last scrap of printed information on the subject, and conducted extensive interviews with the M&M Boys' fellow Yankees Whitey Ford, Yogi Berra and Bob Cerv, the latter agreeing to act as one of the film's technical advisors. Also consulted were the wives and children of Mickey Mantle and Roger Maris; Ralph Houk, Yankees manager from 1961 to 1973; former Yankee first baseman Bill "Moose" Skowron; and Andy Strassberg, longtime friend of both the Mantle and Maris families. Of the above, all but the Mantle family members and Strassberg were portrayed by actors in the film (Strassberg himself showed up on-screen as the fan who caught the 61st home run ball). All were treated respectfully, though Whitey Ford comes off as something of an "enabler" by paying off the various female companions, tradesmen and hotel staffers who might have been offended during Mickey Mantle's drunken rampages; and Yogi Berra speaks in fluent Berra-isms, referring to an "ambidextral" player and reminding his teammates that "90 percent of this game is half mental" in his very first scene!

Less respectful were the characterizations of the people whom the filmmakers regarded as the heavies of the piece, beginning with intractable baseball commissioner

Ford Frick. Described by baseball scholar Alex Holzman as "Babe Ruth's PR flack" and by *Chicago Tribune* columnist Julia Keller as "zealously protective of the slugger's iconic image," it was Frick who publicly proposed the idea of qualifying Maris' record-breaking run with the accursed asterisk. Since he waited to do this until mid–July, when Maris was obviously closing in on Ruth, many latter-day observers feel that this was not so much an homage to Babe as a deliberate slap in the face to Roger. "I never felt it should have been there to begin with," Roger Maris, Jr. told the Associated Press when Fay Vincent belatedly removed the asterisk in 1991. "The only reason I ever felt there was an asterisk was to take away from what he accomplished in 1961." As the *Tribune*'s Julia Keller notes, Frick succeeded in making the word "asterisk" synonymous not only with the Mantle-Maris debacle, but also with any effort to minimize the accomplishments of someone whom the asterisk-imposers happen to disapprove of or dislike. As recently as 2001, *Doonesbury* cartoonist Gary Trudeau has adopted a *talking* asterisk to represent President George W. Bush, whom Trudeau obviously regards as being in the White House only on a technicality.

So if Maris was the hero of *61**, Ford Frick was the logical villain. Surprisingly, the filmmakers aren't as hard on Frick as they might have been, even though the former commissioner was played by veteran movie antagonist Donald Moffat, who portrayed a similar anal-retentive baseball potentate, Colonel Ruppert, in the 1991 TV movie *Babe Ruth* (q.v.). Without backing away from the fact that Frick presumptively robbed Maris of the honor that was truly and fully his, the film shows that the commissioner acted less out of autocracy than fear—fear of how the more virulently violent Yankee fans would react to the "upstart" Maris, and fear of the ever-looming spectre of Babe Ruth. He doesn't even come up with the asterisk idea on his own; having called a conference with several top sports writers to discuss the Maris vs. Ruth controversy and to hammer out a solution, Frick listens in stony silence as the gathered scribes mull over the various pros and cons of Maris' challenge, and finally exhibits a flicker of approval when one of the writers (whom the audience hears but does not see) suggests the "separate record." Only late into the film do we see Frick gloating over the fact that Maris has been unable to hit the 61st within the arbitrary 154-game limit, and by this time he has become less an object of hatred than of piteous contempt, a man so devoid of backbone that he allows Public Opinion to override his own better judgment (in contrast, Ralph Houk is shown courageously refusing to change the batting lineup during the 154th game just to accommodate the Babe Ruth acolytes, and even delivering an inspirational pep talk to keep the dispirited Maris from sitting the game out). After seeing *61**, then-current commissioner Bud Selig expressed the same hesitancy as the filmmakers to paint Frick as an all-out bad guy: "I thought the Ford Frick portrayal was pretty tough, to say the least. I try never to be critical of any of my predecessors publicly. But I will say this. Unquestionably, Fay Vincent did the right thing. Unquestionably. A record is a record."

If the fans were indeed as repulsively terrifying as those seen in this film, one can understand why Ford Frick was running scared. From the beginning of the story, the 1961 Yankee crowd has a habit of turning ugly on a dime, no sooner welcoming Mickey Mantle back for another season than jeering and catcalling because he isn't delivering a home run each time at bat. The shouts of approbation greeting Roger Maris' MVP presentation ceremony soon give way to boos and obscene insults when Maris has the temerity to out-hit Mantle — in fact, the boos persist even when Maris'

homers and RBIs enable the Yankees to keep their Pennant hopes alive. As the season winds down, the fans invariably greet Mantle like a conquering hero and Maris like an invading barbarian. At their worst, the fans are downright psychotic: In addition to the crudely scrawled death threats which pollute Roger Maris' mail, during one ballgame a heavy-breathing yahoo dresses himself up like Babe Ruth, screams foul imprecations from the bleachers above Maris, and ends up hurling a metal chair at the hapless player.

But just as the people behind *61** made an effort to explain Ford Frick's exclusionary decision as largely the result of outside influences, so too are the Yankee fans shown to be manipulated by the "gentlemen" of the press. Miffed that Roger Maris is a man of few words who values his privacy and avoids issuing the sort of colorful statements characteristic of Mickey Mantle, the reporters clearly have it in for Maris the moment he joins the Yankees (one of them quips that "M.V.P." stands for Most Vacant Player). "They gave him a hard time," recalled his teammate Moose Skowron upon seeing the film. "Roger didn't deserve that. He just wanted to be left alone. That's how he was with the writers. He was a quiet guy. But they never left him alone. Everyplace he went he had photographers watching him…. They'd take pictures of him going to the bathroom. Really." In the film, reporters don't exactly dog Maris' trail to the toilet stalls, but they do camp out in front of his family's home in Kansas City — the address of which was supposed to be kept secret — and ambush Roger as he arrives to see his newborn baby for the first time. These journalistic vultures clearly cannot accept the fact that a public man deserves a few private moments, just as Roger cannot understand why he should curry favor with newspapermen who continually tear him down in print for not being Mickey Mantle and for daring to assail the cast-in-stone Babe Ruth Record. In true trickle-down fashion, the nastier the tone of the newspaper coverage, the more hostile the fans in the stands become.

The irony is that most of the reporters don't really give a hang about Maris or whether he breaks the record or not. In an early scene, one ink-stained wretch explains that, with fifteen competing newspapers in New York City alone, if it bleeds it leads—even if the reporters have to start the blood flowing themselves. This, and not any reverence towards the game of baseball or favoritism toward Mickey Mantle, is the reason for the fabricated "feud" between Mantle and Maris, the constant hammering of the "sacrilege" of challenging Ruth, and the excuse for pouncing upon every one of Maris' chance comments and deliberately quoting them out of context. When, for example, Roger modestly explains that he's "not a New York kind of guy," the Press plays up the innocent observation as a gross insult against the Big Apple—and thus another outpouring of public hatred against Roger is a *fait accompli*. Nor do the reporters really want Roger Maris to act like Mickey Mantle; they simply need a whipping boy to boost circulation. Some of the things which the Press would have laughed off had Mantle done them—being photographed with a bevy of beautiful New York showgirls, responding to a sarcastic fan's "Hey, put your 'X' on my ball" by literally signing an "X"—are used as further ammunition in the anti–Maris campaign when *he* does them. The fans may be jerks, but they don't seem to know any better, and at the very least they are sincere in their hostility, misdirected though it is. But most of the reporters in the film are driven by pure cynicism and opportunism, and this truly makes the pen more deadly than the sword (or the thrown chair).

Perhaps the most startling unsympathetic portrayal in *61** is that of Babe Ruth's widow Claire Hodgson Ruth, a woman normally treated on film with the reverence one affords Mother Teresa. Not that actress Rene Taylor goes the Cruella DeVil route as Mrs. Ruth, nor that the lines given her are overtly villainous. Still, the filmmakers' spin on Claire's fierce protection of her husband's name and accomplishments manage to cast the woman in an extremely unflattering light. Introducing herself to Roger Maris' wife Pat on the day that Roger is expected to hit number 61, Mrs. Ruth is pleasant enough at first; but when Pat remarks that she wishes Babe could have lived to see this day, Claire visibly recoils, and in the same calculatedly pleasant tone she replies that, no, Babe was *very proud* of his record, the daggers in her eyes indicating that Maris had better remember to keep his place if he knows what's good for him. And earlier, while watching Maris fail to get past Number 59 during the 154th game in Baltimore, Claire Ruth's heavily lipsticked mouth spreads into a smile—not a beaming smile of pride that her sainted husband's record remains intact, but the sort of smug, self-satisfied smirk one might see on the face of an elderly dowager who has just succeeded in keeping the "wrong kind of person" out of the local country club.

Surrounded by all this antagonism, Roger Maris and Mickey Mantle could not help but emerge from the film smelling like roses. But as much as screenwriter Hank Steinberg admires Maris, and Billy Crystal adores Mantle, *61** acknowledges the chinks in the armor of both men. It would have been dishonest to ignore the fact that Mickey Mantle was an imperfect human being, and the film is unsparing in its re-creations of Mickey's peccadilloes. The filmmakers manage to keep the audience on Mickey's side by pointing out his genuine affection for his friend and roommate Roger Maris and his sincere love of his wife and children, even if he doesn't check in with them by phone as often as he should (and when he does, it is likely to be at 2:30 in the morning). Also, a strong and persuasive motivation is attached to each of his less attractive character flaws. Does he express disproportionate resentment towards his former teammate Joe DiMaggio? Yes, but only because Joltin' Joe rudely snubbed Mickey during his rookie year. And does Mickey burn the candle at both ends, spending his hours off the ballfield bending his elbow, bedding beautiful blondes and raising Holy Hell? Yes, but only because both his father and grandfather died of Hodgkin's disease before the age of 39—and, convinced that he is likewise doomed to a early grave, he is determined to get as much living into his short span on earth as humanly possible, and screw the consequences. (Commendably, the script avoids pointing out the irony that Mantle ended up outliving Maris!)

Conversely, the film's nominal hero, Roger Maris, is not unrealistically portrayed as a paragon. Yes, he *was* a grown-up Boy Scout, selflessly devoted to his family, regarding his body (if not his lungs) as a temple, more concerned with the job of baseball than the glitz and glamour associated with the game, and above all a genuinely modest human being. But for all his virtues, there was the danger that Maris would come off on film as a pompous prig, eliciting yawns and even resentment from the viewers. Addressing this potential problem, the filmmakers contrived to have Maris' rigid personality backfire upon him—and deservedly so. According to 61*, virtually the only ally Roger has among the New York press corps is reporter Milt Kahn, a fictional composite played by Richard Masur. The more the other scribes rag Maris, the more readily does Milt rush to the ballplayer's defense, until he becomes a lone voice in the wilderness, shouting Roger's praises while everyone else is throwing brickbats. Despite this show of support, Roger's understandable distrust of the Fifth Estate spills over into his relationship with Kahn;

having promised to grant an exclusive interview to Kahn on the day of the all-important 154th game, Maris chooses instead to lock himself up in his hotel room and brood over the significance of the event. Offended at being stood up, the normally unflappable Kahn blows his stack, labeling Roger as rude, obstreperous and ungrateful—and the audience is inclined at this point to agree with the reporter, no matter how much abuse we've seen the Press heap upon Maris in the earlier scenes. Building a wall around yourself may be a justifiable defense mechanism, but it can be a pain in the butt for the people who really care about you.

At the same time, neither Hank Steinberg nor Billy Crystal wanted their version of Roger Maris to alienate the audience. Thus, like Mantle, Maris was provided with an inner demon which compelled him to behave the way he did. Halfway through the film, Roger explains that his tightly focused dedication to baseball, and his unwillingness to allow any outside forces or temptations to distract him, is his own personal tribute to his older brother Rudy, a promising ballplayer struck down in his prime by polio.

From the outset, Billy Crystal had vowed that 61* would accurately recreate the era in which it takes place down to the minutest detail. Interviewed on the TV series *Entertainment Tonight*, Crystal noted, "The biggest challenge in making the movie, besides finding the two brilliant actors [to play Mantle and Maris], was recreating the environment that I grew up in and that Yankee fans remember." Since Yankee Stadium no longer looked as it did in the Summer of 1961, the 61* production crew descended upon Detroit's old Tiger Stadium, which had recently been abandoned in favor of a new up-to-date structure. Built in 1912, the ballpark had virtually the same pillars and decks as the Yankee Stadium of four decades earlier. After consulting vintage photographs and newsreels, the construction crew, under the guidance of production designer Rusty Smith, went to work expanding upon what already existed in Detroit to convincingly recreate The House That Ruth Built—at least from August 7 through 21, 2000, when principal photography took place. Even the color of the stadium seats was altered to conform with the vintage Yankee Stadium Look; according to Ross Greenberg, executive producer of HBO's sports division, "It took a crew of 27 men three weeks to spray-paint 49,000 seats." As a crowning touch, the Bronx skyline was digitally added by the special-effects team at Centropolis.

Meanwhile, the costuming and makeup departments were busy assuring that the leading players, supporting actors and extras were properly clothed and coiffed in true conservative 1961 fashion. The art-direction and set-decoration squads replaced all touchtone phones with the antique rotary models, trotted out the shag carpets, Formica tables and "space age" wall decorations for the scenes set in the Maris family home, and constructed the primitive pasteboard backdrops that passed for TV newsrooms in the pre–CNN era. The prop crew printed up hundreds of vintage ballpark souvenir programs, churned out scores of old-fashioned pennants, and dug up as many black and white "tube" televisions (with those noodle-soup antennas) as still existed. And the musical researchers dug up dozens of vintage pieces for background flavor, including the charmingly dreadful novelty songs "The Kid from Red Bank" (Neil Hefti and Count Basie's tribute to Roger Maris) and "I Love Mickey," the latter featuring a tin-ear duet between the real Mickey Mantle and Teresa Brewer. This meticulous attention to detail was practically contagious; when it was necessary for plot purposes to establish that Roger Maris' nervousness had manifested in a dangerous chain-smoking habit, it was shown that

his cigarette of preference was Camels, which the Yankees had been paid to endorse back in 1961.

None of this period flavor would have mattered if the leading actors were not chosen with equal care and authenticity. Fortunately, the two stars so closely resembled Roger Maris and Mickey Mantle that the effect was positively spooky. Barry Pepper, whose previous screen role of note was as the Scripture-quoting sniper in Spielberg's Saving Private Ryan, not only had the voice, facial structure and demeanor of the 27-year-old Roger Maris, but was an excellent natural athlete in the bargain. Thomas Jane, a veteran of such films as The Thin Red Line and The Deep Blue Sea, is not precisely a twin of Mickey Mantle, but he perfectly captures the Mick's crinkly half-smile, good-ole-boy drawl, jaunty cockiness, loose-limbed swagger and rakish charm. Director Crystal painstakingly coached Barry Pepper and Thomas Jane in the movements and vocal inflections of their respective characters, while former Major League outfielder Reggie Smith spent five weeks as the actors' baseball trainer.

Smith had an easier time of it with Barry Pepper, who had actually played ball, than with Thomas Jane, who had apparently never set foot on a diamond in his life—and who, according to Billy Crystal, broke up his audition by asking, "Who's Mickey Mantle?" As HBO's Ross Greenberg recalled, Jane "lied to Billy and told him he'd played. Tom got out there that first day and he couldn't throw, he couldn't hit, he couldn't do anything. But Tom worked really, really hard with Reggie for two or three months [sic]. And by the end he could hit from both sides of the plate, he could throw, he looked good out there."

Of the other actors playing ballplayers, former "brat-packer" Anthony Michael Hall posed a different sort of problem in the role of Whitey Ford. Not that Hall's acting performance or athletic skills were in any way lacking; but whereas Ford was left-handed, Hall was a "rightie." To solve this dilemma, the filmmakers dug back to a device used briefly in the 1942 Lou Gehrig biopic *Pride of the Yankees*: Hall was dressed in a uniform with his character name and team number printed backward; then his ballplaying scenes were "flipped" in the film lab so that he could appear to be a southpaw while still pitching with his right hand (so that the entire stadium didn't have to be built in reverse, Hall's ballplaying scenes were filmed in close-up or tight medium shots).

Otherwise, production moved along with smooth efficiency—though this didn't stop Billy Crystal from experiencing a few bumpy stretches en route. "Doing this picture was tough for me, but in a very good way," Crystal recalled to Tim Wendel. "It put me in touch with amazing feelings toward my dad. He died in 1963. He introduced me to baseball. He taught me how to play and brought me to Yankee Stadium for the first time. The movie is dedicated to him ['For my father, Jack Crystal, who took my brothers and me to our first game at Yankee Stadium, May 30, 1956']. That was a wonderful feeling; not only did I feel that I had Mickey and Roger looking down on us, but also my dad. That summer of '61 was something we shared. We were Yankee freaks. If he'd been a Dodger fan, I might not have made this movie."

One question that nagged everyone during filming was whether or not TV viewers of the early 21st century would regard the forty-year-old M&M saga as relevant, though certain people close to the film harbored no doubts whatsoever. When asked if current audiences would care about what happened so long ago to people so long dead, technical adviser Andy Strassberg responded in the affirmative: "I think the facts are coming out about Roger Maris and what he went through, and I think that [the film] is going to be appealing to a lot of people. And the thing about it is, it's not made up; it really happened." Concurring with this was baseball historian Alex Holzman, who pointed out that the general "Baby Boom Nostalgia" would lend viewer support to the film, adding, "Even now, 40 years after this record was broken, Babe Ruth is still the most single important figure in baseball." Still, the filmmakers knew that there would be those observers, like the reviewer for the cutting-edge periodical *Rolling Stone*, who would dismiss *61** with words to the effect of "Who cares? It's ancient history."

To provide the film with a contemporary slant, Billy Crystal added a framing device, with the widow of Roger Maris recalling her husband's triumph and travails while watching the Cardinals' Mark McGwire preparing to break Maris' record in St. Louis on the evening of September 8, 1998. Thus, the bulk of *61** is a flashback, returning to 1998 only at the very end, with a montage of authentic video clips: McGwire's 62nd homer, his spontaneous hugging of home-run rival Sammy Sosa and the Maris family members in attendance (approvingly described by Bud Selig as a "stunning moment" in his own career as commissioner—take *that*, Ford Frick!), and his emotionally-charged post game press conference, in which Big Mac explains how he insisted upon having the bat with which Roger Maris hit Number 61 delivered to him by the Baseball Hall of Fame so that he could best demonstrate his admiration and reverence for Maris, concluding, "My bat will live next to his—and I'm damn proud of it." Not only do the "bookend" 1998 sequences in *61** provide the proper historical context for those too young to remember the actual events, but they also point out the gratifying contrast between the cruel and retrogressive freezeout of Roger Maris in 1961 and the classy behavior of the teary-eyed Mark McGwire 37 years later. As Billy Crystal explained on

TV's *Entertainment Tonight*, "[T]o me that grounded the movie because it very much became the heart of the picture.... I said, 'That's the heart and guts of this movie.'" (*Chicago Tribune* reviewer Steve Johnson felt that the modern framework was "a clunky device," but even he had to admit that it worked beautifully on screen.)

Since the film is more about the circumstances surrounding Maris' record-breaker homer than the event itself, *61** does not actually contain as much baseball action as it may seem at first glance. But to paraphrase Spencer Tracy in *Pat and Mike*, what baseball action *is* in the film is "cherce." The climactic 154th ballgame in Baltimore is a classic example of collaborative filmmaking at its zenith. Crystal's direction is masterful, focusing attention on what is most crucial to the event and jettisoning all the rest; the acting, from leading players on down to the humblest extra, is flawless; the fluid camerawork, by multiple Oscar winner Haskell Wexler (see notes on *The Babe*), manages to simultaneously convey both nostalgia for the era and the urgency of the moment at hand; and the editing by Michael Jablow (*Little Big League*), deftly juxtaposing the palpable excitement in the ballpark with the wildly contrasting reactions of Pat Maris, Ford Frick and Claire Ruth as they watch the events unfold on television, is worthy of an Eisenstein or a Welles.

So powerful is this sequence that the remaining half hour of *61** pales in comparison—and therein lies the film's only real shortcoming. Running 128 minutes, the film would have been all the more effective had it been just a bit shorter, especially since the premise is set up so early in the proceedings. Granted, it is important to devote a goodly amount of screen time to show how the reporters covering the home-run race went from mild annoyance to full-blown animosity in their treatment of Roger Maris, but after one or two "press-bashing" scenes, things get mighty repetitious mighty soon. And though director Crystal succeeds in conveying how Maris' 61st home run seemed anti-climactic to baseball fans after all the hoopla that had gone before, far too much footage is expended between the film's *real* climax—the Baltimore game—and the closing credits. While it is reassuring to see Mickey Mantle and Roger Maris trade compliments after Ruth's record has been broken, the fact that the two men liked and respected one another has already been established to everyone's satisfaction several times over, and cannot help but seem redundant here—especially since the film, for all intents and purposes, ended back in Baltimore.

And for all the film's vaunted accuracy, Crystal gilds the lily a bit after the 61st home run has taken place. Judging from the cheers of the Yankee Stadium crowd, one might conclude that they have learned to love Roger Maris after all. In truth, however, the New York fans would not truly appreciate Maris until after he was traded to the St. Louis Cardinals—whom he subsequently led to two World Series.

But why quibble over a couple of piddly shortcomings when everything else about the film is so gosh-darned good? *61** is a rare example of a baseball film which clicks on all cylinders: Even if the directing and the other technical aspects of the film had not been first-rate, one could revel in the acting performances. In addition to the aforementioned Barry Pepper, Thomas Jane and Anthony Michael Hall, the casting is well-nigh perfect, with the actors matching their real-life counterparts to the nth degree. An exception might be made in the case of Christopher McDonald, who neither looks nor sounds like "Voice of the Yankees" Mel Allen, but McDonald's bravura performance more than compensates for these lapses in authenticity. Mention should also be made of Jennifer Crystal Foley's quietly effective portrayal of Roger

Maris' stalwart and supportive wife Pat. As the daughter of director Billy Crystal, the actress probably knew that her presence on screen would lead to shouts of nepotism (though Billy claims that the producer who cast Jennifer didn't know her relationship with "the boss"), and this as much as anything else might have inspired her to deliver one of the film's best all-around performances. She was so effective that a few critics, apparently having forgotten the lessons learned by jumping to conclusions after seeing *A League of Their Own* (q.v.) praised Jennifer Crystal Foley for her expertise in portraying the older Pat Maris in the 1998 sequences—and never mind that the older Pat Maris was actually played by veteran actress Patricia Crowley.

After scouring through dozens of print and website reviews, and digesting the comments of fans in an exhausting array of internet chatrooms, this writer can state with a certain measure of assurance that *everybody* enjoyed *61** when it originally aired over HBO on April 28, 2001 (the film had previously been given special theatrical showings in New York, Los Angeles and Maris' hometown of Fargo, North Dakota, on April 21). Most critics were of the same mind as Salon.com's Allan Bara, who, after hypothesizing that *61** was "maybe the best baseball film since *Bull Durham*," went on to remark, "Maybe you had to have been there to really appreciate *61**. On the other hand, *61** might just make you feel as if you were." Equally impressed were the people responsible for handing out the annual Emmy awards, who bestowed nominations upon the film in virtually every category, including best actor (Barry Pepper), best director, best screenwriter and "Outstanding Made for Television Film."

But for Billy Crystal and Hank Stein-

berg the ultimate accolades were delivered by the people closest to the story: the friends, family members and colleagues of Roger Maris and Mickey Mantle. Former first baseman Moose Skowron (portrayed in the film by Dominic Lombardozi) was moved half an hour into the film's screening to whisper, "This is damn good so far"; an hour later Skowron whispered, "This brings back a lot of memories"; and after the closing credits had faded, Moose declared out loud, "I thought it was great. Everything was in there." And, while attending a private preview of the film in Gainesville, Florida, the Maris family (who later were invited by President George W. Bush to watch the "official" TV premiere in the White House) gave *61** their unqualified stamp of approval, with Maris' mother turning to one of the film's technical advisors and murmuring succinctly, "You got it right."

And perhaps, somewhere, Roger Maris was smiling. At long, long last.

Slide, Kelly, Slide

MGM; released March 12, 1927

Directed by Edward Sedgwick. Screenplay by A. P. Younger. Titles by Joe Farnham. Photography: Henry Sharp. Edited by Frank Sullivan. Sets by Cedric Gibbons and David Townsend. Wardrobe by Andre-ami. Technical adviser: Mike Donlin. Assistant director: Edward S. Brophy. 8 reels/7,856 feet; black and white; silent.

Cast: William Haines (Jim Kelly); Sally O'Neill (Mary Munson); Harry Carey (Tom Munson); Junior Coghlan (Mickey Martin); Warner Richmond (Cliff Macklin); Paul Kelly (Frisbie); Karl Dane (Swede Hansen); Guinn Williams (McLean); Mike Donlin, Irish Meusel, Bob Meusel, and Tony Lazzeri (Themselves); Edward Brophy (Joe); John "Beans" Reardon (Umpire); Johnny Mack Brown* (Sarcastic ballplayer).

---

*Johnny Mack Brown, former All-American halfback at the University of Alabama and hero of the 1926 Rose Bowl, made his film debut in Slide, Kelly, Slide. His one-scene, one-line bit was the launching pad for a long and durable screen career, which ranged from leading-man assignments opposite Garbo and Joan Crawford to a string of successful B Westerns for Universal and Monogram. Just thought you'd like to know.

Jim Kelly, rookie pitcher for the New York Yankees, is the sort of fellow who wires ahead to spring training camp to tell the boys that he's on his way and there's nothing to worry about (and never mind that he hasn't actually been signed by the team!). Kelly's brashness does not diminish during training, alienating most of his fellow players. Aging catcher Tom Munson, whose daughter Mary is sweet on Kelly, takes it upon himself to straighten out the young hotshot. But Kelly pays attention to no one, and on the eve of an important game with Chicago he becomes so sore because the rest of the team refuses to back him up that he gets good and plastered. Mary Munson doesn't want Kelly to get canned, so she hides him in her room. When her dad shows up to try to talk some sense to Kelly, the bitter young ballplayer lashes out at him, claiming that he's been carrying "old man Munson" all season. This effectively puts Kelly on the outs with everyone, including Mickey, the hero-worshiping Yankee batboy. Kelly quits the team after being pulled from the World Series lineup by the manager. But the Yankees run out of pitchers just before the deciding series game, so little Mickey is secretly dispatched on his bicycle to retrieve Kelly—and, right on cue, the boy is hit by a car. As Mickey lies in the hospital near death, it becomes clear that he will only recover if Kelly and the manager patch up their differences. At the last moment, a suddenly humbled Kelly shows up at the game, and at the *very* last moment he slides into home for the winning run. As we fade out, Jim Kelly is a hero in everyone's eyes—including those of Mickey, who, just before the victory celebration (get out your hankies), is rolled into the grandstands in a wheelchair.

The genesis of the title *Slide, Kelly, Slide* was a song written in honor of King Kelly, who played for both Chicago and Boston in the early 1880s. A grandstander's grandstander, Kelly was prone to such stunts as substituting himself from the bench while a game was in progress, simply to catch a ball in flight. Kelly's baseball showboating was complemented by his extravagant lifestyle, which culminated with his being fired from the New York Giants in 1893 for overspeculating his paycheck at the race track. The song "Slide, Kelly, Slide" was composed in 1884—the year that King Kelly achieved a .354 batting average—which means that, as a "baseball anthem" of sorts, the tune predated both "Casey at the Bat" and "Take Me Out to the Ballgame."

It's difficult to determine what the first film to bear the name *Slide, Kelly, Slide* was about, since that Essanay one-reeler of 1910 has long since vanished. MGM's still-extant 1927 *Slide, Kelly, Slide*, filmed during the baseball movie cycle that followed Babe Ruth's 1926 comeback, justifies its title with a bit of plot development. In an early scene Jim Kelly is about to score a run home, but he refuses to follow instructions to slide, preferring instead to score while on his feet, and as a result he's tagged out. But when Kelly makes his decisive World Series run in the last reel, he bows to the advice of others and slides in—and, of course, wins the day. Be assured that the movie theater pit orchestras which provided music for silent pictures went into a boisterous rendition of "Slide, Kelly, Slide" at this critical moment—undoubtedly resulting in cheers, whistles and loud applause from the patrons, many of whom were just old enough to remember when that song was new (The film tips its cap to these "oldsters" with an amusingly nostalgic prologue in which a group of heavily moustached 19th century ballplayers stiffly pose for a formal photograph—a vignette later repeated in the 1949 MGM musical *Take Me Out to the Ballgame*).

Slide, Kelly, Slide star William Haines was one of MGM's hottest properties of 1927, popular with the ladies because of his good

Urged on by Sally O'Neill and Warner Richmond, William Haines (center) prepares for his major-league debut in *Slide, Kelly, Slide*.

looks and with the men because of his good-natured bravado. Lest the synopsis of this film make it seem that Haines's character was relentlessly obnoxious, we note that the MGM staff made sure that our hero was humanized by an early scene wherein, just after pulling a practical joke on a pair of Yankees players on the train headed to Florida, Haines is himself snookered by a vampish young lady, who tricks him into paying for her dinner.

Slide, Kelly, Slide was one of several sports-oriented Haines vehicles of the late 1920s; he also appeared as a golfer in *Spring Fever*, a football flash in *West Point*, and a polo player in *The Smart Set*. Haines's baseball picture fell into the tried and true pattern for most of his vehicles: the egocentric

young fellow who redeems himself by tempering his undeniable talent with humility at the end. While Haines's fans ate this sort of thing up, critics became exasperated early on at MGM's cookie-cutter approach to his films; indeed, when Jack Oakie played a cocky young ballplayer who retained that cockiness to the end without being brought down a peg or two (*Fast Company*, 1929 [q.v.]), reviewers welcomed this alternative to the "usual William Haines stuff."

By the time talking pictures came along, audiences had also had their fill of William Haines, shifting their affections to newer, grittier stars like James Cagney and Clark Gable who brought a touch of Depression-era street savvy to the brash roles in which Haines had specialized. Even if

424 *The Slugger's Wife*

he hadn't started losing his audience, however, Bill Haines would have been washed up once it came out in the open that he was carrying on an unabashedly homosexual lifestyle. Happily, Haines was able to cut his losses when his popularity ended, launching a whole new career as a high-priced interior decorator.

But when *Slide, Kelly, Slide* came out, William Haines was on top of the cinema world, and MGM reflected this by sparing no expense on the production. In addition to securing the services of such then thriving ballplayers as Tony "Poosh 'Em Up" Lazzeri and Irish and Bob Meusel (oldtimer "Turkey" Mike Donlin was on hand too, as both actor and technical adviser), as well as major-league umpire John "Beans" Reardon, the studio saw to it that many of the scenes were shot on location (a rare move for MGM) at both Yankee Stadium and at the team's spring training grounds in Florida. Director Edward Sedgwick, a past and future master of ballpark sagas (including *Hit and Run* [1924] and *Death on the Diamond* [1934]), injected a wealth of authenticity into the baseball sequences. Working around the major leagues' prohibition of cameras on the field during the actual playing of games (see notes on *Play Ball*), Sedgwick compensated by adopting the "Eisenstein" approach of rapid-fire editing and montage when staging the film's game scenes. (This approach was also used to excellent advantage in the near-impressionistic sequence wherein little Mickey is struck by a car).

Flying in the face of the "irrefutable fact" that baseball pictures were money losers, *Slide, Kelly, Slide* was one of MGM's most profitable releases of 1927. The powers that were chalked up this success less to the film's plotline than to the audience appeal of William Haines, and to the film's efforts to please the ladies with doses of romance and pathos. The bigwigs would be supported in their opinions by future events; none of the baseball films that followed *Slide, Kelly, Slide* were anywhere near as successful, and, in fact, there wouldn't be another big ballpark "boffo" until the Joe E. Brown baseball comedies of the 1930s.

The Slugger's Wife*

Rastar/Delphi Productions II/Columbia; released March 1985

Executive producer: Margaret Booth. Produced by Ray Stark. Directed by Hal Ashby. Screenplay by Neil Simon. Photography: Caleb Deschanel. Edited by George Villasenor and Don Brochu. Production designer: Michael Riva. Musical producers: Quincy Jones and Tom Bahler. Musical score by Patrick Williams. Song "Love (That's the Way It Goes)" by Quincy Jones, Glenn Ballard, and Cliff Magness. Vocals performed by Rebecca DeMornay, Michael O'Keefe, Lisa Langlois, Loudon Wainwright, III, and Sarah M. Taylor. Costumes by Ann Roth. Sound recording by Jeff Wexler. Production manager: Jerry Baerwitz. Assistant directors: Frank Bueno and Don Yorkshire. Baseball technical adviser: Keith Bodie. Color by Metrocolor. Dolby Sound. 105 minutes. Rated PG-13.†

Cast: Michael O'Keefe (Darryl Palmer); Rebecca DeMornay (Debby Palmer); Martin Ritt (Burly DeVito); Randy Quaid (Moose Granger); Cleavant Derricks (Manny Alvarado); Lisa Langlois (Aline Cooper); Loudon Wainwright, III (Gary); Georgann Johnson (Marie De Vito); Danny Tucker (Coach O'Brien); Lynn Whitfield (Tina Alvarado); Al Garrison (Guard); Nicandra Hood (Nurse); Ginger Taylor (Sherry); Kay McClelland (Peggy); Julie Kemp (Paloma); Dennis Burkley (Chuck); Alisha Das (Lola); Dan Biggers (Preacher); Justine Thieleman (Iris Granger); Marc Clement (Mr. Davis); Tina Kincaid, Martha Harrison, Becky Pate (Baseball Wives); Richard Alan Reiner (Patron at Zelda's); Valerie Mitchell (Waitress at Limelight); Edwin H. Cipot (Cuneo); Stephen H. Steir (Varsity Patron);

*The full title on the release print of this film is Neil Simon's The Slugger's Wife.

†The videotape release of The Slugger's Wife carries these additional technical credits: Special lighting effects in nightclub sequences by John Tedesco/Phoebus. Dog trainers: Michael and Kathy Quattrochi, The Educated Puppy of Atlanta, Georgia.

David R. Yood (Cop in Varsity); Wallace G. Merck (Fan in Limelight); Johnny B. Watson, Jr. (Gateman); Alex Hawkins ("Hawkins"); Mort Schwartz (Man); John B. Sterling (Himself); George Stokes (Stage Manager); Harmon L. Wages (Interviewer); John W. Bradley (Himself); Jerome Olds (Musician); Starshower (Band); Erby Walker, Philip Fontanelli (Waiters); Steve Daniels, Jr., Henry J. Rountree, George Jack Klarman, Collin Fagan, David M. Pallone (Umpires); Kevin James Barnes (Public Address); John Lawhern (Coach Reckon); Douglas Garland Nave, Bill G. Fyte (Catchers); Al Hrabosky, Mark "Bird" Fidrych (Pitchers); Pete Van Wieren, Ernie Johnson (Baseball Narrators); Skip Caray, Nick Charles (Sportscasters); Chico Renfroe, Anthony Peck, Corly B. McPherrin, Paul S. Ryden, Charles Darden, John Buren Solberg, Brad Nessler (Reporters); Helen Dell (Stadium Organist); Ted Turner (Himself); Homer the Dog (Himself). Cut from film: Bernie Carbo, Larry Littleton (Ballplayers).

Darryl Palmer, ace slugger and right-fielder for the Atlanta Braves, falls hard for rock singer Debby Huston when he spots her at the Limelight nightclub, but Debby resists his cloddish attempts at courtship. Finally, Darryl promises the fans of Atlanta that he'll hit two home runs in the next game if Debby will go out to dinner with him afterward. He does, and *she* does, and after several more intimate encounters Darryl and Debby are married. But there are problems almost from the start: Debby wants to seriously pursue her singing career with road trips and recording sessions, but Darryl, obsessed not only with Debby but with the notion that he can only play well when she's at the ballpark, won't let her go. As Darryl begins to approach Roger Maris's sixty-one-homer record, his possessiveness becomes impossible to live with, so Debby walks out on him. After a harrowing period of drunkenness and destruction of private property (not his own), Darryl becomes so morose that the Braves' manager, Burly DeVito, instructs fellow teammates Moose and Manny to go out and get Palmer "laid." This effort at ego building

fails spectacularly, as does DeVito's idiotic scheme to pass off another blonde rock singer as Debby during a hospital visit to Darryl, who's been beaned during practice and thus suffers from temporary blurred vision. On the day that Darryl is expected to make his sixty-second homer (which also happens to be the day that Atlanta may or may not win the pennant), Debby returns from a singing tour to offer moral support. By now, Darryl has grown up enough to rely on his own skills rather than Debby's inspiration, so that when he does achieve his record-breaking four-bagger, he knows he's done it on his own. It is clear at this point that Debby also has learned to stand by her decisions concerning what's best for *her* life and career. Although Darryl and Debby don't reunite at the end, they part as friends, with assurances to one another that they'll "leave the door open" for a future reconciliation.

It must have looked great on paper. Here you have Neil Simon, one of the most successful modern playwrights, and the man responsible for a string of movie hits for Rastar Productions: *The Goodbye Girl, California Suite, Seems Like Old Times, Murder by Death, The Sunshine Boys* and *The Cheap Detective.* To this winning Simon-Rastar combination you add director Hal Ashby, auteur of the cult classic *Harold and Maude* and thereafter responsible for such successes as *Shampoo, The Last Detail, Coming Home,* and *Being There.* Then mix in rising young star Michael O'Keefe, so brilliant as Robert Duvall's son in *The Great Santini* (1979), and new sensation Rebecca DeMornay, who'd all but stolen the show as the wisecracking prostitute in *Risky Business* (1983). And finally, we align all this talent within a baseball story, which is sure to clean up once *The Natural* (q.v.) becomes the smash that everyone expects it to be in the spring of 1984. Put it all together and it spells box office gold mine!

But having a lot of good individual

components doesn't always result in a good unified whole. To paraphrase film historian Joe Adamson, good airplanes might be made that way, but not good movies. And *The Slugger's Wife* wasn't even a good airplane.

Perhaps there was a foretaste of disaster during production. Originally set in Houston, the film's locale was moved to Atlanta, not (as one might suppose) because Columbia Pictures had recently been acquired by the Atlanta-based Coca-Cola company, but because star Michael O'Keefe noted that the Braves had a better home run record in their own ballpark than did the Houston Astros. The Georgia Film and Videotape office, eager to entice future Hollywood productions to Atlanta, gave *The Slugger's Wife* company access to the Office's new studios at the 120-acre Lakewood Fairgrounds, while the real Braves were more than willing to allow the crew to film at Atlanta–Fulton County Stadium. But all this goodwill couldn't stop an onslaught of bad weather; the production was plagued by a series of tornadoes, one of which injured Rebecca DeMornay and her dialogue coach when their trailer was overturned (the actress suffered a black eye, which had to be carefully camouflaged). And when producer Ray Stark sent out a call for ballpark extras, so few Atlantans showed up that Stark had to offer big cash prizes to draw in the locals; and even then the most he could scare up was 600 people, who had to be juggled about to pass as a full house for the pennant race sequence.

Somebody along the line should have taken heed of the radical clash in styles embodied by scenarist Neil Simon—to whom the fast quip and clever turn of phrase was supreme—and director Hal Ashby, whose handling of dialogue wasn't nearly as sure-handed as his visual sense or his sustaining of mood. Leading lady Rebecca DeMornay claimed she was attracted to the script because "it was about the marriage of two opposite types of people. And I thought, how

bizarre that it's a script about two people who are night and day about each other, and Neil Simon and Hal Ashby are doing it together." Bizarre is right. This "marriage" was about as well advised as the thirty-eight-day union of Ernest Borgnine and Ethel Merman in 1965. Whenever Hal Ashby takes advantage of the inbred visual dynamics of a scene, he is weighed down by the heaviness of Neil Simon's repartee. And whenever there's a surefire Neil Simon comic set-up, Ashby finds something else upon which to focus his camera.

All right, a couple of specifics: We see that Darryl Palmer's game has improved once he's smitten by Debby. And we see later on that Darryl is so distracted by his marital strife that he remains standing at the plate after striking out and must be shooed away by the umpire. Well and good. But then the dialogue on the soundtrack *tells* us what we've just seen. Over and over again. Ashby's visuals and Simon's verbiage are for the most part thrown together in the same scene and expected to fight it out.

Or we see Coach DeVito performing a Neil Simon routine that's older than dirt. DeVito asks if his plan to pass off another woman as Debby to a befuddled Darryl makes him a son of a bitch; his two ballplayer companions say "Yes." He asks if his desire to win at all costs makes him an s.o.b.; again, "Yes" in unison. Then he asks if he'll be an s.o.b. if the team *does* win, and one of the players says, "No way." Here you have a factory tested "third time's the charm" gag that could have wrung a laugh on any cheap TV sitcom—but *not* with the mismatched camera angles and utter lack of timing which Hal Ashby invests in this bit. (We won't even bother discussing the mess made of the mistaken identity scene itself.)

During filming, Neil Simon spent all his time on the set rewriting dialogue, then coaching the actors in their delivery. Also during filming, sound technician Jeff Wexler complained that the bad acoustics at

Atlanta's Fairgrounds Exhibition Hall reminded him of "someone's garage." One wonders why Simon was so particular about the lines, or why Wexler cared whether or not the lines could be heard. Though we'd be the last people on earth to presume to tell Neil Simon how to write, it doesn't take a genius to note that *The Slugger's Wife* is just about the worst thing Simon has ever been associated with. Whole reels go by without even half a laugh being raised, and the desperate efforts to convince us that something funny is going on—notably Debby's asking Darryl (after a particularly weak one-liner) if he stays up nights thinking of clever things to say—merely compound the script's lack of real humor. And if the turgidity of the clash of personalities in the Palmer marriage is any reflection on the torment Neil Simon might have been going through over the disintegration of his own marriage to actress Marsha Mason, better that Simon had kept his angst to himself and not ladled it onto the big screen in Metrocolor and Dolby Stereo.

In addition, what *is* this film: a comedy, a drama, a baseball story, or a rock musical? Evidently, the Rastar people were asking themselves the same questions when the 114-minute first cut of *The Slugger's Wife* was completed for potential release around Christmas 1984. Some emergency surgery must have been performed, since the film didn't premiere until March 1985, by which time it had been trimmed by nine minutes. The operation wasn't successful and the patient died all the same: *The Slugger's Wife* looks like it has been edited with a pair of ice skates. During the first fifteen minutes we're never sure if we're supposed to be at the ballpark or at Debby's nightclub concert. Unless we strain to listen to the transitional dialogue on the soundtrack, it appears as though Darryl Palmer is hitting two home runs within thirty seconds of each other. Bits that require a single, uncluttered "take," such as Coach DeVito's

pennant race pep talk (in which he tells his boys that they're playing for commercial endorsements), are ruined by arbitrarily cutting away to other locales. Scenes that could use some editorial help—such as the infantile routine in which Darryl explains the contours of the baseball field by fondling various portions of Debby's anatomy—go on *sans* interruption interminably. And even though Rebecca DeMornay is doing her own singing, and though Michael O'-Keefe had spent six months training with Astros' farm team coach Keith Bodie and one week drilling with the real Atlanta Braves, both stars are usually standing so far away from the cameras while showing off their skills that we might as well be watching their stand-ins. The haphazard editing and mismanaged choice of shots are all the more surprising when one realizes that the executive producer of *The Slugger's Wife*, Margaret Booth, had for many years been editor in chief at MGM.

All of these deficits might not have mattered had the film's stars been brilliant, or at least competent. But it's a toss-up as to who gives the worst performance, Michael O'Keefe or Rebecca DeMornay. DeMornay's whiny, Minnie Mouse delivery of lines and her wimpy demeanor are totally at odds with her character's dogged determination to climb to the top of the rock music heap. At that, the actress is more appealing than Michael O'Keefe who, despite a lame attempt to be charming by serenading his love with an imitation of Gene Kelly warbling "Singin' in the Rain" (replete with water hoses!), makes the already poorly written character of Darryl Palmer one of the most repulsive protagonists in the history of films. O'Keefe/Palmer's violent reaction to his marital breakup—which includes smashing all the windows of a restaurant and drunkenly strongarming a timorous ballpark attendant into participating in a nocturnal batting drill—causes him to appear more psychotic than lovestruck. It's as

Typical of the miscalculations attending *The Slugger's Wife*: Randy Quaid's role as star Michael O'Keefe's teammate was whittled down from a potentially interesting "best friend" part to a glorified stooge. Still, Quaid *does* get to lose the Big Game (photograph courtesy of James L. Neibaur).

schanel had helped develop in the late 1970s—are marvelous. Deschanel even treats us to a rock-steady "skycam" helicopter-eye view of the stadium, a breathtaking effect that he'd originally planned for *The Natural*.

The supporting cast of *The Slugger's Wife* also yields a treasure or two. While some of the secondary actors, notably Randy Quaid and Georgann Johnson, are underused, Martin Ritt, a prominent film director (*Hud*, *Norma Rae*, etc.) who returned to his acting roots in the role of Coach DeVito, is untoppable. Ritt's emotional range, from youthful exuberance over his numerous hare-brained schemes to pull Darryl Palmer out of his slump, to the utter devastation in his face and voice after losing a critical game, makes one wish that Ritt had stepped from behind the cameras more often during his lengthy career.

Also gracing the supporting cast are several real-life sports personalities. Mark "The Bird" Fidrych, the Detroit Tigers' ninety-day wonder of 1976, is rather forgettable at the pitching mound in the early scenes, but onetime Braves pitcher (and future sportscaster) Al Hrabosky is blessed with a number of close-ups in the pennant game finale. The Braves announcers' lineup of John Sterling, Skip Caray, Pete Van Wieren, Ernie Johnson and Nick Charles are all in fine fettle, even when mouthing inanities that none of them would ever use during an actual game—at least not while in their right minds. ("Palmer's out of his slump, and the Braves are

though the homicidal ex-husband in the 1991 thriller *Sleeping with the Enemy* would suddenly turn out to be the film's hero.

Is there *anything* worth watching in *The Slugger's Wife*? Actually, there is. For one, the photography of Caleb Deschanel (who'd also worked on *The Natural* [q.v.]) is first-rate, the deliberate, overexposed quality of the exteriors providing a nice counterpoint to the neon-dominated concert sequences. Though the camera angles used in the baseball scenes are unremarkable, the smooth tracking shots around the bases—rendered free of jiggles and jitters via the utilization of the "steadicam" that De-

happy for it." Wow, no kidding!) And if you're swift enough, you can even spot Braves owner Ted Turner in the grandstands. Reportedly it took ten minutes to film Turner's cameo, which consists of a three-second flash of Atlanta's then-leading citizen shouting, "Come on, Darryl!"

If you've managed to stick through the film long enough to see Ted Turner, then you're in for a treat at the end of *The Slugger's Wife*. For, instead of going the precipitated, banal route of the Braves winning the pennant after Darryl Palmer's sixty-second homer, the script suddenly rears up and offers the unexpected. The Braves *lose* the Big Game, and it's a real last-minute heartbreaker; one which combines a queasy sense of the bottom dropping out of everything with a touch of honest to goodness, "it's about time" humor. Coach DeVito complains that when you lose, a $40 bottle of champagne tastes like Mountain Dew; and there's a great shot of a catering service hastily packing up a victory dinner before the disgruntled team returns to the locker room. This totally unanticipated turn of events is followed by a beautifully handled scene in which Darryl and Debby Palmer, who suddenly sound as though they're actually carrying on a conversation instead of reciting dialogue by rote, avoid the clichéd reunion scene that we've been set up for, opting instead to offer each other good luck and assurances that they *might* get together again once they've learned some more about themselves. For ten whole minutes, *The Slugger's Wife* is a wonderful movie.

It's too bad that by this time many moviegoers who'd plunked down good money to see this film upon its first release had left the theaters in disgust at its previous goings-on, and then went out to warn their friends to steer clear of *The Slugger's Wife*, even if it meant staying five miles away from any movie house unlucky enough to have booked the film. *The Slugger's Wife* wasn't just a disaster; it was probably the principal

reason that Ron Shelton had so many doors slammed in his face when he was making the rounds with his own script for *Bull Durham* (q.v.)—thereby nearly robbing us of that particular Thing of Beauty and Joy Forever. For this reason alone, *The Slugger's Wife* would best be removed from Columbia's vaults and sliced up for protection leader.

Somewhere in Georgia

Sunbeam Motion Pictures Corporation; States' Rights Release, October-November 1916

Directed by George Ridgewell. Screenplay by L. Case Russell, based on a story by Grantland Rice. Photography: Walter Arthur. 6 reels; black and white; silent.

Cast: Ty Cobb, Elsie MacLeod, Harry Fisher, Will Corbett, Ned Burton, and Eddie Boulden.

Ty Cobb, a small-town bank clerk in Georgia, is unhappily embroiled in a triangle involving himself, the bank president's lovely daughter, and an oily cashier. Cobb forgets his troubles on the local baseball field, where he's spotted and signed up by a scout for the Detroit Tigers. While he's away, his girl and his rival plan to marry. When the devious cashier learns that Cobb is on his way home to play an exhibition game, the scoundrel hires a band of thugs to waylay the ballplayer. Though bound hand and foot, Ty manages to wrestle loose and trounce all of his captors. He escapes in a mule wagon, shows up in town just in time to win the game for the local team, wins his girl, and prevents a nuclear attack (just kidding).

Ty Cobb was no showbiz virgin when he filmed *Somewhere in Georgia* in late 1916. The Detroit Tigers' superstar had already toured in a 1911 stock company production of George Ade's play *The College Widow*, produced by Cobb's friend and fellow

Georgian, actor-manager Vaughan Glaser. (Glaser would end his days as a Hollywood character performer, his most memorable role being the blind man who befriends fugitive Robert Cummings in the 1942 Alfred Hitchcock thriller *Saboteur*.) Critics were kind and audiences responsive as Cobb "trod the boards," and his fellow actors reported that the constitutionally illtempered ballplayer was quite cooperative and conscientious. Inevitably, however, the theatrical tour brought out the worst in Cobb when a Birmingham newspaper had the temerity to give him a bad review—resulting in Ty's published riposte that he made more money than the reviewer, "so why should inferiors criticize superiors?"

Ty Cobb was enjoying a baseball comeback after a period of doldrums when he was approached, again by Vaughan Glaser, to star in a film for Glaser's newborn Sunbeam Motion Picture Corporation. Cobb could certainly use the $10,000 he's reported to have received, since he'd recently been fined for barnstorming in New Haven in violation of his Tigers' contract. Ty was suddenly stricken with a rare case of selfdoubt just before his screen test, whereupon Glaser assured the ballplayer that he wouldn't be made to look ridiculous; besides, he assured Cobb, the film's story had been penned by yet another loyal son of Georgia, sports columnist Grantland Rice. *Somewhere in Georgia* was polished off in two weeks, during which time director George Ridgewell praised Cobb's diligence by saying, "I've never had to tell him more than once what I wanted done." The only conflict during shooting occurred over Cobb's timidity at doing a mild romantic scene with leading lady Elsie MacLeod. Ty himself would later dismiss the film as worthless, but recalled that it was fun meeting such movie luminaries as Fatty Arbuckle and Douglas Fairbanks (who, reportedly, wanted to costar in a film with Cobb).

Legend has it that Ty Cobb's only starring feature was horrendous, and that it was universally panned upon its release. It's thus worth noting that the first major review of *Somewhere in Georgia*, printed in the June 8, 1917, issue of *Variety* (the film hadn't made it to New York until nearly a year after its completion), was, despite its ambivalent tone, rather encouraging. While commenting that the story "didn't matter much," *Variety* opined that the film was "going to make a ten-strike with young America," and gave *Somewhere in Georgia* points for invoking the "good, wholesome atmosphere" of the then popular Frank Merriwell college sports novels. Ty Cobb himself (whom the trade paper patronizingly referred to as "Tyrus" throughout the review) was characterized as a "real, liveblooded, cleanlimbed athlete"—not precisely an unqualified rave for Cobb's acting ability, but certainly no condemnation either. *Variety* predicted that the film might not be a financial smash in metropolitan areas but would probably do well on a regional basis. No matter what the gross receipts of *Somewhere in Georgia* actually ended up being, Ty Cobb wouldn't face the movie cameras again until 1929 (a year after his retirement), when he was the subject of a Fox Movietone talking short subject; and knowing the covetous Mr. Cobb, it's a safe wager that he was as nicely overpaid for this ten-minute chunk of cinema history as he'd been for *Somewhere in Georgia*.

Soul of the Game

Gary Hoffman Productions/HBO Pictures; first telecast April 20, 1996

Executive producers: Kevin Kelly Brown, Gary Hoffman, Mike Medavoy. Produced by Robert A. Papazian, Jr. Directed by Kevin Rodney Sullivan. Teleplay by David Himmelstein. Story by Gary Hoffman. Original music: Lee Holdridge. Special music: Terence Blanchard. Photography: Sandi Sissel. Edited by Victor Du Bois. Casting: Reuben Cannon, David Giella.

Production design: Chester Kaczenski. Art director: Marc Dabe. Set decorations: Judi Giovanni. Costume design: Luke Reichle. Makeup artist: Stacye P. Branche. Hair stylist: Ted Long. Production supervisor: Tim Healey. Prod managers: Pattee Roedig, Art Schaeffer. First assistant director: H. H. Cooper. Second assistant director: Jono Oliver. Set design: William L. Camden, Ray Markham. Storyboard artist: Darryl Henley. Supervising sound editor: Dave McMoyler. Dialogue editor: Christopher Assells. Foley artist: Patrick David Cabral. Foley mixer: David Gertz. Music editor: Allan K. Rossen, Carl Zittrer. Special effects: Eddie Colman, Dave Dion, Dennis Dion, Paul Staples. Visual effects supervisor: Johnny Green. Stunt coordinator: Bob Minor. Technical advisor: Joey Banks. Steadicam operator: Chris Haarhoff. Camera operator: Paul Hughen. Film researcher: Deborah Ricketts. Color by DeLuxe. 94 minutes; Dolby Stereo Sound. Rated PG-13.

Cast: Delroy Lindo (Satchel Paige); Mykelti Williamson (Josh Gibson); Edward Herrmann (Branch Rickey); Blair Underwood (Jackie Robinson); R. Lee Ermey (Wilkie); Salli Richardson (Lahoma); Gina Ravera (Grace); Obba Babatundé (Cum Posey); Cylk Cozart (Zo Perry); J. D. Hall (Gus Greenlee); Jerry Hardin (Happy Chandler); Brent Jennings (Frank Duncan); Richard Riehle (Pete Harmon); Armand Asselin (Rip); Joey Banks (Link Rudolph); Paul Bates (Orderly No. 1); Bruce Beatty (Reporter); Guy Boyd (Clark Griffith); Stacye P. Branche (Ella Fitzgerald); Gregg Burge (Bill Robinson); Ed Cambridge (Bellhop); Mimi Cozzens (Jane Rickey); Daniel Estin (Paperboy); Zaid Farid (Clerk); Edith Fields (Nurse); Erika Flores (Girl); Holiday Freeman (Lillian the Secretary); Jesse D. Goins (John Givens, reporter); Tracy Holliway (Marian Anderson); David Johnson (Roy Campanella); Johnny G. Jones (Hotel Manager); Jonathon Lamer (Cardinal); Joseph Latimore (Jesse Williams); William Bruce Lukens (Umpire No. 3); Bob Minor (Goon No. 2); Edwin Morrow (Young Willie Mays); Jon Pennell (Steve Buckley); Alex Rascovar (Boy); Lou Richards (Radio Announcer); Isaiah Washington (Adult Willie Mays); Harvey Williams (Cat Mays); Oscar Williams (Grays Manager); Wayne King, Jimmy Ortega, April Weeden (Stunts).

April, 1945: Encouraged by the fact that the stalwartly racist baseball commissioner Kenesaw Mountain Landis has been succeeded by the more moderate "Happy" Chandler, Branch Rickey, general manager of the Brooklyn Dodgers, sets the wheels in motion for shattering the color line in Major League baseball. Publicly, Rickey announces the formation of the Brooklyn Brown Dodgers, a Negro League expansion team tied in with the "real" Brooklyn club. Privately, Rickey admits to his staff what everyone else already suspects: Using the Brown Dodgers as a smokescreen, he has dispatched his scouts to seek out a perfect candidate to be the first black ballplayer in the National League. At present, the most likely prospects are pitcher Satchel Paige of the Kansas City Monarchs, and catcher Josh Gibson of the Homestead Grays—with Gibson, whose record as a power hitter has earned him the title "The Black Babe Ruth," apparently the front-runner. But Paige, who admits to being 42 years old ("Probably in dog years!" is one associate's derisive rejoinder), is a shameless showboater and team-jumper, while Gibson has a history of mental problems, substance abuse and embarrassing public outbursts. Fully aware that the Dodgers' first black player will be subject to more scrutiny, criticism and outright hostility than anyone else in baseball history, Rickey is not so much seeking out the best ballplayer in the Negro Leagues as he is searching for a man whose reputation, character, integrity and personal discipline are above reproach: "The type of man," explains Rickey to his minions, "that the press will be forced to support." As a result, the K.C. Monarchs' rookie second baseman Jackie Robinson—UCLA graduate, record-breaking college athlete, World War II veteran, and as straight-arrow as they come—finds himself in Rickey's office, discussing the possibility of signing with the Dodgers. An outspoken opponent of institutional racism, Robinson is advised that if he joins the Brooklyn club he will be obliged to "turn the other cheek" for at least three years, by which time it is hoped that the public will be accustomed to seeing black faces on the diamond. Jackie is also told to keep his negotiations with Rickey a secret, causing him no end of anguish whenever he is in the company of Paige and Gibson, each of whom is certain that *he* will be Rickey's first choice—though neither man would ever admit to aspiring to that lofty honor. Despite his powwow with Jackie, Rickey has still not discounted either Satchel or Josh, assuming that he has the luxury of time to make his final decision. But when New York City mayor Fiorello H. LaGuardia announces his intention to impose economic sanctions upon Major League Baseball if the teams have not integrated by the beginning of the 1946 season, Rickey, worried that history will remember him not as a pioneer but as someone who buckled under to political pressure, beats LaGuardia to the punch by immediately signing Jackie Robinson. This is a devastating blow to Paige and Gibson, but both men hope to cut their losses by playing in the annual (and unofficial) post-season game between the Negro and Major League all-stars, an event that is certain to be attended by scouts from all the teams. A few days before the game, Gibson suffers a nervous breakdown and lands in a mental institution. Combining his own celebrity clout with Jackie Robinson's cool-headed diplomacy, Satchel manages to spring Josh from the hospital in time to play for the Negro League All-Stars. Alas, even the fates have conspired against the luckless Gibson; just as the umpire yells "Play ball," the field is drenched in a downpour and the game is cancelled. Though Satchel Paige would eventually join the Cleveland Indians in 1948, Josh Gibson is denied even a belated balm: he dies of a massive tumor at age 36 on January 20, 1947, three months before the Major League debut of Jackie Robinson.

Carrying on the tradition established by *Cobb* (1994) and later perpetuated by such films as *Joe Torre: Curveballs Along the Way* (1997) and *61** (2001), the made-for-cable *Soul of the Game* was of the new breed of baseball biopics which focused on a single, crucial period in the life of the protagonist(s), rather than offering a broadbrush overview of an entire life or career. First telecast by HBO on April 20, 1996, the film offered an intensely personal view of the single most significant sociopolitical upheaval in the history of 20th Century Major League Baseball. *Soul of the Game* comes as close to the *spirit* of truth as any piece of mainstream entertainment on this subject is likely to get, even though many of the film's events are rearranged, telescoped, exaggerated and fabricated for dramatic effect.

The script by David Himmelstein is a vast improvement over the author's previous baseball film, *Talent for the Game* (q.v.), perhaps suggesting that Himmelstein, rather than his two collaborators, can be credited for the isolated moments of excellence in that earlier picture. Director Kevin Rodney Sullivan, a graduate of music videos and later the helmsman of the stylishly incisive theatrical feature *How Stella Got Her Groove Back* (1998), adroitly brings out the best of Himmelstein's teleplay, deftly juggling the many characters, interweaving subplots, backstage intrigues and contrary viewpoints, and coming up with an almost perfectly balanced film.

The most remarkable and satisfying aspect of the film is the seamless matching of characters and actors. The casting is so "right" that the film could stand as a textbook example of how to transform musty historical characters into living, breathing human beings. Even the ages of the three stars are in reasonably close proximity to their real-life counterparts, with the oldest of the three playing the ageless Satchel Paige, the "middle" actor cast as the thirtysomething Josh Gibson, and the youngest in the role of Jackie Robinson (though the actor in question had at least six years on the Robinson of 1945, the discrepancy was not glaringly obvious).

Since the real Satchel Paige was arguably the most colorful personality in the Negro Leagues—certainly he was the most self-congratulatory and publicity-conscious—it is altogether fitting that the film's Paige, 44-year-old Delroy Lindo, steals the show. Born in England to Jamaican parents, Lindo was best known as a stage actor, though his film credits, notably his collaborations with director Spike Lee (*Malcolm X*, *Clockers*, *Crooklyn*), his menacing portrayal of a usurious limo-service owner in *Get Shorty* (1995), and his idiosyncratic guardian angel in *A Life Less Ordinary* (1997), are both extensive and impressive. As Satchel Paige, Lindo has the trademarked swagger, bravado, knowing grins, loose-limbed pitching delivery and unabashed grandstanding down to the tiniest detail. The actor also has an excellent handle on both the "public" and "private" Paige, subtly shifting from one to another and back again without the slightest evidence of strain or spillover. Publicly, Satchel maintains the facade of being utterly in control of his temper and talent, dispensing sage advice to newcomer Jackie Robinson, providing comfort and support to his mercurial colleague Josh Gibson, scoffing at or sidestepping racial slurs and pointed questions about his age, displaying a gregarious *noblesse oblige* when surrounded by his adoring public, and pretending to care not a whit who is chosen as the Major League's first black ballplayer. Privately, Paige is a seething mass of neuroses, desperate for acceptance from white and black fans alike, endlessly worrying that his advancing years or multitude of injuries will bring an abrupt end to his career, and habitually breaking his own self-imposed rule by enviously "looking back" to see the upstart Robinson catching up with him.

Not only does Delroy Lindo do full justice to "both" Satchel Paiges, but he also has two of the film's best scenes. The first occurs early in the action, when rookie Jackie Robinson refuses to be "called in" with the rest of the fielders as Paige prepares to strike out a batter, but instead insists upon remaining in position. Satchel gives Jackie a withering glance and says, loudly but without rancor, "This is *my* game and *my* show!" How right he is—for now.

Later on, Satchel arranges a locker-room meeting with Branch Rickey. Though fully aware that his future in the Majors rests entirely in Rickey's hands, Satch isn't about to betray his anxiousness. After artfully positioning a chair in the middle of the room so that his back will be facing Rickey, he plunks himself down, places a fishing rod in his hands and stretches his legs lazily before him—a meticulously manufactured image of casual insouciance.

Just as Delroy Lindo captures the brash showmanship of Satchel Paige, 32-year-old Blair Underwood does full honor to the sober, businesslike, doggedly unspectacular Jackie Robinson. Best known at the time for his portrayal of no-nonsense attorney Jonathan Rollins on the TV series *L.A. Law*, Underwood never attempts to imitate Robinson's familiar nasally speech patterns, concentrating instead on Jackie's innate dignity, his dedication to both his game and his personal well-being, his smoldering resentment over racial inequality, his grudging but cooperative commitment to keep that resentment under wraps at the outset of his Dodgers contract, and his conscience-stricken embarrassment while trying to hide the knowledge that he would be the "chosen one" and his more experienced colleagues Paige and Gibson were to be shut out.

Even with fewer baseball scenes than either of his costars, Blair Underwood fully realizes Jackie's technique and physical trademarks. In an interview with *Jet* magazine, Underwood observed that, "Mastering

Robinson's running style, which was low to the ground, grasping his particular manner of handling the bat and imitating his pigeon-toed walk was challenging." Since none of the film's stars had played much baseball before filming, they submitted to extensive coaching from Joey Banks, the son of Hall of Famer Ernie Banks (see notes for *Finding Buck McHenry*). Underwood received additional input from actress Ruby Dee, who, though not in *Soul of the Game*, had the unique distinction of playing Jackie Robinson's wife in 1950's *The Jackie Robinson Story* (q.v.) and Jackie's mother in 1990's *The Court-Martial of Jackie Robinson*. Of Dee, Underwood said, "She taught me about his fire inside, his intensity."

Above all, it could be said that Blair Underwood had baseball in his blood. Interviewed by Mike Hammer of *TV Guide*, the actor revealed, "My great-uncle played in the Negro Leagues. He was on the same team with Satchel Paige and Josh Gibson, and one of the reasons I took the part was for him."

We have held off discussing Mykelti Williamson's portrayal of Josh Gibson in order to provide some background information on Gibson himself—who, though generously covered in *Soul of the Game*, really deserves a filmed biography all his own. (For further information on Paige and Robinson, see the separate entries for *Don't Look Back: The Story of Leroy 'Satchel' Paige* and *The Jackie Robinson Story*.) Born in Buena Vista, Georgia, in 1911, John "Josh" Gibson turned pro at age 18, graduating to full Negro League stardom on two Pittsburgh teams, the Crawfords and the Homestead Grays. Because of inadequate, misleading and often contradictory documentation, it is difficult to separate fact from legend, but it is safe to say that Josh Gibson fully deserved the title of "The Black Babe Ruth." Boasting a lifetime hitting record of .391, Gibson has been credited with between 800 and 962 home runs during his

career, though one of his biographers, John B. Holway, has only been able to confirm 236 homers (still an impressive tally, considering that most black teams played only 50 to 80 games per season). As noted in *Soul of the Game*, Gibson's fame and popularly amongst black and white baseball aficionados was second only to Satchel Paige—and there were certain periods, notably the early 1940s, in which Gibson was rated Number One. No less an expert than Dizzy Dean characterized Josh as one of the greatest players alive, and in 1941 the eminent sportswriter Shirley Povich put Gibson at the top of the list of then-active black ballplayers, describing them en masse as "a couple of million dollars worth of baseball talent on the loose," withheld from the Majors only "by the pigmentation of their skin."

The relationship between Gibson and Paige depicted in the film—fellow star players on the color-blind Trujillo All-Stars in the Dominican Republic, trash-talking friendly enemies when on opposing teams, convivial friends during off-hours, Paige doing his best to keep Gibson's spirits afloat during his "dark" periods—is superficially accurate. It should be noted that, despite what we see in the film's opening scenes, the two ballplayers were no longer associated with the Trujillo team in 1945. This bit of dramatic license is, however, justified when, as a means of underlining the exigencies of race relations in America, Satchel and Josh comment on the fact that they are being treated like kings by dictator Rafael Trujillo, while back home the eminently "democratic" President Roosevelt would probably not give them the time of day. It must also be observed that by 1945 the once-strong friendship between Paige and Gibson had deteriorated considerably. One reason for the strained relationship was that Josh Gibson's fame had at last extended to the mainstream white media, notably in a lengthy *Time* magazine profile.

Having long held the opinion that *he* was the only black player worthy of such "crossover" publicity, Paige felt his supremacy being challenged, and his competitive instincts went into overdrive.

The 6'1", 210-pound Josh Gibson was the stuff of which legends are made. One of the most famous bits of Gibson folklore has him knocking a home run out of Yankee Stadium during an exhibition game—a feat that not even Babe Ruth could match. Despite the concerted efforts of dedicated baseball historians the world over, no shred of evidence has ever been found to verify this story, though it is undeniably true that Gibson was one of only two home-run sluggers who ever cleared the fence at Griffith Park in Washington (the other was Mickey Mantle).

Another well-circulated legend states that Gibson was slated to break the Big League color barrier as early as 1942, when he was on the verge of being signed by the Pittsburgh Pirates—only to have this honor unceremoniously yanked away by the lilywhite baseball hierarchy. The facts of the matter are more complex. On the authorization of Pirates president William Benswager, black sportswriter Wendell Smith drew up a list of Negro League players who might be worthy of big-league tryouts; heading that list was Josh Gibson. Outside of Benswager's initial public announcement, however, nothing more was said about the tryouts. Pressed for an explanation, Benswager claimed that Gibson's boss, Homestead Grays owner Cum Posey, had pleaded with him not to "destroy" the Negro Leagues by signing away its top players. According to baseball historian Mark Ribowsky, Posey favored gradual rather than overnight integration of the Majors, so that the best black ballplayers could hold out for higher salaries instead of being immediately thrown into a single, inexpensive talent pool. In *Soul of the Game*, however, the story of Gibson's aborted signing with the Pirates is stripped

of its complexity and is cited primarily to intensify the poignancy of Gibson's climactic freeze-out in favor of the younger, more stable Jackie Robinson.

That "stability"—or the lack of it—was definitely a factor in Branch Rickey's ultimate decision to go with Robinson. Though the film does not delve into the history of Josh Gibson's mental illness, his biographers concur that he suffered his first nervous breakdown in January of 1943. According to his sister Annie Gibson Mahaffey, to whom much of the Gibson folklore can be attributed, the hospitalized Josh was informed that he had a brain tumor. Worried that an operation would turn him into a vegetable, Josh refused to undergo surgery and insisted that the details of his illness not be made public lest anyone pity him. (There is, in fact, no medical record of Gibson's alleged tumor, but this might have been because the doctor honored his wishes to the letter.) Before learning the seriousness of his condition, Gibson was regarded as a friendly, easygoing fellow, despite a periodic drinking problem. After his discharge from the hospital, Gibson returned to baseball, but the old affability was largely absent. Tormented by recurrent seizures, blackouts and sudden violent rages, he turned increasingly to liquor and drugs to assuage the pain. Understandably, both his game and his physical stamina suffered, though he managed to rally during his last year in baseball, not only negotiating the best contract he ever had, but also leading his league in homers and closing out the 1946 season with a .361 batting average.

In still another effort to amplify the pathos of Josh Gibson's exclusion from the White Majors, *Soul of the Game* ignores his triumphant final year in professional baseball, intimating that Gibson's career—and for all intents and purposes, his life—ended with the rainout of an entirely fictional postseason exhibition game in November of 1945. Similarly, the film's printed epilogue, which comments ironically on the fact that Gibson's death occurred only a few months before Jackie Robinson officially broke baseball's color line, does not mention that Josh was posthumously inducted into the Cooperstown Hall of Fame in 1972, the second African American player to be so honored on the strength of his Negro League record (the first, of course, was Satchel Paige)—a fact that might have ever so slightly dispersed the cloud of tragedy and lost opportunities that enshrouded his career.

While there is no verification at hand that Satchel Paige ever acted as Jackie Robinson's unofficial mentor as he does in the film, for the most part *Soul of the Game*'s treatment of Paige and Robinson does not stray too far from the truth. It is a different matter with Josh Gibson; beyond stating factually that he was a brilliant but troubled ballplayer, the script is careless with other particulars of his life. Example: Early in the film, before Branch Rickey has decided upon Jackie Robinson, there is a stunning scene on a Kansas City hotel roof in which Gibson, stripped naked, gazes at a spectacular Fourth of July fireworks display and agonizes over the bad breaks of his past and the uncertainties ahead of him. As pure symbolism—a strong, powerful man humbled and literally stripped bare by events beyond his control—the scene cannot be equaled. In truth, not one of Gibson's friends, associates or family members can ever remember him wallowing in self-pity or uncertainty. As for appearing naked in public, this did indeed happen, but it was *after* he found out that Robinson had been selected for the Dodgers—and it occurred during a drunken bender in San Juan, Puerto Rico. Another aspect of the film not to be taken at face value is the in-your-face

adversarial relationship between Josh Gibson and Jackie Robinson, who, in fact, barely knew or even spoke to one another.

Nowhere does the film part company with truth more frequently than in its depiction of Josh Gibson's love life. Failing to mention his first and only marriage in 1928 to Helen Mason, who died giving birth to his twin sons, the film also ignores Josh's lengthy common-law relationship with a woman named Hattie Jones, a union marked by his frequent and flagrant infidelities. The only one of Josh's "significant others" seen in the film is his wartime mistress Grace Fournier, who remained with him until her husband returned from the Army in 1946. *Soul of the Game* takes great pains to idealize this romance, suggesting that the saintly Grace is the only person who keeps Gibson from falling to pieces during the Bad Times, and even holding out hope in the final scene that she will someday desert her abusive husband and return to nurse poor Josh through his final months on earth. Suffice it to say that in real life, Grace Fournier was no Eleanor Gehrig. Some baseball historians have suggested that it was Grace who got Josh hooked on cocaine during his last years, thereby increasing rather than lightening his burdens.

Though the script's authenticity regarding Josh Gibson might be questioned, the actor playing the role cannot be faulted. 36-year-old Mykelti Williamson, who in 1994 made a vivid impression on filmgoers with his portrayal of the amiable, shrimp-obsessed Bubba in *Forrest Gump*, was physically the ideal choice to portray Gibson. Not satisfied with merely looking the part, Williamson immersed himself in the role, consulting source after source to capture all of Josh's mannerisms and clothing trademarks, notably the familiar rolled-up right

Opposite: **Magazine ad for *Soul of the Game* (1996). Pay no attention to the agent-dictated billing order at the top; Delroy Lindo as Satchel Paige is in the middle of the picture, flanked by Blair Underwood (left) as Jackie Robinson and Mykelti Williamson (right) as Josh Gibson.**

sleeve and angled baseball-cap bill. In many ways, Williamson's task was more challenging than those faced by either of his co-stars, since no films are known to exist of Josh Gibson in action on the ballfield. To fill in the gaps, the actor solicited the help of two of Gibson's Negro League contemporaries, "Prince" Joe Henry of the Indianapolis Clowns and Gene Smith of the Chicago American Giants, to instruct him as to how Josh talked, moved and played. Interviewed by *Jet* magazine, Williamson promised, "This will be the first time an audience will see an authentic portrayal of Josh, and Josh Gibson, Jr., will be watching."

Bypassing the above-mentioned lapses in accuracy, *Soul of the Game* does a terrific job in addressing the issue of Race. Avoiding the overly simplistic, dogmatic political correctness of many films of the 1980s and 1990s in which African Americans were 100 percent virtuous and Caucasians were wholly evil, this film correctly observes that no issue is defined by Absolutes. With the spectacular exception of a slathering bigot in the final exhibition-game sequence, most of the white characters are shown to be decently motivated individuals who tread lightly around integration not because they hate the black man, but because they honestly don't know whether the results will be positive or negative. Nor is Branch Rickey elevated to heroic proportions simply because he is the only white character willing to move expeditiously in bringing black players into Major League baseball. We never know if Rickey is acting out of inherent nobility, if his motivation in grabbing up black talent is purely a matter of economics, or if he is merely an egomaniacal publicity hound eager to cover himself in glory while drawing thousands of curiosity seekers into Ebbets Field. Edward Herrmann (who'd starred in the 1978 baseball film *A Love Affair: The Eleanor and Lou Gehrig Story*) brings to his portrayal of Branch

Rickey the same inscrutable unpredictability that had earned the real Rickey the nickname "Mahatma."

Outside of Rickey, the other white characters are shown to be products of their time, when the separation of races was so entrenched that any other form of social balance was all but imponderable. This deeply ingrained mindset is painfully brought home in a scene that takes place somewhere in the Southwest, as Jackie Robinson accompanies Satchel Paige on a motor trip to their next ballgame. Decked out in a tailor-made outfit and driving a shiny new sedan, Paige pulls up in front of a ramshackle roadside fruit stand, where his impeccably dressed wife Lahoma immediately befriends the raggedy little white girl minding the store. The girl is pleased to have such prosperous-looking customers, and rather enjoys the fuss made over her by Lahoma, who offers to comb the child's tangled hair in "movie star" fashion. But when Lahoma asks if she can use the bathroom in the girl's home, the angel-faced child calmly replies, as if by rote, "My Daddy don't allow no niggers in the house." There is no hatred or malice in the girl's voice, and a second later she is again smiling sweetly, clearly delighted that these strangers have been so nice to her. This brief, heartbreaking vignette addresses the near-insurmountable challenge facing the man who will be chosen to smash baseball's color line far more eloquently than any crowd scene featuring a band of torchbearing redneck cretins spouting reams of race-baiting vitriol.

In only one respect did *Soul of the Game* choose not to address one of the touchier aspects of the race question. It is a matter of record that several black ball-club owners, notably Gus Greenlee of the Pittsburgh Crawfords, resisted the notion of their best players being recruited by the Majors, worried that this would not only cripple the Negro Leagues, but that the white owners' vague promises that the remaining black teams would be converted into farm clubs were just so much hot air (as it turned out, these fears were justified). *Soul of the Game* ignores this resistance, perhaps out of concern that the viewer would conclude that some black ballclub owners tacitly approved of segregation. The only scene relating to this volatile issue occurs between Branch Rickey and J. L. Wilkenson, the *white* owner of the Kansas City Monarchs, here depicted far less sympathetically than he was in the previous Satchel Paige TV biopic *Don't Look Back*.

The concern that the audience would not be able to grasp some of the subtler points of the story might explain the screenwriters' tendency to indulge in the old movie-biography habit of arbitrary namedropping. As if admitting that Jackie Robinson, Satchel Paige and Josh Gibson were no longer household names, an attempt is made to provide recognizable personalities for the average viewer to latch onto by throwing in several other important African Americans of the era, including Ella Fitzgerald, Bill "Bojangles" Robinson, Marian Anderson, and even an adolescent Willie Mays, who shows up just in time to have his baseball autographed by Gibson at the epochal postseason game which closes the story. In all fairness, it should be noted that while the other black celebrities seem to come literally out of left field, Mays is carefully woven into the proceedings as a framing device; he shows up at the beginning and end of the film, recalling the last days of the Negro Leagues to an inquiring reporter. Though Willie Mays' inclusion may at first seem unnecessary, his presence drives home the fact that without the struggles and sacrifices of the Paiges, Gibsons and Robinsons, there might never have been a Mays in the Majors.

Because so much historical ground is covered in *Soul of the Game*, the actual baseball scenes are relatively few, confined mainly to the first twenty minutes, the halfway mark, and the very end of the film. Quality, however, amply compensates for quantity, with director Sullivan and the three main players extracting full value from their comparatively limited opportunities. Rickwood Field in Huntington, Alabama, the oldest active ballpark in the nation and the actual stamping grounds of several top Negro League teams and players (see notes on *Cobb*), stood in for Griffith Park and Chicago's Comiskey Park, while Monarch Stadium in Kansas City was "played" by League Field in Huntingburg, Indiana (see notes on *A League of Their Own*).

If nothing else, *Soul of the Game* proved that black actors playing black ballplayers had come a long way from the minstrel-show buffoonery of *The Bingo Long Traveling All-Stars and Motor Kings* (q.v.). Apparently there were others who felt the same: Delroy Lindo, Blair Underwood, and *Soul of the Game* itself were all nominated for the prestigious NAACP Image Award.

Squeeze Play

Troma Inc.; released 1979

Executive producer: William E. Kirksey. Produced by Lloyd Kaufman and Michael Herz. Directed by Samuel Weil. Screenplay by Haim Pekelis. Additional material by Charles Kaufman. Photography: Lloyd Kaufman. Edited by George T. Norris. Music and lyrics by Rand B. Wohlsetter, Ned Albright, Delmar Brown, Kenwood Denhard, Neil Sheppard, Don Yowell, Joe Bidewell, Steve Sarabande, and Wayne Vicon, among others. Performers include Carol Cass, Scot Paris, and Drew Mosely. Baseball trainer: Roger Kirby. Production manager: William B. Kegg, Jr. Assistant directors: David Alexander and David Hastings. Unit manager: Joe Rosenthal. Associate producer: Ira Kanarick. Production executives: Maris Herz and Patricia Kaufman. "Special thanks" to John G. Avildsen.* Eastman color. 92 minutes; sound. Rated R.

Cast: Jenni Hetrick (Samantha); Jim Harris (Wes); Alford Corley (Buddy); Melissa

Michaels (Betty Lou); Rick Gitlin (Fred); Helen Campitelli (Jamie); Michael P. Moran (Bozo); Sonya Jennings (Max); Sharon Kyle Bramblett (Midge); Zachery (Pop); Diana Valentien (Maureen); Rick Khan (Tom); Lisa Beth Wolf (Rose); Tony Hoty (Sam Koch); Steven W. Kaman (Russ); Brenda Kaplan (Brenda); Kenneth Raskin (Mr. Beasley); Edward D. Phillips (Chester Whatley); Rosemary Joyce (Wanda); Peter Van Norden (Monsieur Pierre); Precious Colquit (Maureen's Mother); Sean McCray (Maureen's Baby); Joyce Anne Finney, Sherry Park (Cheerleaders); Jim Metzler (Second Base); Tom Wiggen (Third Base); Neil Kinsella (Right Field); Kenneth Robert Lane (Home Base Umpire); Vic Hammer (Godfrey); S. Lloyd Kaufman, Sr. (Van Hooten); Allen Harris (Left Field); Irwin Keyes (Bouncer); Bess Lieberman (Teenybopper); Maureen Hughes (Pocketbook Lady); Deborah Jean Templin (Clown); Karen Galanaugh (Woman from Packing); Neil and Marge Marciano (Apartment Hunters); Beatrice Roederer (Beauty Parlor Lady); Linda Ann Watt (Boom Girl); William E. Kirksey (Game Announcer and Narrator of Film); Norman Greenhut (Wet Tee Shirt MC); George Beane (Chic Bartender); Fred Singer, Chuck Dunn, Robert Katz, Eric Perlmutter, Peter Liewant, Sandy Fishman, and Larry Berezin (Animals); Patti Van Cawvenberger, Mary Jan Deutsch, Marilyn Kaufman, Barbara Schweitzer, Sue De Pasquane, Christine Ricci, Carol Kohant, Kathy Kohant, Sheila Kelly, Diana Murphy, Mary Lumosa, Georgina Soborski, Ernest H. Puio (Softball Doubles); Georgina Reisner, Hania Jardin, Susan Tarlton, Inga Thomas, Wendy Stuart, Mary Ann Young, Joanna Jasinka, Susan Wolf, Gail Moore, Gayle West, Sherry Lipsman, Vera Dika (Disco Ladies); and Margie Loren, Abe Levitsky, Abe Gurko, Janet Dailey, Pat Rice McCray, Ben McCray, Marilyn Rosner, Jackie Schneiderman, Meryl Brooks, Alan Moyle, Sheryl Vitale, Patricia S. Kaufman, Maris Herz, Sloane Herz, Steve Lasserman, Nancy Winston, Jay Stern, Cory Ryback, Ed Wolf, and Holly Kegg.

In the little company town of Springborn (its only industry is a mattress factory), the Beavers, an all-male softball team led by macho-man Wes, celebrates each victory in caveman fashion by bedding their womenfolk. The ladies, led by the curvaceous Samantha, rebel at this treatment, going so far as to form their own baseball team, the Beaverettes. A battle for sexual supremacy is fought on the ballfield in the form of a Beaver-Beaverette championship match, and though there's a lot of dirty work on the diamond, romance eventually triumphs over adversity.

I could outline the plot in more detail, but that would mean I'd have to sit through *Squeeze Play* again. The first major financial success from the legendary Troma Inc. exploitation-flick factory (Troma's other contributions to posterity have included *Chopper Chicks in Zombietown*, *Class of Nuke 'Em High* and the *Toxic Avenger* series), this ninety-two-minute paean to breasts, bottoms, belches and (sometimes) baseball is so typical of the sort of R-rated material that kept the drive-in movie industry solvent in the 1970s that it's practically a model of the genre. We are offered several enticing and mostly extraneous flashes of nudity before the opening credits have even faded. The "mildest" gags involve either flatulence or crotch-grabbing; an early line refers to a "hard-fart victory," and during the opening ballgame sequence we see a tight close-up of a catcher's hand flashing signals, the fingers eventually seeking a more pleasurable pursuit within the catcher's nether regions. The battle of the sexes is established with an arbitrary nod to women's liberation (translation: none of the girls wear bras). A wet T-shirt contest transpires out of nowhere, then seems to go on longer than *The Sorrow and the Pity*. The hero is comically, and erotically, humiliated in his bachelor pad, which looks more like an hourly rate motel room. Easy comedy targets include fat black women, fat white motorcyclists, and fat stupid policemen (the top cop is named "Koch," pronounced just as you'd

---

John G. Avildsen was the director of the original Rocky, which is lampooned incessantly in Squeeze Play.

expect). Shameless commercial plugs abound, indicating in the case of *Squeeze Play* that Dannon yogurt, Serta mattresses, Pepsi-Cola and Tropicana orange juice paid for the box lunches on location (the film was shot in exotic, overcast New Jersey). The guys win over the girls at the end of the film because it was mostly guys in their pickups and RVs who paid to see this movie at the drive-in—except for those guys who brought their steady dates, and thus paid *not* to see this film. And at fade-out time everybody who appeared in the picture gets screen credit, which, as an ego massaging device, is a lot cheaper than actually paying any of the extras.

And, of course, there are plenty of opportunities to elucidate the meaning of the title. In baseball, a "squeeze play" is a planned play in which the runner at third waits until the batter bunts, and then heads for home plate. This is explained to us a number of times by the film's sportscaster-narrator (who is also the film's executive producer—no expense spared here), and illustrated by using empty yogurt cartons (plug! plug!) to represent the players. But if there's anyone who needs a more thorough explanation as to the meaning of *Squeeze Play*, then he must have gotten into the theater using his older brother's ID.

Trying to find any value in this sleazy little quickie is like shoveling manure in a stable in hopes of finding a pony. But believe it or not, *Squeeze Play* has a few things going for it. Saddled with material that's about as funny as a urinalysis, the young and very healthy cast members knock themselves out trying to entertain their audience, and occasionally succeed, if through nothing more than sheer, raw energy. And though the direction is atrocious, the staging of the ballgame scenes haphazard, and the camerawork slightly below the level of the home video you took of that 1985 visit to the LaBrea Tar Pits, at least *Squeeze Play* is a movie that *moves* and—once in a great

while—conveys a genuine love of baseball. Taking its extremely intermittent good points into consideration, *Squeeze Play* is far more worthwhile than the dull, meandering *Blue Skies Again* (q.v.), the expensive but hollow *The Slugger's Wife* (q.v.) and the unspeakably awful *Ed* (q.v.).

Squeeze Play's biggest laugh has nothing to do with baseball or bazooms. As the opening credits flash on the screen, we see a tally of the film's "stars." Then we're presented with a special credit which reads "Introducing Rick Gitlin." While it's true that some of the leading players—notably Jenni Hetrick and Al Corley—eventually did go on to bigger things, one wonders how Rick Gitlin was able to keep his humility back in 1979 in the company of such long-established favorites as *Squeeze Play* stars Jim Harris, Sharon Kyle Bramblett, and "Zachery."

Stealing Home

Mount Company Productions/Warner Bros.; released August 1988

Produced by Thom Mount and Hank Moonjean. Written and directed by Steven Kampmann and Will Aldis. Photography: Bobby Byrne. Underwater and aerial photography: Jeff Simon. Edited by Anthony Gibbs. Music by David Foster. Song "And When She Danced (Theme from *Stealing Home*)" by David Foster and Linda Thompson-Jenner; performed by Marilyn Martin and David Foster. Popular songs on soundtrack performed by the original artists. Production designer: Vaughan Edwards. Costumes by Robert DeMora. Associate producer: Chana Ben-Dov. Casting by Bonnie Timmerman. Production manager: Laura J. Medina. Assistant director: Betsy Pollock. Production coordinator: Richard Liebegot. Sound by Garry Alper. Set decorations by Robert Franco. Special effects by J. C. Brotherhood. Color by Technicolor. Dolby Sound. 98 minutes. Rated PG.

Cast: Mark Harmon (Billy Wyatt); Blair Brown (Ginny Wyatt); Jonathan Silverman (Teenage Alan Appleby); Harold Ramis (Alan Appleby); William McNamara (Teenage Billy

Wyatt); Richard Jenkins (Hank Chandler); John Shea (Sam Wyatt); Jodie Foster (Katie Chandler); Christine Jones (Grace Chandler); Beth Broderick (Leslie Jordan); Jane Bruckner (Cheryl); Ted Ross (Brad Scott); Thacher Goodwyn (Billy Wyatt, Age 10); Yvette Croskey (Teenage Robin Parks); Ollie Davison (Robin Parks); Judith Kaban (Laura Appleby); Samuel Chew, Jr. (Nathan Appleby); Miriam Flynn (Mrs. Parks); Dani Janssen (Hooker); Allison Hedges (Robin's Daughter); James Talbot (Carleton Coach); Pat McDade (Umpire); Brooke Mills (Tennis Girl); Peter Bucossi (Frank); Katie Kampmann (Baby Hope); Richard Dauer (Spirit Coach); Helen Hunt (Grown-Up Hope Wyatt).

Onetime minor-league ballplayer Billy Wyatt had quit baseball cold fourteen years ago after an on-field humiliation and has been "on the bum" ever since. Billy returns to the suburban Philadelphia home of his mother when he learns that his former babysitter, Katie Chandler, has committed suicide. Katie's will had stipulated that she be cremated and that Billy would have to dispose of her ashes—he was, in her words, "the only person who would know what to do with them." On the long journey home, Wyatt's mind wanders back to his experiences with Katie: how she flaunted the rules when she'd been his sitter, had taught him how to smoke when he was ten years old, and had advised him on his future sex life; how she'd given him a necklace with a little baseball-shaped ornament as a permanent reminder that baseball was his life, and how Billy had given the necklace to young Robin Parks, to whom he'd lost his virginity as a teenager; how Katie had been there to provide solace to both Billy and his mother when Billy's father died; how Billy and Katie's relationship had deepened into a brief romance; and how, on the last day that Katie saw Billy some twenty years ago, she'd advised him to take an offer to go to baseball training camp. Upon returning home, Billy tries to figure out what Katie meant by saying that he alone would know what to do with her ashes. He is reunited with his old buddy Alan Appleby, whose own "coming of age" occurred about the same time as Billy's, and who is reluctantly pulled into Billy's plan to dispose of Katie's remains. An evening of reminiscences culminates in Billy and Alan squeezing into the baseball uniforms they'd worn at Carleton prep school, breaking into Philadelphia's Veterans Stadium in the dead of night, and staging an impromptu ball game, with Billy rounding the bases while holding the urn containing Katie's ashes. Suddenly Billy remembers a conversation he'd had long ago with Katie while visiting the old Steel Pier in Atlantic City, when Katie confessed that she'd like to take flight like the gulls and fly over the ocean. Billy jubilantly scatters the ashes off the pier and into the sea, an act that galvanizes him into going back into pro baseball. Responding to Katie's long-reaching influence, Billy reclaims the necklace he'd surrendered to Robin Parks so long ago and joins up with the San Bernardino Spirit. We last see Billy Wyatt in a Spirit uniform in the midst of a game, stealing home base just as he'd done at Carleton Prep on the day that he'd received his training-camp offer—while looking on from the grandstands is Alan Appleby, who's gotten a new lease on life himself and who has been united with Robin Parks, the unrequited love of his teen years.

Stealing Home was one of a handful of "little" films made by Jodie Foster in the late 1980s to recharge her acting batteries following her graduation from Yale. Foster is so good, enriching her portrayal of Katie Chandler with a gamut of character traits ranging from cautionless eccentricity to a deep and uncomplicated grasp of human nature, that one is tempted to write about naught but her when discussing this film. Inasmuch as this book is about baseball pictures and not Jodie Foster, we'll look beyond her and analyze *Stealing Home* on its own merits—shaky though these merits are at times.

The film has "personal statement" carved in block letters all over it. Writer-directors Steven Kampmann and Will Aldis (the writing team responsible for the 1986 Rodney Dangerfield vehicle *Back to School*) had sprung from the ranks of Children of the 1960s who in the 1980s had come to feel that they'd lost something in the growth process, and that they had to stop and find it before middle age had set in. This is a concept that millions were able to relate to when *Field of Dreams* (q.v.) came out, but the focus in *Stealing Home* is somewhat narrower. We're asked to empathize with a couple of privileged young suburbanites from the country club/prep school circuit who spend half their time hoping that someone will tell them what to do with their future lives, and the other half trying to score with the girls. Chances are if you shared the same cushy background as the characters in this film you'll get more out of *Stealing Home* than most people; otherwise, the principal feeling one has toward the protagonists of this film is "Get a job! Get a life!"

Stealing Home has been roundly condemned by some reviewers as one of the worst ever baseball films. Actually, once you get past the confusing flashback-flashforward structure set up in the early scenes, the film isn't all that terrible. True, there are major flaws in the screenplay, especially within the flashbacks; one reminiscence told from Billy Wyatt's point of view shows Billy's pal Alan Appleby having his first sexual experience with an obliging "older woman"—something Billy could not possibly have witnessed unless he'd been hiding in the bedroom closet. Also, some plot points and characters are given undue emphasis, then dropped completely. Katie Chandler's various dead-end love affairs with unseen suitors are evidently supposed to set us up for her suicide, but this is never made clear; and much is made of the training-camp offer from the "famous" Bud Scott (played by Ted Ross, whose baseball pic

debut occurred in *The Bingo Long Traveling All-Stars and Motor Kings* [q.v.]), but once Bud Scott gets a line or two out and promises to be an interesting character, we never see him again. And the casting is erratic, to say the least: William McNamara does a fine job as the teenaged Billy Wyatt, but he looks and acts nothing like his "grown-up" counterpart Mark Harmon; while the actors cast as the fathers of Billy and Alan seem far too young to have sired those boys—particularly true in the case of Samuel Chew, Jr., who, as the father of thirty-eight-year-old Alan Appleby (played by Harold Ramis), looks more like Alan's little brother.

Beyond all this, we do have a finely honed performance by Blair Brown as Billy Wyatt's mother, who believably covers an age range from early thirties to mid-fifties. There's also some gorgeous photography, notably in the seashore scenes filmed at New Jersey's Island Beach State Park. And the two times we see Billy Wyatt (man and boy) round the bases during a ballgame are reasonably well staged, though we would like to see more of Mark Harmon (reputedly one of Hollywood's best ballplayers) in action, and rather less of the slow motion and stretch-framing which self-indulgently infests the "stealing home" sequences. Incidentally, when Harmon appears in the lineup of the San Bernardino Spirit (of which the actor was a part owner), those scenes are shot in that California League team's actual stomping grounds of Fiscalini Field, which looks fairly attractive in Technicolor; though again, more of Fiscalini and less directorial showboating in the final scenes would enhance our viewing pleasure, especially since the script has led us to believe that we'd be treated to a longer, more rousing baseball climax.

Some notes worth noting: *Stealing Home* was coproduced by Thom Mount and photographed by Bobby Byrne, both of whom worked on another, infinitely more satisfying up-close-and-personal baseball film of 1988, *Bull Durham* (q.v.). Mark Harmon's three-day stubble and furtive acting style brings to mind *Bull Durham* star Kevin Costner, leading one to speculate that the role of *Stealing Home* hero Billy Wyatt might have been conceived with Costner in mind. Whatever the case, it's certainly no accident that when Mark Harmon steps up to the plate in the last scene, the public address announcer informs us that he's "pinch-hitting for Costner."

The Stratton Story

MGM; released May 12, 1949

Produced by Jack Cummings. Directed by Sam Wood. Screenplay by Douglas Morrow and Guy Trosper, from a story by Douglas Morrow. Photography: Harold Rosson. Edited by Ben Lewis. Art direction by Cedric Gibbons and Paul Groesse. Musical director: Adolph Deutsch. Sound recording by Douglas Shearer. Technical adviser: Monty Stratton. 106 minutes; black and white; sound.

Cast: James Stewart (Monty Stratton); June Allyson (Ethel Stratton); Frank Morgan (Barney Wiles); Agnes Moorehead (Ma Stratton); Bill Williams (Gene Watson); Bruce Cowling (Ted Lyons); Eugene Bearden (Himself, Western All-Stars Pitcher); Bill Dickey (Himself); Jimmy Dykes (Himself); Cliff Clark (Higgins); Mary Lawrence (Dot); Dean White (Luke Appling); Robert Gist (Larnie); Mervyn Shea (Himself, White Sox Catcher); Pat Flaherty (Western All-Stars Manager); Captain F. G. Somers (Giants Manager); Mitchell Lewis (Conductor); Michael Ross (Pitcher); Florence Lake (Mrs. Appling); Anne Nagel (Mrs. Piet); Barbara Woodell (Mrs. Shea); Alphonse Martiel (Headwaiter); Holmes Herbert (Doctor); Lee Tung Foo (Waiter); Charles B. Smith (Theater Usher); Kenneth Tobey (Detroit Player); Roy Partee (Western All-Stars Pitcher); Gino Corrado (Waiter Serving Oysters); Matt McHugh (Slot Machine Patron); Fred Millican (Southern All-Stars Catcher); William Bassett (Stratton Baby); James Nolan, Peter Crouse (Reporters); Pat Orr, John "Ziggy" Sears, Jack Powell, Joe Rue (Umpires); Dwight Adams, George Vico, Louie Novikoff (Detroit Players); Robert Graham, Eugene Persson (Boys); Syd Saylor, George Melford, George Ovey, Cy Stevens, William Bailey, Polly Bailey, Vangie Bielby, Mabel Smaney, Jessie Arnold (Theater Patrons).

In the early 1930s young Texas farmer Monty Stratton is pitching for $3 a game with a sandlot team called the Wagner Wildcats when he's spotted by washed-up major leaguer Barney Wiles. Impressed by Monty's raw skill, Barney tries to talk the boy into trying out for the Chicago White Sox, but Ma Stratton needs Monty to tend the farm. A bargain is struck: Barney will help out with the chores, and as "compensation" will be permitted to train young Stratton. Come early spring, Barney takes Monty to the Sox's California training camp, where manager Jimmy Dykes is convinced to take Stratton on, with Barney retained as pitching coach. As the season approaches, Monty is talked into a blind date one evening with a young girl from Omaha named Ethel, who is bored stiff by baseball but is touched by Monty's sincerity and gallantry. An "introduction" to Bill Dickey of the New York Yankees, culminating in a collision between Dickey's bat and Monty's pitched ball, results in Stratton's being sent to the minors in Omaha for some seasoning. This suits Monty fine, since he can now devote some time to Ethel—"some time" being the rest of his life after he pops the question. Back with the White Sox, Monty strikes out his "friendly enemy" Bill Dickey, and soon Stratton's career is on a roll; he makes it to the All-Star Game and fathers a baby boy, seemingly all at once. But tragedy interferes in November 1938 when Monty accidentally shoots himself in the right leg while hunting; infection sets in, and the leg must be amputated. Stratton spends several bitter months brooding over his bad luck, but eventually he snaps out of it, learning to use his prosthesis by taking his infant son, who is likewise a novice at standing on two legs, for long walks. Life becomes zestful again as Monty manages the farm and keeps in shape by practicing his pitch with Ethel. Barney Dykes stops off to visit Monty en route to a White Sox scouting expedition at a Texas League all-star game, and he invites the Stratton family to join him as his guests. What no one knows is that Monty has made arrangements with the Southern All-Stars coach to return to pitching with this game; he has something to prove to himself, and figures that if he plays in a game where big money and future careers are at stake, he'll have tougher obstacles to overcome. Monty's game is none too good in the early innings, particularly when he waives the use of a pinch-hitter and tries vainly to run to first. But as his confidence grows, his game sharpens. The opposing team tries every trick in the book to beat Stratton, including bunting his pitches out of his reach, but Monty makes a fantastic comeback, not only retiring the other side while on the mound, but managing to hit and run bases with most of his old verve. The Southern All-Stars win the game, and Monty Stratton wins his own personal battle with adversity.

The life story of Monty Stratton (1912–82) had just the right ingredients for a postwar hit. Here was the basically true saga of a never say die amputee who beat the odds and thereafter lived a happy and fulfilled existence. This sort of storytelling had been surefire audience material since the Oscar-winning performance by genuine amputee Harold Russell in *The Best Years of Our Lives* (1946). The fact that Monty Stratton's accident occurred not in the service of his country but in a recreational pursuit was unimportant; like Harold Russell, Stratton served as an inspiration not only to those filmgoers who'd been similarly maimed but to their families and friends, who found it simpler to adapt to the misfortunes of their loved ones after seeing those misfortunes mirrored, and conquered, on the big screen.

So MGM had its story. All it now needed was a big star to take the hoodoo off the baseball angle. It has been frequently reported that MGM contractee Van Johnson was the first choice for Stratton, but that after he banged himself up in a motorcycle accident, the studio considered Gregory Peck, then finally James Stewart. Another legend has it that the studio was deluged with fan mail demanding that Johnson be replaced by Stewart.

Author Donald Dewey's *James Stewart: A Biography* quotes a 1995 interview with Monty Stratton's widow Ethel, in which she stated that Monty had, as a courtesy to MGM, briefly worked out with Van Johnson, only to conclude that the actor was "gun-shy athletically, and would never be convincing as a pitcher. We'd wanted Jimmy [Stewart] from the beginning."

Ronald Reagan claimed in later years that he'd begged his studio boss Jack Warner to loan him to MGM for *The Stratton Story*, only to be vetoed by Warner's decree that, "There are two things movie audiences aren't interested in—baseball and cripples." These words would seem to echo those attributed to MGM chieftain Louis B. Mayer, who, upon initially rejecting the notion of filming Stratton's life story, is alleged to have cited the millions of "pregnant women" who would regard the spectacle of a one-legged ballplayer as "disgusting."

Whatever the circumstances of casting the film, the double-play combination of James Stewart and Monty Stratton worked beautifully, both for the film and for Stewart himself, who, with *The Stratton Story*, enjoyed his first real postwar box office hit. Disdaining the use of a double, Stewart trained five hours a day for three months with a contingent of major-league ballplayers and with Stratton himself, who remained on the set as technical adviser (a rarity for Hollywood of the 1940s, where the "adviser" credit was usually an empty gesture, and the person upon whom it was bestowed was ignored once shooting began).

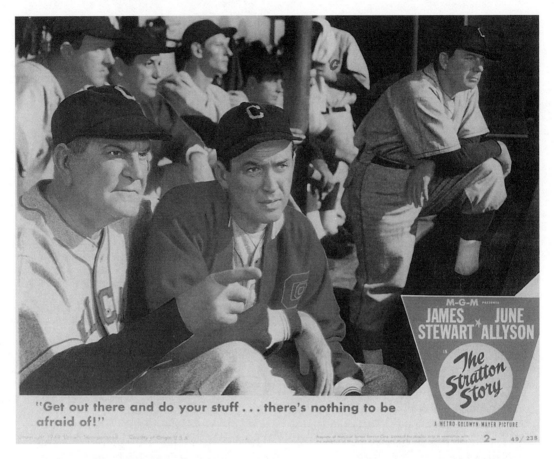

"Get out there and do your stuff . . . there's nothing to be afraid of!"

M-G-M PRESENTS
JAMES STEWART ★ JUNE ALLYSON
IN
The Stratton Story
A METRO-GOLDWYN-MAYER PICTURE

Barney Wiles (Frank Morgan, left) preps Monty Stratton (James Stewart) for his first appearance with the Chicago White Sox in this lobby card from *The Stratton Story*. Former White Sox manager Jimmy Dykes, as "himself," can be seen standing at far right.

The actor also consulted with physical therapists and orthopedic surgeons for the postamputation scenes, and wore a special steel harness to induce his limp.

Jimmy Stewart also carefully plotted out any number of unobtrusive ways to remain seated *before* Stratton's accident, as compensation for the fact that he was a foot taller than his leading lady June Allyson. Incidentally, Allyson had initially resisted the opportunity to play Ethel Stratton and had to be talked into it by her husband Dick Powell. She would later regard Mrs. Stratton as her best part, though it did tend to lock her into "patient and supportive wife" roles for most of her future career; indeed, when Ruby Dee dis-

played a similar (but briefer) predilection for the same sort of roles in *The Jackie Robinson Story* (q.v.) and *Go, Man, Go* (a 1954 film about the Harlem Globetrotters), publicity flacks pigeonholed Dee as "the Negro June Allyson."

Audiences and reviewers alike were happy with June Allyson, Jimmy Stewart, and *The Stratton Story* itself. Douglas Morrow's screen story received the ultimate critical compliment when it was honored with an Academy Award. Morrow managed to keep faith with the facts, although for dramatic impact the chronology of events is telescoped. Stratton's valiant real-life reappearance in uniform after his accident was a one-shot deal during a 1939 White Sox charity game held by the team's manage-ment on Monty's behalf; unfortunately, he was unable to balance his artificial limb with his real one while on the pitcher's mound. Stratton ultimately did return as an active player for the East Texas League, but it was in 1946, after several years' employment as a coach for the White Sox.

While the screenplay by Douglas Mor-row and Guy Trosper tends to adhere to the gospel according to *The Pride of the Yan-kees* (q.v.) in its structure (boy rises from humble surroundings, becomes a baseball star, acquires a cheerleading spouse and a yea-saying older male friend, is stricken down in his prime but makes peace with his tragedy), *The Stratton Story* is remarkably cliché free. In addition, perhaps out of re-spect to the script, musical director Adolph Deutsch likewise steers clear of the obvious by *not once* playing "Take Me Out to the Ballgame." Director Sam Wood also rises to the occasion with one of his best jobs in years (like Stewart, Wood had been in a ca-reer slump of late with expensive but pon-derous pictures like *Saratoga Trunk* and *Heartbeat*). Wood's handling of the base-ball game finale—which runs nearly fifteen minutes—is an artful blend of suspense plus economy of movement; and the di-rector's technique of twenty takes per scene (described in the notes on *The Pride of the Yankees*) serves him well, not only in coax-ing believable performances from former White Sox manager Jimmy Dykes and one-time Yankees star Bill Dickey, but in keep-ing the patented mannerisms of veteran scene-pincher Frank Morgan in check, per-mitting Morgan to turn in one of his most subtle and moving characterizations.

Some recent commentators have taken *The Stratton Story* to task for overglorifying Stratton's impressive but not spectacular career. A closer look at the film reveals that this is not so. Nowhere is it suggested that Stratton is the Second Coming of Ruth, and in fact he is seen to be in need of a lot

of polishing even after making the big leagues. The script is careful to qualify each adulatory remark: Jimmy Dykes says that Stratton has a great future, while lines like, "He's sort of a one-man team!" are deliv-ered by Barney Wiles (Frank Morgan) who, as Stratton's mentor, can be forgiven his hyperbole.

Where *The Stratton Story* falters is in the attempts by MGM to give the picture its studio touch. There is nothing wrong with the use of the studio's own "You Are My Lucky Star" as Monty and Ethel Strat-ton's "special song," but when it pops up in a dinner sequence, the MGM-style night-club is a shade too elaborate and cosmopol-itan for Stratton's Texas home town. And although the studio went to the effort of shooting location footage of games staged in the genuine ballparks of the Chicago White Sox, the Cleveland Indians, the Wash-ington Senators and the Detroit Tigers (foot-age for the most part seamlessly blended in with scenes filmed at L.A.'s Wrigley Field and Gilmore Park), whenever Jimmy Stew-art steps up to the mound, MGM indulges in its standard "who'll notice?" practice of backing up the actor with the fuzziest, least convincing process-screenwork imaginable. (This is the only instance that the computer-colored version of *The Stratton Story* pre-pared in 1989 by Turner Broadcasting is an improvement over the black and white orig-inal; since everything else looks artificial in the pastel hues of "colorization," the medi-ocre process work seems far less obvious.)

The MGM-imposed "improvements" during the final game scene likewise hurt the film's integrity. It is carefully laid out beforehand that the ballplayers will cut Monty Stratton no slack, disability or no disability, and when it becomes clear that the opposition is walking the other players to get to Stratton, Barney Wiles matter-of-factly declares, "That's baseball." But then we're given a lachrymose demonstration that ballplayers really have hearts of gold;

right before ordering his team to bunt Stratton's pitches, the Western All-Stars manager mumbles, "I hate to do this." And just to make sure that we're meant to feel like backward children who have to be told everything twice, after Stratton makes his successful comeback, an anonymous narrator, who hasn't been heard at any time in the past 105 minutes, explains to us that Monty Stratton is an "inspiration" who has "refused to admit defeat." Gee, *thanks*, Mister Wizard.

But why quibble? The very fact that a baseball picture made in 1949 would still have the ability to charm and entertain an audience forty years later absolves *The Stratton Story* of all its minor sins. The additional fact that it is one of the few such pictures to give pleasure to both baseball-hating movie fans and movie-hating baseball fans alike is enough to affirm its "classic" status. And perhaps more significant than the blessings of the viewers was the accolade from the otherwise ultra critical *Baseball News*, which noted upon the release of *The Stratton Story* that, "[n]ot only does Jimmy Stewart imitate Monty Stratton perfectly, but he looks like he really belongs in the big league. He's a major leaguer through and through."

Summer Catch

Tollin-Robbins/Warner Bros; released August 24, 2001

Executive producer: Herbert W. Gains. Produced by Mike Tollin, Brian Robbins and Sam Weisman. Directed by Mike Tollin. Screenplay by Kevin Falls and John Gatins. Story by Kevin Falls. Photography: Tim Suhrstedt. Editor: Harvey Rosenstock. Production designer: John D. Kretschmer. Costume designer: Juliet Polcsa. Casting: Marc Liroff. Music by George Fenton. First assistant director: Timothy M. Bourne. Second assistant director: Rick Clark. Set decoration: Steve Davis. Sound editor: Brian Best. Production mixer: Jeffree Bloomer.

Foley editor: Shawn Siroka. Foley Artist: Laura Macias. Production coordinator: Ingrid Johanson. Casting: Marc Liroff. Sound: Andy Peach. Makeup: Jeff Goodwin, John Elliot, Jr. Baseball coordinators: Mark Ellis, Bill Landrum. Technical adviser: Bill Hughes. Stunt coordinator: Dean Mumford. Titles: Deborah Ross Film Design, Title House Digital. Opticals: Pacific Title. Technicolor; Panavision. 108 minutes; Dolby Digital/DTS/SDDS Sound. PG-13.

Freddie Prinze, Jr. (Ryan Dunne); Jessica Biel (Tenley Parrish); Matthew Lillard (Billy Brubaker); Brian Dennehy (Coach John Schiffner); Fred Ward (Sean Dunne); Jason Gedrick (Mike Dunne); Brittany Murphy (DeDe Mulligan); Bruce Davison (Rand Parrish); Marc Blucas (Miles Dalrymple); Wilmer Valderrama (Mickey "Domo" Dominguez); Corey Pearson (Eric Van Leemer); Christian Kane (Dale Robin); Cedric Pendleton (Calvin Knight); Gabriel Mann (Auggie); Jed Robert Rhein (Pete); Zena Grey (Katy Parrish); Curt Gowdy, Pat Burrell, Dave Collins, Doug Glanville, Ken Griffey, Jr., Jeff Kellogg, Mike Lieberthal, Hank Aaron (Themselves); Dick Allen (Scout in Black Hat); Randi Layne (Vivi Parrish); Tracy Dinwiddie (Lauren); Susan Gardner (Marjorie); Jack Baun (Chris Hunt); Tammy Christine Arnold (Vassar Graduate); Tim Lucason (Hyannis Batter); Kenny Gasperson (Statistician); Mark Robert Ellis (Umpire); Herbert W. Gains (Angry Fan); Thaddeus Hill (Coach Suller); Brock Keene (Chatham Pitcher); Mike Ribaudo (Chatham A No. 1); Matt Hobbie (Chatham A No. 2); Cliff Fleming (Stunt Pilot); John Copeman, Erika Laibson, Tree O'Toole, Dino Muccio, Mike Pridgen (Stunts); Beverly D'Angelo (Domo's Housemother); John C. McGinley (Phillies Scout).

As the best amateur organization of its kind in America, the Cape Cod Baseball League has been a stepping-stone to stardom for many a collegiate ballplayer. For 24-year-old pitcher Ryan Dunne, the first local boy to pitch for the Chatham A's in seven years, participation in the League represents his last chance to crack the Majors. Having been booted off the Framingham Junior College team for brawling, Ryan is told by Chatham coach John Schiffner that he already has two strikes against him—and we all know what happens after Strike Three. Determined not to be a "loser" like his hard-drinking landscaper father Sean and his embittered bartender brother Mike (who had washed out of the League several years earlier), Ryan tries to keep his mind on the game, but there are too damned many distractions. If he isn't being mercilessly hectored by arrogant rival catcher Eric Van Leemer, he is being frustrated in his pursuit of romance with wealthy and ravishingly beautiful Vassar grad Tenley Parrish, whose blue-blooded father strongly disapproves of his daughter's dalliance with the lowborn landscaper's son. Suffering from a surfeit of anger, class envy and self-pity, Ryan can't seem to get his game together, forcing Schiffner to take him out of the regular rotation, even though the coach knows that Ryan has the talent to succeed if only he'd let himself. Fortunately, when things get really tough, Ryan can always depend upon the help and support of his friends and teammates Billy Brubaker, Mickey "Domo" Dominguez and Myles Dalrumple, not to mention his lifelong buds Auggie and Pete. Things take a sharp turn for the better when, after Eric Van Leemer is thrown off the A's for gross misbehavior, Ryan is afforded the opportunity to pitch against the Falmouth Commodores in the biggest game of the season, when all the Major League scouts are sure to be in attendance. Will Ryan be able to take full advantage of this golden opportunity? And what of his relationship with Tenley, who is being forced by her father to leave Chatham for a job with the family business in San Francisco?

Summer Catch was originally conceived in 1996 by producer Sam Weisman, a resident of Chatham, Massachusetts, and one of the biggest boosters of the real-life Cape Cod Baseball League. Established in 1885, the League is an elite nonprofit organization, supported by donations from the local residents, who also provide room and board to the ballplayers throughout the summer season. Truly a breeding ground for big-time baseball stars, the Cape Cod League has produced such distinguished alumni as Thurman Munson, Mo Vaughn and Carlton Fisk. Those college athletes lucky enough to make it into the league play for free, with wooden bats and other "outmoded" equipment, in hopes of catching the eye of one of the many Big League scouts who scope out the League's games each and every year. When they're not on the field, the young players can be found participating in the League's many fundraising activities, including literally passing the hat amongst the spectators.

Convinced that there might be a fascinating movie in the story of the Cape Cod League, Weisman passed along this enthusiasm to producers Mike Tollin and Brian Robbins, whose track record of successes included the cable–TV sports sitcom *Arli$$*, the teen-oriented network series *All That* and *Kenan and Kel*, and the movie money-spinners *Good Burger* (1997) and *Varsity Blues* (1999). Tollin and Robbins had earned their baseball-movie chops with the excellent, multi-award-winning 1998 documentary *Hank Aaron: Chasing the Dream*. Tollin in particular was interested in the possibilities of *Summer Catch*, especially since it would provide him the opportunity to make his feature-film directorial debut (most of the Tollin-Robbins productions, including the subsequently filmed baseball drama *Hardball* [q.v.], were directed by Robbins).

Though it would take the proverbial fly on the wall to determine the division of interests which went into the making of the film, apparently Sam Weisman felt that the story of the Cape Cod League should take front and center. Doing his own version of passing the hat, Weisman secured full cooperation from the League and the residents of Chatham, who donated authentic uniforms, equipment, memorabilia and a wealth of League trivia and minutiae. He

Eric Dalrymple (Marc Blucas), Billy Brubaker (Matthew Lillard) and Ryan Dunne (Freddie Prinze, Jr.) cool down after a hot practice session with the Chatham A's in *Summer Catch*.

also obtained permission to use the name and the uniform number—fifteen—of real-life Chatham A's coach John Schiffner, who was superbly portrayed in the film by the ever-reliable Brian Dennehy. One of the few aspects of the League that Weisman could not precisely duplicate in the film was the Massachusetts setting itself; the filming schedule would extend from April to June 2000, during which time Chatham's Veterans Field would be occupied by the actual League members. Thus, production moved to Southport, North Carolina, not far from the Wilmington studios of Screen Gems Productions. An old abandoned Little League field was renovated and dressed up as an identical twin to Veterans, right down to the press-box banner for Chatham radio station WQRC-FM.

During the period that the coast of North Carolina was being temporarily made over into Cape Cod, Weisman sent out a two-state call for ballplayers to appear in the film. Mark Ellis, one of the picture's three baseball coordinators (along with Bill Landrum and *A League of Their Own*'s William Hughes), whittled down the 300 auditionees to the 35 players seen in the film, then subjected the finalists to four weeks in a genuine baseball camp. The experience was extremely beneficial to these background players, several of whom went on to play professional and semi-pro baseball the following year.

Meanwhile, Mike Tollin and Brian Robbins were focusing on what they regarded as the most important element of *Summer Catch*—the behavior of, and relationships between, the central characters. In an interview with *Sports Illustrated*, Tollin insisted that the film was not about baseball but about "believing in yourself, about fear of success, about people who are their own worst enemies." Tollin and Robbins also wanted to replicate the formula of their previous hit *Varsity Blues*, in which an "underdog" football player with a smartass attitude learned to become a star athlete and team leader in spite of himself. Above all, the producers needed a vehicle for current

Hollywood heartthrob hunk Freddie Prinze, Jr., who had recently vaulted to full-scale stardom in such blockbusters as *I Know What You Did Last Summer* (1997) and *She's All That* (1999).

Perhaps Sam Weisman was right. Perhaps there is a fascinating film in the story of the Cape Cod League. In the meantime, we'll have to settle for dreck like *Summer Catch*.

This is the sort of film in which characters in their early twenties comport themselves like horny high-schoolers. This is the sort of film in which the male and female leads spend half their time in various states of undress, whether justified by the script or not. This is the sort of film in which we know we're in a rich person's house because we hear classical music on the radio. And this is the sort of film in which we hear dialogue like, "You want the Big Leagues? You've got to take big risks!" "You've got a bat full of talent and a head full of crap"; "This ain't just about a paycheck, it's about having pride in what you do"; and this precious gem from the confrontation scene between the blue-collar hero and the wealthy girl's snobbish daddy: "You stepped over a boundary here, son."

And just in case the audience might miss something, every plot point is established, re-established and re-re-established until one gets the feeling that the script was turned out by a berserk laser printer. So many people tell the sullen hero that he's got to stop wallowing in self-pity and begin believing in himself that they practically have to stand in line and take numbers.

The film serves up several "hilarious" running gags for those not interested in baseball, romance or self-pride. It is hard to determine which of these gags is the least amusing: the efforts by League rookie Mickey "Domo" Dominguez to avoid seduction at the hands of his gorgeous fortysomething housemother (an unbilled Beverly D'Angelo), who does strange things with cucumbers and grapes; team member Miles Dalrymple's obsession with dating, and bedding, overweight women; or the efforts by Tenley Parrish's precocious kid sister to become the Chatham A's mascot by costuming herself as a lobster, a clam and a one-legged pirate. One gag, repeated only twice, admittedly does raise half a laugh: After separate drunken evenings with local hot-to-trot waitress DeDe Mulligan, both Ryan Dunne and his buddy Billy Brubaker awaken the next morning to discover that they're wearing DeDe's orange thong underwear. Alas, even this ribald bit is a letdown, especially for Freddie Prinze, Jr. fans; reportedly, Prinze's then girlfriend refused to allow his bare backside to be shown on screen, thus the services of a "stunt butt" were required.

And how about the baseball scenes? Well, it's fun to see venerable sportscaster Curt Gowdy back in harness as the Chatham A's play-by-play announcer, and equally enjoyable to see 1972 MVP Dick Allen and all-time home run king Henry Aaron making brief sideline appearances. Also, the real-life ballplayers obviously know what they're doing on the field. And then there's Freddie Prinze, Jr. Despite breathless publicity-release reports about how the actor had "loved" baseball since growing up watching the Albuquerque Dukes, and how he worked day and night to measure up to the role of Ryan Dunne, the fact remains that Prinze is probably the least convincing movie ballplayer since Anthony Perkins as Jimmy Piersall. When *Summer Catch* was previewed in March of 2001 (at an unwieldy length of 123 minutes!), customers carped that director Mike Tollin could not camouflage the fact that Prinze's "95 MPH" pitches were actually slower than molasses in January—this despite Tollins' yeoman efforts to divert audience attention by filming each of Prinze's baseball scenes from a variety of bizarre camera angles (in one shot, the camera is positioned at ground level, pointing upward at Prinze, as though the pitching mound has suddenly acquired an orchestra pit). By the time the film was officially released nearly six months later, all of Prinze's pitching sequences had been heavily gone over in the editing room to sustain the illusion of Ryan Dunne's "dynamite" pitching arm. But to no avail; Prinze still ran a distant third to the above-average ballpark performances of his costars Corey Pearson, cast as nominal villain Eric Van Leemer, and Matthew Lillard, playing Ryan's spacey buddy Billy Brubaker. It is embarrassing enough when the star is out-pitched by the bad guy; but when even the comedy-relief character is a better ballplayer, it has to be the final plateau of humiliation.

The overall believability of *Summer Catch* can best be summed up by describing the climax. On the verge of pitching a perfect game before an approving audience of Major League scouts, the previously noncommittal Ryan Dunne suddenly realizes that he's deeply in love with heroine Tenley Parrish and doesn't want her to leave for San Francisco. To prove the length, breadth and depth of his ardor, he *pulls himself out of the game* to chase after Tenley, who is just about to board a California-bound plane. Upon his arrival at the airport, Ryan is swarmed by his fellow teammates, bearing the great news that the A's have won the game without his services. Also on hand is a scout for the Philadelphia Phillies (played by John C. McGinley, who, like Beverly D'Angelo, wisely declined an on-screen credit). By rights, the scout should dismiss Ryan with a curt, "If you're willing to run out of a crucial game at the bottom of the seventh, we certainly aren't about to offer you a Big League contract!" while Tenley should brush off our hero with a tearful, "If you can turn your back on the biggest opportunity of your career, how can I be sure that you'll show up for our wedding?" Instead, Ryan not only gets the girl but also the contract, ending up pitching opposite

Ken Griffey, Jr., during the closing credits! And next week, boys and girls, we'll tell you all about what happens when you put your baby teeth under your pillow.

Freddie Prinze, Jr.'s performance as Ryan Dunne evokes the words of Gertrude Stein: "There's no *there* there." Of the supporting actors, the graceful and charming Jessica Biel (a long-time regular on the popular TV drama *Seventh Heaven*) seems far too intelligent to be mouthing the idiocies provided her by the script, while Wilmer Valderrama, the gifted young comic actor who played the excitable exchange student "Fez" on the hit sitcom *That 70s Show*, is wasted in the peripheral role of the virginal Domo. The same can be said of Marc Blucas, a.k.a. "Riley Finn" on TV's *Buffy the Vampire Slayer*, here cast as the cellulose-obsessed Eric Dalrymple. On the plus side, Matthew Lillard deftly steals every scene he's in as Ryan's surfer-dude best friend Billy Brubaker, who needs a roll in the hay with the town's "fast" girl before he can overcome his aversion to wooden bats. Inasmuch as this was the third screen teaming of Freddie Prinze, Jr., and Matthew Lillard (their previous films together were *She's All That* and *Wing Commander*), Prinze would have been well advised to stop playing Dean Martin to Lillard's Jerry Lewis if he ever hoped to get critics and filmgoers to pay closer attention to *him*.

Not since the deplorable *Ed* (q.v.) had film reviewers exhibited such unanimity of adverse criticism. To quote two of the many: "In baseball slang, a 'can of corn' is a high lazy ball to the outfield. The baseball movie *Summer Catch* is the cinematic equivalent of that can of corn—a movie going nowhere and filled with far too much corn..." (Kirk Honeycutt, *The Hollywood Reporter*). "A passed ball, a booted grounder, a balk with bases loaded.... There aren't enough metaphors of lousy baseball to adequately describe this lackadaisical romance" (Gene Seymour, *Newsday*). But perhaps Jay

Carr of the Boston *Globe* summed it up most eloquently when he described *Summer Catch* as *"Bull Durham* for Dummies."

Swell Head

Columbia; released May 1935

Directed by Ben Stoloff. Screenplay by William Jacobs, from a story by Gerald Beaumont. Photography: Joseph A. Valentine. 62 minutes; black and white; sound.

Cast: Wallace Ford (Terry McCall); Dickie Moore (Billy Malone); Barbara Kent (May Malone); J. Farrell McDonald (Umpire); Marion Byron (Bessie); Sammy Cohen (Casey Cohen); Frank Moran (The Rube); Mike Donlin (Brick Baldwyn); Bryant Washburn.

Original title: *Called on Account of Darkness*

Terry McCall, a small-town home run king whose overbearing arrogance imperils his romance with waitress May Malone, is hit on the head by a baseball during a game and goes blind. Terry shuts himself off from the world and disappears from view; he is found by May's kid brother Billy, whose hero worship restores Terry's self-esteem. Eventually, Terry regains his sight and returns to the waiting arms of May Malone.

Swell Head, a six-reel gabfest almost devoid of any action on or off the ballfield, was released in the spring of 1935 but was actually filmed anywhere from two to three years earlier. This is confirmed by three pieces of evidence: (1) prominent in the cast was Jewish comedian Sammy Cohen, whose particular brand of ethnic humor had been all but purged from the screen after the 1934 Production Code decreed a ban on certain racial stereotypes in films; (2) contemporary reviewers commented that child actor Dickie Moore appeared not to understand his lines in *Swell Head,* a curious observation in that Moore was ten years old in 1935 and had already been showcased in over forty-five films, including a full season with Hal Roach's *Our Gang,* wherein Dickie

was the most articulate kid in the bunch; and (3) it would have been difficult beyond measure for ex-ballplayer Mike Donlin to have been cast in a featured role in a 1935 film, especially since he'd been dead for nearly two years.

Take Me Out to the Ballgame

MGM; released March 9, 1949

Produced by Arthur Freed. Directed by Busby Berkeley. Screenplay by Harry Tugend and George Wells, based on a story by Gene Kelly and Stanley Donen. Photography: George Folsey. Edited by Blanche Sewell. New songs ("Yes, Indeedy," "O'Brien to Ryan to Goldberg," "The Right Girl for Me," "It's Fate, Baby, It's Fate" and "Strictly USA") by Betty Comden, Adolph Green, and Roger Edens. Musical numbers staged by Gene Kelly and Stanley Donen. Art direction by Cedric Gibbons and Daniel B. Cathcart. Set decoration by Edwin B. Willis and Henry R. Grace. Color director: Natalie Kalmus. Recording director: Douglas Shearer. Special effects by Arthur Newcombe. Montage sequences by Peter Ballbusch. Costumes by Helen Rose and Valles. Hairstyles by Sydney Guilaroff. Makeup by Jack Dawn. Associate producer: Roger Edens. Color by Technicolor. 93 minutes; sound.

Cast: Frank Sinatra (Dennis Ryan); Esther Williams (K. C. Higgins); Gene Kelly (Eddie O'Brien); Betty Garrett (Shirley Delwyn); Edward Arnold (Joe Lorgan); Jules Munshin (Nat Goldberg); Richard Lane (Michael Gilhuly); Tom Dugan (Slappy Burke); Murray Alper (Zalinka); Wilton Graff (Nick Danford); Mack Gray, Charles Regan (Lorgan's Henchmen); Saul Gorss (Steve); Douglas Fowley (Karl); Eddie Parkes (Dr. Winston); James Burke (Cop in Park); The Blackburn Twins (Specialty); Gordon Jones (Senator Catcher); Frank Scannell (Reporter); Henry Kulky (Burly Acrobat); Dorothy Abbott (Girl Dancer); Virginia Bates, Joi Lansing (Two Girls on Train); Jackie Jackson (Kid); Si Jenks (Sam); Jack Rice (Hotel Clerk); Ed Cassidy (Teddy Roosevelt); Dick Wessel (Umpire); Sally Forrest (Dancer); Jack Bruce, John "Red" Burger, Aaron Phillips, Edward

Cutler, Ellsworth Blake, Harry Allan, Joseph Roach, Hubert Kerns, Pete Kouy, Robert Simpson, Richard Landry, Jack Boyle, Richard Beavers (Members of the Wolves); Mitchell Lewis (Fisherman); Esther Michelson (Fisherman's Wife); Almira Sessions, Isabel O'Madigan, Gil Perkins, Robert Stephenson, Charles Sullivan, Edna Harris (Fans).

It is 1906: The Wolves are the champion baseball team of the nation, thanks in no small part to the double-play combo of "O'Brien to Ryan to Goldberg." But while Nat Goldberg is dutifully attending spring training in Florida, Eddie O'Brien and Dennis Ryan are knocking 'em dead as a song and dance act in vaudeville. Eddie would be perfectly content to stay in show business and dally with the beautiful chorus girls, while Dennis is a baseball man down to his toes, and a man who undergoes a severe bout of bashfulness whenever he comes near anything in skirts. When O'Brien and Ryan arrive in Florida, they learn that the Wolves have been inherited by a new owner named K. C. Higgins, who, to everyone's surprise but the audience, turns out to be a lovely young lady. Dennis is immediately smitten by the beauteous K. C., especially after watching her field a grounder during training, but Eddie chafes at the new owner's insistence that he stick to training and observe the 10 P.M. curfew. Eddie pitches some woo at K. C. in hopes of weakening her adherence to team discipline, a device that to the ultimate astonishment of both O'Brien and Higgins blossoms into a genuine romance. Meanwhile, Dennis is "squired" by hoydenish Shirley Delwyn, an entertainer who works in a night club owned by gambler Joe Lorgan. Lorgan has bet heavily against the Wolves in the upcoming pennant race, and to cinch his bet he offers Eddie a leading role in an upcoming musical production—knowing full well that the rigors of rehearsal will cause Eddie's game to suffer. When K. C. learns of Eddie's moonlighting, she as-

sumes it's because he wants to make time with the chorines and she promptly fires him; whereupon Lorgan, his plan reaching full fruition, likewise cans Eddie. O'Brien, being down but not out, gets his fans to rally round him, forcing K. C. to reinstate him during the Big Game. Lorgan decides to do O'Brien in, but Shirley overhears his plans and tells Dennis to get Eddie out of harm's way, which Dennis does by knocking Eddie out with a pitched hardball. The crooks are routed, and Eddie awakens to find himself in the arms of a forgiving K. C.; but when Eddie discovers that Dennis had beaned him, he sets out to pummel his teammate. Seeking escape, Dennis knocks a home run out of the park, which will allow him to run the bases and thus stay out of Eddie's reach. Eddie pursues Dennis around the diamond by clubbing his own homer, and before he's able to thrash poor Dennis, both players are carried off in a victory march by the exultant fans.

Take Me Out to the Ballgame came about as an act of self-defense on the part of Gene Kelly. Following the financial success of the Kelly–Frank Sinatra vehicle *Anchors Aweigh* (1945), MGM producer Joe Pasternak wanted to create a follow-up musical in which Kelly and Sinatra, again cast as sailors, convert an old aircraft carrier into a nightclub. Kelly disliked not only the concept but the outdated approach taken by the proposed script, so he and his assistant choreographer, Stanley Donen, worked up their own scenario, one that would keep its stars far, far away from any sort of naval uniform.

Though there was a precedent set as far back as 1902 for baseball players touring in vaudeville during the off-season, Gene Kelly's inspiration for *Take Me Out to the Ballgame* sprang from the star's enjoyment of the buffoonery of "baseball clown" Al Schacht. In Kelly and Donen's original story treatment, Kelly, Sinatra, and Brooklyn Dodgers manager Leo Durocher would play three ballplayers on an early twentieth-century team. The double-play combination of "O'Brien to Ryan to Shaughnessy," a play on columnist F. P. Adams's ode to "Tinker to Evers to Chance," would provide not only a foundation for the plot but a golden opportunity for a dazzling dance number. "I've worked out an Irish jig that Sinatra and Durocher will be able to dance and which will carry on the myth of Frank's terpsichorean ability," explained Kelly in his treatment. The romantic angle was intended by Kelly to be handled by songstress Kathryn Grayson as team owner "C. B. Higgins." Kelly and Donen's story concept was sold not to Joe Pasternak but to another MGM musical producer, Arthur Freed, who bought it to keep the notoriously mercurial Gene Kelly happy in his work. Stanley Donen, who'd been in Hollywood as long as Kelly but had yet to break into the big-bucks category, was astonished when MGM paid $25,000 for the seven-page story treatment.

Arthur Freed made several changes, the first of which was to replace Kathryn Grayson with Judy Garland. George Wells was assigned to fashion a screenplay from Kelly and Donen's notes, while Harry Warren and Ralph Blane were conscripted to write the songs. Garland, however, was going through one of her physical and mental downers, so the part of C. B. Higgins (now "K. C. Higgins") went to MGM's aquatic star Esther Williams. Harry Tugend was brought in to refashion the script to suit Williams's talents; this meant shoehorning in a brief swimming pool sequence (in which the actress wore a one-piece bathing suit that was hardly *de rigueur* in 1906!) and cutting down on the leading lady's singing and dancing. Many of the specialties designed for Judy Garland were now transferred to second lead Betty Garrett. Leo Durocher's part was likewise transferred to a more experienced musical comedy man, Broadway actor Jules Munshin, though it appears in the com-

pleted film that the role of "Nat Goldberg" may have been concocted with Phil Silvers in mind. Finally, the songwriting combo of Warren and Blane was succeeded by Freed's associate producer Roger Edens and by Broadway transplants Betty Comden and Adolph Green. Comden and Green were established song satirists—just the sort needed to fashion the mock turn of the century tunes required in *Take Me Out to the Ballgame*—though as it turned out, their songs were more in keeping with the then current Rodgers and Hammerstein school. (Asked nearly forty years later to assess her contributions to the film, Betty Comden, speaking for both herself and Adolph Green, said only, "It's not one we like to talk about.")

In her autobiography, Esther Williams recalls *Take Me Out to the Ballgame* as an unhappy shoot, noting that Gene Kelly and Stanley Donen never let an opportunity pass to remind her that she wasn't Kathryn Grayson or Judy Garland. Kelly and Donen's palpable disdain and endless needling finally forced Williams to pull rank, reminding them that she was currently one of MGM's biggest box-office draws—if not *the* biggest—and that they'd better start acting like grownups or she might have *them* replaced. Conversely, Williams found a friend and confidante in costar Frank Sinatra, whose kindness and courtesy went a long way towards assuaging her wounded ego (Betty Garrett has also recalled that Sinatra went out of his way to be friendly and cooperative, generously insisting that Garrett be given flattering close-ups whether the script called for them or not). For his part, Stanley Donen regarded Williams' casting as "a mistake," claiming that her nearsightedness caused her to clumsily ruin several takes—a complaint that no one else at MGM ever made, before or after.

Freed's choice of director Busby Berkeley was sentimentally motivated. Once a film musical maestro, Berkeley's overdictatorial demeanor and severe personal problems had kept him out of MGM since he'd been fired from the 1941 Freed production *Girl Crazy*. The producer wanted to give the troublesome but undeniably gifted director-choreographer—who hadn't made a picture in five years—one last shot at retaining his stature with *Take Me Out to the Ballgame*. Gene Kelly wasn't pleased with this turn of events, making the same complaint he'd made about Pasternak's long-gone "aircraft carrier" musical, that the Berkeley style was woefully out of date. However, Kelly would later concede gratefully that Berkeley taught him a method of counting out musical beats during production numbers that would allow Kelly to coordinate his dancing with the camera movements, and that Berkeley, worn out by the rigors of keeping the rest of *Ballgame* coherent, gave Kelly and Stanley Donen free rein in staging the choreography. While Busby Berkeley's direction did suffer from his cumbersome use of slow pans and 1930s-style compositions, he invested in *Take Me Out to the Ballgame* enough entertainment value to cop *Photoplay* magazine's Blue Ribbon award for best direction—at least best direction for the week that *Ballgame* went into release.

Well, three paragraphs have come and gone without even alluding to the baseball angle, so let's get back on track. Gene Kelly later recalled that, "[t]he fact that we'd totally ignored the foreign market and blissfully refused to realize that few people outside America knew or cared what a ball game was ... was irrelevant. We thought it was a funny idea and that's all that mattered." That blissful refusal to pay homage to the foreign market wasn't reflected by the MGM front office, which retitled *Take Me Out to the Ballgame* as *Everybody's Cheering* for its British release. And for all its banter about baseball and the slapstickery around the bases at the finale, *Ballgame* taps what was regarded in 1949 as a richer vein

of humor than ballplaying with its endless jokes about Frank Sinatra's skinniness and his character's shyness around women (this latter conceit gets bigger laughs than anything else when *Take Me Out to the Ballgame* is theatrically revived today).

There are precisely two full-out "game" sequences in this film, one of which disintegrates into a fistfight; the rest of the Wolves' season is depicted through the marvelously assembled montages of Peter Ballbusch, whose off-center camera angles and documentary-style editing have an urgency and vitality that the rest of the film can't quite match. With the exit of Leo Durocher, MGM lost the one real link to the actual playing of the game. We see Frank Sinatra step up to the plate and daintily daub a ball, which results in a three-bagger (movie magic at work!). Esther Williams "impresses" the Wolves by picking up a ground ball that a seven-year-old kid could have recovered blindfolded. And for all the film's talk about "O'Brien to Ryan to Goldberg" (including one of the film's best musical setpieces), why couldn't we have seen that double-play combination in action at least once? Or, failing that, why couldn't the story have been pumped up with some of the tensions prevalent in the real-life combo of Joe Tinker, Johnny Evers, and Frank Chance, who, despite a seemingly copacetic record of over fifty double plays between 1906 and 1909, reportedly hated each others' guts?

So little baseball occurs during the film that by the time we're treated to the ludicrous climax—in which Gene Kelly horns into the batting order to slug out a home run *before* Frank Sinatra has even touched home plate—we're grateful that the filmmakers have seen fit to include any baseball at all, even something as goofily contrived as this. That this finish is not the rouser that it was supposed to have been was recognized by Arthur Freed, Stanley Donen, and Comden and Green, who cooked up

Very much a posed shot from *Take Me Out to the Ballgame*; in the film itself, Frank Sinatra, Gene Kelly and Jules Munshin perform the "OBrien to Ryan to Goldberg" number in a hotel restaurant.

a musical finale wherein Kelly and Sinatra inform us in song that all the romances have come to fruition in the story, adding an "it's all a put-on" touch by referring to one another, and to Esther Williams and Betty Garrett, by their real names instead of their character names.

Rather than continue heaping on adverse criticism by juxtaposing Gene Kelly's complaint about the "old-fashioned" notions of Joe Pasternak and Busby Berkeley with the banality of Kelly's own screen story (that chestnut about the female club owner wasn't new when seen in *The Bush Leaguer*, 1927 [q.v.]), we should observe with praise and awe that *Take Me Out to the Ballgame* has one ingredient that could have added zing to many a future baseball epic. Gene Kelly's character of Eddie O'Brien is, without being totally repellant or charm-

less, one of the most self-serving, unregenerate heels ever depicted in a film about ballplayers. O'Brien is obviously out for Number One from fade-in to fade-out: His crocodile tears over "letting the boys down" when his nocturnal rehearsing begins to hurt his game are shed more for his own bruised ego, and when he campaigns for his comeback with the Wolves, he does so by shamelessly exploiting the affections of his youthful fans. When O'Brien finally wins the girl, he can't give up his own competitive instincts long enough to stay in K.C.'s arms and not go gunning for the luckless Dennis Ryan. This "Pal Joey" quality in Gene Kelly's performance is extremely effective and plays as freshly today as it did four decades ago. It would have been fascinating to see Kelly portray "Prince" Hal Chase, whose admirable hitting record in the early part of the century was matched only by his ability to ruin the morale of every team he joined due to his selfishness and duplicity, and whose ruthlessness in pursuing the fast and easy buck resulted in innumerable game-fixing schemes and his ultimate blacklisting from professional baseball.

That's quite a note on which to end our discussion of something as basically lighthearted as *Take Me Out to the Ballgame*, which, despite its shortcomings, worked quite well within its own musical comedy limitations. We can be grateful that the picture was enjoyable enough for 1949 audiences to garner a box office gross in excess of $4 million. It was the success of *Take Me Out to the Ballgame* which encouraged Arthur Freed to regroup Gene Kelly, Frank Sinatra, Jules Munshin, Betty Garrett, and Comden and Green for their next project: the brilliant and innovative *On the Town*.

Talent for the Game

Paramount; released October 1991 (test marketed earlier that year)

Produced by Martin Elfand. Executive producer and unit production manager: David Wisnievitz. Directed by Robert M. Young. Screenplay by David Himmelstein, Tom Donnelly and Larry Ferguson. Photography: Curtis Clark. Edited by Arthur Coburn. Music by David Newman. Production designer: Jeffrey Howard. Costume designer: Erica Edell Phillips. Set decorator: Thomas D. Roysden. Production coordinator: Susan W. Dukow. Supervising sound editors: Cecilia Hall, George Watters, II. Supervising Foley editor: Victoria Martin. Additional orchestrations by Randy Miller. Additional music by the original artists. Makeup by Frank Carrisosa. Hairstylist: Janis Clark. Location manager: Bruce Lawhead. Additional casting by Central Casting (Los Angeles) and Debi Tagliaferro and Rich Farver (Idaho). Color by Technicolor. Dolby Sound. 91 minutes. Rated PG.

Cast: Edward James Olmos (Virgil Sweet); Lorraine Bracco (Bobbie Henderson); Jeffrey Corbett (Sammy Bodeen); Jamey Sheridan (Tim Weaver); Terry Kinney (Gil Lawrence); Thomas Ryan (Paul); Felton Perry (Fred); Tom Bauer (Rev. Bodeen); Janet Carroll (Rachel Bodeen); Daniel A. Hard (Burns); Murphy Sua (Dick Bortner); David Riley (Toby Corry); James Keane (Ray Coffey); Zachary I. Young (Rudy Coffey); Phillip M. Pote (Cal Murphy); Ken Medlock (Scooter Eaton); Tom La Grua (Frank Carbo); Alan J. Krick, Henry Ford Robinson (Umpires); Bill Higham (Bob Morgan); Todd Cantamessa (Lester); Kent Welborn, Mark David Sudaska (Coaches); Karl Grey (Dwayne Seybolt); Tamara Lynne Thompson (Martha Jo Seybolt); Harold Gower (Grandpa Seybolt); Adam Stellman (Boy); Kathy Gecas (Girl); John Yajko (Riggs); Caroline Barday (Blonde Secretary); Fernando Gubillas, James Guy O'Neal (Paramedics); Jeff Barnett Howard (William); Allan Malamud, Paula McClure, Rick Garcia, Carole Ann Borys (Reporters); Candy Trabuccos (Bobbie's Assistant); Leslie Bevis (Marla); Dennis Boutsikaris (Rossi); Patrick D. Rummerfield (Mine Safety Supervisor); D. E. Wells (Bus Driver); Tammie Erickson (Tractor Driver); Steve Robles (Waiter); Kathryn Wilde (Office Woman); Reina Elizabeth Jovil (Motel Housekeeper); Mike Brito (Scout); Byron Shantz (Press Box Reporter); Meline A. Grieger, Steven Jae Johnson, Frank Carrisosa (Fans); Jimmie Davis, Jr. (Baseball Trainer); Bobby Tolan, Darrel Thomas, Lenny Randle, Barry Moss, Frank Mendosa, John E. Coleman, Danny Davidsmeier (Angels); Sean Collins, Todd Crus, John D'Aquisto, Damon Farmar, Chuck Fick, Victor Hithe, Lee Lacy, Rudy Law, Phil Lombardi, Steve Ontiveros, Steve Springer, Tony Tarasco, Dejon Watson (Ballplayers); and Ken Brett.

Virgil Sweet roams the rocks and rills of the farm states as a scout for the California Angels, ever in pursuit of a "phenom"—a natural-born ballplayer with skill from God who will pull the Angels out of their slump. After a particularly disappointing scouting foray, Virgil learns that the team has been sold to billionaire ad executive Gil Lawrence, who wants to cut costs by eliminating the scout system and relying on computer statistics. In the company of his girlfriend, the Angels' junior exec Bobbie Henderson, Virgil heads to Idaho to check out a prospect. His car breaks down just outside a flyspeck community, where, by the sheerest coincidence (the only kind of coincidence there is in a movie like this), Virgil spots young Sammy Bodeen, a minister's son whose sandlot pitching displays an inborn "talent for the game." It takes some doing to wrest Sammy away from his family, but soon Virgil is on his way to Anaheim with his "phenom" in tow. Sammy falters during a tryout session, but starts performing like a seasoned vet when Virgil agrees to catch for him. New owner Gil Lawrence, his ad-man instincts working overtime, decides to promote Sammy as a "miracle man." Lawrence arranges for the boy to make his pro baseball debut as a starting pitcher, and sees to it that Sammy's name and face are plastered on billboards all over metropolitan L.A. Intimidated by both the undue media attention and the hostility of the other Angels, Sammy disappears shortly before the Big Game, only to be talked back into the stadium by his mentor Virgil who, as a reward for Sammy's discovery, has been made the team's assistant general manager. Alas, the night of Sammy's premiere threatens to be as dismal an evening as has ever been endured by anyone in any ballpark, anywhere. Sammy's pitches are batted, bunted, and blasted with the greatest of ease by the K.C. Royals lineup, and after an inning of this, a disgusted Gil Lawrence orders team manager Tim Weaver to yank the rookie. Virgil angrily denounces Lawrence's fickle attitude and quits the Angels, and when Lawrence refuses to back down, everyone else walks out on the owner as well. To bolster Sammy's confidence, Virgil dons a uniform and surreptitiously "subs" for the real Angels catcher, whereupon the boy begins to play like the Messiah of Baseball. As a result of his excellent first showing, Sammy Bodeen is signed on for a long hitch with the Angels, while Virgil Sweet and Bobbie Henderson walk off together, basking in the glory of a true blue Technicolor miracle.

Talent for the Game was given a trial run by Paramount with a few scattered Southern playdates in the spring of 1991. Audiences were cool and critics were ice cold (total box-office gross was a puny $336,396), so Paramount withdrew the film, releasing it directly to home video in late October.

There's evidence aplenty that a lot of heavy cutting took place somewhere along the line. The film's pace pokes along languidly for about an hour or so, then hastily wraps up everything in a little over twenty minutes—suggesting that *Talent for the Game* was supposed to have run considerably longer than its present ninety-one minutes. Also, there's a scene at the beginning where Virgil Sweet, whose baseball career had been cut short by an unspecified injury, appears on the verge of collapse. Nothing further comes of this, but the closing credits list two actors as "paramedics," neither of whom appears in the film, which would seem to indicate that *Talent* had once included something darker than its current upbeat denouement.

What was left on-screen included a couple of performances above reproach from Edward James Olmos as Virgil Sweet and Jeffrey Corbett as Sammy Bodeen, as well as a faultlessly photographed and masterfully staged baseball-game climax. This is the best we can do in the way of praise, because this is the best *Talent for the Game* can do in the way of quality and credibility.

Let's take some time to analyze that credibility, since if you aren't willing to suspend your disbelief while watching a movie, chances are you won't be willing to overlook its flaws.

Virgil Sweet is supposed to be a veteran scout, and thus would be expected to assess the talents of various prospects in conditions comparable to those found in actual ballgames. Yet when we first see Virgil, he's checking out a young pitcher in a deep, dank coal mine! Why? Because this is the only time off the aspiring player has. Just where in the United States of 1991 is there a mining town that forces its residents to work seven days a week?

Sammy Bodeen tells Virgil that he's wanted to be a ballplayer more than anything all his life. So why has he kept his mouth shut and his talents confined to a few close friends until an outsider happens to stumble upon him? Are there no school teams or semi-pro clubs in the whole of Idaho? And even allowing for the fact that Sammy's father resists the notion of the big leagues, would not at least one of Sammy's pals have told tales of the boy's remarkable baseball skill to someone outside of Genessee County, so that Virgil would have happened upon Sammy in the course of business rather than by pure dumb luck? (The answer, of course, is that the script has contrived to send Virgil on a quest for a "phenom" who must appear literally out of nowhere. Please note that word "contrived.")

Angels owner Gil Lawrence (played with all caution thrown to the wind by Terry Kinney) is a billionaire and thus is wealthier than anyone watching the film. Ta-da! Instant bad guy! Not content with this, the script strains to make us despise Lawrence by showing him disdainfully riding his mile-long, air-conditioned limousine onto the ballfield while his poor working-stiff players sweat through a practice session. Also, Lawrence is forever puffing on an expensive cigar, which he uses to ostentatiously blow smoke upon his inferiors. And just so we don't miss the point, Lawrence's first line is "I don't much like these games." A team owner who doesn't like baseball? He might as well be shown drowning kittens.

And how did Gil Lawrence become a billionaire? We're told he's an advertising man of genius caliber. Yet his idea of a "wow" introduction for Sammy is to have the ballplayer lowered on piano wire from the mists of a dry ice–induced cloud before an assemblage of reporters. After trying to curry favor with the press with this little piece of flimflam, Lawrence ducks their questions about Sammy with obfuscations and stonewalling; when one reporter asks if Sammy shouldn't first go to the minors for some seasoning, Lawrence endears himself to the media by responding, "Do you have a point?" And later, Lawrence looks on in hushed, approving reverence at the ad campaign mounted to promote Sammy—a stiffly posed photo of the rookie standing before a field of wheat (this couldn't *possibly* be a subtle dig at the promotional campaign for *Field of Dreams*? [q.v.]). Until *Talent for the Game*, I had absolutely no idea that comporting yourself in the manner of Gil Lawrence would turn you into a billionaire. I've never made a dime out of being obnoxious and ridiculous.

It's not easy to swallow the premise that Lawrence would spotlight Sammy by having him pitch in the first inning of his very first game; but had we left it at that, the sequence might have got by. No such luck. Sammy plays very poorly his first time out, which, in any real-life situation, would be utterly forgivable, given the pressure that has been put upon him prior to his debut. But Gil Lawrence isn't having any. He orders the manager to tear up Sammy's contract after his first game. Better than that, he orders the contract to be torn up after the *first inning*. Not only has this never happened in major-league baseball, it would never, ever happen in Lawrence's supposed field of expertise, that of advertising. The Edsel, the eight-track stereo, and the "new Coca-Cola" were all given longer test periods—and with far less justification—than poor Sammy Bodeen.

We could go on and on like this. During Sammy's tryout, Virgil calms the boy down by discussing the pleasures of eating sushi. Sammy's first game is carried on television, a broadcast dutifully witnessed by

Sammy's friends and family back in Idaho—where, in 1991 at least, one seldom had the opportunity to watch a relatively unimportant California Angels night game, cable television notwithstanding. In the middle of Sammy's tepid first inning, half the spectators head for home, evidently disregarding how much they'd paid to attend the game. And not one person in the entire stadium notices something amiss when Virgil strolls onto the field during the final scene disguised as the Angels' catcher, not even the team's TV play by play announcer, who would presumably be fairly familiar with the genuine California lineup. On and on and on and on...

So much for credibility. As for quality, we needn't say anything more than those three bloodcurdling words which strike terror in the hearts of all true baseball movie buffs: slow motion photography.

Early in this film Virgil Sweet says to a would-be ballplayer who's been told he'll "maybe" make it someday that, "The road to heaven is paved with maybes." Unfortunately, the road taken by *Talent for the Game* is the more familiar concourse paved with good intentions.

They Learned About Women

MGM; released January 31, 1930

Directed by Jack Conway and Sam Wood. Screenplay by Sarah Y. Mason. Dialogue by Arthur "Bugs" Baer. Titles for the silent version by Alfred Block. Story by A. P. Younger. Photography: Leonard Smith. Edited by James McKay and Thomas Held. Songs: "Daugherty Is the Name" by Van and Schenck; "Harlem Madness," "He's That Kind of Pal," "Ain't You Baby?" "A Man of My Own," "Does My Baby Love?" "There'll Never Be Another Mary," and "Ten Sweet Mamas" by Jack Yellin and Milton Yegger. Art director: Cedric Gibbons. Dance director: Sammy Lee. Recording engineers: Douglas Shearer and Robert Shirley. Wardrobe by David Cox. 95 minutes; black and white; sound (also released in a silent version).

Cast: Joseph T. Schenck (Jack Glennon); Gus Van (Jerry Burke); Bessie Love (Mary); Mary Doran (Daisy Gebhardt); J. C. Nugent (Stafford); Benny Rubin (Sam Goldberg); Tom Dugan (Tim O'Connor); Eddie Gribbon (Brennan); Francis X. Bushman, Jr. (Haskins).

Jerry Burke and Jack Glennon, a couple of players for the Blue Sox baseball club, capitalize on their popularity with an off-season vaudeville tour. Both teammates are sweet on Mary, whose affections lean in Jack's direction. When the vampish Daisy threatens to break up the boys' friendship and destroy their dual careers, Mary pretends to be in love with Jerry, sacrificing her true feelings to keep our heroes together. But Mary winds up with Jack at the end, and both Jerry and Jack return to the Blue Sox just in time to win the World Series.

They Learned About Women is occasionally referred to as the inspiration for the 1949 MGM opus *Take Me Out to the Ballgame* (q.v.); some film historians have taken this notion one step farther by suggesting that *Ballgame* is a remake. As noted in the entry on the 1949 film, however, *Ballgame* star Gene Kelly cited as his inspiration the antics of baseball clown Al Schacht, whereas the earlier film was based on the novelty vaudeville act performed by Waite Hoyt of the New York Yankees and Mickey Cochrane of the Philadelphia Athletics. Besides, *They Learned About Women* hadn't been at all successful when it was first released, hadn't yielded a single hit song, and had been out of circulation for over sixteen years when Kelly and Stanley Donen came up with their *Ballgame* treatment. Even though both films were made by MGM and Kelly could have conceivably asked for a screening of the 1930 film, it's unlikely that *They Learned About Women* would have had such an impact in Gene's memory that he'd want to remake it.

The two gossamer strands connecting MGM's brace of baseball musicals were the

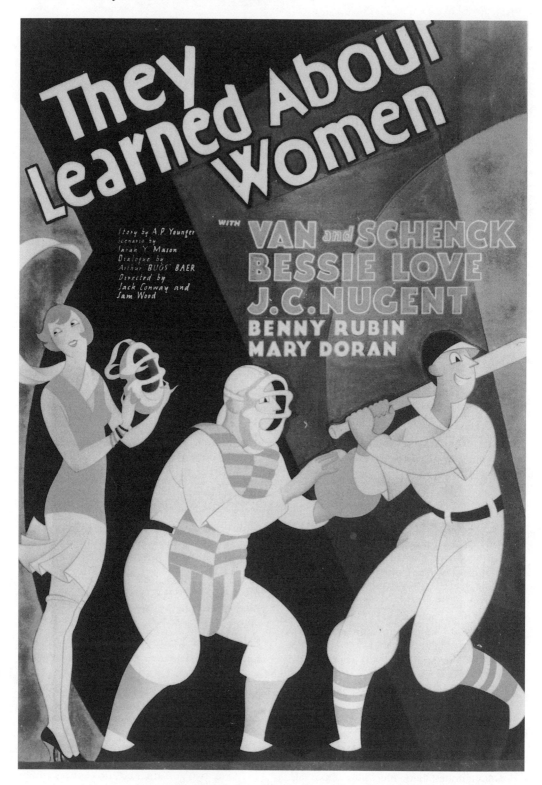

Vintage jazz-age poster art for *They Learned About Women*.

appearances in both films of prolific character actor Tom Dugan (best remembered for his Hitler imitation in 1942's *To Be or Not to Be*) and the fact that both films concerned themselves with ballplayers who doubled as vaudeville entertainers. This latter plot point was needed in *They Learned About Women* to justify the presence of its stars, the celebrated nightclub song and snappy patter duo of Van and Schenck. The baseball gimmick in the 1930 film may have come about because Joseph T. Schenck (no relation to United Artists production executive Joseph Schenck) was a consummate fan of the game who'd once captained the vaudeville "All-Stars" baseball team.

Other than its World Series angle, *They Learned About Women* was all too typical of the stagebound musical comedies churned out by Hollywood between 1929 and 1931—right down to the inevitable presence of leading lady Bessie Love, who appeared in just about every musical that MGM produced in the swaddling years of talking pictures as a result of her star turn in the studio's first full-fledged talkie, the Oscar-winning *Broadway Melody* (1929). Bessie was even obligated to reprise her *Broadway Melody* plight of giving up the guy she was really in love with so that the show could go on. For the "tired businessmen" in the audience who weren't interested in the baseball stuff or the romance business, Bessie Love highlighted her *They Learned About Women* appearance with a brief scene in which it was implied (via silhouette) that she was stripping down to her birthday suit. Even Esther Williams, the far more pulchritudinous female lead of *Take Me Out to the Ballgame*, couldn't top that.

For a baseball story, *They Learned About Women* is strangely claustrophobic; most of the picture takes place in a succession of fleabag hotel suites, tacky vaudeville theaters, cramped train compartments and dingy locker rooms. Of some sociological interest is the presence of Benny Rubin (see notes on *Hot Curves*) and the aforementioned Tom Dugan as an ersatz comedy team, with Rubin's Jewish-dialect jokes playing off Dugan's Irish blarney. This musty brand of humor is about as relevant to audiences of the 21st Century as the puns of Aristophanes, though not nearly as funny. On the other hand, the picture does yield a handful of unexpected delights, among them the musical number "Ten Sweet Mamas," sung by a chorus of ballplayers as they take their showers, and the closing scene wherein Jerry (Gus Van) takes advantage of a rain delay during the deciding Series game to reunite Jack (Joe Schenck) with Mary (Bessie Love).

As mentioned, *They Learned About Women* was a financial dud, utterly forgotten by all but the most fanatical movie musical buffs; in fact, the picture came and went so quickly upon its initial release that neither *Variety* nor the *New York Times* bothered to review it! Then in the mid–1990s, the film suddenly went back into circulation thanks to media mogul Ted Turner, whose TNT and TCM cable services made a practice of exhuming old and long-neglected treasures from the vast MGM library which Turner had purchased *in toto* a few years earlier. Around the same time, *They Learned About Women* was given limited distribution on laserdisc; as a result of these developments, more people ended up seeing the film seventy years after its release than when it first came out. But whether or not *They Learned About Women* would have made major movie stars of Van and Schenck remains a moot point, since Joseph T. Schenck died shortly after its completion.

Tiger Town[*]

Thompson Street Pictures/The Disney Channel; first telecast October 9, 1983

Produced by Susan P. Landau. Written and directed by Alan Shapiro. Additional story material by Bobby Fine. Photography: Robert Elswit. Edited by Richard A. Harris and John F. Link. Musical editor: Ted Roberts. Musicians: Eddy Manson, Mel Tax, Abe Most, Tony Terran, Chauncey Walsh, Mundell Lowe, Louis Kabok, Clare Fisher, and Victor Feldman. Assistant directors: Steve Novack and Mary Ellen Woods. Production manager: Joanne Mallas. Production associate: Forrest Murray. Storyboard artist: Bill Bryan. Technical adviser: Gates Brown. Stunt coordinator: Sandra Gimpel. Makeup by Felice Fassmacht. Title design by Dan Curry. Casting by Lynn Kessel (New York) and Nancy Kelly (Detroit). Color by TVC. 76 minutes; sound.

Cast: Roy Scheider (Billy Young); Justin Henry (Alex); Ron McLarty (Buddy); Bethany Carpenter (Nancy); Noah Moazezi (Eddie); Lindsay Barr (Peanut Vendor); Dave Bokas (Crusty Man); Chris Bremer (Loud Kid); Kate Delozier (Little Girl); Jack Fish (Stadium Guard); Gerald L. Monford (Lunchroom Kid); Leon Smith (Druggist); Ralph Valatka (Hot Dog Vendor); Larry Williams (Bus Driver); Whit Vernon (Mr. Cullen); Von Washington (Souvenir Vendor). And as themselves: Al Ackerman (WWJ Sportscaster); Sparky Anderson (Detroit Tigers Manager); Ernie Harwell and Ray Lane (WJR Radio Announcers); Mary Wilson (National Anthem Singer).

Veteran Detroit Tigers right-fielder Billy Young would like to play in just one World Series before his retirement, but from the looks of the recent batting slump suffered by himself, and the fifteen-year slump endured by the Tigers, his series chances aren't too promising. Billy's biggest fan is young Alex, whose love of baseball extends to his having to be woken up each morning for school with a recorded rendition of "The Star Spangled Banner" and his mother's shout of "Play ball!" Alex despairs at the Tigers' bad breaks but is encouraged by the advice once given to him by his late father: "If you really believe deep in your heart, there's always hope and you can make it happen." While attending a Tigers-Royals game, Alex decides to implement his father's philosophy; as Billy Young stands at bat, Alex folds his hands, shuts his eyes tight, and "wills" Young to hit a home run. Wham! Out of the park!! And when Alex undergoes the same ritual at the next day's game, Billy Young cracks out another homer. Both Young and the Tigers pull out of their losing streak and enter the pennant-race mainstream. The media is astounded, Billy chalks it up to the good luck charm he wears around his wrist, but only Alex is cognizant of what he thinks is the "secret" of Detroit's success; and the boy's opinion seems confirmed by the fact that the Tigers lose whenever Alex isn't at the ballpark. Alex's mother becomes concerned that her son is cutting school to attend the ballgames, but after Billy Young is beaned when Alex prematurely leaves a game, she too decides to put some stock in Alex's "willing" powers. On the day of the deciding pennant game with the Orioles, Alex is about to make a beeline to Tiger Stadium when he's detained and harrassed by the school bully—while at the stadium Billy Young's game suffers. Finally escaping from his tormentor, Alex makes a mad dash to the ballpark, commandeering a little girl's bicycle and hitching a ride on the back of a bus along the way. He arrives at the park just in time for Billy Young's last-stand play in the ninth with the bases loaded, and just after Billy—deciding to rely on pure skill rather than any "outside" influence—has tossed his good luck bracelet to the ground. Billy connects with the ball the moment that Alex shows up; and while we're never sure whether or not Alex's presence was really the deciding factor, Billy scores the winning home run.

*Winner of the National Cable Television Association's Award for Cable Excellence for Best Dramatic Feature Film of 1984.

Created as a pay TV service on April 18, 1983, the Disney Channel wasted no time in providing subscribers with fresh, first-rate entertainment. *Tiger Town*, which premiered on October 9, 1983, was the first feature film produced exclusively for the Disney Channel; not only was it one of the studio's best products in years, but it was also one of the finest baseball pictures turned out by any company at any time.

As Billy Young, *Tiger Town* star Roy Scheider so dominates every scene he's in that only after the film has ended does it dawn on us that Scheider has spoken only a dozen or so lines in the whole seventy-six minutes. The actor looks just right when prepping himself at the plate, and he doesn't let us down when we see him in action— mainly because he doesn't really have to play baseball at all. The unswerving hand of first-time director Alan Shapiro, the mathematically precise editing of Richard A. Harris and John F. Link, and the richly evocative photography of Robert Elswit (who four years later would surpass his work on *Tiger Town* with an even better baseball yarn, HBO's *Long Gone* [q.v.]) all combine to "pinch-hit" for Scheider in the ballgame scenes. Whenever there's a strike, a ball, or an RBI, it is conveyed montage style with quick full-figure glimpses of Scheider, close-ups of his hands and then his face, tight shots of the fans in the stands, tighter shots of scorecards, programs, pennants, and edible concessions, and ever so brief flashes of the Tigers scoreboard—all bundled together by the ongoing play by play narration of "Voice of the Tigers" Ernie Harwell. Much of the credit for the masterful design and execution of *Tiger Town*'s baseball sequences must go to Disney's long-standing practice of meticulously preparing an artist's storyboard for each of its live-action films, in the tradition of the studio's feature length cartoons.

While the basic storyline flirts and dallies with the obvious, *Tiger Town* comes off as original and spontaneous, principally by avoiding drawn-out dialogue sequences and telling most of its story visually. One of the best scenes occurs after the death of Alex's father (a wholly unexpected and brilliant vignette in itself). The disconsolate Alex makes a return visit to Tigers Stadium which, despite the cheers and jeers of the fans and the poor performance of the home team, had always seemed a warm and convivial gathering spot when visited by the boy in the company of his father. Now that Alex is alone, however, the stadium becomes a thoroughly hostile environment, festooned with animal-like behavior and overrun with oversized, glowering adults who tower threateningly over Alex like Ulysses' Cyclops. Few films made either for television or for theaters have conveyed the utter loss, loneliness, and terror attendant to the death of a parent as successfully as *Tiger Town*.

The little touches that make the difference between a pedestrian film and a superlative one abound. For example, we see the mounting "Tiger fever" in Detroit mirrored by a series of swift location shots of the metropolis at work and at play (*Tiger Town* was filmed in its entirety in the Motor City), alternating with snatches of Billy Young being interviewed, making spot promotional TV announcements on behalf of the Tigers, and starring in a gloriously goofy (but realistic) shaving-cream commercial—while the soundtrack booms forth an inspirational chorus of "Go Get 'Em, Tigers," a tune played during the team's painfully infrequent real-life pennant races. In its own tight-budget way, *Tiger Town* is every bit as successful in detailing the mania that grips a city on the threshold of a series bid as the more elaborate 1989 theatrical feature *Major League* (q.v.).

The potentially sticky "fantasy" aspects of the plot are handled with equal aplomb. While it would have been standard operating procedure for Disney to play up Alex's willpower as though it was irrefutably the real thing, the script is careful to leave open the possibility that Alex's mental magic may all be in his own imagination, and that Billy Young's off and on performance is merely coincidental to Alex's presence at the stadium. Indeed, the final scene shows us Billy hitting his winning homer a fraction of a second *before* Alex arrives to see his idol play. Alan Shapiro's *Tiger Town* screenplay manages to have its cake and eat it too, without disappointing either the realists or the fantasists in the audience.

We regret to report, however, that *Tiger Town* is some distance from an unqualified success. One of its drawbacks is admittedly a minor one. Though Justin Henry (as Alex) proves that his excellent 1979 performance in the Oscar-winning *Kramer vs. Kramer* was no fluke and that the kid had the stuff to carry a film, some of the other child actors are less convincing. Writer-director Shapiro adroitly played against cliché by making school bully Eddie not a physical monster but a sweet-faced little cherub who stands nearly a head shorter than Justin Henry; but this gimmick fails to pay off, due to the overly cute and inadequately menacing performance by Noah Moazezi as Eddie.

Inflicting far more injury on *Tiger Town* was the decision to turn the film into a traditional "Disney Movie" some twenty minutes before the end by grafting on a protracted and totally unnecessary chase sequence. The film treats the audience to scenes of Alex careening through town on a bicycle, knocking over pedestrians, causing bags of groceries to cascade all over the pavement, and precipitating a horn-honking, near calamitous traffic jam. Making matters worse is Alex's boorish and irresponsible behavior. He trades his belt for a little girl's bicycle on the promise that the vehicle will be returned, but then he abandons the bike on a hill, miles from its owner. Alex then hops a ride on the back of a bus—the sort of behavior that can be eagerly

(and fatally) imitated by the kiddie viewers. And when he finally reaches Tiger Stadium, Alex quickly rouses the child strangler deep within all of us by pushing and shoving his way into the crowd and barking, "Get outta my way!"

In spite of its "feel good" climax, *Tiger Town* never completely recovers from that gratuitous chase sequence, which is a real shame. For in its first hour, *Tiger Town* is a model of what a good baseball picture should be: funny, sad, suspenseful, heartwarming, and drenched through and through with a boundless love of the game and the people who play it.

Trading Hearts

Vista Organization/Cineworld Enterprises; released July 1988

Produced by Josi W. Konski. Directed by Neil Leifer. Screenplay by Frank Deford. Photography: Karen Grossman. Edited by Rick Shaine. Music editor: Joseph S. DeBeash. Music supervisor: Ron Gertz. Original music by Stanley Myers. Art director: James R. Bilz. Set decorations by Regina McLarney. Production design by George Goodridge. Production coordinator: Rosalyn M. Mayer. Stunt coordinator: Roberto S. Messina. Assistant directors: Jim Bingham, Scott "Chip" Laughton, and Robert Leveen. Casting by Nina Axelrod. Casting directors: Dee Miller (Miami); Joel Blumenau (Los Angeles); and Brad Davis (Extras). Baseball technical adviser: Joe Johnson. Hair makeup by Jaren Millard. Costume design by Franco Carelli. Title design by Tom Bentkowski. Color by Deluxe. 88 minutes; sound. Rated PG.

Cast: Raul Julia (Vinnie Icona); Beverly D'Angelo (Donna Nottingham, a.k.a. "Amber Flaxen"); Jenny Lewis (Yvonne Rhonda Nottingham); Parris Buckner (Robert Nottingham); Robin Caldwell (Patricia Nottingham); Robert Gwaltney (Ducky); Honorable Edward I. Koch (Tourist Husband); Jeffrey "Ed" Miller (Ted); Ruben Rabasa (Pepe); Earleen Carey (Pearl); William Fuller (Sheriff); Mark Harris (Ralph); Frank Logan (Skip); Sandy Mielke (Ray Bob); Alexander Panas (Benjie); Arnie Ross (Deputy);

Janice Tesh (Shirley Louise); William Wohrmann (Malone); D. J. Blakely (Heckler 1); Scot Alan (Heckler 2); Tom Kouchalakos (Bartender 1); Frank Deford (Bartender 2); Richard Baron (Stranger); Ruth Farley (Nottingham Maid); Rhonda "Ru" Flynn (Female Tourist); Barry Hober (Male Tourist); Richard Kosters (Truck Stop Attendant); Neil Leifer (Bar Patron); Darcy Schaffer (Bar Hostess); Don Wellington (Office Boy); Jody Wilson (Tourist Wife).

Florida, 1957: Donna Nottingham and her preteen daughter Yvonne have to keep on the move so that Donna's wealthy ex-husband can't take Yvonne away to live with him. Right now mother and daughter are living in a trailer, Yvonne keeping the wolf from the door by working at a rundown alligator farm and Donna aspiring to a singing career by appearing at the Park Motel dining room as a "tweener" (an unknown performer who keeps the audience happy between the bigger acts), using the *nom de stage* of "Amber Flaxen." One of the motel patrons is Vinnie Icona, former pitcher for the Boston Red Sox who doesn't have it anymore and has been released during spring training. Vinnie takes an instant liking to Donna, but she is turned off by his pugnaciousness and his self-pitying demeanor. Yvonne, on the other hand, is a baseball nut from the word go; she befriends Vinnie and tries to act as matchmaker between the ballplayer and her mother. The usual complications ensue, culminating with Donna and Vinnie patching up their differences. While Vinnie is keeping an eye on Yvonne during one of Donna's singing engagements, detectives arrive to take Yvonne away to her father. The plucky kid sneaks out to the car and, despite the fact that she's a long distance from sixteen, drives away with a nonplussed Vinnie in the passenger seat; suddenly Vinnie is pursued as Yvonne's kidnapper, though, truth to tell, it is the other way around. Yvonne suggests that Vinnie hide out by taking a pitching job with the Havana Sugar Kings, a Cuban

team with a training camp in the Everglades. But Vinnie can't stay incognito long and tips his hand by visiting the bar where Donna is currently singing. After a contretemps with a heckler, Vinnie pulls Donna off the stage and takes her with him to training camp, where Yvonne has been "adopted" as a bat girl. An evening in bed intensifies Vinnie and Donna's relationship, as well as Donna's new resolve that she really can't make it as a singer and that she'll put her fate in Vinnie's hands. But during an exhibition game between the Sugar Kings and the Boston Red Sox, Vinnie pitches very badly against his old team and realizes that it is he, not Donna, who should hang it up and look for another line of work. As Vinnie walks off the field, detectives show up again to strong-arm the ballplayer into giving up Yvonne to her natural father. Donna blames Vinnie for the loss of her daughter and walks out on him. Months pass: Robert Nottingham is aware that Yvonne is not happy in her new environment; Vinnie tries to make a go as a stockbroker; and a desperate Donna takes a job as a stripper at a skuzzy burlesque house. Once again, Yvonne tries to be "Miss Fixit" by writing a letter inviting Vinnie to the Nottingham mansion. Just as we all knew it would, the story ends happily. Nottingham agrees to allow Donna to share custody of Yvonne; Vinnie "rescues" Donna from her humiliating job at the burleycue; and Vinnie, Donna, and Yvonne launch an elaborate new alligator farm with a $10,000 check that was purportedly a gift from Nottingham but was actually the handiwork of master forger Yvonne.

Trading Hearts was filmed in Greater Miami in 1987 under the title *Tweeners*, a reference not only to Donna Nottingham's aforementioned "filler" status as a nightclub singer but to Vinnie Icona's crossroads stance between baseball and a civilian profession. The original title suited the finished product: Most of the participants in this picture behave as though they're biding their time between jobs that they'd rather be doing.

The screenplay, by *Sports Illustrated* writer Frank Deford, must have read infinitely better than it played for its producers to have put up good money to make the film. Under the single-cylinder direction of another *Sports Illustrated* alumnus, photographer Neil Leifer—who admittedly does have an unerring eye for late 1950s period detail—*Trading Hearts* is so laid back that at times it's practically comatose. The baseball scenes are about as thrilling as watching grass grow, while the ballgame spectators are so noncommittal that none of them pays the slightest attention when Vinnie walks off the Sugar Kings' field and is beaten up in full view of the crowd by two detectives. The one scene where action actually rears its head is a 1970s-style "free spirit" passage in which Vinnie and Yvonne race through the Everglades on a propeller boat. It's all very prettily photographed and cunningly edited, and it all has nothing to do with the movie.

As Vinnie Icona, Raul Julia is physically impressive and admirably successful in hiding his natural Hispanic cadence with a thick Brooklyn dialect, but his ballplaying is at best junior college level. We can believe that he's washed up in the majors, but it's asking a bit much for us to believe that he ever got to the majors in the first place. Beverly D'Angelo's dilemma is the opposite of Raul Julia's; as Donna "Amber Flaxen" Nottingham, she is much too good a singer for us to accept that the best job she can obtain by the end of the film is a bubble-bath strip act in a sleazy dive. As for precocious little Jenny Lewis (who later essayed variations of worldly-wise Yvonne Nottingham in *Troop Beverly Hills* and *The Wizard*), the less said the better. Suffice it to say that Lewis galumphs through *Trading Hearts* as if she'd just flunked an audition for the role of Pippi Longstocking.

There are islands of salvation here and there. As Robert Nottingham, Parris Buckner tackles a character that could have been a stock stuffed-shirt villain and convinces us that he's basically a decent guy beneath his immaculately tailored wardrobe. Buckner is rewarded with the film's most satisfying moment: As the swaggering Vinnie Icona threatens Nottingham with the standard "these hands are licensed as lethal weapons" palaver that he's used throughout the film to avoid physical combat, Nottingham calmly decks Vinnie with a single, well-aimed blow. If you can't endure *Trading Hearts* long enough to see Vinnie's comeuppance, at least try to stick out the opening alligator farm sequence. That abrasive tourist who is doing such an on-target imitation of former New York City mayor Edward Koch turns out not to be "What's His Name the Actor" who spent most of the 1980s portraying Koch-like characters, but the genuine "hizzoner" himself.

Trading Hearts never got a theatrical release; the film went straight to video in July 1988, and can be found with the greatest of ease at any of your local rental shops. But caveat emptor: One nationwide video-rental chain stocks the film in its "Family" section, basing this categorization on the cassette box liner notes which characterizes the film as "for the whole family." Right. During the course of the film's eighty-eight minutes, eleven-year-old Yvonne Nottingham drives a car with reckless abandon; forges Vinnie Icona's autograph to sell to her friends, as well as her father's signature on a $10,000 check; expresses her desire to one day develop "knockers" proportionate to her mother's; and, upon discovering that her Mom and Vinnie have spent the night together, gleefully jumps into bed with them. If this is for the whole family, then I hope I'm never sitting behind that particular family at the movies.

Trifling with Honor

Universal; released May 28, 1923

Directed by Harry A. Pollard. Screenplay by Frank Beresford and Raymond L. Schrock. Adapted by Raymond L. Schrock from the story "His Good Name" by William Slavens McNutt, published in *Collier's* Magazine, July 22, 1922. Photography: Jack Brown. 8 reels/7,785 feet; black and white; silent.

Cast: Rockliffe Fellows (The Gas Pipe Kid/Bat Shugreve); Fritzi Ridgeway (Ida Hunt); Buddy Messinger (Jimmy Shugreve); Hayden Stevenson (Kelsey Hunt); Emmett King (Judge Drury); William Welsh (Warden); Frederick Stanton (Luke Clotz); William Robert Daly (The Kid's Father); Jim Farley (Murray Jessop); Sidney De-Gray (Dud Adams); John Hatton (Jimmy, age 8); Mike Gaffner (Landlord).

[Working Titles: *His Good Name*; *Your Good Name*]

The "Gas Pipe Kid," a recent parolee, is thrown back in jail after beating up the landlord who threatened to evict the Kid's widowed father. With the aid of Ida Hunt, the Kid escapes from the courtroom while his trial is in progress and spends the next several years building up a whole new identity as Bat Shugreve, a champion baseball star who is the epitome of clean living both on the field and off. Newsman Kelsey Lewis sends his stenographer to get an interview with the noble but secretive Bat Shugreve. As these things sometimes happen around the third reel, the stenographer is Ida Hunt, and when she meets the former Gas Pipe Kid their romance rekindles and she agrees to keep his secret. Blackmailers get wind of the truth about Bat Shugreve and try to pressure the ballplayer into throwing a game. But Shugreve goes to Judge Drury with the whole story and the bad guys are hauled off to the pokey. Shugreve, a.k.a. the Gas Pipe Kid, fully expects to be incarcerated as well, but the judge, whose last name isn't Landis, rules that the ballplayer is more valuable to the youth of America as a free man.

Trifling with Honor may have been better than its title, but reviewers in 1923 weren't completely convinced. The general complaint was that the film was eight reels of merciless hokum, helped not at all by the Keystone-like comedy of its early eviction sequence. The quick-as-a-wink climactic baseball scenes were by and large harvested from stock footage of a game featuring the two Pacific Coast League teams from Los Angeles and Vernon, California. The star of *Trifling with Honor* was Rockliffe Fellows, a big bear of a man who is best known to modern-day movie fans as the softhearted bootlegger whom Groucho Marx promises to simultaneously attack and defend in *Monkey Business* (1931).

Warming Up

Paramount/Famous/Lasky; released August 4, 1928

Presented by Adolph Zukor and Jesse Lasky. Directed by Fred Newmeyer. Screenplay and adaptation by Ray Harris. Story by Sam Mintz. Titles by George Marion. Photography: Ed Cronjager. Song "Out of the Dawn" by Walter Donaldson. Technical adviser: Mike Donlin. 8 reels/6,509 feet: black and white; silent, released with music and sound effects.

Cast: Richard Dix (Bert "Beeline" Tolliver); Jean Arthur (Mary Post); Claude King (Mr. Post); Philo McCullough (McRae); Billy Kent Schaefer (Edsel); Roscoe Karns (Hippo); James Dugan (Bill); Mike Donlin (Veteran); Wade Boteler (Bit Man); and members of the New York Yankees, including Mike Ready, Chet Thomas, Joe Pirrone, Wally Hood, Bob Murray, and Truck Hannah.

Small town pitcher Bert Tolliver is given a spring training tryout with the big-league Green Sox, where he becomes an object of ridicule after falling for a gag in which he's convinced via a bottle of iodine that he's beaned a teammate and drawn blood. Tolliver becomes obsessed with the idea that mean-tempered Green Sox player

Richard Dix (left), looking a bit long in the tooth for a rookie, is given some pointers in
Warming Up.

McRae is jinxing him, and consequently the rookie is washed up. He heads for the local amusement park to forget his troubles, where he wins a concessionaire's job after amazing the other customers with his pitching display at the "win the kewpie doll" booth. Witnessing one of Tolliver's demonstrations is Mary Post, daughter of the Green Sox owner; Mary arranges behind the scenes to get Tolliver hired by the team, all the while keeping her identity a secret from Bert. The gangling young player soon earns fame, a fan following, and the nickname of "Beeline" Tolliver. When the Green Sox inevitably enter the series race, Tolliver learns to his dismay that former teammate McRae is playing for the opposition. Led to believe that McRae is not

only still jinxing him but that his rival has stolen the affections of Mary, Tolliver walks McRae and is benched for the balance of the series. But necessity dictates that Tolliver pitch during the last game. Just before facing McRae again, Bert spots Mary in the stands; the girl mouths the words "I'm yours forever," echoing the affectionate message written on the kewpie doll that Bert had won for Mary back during her amusement park visit. "Beeline" Tolliver strikes out McRae, and the series is claimed by the Green Sox.

Variety devoted nearly a full page to its June 27, 1928, review of *Warming Up*—not to praise but to bury. The kindest thing the trade paper had to say about the film was that it was "the most asinine concoction ever trotted out for the edification of that mythical 12-year-old audience the boys have invented."

The most potent complaint made by *Variety* concerned the plot contrivance involving the villainous McRae's defection to an opposing team. When *Warming Up* was trade shown in June, the team depicted in the film was the New York Yankees. The plotline would have the audience believe that McRae had originally belonged to the National League's Pittsburgh Pirates, but had been traded to the *American* League Yankees—something that just plain wouldn't happen in 1928. The filmmakers compounded their booboo by arranging for the Pirates to exercise their option on McRae by claiming his services just before the World Series (a turn of events explained by the hastily inserted close-up of a telegram), thus paving the way for the last-reel showdown between hero and heavy. *Variety* noted with jaundiced irony that former New York Giant "Turkey" Mike Donlin hadn't exactly earned his money as the film's technical adviser by letting the Yanks-to-Pittsburgh crossover pass by unnoticed; curiously, the review heaped no scorn upon the director of *Warming Up*, Fred Newmeyer, who had himself played professional baseball with the Denver Association from 1909 to 1913.

Evidently, Paramount took heed of *Variety*'s admonitions. According to the synopsis provided in the early 1970s by the American Film Institute, by the time *Warming Up* went into general release in August 1928, the Yankees had metamorphosed into the fictional "Green Sox," which apparently operated as a league unto itself. This still didn't make the film any better; despite the drawing power of star Richard Dix and the sprightly performance by comparative newcomer Jean Arthur (light-years away from her big-time stardom in the 1930s), *Warming Up* was strictly cold potatoes at the ticket booth.

Of some faint historical significance is the fact that Paramount outfitted the silent *Warming Up* with a music and sound-effects accompaniment recorded on disc by the Victor Talking Machine Company—thus making the picture Paramount's first "sound" release. There was nothing special about the film that warranted this honor; it just happened to be the release at hand when Paramount executive Walter Wanger came up with the idea of emulating Warner Bros.' *The Jazz Singer*.

This hybrid effort at entering the talkie sweepstakes of the late 1920s drove a further nail into the coffin of *Warming Up* once the fans caught on that the sounds had been synchronized with the same "accuracy" that Paramount had bestowed upon McRae's trade to Pittsburgh. When a batter knocked out a homer in one scene, for example, you didn't hear the crack of the bat until two seconds later. That's assuming, of course, that you were still in the theater by the time anyone stepped up to the plate.

A Winner Never Quits

Blatt-Singer Productions/Columbia; originally telecast April 14, 1986

Executive producers: Daniel H. Blatt and Robert Singer. Produced by James Keach and Lynn Raynor. Directed by Mel Damski. Screenplay by Burt Prelutsky. Photography: Joseph Biroc. Edited by Michael A. Stevenson. Music by Dana Kaproff. Production design by Paul Peters. Art director: Ross Bellah. Costume designer: Gary Hunt. Associate producers: Pixie Lamppu and Frank Pace. Casting by Judith Weiner and Associates. Production manager: Bill Carrell. Assistant directors: Nick Smirnoff and Hope Goodwin. Color by Metrocolor. 100 minutes; sound.

Cast: Keith Carradine (Pete Gray); Ed O'Neill (Whitey Gray); Huckleberry Fox (Nelson Gary, Jr.); Mare Winningham (Annie); Dennis Weaver (Joseph Wyshner); Jack Kehoe (David Bloom); Fionnula Flanagan (Mrs. Wyshner); Steve Rees (Young Pete Gray); Charles Hallahan (Nelson Gary, Sr.); Andrew Lubeske (Young Whitey); G. W. Bailey (Tatum); Dana Delany (Nora); Mary Jo Deschanel (Mrs. Gary); Jeff McCracken (Sheldrake); Jim Morgan (Hatfield); David Haid (Henderson); Brad Sullivan (Taylor); Lulu Downs (Josie); Peter Hobbs (Dan McGregor); J. J. Johnston (Trainer); Art LaFleur (John Stewart); Macon McCalman (Dr. Wilson); Tom Turbiville (First Man); Jim Boyd (Second Man); John Hosteter (Sergeant); James Troesh (Phil Nolan); Regi Green (Veteran); Ted Henning (Brock); Phillip L. Stone (Announcer); Robert Benson (Child Shortstop); Patrick Beall (Child Catcher); Bryan Coley (First Captain); Jamey Lee Moore (Third Man); Mike Quarry (Kid Falco); Charles Joseph Fick (Second Baseman); Walter Robles (Masher); Al Silvani (Referee).

The story opens in the early 1930s in the mining town of Nanticoke, Pennsylvania. Like most kids, Whitey Wyshner balks when ordered by his mother to let his younger brother Pete play baseball with him, but Whitey's reason is to him a practical one: Pete has lost an arm in an accident and the kids on the other team have no qualms about taking advantage of Pete's handicap. Whitey works out with Pete to improve the younger boy's game, advising him to "get angry and stay that way" because no one's going to give a "one-armed Litvak" a break: "Anything you're going to get, you're going to have to fight for." Pete takes these words to heart, and soon he's playing better and more competitively than anyone in his community. As the Wyshner boys mature, Whitey decides to pursue a boxing career under the name of Whitey Gray, and hero-worshiping Pete also adopts the new surname. When Whitey incurs a serious and permanent brain injury during a particularly brutal bout, Pete takes it upon himself to pick up his brother's cudgel and excel at professional sports. His superior pitching skill earns the twenty-eight-year-old Pete a spot with the Class-A Memphis Chicks in 1943, though it's made abundantly clear to him that he's been taken on

mostly as a "freak attraction" and a wartime morale booster. As a byproduct of Whitey's pre-injury advice and life's hard knocks, Pete develops a tough hide and a cynical demeanor, determining never to let anyone get close to him. This resolve weakens a bit when he meets waitress Annie, who isn't the least self-conscious about Pete's handicap nor starstruck by his baseball fame, but likes Pete for himself. Not that Pete goes out of his way to be likable; when he's urged to visit the local VA hospital as an "inspiration" for recent amputees, Pete refuses to become a sentiment-baiting public spectacle. When the Memphis Chicks learn that young Nelson Gary, Jr., a baseball fan from California who's likewise lost an arm, is anxious to meet Pete, the team arranges a meeting as a publicity gambit; but Pete is a no-show at the testimonial dinner for Nelson—"I ain't nobody's hero, and never said I was." His seeming lack of consideration for the boy grows from his hatred of contrived sentimentality; Pete is perfectly willing to meet and talk to Nelson so long as the media keep their noses out of it. Pete and the boy become close friends, practicing catch whenever time permits and sharing each other's innermost thoughts. The friendship is beneficial to both of them: Pete's closed-off attitude toward people opens up a bit (he humanizes enough to propose to long-suffering Annie) and his game improves with Nelson in his corner, while Nelson's confidence in himself and his own baseball talent is strengthened. In 1945, with the war depleting the manpower in big-league baseball, Pete is hired by the St. Louis Browns. After Pete warms the bench during most of the season, his bitterness resurfaces, but the pitcher is encouraged to stick things out by his father, who is proud that his son has become somebody on his own initiative. Thus it is that Pete Gray finally realizes his childhood dream of playing in the major leagues; and the courage and persistence which he displays on the

For as long as Americans play the game of baseball and honor its heroes, the story of Pete Grey will be remembered with pride... and a smile.

A Winner Never Quits

Starring Keith Carradine, Mare Winningham and Dennis Weaver
Written by Burt Prelutsky   Directed by Mel Damski
ABC Monday Night Movie 8 PM ⑦ ⑫ ⑬ ㉗

TV Guide ad for *A Winner Never Quits* (1986).

ballfield is transmitted to Nelson Gary, Jr., who in the late 1950s becomes a top ball-player in the San Diego League.

Pete Gray's minor-league career with the Memphis Chicks, during which he attained a batting average of .333, stole 63 bases and was elected his league's MVP, was far more impressive than his 77-game tenure with the St. Louis Browns. *A Winner Never Quits* takes this into consideration by concentrating almost exclusively on Gray's years with Memphis. It isn't really important to point out that his major-league performance was unremarkable; the fact that Pete Gray made it to the majors at all is the crux of the climax, so no further detailing is necessary.

Actually, it wasn't really the life of Pete Gray that inspired this made-for–TV film, but the story of Nelson Gary, Jr., the youthful amputee who befriended Gray, who was in real life a high school friend of the film's coproducer, actor James Keach. The scenarist of *A Winner Never Quits*, Burt Prelutsky, had previously shown a knack for demonstrating the "trickledown" inspiration that an indefatigable handicapped person can have on children with his script for another true-life baseball TV movie, *Aunt Mary* (1979) (q.v.). In *A Winner*, Prelutsky sidesteps the excess of syrup that had weakened *Aunt Mary* by accurately depicting Pete Gray as an irascible loner who behaves graciously only on his own time, not when the nonhandicapped establishment tells him to do so. The script's only faltering moments occur during the scenes with Pete's Slavic father (played by Dennis Weaver), who is drawn as a fractured–English old country type more suited to something as antediluvian as *The Pride of the Yankees* than a film made in the 1980s.

The baseball scenes are expertly staged at Joe Engel Stadium in Chattanooga, Tennessee, with extra-tight close-ups effectively complementing the action long shots; and, as a bonus to fans, there is a snippet or two of authentic 16-millimeter color footage of the old Yankee Stadium in the closing scenes. As Pete Gray, Keith Carradine is a marvel to behold, playing baseball with one arm literally tied behind his back. His performance is even more outstanding during a brief pool-hall scene, shot in a single take, where he balances the cue in his "good" hand and clears the table. Carradine carries the dramatic load of *A Winner Never Quits* with his usual finesse, bolstered by above-average assistance from an excellent supporting cast. Prominent among the featured players are two incipient TV series stars: *Married with Children* star Ed O'Neill as Pete's mentally impaired older brother, and *China Beach* star Dana Delany as a nurse whose desultory romance with Pete Gray is motivated more out of self-righteousness than genuine attraction.

A Winner Never Quits is one of the handful of baseball biopics that so thoroughly captures the thrill of the game and the essence of its real-life protagonist that it can be forgiven its occasional lapses in accuracy and chronology. But sometime in the future, guys, can we please please *please* put a moratorium on that slow-motion photography accompanied by the sound effect of a heartbeat?

The Winning Team

Warner Bros.; released June 1952

Produced by Bryan Foy. Directed by Lewis Seiler. Screenplay by Ted Sherdeman, Seeley Lester and Merwin Gerard. Story by Seeley Lester and Merwin Gerard (originally titled "Alex the Great"). Photography: Sid Hickox. Edited by Alan Crosland, Jr. Music by David Buttolph. Art director: Douglas Bacon. Set decoration by William Kuehl. Costumes by Leah Rhodes. Special effects by Hans Koenekamp. Makeup by Gordon Bau. Technical advisers: Mrs. Grover Cleveland Alexander, Bob Lemon, Jerry Priddy, and Jigger Statz. 98 minutes; black and white; sound.

Cast: Doris Day (Aimee Alexander); Ronald Reagan (Grover Cleveland "Pete" Alexander); Frank Lovejoy (Rogers Hornsby); Eve Miller (Margaret Killifer); James Millican (Bill Killefer); Rusty Tamblyn (Willie Alexander); Gordon Jones (George Glasheen); Hugh Sanders (Joe McCarthy); Frank Ferguson (Sam Arrants); Walter Baldwyn (Pa Alexander); Dorothy Adams (Ma Alexander); Bob Lemon, Jerry Priddy, George Metkovitch, Hank Sauer, Peanuts Lowry, Irv Noren, Al Zarilla, Gene Mauch (Themselves, Ballplayers); Bonnie Kay Eddie (Alex's Sister); Jimmy Dodd (Fred); Fred Millican (Catcher); Pat Flaherty (Bill Klem); Tom Greenway (Foreman); Frank McFarland (Johnson); Arthur Page (Preacher); Thomas Browne Henry (Carlson Carleton, Lecturer); Larry Blake (Detective); Frank Marlowe (Taxi Driver); Kenneth Patterson (Dr. Johnson Conant); Glenn Turnbull, John Hedloe (Reporters); Henry Blair (Batboy); Gordon Clark (Pianist); John Kennedy (Announcer); Allan Wood (Usher); Alex Sharp (First Baseman); William Kalvino (Batter); Robert Orrell (Catcher); Russ Clark (Whitey); Tom Dugan (Candy Store Proprietor); Eddie Marr (Carny Barker); Walter Appler (Desk Clerk); Art Gilmore (Radio Sports Announcer); Paul Panzer (Central City Fan).* [Working title: *The Big League*].

This Hollywoodization of the life of Grover Cleveland Alexander (1887–1950) begins during Alexander's days as a telephone lineman in Nebraska. Alex has promised his fiancée Aimee Arrants that he'll settle down and become a farmer, but the siren call of bush-league baseball is too much to resist. He is hired to pitch for the Galesburg Triple-A team, a job he intends to hold until he's made enough money to marry and settle down. But Alex is hit on the head by a batted ball during one game, which causes him to endure double vision and dizziness. Even though it looks like he's through, his contract is sold to the Philadelphia Phillies. Pride dictates that Alex at least try to whip himself back into shape; his diligence pays off when his blurred vision miraculously disappears and he's able to pitch better than ever. Wife Aimee, previously resistant to Alex's baseball career, now becomes his biggest booster and inspiration. During his rookie year with Philadelphia, Alex totes up a remarkable record of twenty-eight wins with thirteen shutouts. He is called to fight in World War I just before he's to be traded to the Chicago Cubs in 1917, and while on the battlefield his double vision and dizziness recur. During his first Cubs game after the war, Alex collapses on the field. In conference with the team doctor, the pitcher learns that his disorder has returned and that the seizures will increase unless he retires. Alex swears the doc to secrecy, telling neither his team nor wife Aimee of his affliction. As the dizzy spells overcome him, Alexander turns to the bottle. Thanks to the gossip mill, Alex is branded an "alky," and before long he's washed up both in baseball and, briefly, in marriage when Aimee walks out on him in frustration. Alex drops out of sight, playing with the barnstorming House of David team until his fainting spells lose him that job and ultimately

*Trivia alert! The cast of The Winning Team is filled to overflowing with baseball movie veterans. The ubiquitous Pat Flaherty (see notes on Death on the Diamond) is on hand in the role of famed umpire Bill Klem. Rusty Tamblyn, who was "introduced" in 1949 in The Kid from Cleveland, portrays Grover Cleveland Alexander's kid brother. Fred Millican, a minor-league catcher who appeared under his own name in The Stratton Story, shows up in The Winning Team as still another catcher. Frank Ferguson, appearing in this film as G. C. Alexander's father-in-law, was later cast none too convincingly as a former baseball superstar in Big Leaguer (1953). Gordon Jones, previously a catcher at the turn of the century with whom Gene Kelly engaged in a donnybrook in Take Me Out to the Ballgame (1949), has a far larger part in The Winning Team as Alexander's first professional manager, while Tom Dugan, the long-suffering coach in Take Me Out to the Ballgame, is assigned in The Winning Team the far smaller role of a candy store owner who places bets on the side. Hugh Sanders, a lowly bush-league manager in The Pride of St. Louis (1952), "graduates" in The Winning Team to the role of Cubs manager Joe McCarthy. And in the very first scene of The Winning Team, the young buck who tells G. C. Alexander about a big upcoming game is Jimmy Dodd, who two years earlier had been the younger buck who brought Jackie Robinson's resume into the UCLA sports department office in The Jackie Robinson Story, and who, as anyone over the age of forty-five will tell you, would later croon his way into America's heart as the "head mouseketeer" on the original Mickey Mouse Club.

reduce him to touring with a tawdry traveling sideshow. But with the help and support of his forgiving wife and his old friend Rogers Hornsby, Alexander finally secures a comeback in 1926 when he's hired by Hornsby's St. Louis Cardinals. Grover Cleveland Alexander demonstrates how completely he's conquered his affliction during the 1926 World Series, when he strikes out the New York Yankee Tony Lazzeri and leads the Cards to victory.

If you've been reading this book straight through from "A" to "W," you'll remember we noted in the essay on MGM's *The Stratton Story* that Ronald Reagan had implored his boss Jack Warner to be allowed to portray Monty Stratton, and that Warner had nixed the idea because no one ever went to see movies about baseball or cripples. Once the money started rolling in for *The Stratton Story*, Warner was less firm in his convictions, though it did take nearly two years for the producer to mount his own "crippled baseball player" project; but this time Ronald Reagan got his crack.

Like Monty Stratton, Grover Cleveland Alexander worked up from the "bush" ranks, performed impressively in his formative major-league years, suffered a setback due to medical reasons, then made a remarkable comeback. Also like Stratton, Alexander reclaimed his glory with his loving wife at his side. But unlike amputee Monty Stratton, Alexander's impairment was not physical but neurological, and in part psychological: Alexander was an epileptic, one who unfortunately tried to assuage his affliction by drinking. Also unlike Stratton, Hollywood was freer and easier with the facts of Alexander's life.

The Winning Team may have been conceived in the image of *The Stratton Story*, but in terms of quality, that's where all resemblance ended. Where the Stratton biopic was for the most part restrained and dignified, the Grover Cleveland Alexander story wallows in the obvious and the maudlin, complete with a strident musical score crashing down upon us whenever something of the slightest significance takes place. And while *The Stratton Story* at least made an effort to steer clear of baseball biopic clichés, *The Winning Team* has all those clichés down to a science. We're offered everything from a shot of a sick kid in a hospital bed listening to the 1926 Series on his radio, to the moth-eaten passage-of-time routine as reflected in Mrs. Alexander's scrapbook of her husband's career.

And, oh, that Mrs. Alexander! *The Winning Team* goes above and beyond the concept of the wife being the spiritual strength of her man. If we take this film at face value, Aimee Alexander (played very well by top-billed Doris Day, who surprisingly sings only once in the picture) emerges as the one and only reason that her beloved Alex was able to make his spectacular comeback. She's the cheering section of his triumphs and the wailing wall of his disasters. ("God sure must think a lot of me, to have given me you," Alex sighs lugubriously at one point.) And in the final scene, it looks as though Alexander may falter and not come through with his strike-out of Tony Lazzeri until faithful Aimee, in true "curfew shall not ring tonight" fashion, makes an eleventh-hour appearance at the ballpark. How the script for *The Winning Team* (note that word "team"—it doesn't mean the Phillies, Cubs, or Cards) came to be a "Hosanna to Aimee in the Highest" is understandable. Just look at the opening credits. There it is. "Technical adviser: Mrs. Grover Cleveland Alexander."

When we concentrate on Mr. Grover Cleveland Alexander himself, the story isn't too bad. It's what the script *doesn't* tell us that makes an even better story. In the film, Alexander's neurological disorder is diagnosed merely as double vision. Never once does the film inform us that Alexander has epilepsy—he just sees two of everything once in a while, and that's why he

The Winning Team: Grover Cleveland Alexander (Ronald Reagan, left) and Rogers Hornsby (Frank Lovejoy) strike a pensive pose before a process-screen crowd.

drinks himself blotto. Ronald Reagan himself felt that not mentioning Alexander's affliction by name was a major mistake; he didn't agree with Warner Bros.' rationale that it would be offensive to explicitly label Alexander as an epileptic. Reagan was quite right in predicting that the vagueness of his character's illness would confuse audiences, leading them to conclude that Alexander couldn't handle a simple case of double vision—a problem not all that uncommon in 1952—and that the ballplayer was a stupidly proud man who used liquor as a crutch. Nor does the script help things any by obscuring the amount of alcohol being consumed. A doctor comments that some of Alex's fainting spells *may* have been booze related, a statement that further clouded the issue—an especially fatal flaw in an era of filmmaking where clear-cut cause and effect was preferred by the audience.

The film's climax likewise tells us only a fraction of the facts. Yes, it's true that during the 1926 Series "Pete" Alexander struck out Tony Lazzeri with the bases loaded and two out. As far as *The Winning Team* is concerned, the series is over at this point and Alexander is triumphantly carried off the field on his teammates' shoulders. The film tactfully ignores what really happened next. Right after retiring Lazzeri, Alexander nearly blew the game by walking Babe Ruth—a loss avoided only by Ruth's being called out after clumsily trying to steal second.

Throughout the film, the facts are realigned to satisfy Hollywood's happy ending obsession. *The Winning Team* accurately displays a washed-up Alexander playing for the House of David (a buffoonish contingent of ex-stars and wannabes who showed up on the field sporting long black beards), then moving farther down the ladder as the central attraction of a flea circus. The basic circumstances are correct, but the chronology isn't: Alexander's humiliating career of trading on his past success occurred *after* the 1926 Series, not before. According to the film, Alexander rose from the depths for his big comeback, when in truth the House of David to sideshow route was how the pitcher scratched out a living for the remainder of his life.

The most heartrending aspect of Alexander's last days would probably not have been filmed even if Warner Bros. had been interested in presenting a realistic portrayal, simply because the full facts weren't known until long after 1952. Sam Breaden, the former owner of the Cardinals, sent Alexander a weekly check out of his own pocket to keep the old trouper from starving. Breaden doctored Alexander's checks to make it appear that they'd been issued by the office of the National League, convincing the proud ex-ballplayer that the money was coming from the league's pension fund.

The Winning Team may be a lost cause in terms of accuracy (this extends even to the Alexanders' "special song," a tune titled "I'll String Along with You," written for the Dick Powell vehicle *Twenty Million Sweethearts* in 1934, several years after the events in *The Winning Team* took place), but it satisfies on the level of amiable, unsophisticated entertainment. One pleasantly nostalgic touch is the use of 1920s-vintage photographs and newsreels taken of the old Yankee Stadium as "back projection" in the World Series scenes—a bit of special effects largesse unusual for the pinchpenny Bryan Foy unit which produced *The Winning Team* for Warner Bros.

The film's biggest plus is the likable, unpretentious performance of Ronald Reagan as Grover Cleveland Alexander, which almost compensates for the fact that he's way too old for the role. For his pitching scenes, Reagan trained two hours a day for three weeks with the Indians' Bob Lemon and the Tigers' Jerry Priddy (both of whom also appeared in the film, along with several other current and past big leaguers), as well as a contemporary of Alexander's, former Chicago Cub and Brooklyn Dodger Arnold "Jigger" Statz. The extra effort paid off; while Reagan is not as limber as Jimmy Stewart in *The Stratton Story*, his ballplaying skill is certainly head and shoulders above anything Gary Cooper did in uniform in *The Pride of the Yankees* (q.v.). And for a fellow who purportedly never touched a drop, Ronnie does a dead-center interpretation of drunkenness when the script calls upon him to dramatize Alexander's downfall.

The Winning Team was a satisfying culmination to Ronald Reagan's lifelong fascination with professional sports, which had led to his first media job in the '30s as a sportscaster for Des Moines radio station WHO, and which had in 1940 been vicariously satiated through his portrayal of football legend George Gipp in *Knute Rockne, All American*. The role of Alexander certainly *had* to have been heaps more rewarding to Reagan than his short-lived association in the late 1940s with the Movie Star World Series, an event organized to raise funds for the City of Hope; Reagan got no farther than a run to first before he tripped and broke his leg.

There. See how easy it is to write about *The Winning Team* without once mentioning Iran-Contra or Bonzo? Oh, wait, here's an entry for the *Twilight Zone* department: More than one observer has commented on the cute coincidence that future president Ronald Reagan plays a man named after former president Grover Cleveland. But no one has noted that if Ronald Reagan had gotten the lead in *The Stratton Story* like he'd wanted, he would have played a man whose full name was Monty Franklin Pierce Stratton.

Baseball Short Subjects

Up until 1914, every baseball movie (and virtually every movie, for that matter) was a short subject, often running as little as 150 feet—about two to three minutes of screen time.

The earliest film with a baseball theme that anyone has been able to pinpoint was *The Ball Game*, released by the Edison Company May 20, 1898. This very brief effort showed highlights of a game between two nonprofessional teams from Newark, New Jersey, and Reading, Pennsylvania. The film was principally shown at kinetoscopes, the peep show parlors which predated public movie houses. Even at this early date the Edison people knew the value of hard-sell promotion: In the company's film catalog, *The Ball Game* is effusively described as "Very exciting. Man on the coaching line yells, and umpire runs up and makes decision. Small boy runs past back of the catcher close to the grand stand, where there is great commotion. A most excellent subject, treated brilliantly."

Later in 1898, another film—the title of which has been lost to the ages—depicted a group of U.S. Cavalry soldiers tossing a ball around at training camp, prior to their being shipped to the Spanish-American War in Cuba. This vignette was most likely staged for the benefit of the camera, the giveaway being a dog that ran into the action on cue, grabbed the ball, and was then pursued by the soldiers.

Edison was back in 1899 with *Casey at the Bat*, which utilized the title of the Ernest Lawrence Thayer poem and nothing else. Filmed in Edison's own West Orange, New Jersey, backyard, the "storyline" involved a batter striking out and then arguing with the umpire. The whole affair was filmed in one shot from behind home plate, revealing only Casey, the ump, the catcher, and—in barely visible long shot— the pitcher.

In 1903 the Lubin Company of Philadelphia released a little gem titled *Game of Base Ball* (how *did* they come up with these titles?). This was virtually a newsreel, depicting a game between the Philadelphia Athletics (the champion ball club of 1902) and the Baltimore team. The players were filmed full-figure at their positions, with special emphasis placed upon pitcher Rube Waddell. Lubin distributed *Game of Base Ball* with a companion featurette, the provocatively titled *Crowd Leaving Athletic Base Ball Grounds*.

The year 1906 was a watershed for baseball shorts, offering the first fully dramatized subject and the first glimpses of an actual World Series match. The drama— actually a comedy—was Edison's *How the Office Boy Saw the Ball Game*, wherein the

481

hero brashly ducked out of work, only to find himself seated next to his baleful boss at the ballpark (a plot device that Harold Lloyd reactivated in *Speedy* [1928]). The Series picture was Selig Polyscope's *The World Series Baseball Games—White Sox and Cubs*, released shortly after the big event on October 27, 1906. The game sequences were frustratingly filmed in extreme long shot; the best scenes in this 600-foot epic involved the pregame parades and festivities.

Rounding out 1906 was American Mutoscope and Biograph's *Play Ball on the Beach*, filmed before a wrinkly backdrop representing the shores of New Jersey. The plot, based on a vaudeville sketch of the period, involved a group of players enraged over an umpire's bad call, but the principal attraction of *Play Ball on the Beach* was the presence of several pretty young ladies attired in fetching (albeit totally unrevealing) bathing costumes.

The year 1907 offered Lubin's 175-foot *Base Ball Game*; Vitagraph's 280-foot *One Man Baseball*, based on a popular vaudeville turn (we don't know who appeared in this picture, but it might have been "Slivers," a circus clown whose specialty was a solo ballgame routine); and Winthrop Moving Picture Company's self-explanatory *Christy Mathewson, N. Y. National League Baseball Team*. This last film, reportedly part of a series of one-reelers produced by Winthrop featuring baseball heroes, had as its highlight a shot of Christy Mathewson performing his standard pregame stunt of driving onto the ballfield in his new automobile—a piece of surefire showmanship that would later be echoed in *Alibi Ike* (1935), *Bang the Drum Slowly* (1973), and even *The Bad News Bears in Breaking Training* (1977).

Released in November 1907, the 350-foot *How Brown Saw the Baseball Game* (copyrighted as *How Jones Saw the Base Ball Game*) has often been referred to as the Lubin Company's answer to the previous season's Edison comedy *How the Office Boy Saw the Ball Game*. Actually, the Lubin picture was more a trick film in the tradition of Georges Méliès. Mr. Brown goes to the ballpark after having consumed mass quantities of alcohol, and as a result he witnesses the game in reverse motion, with the players running backward and with the baseball magically jumping back into the catcher's mitt. At the conclusion of this "screamingly funny farce" (Lubin's own assessment), Mr. Brown's friend escorts him home, only to be beaten soundly by Mrs. Brown, who is convinced that the good samaritan was responsible for her husband's condition.

Amidst such long-forgotten 1908 endeavors as *The Baseball Fan* (filmed by Essanay at a Chicago White Sox game) and *Baseball* (producer unknown), the Essanay company released the first of its annual World Series highlights reels. Essanay production head G. M. Anderson (who that same year became the movies' first cowboy star under the alias of Broncho Billy) negotiated the contract that allowed his camera crews to record the big event. Advertised as "authorized" World Series digests, these one-reelers proved extremely lucrative not only to Essanay but to the competing teams, both of whom received a portion of the profits. The Series pictures ultimately grew to two reels in length, becoming an Essanay mainstay until movie rights to the games were sold to Selig in 1913. With so much film at his disposal, the crafty G. M. Anderson economically utilized leftover Series footage to pep up several fictional one-reelers, notably *Take Me Out to the Ballgame* (1910), which related a shaggy-dog story about a fan who becomes so engrossed in his team's victory that he abandons his wife at the ballpark (*plus ça change...*).

While Essanay was raking in bucks with its Series documentaries, audiences were treated to the first fictional ballgame film with a noncomic plotline. *His Last Game* (1909), a single-reeler released in December by I.M.P. (the precursor to Universal Pictures), told the tale of a Native American ballplayer who hits a home run after refusing a bribe. If nothing else, *His Last Game* was proof positive not only that Indians frequently appeared as heroes in early silent pictures, but also that fixed games were commonplace in the pre–Black Sox era.

Francis Ford, an early matinee idol and director of note (he was the elder brother of John Ford), was the leading player of Méliès's 950-foot *Baseball, That's All*, released in September 1910. Anticipating the William Bendix vehicle *Kill the Umpire* by four decades, *Baseball, That's All* was an amusing yarn (penned by one D. Reichgott) about a clerk whose obsession with the game nearly costs him his job and his wife. A second 1910 baseball comedy, *Bumptuous Plays Baseball*, was offered by the Edison Company in October. As its title suggests, this little gem featured a fat man (John R. Cumpson) romping around the diamond. Released as a 645-foot split-reeler in tandem with a 345-foot vignette entitled *The Farmer's Daughter*, *Bumptuous Plays Baseball* was well enough received to be virtually remade by the Essanay company as *Baseball Star from Bingville*, released in June 1911. The year 1910 also saw two more baseball shorts, Essanay's *Slide, Kelly Slide* and the same company's aforementioned *Take Me Out to the Ballgame*.

In addition to *Baseball Star from Bingville*, 1911 yielded a brace of one-reelers from the Thanhouser Company: *Baseball and Bloomers*, featuring William Garwood and a bevy of female ballplayers, and *The Baseball Bug* ("bug" was the word used instead of "fan" in those days), which spotlighted John W. Noble and Florence LaBadie. *The Baseball Bug* was the tale of a swellheaded, small-town amateur ballplayer cut down to size by his long-suffering wife, who arranges a match between her husband and several professionals. In what may be the first examples of guest star appearances in a non-documentary baseball picture, the pros rounded up by the wife included famed pitcher Chief Bender and two of Bender's old Philadelphia Athletics teammates, Rube Oldring and Jack Coombs (film historian Jack Spears has alluded to a fourth major leaguer appearing in this film).

Likewise issued in 1911 was another celebrity featurette. Kalem's *Hal Chase's Home Run* starred the titular New York Yankees first baseman who, in the pre–1910 years, had been the biggest audience draw in his league, and who—as mentioned in our notes on MGM's *Take Me Out to the Ballgame* (1949)—frequently compromised his undeniable talent through cheating and bribery. The plot of *Hal Chase's Home Run* concentrated on a friend of Chase's, yet another baseball nut whose preoccupation is imperiling his love life. In this instance, the friend's fiancée, who despises baseball, has threatened to call off the engagement unless the Yankees win the pennant (we just describe these stories, folks, we don't explain them). Chase saves his buddy's future happiness by hitting a pennant-clinching home run in the bottom of the ninth. Had this picture been closer to real life, the duplicitous Mr. Chase would probably have paid off the opposing pitcher to throw the game.

Other than the annual Essanay World Series reel and the occasional nonfictional glimpses of baseball celebrities, 1912 offered only Selig's *The Pennant Puzzle*, wherein a fan's fascination with a board-game puzzle eventually overtakes his fellow fans, the ballplayers on the field, and the cops, all of whom drop what they're doing to kibitz the puzzle player. (Over twenty years later this plot was reheated for Laurel and Hardy's two-reel talkie *Me and My Pal*.) *The Pennant Puzzle* can be regarded as the genesis of Selig's later Mudville comedies, especially since the 1912 picture featured future Mudville star John Lancaster.

The year 1913 gave the world a few more star shorts. Patheplay's *Baseball's Peerless Leader* featured Chicago Cubs first baseman Frank Chance, minus Tinker and Evers but in the company of actors Ned Burton and Gwendolen Pates. In this one, Chance's ballpark skill is somehow linked to a trivial romantic subplot. The Philadelphia Athletics' Frank "Home Run" Baker had his moment before the camera in Selig's *A Short-Stop's Double*, while the New York Giants' Rube Marquand reportedly capitalized on his nineteen straight wins of the previous season in a film titled—what else?—*Nineteen Straight*. (The producer and supporting cast is unknown, though in later years Marquand remembered that he'd once costarred in a film with his then wife, vaudevillian Blossom Seeley.) And Giants manager John McGraw and his star player Christy Mathewson could be seen supporting Harry Millarde, Marguerite Courtot and Henry Hallam in *Breaking Into the Big League*, the first of Kalem's annual baseball specials in which bona fide athletes bolstered the histrionics of the studio's acting stable. *Breaking Into the Big League* ran two reels; it was released in some markets as a unified twenty-minute short, and in others as two separate one-reelers.

Also in 1913, audiences were treated to Vitagraph's one-reel version of *Casey at the Bat*, directed by James Young (husband of silent-film leading lady Clara Kimball Young) and featuring the hulking Harry T. Morey in the title role, with future star Norma Talmadge in support. Majestic Pictures scrutinized another aspect of the game with its September 23 release, *The Baseball Umpire*.

The main event of the 1913-14 movie season was the acquisition by Selig Polyscope of the rights to the annual World Series reels from Essanay. Selig lengthened these films from two reels to four over the next few years, extending their scope of on-screen celebrities to include the nonplayers in the stands: The 1915 edition, subtitled *Boston vs. Philadelphia*, featured President Woodrow Wilson in the company of his fiancée Edith Galt. This 1915 effort additionally made film history by being the first baseball film where the camera was positioned behind home plate, rather than offering an overhead or side view of the game. (Although this particular angle had been anticipated as far back as 1899 in *Casey at the Bat*, the 1915 Series film was the first instance that a *real* game was recorded from the vantage point of the home-base umpire.)

The one surviving Selig Series picture, supervised by J. C. Wheeler and released through K.E.S.E. Films on October 16, 1916, was allowed to run a full five reels (suitable for reediting into five one-reelers, depending on the individual needs of the exhibitors). *World Series 1916: Boston vs. Brooklyn* was an invaluable record of how baseball was played in the pre–World War I era; director Wheeler utilized eight cameras to film the action from all available angles, even allowing for a shot or two of the Dodgers fans playfully throwing seat cushions onto the field. This particular film was also the last in the series; Selig went bankrupt a year or so later, and thereafter all World Series coverage was confined to the standard weekly newsreels.

Back to 1914, the year of the first dramatic baseball feature film, *Little Sunset*. Short subjects dwelling upon the game still flourished, among them Biograph's *Baseball, Grand Old Game*; Lubin's *Baseball and Trouble*; Powers's *The Baseball Fan*; and Joker's *Baseball Fans of Fanville*, starring prolific comic actor Billy Franey. Christy Mathewson was back in Bison's *Love and Base Ball*, a bucolic two-reeler about a farm boy's rise to big-league fame. "Home Run" Baker was also on hand for *Home Run Baker's Double*; this mistaken identity farce, directed by Kenean Buel, was the second of Kalem's annual baseball specials, and, like the first (*Breaking Into the Big League*), costarred Marguerite Courtot and Henry Hallam.

Also in 1914, two new series were inaugurated. Selig, with its recently acquired World Series shorts adding to its coffers, expanded its baseball coverage to include a group of shorts showing ballplayers at spring training and pursuing their off-season jobs as farmers, streetcar conductors, lumberjacks, etc. This Selig series rounded out its human interest stuff with highlights of major games, one such highlight offering the spectacle of angered fans rioting after an umpire's unpopular call. Vitagraph likewise launched a series of baseball shorts, sporadically issued under the umbrella title *Baseball Stars*, with emphasis on the novel and bizarre: An early entry featured a match between a visiting Chinese team and a contingent of lovely "Bloomer Girls" (the girls won).

Another film series, this one a group of humorous baseball shorts, was produced by Hans Moss in 1915 and released by Universal-Jewel the following year. These one-reelers were adapted for the screen by Ring Lardner from his own "Jack Keefe" stories (a.k.a. "Busher's Letters"), previously published in the *Saturday Evening Post*. Faithful to their source material, each episode incorporated the word "Busher" in the title: *The Busher Breaks In*, *The Busher Comes Back*, etc. Unfortunately, none of these films is currently available, so we'll have to settle for the feature-length *The New Klondike* (q.v.) as the earliest existing cinematic sampling of the prolific Ring Lardner.

Spit-Ball Sadie, a one-reel comedy put together by fledgling producer Hal Roach for his own Phunphilm company, was released by Pathé on July 12, 1915. This knockabout farce concerned a man who disguises himself as a woman and joins up with a girls' baseball team. When our hero's ruse is revealed, he is saved from the wrath of the girls by the pretty team manager. *Spit-Ball Sadie* may or may not have featured twenty-two-year-old Harold Lloyd, who was then Roach's biggest—and only—star.

It was series time again in 1916 with the introduction of "Baseball Bill," a character portrayed by Universal/Victor's number one comedy attraction, Smilin' Billy Mason, who'd once toured vaudeville in one of those "one man ballgame" sketches. The six one-reel *Baseball Bill* comedies, written and directed by Mason, Al Russell, John Stepping and Craig Hutchison, were released between 1916 and '17. Titles included *Baseball Bill*, *Flirting with Marriage*, *The Black Nine*, *Baseball Madness*, *A Box of Tricks* and *Strike One*. Since the rotund, affable Smilin' Billy was pretty much the whole show, few noticed the appearance in *Baseball Madness* (1917) of seventeen-year-old Gloria Swanson (apparently not even Swanson noticed; the film is not mentioned in her autobiography).

Comedy dominated the baseball picture scene in 1916. In addition to its *Baseball Bill* efforts, Universal released Nestor's one-reel *Kill the Umpire*, starring the long-running (and now long-forgotten) comedy team of Eddie Lyons (the handsome one) and Lee Moran (the other one). And Mutual Films, soon to be the home base of Charlie Chaplin, contributed *Love, Dynamite and Baseballs*. This lively little two-reeler starred Jack Dillon (who also directed) as a major-league pitcher who thwarts a gang of society crooks by pitching dynamite-loaded baseballs at them—a unique if somewhat impractical method of crime control. Supporting Jack Dillon was the lovely Priscilla Dean, whose best cinematic efforts lay ahead of her in the 1920s.

The 1917 product included a pair of Selig one-reelers loosely bundled together as the Mudville series, featuring John Lancaster and Lee Morris as a pair of dimwitted ballplayers. The first Mudville short, *The Bush Leaguer*, spotlighted Lee Morris who, after learning a trick or two from a traveling hypnotist (William Hutchison), mesmerizes the opposing team into making a number of bonehead plays. *Baseball at*

Mudville resurrected the central situation of *Spit-Ball Sadie* (1915) by featuring a barnstorming team of roughnecks who disguise themselves as the red-wigged "Milligan Bloomer Girls" and regularly make mincemeat out of local male ballclubs (a routine still viable enough in 1963 to be used on the cartoon series *The Bullwinkle Show*). Naturally, Lancaster and Morris's team is far too gentlemanly to rough up these formidable "ladies"—that is, until the deception is uncovered when one of the Bloomer Girls loses "her" wig.

As in 1916, baseball comedies were plentiful in 1917. Metro's *Her First Game* headlined the popular polite comedy duo, Mr. and Mrs. Sidney Drew. The plot situation was one that would be endlessly repeated for the next seven decades: Mrs. Drew drives her husband and everyone around her crazy with her silly questions and sillier reactions on the occasion of witnessing her first ballgame. Adding to the film's appeal was its being shot at the New York Polo Grounds, with Yankee first baseman Wally Pipp on hand in a brief bit as himself. Equally comic in an earthier manner was Jaxon's *Play Ball*, featuring Walter Stull and Bobby Burns as the Mutt and Jeff team "Pokes and Jabbs." In this effort, "Pokes" dreams that he hits a ball out of the park which ends up clobbering a safecracker.

Over the Fence, a Hal Roach one-reeler released by Rolin/Pathé on September 9, was perhaps the most memorable of 1917's baseball comedies, not because of its pedestrian plot (two tailors find a pair of ballgame tickets in the pocket of a coat and somehow wind up in the game themselves, with the better looking of the two scoring the winning run), but because it was the first film in which Roach's star player Harold Lloyd eschewed the heavy Chaplinesque makeup he'd previously worn onscreen. In *Over the Fence*, Lloyd introduced the bespectacled All-American Boy charac-

ter that would earn him worldwide fame within the next few years. The film included a rare movie appearance by Harold Lloyd's father who, like his son, was an enthusiatic baseball fan.

Also making the rounds in 1917 was Edison's *Shut Out in the Ninth*, a two-reeler written by Edward H. Griffith and Sumner Williams and featuring a cast of teenagers. The baseball angle was merely a new coat of paint for the old saw about two young sprouts (Howard Brooks and Andy Clark) who use an athletic event to vie for the affections of a toothsome young lass (Peggy Adams).

The contrivances of *Shut Out in the Ninth* seemed pretty pale when compared to the authentic baseball footage in Athletic Feature Films' *Baseball Revue of 1917*, another "convertible" film that was exhibited as either a five-reel feature or five one-reel featurettes. In this (apparently) one of a kind endeavor, Athletic Films' president Marty McHale photographed all the major-league teams then in existence, with two full reels devoted to the 1917 Red Sox–Giants World Series. Appearing on camera was Tris Speaker, vice president of Athletic Films, in the company of a remarkable array of talent: John McGraw, Ty Cobb, Christy Mathewson, Honus Wagner, Walter Johnson, Eddie Collins, Connie Mack, Frank "Home Run" Baker, Babe Ruth, Grover Cleveland Alexander, Miller Huggins, Smokey Joe Woods, Hughie Jennings, Larry Doyle, Rube Marquand, Chief Bender, Big Ed Walsh, Jim Thorpe, Buck Herzog, Benny Kauf, Clarence Rowland, George Stallings, Fielder Jones, Stuffy McInnis, Jack Coombs, and Heinie Zimmerman. There were also poignant (in retrospect) glimpses of two Black Sox conspirators soon to be banished, Eddie Cicotte and Shoeless Joe Jackson.

With the exception of *Home Run Ambrose*, an L-KO two-reel comedy starring Mack Swain as the latest in a long line of overweight ballplayers, 1918 was notably barren of baseball pictures, with the Great War occupying the minds of most movie-goers. Almost as skimpy in the short-subject category was 1919, yielding only *Baseball and Bloomers*, a semidocumentary produced by publisher–health expert Bernarr Mac-Fadden's Physical Culture Photoplays; *Baseball: An Analysis of Motion*, an instructional short subject utilizing slow-motion photography to illustrate its thesis; and *Home Run Bill* (Nestor/Universal), another Smilin' Billy Mason opus which might very well have been filmed a year or two earlier as part of the *Baseball Bill* series.

Educational Pictures—a concern which belied its name by specializing in slapstick comedies—scored a real coup in 1920 with its *Babe Ruth Instructional Films*. The studio tooted its horn for this new series with full-page trade ads, prominently displaying a painstakingly detailed pen and ink sketch of Babe's countenance, and to all the world it seemed as though the pair of one-reelers that followed—*How Babe Hits a Home Run* and *Play Ball with Babe Ruth*—had been produced with Ruth's full cooperation and endorsement. Well, maybe all the world labored under that belief, but it was news to Babe. The Educational films had been assembled from newsreel footage of Ruth in action, without his knowledge and with nary a penny going to the star. Ruth and his business manager, Christy Walsh, sued Educational for $250,000; Educational countersued for libel, insisting that the films had been legally purchased from the original copyright owners. Babe ultimately lost out when the judge ruled that, as a public figure, Ruth could be photographed without his permission—thereby setting a precedent protecting future newsreel and documentary producers from potential legal action. The suits and countersuits were withdrawn, and so were the *Babe Ruth Instructional Films*—but not before Educational had made a comfortable profit.

The years 1921 and 1922 were notable in their paucity of baseball films, shorts as well as features. Moe Howard, senior member of the Three Stooges comedy team, recalled late in life that he'd appeared in a series of twelve two-reelers in the early 1920s starring the great shortstop Honus "Hans" Wagner. Since this allegedly occurred between the time that Moe had worked with his brother Shemp in vaudeville in the late 1910s and the time that Howard became a "stooge" of comedian Ted Healy in 1922, the Wagner shorts would have to have been produced sometime in 1920 or 1921. Even allowing for the swiftness with which low-budget silent shorts were cranked out, however, Moe's claim that a full dozen films had been produced seems improbable; nor is there any further information about these shorts beyond Howard's printed reminiscences.

The year 1923 offered what amounted to a major disappointment. *Giants vs. Yanks*, released May 13 by Pathé, was the latest two-reeler starring Hal Roach's recently organized "Our Gang"; in this instance, the kids were Mickey Daniels, Allen "Farina" Hoskins, Jackie Condon, "Sunshine Sammy" Morrison, Jackie Davis (brother-in-law of Harold Lloyd), Andy Samuels, and Joe Cobb. What promised to be an irresistible combination of these slapstick-inclined urchins and baseball (the title was meant to invoke memories of the recent Subway Series between New York City's two major league teams) rapidly fizzled after a few random gags. Most of the picture involved Mickey Daniels's inventive methods of washing clothes and an enforced visit to a wealthy family's quarantined house. The one fascinating aspect of *Giants vs. Yanks* was sociological, in that the film depicted an integrated ballgame involving black and white youngsters—long, long before such games became commonplace among adults. In fact, little "Farina" acts as the umpire!

One would have thought that, given

the fanatical devotion to baseball by the youth of America, "Our Gang" would have made up for the skimpiness of the ballgame scenes in *Giants vs. Yanks* with a slam-bang baseball follow-up. This, alas, was not to be. Throughout the twenty-two-year career of this kiddie contingent, baseball was merely a peripheral ingredient, popping up fitfully in such later "Gang" pictures as *Official Officers* (1925), *Kiddie Cure* (1940), *1-2-3 Go* (1941), and *Rover's Big Chance* (1942). One 1938 one-reeler *The Awful Tooth* never got any farther than displaying a ball and catcher's mitt.

The next baseball comedy short had a bit more ballpark activity than *Giants vs. Yanks*, if not more coherence. Mack Sennett's *Butterfingers*, distributed by Pathé in 1925, starred Billy Bevan as an ace pitcher who, before the first reel has ended, finds himself in the bathtub of another man's wife (the Sennett films made a point of avoiding subtlety). The husband, who happens to be a rival ballplayer in cahoots with a gambling ring, promises not to fracture Bevan if Billy will agree not to pitch in the Big Game. As the two-reeler hastens toward its conclusion, the ball used in the game falls in a bucket of tar and is retrieved by outfielder Bevan. Billy's rival is about to run home but is slowed down when his spiked shoe becomes stuck to the third-base plate. Alas, Billy can't throw in an easy out, since the tar has fused the ball to his fingers. The rival limps toward home, Billy runs to catch him, there's a cloud of dust, and when the air clears, we see the rival with the tar-covered ball embedded in his hair. It has been said that the director of *Butterfingers*, Del Lord, had a tendency to film the last scene of a comedy first, and then to figure out how to build up to that climax. I'd liked to have been at the story conference where Lord exclaimed, "How's this? A fat guy with a baseball in his hair!"

Around the Bases, a two-reeler released by Universal in December 1926, was one of that studio's "Collegians" series, which concentrated on the athletic and comic aspects of campus life. George Lewis, who starred in this series into the sound era (and who later kept busy as a serial villain), was top billed as a college baseball whizz, his on-field performance bombarded from all sides by the freshman vs. seniors routines and romantic subplots indigenous to the "Collegians" shorts. The screenplay for *Around the Bases* was attributed to Carl Laemmle, Jr., son of Universal's president; if we can believe this credit tag, Junior Laemmle was one of the few eighteen-year-old screenwriters in Hollywood.

Outside of the requisite newsreels and real-life sports films, the remaining silent baseball shorts were slapstick farces. Educational Films was on hand in August 1927 with *Batter Up*, produced by Jack White, brother of Columbia Pictures' future two-reeler maven Jules White. Around the same time, Larry Darmour Productions cranked out *Mickey's Athletes*, starring a very young Mickey Rooney as comic-strip artist Fontaine Fox's tough-kid creation, Mickey "Himself" McGuire. This "Our Gang" clone had a wonderfully edited ballgame climax, but the majority of the gags concerned a spooky old house inhabited by a zany magician (excerpts of this last sequence made the 8-millimeter home movie rounds for decades under the title *The Haunted House*).

Discounting the experimental 1922 DeForest Phonofilm "talkie" of DeWolf Hopper reciting "Casey at the Bat" and the 1929 Fox Movietone interview with Ty Cobb, the first audible baseball short was Mack Sennett's *Clancey at the Bat*, released by the inescapable Educational Pictures on November 3, 1929. Harry Gribbon was headlined as a goonish ballplayer in need of practice, with Sennett's top star Andy Clyde as Gribbon's coach. Surprisingly, considering that Sennett had since 1912 maintained Hollywood's busiest comedy studio, *Clancey* was only Sennett's second full-out

DeWolf Hopper tears a passion to tatters in this 1922 "De-Forest Phonofilm" rendition of *Casey at the Bat.*

baseball picture (the aforementioned *Butterfingers* was first); this fact is doubly surprising given that Sennett's first star back in 1912 was Fred Mace, who, previous to his screen career, had been seen on Broadway in 350 performances of the musical extravaganza *The Umpire*. Perhaps to compensate for lost time, the Sennett studio slapped together two more ballpark laugh spinners in the early talkie years: *Slide Speedy Slide* (1931), a girl's-team pastiche featuring pint-sized Daphne Pollard, with *Clancey at the Bat* director Earl Rodney among the scenarists; and *The Loud Mouth* (1932), directed by Del (*Butterfingers*) Lord, starring Matt McHugh as an obnoxious fan.

The year of *The Loud Mouth*, 1932, was an unusually busy one for baseball featurettes. Comedies included RKO-Pathe's *Stealin' Home*, a two-reeler entry in the studio's "Rufftown" series starring James Gleason, Eddie Gribbon, and (as Jackie Gleason designated her) the ever popular Mae Busch. This short tale of an egocentric tank-town pitcher was based on a story by Arthur "Bugs" Baer, the sports humorist responsible for the subtitles of the 1920 Babe Ruth vehicle *Headin' Home*, and was scripted by Ralph Cedar—best remem-

bered for his second-unit direction of filmed chase sequences (notably the memorable car chases in W. C. Fields's features *The Bank Dick* and *Never Give a Sucker an Even Break*). A second 1932 two-reeler, Hal Roach/ MGM's May 14 release *Too Many Women*, was an entry in Roach's "Boy Friends" series, a group of teenage comedies featuring "Our Gang" alumni Mickey Daniels and Mary Kornman, with bucolic character actor Grady Sutton and future director Gordon Douglas in support. *Too Many Women* dealt with a star pitcher (eighteen-year-old Mickey Daniels, also seen in Roach's *Giants vs. Yanks* [1923]) who goes into a slump when his waitress sweetheart gets married. The film's principal appeal to audiences in 1932 (and, incidentally, to film buffs of future generations) was a captivating sequence in which Daniels and Mary Kornman page through an old photo album, wherein the pictures "come to life" via clips of Daniels's and Kornman's silent "Our Gang" appearances.

The jewel in 1932's crown was Universal's *Babe Ruth Baseball Series*. Unlike Educational's late and unlamented series of 1920, these Universal one-reelers were produced with Babe's full endorsement and participation, and were filmed under the auspices of Ruth's longtime business manager Christy Walsh, who saw to it with his standard self-aggrandization that his own name was plastered all over the screen credits. In all six of these shorts Babe was seen giving youngsters pointers on the game within the framework of fragmentary plotlines. Best of the batch, and the one short that seems to have resurfaced with more regularity than the rest (both on-screen and in the form of publicity stills), was *Perfect*

Catch-all lobby card for one of Universal's *Babe Ruth Baseball Series*.

Control. In this little nugget a schoolboy dozes off in the classroom and dreams that Babe shows up to take the boy and his classmates out to the ballpark. Character comedian Franklin Pangborn, playing the prissy, bespectacled schoolteacher, also appears in the boy's daydream as Babe's catcher. Other titles in the Universal series included *Play Ball, Slide, Babe, Slide, Just Pals, Fancy Curves* and *Over the Fence*.

Back at Educational Films, Frank Coghlan, Jr., who'd previously lent strong support to William Haines in the 1927 feature *Slide, Kelly, Slide*, starred in the 1933 two-reeler *What's to Do?*, part of the studio's short-lived "Frolics of Youth" series. Coghlan played Sonny Rogers, teenaged star of his neighborhood baseball team. In an early sequence, Sonny, sidelined by a bad cold, disobeys doctor's orders and sneaks out of his bedroom window to score a winning homer while still garbed in his nightgown. He then dives back into his bed via the selfsame window, and neither the doctor nor his parents are any the wiser—at least, not until Sonny is ratted out by his pesky kid sister, played by four-year-old Shirley Temple.

Our next attraction, Vitaphone/Warner Bros.' two-reel *Dizzy and Daffy*, made its debut on December 15, 1934. Per its title, the stars of this film were the St. Louis Cardinals' Jerome "Dizzy" Dean and his brother Paul "Daffy" Dean, fresh from their 1934 World Series triumph. The Jack Henley-Dolph Singer screenplay spins a fanciful tale of how the Dean boys rose from the bushes to the majors with the help of a nearsighted pitcher (Coke-bottle glasses and all), played by Shemp Howard. The scenarists' web of deception further informs us that it was Shemp who gave the brothers their nicknames!

It isn't really fair to assess the Dean brothers' acting ability in this film, except to say that they're endearingly awful. The most naturalistic performance is offered by "Daffy" Dean, who manfully stifles a giggle whenever Shemp Howard goes into one of his time-tested routines. The bulk of the thespic responsibilities in *Dizzy and Daffy* is handled by Shemp, who is quite funny, and by movie bad guy Richard Cramer, here essaying the benign role of the Deans' tank-town manager. Unfortunately, the short is hampered by the interminable comedy of Roscoe Ates, who, in a triumph of poor taste, is cast as a stuttering umpire. By the time Ates grabs a microphone and stammers his way through a play by play broadcast, even the most docile audience member is inclined to inflict extensive damage upon the movie screen.

Its low humor aside, *Dizzy and Daffy* is a priceless record of the Deans in action, with some particularly choice close-up shots of Dizzy's windup and delivery. Daffy isn't quite as athletically extroverted as his brother, but this film should put to rest rumors that his presence on the Cardinals' line up was a mere publicity ploy to build up Dizzy; the younger Dean is fabulous when subbing for Ole Diz in the film's climactic Series scenes. As an added visual treat, director Lloyd French utilizes a gimmick previously (and less effectively) seen in the Joe E. Brown feature *Fireman Save My Child* by having Dizzy Dean pitch the ball directly at the camera. Even after nearly seven decades, the velocity of Dean's pitches can prompt the viewer to duck! (It's possible that cinematographer Robert Elswit saw *Dizzy and Daffy* at one time or another, since he recreates the pitch to the camera bit verbatim in *Tiger Town* [1983].)

Distributed by Fox Films on February 22, 1935, Educational Pictures' *One Run Elmer* was one of that studio's sixteen cheaply made two-reelers starring the immortal Buster Keaton, here making a comeback after his career hit rock bottom in 1933. Once its wearisome first reel—involving a price war between two competing gas station proprietors in the middle of the desert—has been dispensed with, *One Run Elmer* regales its audience with a genuinely hilarious amateur baseball game between the Bearcats (for whom Keaton is catcher) and the Rattlers (captained by Harold Goodwin, Buster's rival for the affections of the ravishing Lona Andre). In concert with screenwriter Glen Lambert and director Charles Lamont, Keaton dishes up one great sight gag after another, ranging from Buster's unorthodox method of scoring a home run by leaping in the air and using his outstretched feet to knock over the opposing catcher, to a batter smashing an apple—which has been substituted for a baseball—into a million pieces, forcing Buster and his teammates to hastily reassemble the fruit in order to tag the batter out. The exuberance of the finale in *One Run Elmer* leaves one wishing that Buster Keaton had been able to produce an all-stops-out baseball comedy while in his prime, instead of while working for eating money at that lowest echelon studio, Educational Pictures. (Note: This two-reeler was shot in the desert surrounding Chatsworth, California, which, after being subdivided and dotted with split-level houses, served as the locale for *The Bad News Bears* [1976].)

As in the mid–1920s, comedies predominated the milieu of baseball shorts in the mid–1930s. Vitaphone/Warner Bros.' two-reel *Slide, Nellie, Slide* (1936) dealt with (as if there was any doubt) female ballplayers; Bert Granet, later a powerful production executive, wrote the script and essayed a supporting role. The old reliable girls' baseball angle was further recycled in October 1937 with Columbia's *Gracie at the Bat*, starring Andy Clyde (Columbia's most popular two-reeler attraction next to the Three Stooges) as a grizzled old ball team manager hired to guide the destinies of a woman's softball club. Directed by Sennett veteran Del Lord (who'd also commandeered the previously mentioned *Butterfingers*), *Gracie* made good use of leftover costumes and props from the 1937 Columbia feature *Girls Can Play*, even featuring one of that film's bit players, Ann Doran, as a member of Andy Clyde's team (Doran also showed up in the later baseball outings *The Babe Ruth Story* [1948] and *The Kid from Cleveland* [1949]). As was customary with Columbia's "they'll love it twice" mentality, the studio's short-subject unit put Clyde through much the same paces in a later two-reeler, released in October 1941, *Lovable Trouble* (again directed by Del Lord), wherein Andy is called upon to coach a team of gorgeous showgirls, among them the ubiquitous Ann Doran.

Practically the only baseball comedy of this period that *didn't* spotlight a girl's team was MGM's one-reel *Opening Day* (November 1938), in which humorist Robert Benchley performed the latest variation of his standard after-dinner speaker characterization. In this "MGM Miniature," Benchley long-windedly substitutes for the local mayor during the annual ceremony of tossing out the first ball at the first game of the season—and in the process reveals everything he doesn't know about baseball.

Two years prior to *Opening Day*, filmgoers bore witness to one of the strangest baseball shorts ever made, Vitaphone/Warner Bros.' *Home Run on the Keys* (1936). Within its ten-minute life span, this pocket epic offers the recently retired Babe Ruth reminiscing over his controversial "called shot" of the 1932 World Series (see notes on *The Babe*, *The Babe Ruth Story* and *Elmer the Great*), and then rendering—or, more accurately, rending—the film's title song, penned by "Kitten on the Keys" composer Zez Confrey who, with his collaborator Byron Gay, also appears in the film. During the first half of *Home Run*, Babe not only muses over the called shot, which he attributes to "the good Lord and good luck," but also reenacts the moment. Since this is probably Ruth's longest sustained commentary on the subject of his preordained home run, portions of *Home Run on the Keys'* soundtrack have popped up for years in baseball documentaries, invariably represented as snippets from a "genuine" interview. As for Babe's musical performance (which supposedly takes place during a radio broadcast following an incongruous presentation of "The Beach at Bali-Bali" by the preteen DeMarco Sisters), it's perhaps best not to dwell too long or too critically. Anyway, he doesn't stink.

Columbia Pictures was back at the helm on February 16, 1940, with *The Heckler*, a deft reworking of Sennett's *The Loud Mouth*, directed by the ineluctable Del Lord and featuring the studio's "quadruple-threat" comedy star (actor, writer, producer, and director) Charley Chase. The ballgame sequences in this two-reeler were miserly, consisting mostly of mildewed stock footage and a closeup or two of star player Oley Margarine (played by Bruce Bennett, later the truculent, doomed pitcher in the 1951 MGM feature *Angels in the Outfield*). But this matters not a whit, since the emphasis in *The Heckler* is on Chase, here playing a composite of all the irritating and obnoxious baseball fans that have festered in the grandstands since the beginning of the sport. Charley declares his presence by jabbing his elbows into his neighboring fans, swatting them on their backs and laughing uproariously at their irritation. He sprays the stands with a shaken-up carbonated beverage, "excusing" himself by bellowing, "That's all right. It's a *soft* drink!" He tosses peanut shells into the toupees of the unfortunate fans sitting in the lower stalls, drops a mustard-laden hotdog into the lap of a lady spectator, loses the contents of an ice cream cone in a gentleman's pipe, and

Andy Clyde seems fascinated with Ann Doran (wearing hand-me-downs from *Girls Can Play*) in *Gracie at the Bat* (courtesy of Ted Okuda).

repairs a hole in his seat cushion by "borrowing" a band-aid from the neck of the guy sitting in front of him. And, in a device designed by screenwriter John Grey to bring a pair of game-fixing gangsters into the plot, Charley continually throws the home team off their game by heckling the players with his trademarked cry, "Watch him *miss it!*" Though the short loses steam when the plot takes over, things brighten up with a surrealistic climax wherein Charley uses his heckling talents to save himself from being shot to death at close range. While not the best baseball comedy of all time, *The Heckler* is without question one of the most consistently funny shorts ever assembled at Columbia, not to mention one of Charley Chase's most hilarious performances.

The Heckler was remade virtually scene for scene in 1946 as *Mr. Noisy*, and while Edward Bernds' direction doesn't quite match the breathless pace of Del Lord's, the later film is an improvement on the original, particularly in Columbia's casting choice of Shemp Howard in the title role. As brilliantly as Charley Chase played the heckler, one always felt that Chase was standing outside the character and commenting upon it, as if to say, "Look at me. Am I not the complete creep?" Shemp Howard, though nowhere near as versatile as Chase, is nonetheless far better cast as "Mr. Noisy"; Shemp *inhabits* the role, making the audience believe that he is genuinely and utterly the Neanderthal that he portrays. By the time of the final fade-out, the viewer is overwhelmed by the urge to climb into the screen and strangle the life out of the cretinous Mr. Howard.

Mr. Noisy represented Hollywood's last live-action baseball comedy short. Thereafter, most glimpses of the game were concentrated within newsreel highlights narrated by such commentators as Fox Movietone's Ed Thorgeson and Hearst/MGM's Bill Stern in *News of the Day*. Occasionally throughout the 1930s and 1940s, series like RKO's *Sportoscopes* and Paramount's *Grantland Rice Sportlight* (which was good for 206 installments!) touched upon baseball, but as historian Leonard Maltin has pointed out, "[m]ost of the sports reels ... tried to stay away from familiar games like baseball and football, figuring that audiences would prefer something more offbeat."

This was also true of MGM's wide-rang-ing *Pete Smith Specialties*, which began as purely a sports-highlights series in 1931 but which would eventually cover a multitude of unusual subjects in and out of sports until the cessation of the series in 1955. Occasionally, the *Specialties* would offer a traditional reel like *Sports Quiz* (September 1944), in which the New York Giants' Carl Hubbell joined several other sports greats in demonstrating their winning techniques. For the most part, however, the Pete Smith films were characterized by such titles as *Donkey Baseball* (March 1935), which lived up to its title by showing a number of familiar slapstick-comedy supporting actors (Eddie Baker, Bobby Dunn, etc.) playing ball while sitting on their donkeys (filmed at Hal Roach Studios, this one-reeler also prominently displays a political banner for Roach's mother, who was running in an upcoming municipal election!); and *In Case You're Curious* (November 1951), which emphasized little-known facts about "baseball, beverages, and broken glass." Then there was *Early Sports Quiz* (March 1947), in which Smith posed questions to the audience about various antiquated rules and regulations of popular sports—revealing, among other things, that it was once customary to tag a ballplayer "out" by hitting the hapless player with a thrown ball.

The best Pete Smith–produced baseball effort was *Diamond Demon* (February 1947), directed by David Barclay (the pseudonym for Dave O'Brien, stuntman star of Smith's comedy reels) and featuring the astonishing comic calisthenics of baseball trickster Johnny Price. Significant in the overall scheme of film history was the fact that Pete Smith pulled the brilliant cinematographer William Daniels (who'd lensed such classics as *Greed*, *Grand Hotel*, and *Dinner at Eight*) out of a retirement forced upon him by contractual difficulties to photograph *Diamond Demon*. Smith was careful to praise William Daniels's superlative camerawork in his narration of the short, leading

Daniel Kerry (left) and Wally Rose prepare to give moviegoers what they've paid to see as they take aim at Shemp Howard in *Mr. Noisy* (courtesy of Ted Okuda).

to Daniels's triumphant return to Holly-wood, topped off one year later with a Best Black and White Cinematography Oscar for Universal's *The Naked City.*

As double features, and then television, diminished the market for theatrical shorts, the number of baseball featurettes dropped proportionately. World Series wrap-ups continued to be produced for the 8 and 16 millimeter home-movie market into the 1970s, and on videocassette into the 1980s and beyond. Those shorts that did pop up sporadically in theaters were usually designed for dual markets: *The Glory of Their Times* was released to movie houses and syndicated to local TV stations almost simultaneously in 1970, and *Baseball the Pete Rose Way* could similarly be seen

both theatrically and on home video in 1986. *When It Was a Game* (1991), the first of two marvelous assemblages of color home-movie footage of baseball teams in the 1930s and 1940s, might once upon a time have gone directly to the cinema circuit; instead, it premiered on HBO, a pay cable TV service. That's where the money was, and that is where it remains to this day. (Not that there's anything wrong in this; without TV, would Ken Burns have ever dreamed of tackling his brilliant, all-inclusive PBS miniseries *Baseball* [1994], unquestionably the best-ever nondramatic film treatment of the subject?)

We haven't gone into great detail on one of the most prolific sources of baseball-oriented shorts, the animated cartoon, simply because that source *is* so prolific. Virtually every cartoon studio in existence since the 1910s has ground out its quota of ballpark comedies, but only a handful are worth remembering. Most of these shorts were content to haul out their own set of clichés, time after time: The "twister" pitch, accomplished by literally winding up the arm like a corkscrew; the ball that zooms through the air with such force that it bores a hole into the bat, the catcher's mitt, or the catcher himself; the home run king who "elasticizes" the baseline as he rounds the diamond; the anthropomorphic giraffe in the outfield who catches the pop fly in his (her?) mouth; the dynamite-loaded baseball, usually accompanied with the remark, "He'll get a *bang* out of this!"; and the inevitable "slow-motion" sequence, capturing the players in silly poses with grotesque facial expressions. In the late 1920s and early 1930s there was the additional cliché of featuring a snub-nosed caricature of Babe Ruth, which could sometimes be funny (as in Ub Iwerks's 1933 "Willie Whopper" cartoon, *Play Ball*) but was usually tossed in for a quick "shock of recognition" chuckle and nothing more (as in the 1931 Van Beuren release, *Big Game*).

Once in a while animators would strive for something different but would be laid low by unsatisfactory execution. Famous Studios/Paramount's *Abner the Baseball* (1961) had the amusing concept of telling the story of the game from the baseball's point of view (the little round orb's voice was supplied by Eddie "The Old Philosopher" Lawrence), but at a length of two reels this cartoon was much too attenuated and far too leisurely paced to make a real impact.

Amidst such pedestrian efforts as Max Fleischer's *The Twisker Pitcher* (a 1937 Popeye cartoon that was actually funnier when excerpted in *Customers Wanted* [1939], with a fresh supply of ad-libbed mutterings from Jack Mercer, the voice of Popeye) and Wal-

ter Lantz's 1942 *The Screwball* (which suffered from a hazy continuity wherein Woody Woodpecker spends the first half of the cartoon trying to sneak in to watch a game, then devotes the second half to playing for the local team), the animation field offered a memorable moment or two. Pat Sullivan and Otto Messmer's silent *Felix Saves the Day* (1922) was bolstered by the novelty of Felix the Cat acting as lucky mascot for the New York Yankees, and was released shortly after the first of the Yankees' three consecutive World Series clashes with their neighbors, the Giants. Warner Bros.' *Buddy's Bearcats* (1934) was for the most part unremarkable, but it did feature a caricatured Joe E. Brown as a radio announcer, some twenty years before Brown really *did* man the microphone in such a capacity for the New York Yankees.

Buddy's Bearcats was one of several Warner Bros. baseball cartoons, the majority of these being real letdowns considering the talent pool at that animation house. *Boulevardier from the Bronx* (1936) features a barnyard ball game played by scrawny-looking chickens, with bragadoccio "Dizzy Dan" as star player (that's about as amusing as it gets); *Porky's Baseball Broadcast* (1940) is funny only if you found the stuttering sportscaster gag in the live-action *Dizzy and Daffy* (1934) funny; and *Gone Batty* (1954)—despite a hilarious opening in which a tiny, effete ballplayer responds to the brute strength of his gargantuan opponent by murmuring "I don't like you!"—wastes six minutes of screen time with a series of flat gags about a ballplaying elephant. Conversely, *Baseball Bugs* (1946), directed by Friz Freleng, is one of the best sports cartoons to come out of any studio. Bugs Bunny is in rare form in this picture, confounding his King Kong–like opponents by playing all the positions himself, flummoxing the umpire ("Yer out!" "I'm safe!" "Yer out!" "I'm out!" "Yer safe!" ad infinitum), and racing across Manhattan to catch a long ball atop the Empire State Building, with the Statue of Liberty declaring a fair catch.

Walt Disney, the league leader in the animation field, produced a few scattered baseball cartoons, with one of these, the 1942 Goofy vehicle *How to Play Baseball*, achieving the honor of being handpicked by Samuel Goldwyn to play on the world premiere bill with Goldwyn's *The Pride of the Yankees*. Disney's baseball *pièce de résistance* was the "Casey at the Bat" section of his studio's 1946 omnibus feature *Make Mine Music* (this sequence was released as a separate short in 1954). Of all the screen adaptations of "Casey," the Disney version, directed by Clyde Geronimi, comes closest to matching the satiric hyperbole of Ernest Lawrence Thayer's original ballad. The gags, ranging from a bat becoming entangled in one of the players' 1890s-style wax mustaches to "the force of Casey's blow" being dramatized with hurricane-like dimensions, are first-rate and much faster paced than most Disney cartoons of this period. Adding to the fun is a hurdy-gurdy theme song by Ray Gilbert, Ken Darby and Eliot Daniel, "Casey the Pride of Them All," in which one lyric describes our hero as "The Sinatra of 1902"; and best of all is the unbridled "singing narration" of five-alarm voiced Jerry Colonna. Unfortunately, the reputation of Disney's *Casey* has suffered in the last thirty-five years or so, due in part to the studio's half-hearted 1954 animated "sequel" *Casey Bats Again* (in which Casey manages a ball club comprised of his feisty young daughters), but mainly because the original *Casey* was most often featured on Disney's weekly NBC series, where Colonna's voiceover was replaced by the Mittel-European tones of Professor Ludwig Von Drake (Paul Frees), possibly the most doggedly unfunny Disney character of all time.

This writer's candidate for the best baseball cartoon ever put on celluloid is director Tex Avery's *Batty Baseball*, released by MGM in April 1944. This five-minute spectacular moves so swiftly that we're a full minute into the action before a character pauses to comment that we haven't even seen the MGM lion or the production credits! As was typical of the Tex Avery *ouevre*, *Batty Baseball* is chock full of outrageous visual puns, wheezy verbal gags, wartime references (the entire outfield is replaced by a field of "1-A" signs) and overcharged sexuality (a "curve ball" plots such a voluptuously feminine path that the men in the grandstands wolf-whistle in unison). All the jokes, even the most atrocious, are played full out with such shameless energy that Avery virtually dares you not to laugh. The best bits include the name of the stadium, "W. C. Field" ("The guy who thought up this corny gag isn't with us any more," we are assured via subtitle); the fan who screams "Kill the umpire!" then turns a rancid shade of green when his orders are carried out literally; the pitcher warming up in the bullpen by being cosseted by a couple of full-figured sweater girls; another pitcher with a bombsight on his shoe; the pompous umpire who dusts off home plate, then is tipped by the batter; and the closing gag, in which the man at bat inadvertently clubs to death an overenthusiastic catcher, whose demise is depicted off-screen by the sound of breaking glass. *Batty Baseball* fades out as the announcer asks for "a brief moment of silence," while the catcher, winged and flying heavenward, passes by the camera, holding a sign which reads "Sad ending, isn't it?"

A sad ending for the cartoon catcher perhaps, but a delightful finish for our brief journey through the world of baseball short subjects.

Baseball in Non-Baseball Films

This section represents a lot of "hard calls." If we were to list every film in which someone wields a bat, we'd have to include such pictures as *Walking Tall* (the saga of bat-happy sheriff Buford Pusser) and *The Untouchables* (in which Robert De Niro, as Al Capone, demonstrates the slugging technique he'd picked up in *Bang the Drum Slowly* [1974] by crushing the skull of an unfaithful Capone hireling). If we were to tally every film where a ball was tossed or hit, this would qualify *Test Pilot* (1938), *The Chosen* (1982), *A Soldier's Story* (1984), *Superman IV* (1984), *Memphis Belle* (1991), *Pearl Harbor* (2001), and even the 1969 Castro documentary *Fidel* as peripheral baseball pictures. If we were to cite any film in which baseball stars and stats are mentioned, we'd be obliged to comment upon everything from *The Devil with Hitler* (1943) to *City Slickers* (1991). And how would we categorize the production number "The Umpire is a Most Unhappy Man" in the 1949 musical *I Wonder Who's Kissing Her Now?*, or the roundabout manner in which the 1969 "Miracle Mets" enable a firefighter to communicate with his son thirty years in the future, thereby foiling an elusive murderer in the 2000 fantasy *Frequency*? And do we *have* to bring up the mongrelized "game" which forms the basis of the looney 1998 comedy *BASEketball*?

Let this section serve, then, as a roll call of non-baseball films in which baseball is actually depicted in some way or another—either through the existence of baseball elements that have some bearing on the plot, or by the presence of a ballplayer or related sports personality in the cast—rather than merely referred to in passing.

There are some films listed herein that could conceivably qualify as bona fide "baseball pictures"—almost. Buster Keaton's 1927 silent feature *College* (Schenck/United Artists) is frequently catalogued as one of Hollywood's best baseball films, simply because of a prolonged and very funny sequence in which college freshman Buster first distinguishes himself by his ineptitude during a practice session, then later plays the game like the professional-level athlete that Keaton was in real life. But *College* covers virtually every campus sport, from hurdling to javelin throwing, so it is no more a baseball film pure and simple than Buster's 1928 *The Cameraman* (MGM), which contains a delightfully extraneous vignette wherein the star pantomimes a one-man game in a deserted Yankee Stadium.

Similarly, *Jim Thorpe–All American* (1951, Warner Bros.) could in a less exacting assessment pass muster as a baseball picture, since it was the fact that Thorpe (enacted by Burt Lancaster) had once played baseball for money that obligated the Olympic committee to strip the athlete of his 1912 Olympic medals. As with *College*, however, *Jim Thorpe* deals with far too many different sports to be pinpointed as solely a baseball epic—in fact, if you were to ask anyone who's seen the film, it's likely that that person's most vivid memory would be of Burt Lancaster in a football uniform.

Most video rental shops categorize the Richard Pryor vehicle *Brewster's Millions* (1985, Universal) as a baseball movie because Pryor plays an end-of-pier major leaguer who must spend several million dollars within a given period of time in order to inherit an enormous fortune, and one of his schemes includes expunging great wads of dough to finance a game between his bottom of the barrel team and the league's champs. But Pryor's film was actually the *seventh* screen version of a pre–World War I stage farce in which the protagonist was originally a young lawyer. In the 1945 *Brewster's Millions*, Dennis O'Keefe portrayed the hero as an impoverished G.I., just back from World War II. Does this make *Brewster's Millions* a service comedy?

Two pictures that have often been listed as baseball movies were both released by the inappropriately named Epic Productions. 1989's *Night Game*, starring Roy Scheider (say it ain't so, Roy!), is a "slasher" film about a looney-tune who slices and dices his victims whenever the Houston Astros play a home game at night. There's a shot of the Astrodome filled to capacity at the beginning of the film, and a similar shot at the end. In between we're forced to endure a gruesome array of bloody murders and a relentless series of rip-offs from such films as *Lady from Shanghai* and *Psycho*. It's hard to imagine anything worse than *Night Game* until you've seen Epic's second "baseball" flick, *Bloodgame* (1990), featuring a no-star cast in an excruciating horror yarn about a sexy female team ("Babe's Ballgirls") which makes the mistake of visiting a backwoods community populated exclusively by homicidal morons. In the opening ballgame sequence the girls, attired in cutoffs and halter tops, play ball with the expertise of dayschool children, fending off the poor sportsmanship and the roving fingers of their yahoo opponents with such Noel Cowardlike repartee as "You asshole!" We're a long way from *A League of Their Own*.

The 1980 TV movie *The Comeback Kid* from ABC/Circle Films is one of a handful of films in this section that could arguably have been included in the alphabetical main body of the text. It is, after all, the story of Bubba Newman (John Ritter), a San Diego–based major leaguer who goes on a drunken binge after being sent to the minors, then spends most of the rest of the film trying to make his titular comeback. *The Comeback Kid* does open with a well-photographed night game sequence (including that favorite visual cliché of 1980s baseball films, the series of super-tight close-ups of the pitcher's hands, feet, and eyes), and Bubba Newman does make sporadic visits to his old teammates, even taking part in two brief batting practice scenes. But the plot of the film is preoccupied with Bubba's being hired by an attractive social worker (Susan Dey) to coach a track team composed of surly street kids and problem children. Thereafter, despite such deliberate echoes of *The Bad News Bears* as the hardbitten youthful ringleader who eventually joins the track team, and the vignette in which the kids find the inebriated hero sleeping it off in the middle of the playground, *The Comeback Kid* is a story of regeneration and reform (regeneration for Bubba, reform for the kids) played out with practically no bats, balls, or gloves in sight.

In fact, the film goes out of its way to *renounce* anything to do with baseball. Bubba steals a check meant to buy equipment for the kids in order to finance his return to the major leagues, then deserts his youthful team just when they need him most when he gets a chance to play ball—this action indirectly causing one of the children to be killed after riding his bike into heavy traffic. As for Bubba's former teammates, they're depicted as leering, lascivious, drink-sodden, arrested-development cases who can't function in a world of adult responsibilities and lasting human relationships. The film seems to be arguing that only through working nonprofessionally with underprivileged children can Bubba "purify" himself. Together with the 1996 theatrical release *The Fan*, *The Comeback Kid* qualifies as one of the few *anti*-baseball movies ever made, and this, as much as the fact that it isn't really very good, is reason enough for any baseball fan to seek entertainment elsewhere when the film pops up on TV nowadays. It's entirely possible that *The Comeback Kid* might have remained permanently on the shelf after its initial 1980 release had not its supporting cast included future movie heartthrob Patrick Swayze.

The Comeback Kid was one of many non-baseball pictures to feature a ballplayer—professional or recreational—as a leading character. Examples of this sort of film stretch as far back as 1915. *The Grandee's Ring*, produced that year by Interstate Feature Film Company and distributed by Picture Play Film Corporation, was a five-reeler about a wealthy rancher's tomboyish daughter Shirley (Helene Wallace), who is kidnapped, along with high-born Mexican Carlos La Barbara (Kenneth MacDougall), by border bandidos. Carlos escapes, rescuing Shirley in the process. A professor visiting Shirley's father is so impressed by this deed that he gets Carlos enrolled at Watson College (talk about scholarships!), where the young Mexican and his roomie Jack Foster excel at baseball. Shirley falls for both boys, but in a dream she realizes that Carlos is the better man. We'd say that *The Grandee's Ring* pulls a cliché reversal when Jack hits a winning run but loses Shirley to

Carlos all the same, except that the "win the ballgame, win the girl" cliché hadn't been developed yet in 1915—at least not in the movies.

The Varmint (1917, Morosco/Paramount) starred Jack Pickford (Mary's younger brother) as the standard braggart collegiate who comes to maturity within the perimeters of team sports. Jack's college baseball career is curtailed when his careless antics result in his being booted from the team, but he redeems himself at the end during a football game. Directing *The Varmint* was William Desmond Taylor, whose spectacular, still-unsolved 1922 murder has overshadowed the consistent high quality of his film work.

The year 1919 offered three features with baseball inclined protagonists. *The Final Close-Up* (Famous Players/Lasky) was the tale of a millionaire's son (Francis MacDonald) who, after being fired from his reporter's job, pitches briefly on the ball team of a fashionable seaside hotel before moving on to new adventures. *Muggsy* (Triangle) spotlighted Jackie Saunders as a hoydenish young girl who plays baseball—and swears—as heartily as any of "the guys." This intriguing plot device was merely a prologue for the film's principal storyline: Jackie disguises herself as a boy when she's sent to live with her wealthy uncle, who hates women. Guess what all *this* was leading up to!

The oddest of the 1919 trilogy was *The Greater Victory*, a five-reel melodrama produced by the U.S. Vocational Education Commission, with funding provided by the Benevolent and Protective Order of the Elks. In this thick and chewy slice of postwar propaganda, Bill and Ted are two young small-town ballplayers, both stuck on the same girl. Both are drafted into the U.S. Army, though wastrel Bill dons a uniform with great reluctance. In France, Bill and Ted's "excellent adventure" becomes a "bogus journey" when Ted loses an arm and Bill a leg. Back home, Ted sagaciously enters a government vocational course, becomes a mechanic, works his way up to factory supervisor, and marries his sweetheart. But Goofus—er, Bill—feeling sorry for himself, drifts into boozing and gambling. Bill kills a man during a $5 robbery, and just as he's about to be executed, he wakes up; it's all been a horrible dream, except for the missing-leg part. Bill hobbles over to the government vocational offices to take rehabilitative courses himself. But since the protagonists of *The Greater Victory* are Bill and Ted and not Monty Stratton and Pete Gray, neither boy ever plays baseball again.

Cowboy star Tom Mix took to the diamond in the early reels of *Stepping Fast* (1923, Fox). The ballgame scenes in this film were directed by Edward Sedgwick, something of a trial run for Sedgwick's later baseball pictures *Hit and Run* (1924, Universal), *Slide, Kelly, Slide* (1927, MGM) and *Death on the Diamond* (1934, MGM).

In 1926, Producers' Distributors Corporation came out with *Young April*, a typical "princess in an arranged marriage of state" confection, with Bessie Love starring as the "arranged" princess. As a clue that American democracy has doomed the upcoming royal wedding, we first see Bessie attending a Stateside girls' school, where she demonstrates her "Americanization" by participating in a vigorous softball game. When the camera follows Love around the bases at one point, there's every indication that the actress could have successfully pulled off a full-fledged baseball film (other than her appearance as a nonparticipant in the 1930 ballpark musical *They Learned About Women*) had she been given the chance.

After *Young April* there was a period of ten years before there'd be another feature-length picture headlining a baseball player that wasn't itself devoted to the game. Based on the novels by Burt L. Standish (a.k.a. Gilbert S. Patton), the 1936 Universal serial *The Adventures of Frank Merriwell* focused

on an all-round college athlete (played by Donald Briggs) who manages to rescue his kidnapped scientist father, and defeat a veritable regiment of villains, just in time to score a winning run for the Yale team in the final chapter. Marginally more credible were the 1938 Warner Bros. comedies *Brother Rat* and its 1940 sequel *Brother Rat and a Baby*, with Eddie Albert re-creating his stage role of a Virginia Military Institute baseball flash whose game—and future career—is nearly scuttled by a secret marriage. *Brother Rat* was remade by Warners in 1952 as a musical entitled *About Face*, with Eddie Bracken, himself a reasonably talented amateur ballplayer, in the Eddie Albert role.

Frank Capra's *Meet John Doe* (1941, Warner Bros.) starred Gary Cooper as Long John Willoughby, a minor-league pitcher who goes on the bum after his arm gives out (Long John's previous vocation is reflected in the passages from "Take Me Out to the Ballgame" heard during the main credits). Before the baseball angle is absorbed by Capra's trenchant story of how media manipulation can both create a folk hero out of thin air and very nearly cause the United States to surrender to fascism, *Meet John Doe* offers a glimpse or two of Gary Cooper "practice pitching" a nonexistent ball to fellow bindlestiff Walter Brennan, and, incidentally, exhibiting a lot more form than he would as Lou Gehrig in *The Pride of the Yankees* (1942; which likewise costarred Brennan).

Another 1941 release, Universal's *Mr. Dynamite*, starred Lloyd Nolan as a Brooklyn pitcher who, in "Frank Merriwell" fashion, manages to attend a crowded amusement park, mop up an espionage ring, and win the heroine (Irene Hervey), with enough time left over to make it to the ballpark for the World Series. B-picture historian Don Miller has observed that Lloyd Nolan successfully "conveyed the impression that he very well could have been a star pitcher" without ever being seen on a ballfield or in uniform, a quality that Nolan carried over into his next baseball B-picture assignment, 20th Century–Fox's *It Happened in Flatbush*.

Flatbush was released in 1942, the same year that Allan Jones portrayed a ballplayer who had to choose between the major leagues and a singing career in Universal's *Moonlight in Havana*. This sixty-minute mini-musical had the distinction of being directed by Anthony Mann, who graduated to such prestige assignments as *Winchester 73*, *The Glenn Miller Story* and *El Cid*. Another 1942 effort, *Taxi, Mister*, was a Hal Roach/United Artists "streamliner" (running 45 minutes or so, deliberately designed by Hal Roach as a companion feature for overlong films on double bills) starring William Bendix, the screen's future Babe Ruth, as a cloddish cabdriver who pitches for the "Flatbush" sandlot baseball team. The film's closing sight gag, in which Bendix knocks out villain Sheldon Leonard with a well-aimed curveball, was the latest exhumation of a "distance" gag that producer Roach had previously trotted out in such comedies as Max Davidson's *Pass the Gravy* (1927), Our Gang's *Divot Diggers* (1936) and Laurel and Hardy's *Swiss Miss* (1938). (Joe Sawyer, who appears in *Taxi, Mister* as Bendix's best pal and catcher, later did a "stumble-on" in 1946's *Deadline at Dawn* [RKO], playing Babe Dooley, a former big-leaguer who has degenerated into a drunken derelict.)

Block Busters (1944, Monogram) was one of producer Sam Katzman's "East Side Kids" quickies, providing a respite to the series' usual city streets locale by allowing Leo Gorcey, Huntz Hall, and company to take to the diamond as a ball team sponsored by an East Side deli owner (played by Bernard Gorcey, Leo's father). Most of the humor would have been better suited to a two-reeler, such as the rickety routine in which Huntz Hall lets three pitches go by him while he's warming up. The ballpark setting in *Block Busters* was also utilized for a reworking of a plot device previously seen in the 1926 silent *Young April*: the assimilation into American society of a foreign youth (in this case, a French refugee) through the love of baseball.

Boys' Ranch (1945, MGM) stars James Craig as baseball star Dan Walker, who no sooner polishes off the opposition in the traditional Big Game (staged, as usual, in Los Angeles' Wrigley Field) than he announces his retirement to the craggy-but-goldenhearted team manager. After the two men trade words so benign and friendly that they make the "Andy Hardy" films sound like the collected works of David Mamet, Walker heads off to fulfill his lifelong dream of setting up a ranch in Texas to help potential juvenile delinquents find a more uplifting purpose in life. The baseball angle is promptly dispensed with so that the rest of the film can be used to show off MGM's stable of adolescent talent, including Jackie "Butch" Jenkins, Skippy Homeier and Darryl Hickman. Spending almost as little time in uniform as James Craig was Dan Dailey (future star of *The Kid from Left Field* and the Dizzy Dean biopic *Pride of St. Louis*) in the Technicolor musical *Give My Regards to Broadway* (1948, 20th Century–Fox). Cast as a talented but recalcitrant song-and-dance man, Dailey quits his family's variety act to pursue a baseball career, prompting his veteran-trouper father (Charles Winninger) to admit that vaudeville is dead and to allow his children to pursue careers of their own choosing. (Had Dan Dailey's character seen 1930's *They Learned About Women*, he might have found time for both baseball and showbiz, but that would have robbed him of his showy last-reel confrontation with dear old dad.)

Moving ahead six years, we find James Stewart, who, of course, had once played Monty Stratton, donning another baseball uniform for the opening scene of Paramount's *Strategic Air Command*. It isn't long before a high-powered B-36 streaks over Al Lang Field in St. Petersburg, Florida, where Stewart, in the role of third baseman Dutch Holland, is in winter training with the St. Louis Cardinals. The aircraft's appearance is followed by the arrival of an Air Force general, played by James Millican (who in 1952 portrayed Grover Cleveland Alexander's Phillies teammate Bill Killefer in *The Winning Team*). The general is there to tell Dutch Holland that he's been called back to the Air Force Reserves. While real-life reserve officer Jimmy Stewart would have dropped his glove and climbed into the cockpit in the twinkling of an eye, the script of *Strategic Air Command* requires Dutch Holland to be bitter over this interruption of his soaring baseball career. Baseball movie fans were bitter as well, since the first time Stewart is seen in a Cards uniform is also the last time in this particular film—though if you stick with the story you'll encounter yet another echo of *The Winning Team* in the person of Frank ("Rogers Hornsby") Lovejoy, playing the top brass of *Strategic Air Command*.

Now we zoom forward to 1974, where the only ballplayer in a nonballplaying picture is future talkshow host David Hartman. The actor plays the title role in Universal's made-for–TV *Lucas Tanner*, which functioned as the pilot film for Hartman's short-lived series about a onetime major leaguer who becomes a deeply committed high school teacher after the death of his wife and son.

Another quantum leap plants us in 1981, where we regretfully stumble upon *Chu Chu and the Philly Flash* (20th Century–Fox). In this award loser, Alan Arkin plays a derelict ex-ballplayer who roams the streets in a tattered and torn Phillies uniform, and who teams with an erstwhile Carmen Miranda imitator (Carol Burnett) to foil a gang of crooks. Almost mesmerizing in its utter lack of humor or any other entertainment value, *Chu Chu and the Philly Flash*

was scripted by Alan Arkin's wife, and since any comment made upon that fact by this writer would be construed as sexist, let's just drop the whole thing.

Nick Nolte is Doc, a big leaguer turned marine biologist, in *Cannery Row* (1982, UA/MGM), a benighted Steinbeck adaptation written and directed by David S. Ward, of *Major League* fame. Of less aesthetic value was another 1982 product, *Zapped!* (Embassy), a horny-teenager fiasco featuring Scott Baio as a young man with telekinetic powers. Baio "wills" a baseball to move his way during a high school game, but this is secondary to his preoccupation with removing the clothes of his female classmates. And it was back to the ranks of the unemployed in *Ironweed* (1987, Tri-Star), a beautifully acted but thoroughly depressing adaptation of William Kennedy's Pulitzer Prize–winning novel about Depression era street people. Jack Nicholson stars as an alcoholic ex-ballplayer who tries with all his might to shut out haunting memories of the tragedies that ruined him. Also in the cast is Michael O'Keefe, here served with better material than he'd been saddled with in *The Slugger's Wife* (1985), and Margaret Whitton, soon to be the rich bitch owner of the Cleveland Indians in *Major League*.

Examples of baseball players in films focusing on matters other than baseball in the late 20th and early 21st century include Howard Dell as New York Yankees slugger Cash Manley in the made-for-cable chiller *Mean Streak* (1999, Showtime). As he draws ever closer to beating Joe DiMaggio's 56-game hitting streak, the African American Manley finds himself the focus of a campaign of terror conducted by an unknown serial killer who hacks the thumbs off his black victims and mails them to Manley as a warning to leave DiMaggio's record unsullied. Though it sounds like a variation on 1996's *The Fan*, *Mean Streak* spends most of its time exploring the character of investigating detective Lou Mattoni (Scott Bakula of *Major League: Back to the Minors*), who is forced to confront his own deeply ingrained racism while protecting Manley and trying to prevent further bloodshed. On a lighter note, we have the independently produced theatrical feature *The Broken Hearts Club: A Romantic Story* (2000, Banner/Columbia), with John Mahoney, who previously appeared as Kid Gleason in *Eight Men Out*, cast as Jack, the manager of a West Hollywood amateur men's softball team. What makes this film truly unique is that every member of the team is gay, Jack included. Before *The Broken Hearts Club* begins its plot proper, the audience is treated to an uproarious opening scene in which the team members hold a contest during an informal ballgame to determine who among them can exhibit the "straightest" behavior for the longest period without lapsing into an "O.G.T."—Obviously Gay Trait. (And you thought the Major League umpires were tough....)

Worthy of only the briefest of mentions is that disturbing subgenre in which ballplayer characters are cast in the most unsympathetic and repellant of lights. To cite four particularly odious examples, there is the former big leaguer-turned-homicidal maniac (Michael Pataki) who, along with two fellow asylum escapees, terrorizes a girl's school (before he is beaten to death by the female students!) in the 1973 sexploitationer *Carnal Madness*; washed-up ballplayer Roger (Richard Masur), who, upon establishing a second career as a murderous drug dealer, succeeds in corrupting virtually ever member of a big-city vice squad in Burt Reynolds' *Rent-a-Cop* (1988, King's Road Films); liquor-besotted major leaguer Bud Valentine (Skeet Urich), who, while trying to rape amnesiac heroine Patty Vare (Winona Ryder), causes a disastrous traffic accident in the muddled psychological thriller *Boys* (1996, Touchstone); and invalided ballplayer Henry Mulhill (Luca

Bercovici), who, after leeching off his hardworking bartender wife Tanya (Lara Flynn Boyle) while waiting for his insurance settlement, caddishly refuses to share the money with her when the check finally arrives, thereby setting in motion the *Double Indemnity*–style plot convolutions of *The Big Squeeze* (1996, Zeta/First Look Pictures).

There will undoubtedly be future films with "proxy" baseball roots by virtue of the presence of ballplaying lead characters. Equally likely are future productions featuring characters who inhabit baseball's sidelines—notably sports reporters, fans, and players' relatives.

Sportswriters and sportscasters have made scattered cinematic appearances over the last six decades. *Young Man of Manhattan* (1930, Paramount) starred future director Norman Foster as a hotshot reporter sent to St. Louis during the course of the film to cover a World Series match. *Panic on the Air* (1936, Columbia) plunked Lew Ayres into a radio studio as a sports announcer tracking down a gang of miscreants who've been fixing baseball games. The most fondly remembered of Hollywood's prewar sportswriters was Spencer Tracy in the 1942 MGM production *Woman of the Year* (cowritten by Ring Lardner, Jr.). In a justly famous sequence, Tracy, down to earth as usual, offers snooty political columnist Katharine Hepburn an impromptu play by play of her first baseball game—a scene skimmed over in the 1978 TV-movie remake of *Woman of the Year*, which starred Joseph Bologna and Rene Taylor.

Walter Matthau's re-creation of his stage role as slovenly sportswriter Oscar Madison in Neil Simon's *The Odd Couple* was expanded in Paramount's 1968 screen version to include a short sequence at Shea Stadium, where Matthau is seen discussing matters of importance with real-life sports reporter Heywood Hale Broun. Woody Allen, who, like Walter Matthau, was a bone-deep baseball nut (remember his routine about thinking of ballplayers during intercourse?), conceived a lengthier "sports comment" scene for his 1987 *Radio Days* (Orion). In this unbearably funny lampoon of 1940s radio sports prevaricator Bill Stern, we see and hear one "Bill Kerns" spinning an incredible tale of a ballplayer who loses an arm, a leg, and finally his sight, but keeps on playing because "he has heart." Even death does not slow down Kern's hero, who goes on to win eighteen games in "the Big League in the sky."

With the obvious exception of *The Fan* (1996), there haven't been any feature films about baseball told completely from the fan's point of view, though songwriter Harry Ruby's puppylike devotion to the game was well documented in MGM's 1950 musical biography *Three Little Words*. In recent years, however, at least one "fan" has won an Academy award. This was Raymond Babbitt, the autistic savant portrayed by Dustin Hoffman in *Rain Man* (1988, United Artists). Raymond's fascination with baseball is reflected by the pennant-studded decor of his little room at the Cincinnati sanatorium where we first meet him; by his encyclopedic tally of baseball statistics; and by his obsessive, ceaseless repetition of Abbott and Costello's "Who's on First" routine from the 1945 Universal picture *The Naughty Nineties* (represented by a film clip near the end of *Rain Man*).

Relatives of baseball players were inadequately served in *Ladies Day*, which, as noted in a previous chapter, has the most intimidating group of baseball wives that you're ever likely to see. Nine years earlier, Jack Holt played an influential businessman who tries to manipulate his kid brother's grades so that the boy will qualify for his school's baseball team in Columbia's *I'll Fix It*. But for the most part, baseball relatives were confined to movieland's notion of parental pressure brought to bear on participants of Little League baseball. Outside of such baseball-dominated films as *The*

Great American Pastime (1956), the *Bad News Bears* trilogy of the 1970s, and 2000's *Perfect Game*, throwaway sequences in films like *Boys' Night Out* (1962) and *Critics' Choice* (1963) touched gingerly, and without great depth, on the manner in which frustrated athletes live vicariously through their children.

This theme was explored more thoroughly as one of the many plot strands in director Ron Howard's *Parenthood* (1989, Universal), in which Steve Martin is so concerned with being a "pal" to his son (Jasen Fisher) that he refuses to acknowledge that the boy is having as much trouble coping with life as dear old Dad himself. Martin tends to frame everything in terms dictated by his one lasting childhood memory, that of being left alone by his father while attending a St. Louis Cardinals game on his birthday. Determining that he'll never shut out his own children in such a callous manner, Martin over-organizes his son's activities, all but forcing his kid to participate in sports, convincing himself that this is what parental commitment means.

In a marvelous opening sequence, a small-boy version of Steve Martin's character discusses his past and future family problems with a ballpark usher while that fateful Cards game is in progress, and it's only after a moment or so that we realize the entire conversation is taking place in Martin's mind, as he drifts back to his youthful trauma while attending a game as an adult with his own children. This sets up another daydream sequence later on, when Martin watches his son during a Little League match, imagining that the boy will pull off the winning play and then go on to the happy, carefree adult life that Martin feels he himself has missed. When the boy not only fails to come through on the diamond but pulls a boner that loses the game, Martin's visions turn hilariously bleak: He sees his grown-up son as a sniper shooting at innocent passersby from a clock

Though Abbott and Costello's "Who's on First" is considered the quintessential marriage of baseball and show business, this classic bit of ballpark humor was never actually performed in a movie *about* baseball. However, Abbott and Costello did at one point in the 1940s draw up plans to costar with Joe DiMaggio in a film that was to have been titled ... guess what (courtesy of James L. Neibaur).

tower, all because he'd blown that one game!

In a similar vein, several films have suggested that being a good father is synonymous with faithful and unswerving attendance at Little League games. One of the earliest examples of this occurs in *Executive Suite* (1954, MGM), in which businessman Mac Walling (William Holden) is torn between his son's ballgames and corporate intrigue at the office; ultimately Walling proves himself a "regular guy" by finding time for his paternal obligations. In Steven Spielberg's misfire "Peter Pan" sequel *Hook* (1991, Amblin/Tri-Star), the grown-up Peter (Robin Williams) learns to regret not showing up for his son's Big Game when his old nemesis Captain Hook (Dustin Hoffman) endeavors to win the boy's affection by staging an unorthodox ballgame of his own, merrily murdering any pirate-player who has the temerity to steal a base. And in the made-for–TV *Hi Honey, I'm Dead* (1991, FNM Films), neglectful dad Brad Stadler (Kevin Conroy) is doomed to be killed and reincarnated as Arnold Pishkin (Curtis Armstrong) as punishment for missing *his* son's turn at bat. (Bet now you'll think twice when your own kid asks you to sell those fund-raising chocolate bars at the office, hmmmm????)

Let's move on as though the Little League game in *Problem Child* (1990), in which a pathologically destructive kid (Michael Oliver) incapacitates an opposing player by applying a bat to the business end of the pelvis, never happened. We'll just backtrack to a youth-oriented ballgame with happier results in Neil Simon's *Max Dugan Returns* (1983, 20th Century–Fox). In this picture's slow-motion climax, teenager Matthew Broderick hits a home run as a loving tribute to his jailbird grandfather (Jason Robards), who's left town to start life anew. The batted ball flies out of the park and lands at grandpa's feet, strengthening the old guy's resolve to go straight. Charlie Lau,

onetime batting coach for the Kansas City Royals, appears in this sequence.

And then there's the Little League player who saved civilization. Keep reading, it gets better. *Amazing Grace and Chuck* (1987, Tri-Star) is a "once upon a time" melange about a young boy named Chuck (Joshua Zieleke)—his team's star pitcher—who sits down in the middle of a game and refuses to play again until the world powers disarm all their nuclear devices. Chuck becomes a pariah to both friends and family until a famous basketball player named "Amazing Grace" (Alex English) likewise puts a hold on his career until mankind divests itself of its weaponry. Soon thousands of pro athletes join Chuck's cause, and this does not sit well at all with an evil business mogul who has a lot of money sunk in the sports industry. The villain has Amazing Grace killed in an "accident," as transparent as glass, whereupon Chuck inaugurates a second protest by refusing to speak. Before long, virtually all the kids in America have become "silent children," a turn of events that in any real-life circumstance would have encouraged the great nations to step up their stockpiling of nuclear arms. Not here. Thanks to the levelheadedness of President Gregory Peck and his Russian counterpart, a firm no-nuke pact is signed. The film ends with Chuck picking up his baseball game where he left off, while hundreds of members of the media—not to mention all the heads of the world powers (including kinder and gentler President Peck)—crowd the grandstands.

Many people are crazy about this film, while just as many people ran screaming from the theaters when it first opened; *Amazing Grace and Chuck* must therefore be seen to make one's own assessment. But be warned! The film runs (or walks) for 116 minutes; Elmer Bernstein's musical score isn't quite as subtle as the storyline; and, despite the presence of cinematographer Robert Elswit, who'd previously done exceptional work on the baseball features *Tiger Town* and *Long Gone* (the star of which, William L. Petersen, plays Chuck's father in this film), we see approximately two baseballs pitched in *Amazing Grace and Chuck*—and one of those is freeze-framed. To read more about this masterpiece, wait until someone publishes a book called *The Great Fuzzy-Headed Liberal Films of the 1980s*.

And let us not forget the pivotal Little League game in *Simon Birch* (1998, Caravan/Hollywood Pictures), in which the physically handicapped title character (played by Ian Michael Smith), who believes that his stunted growth is somehow a "Gift From God," slugs out a foul ball which ends up killing the mother of his best friend. This tragically embarrassing blooper somehow enables Simon to fulfill his avowed destiny as a soldier in the Army of the Almighty!

Amazing Grace and Chuck and *Simon Birch* straddle two categories; they are both Little League films (after a fashion), and both are films in which a single game, or single series of games, has some bearing on the plot. Pictures in this latter "crucial game" category include, of all things, a prison comedy, *Up the River* (1930, Fox). This improbable effort revolves around two convicts (Spencer Tracy, in his film debut, and Warren Hymer), star players of their prison baseball team, who escape to help a pal (Humphrey Bogart in his second film appearance) on the outside, then willingly return to jail after performing their good deed, there to guide their team to victory. *Up the River* was remade in 1938, with the team sport in question changed to football, in keeping with 20th Century–Fox's late 1930s preoccupation with the gridiron (as witnessed by *Pigskin Parade*, *Life Begins in College*, and *Hold That Co-Ed*). The 1930 *Up the River* was directed by John Ford, whose only other association behind the camera with baseball was manifested in two television films, *Rookie of the Year* (Screen Director's Playhouse, 1956, starring John Wayne)

and *Flashing Spikes* (Alcoa Premiere, 1962, starring Jimmy Stewart and L.A. Dodger Don Drysdale, with John Wayne back for a cameo role).

A second soft-hearted crook farce, *Larceny Inc.* (1941, Warner Bros.), opens with still another prison ballgame. Inmate Edward G. Robinson forces a winning run by indulging in a bit of masochistic gamesmanship that was duplicated forty-five years later by William L. Petersen in *Long Gone*, a film made for cable TV.

On to 1943: With a title like *Whistling in Brooklyn*, it was perhaps inevitable that this particular MGM Red Skelton farce would feature an Ebbets Field sequence, with L.A.'s Wrigley Field standing in for Ebbets, and with several of the Brooklyn Dodgers, including manager Leo Durocher, playing themselves. Inevitable it was indeed, with Red—as a bumbling radio sleuth known as "The Fox"—attempting to elude a gang of criminals by donning a beard and posing as a member of the Battling Beavers, a hirsute House of David–style team. And equally inevitable was the moment in which Skelton uses his false set of whiskers to catch a pop fly. But the sequence's biggest laugh belongs to Durocher, who dismisses Skelton with the Groucho-esque comment, "I never forget a face, but in your case I'm willing to make an exception."

Living It Up (1954, Paramount), a very loose remake of *Nothing Sacred* (1937), stars Jerry Lewis as a young man erroneously diagnosed as being near death by doctor Dean Martin. The storyline dictates that Jerry be feted by the city of New York for his bravery in the face of doom; one of the honors bestowed upon our hero is the privilege of tossing out the first ball of the season at Yankee Stadium. Jerry carries this off with such enthusiasm that he messes up the Yanks' batting order! Of less relation to the plot was Jerry Lewis' baseball episode in *The Geisha Boy* (1958, also Paramount), where his incessant heckling upsets the dignity of a Japanese ballgame—not to mention the 1958 Los Angeles Dodgers, who receive special billing in the opening credits. In this one, Jerry winds up with a baseball lodged in his mouth, undoubtedly to the great amusement of all his disciples at *Cahiers du Cinéma.*

Nearly as urbane and sophisticated was *Horizontal Lieutenant* (1962, MGM), where officer Jim Hutton performs so ineptly at an army baseball game that he's transferred to a flyspeck island in the South Pacific. But all was not lost in a sea of slapstick in 1962, a year which yielded one of the best ever ballpark sequences put on film in Blake Edwards's *Experiment in Terror* (Columbia). The climax of this melodrama occurs during a Giants-Dodgers night game at San Francisco's Candlestick Park (stock footage of Don Drysdale, Felipe Alou, Harvey Kuenn, Wally Moon and Mike McCormick can be seen in this sequence, while the voice of announcer Vin Scully is heard calling the play-by-play). Ross Martin, the film's resident psychotic extortionist-kidnapper, tries to escape from the law with a purseful of ransom money by losing himself in the crowd of departing fans. But as FBI agent Glenn Ford and the police close in, Martin scurries to the middle of the deserted, floodlight-drenched diamond, where he is mowed down by a shower of bullets. The scene works both as a thrilling conclusion to a nail-biting cat and mouse tale, and as a faithful representation of the chaotic euphoria that often accompanies night games in a major metropolis with an enthusiastic baseball-fan contingency.

Far funnier within the category of cops at the ballgame was the Anaheim Stadium climax of *The Naked Gun* (1988, Paramount), a detective spoof concocted by those inimitable *Airplane!* boys, Jim Abrahams and Jerry and David Zucker. Through an incredible series of circumstances that we're not about to detail here, star Leslie Nielsen (as thickheaded police lieutenant

Frank Drebin) finds himself masquerading first as an opera singer engaged to sing the national anthem at an Angels-Mariners game, then as a "dirty dancing" umpire who moonwalks across the field (courtesy of a deliberately obvious stunt double) after calling a strikeout. Topping the sequence, Nielsen is seen proposing to his lady love Priscilla Presley on the ballpark's giant TV screen, to the accompanying sighs and tears of a capacity crowd. Bounding this activity is a limitless supply of sidesplitting cartoon-like vignettes, ranging from the glimpse of a coach using semaphore to signal his players, to the shot of everyone—including the players' wives—expectorating great obscene gobs of tobacco juice. Oh, yes. Also in this scene, Reggie Jackson is hypnotized and programmed to assassinate Queen Elizabeth. *This Week in Baseball* it isn't.

Another Big Game, this one played out on a high school field, figures in the opening and closing scenes of *Mr. Destiny* (1990, Touchstone), a dismal variation on *It's a Wonderful Life.* James Belushi, playing a man unhappy with his dead-end job and mundane existence, has convinced himself that his life would have been peaches and cream had he just won that one crucial high school baseball game. Enter "Mr. Destiny" (Michael Caine, in one of his 627 movie appearances in 1990), who gives Belushi a chance to see what his life would have been like if indeed he'd been victorious in that ballpark long ago. That's right, folks: Always beware what you wish for, because you just might get your wish. The wealthier Belushi is far worse off, even unto being pursued by the police on a murder charge! Things turn out all right in the end, of course—except for moviegoers who once more had to endure the spectacle of a first-rate performer like Jim Belushi mired in tenth-rate material. Even an adroit closing bit—where Michael Caine appears just after the baseball defeat when Belushi was a boy to assure the disconsolate teenager that things have a way of working out for the best—fails to make up for the drearily contrived storyline that has gone before.

One category of "incidental baseball" movies is a relatively recent and sparsely populated one: films in which a famous baseball player of the past is depicted in circumstances that prevent his going anywhere near a ballfield. *Insignificance* (1985, Zenith), adapted by Terry Johnson from his own play, is a sort of pop-culture *No Exit*, featuring characters representing Albert Einstein, Joseph McCarthy, Marilyn Monroe, and Joe DiMaggio, who sit around in a Manhattan hotel room in 1953 to commiserate on the insignificance of fame in an atom-dominated society. Gary Busey portrays the *a clef* DiMaggio, known merely as "The Ballplayer," in this fascinating if stagey piece of speculative fiction.

More to the point was Andre Braugher's portrayal of baseball's first black major leaguer in the made-for-cable film *The Court-Martial of Jackie Robinson* (1990, Turner). This intense dramatization of a wartime incident involving Robinson's rebellion against "Jim Crow" laws while serving in the U.S. Army suggests that Jackie's courage and bearing in the face of a court-martial were the deciding factors in his being chosen to break baseball's color line. Ruby Dee, who'd played Jackie's wife in *The Jackie Robinson Story* (1950), portrayed Robinson's mother in the 1990 film.

So. Does that cover everything? Not quite. Except for a handful of titles like *Max Dugan Returns* and *The Naked Gun* described in the above notes, we haven't discussed those films wherein real-life baseball personalities have appeared and sometimes acted. There's no point in annotating the showbiz careers of people like John Beradino, Chuck Connors, or Bob Uecker, since these worthies had hung up their uniforms long before settling down in front of the cameras (except for Beradino, who in *The Kid from Cleveland* flirted with acting a few

years before taking up that profession full-time). Therefore, let's give a thumbnail sketch of some essentially *non-*acting ballplayers who've honored moviegoers with cameo roles over the years.

In addition to the aforementioned appearances of Mickey Mantle and Roger Maris in *Safe at Home!*, the heroes of 1961 could be spotted along with Yogi Berra in *That Touch of Mink* (1962, Universal), which starred Cary Grant and ardent baseball devotee Doris Day. In a fleetingly amusing vignette, Doris manages to get Mantle, Maris, and Berra on the bad side of the umpire during a Yankees game, whereupon all three players are sent to the showers—without Doris, of course. This was 1962, not 1972. (Eighteen years after *That Touch of Mink*, Mantle and Maris contributed a much shorter token appearance in the 1980 Rastar/Columbia domestic drama *It's My Turn*, this time in the company of Bob Feller and Elston Howard.)

Thanks to multiple *Late Show* and cable–TV screenings, the baseball star cameos in *That Touch of Mink* were for many years the best known of such appearances. More recently, however, three other ballplayers' guest shots have resurfaced and enjoyed fairly wide exposure.

The first was Babe Ruth's extended appearance in the Harold Lloyd silent comedy feature *Speedy* (1928, Lloyd/Paramount), directed by Ted Wilde, the man responsible for Ruth's starring vehicle *Babe Comes Home* in 1927. After establishing that Lloyd is a baseball fan to the manor born (whenever there's a major-league game in progress, Harold keeps score for his pals at the soda shop by using pretzels and doughnuts to represent numbers), the plot contrives to have the star employed by a taxicab company, with one of his first fares being the Babe himself. Characteristically, Ruth is late for a game at Yankee Stadium, compelling Harold to rush his charge through heavy cross-town traffic. It's not a smooth journey at all, given Harold's propensity for turning around while driving to chat with his back-seat celebrity passenger. Looking more like a prosperous business executive than the Sultan of Swat, Babe does a credible job reacting in horror as the taxi barely misses disaster at every turn. It's highly probable that Babe Ruth agreed to do this scene (shot on location in New York, by the way) to tweak the nose of Yankees manager Miller Huggins, who reportedly was terrified of taxicabs.

Republic's 1937 *Manhattan Merry-Go-Round*, a harmless musical comedy about an amiable racketeer (Leo Carrillo) who takes over a record company, has become a cable–TV and home-video staple ever since lapsing into public domain. Amidst such legitimate musical acts as Louis Prima, Gene Autry, Cab Calloway, and Ted Lewis, who should appear in this film but Yankee Clipper Joe DiMaggio! And as a bonus, Joe sings—I think. (No, he doesn't sing "Let's Have Another Cup of Coffee.") As a footnote, DiMaggio completists are advised to also catch Joltin' Joe's cameo as himself in the G-rated circus picture *The First of May* (2000).

The diligence of the archivists at Blackhawk Films, at one time the largest purveyor to the 8 and 16 millimeter movie collectors' market, resulted in the late–1970s reappearance of *Rawhide* (1938, Sol Lesser/20th Century–Fox), a fifty-nine-minute western ostensibly starring singing cowboy Smith Ballew but actually bestowing top billing upon Lou Gehrig. Gehrig plays himself—that is, he plays a character named "Lou Gehrig" who, according to the script, is a rancher being pressured to surrender his land to a band of crooks. Gehrig's sister (Evalyn Knapp) joins forces with a lawyer (Ballew), who enlist the aid of Lou and his fellow ranchers to rout the bandits. During the climactic battle, Gehrig puts his baseball skills to practical use in subduing the heavies.

In real life a devotee of B-westerns, Gehrig was none too comfortable as a cowboy actor, as evidenced by his stiff-legged stance, high school pageant gestures, constipated grin, and overemphatic dialogue recitals. But he's an impressive screen presence; thanks to his muscular physique, he seems far mightier and more capable of fending for himself than any of his costars—including nominal leading man Smith Ballew. Producer Sol Lesser wanted to use *Rawhide* as a launching pad for Lou Gehrig's film career, but the Iron Man deferred to his first love and returned to the Yankees.

And then there's Satchel Paige, giving a good account of himself in the small role of a cavalry sergeant in the 1959 western *The Wonderful Country*; Houston's Bo Belinsky, trapped among surfers and beach bunnies in 1967's *C'mon, Let's Live a Little*; Dodgers catcher John Roseboro, sleepwalking along with Jack Webb as a detective in the 1966 TV-movie *Dragnet*; Vida Blue of the Oakland As, steering clear of star Jim Brown in the 1972 actioner *Black Gunn*; Cleveland Indian Leon Wagner, not playing the title role in director John Cassavetes' *A Woman Under the Influence* (1974); Yankees outfielder Roy White, managing to live through his brief bit in the Mississippi-filmed thriller *The Premonition* (1976); 1978's Most Valuable Player, Bucky Dent of the Yankees, as "Kyle Jessop" in the 1979 made-for–TV jigglefest *The Dallas Cowboys Cheerleaders*; a pre-diet Dodgers manager Tommy Lasorda in the all-star bomb *Americathon* (1979), followed by *post*-diet appearances in the Rodney Dangerfield vehicle *Ladybugs* (1992, as "Coach Canoli") and *All Saint's Day* (1998), which Lasorda wrote, produced and directed; and Willie Mays, taking up space with fellow pop icons Morey Amsterdam, John Cameron Swayze, Myron Cohen and G. Gordon Liddy in the 1985 "Wilderness Family" spoof *When Nature Calls*.

Don't head for the parking lot just yet: We haven't mentioned former Red Sox pitcher and Cy Young Award winner Roger Clemens as "Skidmark" in the Farrelly Brothers' gloriously smutty bowling comedy *Kingpin* (1996); the Cubs' record-smashing Sammy Sosa in the David Schwimmer starrer *Kissing a Fool* (1998), largely filmed on location in Chicago; and the Dodgers' Steve Garvey, MVP of 1974—who, evidently entertaining thoughts of being the new Chuck Connors or John Beradino, tackled character roles in such masterpieces as *Direct Hit* (1994), *Bloodfist VI: Ground Zero* (1994) and *The Ice Cream Man* (1995).

Maybe it's time that someone wrote a full-length study of "instant movie stars"— nonactors, such as athletes, who've been called upon to fill up space before the cameras. I said it's time that *someone* wrote that book—not me! I'm outta here and off to Miller Park. Sure, the Milwaukee Brewers haven't won a pennant since 1982. But the century is still young.

Bibliography

Abrahams, Peter. *The Fan.* New York: Warner Books, 1995.

Alexander, Charles C. *Ty Cobb.* New York: Oxford University Press, 1984.

Alibi Ike, Pressbook, 1935. United Artists collection, Microfilm 448, reel 1. Wisconsin Center for Film and Theatre Research, Madison, WI.

Allen, Lee, and Tom Meany. *Kings of the Diamond.* New York: Putnam's, 1965.

Allen, Maury. *Roger Maris: A Man for All Seasons.* New York: Donald I. Fine, 1986.

The American Film Institute Catalog of Motion Pictures (three volumes): *Feature Films 1921–1930.* New York: R. R. Bowker, 1971. *Feature Films 1961–1970.* New York: Bowker, 1971. *Feature Films 1911–1920.* New York: Bowker, 1990.

Angell, Roger. "Scout." Reprinted in *Five Seasons: A Baseball Companion.* New York: Simon and Schuster, 1977.

Angels in the Outfield. Studio Pressbook, 1994.

Ardolino, Frank. "Ceremonies of Innocence and Experience in *Bull Durham, Field of Dreams,* and *Eight Men Out.*" *Journal of Popular Film and Television,* Summer 1990.

Armstrong, Douglas. "Meet David Ward, the Boss of the *Major League* film, and Find Out What He Plans." *Milwaukee Journal,* July 17, 1988. (Plus follow-up *Major League* articles in the *Journal,* written by various staffers.)

Arnold, Edwin T., and Eugene L. Miller. *The Films and Career of Robert Aldrich.* Knoxville: University of Tennessee Press, 1986.

Asinof, Eliot. *Eight Men Out.* New York: Henry Holt, 1963.

The Babe. Studio Pressbook. 1992.

Babe Comes Home. Pressbook, 1927. United Artists Collection, Microfilm 448, reel 10A. Wisconsin Center for Film and Theatre Research, Madison, WI.

Barth, Jack. "Roadside Hollywood." *US Magazine,* July 11–25, 1991.

Beck, Jerry, and Will Friedwald. *Looney Tunes and Merrie Melodies.* New York: Henry Holt, 1989.

Benson, Michael. *Ballparks of North America: A Comprehensive Historical Reference to Baseball Grounds, Yards, and Stadiums.* Jefferson, NC: McFarland, 1989.

Berg, A. Scott. *Goldwyn: A Biography.* New York: Borzoi/Knopf, 1989.

Biskind, Peter. *Seeing Is Believing: How Hollywood Taught Us to Stop Worrying and Love the Fifties.* New York: Pantheon, 1983.

Bodeen, De Witt. "Charles Ray." *Films in Review,* November 1968.

Bogle, Donald. *Toms, Coons, Mulattoes, Mammies and Bucks.* New York: Frederick Ungar/Continuum, 1973; revised edition, 1979.

Bohjalian, Christopher A. *Past the Bleachers.* New York: Carol & Graf Publishers, 1992.

Brashler, William. *The Bingo Long Travelling All-Stars and Motor Kings.* New York: Harper and Row, 1973.

Brooks, Tim, and Earle Marsh. *The Complete Directory to Prime Time Network and Cable TV Shows, 1946–Present.* 6th ed. New York: Ballantine Books, 1995.

Brown, Garret. "It's a Bird, It's a Plane, It's a—Camera?" *American Film,* September 1983.

Brown, Joe E., with Ralph Hancock. *Laughter Is a Wonderful Thing.* New York: A. S. Barnes, 1956.

The Bush Leaguer. Pressbook, 1927. United Artists collection, Microfilm 448, reel 10A. Wisconsin Center for Film and Theatre Research, Madison, WI.

Byrne, Bridget. "Hits, Long Runs and Flops." Entertainment News Service. Published in *Milwaukee Journal*, October 6, 1991.

Campanella, Roy. *It's Good to Be Alive.* New York: Signet, 1959.

Cantwell, Robert. "Sports Was Box-Office Poison." *Sports Illustrated*, September 15, 1969.

Capra, Frank. *The Name Above the Title.* New York: Macmillan, 1971.

Casper, Joseph Andrew. *Stanley Donen.* Metuchen, NJ: Scarecrow, 1983.

Chanko, Kenneth M. "Reviews of *Major League* and *Field of Dreams.*" *Films in Review*, August/September 1989.

Cobb. Studio Pressbook, 1994.

Cobb, Ty, with Al Stump. *My Life in Baseball: The True Record.* Garden City, NY: Doubleday, 1961.

Coghlan, Frank, Jr. *They Still Call Me Junior: Autobiography of a Child Star, with a Filmography.* Jefferson, NC: McFarland, 1993.

Cook, Bruce. "The Saga of *Bingo Long and the Travelling Motor Kings.*" *American Film*, July/August 1976.

Corliss, Richard. "Cover Story: Pursuing the Dream." *Time*, June 26, 1989.

Cotter, Bill. *The Wonderful World of Disney Television: A Complete History.* New York: Hyperion Books, 1997.

Coyle, Daniel. *Hardball: A Season in the Projects.* New York: G. M. Putnam's Sons, 1993.

Davis, Ossie, and Ruby Dee. *With Ossie and Ruby: In This Life Together.* New York: William Morrow, 1998.

Dewey, Donald. *James Stewart: A Biography.* Atlanta, GA: Turner Publishing, 1996.

"Dialogue on Film: Alan J. Pakula." *American Film*, November 1985.

Dickens, Homer. *The Films of Gary Cooper.* Secaucus, NJ: Citadel, 1971.

Dooley, Roger. *From Scarface to Scarlett: American Films in the 1930s.* New York: Harcourt Brace Jovanovich, 1979, 1981.

Dougan, Andy. *Untouchable: A Biography of Robert De Niro.* New York: Thunder's Mouth Press, 1996.

Dudek, Dwayne. "Weary Reeves Wears Game Face for 'Hardball.'" *Milwaukee Journal-Sentinel*, September 17, 2001.

Eames, John Douglas. *The MGM Story: The Complete History of Fifty Roaring Years.* New York: Crown, 1975.

_____. *The Paramount Story.* New York: Crown, 1985.

Easton, Carol. *The Search for Sam Goldwyn: A Biography.* New York: William Morrow, 1976.

Ebert, Roger. *Chicago Sun-Times* film reviews and interviews, 1991–present. Ed. Studio Pressbook, 1995.

Edelman, Rob. *The Great Baseball Films: From Right Off the Bat to A League of Their Own.* Secaucus, NJ: Carol Publishing Group, 1994.

Elmer the Great, Pressbook, 1932. United Artists collection, Microfilm 448, reel 3. Wisconsin Center for Film and Theatre Research, Madison, WI.

Enright, Ray, Robert Lord, Arthur Caesar, and Lloyd Bacon. *Fireman Save My Child.* Story treatment and screenplays. 1931–32. United Artists Collection, Box 112, folder 1.2. Wisconsin Center for Film and Theatre Research, Madison, WI.

Entertainment Weekly. Film reviews, 1991–present.

Eyles, Allan. *James Stewart.* New York: Stein and Day, 1984.

Feller, Bob, with Bill Gilbert. *Now Pitching: Bob Feller.* Secaucus, NJ: Birch Lane/Carrol, 1990.

Field, Leslie A., and Joyce Field, editors. *Bernard Malamud and the Critics.* New York: New York University Press, 1970.

Fireman Save My Child. Pressbook, 1932. United Artists collection, Microfilm 448, reel 3. Wisconsin Center for Film and Theatre Research, Madison, WI.

For Love of the Game. Studio Pressbook. Universal Studios Website, 1999.

Fordin, Hugh. *The World of Entertainment: Hollywood's Greatest Musicals.* Garden City, NY: Doubleday, 1975.

Frommer, Harvey. *Rickey and Robinson: The Men Who Broke Baseball's Color Line.* New York: Macmillan, 1987.

Gardner, Martin. "Casey at the Bat." *American Heritage*, October 1967.

Garrett, Kelly. "Baseball Movies: The Best, the Bench and the Bios." *Sport*, March 1990.

Gehrig, Eleanor, with Joseph Russo. *My Luke and I.* New York: Crowell, 1976.

Geist, Kenneth L. *Pictures Will Talk: The Life and Times of Joseph L. Mankiewicz.* Foreword by Richard Burton. New York: Charles Scribner's Sons, 1978.

Geraghty, Tom. *Elmer the Great*, screenplay, 1933. United Artists Collection, Box 112, folder 1.2. Wisconsin Center for Film and Theatre Research, Madison, WI.

Gerosa, Melina. "Actor William Russ: Heading for the Majors." *Entertainment Weekly*, September 6, 1991.

Good, Howard. *Diamonds in the Dark: America, Baseball and the Movies*. Lanham, MD: Scarecrow Press, 1997.

Goodman, Gloria. *The Life and Humor of Rosie O'Donnell: A Biography*. New York: William Morrow, 1998.

Grobel, Lawrence. *The Hustons*. New York: Charles Scribner's Sons, 1989.

_____. "Kurt Russell Yells Fire in Crowded Theatres!" *Entertainment Weekly*, July 14, 1991.

Gunselman, John. "Batter Up." *American Cinematographer*, October 1999.

Hageman, William. "The Record That Broke the Man." *Chicago Tribune*, April 27, 2001.

Haines, William Wister. *Alibi Ike*. Various screenplay drafts, 1935. United Artists Collection, Boxes 11 and 12, folder 1.2. Wisconsin Center for Film and Theatre Research, Madison, WI.

Hardball. Studio Pressbook, 2001.

Harmetz, Aljean. "My Son the Movie Star." *American Film*, March 1976.

Harris, Mark. *Bang the Drum Slowly, by Henry Wiggen: Certain of His Enthusiasms Restrained by Mark Harris*. New York: Alfred A. Knopf, 1956.

_____. "Robert De Niro/Michael Moriarty: Obedience to Self," in *Close-Ups: The Movie Star Book*, edited by Danny Peary. New York: Workman, 1978.

Haskins, Jim. *Richard Pryor: A Man and His Madness*. New York: Beaufort, 1984.

Hayes, David, and Brent Walker. *The Films of the Bowery Boys: A Pictorial History of the Dead End Kids*. Secaucus, NJ: Citadel, 1982, 1984.

Hemphill, Paul. *Long Gone*. New York: Viking, 1979.

Higham, Charles, and Joel Greenberg. *The Celluloid Muse*. Chicago: Henry Regnery, 1969.

Hirschhorn, Clive. *Gene Kelly*. New York: St. Martin's, 1974; revised edition, 1984.

_____. *The Columbia Story*. New York: Crown, 1989.

Holway, John B. "Background: Satchel Paige." *TV Guide*, May 30, 1981.

_____. *Josh and Satch: The Life and Times of Josh Gibson and Satchel Paige*. Westport, CT: Meckley Publishing, 1991.

Hunter, Allan. *Walter Matthau*. New York: St. Martin's, 1984.

"Jackie Robinson: Star Ballplayer Stars in a Movie." *Life* (cover story), May 8, 1950.

James, Bill. *The Bill James Historical Baseball Abstract*. New York: Villard, 1985.

Jewell, Richard B., with Vernon Harbin. *The RKO Story*. New York: Arlington, 1982.

Johnson, Steve. "'61*' Hits a Home with Baseball Fans." *Chicago Tribune*, April 27, 2001.

Jones, Allen. "The Slugger's Wife." *On Location*, July 1984.

Jones, Ken D., Arthur F. McClure, and Alfred E. Twomey. *The Films of James Stewart*. New York: A. S. Barnes, 1970.

Kahn, Roger. "Background: Roy Campanella." *TV Guide*, February 16, 1974.

Katz, Ephraim. *International Film Encyclopedia*, rev. ed. New York: Macmillan, 1994.

Kay, Laura Smith. "Talking with Matthew Perry." *People* magazine, June 1, 1998.

Keller, Julia. "The Asterisk's Impish History." *Chicago Tribune*, April 27, 2001.

Kinsella, W. P. *Shoeless Joe*. Boston: Houghton Mifflin, 1982.

Klapisch, Bob. "Brains on the Bench: Torre Keeping His Cool in Postseason Heat." *The Bergen Record*, October 19, 1996.

Kray, Robert, and Michael Haney. "Caleb Deschanel, ASC, and *The Natural*." *American Cinematographer*, April 1985.

Lahue, Kalton. *Bound and Gagged*. New York: Castle, 1968.

Lardner, Ring. *The Ring Lardner Reader*. Edited by Maxwell Geismar. New York: Charles Scribner's Sons, 1963.

_____, and George M. Cohan. *Elmer the Great: A Comedy in Three Acts*. 1928. United Artists Collection, Box 112, folder 1.2. Wisconsin Center for Film and Theatre Research, Madison, WI.

Lardner, Ring, Jr. "Foul Ball." *American Film*, July/August, 1988, pp. 45–49. (Includes sidebar by Susan Linfield, "Studs Terkel: World Serious.")

Leahy, Michael. "A Little-Known Actor Puts on the Pinstripes to Play Baseball's Most Famous Superstar." *TV Guide*, October 5, 1991.

LeFlore, Ron, with Jim Hawkins. *Breakout*. New York: Harper and Row, 1978.

Lenburg, Jeff, Joan Howard Maurer, and Greg Lenburg. *The Three Stooges Scrapbook.* Secaucus, NJ: Citadel, 1982.

Leonard, John. *New York* magazine TV reviews, 1993–present.

Little Big League. Studio Pressbook, 1993.

Mair, George, and Anna Green. *Rosie O'Donnell: Her True Story.* Secaucus NJ: Carol Publishing Group, 1997.

Major League II. Studio Pressbook, 1994.

Major League: Back to the Minors. Studio Pressbook, 1998.

Malamud, Bernard. *The Natural.* New York: Harcourt, Brace, 1952.

Malden, Karl, with Carla Malden. *When Do I Start?: A Memoir.* New York: Simon and Schuster, 1997.

Maltin, Leonard. *The Great Movie Shorts.* Foreword by Pete Smith. New York: Crown, 1972.

_____. *The Great Movie Comedians.* New York: Crown, 1978.

_____, editor. *Hollywood Kids.* New York: Popular Library, 1978.

_____. *Of Mice and Magic.* New York: New American Library, 1980; revised edition, 1987.

_____, editor. *Leonard Maltin's TV Movies and Video Guide.* New York: Signet & Plume, 1969–present.

_____, and Richard W. Bann. *The Little Rascals: The Life and Times of Our Gang* (revised and updated edition). New York: Crown Trade Paperbacks, 1977, 1992.

Manchel, Frank. *Great Sports Movies.* New York: Franklin Watts, 1980.

Mantle, Mickey, with Herb Gluck. *The Mick.* Garden City, NY: Doubleday, 1985.

Mapp, Edward, editor. *Directory of Blacks in the Performing Arts.* Metuchen, NJ: Scarecrow, 1990.

Marill, Alvin H. *Movies Made for Television: The Telefeatures and the Mini-Series, 1964–1986.* New York: Dateline/Zoetrope, 1987.

Marshall, Gary, with Lori Marshall. *Wake Me When It's Funny: How to Break Into Show Business and Stay There.* Massachussetts: Adams Publishing, 1995.

Martin, Len D. *The Republic Pictures Checklist: Features, Serials, Cartoons, Short Subjects and Training Films of Republic Pictures Corporation, 1933–1959.* Jefferson, NC: McFarland, 1998.

McBride, Joseph. "Sports No Longer Poison." *Variety,* January 5, 1977.

McCallum, Jack. "Reel Sports." *Sports Illustrated,* February 5, 2001.

McCay, Keith. *Robert De Niro: The Hero Behind the Masks.* New York: St. Martin's, 1986.

McClelland, Doug. *Hollywood on Ronald Reagan: Friends and Enemies Discuss Our President.* Winchester, MA: Faber and Faber, 1983.

McEntire, Reba, with Tom Carter. *Reba: My Story.* New York: Bantam, 1994.

McGurk, Margaret A. "Moviemaker Pitches 'Perfect Game.'" *Cincinnati Enquirer,* April 16, 2000.

Meryman, Richard. *Mank: The Wit, World and Life of Herman Mankiewicz.* New York: William Morrow, 1978.

Michael, Paul, editor-in-chief. *The Great American Movie Book.* Associate editor, James Robert Parish. Contributing editors, John Robert Cocchi, Ray Hagen, Jack Edmund Nolan. Englewood Cliffs, NJ: Prentice-Hall, 1980.

Miller, Don. *B Movies.* New York: Curtis Paperbacks, 1973.

_____. *Hollywood Corral.* New York: Popular Library, 1976.

Mills, Bart. "Stephen Lang Gives the 'Babe' His Best Shot." *Chicago Tribune TV Week,* October 6, 1991.

Monaco, James M. *American Film Now: The People, the Power, the Money, the Movies.* New York: Zoetrope, 1979 (updated 1984).

Mote, James. *Everything Baseball.* Englewood Cliffs, NJ: Prentice-Hall, 1989.

Nash, Jay Robert, and Stanley Ralph Ross. *The Motion Picture Guide.* Chicago: Cinebooks, 1985 (plus annual updates).

Nelson, Kevin. *The Greatest Stories Ever Told (About Baseball).* New York: Perigee/Putnam, 1986.

The New York Times Film Reviews, 1913–1968. New York: New York Times and ARNO, 1970 (plus annual updates, 1969–present).

Oakie, Jack. *Jack Oakie's Double Takes.* San Francisco: Strawberry Hill, 1980.

Okrent, Daniel, and Steve Wulf. *Baseball Anecdotes.* New York: Oxford University Press, 1989.

Okuda, Ted, with Edward Watz. *The Columbia Comedy Shorts: Two-Reel Hollywood Film Comedies, 1933–1958.* Foreword by Emil Sitka. Jefferson, NC: McFarland, 1986.

Osborne, David. "John Sayles—From Hoboken to Hollywood and Back." *American Film,* October 1982.

Paige, Leroy "Satchel," with David Lipman.

Maybe I'll Pitch Forever. Garden City, NY: Doubleday, 1962.

Parish, James Robert. *Rosie: Rosie O'Donnell's Biography.* New York: Carroll & Graf, 1997.

_____, and Alvin H. Marill. *The Cinema of Edward G. Robinson.* Research associates, John Robert Cocchi, Florence Solomon, and T. Allan Taylor. New York: A. S. Barnes, 1972.

_____, and William T. Leonard, with Gregory W. Mank and Charles Hoyt. *The Funsters.* Research associates, John Robert Cocchi and Florence Solomon. New Rochelle, NY: Arlington House, 1979.

Pastime. Studio Pressbook, 1991.

Peary, Danny, editor. *Cult Baseball Players: The Greats, the Flakes, the Weird and the Wonderful.* New York: Simon and Schuster, 1990.

Perfect Game. Studio Pressbook. Disney Studios Website, 2000.

Pfeiffer, Lee, and Michael Lewis. *The Films of Tom Hanks.* Secaucus, NJ: Citadel, 1996.

Piersall, Jimmy. *The Truth Hurts.* Chicago: Contemporary, 1985.

Pirone, Dorothy Ruth, with Chris Martens. *My Dad, the Babe: Growing Up with An American Hero.* Boston: Quinlan, 1988.

Pitts, Michael R. *Poverty Row Studios, 1929–1940: An Illustrated History of 53 Independent Film Companies, with a Filmography for Each.* Jefferson, NC: McFarland, 1997.

Reagan, Ronald, with Richard G. Hubler. *Where's the Rest of Me?* New York: Duell, Sloan and Pearce, 1965.

Reid, Dorothy, and Francis Cockrell. *Rhubarb,* screenplay, with related correspondence to and from George Seaton, 1950–51. George Seaton Collection, Box 19. Wisconsin Center for Film and Theatre Research, Madison, WI.

Reidenbaugh, Lowell. *Take Me Out to the Ball Park.* Illustrations by Amadee. St. Louis: Sporting News, 1983.

Reilly, Adam. *Harold Lloyd: The King of Daredevil Comedy.* Foreword by Gene Stavis. New York: Collier/Macmillan, 1977.

Ribowsky, Mark. *The Power and the Darkness: The Life of Josh Gibson in the Shadows of the Game.* New York: Simon and Schuster, 1996.

Richman, Sidney. *Bernard Malamud.* New York: Twayne, 1966.

Ritter, Lawrence S. *The Glory of Their Times.* New York: William Morrow, 1966; enlarged edition, 1984.

Robbins, Jhan. *Everybody's Man: A Biography of Jimmy Stewart.* New York: G. P. Putnam's Sons, 1985.

Roberts, Randy. *Papa Jack: Jack Johnson and the Era of White Hopes.* New York: Free Press/Macmillan, 1983.

Robinson, Jackie, with Arthur Duckett. *I Never Had It Made.* New York: G. P. Putnam's Sons, 1972.

Robinson, Ray. *Iron Horse: Lou Gehrig in His Time.* New York, London, 1990.

Rookie of the Year. Studio Pressbook, 1993.

Rosenberg, Bernard, and Harry Silverstein. *The Real Tinsel.* London: Collier Macmillan, 1970.

Sarandon, Susan. "My Annie Savoy's Red-Hot Rules for Better World Series Viewing." *TV Guide,* October 15, 1988.

The Scout. Studio Pressbook, 1994.

Shaara, Michael. *For Love of the Game.* New York: Carol & Graf Publishers, 1991.

Shatzkin, Mike, editor. *The Ballplayers: Baseball's Ultimate Biographical Reference.* Managing editor, Stephen Holtje. Created and developed by Mike Shatzkin and Jim Charlton. New York: Arbor House/Morrow, 1990.

Shlain, Bruce. "Power Hitter." *Rolling Stone,* July 14–28, 1988.

Shrake, Edwin. "The Film-Flam Men." *Sports Illustrated,* June 3, 1974.

Siebert, Charles. "It's the 1919 World Series, and Catching for the Reds Is Yours Truly." *Esquire,* August 1988.

Silverman, Jeff. "The Cockeyed World of Ron Shelton." *American Film,* December 1989.

Silverman, Stephen M. *Dancing on the Ceiling: Stanley Donen and His Movies.* With an introduction by Audrey Hepburn. New York: Knopf/Random House, 1996.

Sloate, Alfred. *Finding Buck McHenry.* New York: HarperCollins, 1991.

Slotek, Jim. "Things That People Buzzed About in '97." *Toronto Sun,* December 31, 1997.

Smith, Curt. *America's Dizzy Dean.* St. Louis: Bethany, 1978.

_____. *Voices of the Game: The First Full Scale Overview of Baseball Broadcasting, 1921 to the Present.* South Bend, IN: Diamond Communications, 1987.

Smith, H. Allen. *Rhubarb.* Illustrated by Leo Hershfield. New York: Doubleday, 1946.

Sobol, Ken. *Babe Ruth and the American Dream.* Introduction by Dick Schaap. New York: Random House, 1974.

"*Soul of the Game* Tells How Blacks Broke the Color Barrier." *Jet* magazine, April, 29 1996.

Spada, James. *The Films of Robert Redford.* Secaucus, NJ: Citadel, 1976; revised edition, 1984.

Spears, Jack. "Baseball on the Screen." *Films in Review,* April 1968. (Plus follow-up "Letters to the Editor" comments in subsequent issues by William K. Everson, George Geltzer, Don Miller, and Frank Leon Smith.)

Stump, Al. *Cobb: The Life and Times of the Meanest Man Who Ever Played Baseball.* Foreword by Jimmy Reese. North Carolina: Algonquin Books of Chapel Hill, 1994.

Swindell, Larry. *The Last Hero: The Biography of Gary Cooper.* Garden City, NY: Doubleday, 1980.

Summer Catch. Studio Pressbook. Warner Bros. Studios Website, 2001.

Taylor, Lawrence, and Louis Pollock. *The Jackie Robinson Story.* Story treatment and screenplays, written with Arthur Mann, 1949-50. Herbert Biberman and Gale Sondergaard papers, Box 93, folder 13; and United Artists Collection, Box 5, folder 2. Wisconsin Center for Film and Theatre Research, Madison, WI.

Thomas, Tony. *A Wonderful Life: The Films and Career of James Stewart.* Secaucus, NJ: Citadel, 1988.

_____, and Aubrey Solomon. *The Films of 20th Century-Fox: A Pictorial History.* Secaucus, NJ: Citadel, 1979.

Thorn, John, and Bob Carroll. *The Whole Baseball Catalog.* New York: Simon and Schuster, 1989.

Time magazine. Film reviews, 1991–present.

TV Guide. Made-for-TV movie reviews and related articles, 1991–present.

Uebelherr, Jan. "Wausau Native Comes 'Home'; Film's Premiere Set for County Stadium." *Milwaukee Journal-Sentinel,* October 5, 2000.

USA Today. Film reviews, 1991–present.

Variety. Film Reviews, 1916–present.

Wagenheim, Kal. *Babe Ruth: His Life and Legend.* Maplewood, NJ: Waterfront, 1990.

Wallop, Douglass. *The Year the Yankees Lost the Pennant.* New York: Norton, 1954.

Weiner, Thomas. "An Actor and a Gentleman." *American Film,* April 1983.

_____. "Rebecca DeMornay—On Deck." *American Film,* April 1985.

Wetzsteon, Ross. "Too Close for Comfort." *American Film,* May 1984.

Williams, Esther, with Digby Diehl. *The Million Dollar Mermaid.* New York: Simon & Schuster, 1999.

Willis, John, editor. *Screen World.* Annual editions 1981-1999. New York: Crown.

Wolff, Rick, editorial director. *The Baseball Encyclopedia* (tenth edition). New York: Macmillan, 1996.

Wolfley, Bob. "Selig Doesn't Spare Praise for '61*.'" *Milwaukee Journal-Sentinel,* April 29, 2001.

Selected Websites

All-American Girls Professional Baseball League. http://www.AAGPBL.org

All-Movie Guide. http://www.allmovie.com

Amercian Studies Program at the College of William and Mary. http://www.indiana.edu

Baseball Archive. http://www.baseball.com

Best Digest. http://www.bestdigest.com

Black Baseball's Negro Baseball Leagues. http://www.blackbaseball.com

CANOE. http://www.canoe.ca

CBS-Sportsline. http://www.cbs.sportsline.com

Cigar Aficionado. http://www.cigaraficionado.com

Coming Attractions. http://www.ign.com

Film.com. http:// www.film.com

HBO.com. http://www.hbo.com

Internet Movie Database. http://www.imdb.com

Mr.Showbiz.com http://www.mrshowbiz.com

Movie Magazine International. http://www.shoestring.org/mmi_revs

Movie Mirrors Index. http://www.san.beck/org/MM

NETFLIX. http://www.netflix.com

Salon.com. http://www.salon.com

Shadowball Site. http://www.library.thinkquest.org

Show Biz Data. http://www.showbizdata.com

Silents Majority. http://www.mdle.com./Classic Films

Society for American Baseball Research. http://www.sabr.org

True Baseball. http://www.truebaseball.com

World Entertainment News Network. http://www.wenn.com

Index

Numbers in boldface refer to photographs.